PANDA GUIDES

THINK CHINA   THINK PANDA

BEIJING

THIS EDITION WAS RESEARCHED AND WRITTEN BY

**Robert Linnet
Trey Archer
Emily Umhoefer
Grant Dou**

How to Use this Book

1. **Overview** – The Overview is the place to start. Here you can learn about the history and culture of Beijing, and decide which season is best for your trip and which festivals are going on during your visit. There are plenty of fun facts as well, including the Beijing reading and movie list.

2. **Hot Topics** – Mentally prepare with Hot Topics. Everything you need to know about how to travel with kids, protect yourself against pollution, stay safe and healthy, and more is touched on in this chapter. There are also a few sample itineraries to help with planning your trip.

3. **Getting Prepared** – Pack those bags, get your visa and buy a ticket through the help of our user-friendly Getting Prepared section.

4. **Top Attractions & Other Attractions** – Learn about Beijing's many world-class attractions through vivid descriptions, histories and vibrant full-color pictures. If your trip is limited in time, the hardest part will be narrowing down the list! It's also a good idea to bring this guidebook to these sites to stay fresh on their details – it's certainly cheaper than hiring an overpriced tour guide.

5. **Side Trips** – If you have time to spare after seeing it all, go for one (or a few) of our Side Trips. Whether it's an overnighter to the ancient Wall Street of China at Pingyao, a glorious imperial palace at Chengde, or a beach retreat at Beidaihe, we've got options for every kind of traveler.

6. **Sleeping** – Book the perfect lodging via the Sleeping chapter. You can even use the customized pull-out city map to ensure your hotel or hostel is close to all of your desired sights. To save cash, choose a place with a Panda Partnership. Each location with the blue ribbon offers discounts when you flash this Panda Guides guidebook.

7. **Eating and Drinking & Nightlife** – Reserve a five-star restaurant or do as the locals do and chow down at a hole-in-the-wall using our comprehensive restaurant list. After your meal, paint the town red at the city's hottest bars, clubs and live music venues. Be sure to see which ones offer discounts (again, look for the blue discount ribbon). It'll save you a pretty penny.

8. **Distractions** – When you need a break from all the sightseeing, flip through Distractions to see which massage parlor can best spoil you. Perhaps a cooking class, camping trip, or even a cycling tour is calling your name? We have tons of pleasant activities to "distract" you along the way.

9. **Travel Resources** – Lost your passport and need a new one? Decided to continue traveling and need visas for other countries? Travel Resources can be your best friend and a lifesaver if a problem arises.

10. **Mandarin Phrasebook** – By speaking the local lingo and learning more about one of the world's oldest and most fascinating languages, not only will you enlighten your soul, but you'll also find traversing the town a lot easier. Get started in our Mandarin Phrasebook.

Table of Contents

Beijing Overview.................................8
Getting Prepared 31
Transportation 40
Top Attractions 49
   The Great Wall 50
   The Forbidden City 62
   Summer Palaces &
   University Area.................................71
   Temple of Heaven &
   the Prayer Altars 78
   Tian'anmen Square &
   Surrounding Area...............................86
   Shichahai Area 98
   Beihai Park.......................................107
   Hutongs 110
   Lama Temple Area.........................116
   798 Art District 123
   Olympic Legacies 127
Other Attractions...............................131
Sleeping...193
Eating...205
Drinking & Nightlife 243
Shopping...252
Distractions..263
Side Trips from Beijing....................266
   Tianjin 267
   Pingyao...270
   Beidaihe..273
   Chengde 275
Travel Stories 278
Hot Topics..290
   Sample Itineraries.........................290
   Air Pollution in Beijing 301
   Food & Water Safety....................305
   Toilets in Beijing 307
   Smart-phone Apps........................309
   Scams...312
   Culture Shock for Travelers 318
   Etiquette &
   Taboo in Chinese Culture 323
   Internet & Phone Access 327
   Traveling with Kids 329
   Beijing on a Budget.......................334
Mandarin Phrasebook....................336
Glossary 345
Travel Resources.............................347
Index 350

Beijing Overview

Běijīng (北京) first emerged as a national leader some 2,000 years ago. It was originally called Yànjīng (燕京) when it was established as the capital of the State of Yan, and for this reason you'll see Yanjing Beer across town; it's one of the favorite brews amongst the locals. After the fall of Yan, during the later Han and Tang Dynasties, Beijing lost its status as a capital, but it remained a major prefecture of northern China.

In 938, Beijing was conquered by a nomadic people called the Khitans, who declared it the capital of their Liao Dynasty (907-1125). Later, the Mongols seized the city in 1215, and in 1264 Kublai Khan (grandson of Genghis Khan) made Beijing the capital of China, naming it Great Capital (Dà Dū; 大都).

After Kublai moved his capital from Karakorum in Mongolia to Beijing (a move to gain more control over the Chinese heartland), the empire encompassed most of East Asia. Beijing, under the rule of the Khans of the Mongolian Yuan Dynasty (1260-1368), developed into a major world city, and it was during this time that it saw the rise of the Bell and Drum Towers, the hutongs, the city wall, and many other monuments that still grace the historic landscape.

After the fall of the Yuan Dynasty in 1368, the emperors of the ensuing Ming Dynasty (1368-1644) moved the capital to the southern city of Nánjīng (南京). However, in 1403 the Ming Emperor Zhū Dì (朱棣), also known as Emperor Yǒnglè (永乐), moved it back to Beijing and gave the city its current name (Nanjing means Southern Capital, while Beijing means Northern Capital). The Ming period was Beijing's golden era, a time when the Forbidden City, the Temple of Heaven, an enormous section of the Great Wall, and many other Beijing landmarks were built. During Ming rule, Beijing prospered into a massive city, becoming the religious and cultural center of Asia and one of the biggest cities in the world.

In 1644, the Manchu descendants of the Khitans overthrew the declining Ming Dynasty and established the Qing Dynasty (1644-1912). The Manchu imperial court, taking full advantage of the Ming's ambitious building projects, moved into the Forbidden City and contributed to Beijing's aura by constructing the Summer Palace and Old Summer Palace. These palaces served as retreats from the steamy Beijing summer heat for the emperors and their entourages.

It was also during the Qing Dynasty that Western countries established foreign legations in the Qiánmén (前门) area, south of the Forbidden City. China was notorious for closing its gates to the world, but that all changed after the Opium Wars of the mid-1800s, when the country was forced by France and Britain to open its doors.

With Christian missionaries and businessmen flooding into China and the disarray of the Qing Empire, frustrated and unemployed locals banded together in the name of nationalism to eject the foreigners. Foreign churches, embassies and businesses suffered violent and deadly attacks around Beijing during the Boxer Rebellion of 1900, as the Boxers – known as such because of the martial arts they practiced – tried to rid their land of all things foreign.

In the end, a force of eight world powers (the UK, the US, Japan, Russia, Austria-Hungary,

Map of Beijing during the Ming Dynasty

France, Germany and Italy) intervened militarily to quell the radical Boxer Rebellion. The Eight-Nation Alliance succeeded and eventually forced Empress Dowager Cixi (who originally supported the Boxers) to sign a series of unfavorable treaties – a move that eventually lead to the Qing's demise.

The Qing Dynasty came to an end in 1912, and China fractured into a land of competing warlords. The Kuomintang political party (KMT, or Nationalists) under the guidance of Sun Yat-sen (the first president of China) took power and moved the capital back to Nanjing in 1928, renaming Beijing to Běipíng (北平; Northern Peace). Beijing still remained an important city during the years of KMT rule, but it returned to the front stage after the Nationalists were first weakened by the ferocious Japanese invasion and then defeated by a communist insurgency led by Mao Zedong. On October 1, 1949 Mao stood on the balcony of Tian'anmen Tower and proclaimed the founding of the People's Republic of China with its capital in Beijing. Since then, Beijing has been the nation's political, cultural and educational hub, and it's considered the ideological center of the Chinese nation.

Today, Beijing is often described as a city of curious contrasts. This sprawling metropolis of more than 20 million people is one where you and your neighbor might still use a communal outhouse. It's a center of bold, outspoken modern art, but you still can't access Facebook or get uncensored internet searches. There are more Gucci stores than days of the week, but shoppers in these high-end venues walk in wearing rubber ducky pajamas. Hard science and technology are lauded as the road to prosperity, and yet people will still pay out the nose to avoid having an unlucky 4 in their phone number.

Make no mistake, these endless juxtapositions are more than just contrasts – they're conflicts. The destruction of Beijing's ancient hutong alleyways is merely the most visible symbol of a culture that is being torn down, papered over, imported, exported and rebuilt at a whiplash-inducing pace. Alongside old pleasures like tranquil walks at the Temple of Heaven, blue skies over the ancient towers of the Great Wall, and perfectly prepared portions of Peking Duck, Beijing offers hordes of office workers fighting their way through jam-packed subways, while intractable pollution clouds blot out the sun for days at a time and massive abandoned shopping malls glisten with wasted marble and glass.

Beijing's contradictions can be seen in the people as well since much of local life takes place in public: men get haircuts on the curb, elegant old women practice ballroom dancing in the park, and young people, escaping the lack of privacy that results from multiple generations living under one roof, take their courtship to the streets. At the same time, thanks to the internet and Western TV and movies, the average Chinese high-schooler may be just as vampire-obsessed, social media-happy and NBA-gripped as their American or European counterparts. Personal appearance is also seen as an important means of self-expression, just as in the West, and tattooed punk rockers and gold-plated iPhone fashion cases attract no special attention on the street.

For now, Beijing is the political center of the world's emerging superpower, and it's doing everything in its might to keep the country steaming ahead on this trajectory. Already the policy changes decided in its walled compounds and massive ministries resonate not only throughout China, but to the furthest corners of the globe. No one knows for sure where Beijing will lead the country of China, but if history is any indicator, you can be sure that any major events will probably happen right here in the capital.

It's hard to say what Beijing is for sure, except that it's gritty, it's thrilling, and it's the perfect time to visit, because in this moment the past and the future are equally visible. So what are you waiting for? Come now, because this place changes in the blink of an eye.

This is Beijing!

Politics

Wang Anshun

One aspect of Beijing culture is the appearance of its leadership: nine times out of ten, you can count on a politician being a middle-aged man in a dark suit in the back seat of a Benz with dyed jet-black hair. It's said that gray hair is a sign of vulnerability, so Chinese politicians hit the salon to maintain a coal-black coif. The mayor of Beijing, a 56-year-old Communist Party member named Wáng Ānshùn (王安顺), is no exception. Wang took office in January 2013 after serving the Party in Jilin Province, Gansu Province, and Shanghai. Upon his election, Wang told news outlets that he vowed to do more to manage Beijing's recurring air pollution problem, saying, "The current environmental problems are worrisome." Surprise, surprise! So far the hazardous levels of air pollution only seem to have gotten worse.

Though he runs a city of more than 20 million, Wang and his nine vice-mayors are overshadowed by Guō Jīnlóng (郭 金 龙), the Party Secretary of the Beijing Municipal Committee, who is the highest-ranking official in the government of Beijing. Also in the mix are the national-level politicians who live and work in Beijing, like China's newly appointed president, Xí Jìnpíng (习 近 平), who is considered by some observers to be a relatively conservative politician who is likely to support stronger government controls and make no real effort to increase transparency.

The real thorn in the government's side is the internet, which certainly didn't invent political dissent, but has made it much easier to spread. As the Great Firewall of China maintains an ever-growing list of blocked sites and search terms, Chinese netizens have taken to Twitter-style micro-blogging sites such as www.weibo.com to spread news, gossip and opinions that travel fast and far before censors can kick in.

For these reasons, it should be no wonder that Beijing, as the heart and soul of Chinese politics, is the epicenter of China's large and somewhat influential group of micro-blogging crusaders. Recently, however, the government passed anti-defamation legislation to issue prison sentences for any netizen – blogger or otherwise – who posts an "inaccurate rumor" that goes viral. What makes the new law especially draconian is the fact that China's version of "viral," in this instance at least, is if the "rumor" is reposted 500 times or more and is viewed by at least 5,000 people; decidedly low numbers. Since the law was passed in the summer of 2013, dozens have been detained, internet censorship is tighter than ever, and blogging site Weibo has seen a 70% drop in usage since its peak in 2012.

Economy

While Beijing's southern counterpart Shanghai has a reputation as China's financial hub, the capital is giving it a serious run for its money. Many heavy industries and factories have been pushed out of Beijing – Beijing Capital Steel, once one of the biggest employers and biggest polluters in town, has been relocated to Tángshān (唐 山) in Héběi (河 北) Province – as the city attempts to ditch the "Made in China" manufacturing-based image of Chinese business and refashion itself as a center of white collar entrepreneurship and innovation.

Beijing is home to 44 Fortune 500 companies, more than any city in the world except Tokyo, and 279 Fortune 500 companies have invested in more than 637 projects in Beijing. The action is clustered in several areas. The Central Business District on the east side of town has become a hub of corporate headquarters, high-end malls, and housing to serve the business community. Financial Street (Jīnróng Jiē; 金融街), known as Beijing's Wall Street, is another hotspot for growth, as is Zhōngguāncūn (中关村), which is often called "China's Silicon Valley."

All of this investment led to a blistering 9% growth in GDP between 2011 and 2012. The rosy picture is occasionally interrupted by complaints over corruption and the growing inequality between rich and poor, and sky-high real estate prices have Beijingers' income stretched thin. But in a country with extreme poverty and economic restriction only in its recent past, rising living standards go a long way toward neutralizing discontent.

Food

Peking Duck may be the most famous of the capital's culinary offerings, and with its crisp red skin, tender meat, and huge array of sauces and accompaniments, it's easy to see why. But a fancy duck dinner doesn't quite capture the real food scene in Beijing, where a wide variety of cheap, filling, and delicious fare is the default. Whereas rice is the staple food in southern China, northerners tend to go for bread and noodles. For breakfast, Beijingers tuck into *yóutiáo* (油条, fried dough sticks) and wash it all down with hot soy milk. *Bǐng* (饼), a thin pancake-like bread, appears in all forms, from the crunchy *jiānbǐng* (煎饼) to meat-stuffed *ròubǐng* (肉饼), and from *jiǔcài bǐng* (韭菜饼) stuffed with cabbage, chives, leeks, and egg to *dàbǐng* (大饼) sprinkled with sesame seeds.

Beijing is a dining out kind of town. There are 60,000 restaurants here and many of them overflow out onto the sidewalks. Roasted sweet potatoes are for sale on practically every corner, along with boiled corn and, in the summer, slices of pineapple or melon on a stick. You can't take two steps in Beijing without passing a place selling *chuan'er* (chuàn'er; 串儿) – meat kebabs, usually lamb – *jiǎozi* (饺子; dumplings), *bāozi* (包子; steamed buns with meat or veggie filling), or *mántóu* (慢头; steamed bread rolls). Food from other areas of China is well-represented in Beijing too (spicy Sichuan, sweeter Shanghai, hearty Mongolian hot pot, etc), and there are even Western imports like KFC and Pizza Hut. For more information on dining in Beijing, see page 205.

Hutongs

What is a hutong? Well, in short they are ancient alleyways originally built by the Mongolians around 800 years ago. The original hutongs were shaped and formed over the Yuan, Ming and Qing Dynasties by *siheyuan* (four-sided courtyard houses). Over time and subsequent population booms, the hutong neighborhood planning structure soon formed into a fascinating maze of narrow alleyways, while many *siheyuan* were divided up into sections to fit different families. The communists of the '60s and the capitalists of today have had a field day bulldozing these classical streets and houses to make room for the new.

A saying among Beijing old-timers is, "There are 360 large hutongs and as many small hutongs as the hairs on an ox." That may have been true 60 years ago, but it's less true every day, as the city continually razes these ancient alleyways to construct higher-density neighborhoods with more modern amenities. In fact, in 1949 the city had 3,050 hutongs, and in 2004 the count numbered only 1,300. Today, it's estimated that less than 1,000 remain.

Among the dusty and ramshackle dwellings crammed into many hutongs, there are some real gems, like beautifully preserved ancient courtyard homes complete with elaborately painted façades and glazed tile roofs. Some hutongs, like Nánluógǔ Xiàng (南锣鼓巷), Wǔdàoyíng (五道营), and Fāngjiā (方家), have been almost completely co-opted by bars, restaurants, boutiques, and shops catering to tourists, expats, and wealthy Chinese. Do a little wandering and you can easily find yourself on a relatively untouched street, with laundry hung out to dry, folks gathered chatting on stoops, and grandparents working out on low-tech public pull-up bars.

Population

According to ubiquitous government posters, the Beijing spirit is "Patriotism, Innovation, Inclusiveness and Virtue." But what it means to be a Beijinger has become harder to pin down with the influx of an estimated 7 million plus migrant workers to the capital. Though they build the subways, staff the restaurants, nanny the children, and generally subsidize the increase in living standards for the middle-class by working for scandalously low wages, they're derided as *wàidìrén* (外地人 ; outside place people) and are blamed for everything from overpopulation to pollution. Making matters worse, because the government distributes social benefits through a residence permit called *hùkǒu* (户口) that is tied to one's place of birth, these migrants have little access to health-care or education once they leave their hometown since they don't hold a Beijing *hukou*.

At last count, Beijing's population numbered over 20 million, making it one of the most highly populated cities in the entire world. As if this 20 million figure wasn't impressive enough, the reality of Beijing's population may be even bigger thanks to these migrant workers. The city's true headcount is notoriously difficult to grasp because of the transient and unregistered nature of its migrant population, but one unofficial counting method that has been suggested measures the number of Beijing transportation smartcards issued, which Beijing's Municipal Commission announced is now over 40 million. Even accounting for tourists (most of whom don't use them) and other visitors, that number is certainly far higher than the 20 million usually put forth. Despite serious air pollution and extremely high property prices, by some estimates more than 500,000 newcomers arrive in Beijing every year.

The curious demographics of Beijing's population have also been shaped in other ways. Beijing is a city of only "one child," thanks to the One Child Policy that was introduced in 1979 to control China's mushrooming population. The result is what some call "Little Emperor Syndrome," where every child is an only-child and therefore subject to a confusing mix of smothering adoration and painfully high expectations for success. A preference for male children led to widespread selective abortions, causing men to outnumber women so badly that by 2020 it's estimated that more than 24 million Chinese men may be unable to find a spouse. So, Beijing, along with other Chinese cities, is full of single males and spoiled children. Yikes!

China boasts 56 ethnicities among its population, though Han Chinese are by far the majority. In Beijing, the Han nationality makes up 96.5% of the total, while the other 55 ethnic minorities total about 300,000 and are mostly Manchu, Hui, and Mongolian. Beijing's population also includes a growing number of foreigners. As many as 200,000 from dozens of countries are attracted by adventure and opportunity in industries ranging from English teaching to management consulting and international politics. Though generally welcomed, expats are subject to occasional police "crackdowns" when global politics demand a demonstration of China's power.

Beijing's top notch universities have attracted some of the brightest individuals from around the country, and the city's boom economy has lead many recent graduates to stick around and work. For this reason, most of the people you meet in Beijing aren't actually from Beijing; you can find Chinese from Xinjiang to Shanghai here. Unfortunately, there isn't enough opportunity to go around Beijing's (and in general China's) enormous population, leading many graduates to settle for menial jobs in the proverbial "ant colony." This new subculture known as "the ant tribe"— coined because they live in such cramped, claustrophobic conditions with as many as a dozen sharing small apartment spaces — are young educated college grads working low-skill, low-wage jobs in Beijing. The competition in this city is so high that the ants are making less than minimum wage and are forced to live on a shoestring budget. Beijing's most famous ant colony is in the neighborhood of Tangjialing.

The Car Boom

Once a model of *feng shui* harmony and proportion emanating from the central Forbidden City, the layout of the city itself is now dominated by concentric ring road highways, numbered from two (the innermost) to the soon-to-be-constructed seven — an epic 950 km (590 mi) circle that will travel all the way south to Tiānjīn (天津) and into neighboring Hebei Province. Why so many roads? Well, there are a whole lot of cars, so many that the government was forced to institute a monthly lottery process to determine who has the right to drive on any given day.

How many cars are there today? At last count in 2012, the number reached just over 5 million. That's one car for every man, woman and child in the entire country of Finland! And you can bet that number is rising each day. In February 2013, 1.42 million applicants competed for 18,511 plates. Even with the quota, experts expect to see 6 million cars on the road by 2015.

Tourism

Of the 45 UNESCO World Heritage Sites in China, Beijing boasts an impressive six of them: the Forbidden City (pg 62), the Summer Palace (pg 71), the Temple of Heaven (pg 78), the Great Wall (pg 50), the Ming Tombs (pg 138), and the Peking Man Site (pg 139).

The United Nations World Tourism Organization predicts that China will become the number one international tourism destination by the year 2020 – it's already third, behind France and the United States, despite the fact that it has only accepted visitors since the late 1970s. Some 26.3 million foreigners came to China in 2013, and 3.9 million of them made their way to Beijing (the number for Shanghai was 5.1 million). Where do the masses of visitors hail from? In 2013, Americans constituted the largest number with 747,587 checking out China's capital, followed by South Koreans, and Japanese with 377,105 and 248,751, respectively. Germans (230,317) and Brits (175,425) rounded out the top five.

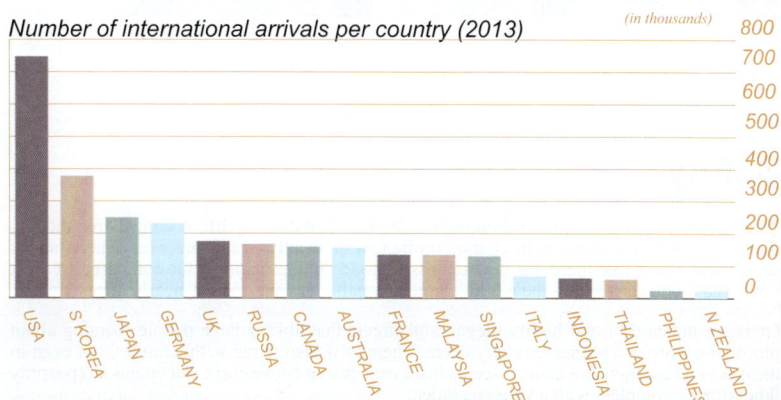

Number of international arrivals per country (2013) (in thousands)

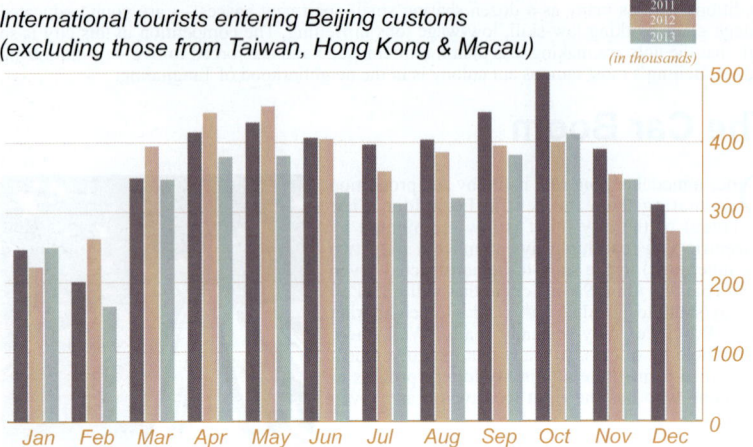

International tourists entering Beijing customs (excluding those from Taiwan, Hong Kong & Macau)

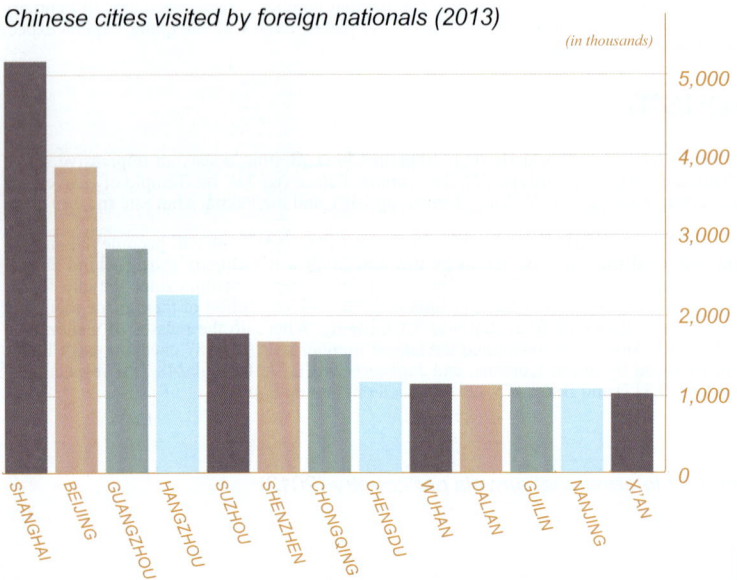

Chinese cities visited by foreign nationals (2013)

Safety

In regards to crime, Beijing is extremely safe. This is not to say life is danger-free though, since crossing the street with chaotic traffic can be deadly, scams are everywhere, and it seems that every day there are new reports of food contamination. But compared to most cities and towns throughout the world – large or small – violent crime is nearly nonexistent.

Guns are unheard of and highly illegal, and streets that always have people roaming about means there are eye witnesses everywhere. The city is also wired with cameras, but even in the places where there are none, it seems that every citizen between six and 96 has an (possibly fake) iPhone complete with a video recorder.

The most prominent crime that any Beijing visitor needs to watch out for is surely thievery, especially pickpockets. Make sure your backpacks and purses are zipped up tight and hold them in front when you're in a crowded place. Watch your pockets while you're compressed into the subway car with 10,000 people, and consider keeping your cash in a money belt under your clothes, or at least in a place on your torso where you can see it. Finally, though this might sound obvious, don't drink so much that you fall down the stairs, crash your bike or tumble into the gutter. There are plenty of party spots in Beijing, and we all know accidents can happen when people are intoxicated. Be sure to pace yourself and remember to ask, "Do I really need another shot right now?"

Another way tourists lose their hard-earned cash is through scams. They are waiting in most of the crowded Beijing tourist locations, so make sure to check out our full list of scams on page 312 in Hot Topics.

Beijing Layout

Beijing Districts

Beijing sits on the North China Plain at roughly the same latitude as Philadelphia. The Xishan and Yanshan mountain ranges curve around the city to the north and west, shielding it from the winds and sands of the Gobi Desert. Despite this natural barrier, spring sees sandstorms whipping dust into Beijing just as the city thaws from the bone-dry freezing winter. The generally pleasant spring weather leads to wet hot monsoon-influenced summers, followed by crisp blue-sky autumns.

Beijing is an overwhelmingly flat city (hence the popularity of bicycles for getting around). The tallest point in downtown Beijing, Coal Hill (Méi Shān; 煤山) in Jingshan Park (pg 70), is only 88 m (289 ft) high. A series of lakes dot the landscape of central Beijing – the three northernmost lakes of Xīhǎi, Hòuhǎi and Qiánhǎi are collectively known as Shíchàhǎi (pg

Corner tower of the Forbidden City; the Forbidden City and Tian'anmen Square lie in the middle of Xicheng and Dongcheng, meaning you can easily reach them from both districts

98) and are heavily visited and lined with hookah bars, rickshaw drivers, and souvenir stands. Just to the south, the lake of Běihǎi is surrounded by a lovely park, while Zhōnghǎi (中海) and Nánhǎi (南海) are within Zhōngnánhǎi (中南海), a private residence compound for China's political leaders. In the northwest, mountains and grand forests characterize the land, but if you continue north just outside of the city you'll reach the Great Wall (pg 50) and then the barren desert sands of the Gobi.

There are 16 districts in Beijing. While that number sounds overwhelming, don't sweat it, most of them are rural areas where you probably won't be going (unless you want to spend some time out by the Great Wall). The Forbidden City is the geographic apex of the city, meaning all ring roads and metro lines run around it. Inside the Second Ring Road (which more or less follows Line 2 of the metro), the Forbidden City divides two of the city's most popular districts: Xicheng (West City) and Dongcheng (East City). It doesn't take a genius to figure out which of these districts lies on either side of the Forbidden City. A little bit outside of Xicheng is the Haidian District, and to the east of Dongcheng is the Chaoyang District. To keep it simple, you can find just about everything you need in these four districts, but each one possesses it's own unique flair and personal touch:

Dongcheng District (东城区): This is hutong central, but the areas directly to the east of Tian'anmen Square are going through a fairly massive makeover as luxury hotels, tourist massage parlors and expensive restaurants are becoming the name of the game. Still, if you wander just off the main drags, you can easily catch the essence of Old Beijing in its surviving hutongs.

Best Attractions: Tian'anmen Square & Surrounding Area (pg 86), Lama Temple Area (pg 116), the Hutongs (pg 110), Forbidden City (pg 62)

Best Drinking: Cuju (pg 245), Zajia (pg 247), Temple & Dada (pg 250)

Best Eating: Nanluogu Xiang (pg 101), Mr Shi's Dumplings (pg 216), Argo (pg 236)

Xicheng District (西城区): The west side of the Forbidden City is a mixed bag. On one hand you've got your old crumbling hutongs that haven't seen the renovations that the east side is getting. On the other hand, along Financial Street, modern skyscrapers and transparent buildings mark the tree lined avenues. In the middle of it all are the Shichahai lakes. Xicheng is a great place to relax and chill by the water and get lost in its labyrinth of ancient hutongs.

Best Attractions: Tian'anmen Square & Surrounding Area (pg 86), Drum and Bell Tower (pg 100), Beihai Park (pg 107), Shichahai Area (pg 98), Forbidden City (pg 62)

Best Drinking: Shichahai Bar Street (pg 100)

Best Eating: The Box (pg 229), 4 Corners (pg 234)

Haidian District (海淀区): To the northwest of Xicheng is Haidian, and the further into it you travel, the more you get away from the center of the action… that is, until you reach the college town at Tsinghua University and Peking University at Wudaokou (on subway Line 13). Here, you'll find cheap bars and restaurants, mostly with a funky international vibe that has been greatly influenced by the local and expat student populations. There are even the treasures of the Summer Palace, the Old Summer Palace, and tons of great nature and hiking

trails far from the concrete jungle.

Best Attractions: Summer Palaces and University Area (pg 71), Fragrant Hills Park (pg 172)

Best Drinking: Propaganda (pg 248), Wudaokou Beer Garden (pg 247)

Best Eating : Around Wudaokou for Japanese and Korean (pg 244), East is Red (pg 240)

Chaoyang District (朝阳区): Chaoyang is without question one of the nicest areas of town, and for this reason it's no wonder so many of the local expats choose to call this place home. You're not going to find any hutongs, rolling mountains or ancient palaces, but if you're looking to raise the bar and experience the finer side of Beijing, this is where you want to start.

Best Attractions: CCTV Building (pg 162), Chaoyang Park (pg 172), 798 Art District (pg 123), Olympic Legacies (pg 127)

Best Drinking: In and around Sanlitun Village & Bar Street (pg 243), Heaven Supermarket (pg 244)

Best Eating: Haidiliao (pg 215), Lei Garden (pg 215), Quanjude (pg 217), Duck de Chine (pg 218)

Crazy Beijing

"It's big, it's polluted, it's crowded, and it's either too cold and dry or too wet and hot. But somehow it still manages to be my favorite city in the world!"

Anyone who knows China is aware that this country is just one big (and often hilarious) contradiction. With Beijing being the center of it all, sometimes you just can't help noticing some of the quirky shenanigans that happen in this city day in and day out. Some are funny, and some make the average local or expat want to pull their hair out, but no matter what your take is, they are the aspects that make Beijing the place that it is.

Where's the restroom?

Beijing has some of the highest rent prices in the world. The only problem is if you plan on living in the hutongs you're likely going to pay hundreds of dollars a month for a studio that doesn't even have a bathroom. Get ready to pop a squat with your neighbors and even their kids in the communal pot down the road in sub-zero winter temps!

How much did you say the rent was again?

Even if you do find a modern apartment with its own bathroom, chances are you're still going to have to share it with at least one complete stranger. But if you get really, really lucky, then you may just find one all for yourself. Of course, if you live near the center of the city, rent will be higher, but even if you live an hour outside of town, you're still going to be paying close to US$500 per month for a small studio.

For this reason, a favorite conversation topic amongst local Beijingers is rent prices, and you can always see a group of people outside real estate companies complaining about the prices they have listed on their front windows. If you speak Chinese, don't be scared to strike up a conversation about rent with a local, it'll make their day! Especially when you compare housing prices here to the ones back home.

Don't forget your gas mask!

China is the world's number one investor in green energy, and yet in some miraculous way toxic clouds of pollution choke the major cities' airways. It's amazing how Beijing, one of the country's most important places, manages to suffer the most from this serious problem. And if pollution wasn't enough to hack a lung up, sand storms from the Gobi blow in during the spring, sandblasting cars, skin and eye balls alike. How many other major cities in the world still have sand-storms?

What skyline?

Beijing has more than 20 million people, so where are all the buildings? If you stand in the center of town, right in the middle of the hutongs, you'll notice that you aren't in a pile of massive skyscrapers. In other world metropolitan zones like New York, Tokyo and Hong Kong, you'd be overwhelmed with the height of the buildings surrounding you on each side. This is not the case in Beijing. The center is comprised of modest, one or two story buildings in the hutongs, making much of downtown feel like rural Hebei Province with a fantastic village-in-a-city vibe.

That's the skyline?

OK, so there is a skyline, but it's far to the east, after the Third Ring Road, and once you do lay your eyes upon it, you won't help but chuckle at the CCTV Building that locals have affectionately called the "Big Underpants" (see pg 162 to find out why). If a giant tower shaped like a raggedy pair of underwear wasn't enough, the municipal government has just announced plans to erect a gigantic structure that resembles an enormous… well, let's just say it'll be the most phallus-shaped icon in China.

Yes, this is Beijing's newest building, the new headquarters for the esteemed People's Daily. Ironically, it will join other Beijing modern structures such as the Bird's Nest and Big Underpants.

Where can I park my ride?

With so many cars and a massive shortage of parking spaces, sidewalks, street sides, parks, playgrounds, and even the entrance gates of apartment complexes have become parking lots. If you're not driving a car, you're probably on a bike, electric scooter, or motorcycle, and you can bet your last *baozi* that these machines will be squeezed inbetween cars for an awkward metal jigsaw puzzle. Besides making bike transportation a hassle, it can even turn walking down the street into a game of Tetris.

The Olympics…

China may have won a ton of medals in that fateful summer of 2008, but a lot of the town's citizens lost their houses due to the billions spent on the makeover. The municipal government went on a rampage, kicking old folks out of their ancient houses, only to tear them down to make the city look "more modern for the foreign eye." There were a handful of other controversies surrounding the Olympics as well, and the Bird's Nest Stadium still sits mostly idle. Now, with Beijing lobbying to host a Winter Games, some of the locals are left saying, "Oh no, not again!"

Home, sweet home!

Despite all of Beijing's ups and downs, at the end of the day most Beijingers still love the city and are proud to be a local. Maybe it's the thousands of years of history and culture or the never ending diversity of international and Chinese restaurants. Maybe it's the economic opportunities this great city has brought to many, or the numerous fun and unique activities just an arm's reach away. Whatever it is, there is something truly special about Beijing, and anyone who lives here long enough forms a love-hate relationship with the city – riding their bike through chaotic traffic in the middle of a sand storm, asking the person in the next stall over for an extra square of toilet paper, and making fun of the government's new blue-prints for the next "building of the future."

Holidays & Festivals

Public Holidays in the PRC				
Festival	Date	Legal Holidays	2014	2015
New Year's Day	Jan 1	1	Jan 1 – 3	Jan 1 – 3
Spring Festival	Follows the lunar calendar	3	Jan 30- Feb 5	Feb 18- Feb 24
Tomb Sweeping Festival (Qingming)	Apr 4 or 5	1	Apr 4- 6	Apr 4- 6
May Day	May 1	1	May 1- 3	May 1- 3
Dragon Boat Festival	Follows the lunar calendar	1	May 31- Jun 2	Jun 20- 22
Mid-Autumn Festival	Follows the lunar calendar	1	Sep 6- 8	Sep 26- 28
National Day	Oct 1	3	Oct 1- 7	Oct 1- 7

When Chinese New Year rolls around, the entire country buckles its seatbelt for the world's largest annual human migration. Train tickets sell out in a matter of seconds, buses overflow with travelers toting huge suitcases full of gifts, highways become parking lots, and drivers get out of their cars to walk dogs and do pushups while waiting for the traffic to budge an inch. For the masses of migrant workers and college students far from their hometowns, this trip may be the only time they make it home all year.

The majority of Chinese holidays unfold on a lunar calendar, and nowhere are they more vibrant than in Beijing. Chinese New Year (also known as Spring Festival; Chūn Jié; 春节) sees the city erupt with fireworks launched by local Beijingers (though the authorities have tried to restrict these homemade displays, you wouldn't know it from looking at the sky). It's as big as Christmas in the West, but it falls sometime between late January and mid-February and lasts about half a month. The New Year celebration concludes 15 days after it begins with the Lantern Festival (Yuánxiāo Jié; 元宵节), featuring a parade and a lion dance to honor the first full moon, and a whole lot of *yuánxiāo* (元宵; sticky rice dumplings with sweet fillings) are eaten up over the holiday.

In early April comes the Tomb Sweeping Festival (Qīngmíng Jié; 清明节), which was traditionally a time to visit ancestral gravesites to clean them and make offerings. These days, it's more likely to be celebrated with a spring outing of some sort. May Day (Wǔyī Guójì Láodòng Jié; 五一国际劳动节) on May 1st brings a three-day national holiday, while June's Dragon Boat Festival (Duānwǔ Jié; 端午节), honoring ancient poet and patriot Qū Yuán (屈原), brings high-spirited boat races and *zòngzi* (粽子; sticky rice dumplings).

For the Mid-Autumn Festival (Zhōngqiū Jié; 中秋节), usually taking place in September, families reunite and eat moon cakes, round pastries filled with rich red bean paste or the yolks of duck eggs. Revelers worship the Chinese goddess Cháng'é (嫦娥), who is said to inhabit the moon after taking her husband's elixir of immortality to keep it from a thief. The public holiday National Day (Guóqìng Jié; 国庆节) celebrates the October 1st founding of the People's Republic of China with a massive party in Tian'anmen Square, and the party extends for a full seven days, sometimes known as Golden Week (we do not suggest attempting to travel in China during this week).

Western holidays like Valentine's Day, Mother's Day and Christmas have also caught on to some extent, though really only as opportunities for commerce.

Unique Beijing Festivals

There are countless only-in-Beijing festivals and events to watch out for, and while there are certainly too many to mention in just a few breaths, we have drawn up a few of our favorites to wet your appetite.

Huangyaguan Great Wall Marathon

When: Third Saturday of May
As if hiking the rugged hills of the Great Wall was not difficult enough, a marathon is organized every summer. Beginning at Huangyaguan, near the city of Tianjin, the race also features a half marathon, a 10k and a 5k. Registration begins in July.

Red Leaf Festival

When: October 15 to November 7
Held in the beautiful Fragrant Hills Park on the east side of Haidian District, the Red Leaf Festival celebrates the magnificent colors and scenery that saturate the hillsides of eastern Beijing every autumn. Come for beautiful flower displays and food.

White Cloud Temple Fair

When: January and March
January sees an excellent temple fair at the Baiyun Temple (also known as the White Cloud Temple), that fills the grounds with craft makers, performers and snacks of all kinds. The temple holds another festival during March to honor the birthday of its founder, Qiu Chuji.

798 Art Festival

When: End of September
Located in the 798 Art District in Beijing's affluent Chaoyang District, the 798 Art Festival is one of China's premier art shows.

Beijing International Beer Festival

When: August 15 to 31
Though it certainly doesn't hold up to the Oktoberfest of Munich that it purports to emulate, the Beijing International Beer Festival definitely puts on a respectable show, with international beers, a carnival atmosphere and plenty of drinking contests.

Beijing Chrysanthemum Exhibition

When: September 26 to November 16
One of the four traditional flowers of China, chrysanthemums come into a fantastic bloom every autumn in Beijing, and you can catch some outstanding displays of them at parks around the city. The best places are at Beihai Park and the International Flower Port.

Temple Fairs

A range of temple fairs erupt around Beijing throughout the year. Some temples have their own special events to celebrate a late monk's birthday or some other special event, but nearly every temple holds celebrations during Chinese New Year/Spring Festival.

Bottoms up at the Beijing Brew Fest

Weather

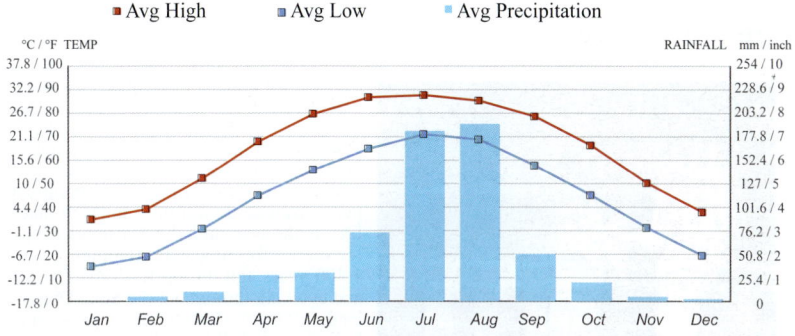

Beijing Average Temperature & Precipitation

Beijing's weather is schizophrenic, and anyone here will tell you that seasons can often transition over the course of one week. The winters (December to February) are dry with little (or no) snow, and temps hover around the freezing mark. It's also during the winter that pollution levels soar since most folks keep warm by using coal as their preferred heating fuel. Summers (June to August), on the other hand, will make you believe you're in a Brazilian rainforest: they're hot and humid, and torrential downpours and thunderstorms are common. The spring (March to May) and autumn (September to November) periods, both lasting about three months, are the most pleasant times to visit since temperatures are moderate and humidity and thunderstorms are tame.

Shichahai Summer vs Shichahai Winter

The Arts

Peking Opera

The most famous of Beijing's traditional musical styles is by far Peking Opera (Jīngjù; 京剧). Known also as Beijing Opera, this timeless art still holds a notable amount of interest among the Chinese today, and it's quite easy to find traditional performances around the capital in places like teahouses and the National Center for the Performing Arts. Beginning some 1,300 years ago during the Tang Dynasty and evolving throughout the Song Dynasty, Beijing Opera came to encompass songs, ballads and folklore through a loosely related set of dazzling skills, including martial arts, acrobatics and stylized dance. Face painting and the wearing of elaborate masks evolved as well, mimicking a practice begun by soldiers attempting to intimidate their enemies.

Mixed sex performance groups were banned for hundreds of years, leading to a tradition of actors taking on the roles of the opposite sex and ultimately bringing this practice to the level of a stylized performance technique. One of the most famous Beijing Opera performers of the 20th century (and truly of any century) is Mei Lanfang. Known for his perfection of the female role, he was ultimately immortalized when his feminine performance techniques were adopted into their own school.

Beijing Opera is considered far and wide as the elite of Chinese operatic styles, which boast at least one different style for every provincial region of China. Peking Opera makes use of three of China's most traditional and spiritually haunting instruments, the *erhu*, the *jinghu* and the *yueqin* (all of which are stringed instruments). The *erhu* is two stringed and set to a low register, while the *jinghu*, another two-stringed piece, is set to a higher tuning and plays much like a Chinese viola. The two often work in concert and can produce some of the most stirring music of traditional China. Sometimes played individually and often accompanied by the four-stringed guitar-like *yueqin*, these instruments make up the quintessential sounds of ancient Chinese music and are staples in Beijing's traditional opera.

Music

For those expecting to find their way to a new punk rock, rock, metal or blues club every night and witness the sonic power of Beijing's most uproarious rockers, you will be happy campers. China may have caught on to the rock and roll scene several decades late – almost entirely the fault of the oppressive Cultural Revolution – but these days Chinese rock is a force to be reckoned with (especially at the underground level), and nowhere else is that more prevalent than in Beijing.

Unlike some cities that double as both political capitals and financial capitals (e.g. Paris, London), Beijing is solely a seat of political power (the financial capital is Shanghai). This is a massive fuel for the fire of underground rock and punk

rock in Beijing, where the stifling pressure of the iron-fisted ruling party is felt here more than anywhere else in China, giving rise to alternative (and at times) revolutionary music. Because outspokenness and government criticism is so muted, most of these bands must play at night in small local spots, and few can do more than make a poor-man's living off of the income from continuous gigs. Between the silencing power of the government and the piracy epidemic that grips much of the country, making music by selling CDs is not possible. If you're into seeing some rock groups in Beijing, a few names to keep an eye out for are Brain Failure and Subs, the new wave sounds of the Re-TROS, or noise-pop from Snapline. For some outstanding Blues that sounds like its straight out of the Mississippi Delta, check out the Western trained sounds of the Big John Blues Band, who usually play at their home venue CD Blues near Ritan Park. See page 250 for music venues.

Hip hop is in a nascent stage, but it and electronic music are beginning to take off as well, and there is no shortage of rap or DJs in Beijing. The biggest name is Mickey Zhang, which you can easily spot on fliers around town, but it's a piece of cake finding electro, house, techno, drum and base or trance just about anywhere downtown on any given weekend.

Visual Arts

Socialist Realism

As the traditional aesthetics that had governed Chinese arts for thousands of years went into rapid decline during the rise of communism, propaganda campaigns aimed at confronting and gilding the plight of the lower classes were commissioned to fill the artistic void. So hijacked was the art scene in Beijing after 1949 that anything unrelated to promoting the party was banned outright. A huge influx of foreign techniques and concepts filled an aesthetic scene that had been homegrown and focused on the natural and ethereal worlds for countless generations, and overnight the Chinese infatuation with mystical and metaphysical topics was pounded into cold hard realism, stating the concrete and ruminating on detail.

Soviet art was imported wholesale, and nothing was left untouched by the hammer and sickle. Traditional Taoist and Buddhist dreamscapes were replaced by blazing red suns, burly peasants and industrial scenes with Maoist or Stalinist quotations. New buildings were designed in monolithic granite and marble faces, cordoned with fences and topped with red stars. Sculpture drew from purported scenes of peasant struggle against landlords or marches of the PLA. All interpretation of beauty was legislated to be seen through the eyes of Marxism; anything not complying was removed.

Propaganda Art

Littered across quirky shops, touristy streets and the canvases of modern artists today, propaganda art was first forced into the aesthetics of China after the founding of the PRC in 1949. Most propaganda posters focused on scenes of the working class with men and women proudly raising tools against backdrops of smoke stacks and machinery, but also included a plethora of wild imagery, including the crushing of counterrevolutionary activity, the success of the Cultural Revolution and the Great Leap Forward, Maoist ideals, fat and "well-nourished" Chinese babies, and the "utopias" of China and North Korea. However, propaganda art went into rapid decline after the death of Mao and during the 1980s under the reforms of Deng Xiaoping. Nearly all of what you will find today are reproductions that are sought for their kitschy appeal.

Modern Art Movements

Most post-1989 art ruminated on the loss suffered that summer at Tian'anmen and became obsessed with feelings of isolation and socioeconomic issues. Consumer culture became a hot topic, as did social change and materialism. Many works, like those of Yue Minjun, became extremely cynical through pieces such as his stirring set of masks feigning joy through horrible pain. After an initial mass exodus of artists to the West, many of them returned a decade later, bringing with them a smattering of new inspiration and ideas from their journeys in places like Paris, London, Rome and New York City. The government's grip on expression ever-so-slowly loosened throughout the 90s, and though censorship certainly remains, it has slackened the reigns enough to allow a burgeoning and avant-garde art scene in much of modern China (though, things may be tightening once again under the new leadership of President Xi Jinping).

Today, the most nascent and modish scenes are blossoming in Beijing's 798 Art District. Ai Wei Wei, perhaps best known in the West for his outspoken dissidence, has been an integral part of 798. His works range from helping to design the Bird's Nest Stadium in Beijing – which he has distanced himself from and called "a fake smile of bad taste" – to his temporary exhibition of a million hand-painted porcelain sunflower seeds that graced the floor of the Tate Modern Art Museum in London. Like many outspoken artists, writers or bloggers, Ai's studios have been repeatedly shut, and he is harassed under the guises of operating "illegal buildings" (as was said when his Shanghai studio was ruined) or charges of "tax evasion" (when his Beijing home was raided).

Literature

As the Qing Dynasty was on its way out and two revolutionary forces – the Nationalists and the Communists – competed for control of the country, many Chinese were fueled by new ideas of the importance of the common person. Through the fire of an exciting spirit of a new China, the author Lu Xun broke free of the haughty grip of Classical Chinese and in 1918 wrote "A Madman's Diary" in vernacular (common) Chinese. It was as revolutionary as it was stunning; in one piece he had broken the shackles of thousands of years of literary elitism and invited millions of commoners to the reading party. His work singlehandedly changed literature in China, and from its publishing on, all works would be written just the way normal people spoke and thought.You can visit Lu Xun's former residence (pg 132) in Beijing.

Unless you can read Chinese, your options for reading contemporary Chinese authors are very limited. One sure-fire option is the short story writer Zhu Wen, whose 2007 collection *I Love Dollars and Other Stories of China* has been published in English and is a fantastically humorous criticism of the get-rich movement in China and its many absurdities.

Mo Yan (pictured on the left) won the Nobel Prize in 2008 for his fascinating, and at times heart-wrenching, novel *Life and Death are Wearing Me Out*. It's about a kind and wealthy land-owner who is reincarnated as various farm animals upon his death and he experiences the development of China since the '50s through their eyes.

Beijing Reading List

You'll get more out of your trip if you do some reading about Beijing before you arrive. It doesn't have to be a dry history tome, either – there are plenty of contemporary novels and non-fiction that will get your imagination going.

Last Days of Old Beijing, Michael Myer

An American takes a position at a local public school and quickly becomes a fixture in his rapidly crumbling hutong neighborhood. Despite the understated humor, it provides a fascinating perspective on the constant changes to the capital's landscape and outlook.

Wild Swans: Three Daughters of China, Jung Chang

While it's not specifically Beijing-focused, this classic memoir, which has sold more than 13 million copies, captures the scope of recent Chinese history by following three generations of women in one family as they overcome war, the Cultural Revolution, and the frantic and competitive world of modern China. Gripping and personal, it's a great history lesson. Be aware that this book is banned in China.

The Last Empress, Anchee Min

This work of fictionalized history takes one of the most notorious women in Chinese history, the Empress Dowager Cixi, and creates a powerful first-person narrative that makes her surprisingly relatable. Cixi's position, trapped between those who wanted to open China to the West and those who wanted it to remain cloistered, echoes on some level the current struggle within the Communist Party.

Beijing Coma, Ma Jian

One of China's best-known novelists takes on the Tian'anmen Square events with a well-crafted metaphor for the country's relationship with that day. A student activist wounded in the square remains in a coma, unable to move on or forget, but also unable to express himself.

Rickshaw Boy, Lao She

This famous satirical novel, published in 1936, helped initiate Chinese literature in its modern form – previously, elevated Classical Chinese was the dominant language of writing. The natural style of expression combines with wry observation and vivid description to create a haunting story of hard labor and misfortune in Beijing.

Film

Film in China actually goes all the way back to 1905, when the first home-grown Chinese movie, *Conquering Jun Mountain,* was filmed in Beijing. Apart from *Conquering Jun Mountain,* which was simply an excerpt from Beijing Opera, the capital of the Chinese film industry was the set in the exotic flair and sophistication of Shanghai, which opened its first cinema in 1908. The industry grew to cover over 140 Shanghai theaters until its climax in the 1930s (peaking with the 1937 comedy about three unemployed university graduates, *Crossroads*), but declined under the Japanese invasion that began the Sino-Japanese War and WWII in Asia.

Creative film further declined under the watch of the Communist Party, who regulated it to glorify the Party and produce propaganda at breakneck speed and efficacy. The filmmakers who weren't already sent running to the West by the Japanese packed up their bags and headed to Hong Kong. Filmmaking in the Mainland came to a full standstill as only eight movies were made between 1966 and 1977.

Two years after the death of Mao Zedong, the reopening of the Beijing Film Academy precipitated the birth of the esteemed and internationally acclaimed "Fifth Generation." The cinematic creations of the Fifth Generation began to move away from the colorless and stern visage of communist complexion and churned out beautifully conceived tragedies that (while they often garnered less interest in the Mainland) blew the socks off of movie goers and critics in the West. Some of the best known and stalwartly appreciated early films of the Fifth

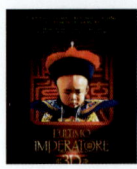    

Generation directors are Chen Kaige's *Yellow Earth* (1984), Zhang Yimou's *Red Sorghum* (1987), and Tian Zhuangzhuang's *The Horse Thief* (1986).

These days, contemporary Chinese film is driven largely by a market – domestic and international – with an insatiable hunger for historical pieces, mostly in the vein of martial arts action or heroic war tales. While much of the rest of China's film industry is dominated by sappy love dramas and superficial stories of spoiled socialites, others boldly approach deeper social issues. See our list below for some excellent recommendations of films about Beijing.

Beijing Films

The Last Emperor (Mòdài Huángdì; 末代皇帝) (1987) – Bernardo Bertolucci's seven-Oscar-winning film chronicles the life of China's last emperor, Puyi, as his life is transformed by the end of dynastic rule in China and the ascension of the Communist Party.

Farewell My Concubine (Bàwáng Biéjī; 霸王别姬) (1993) – Chen Kaige's masterpiece follows the lives of two friends from Beijing's School of Opera as they struggle through the political and social mayhem that gripped China from 1920 to the Cultural Revolution.

In the Heat of the Sun (Yángguāng Cànlàn de Rìzi; 阳光灿烂的日子) (1994) – Directed by Jiang Wen, this stirring and surreal piece is about frenzied Beijing youth during the final days of the Cultural Revolution.

Beijing Bicycle (Shíqīsuì de Dānchē; 十七岁的单车) (2003) – Following the young courier Guo as he tracks his stolen mountain bike throughout Beijing, Wang Xiaoshuai's colorful and mesmerizing story is a top pick.

Lost In Beijing (Píngguǒ; 苹果) (2007) – Directed by Li Yu, this film, which was too steamy for Chinese censors, depicts the story of a female massage parlor worker and her love triangle with her boss and his wife. It all takes place as Beijing changes at a frenetic pace, and the twists and turns make it a great choice.

Language

Mandarin

It's difficult to identify a Chinese language because the ten main dialects that would comprise it – Mandarin, Jin, Wu, Hui, Gan, Xiang, Min, Hakka, Cantonese (or Yue), and Ping – are actually considered separate languages by many linguists. In fact, the line between dialect and language is quite blurry, but for the sake of simplicity we will discuss these varieties of Chinese as different Chinese languages. Within each of these languages, dozens of dialects can be found, many of which can vary by village. This means that two speakers of Jin from different villages of Shanxi Province may have a difficult time understanding each other because their local dialects are different, even though they speak the same language, and this problem would be further complicated if these two people traveled to a region of China where another language, like Cantonese, is dominant.

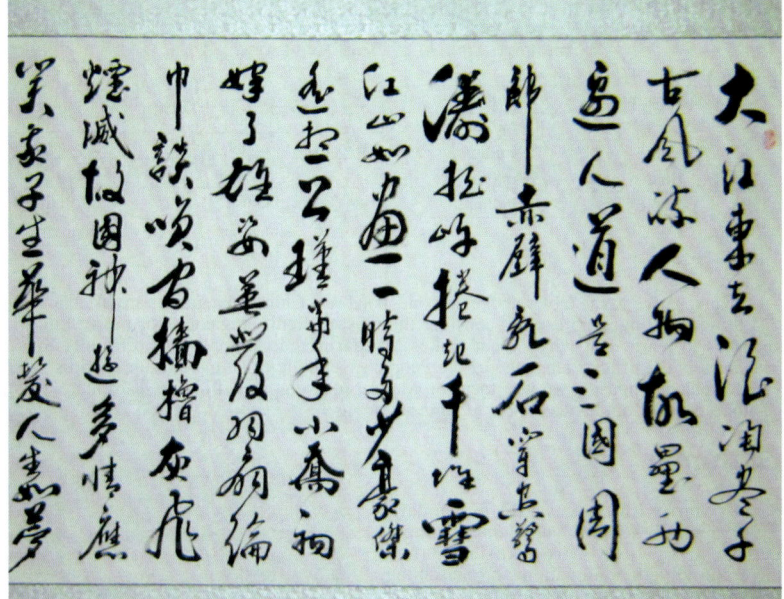

Though Beijing is largely a city of immigrants, the only language you'll really need to be concerned with here is Mandarin. The dominant language for a vast stretch of China from the northeast to the southwest (and up into some regions in the northwest), Mandarin first came about in the Ming Dynasty as the official language of the Han imperial court. Today, there are numerous dialects of Mandarin, but the one that is China's official language today is called Pǔtōnghuà (普 通 话) – or "Common Speech." Developed and instituted by the Communists, Putonghua is based off the Beijing dialect, and though it incorporates some elements from other Mandarin dialects, it is extremely similar to the common Beijing dialect (called Běijīnghuà; 北京话), but not exactly the same. The similarities mostly come in the form of tones (which can vary in other dialects of Mandarin) and vocabulary, but slang and colloquialisms of Beijinghua are unique to the local dialect. Since Putonghua is generally called Mandarin in the West, from here on out we will simply refer to it as Mandarin.

Mandarin is the standard communication tool for China's many speakers of different languages and dialects. For example, if a native of Chengdu, Sichuan Province and a native of Xi'an, Shaanxi Province met, communication would be almost impossible because of how different their dialects are. If they spoke Mandarin, however, communication would be no problem because this dialect is the standard speech throughout the country.

When people from different regions of China speak Mandarin, they invariably have a local accent. It's easy to differentiate a Beijing/northeastern accent due to the use of the hard "er" (儿) sound. Visitors are shocked when they come to Beijing and hear locals speaking like pirates since it sounds so different from what they are used to hearing from Chinese movies (most of which were produced in Hong Kong and use Cantonese, not Mandarin). If you travel to other parts of the nation, you may notice that Mandarin speakers in other regions tend to drop this hard "er" sound. So, when asking "where?" a Beijinger will say *na'er* (哪儿) and a southerner will say *nali* (哪里).

Despite the differences, the Beijing accent of Mandarin is the one taught in schools and universities across the globe. For this reason, Beijing is perhaps the best place for foreign exchange students to learn Mandarin.

Mandarin 101

Top 5 most widely spoken languages in terms of native speakers		
1	Mandarin	955 million
2	Spanish	407 million
3	English	359 million
4	Hindi	295 million
5	Arabic	293 million

Top 10 hardest languages for native English speakers to learn (in no particular order)			
1	Basque	6	Mandarin
2	Arabic	7	Japanese
3	Cantonese	8	Estonian
4	Finnish	9	Polish
5	Hungarian	10	Korean

As you can see in the tables above, not one, but TWO Chinese languages are listed among those that linguistic experts consider the most difficult languages for native English speakers to learn. But why? What makes Mandarin and Cantonese so difficult? Since Mandarin is the official language of the People's Republic of China and the world's most widely spoken language, we will focus on Mandarin. If you would like to learn more about Cantonese, check out Panda Guides *Hong Kong*.

Grammar

Let's start with the easy stuff. Mandarin grammar is actually surprisingly simple. Unlike many Indo-European languages, there are no verb conjugations, no masculine, feminine or neutral forms, and no cases. In its most basic forms, Mandarin's past tense simply requires that you add *le* (了) to a verb or to the end of the sentence. To speak in the future tense, simply add *huì* (会) before the verb. Apart from a few other words like "already" (yǐjīng; 已经), the past participle "have" (guò; 过), or "going to" (jiāng; 将), there aren't many other verb tenses for basic communication.

Example:

I go. – Wǒ qù. – 我去。

I went. – Wǒ qù le. – 我去了。

I have gone. – Wǒ qù guò. – 我去过。

I already went. – Wǒ yǐjīng qù le. – 我已经去了。

I will go. – Wǒ huì qù.- 我会去。

I am going to go. – Wǒ jiāng qù.- 我将去。

Notice that the character 去 (to go) stays the same, unlike in English where the verb "to go" transforms to "went," "gone" and "going to go." With these few simple words, you can easily inflect your sentence for past, present and future with ease. But don't get too confident; if the entire language was so easy, everyone would be speaking Mandarin.

Tones

This is the aspect of Mandarin that is particularly difficult for foreigners because these kinds of tones don't exist in English or other Western languages. The majority of the world's languages – including English – do indeed use tones, but few use them to distinguish different words and morphological meanings. Whereas English uses tones to show things like questions ("Him?" vs "Him!"), or emotions like anger, urgency, worry and others, Chinese uses tones for these and word-level meanings. In Mandarin, there are four tones and one neutral tone that distinguish meanings among the language's endless homophones (words that are pronounced the same but have two different meanings, like "bow" as in ribbon and "bow" as in a bow and arrow) and homonyms (words that sound similar to one another but have different meanings, like "scents" and "sense.")

In Mandarin, there are many more homophones and homonyms than in English or other Indo-European languages, and tones are the only ways to differentiate meanings. For example, "yanjiu" is the phonetic pronunciation for the Chinese word "to study" (yánjiū: 研究). However, this homophone sounds almost exactly the same as the word "smoking and drinking" (yānjiǔ; 烟酒). The only difference between these two very different words are their tones. For studying, *yanjiu* has *yan* in the second tone and *jiu* in the first tone. For drinking and smoking, *yan* is in the first tone and *jiu* is in the third tone.

These goofy homophones and homonyms make it easy for a student to nonchalantly tell his or her parents about college life. Instead of downplaying the boredom of diligent student life by saying, "eh, studying is studying," with the nimble shift of a tone, the student is actually telling his or her folks that "studying is drinking and smoking."

Characters

If the tones, homonyms and homophones weren't already brain-busters, then characters most certainly are. There are tens of thousands of Chinese characters, but luckily most of these are not used in common written language. Today, you need to memorize around 3,000 characters to be truly literate, but the average educated Chinese person knows more than 5,000. With so many characters, the paring of different characters together to make compound words, and some characters having more than one pronunciation, it's no wonder Chinese students cannot fully read until their early teens.

Apart from reading, writing is perhaps the most difficult attribute of all. The mere fact that you need to memorize thousands of characters is daunting; what makes them even harder is that these characters are comprised of multiple strokes. For example, the character for "person" is rén (人) and only takes two stokes. However, the common word for "to wipe" or "to clean" (cā; 擦) has 17 strokes! And if you mess up, it's wrong, plain and simple. Unlike baseball, where it's "three strikes and you're out," in Mandarin it's one stroke and you're out!

> We could go on and on about the difficulty of Mandarin, but why waste your valuable study time. Go to our phrasebook on page 336 to learn some phrases along with some other useful information about Mandarin to get you speaking the local lingo like a pro!

Beijingers in Their Own Words

We asked a few Beijingers – some natives, some transplants – what's unique about the character of Beijing and why travelers should put it on their list.

Ken, 30, Chinese

Ken is my English name – it's important for me to have one because I work in a wine shop and many of the customers are foreigners. I love my job for the same reasons I love Beijing. It's busy, it's loud, and there are new people every day.

David, 35, American

What attracted me to Beijing? I'll probably get in trouble if I don't say it was my wife. We met during college in the US, where she was studying abroad. I was taking Chinese classes and thought I would try out what I had learned on the cute Chinese girl in the cafeteria… One thing led to another and now we're married with two kids, living in Beijing. As an American, I sometimes still feel like a tourist in this city, so I know exactly what to say when people ask me if they should come to Beijing: Yes. The warmth and humor and curiosity of the Chinese people is a wonderful thing to experience, and the unique moment that Beijing occupies now – somewhere between the past and the future as we see it – will make your visit so fascinating. Imagine being able to visit the US 100 years ago, when it was in a similar position between its rural past and industrial future. I'm not saying a visit to Beijing is like time travel, but it can feel darn close.

Gao Pan, 59, Chinese

I was born and have lived my whole life here in this courtyard house. Now my wife and I live in one of the rooms and rent out the rest. We don't have a lot of money, but this property is worth a lot. When our children come and visit us they say we should sell it and move to a better place, an apartment that's private and modern and clean. They don't like going to use the toilet out in the hutong with everybody else. But listen, I see my neighbors every day and talk to them, I know all their children and grandchildren. We sit outside at night and smoke cigarettes and tell stories and let our dogs run around. For me living here is important, not just because our lifestyle is disappearing from Beijing, but because it's disappearing everywhere in the world. People are too interested in technology and not interested in each other. I hope that travelers will come and see the way we live in the hutong and think about what's important in life.

Elliot, 25, Canadian

I was working as a journalist in Vancouver writing about politics, but I was getting bored. It seemed to me like the really exciting stories were happening outside of Canada. I moved to China two years ago and haven't looked back. Beijing is the number one place that I recommend when friends and family ask me where they should spend their next vacation. Maybe I'm biased, but seriously — I could build an amazing itinerary based on food alone, not to mention the opportunity to explore the culture, art, and history of this place.

Liu Laoshi, 22, Chinese

Liu Laoshi means Teacher Liu, and that's what my students call me. I work for a private Chinese teaching institute. Most of my students are about my age, and I love chatting with them about pop culture – we know a lot of the same celebrities! If someone asked me why they should come to Beijing, I would tell them that China is one of the most powerful countries in the world, maybe the most powerful – and they should get to know its people and its traditions the same way that we have always studied the culture of the West. All the countries in the world are going to be working together in the future and it's better if we know each other firsthand, not just through our governments.

Tiziano, 46, Italian

It's been two years since my family and I left our home for Beijing, where I had a great job offer. Everyone said we were crazy to leave all the food and charm and character of Italy for the dusty Chinese capital. They couldn't have been more wrong. Sure, there are some polluted days, but the opportunities – both economic and cultural – are fantastic. Even someone visiting the city for a few weeks will get the sense that Beijing is a fast-changing place where it's easy to make your mark.

Jiajia, 15, Chinese

Everyone complains that my generation has forgotten our real roots and is obsessed with money and technology. I really don't think that's true. Maybe some people spend the whole weekend at the mall, but I'd rather be out exploring the temples and parks all over the city. I love studying some more traditional aspects of Chinese culture, like painting and tea. None of my friends think it's a waste of time – they think it's cool that I am interested. I love living in Beijing because even though it's a really modern place in some ways, ancient history is here too.

Emma, 23, Irish

My passion is food. I was in culinary school in the UK when my parents proposed a family vacation to China. I wasn't excited at all – I wanted to go somewhere known for its cuisine, and thanks to the gloppy and greasy Chinese food I had back home, I was pretty sure China wasn't that. Fast forward three years and I'm living in Beijing full-time, co-owner of a small café and taking as many classes as I can to learn the ins and outs of Chinese cooking. The range of dishes here – from eye-wateringly spicy *mala* soup to delicate, fragrant fish and 1,000 ways of serving tofu – makes me excited to get up every day and plan what I'm going to eat. It's a foodie's dream. Any visitor to Beijing is bound to have an unforgettable dining experience.

Getting Prepared

Before you book:
Imagine your trip and put together an itinerary

Before you spend a single dime or book anything, take the time to let your imagination run wild. What do you want your trip to Beijing to be? A serene and luxurious retreat, with mornings spent exploring temples, afternoons whittled away in teahouses, and nights spent indulging in five-star cuisine? An outdoor experience where you sleep under the stars on the Great Wall, zoom around town on a bicycle, and take a dip in the Imperial Lakes alongside the Speedo-clad old-timers? Or a city-slicker's tour where you eat all the street food you come across and penetrate the local punk rock scene?

Beijing has something for everyone, no matter what your interests are. If you need help getting your imagination going, check out a few local English-language websites to get a good sense of what's going on in town: The Beijinger (**thebeijinger.com**), **echinacities.com**, City Weekend (**cityweekend.com.cn**) and Time Out Beijing (**timeoutbeijing.com**) are four of the most popular rags. Rent movies about China or buy the latest China bestseller to learn about the place you'll be visiting (see our favorites on pg 25 & 26). Another good way to get psyched is to get in touch with people you know who have visited or lived in China. Just explore and have fun with the idea of your trip before you have to get down to details.

When you're ready to start planning for real, the first decision you should make is whether or not to use a travel agent or tour company. The internet makes it easy to book plane tickets and make dinner reservations, so the idea of paying someone to plan your trip might seem outdated or silly. We suggest grabbing your Panda Guides book and thumbing through to build a trip that's perfectly catered to you.

On that note, we've created some great sample itineraries to help you get the most out of Beijing. See page 290 to check out our recommendations.

Step 1: Air Ticket & Accommodation	Step 5: Customs Regulations
Step 2: Getting a China Visa	Step 6: Female, Gay & Disabled Travelers
Step 3: What to Take With You	Step 7: Religious Services in Beijing
Step 4: Money During Your Visit	Step 8: Emergency Card

1 Air Ticket & Accommodations

Once you know when you want to go, the first step is to book an airline ticket. Your best bet for finding a good deal is to use a website that searches many airlines at once, like Kayak (**kayak.com**), Orbitz (**orbitz.com**) or Expedia (**expedia.com**). Kayak is particularly useful if you have slightly flexible travel days because it allows you to search for a range of departure dates. You can often save hundreds of dollars by leaving on a Tuesday instead of a Monday, for example, and Kayak helps you discover these opportunities.

If you're tempted to buy a one-way ticket and leave the length of your trip flexible, note that when you apply for your Chinese visa you will need to provide proof of a round-trip air ticket to demonstrate your intent to return to your home country. However, if you have a Letter of Invitation from a business, institution or individual in China, you do not need to show proof of a round-trip ticket. For more on visa application requirements, see the visa section below.

Once you have booked your flights, start thinking about accommodation. What's your budget and where would you like to stay? Most travelers will best maximize their time in Beijing by staying somewhere inside the Second Ring Road – it's more central and vibrant, and close to many of the main attractions. See our Sleeping listings (**pg 193**) to get a sense of your options.

If you'd rather not commit to a long stay in one hotel or hostel before you arrive, that's fine. But unless you have a Letter of Invitation, your visa application will need to provide proof of accommodation for at least the first night you're in China. If you're not sure where you want to stay yet, just book an inexpensive hostel online and print out the confirmation for your visa application. You won't have to follow through on the reservation if you don't want to.

2 Getting a China Visa

The following visa procedures are applicable only to citizens of the United States. For details on applying for a China visa from other countries, see our website at **www.pandaguides.com**.

Passport status

If you don't already have a passport, you'll need to get one as soon as possible. Expedited service takes two to three weeks, while regular processing takes five to six weeks. Add that to the time you'll need for processing your China visa and you should plan to begin this process at least two months before you plan to leave. See **travel.state.gov/passport** for details on how to apply for a passport.

If you already have a passport, check to make sure that it has at least six months of validity remaining before it expires. You won't be granted a visa with less than six months. If you're applying for a year-long tourist visa, you'll need 18 months of validity remaining.

Visa application

Once you've got your passport sorted, it's time to apply for a tourist visa, also called an L visa. But should you do it by yourself, or use a visa service agency? If you live in or near Washington DC, New York, San Francisco, Los Angeles, Houston, or Chicago, you have the option of applying for your visa in person at the local Chinese consulate. Go to **www.china-embassy.org/eng/** to find the locations of these processing centers.

If none of those cities are convenient for you, or if you'd rather not go and wait in line, you can hire a visa service agency to do it for you. In that case, you would bring your passport and visa application to them so that they can present it in person at the consulate. There are many reliable and efficient companies to choose from – the China Visa Service Center (**mychinavisa.com**) has a good reputation and an organized website. These agencies invariably charge a fee on top of the cost of the visa. When you apply for a visa, you'll submit your passport and a number of supporting documents. See below for a complete list of the requirements as of the time of research.

How much does a visa cost?

Number of Entries	Visa Validity	2nd or 3rd Day Pickup	4th or 5th Day Pickup
Single Entry	3 months	US$160	$140
Double Entry/Multi-Entry	6 months	US$160	$140
Multi-Entry	12 months	US$160	$140

As you can see, the cost is the same no matter how many entries you choose, so go ahead and request 12 months multiple-entry, even if your trip will not be that long. You may not always get the longer validity, but it's better to aim high. In the event of unforeseen circumstances it's better to have too long of a visa than to try to negotiate an extension at the last-minute.

What goes into my visa application? — BASIC DOCUMENTS

1) Passport – You should submit your original passport that is valid for at least another six months and a photocopy of the passport's information and photo page. Your passport must also have at least one blank visa page.

2) Visa Application Form – Truthfully and completely fill out the Visa Application Form of the People's Republic of China (V2011A), which is available online at **china-embassy.org/eng/**. It's a straightforward form, but be sure to type or print neatly. In the "Itinerary in China" section, if you're planning to travel to the politically sensitive areas of Tibet or Xinjiang, don't include that in your list of intended destinations; no one will check up on it. (There is a separate travel permit for Tibet and you must go with an official tour guide, but you need a China visa first, and mentioning Tibet on this application might create a needless red flag.)

> There are a few gray areas when it comes to "truthfully" completing your visa application. There is a section that asks you to disclose your criminal record – some US citizens have chosen not to include that information in their application. It's not completely clear what impact your criminal record can have on the status of your application, and it's ultimately a personal choice to disclose or not disclose it. Another ambiguity applies to journalists or "staff of media," as the form designates them, who may have a difficult time getting a tourist visa if they disclose their real occupation on the form. Some applicants choose to get around this by writing something else, though again, it's not clear how that choice may affect your application.

3) Photo – Attach one passport-size color photo to your Application Form. The 48 mm x 33 mm photo should be a recent, front view picture taken without hats or head coverings. You can get these photos taken cheaply at many national drugstore chains like Walgreens and CVS.

4) Certificate of Name Change – If the name in the new passport is different from that in a previous one, the official name change certification document should be submitted.

5) One of the following supporting documents is required:

An Invitation Letter for Tourist Group or Invitation Letter for Tourist by a duly Authorized Tourism Unit.

An Invitation Letter issued by a company, corporation, institution or individual in China. If the Invitation Letter is issued by an individual in China, a photocopy of the individual's ID is required.

OR

A photocopy of your roundtrip airline ticket and hotel reservation.

If you have a tour group they may provide you with an Invitation Letter, but for most visitors the easiest supporting document to provide is the proof of airline ticket and hotel reservation. However, if you would prefer to submit an invitation letter from a company, group or a friend already in China, the letter must include all of the following:

(A) Personal information of the applicant: name, gender, date of birth, etc.

(B) Information concerning the applicant's visit to China: purpose of the visit, dates of arrival and departure, places to visit, relationship between the applicant and the inviter, and who will bear the cost of the applicant's accommodation in China.

(C) Information of the inviter: name of the business/institute or individual, phone number, address and, if applicable, seal and signature of their legal representative.

(D) A photocopy of the inviter's ID: if they are Chinese, their national ID; if they are a foreigner, their residence permit.

For non-US citizens only, these documents should be included with your application:

Proof of US Residency Status – Third country citizens also need to provide the original and a photocopy of proof of US residency (work or study), proof of residency in the consular district (e.g. ID, water or electricity bills, tenancy agreement, etc) or a valid US visa.

Previous Chinese Visa – Those who have obtained a Chinese visa before (when applying for a visa with a new passport) should submit a photocopy of the original passport's information/photo page and the page containing the previous Chinese visa.

Original Chinese Passport – First-time applicants whose former nationality was Chinese, or who were born in China (including Hong Kong, Macao and Taiwan), need to submit their original Chinese passport and a photocopy of the passport's information/photo page and extension page (if applicable).

It might seem like a lot of documents to assemble, but it's relatively straightforward as long as you leave yourself enough time.

How long will it take to get my visa?

If you submit your application in person, the processing time is usually four business days, or two to three business days if you pay for expedited service. Some consulates have processed same-day applications in the past for an additional fee, but as the volume of applications has increased this is not always an option. When you work with an agency, the same processing times should apply, plus the time it will take to send your application and receive it back in the mail.

3 What to Take With You

What to pack

What you pack is highly personal and depends on the length and season of your trip, not to mention the activities you have planned, so we won't bore you with a detailed universal packing list. But here are some general suggestions, followed by a few recommendations for non-essential items, that can make a big difference in your trip.

First and foremost, don't overpack. The hassle of lugging a massive bag through the crowded streets of Beijing will quickly cancel out the convenience of bringing your entire closet, and if you forget something, you can almost certainly replace it here, probably for cheap.

Look up and follow the weather in Beijing for the weeks leading up to your trip. Winter can be bone-chillingly cold and windy, and by the end of May temperatures can hit 30 ºC (86 ºF). Try to pack accordingly, though again, don't stress – if you find there's something you wish you had packed, buy it here.

Beijing is not a very formal city, so unless you have a lot of meetings or fancy galas planned, one or two "nice" outfits should be more than enough.

Pack a duffel bag that you can fold up and keep in your luggage – if you buy a lot of souvenirs or hit the clothing markets, you'll have a way of transporting your loot home.

Washing machines are common in China, but driers are not, and it can take more than 24 hours for clothes to air-dry in the humid seasons. Factor that drying time in when you're considering how many outfits to bring.

Check your airline's baggage allowance so you don't get smacked with excess baggage fees.

If you're traveling with kids, packing becomes a bit more complicated: see our section on page 329 for more information on traveling with kids.

China runs on 220 volts with a variety of plug types. The most common are the two-prong straight plug (USA style; top of photo at left) and three-prong angled (bottom of photo at left). Most laptops, camera chargers, phone chargers, and other electronics will plug into Chinese sockets with no problem. If your devices are not rated for 220V or if you have other plug shapes (including a two-prong straight plug where one plug is slightly larger than the other), you'll need to purchase an adapter. Power strips are widely available for very cheap in Beijing, and they can accept just about any plug in the world.

None of the following items are technically essential, but they may come in handy, so consider bringing them.

E-reader or paper books: Traveling in China often means long bus or train rides, not to mention your long flights there and back. Reading material can turn boring "lost" transit time into a fun and relaxing experience.

Earplugs: In a sleeper train or a hostel or hotel, you're bound to hear a lot of sounds that can steal much-needed sleep. Pop some earplugs in and forget all about it.

Ziploc bags: Keep your passport in one to protect against damage. You'll no doubt find many other uses for these throughout the trip.

Pocket-sized dictionary or smart-phone with dictionary app: When you need just a few words of Chinese, a dictionary is a lifesaver, even if you have to point (see our Mandarin phrasebook on pg 336).

Reusable water bottle: A Nalgene or other hard plastic bottle is a good way of keeping water with you at all times while reducing waste created by disposable plastic bottles. Remember to only fill with boiled or purified water; no tap!

Flashlight: Packing or unpacking in the dark, wandering down a dark and charming hutong late at night... these are only a few times when a flashlight might come in handy.

Money belt: The jury is out on money belts. Some travelers swear by the under-the-clothes variety for protecting their cash, while others think it's a hassle. If you don't have the under-the-clothes type, you might just attract additional attention to your money. Either way, staying alert and keeping your money in a secure location (e.g. in your front pocket instead of your back) is the best way to stay safe.

Camera: It should go without saying, but you might be kicking yourself (and us) if we didn't throw this one in there just in case. If you have a smart-phone, you may not need this. However, keep in mind that China's scenery is extremely photo-worthy, so if you have a high-end camera and love photography, you may want to consider bringing it.

Apps

Got a smart-phone? There is a grab bag of useful apps that you can throw on your phone to keep you updated on certain useful and important events around town. From those giving daily weather and air pollution updates to others covering currency exchange and Chinese language, apps are the future, and the future is in Beijing. See page 309 for a list of these apps and how to find them.

Health Insurance

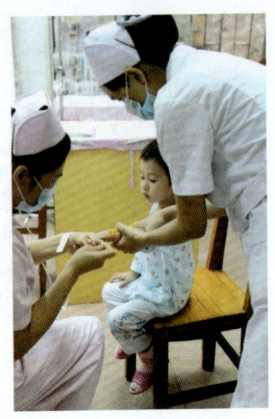

The most important thing you pack might not be in your suitcase. Many people believe that their existing health insurance policy will cover them worldwide, but that's usually not the case. Contact your insurer to confirm what coverage, if any, they provide while you're traveling in China. Some major insurers, like Blue Cross Blue Shield, do have networked providers throughout China. Obtain this information in writing before you depart.

If your regular insurance coverage does not extend overseas, consider purchasing a travel insurance policy. Ask your insurer to recommend one, or check out the policies offered by International SOS (**internationalsos.com/en**).

Some types of travel insurance include emergency evacuation coverage but do not cover the actual medical costs of treatment. You may need additional medical insurance to cover these situations. Read any potential policy carefully to understand exactly what it covers. Understand whether you can use any doctor or if you must use one who is in your network.

Most Chinese hospitals require cash. Even if you have medical insurance, you may have to pay first then apply for reimbursement. A few hospitals in major cities may accept credit cards, but don't put all your eggs in one basket. Make sure to get a receipt for all services or you may not get a reimbursement.

4 Money During Your Visit

Chinese currency: Renminbi (人民币)

Abbreviated as RMB, *renminbi* means "the people's currency." The main unit of the RMB is the *yuán* (元) – for example, a bottle of water might cost three *yuan*. In Beijing, the word *yuan* is interchangeable with the word *kuài* (块), and you'll usually hear prices quoted as *kuai* instead of *yuan*. The largest bill in circulation is the red ¥100 (about US$16, see picture on the following page), followed by ¥50, ¥20, ¥10, ¥5, and ¥1. Below ¥1, there are a series of coins and smaller-sized bills worth ¥0.5 and ¥0.1. These are called *jiǎo* or, more commonly, *máo* (i.e. ¥0.5 is five *mao*).

Though ATMs will only dispense ¥100 bills, you'll find that shop owners and cab drivers sometimes balk at taking one – they may not have enough change. While traveling in China, it's a good idea to keep a supply of ¥100 bills and a good mix of smaller bills.

Exchange Rates (at time of research)

Australia	AU$1	¥5.7
Canada	CA$1	¥5.9
Euro Zone	€1	¥8.1
Hong Kong	HK$1	¥0.8
New Zealand	NZ$1	¥4.8
Singapore	SG$1	¥4.8
UK	UK£1	¥9.5
USA	US$1	¥6.1
For up-to-date currency exchange rates, see **www.xe.com**.		

One Hundred Yuan Note

"People's Bank of China" written in five different languages. Clockwise from top: Chinese pinyin, Tibetan, Zhuang, Uighur, and Mongolian

Credit & debit cards

China is a heavily cash-based economy. Outside of big international hotels and some stores, don't expect to swipe a credit or debit card. Luckily, almost all foreign ATM cards work in China, though you will incur fees for international withdrawals. If you're concerned, check with your bank. If you plan on using your credit or debit cards while you're abroad, make sure to notify your bank of your travels before you leave so that your purchases do not activate a fraud warning.

Cash

There are a number of ways to get cash during your trip. First, you can bring an amount of your home currency and exchange it once you arrive at the airport, but the rates will most definitely be inflated. You can also exchange cash at a branch of the Bank of China, though foreigners are restricted to exchanging US$500 worth of currency per day. Second, you can withdraw cash from an ATM once you arrive – ATMs are very common in Beijing, especially downtown and near tourist attractions.

Traveler's checks

These can be cashed at international hotels and branches of the Bank of China. Though they do offer more security in the event of theft, the ease of using debit cards to withdraw cash at ATMs has made them less popular in recent years, and you might need to go out of your way to cash them.

5 Customs Regulations

Generally speaking, the customs enforcement at the airport is hands-off. When arriving or departing, you must walk through the "green channel" (nothing to declare) or the "red channel" (something to declare). If you're unsure about declaring something, err on the side of caution and choose the red channel.

What can I bring into China?

400 cigarettes, 1.5 L of alcohol, and 50 g of gold or silver are allowed in without any duty.

No fresh fruit or meat is permitted. Any amount of foreign currency can be brought in, but more than US$5,000 (or the equivalent) must be declared. Guns, knives, explosives, and other weapons are obviously prohibited. Electronics like TVs and computers will need to be declared.

What can I take out?

Pretty much anything except weapons, pornography and produce, and pirated DVDs and CDs will likely be confiscated. Antiques that you bought in China need a certificate and red seal to clear customs. Anything before 1949 is considered an antique and needs this documentation, and objects from before 1911 cannot be legally exported, period.

6 Female, Gay & Disabled Travelers

Female travelers

Beijing is a very safe place for solo female travelers. In addition to its very low crime rate in general, there's far less of a macho, alpha-male attitude here than in some other countries (or cities), and the Chinese tend to give females a relatively high degree of respect. Of course, take the usual precautions and consider carrying a whistle or other noisemaker in the event of a threatening situation. Try to choose accommodation that is centrally located and well-trafficked.

Gay & lesbian travelers

You may have heard that homosexuality was classified as a mental disorder in China until 2001. While it's still hardly the equal rights capital of the world, there is a very active, well-educated, open-minded younger generation that is piecing together a good gay scene in Beijing. There's no gay neighborhood, per se, but most nightlife is very Western and open. Check Utopia's site at **utopia-asia.com/tipschin.htm** for more detailed listings, but here are a few recommendations:

Destination

This very "clubby" club has two floors of drinking and dancing, with a mostly male crowd. ¥60 cover. Beijing's best-known gay "destination."

> Hours: 20:00-2:00 (Sun-Thu); 20:00-late (Fri-Sat)
> Address: 7 Gongti Xilu, Chaoyang District (朝阳区工体西路 7 号)
> Phone: 6552 8180

Alfa

This slightly classier but still wild spot has a weekly gay night on Fridays. ¥30 gets you a free drink and two-for-one specials all night. Mostly male.

> Hours: 18:00-3:00
> Address: 6 Xingfu Yicun, in the hutong opposite the north gate of Workers' Stadium (朝阳区幸福一村 6 号工体北门对面的胡同里).
> Phone: 6413 0086

Mesh

Inside the swanky Opposite House hotel, this low-key lounge hosts a sophisticated gay night on Thursdays with creative cocktails in a sexy setting. Free entrance, two-for-one drinks from 17:00-20:00.

> Address: 1/F, The Opposite House, Bldg 1, 11 Sanlitun Lu, Sanlitun Village, Chaoyang District (朝阳区三里屯路 11 号).
> Phone: 6417 6688

Travelers with disabilities

Regrettably, Beijing is a bit of a minefield for travelers who are wheelchair-bound or have mobility disabilities. Airports, railway stations, and subway stations are basically barrier-free and up to Western standards, but elsewhere crowded sidewalks and high curbs make navigating the streets a challenge, and ramps and elevators are not nearly as common as in the West. Visiting sights like the Forbidden City or Summer Palace involves a lot of walking and stepping over uneven doorways, but a limited number of wheelchairs are available to rent at the ticket gate. If you bring your own wheelchair, ideally it would be lightweight and collapsible to facilitate fitting it in the trunk of a taxi. Travelers with sight or hearing disabilities should also take extreme caution when crossing the street because cars move fast and almost never yield to pedestrians.

7 Religious services in Beijing

Christian

Beijing International Christian Fellowship is a family of more than 20 evangelical and Protestant congregations, with two locations: 21st Century Auditorium, offering English services at 9:00 and 11:00 on Sundays (40 Liangmaqiao Lu, 朝阳区亮马桥路40号); or in Haidian District at 2 Kexueyuan Nanlu (科学院南路2号), with English services at 10:00 and 18:00 on Sundays. Check their website **www.bicf.org** for more info.

Capital Community Church meets in suburban Shunyi at 10:00 on Sundays. Similar to most non-denominational churches in the US.

> Address: 1A Shunhuang Lu, Shunyi District (顺义区顺黄路甲1号)
> Website: www.capitalcommunitychurch.net

Jewish

Kehillat Beijing International Jewish Community offers Friday night shabbat services open to all.

> Address: Capital Mansion, 6 Xinyuan Nanli (京城大厦．新源南里6号)
> Website: www.sinogogue.org

Chabad House has welcoming Friday night services and a Kosher restaurant.

> Address: Fangyuan Xilu, next to the south gate of Side Park (芳园西路，四得公园南门旁)
> Website: www.chabadbeijing.com.

Muslim

Niujie Mosque has sessions on Friday around 13:00 which have been known to draw more than 500 people.

> Address: 88 Niujie Zhonglu (牛街中路88号)
> Phone: 6353 2564

8 Emergency Card

It's a good idea to carry an emergency card with you – just in case. We have provided one, which includes Chinese and English, and we encourage you to make copies to suit your needs.

My info	Help
My name 我的名字：	My nationality 我的国籍：
My address 我的地址：	
My phone number 我的电话号码：	
For emergency, please contact 紧急情况请联系：	

Transportation

Airport

Beijing Capital International Airport (Běijīng Shǒudū Guójì Jīchǎng; 北京首都国际机场; IATA code: PEK) will probably be the first stop on your trip to Beijing. PEK is the second-busiest airport in the world after Atlanta, and its Terminal 3 is the fifth-largest building in the world by area. Most international flights arrive at and depart from Terminal 3. Banks and an ATM are available on your right as you exit customs, and this is a good place to withdraw or exchange money.

Getting Out of the Airport

The airport is 25 km (15.5 mi) from central Beijing, so unless you're one of the lucky people with a driver holding a sign with your name on it in the arrivals area, you'll need to figure out how to get into town. Here are your options:

Airport Express

The airport express train is the fastest and most economical way to get into the city from the airport between 6:35 and 23:10. A one-way trip takes 15-20 minutes and sets you back ¥25 (about US$4), and trains depart about every 10 minutes. After picking up passengers in Terminals 2 and 3, the train heads into downtown Beijing, where it makes two stops: Sanyuanqiao (三元桥) and Dongzhimen (东直门). At Sanyuanqiao Station, you can transfer to the regular Beijing subway system Line 10, and at Dongzhimen Station, you can transfer to Line 2 or Line 13. The metro has extensive English signs and it should be easy to navigate even if it's your first time in the city.

Taxi

If your destination is not near a subway stop, or you have a lot of big heavy bags, taxis are a good choice. Follow the signs in the terminal, make a beeline for one of the official taxi stands, and ignore anyone who approaches you in the terminal offering taxi or limo service. These are illegal cabs and they will surely charge you much, much more than you need to pay. A legal, metered taxi to the city center should cost about ¥100, including tolls. Tipping taxi drivers is not common in Beijing.

Bus

We don't recommend bus transport from the airport, as the options are limited and tricky to navigate, and luggage can make the trip a pain. However, the airport does offer a shuttle bus service for ¥16 to destinations throughout the city. Inquire at Gate 11 if you're interested in these buses. If your final destination is not Beijing, there are longer-distance buses to nearby cities Tianjin (天津; ¥82; 2.5 hours; every 45-60 minutes from 7:30 to 23:00), Tanggu (塘沽; ¥94; 3 hours; departing at 10:30, 13:00, 18:30 and 20:30), Qinhuangdao (秦皇岛; ¥128; 4 hours; departing at 9:00, 11:00, 13:00, 15:00, 17:00 and 20:00), Langfang (廊坊; ¥40; 2 hours; every 2 hours from 10:30 to 20:30), Baoding

(保定; ¥95; 3.5 hours; departing at 10:10, 11:40, 14:10, 16:10, 18:10 and 20:10), and Tangshan (唐山; ¥80; 3 hours; every 2 hours from 10:15 to 20:15).

Travel within Beijing

Before we get into your transportation options, you should know that although some Beijingers speak conversational English, it's less common than you might think, and you should never count on finding a taxi driver or passer-by who knows English well. And, unless you have some experience studying Chinese, don't put too much faith in your ability to pronounce Chinese place names and be understood by the locals. The pinyin romanization of Chinese characters may not get you very far either. Your best bet is to have the name of the place you want to visit written out in Chinese characters – whether you use this guidebook, an app on your smart-phone, or have someone at your hotel or hostel write it out for you.

Yikatong Smartcard

Like New York's MetroCard or London's Oyster Card, Beijing has a rechargeable smartcard for its transit system – it's called Yīkǎtōng (一卡通; one card pass). There are several advantages to getting one as soon as you arrive. First, it'll save you the trouble of waiting in line to buy a ticket every time you get on the subway (and those lines can be long and slow). Second, if you decide to take the bus during your trip, Yikatong users get a 60% discount on fares. This discount might seem less compelling when you realize it reduces the normal fare of ¥1 (about US$0.16) to ¥0.4 (US$0.06). Your Yikatong also entitles you to rent public bicycles for the very cheap rate of ¥10 per day (more on that in the Bicycle section). The Yikatong advertises that you're able to pay taxi fares with the card too, but it's not actually possible in practice, whether because of unwilling drivers, broken card readers, or some other hiccups.

There's a ¥20 deposit on the card that'll be refunded if you return it to a designated location. Conveniently, the card can be both purchased from and returned to the Airport Express stop in Terminal 3, so if you plan to use public transit during your trip, we recommend that you purchase the Yikatong as soon as you arrive at the airport.

Subway

The subway is probably your best bet for getting around town. The advantages (cheap, convenient, easy to navigate, fast) definitely outweigh the disadvantages (can be crowded, closes early).

Except for the Airport Express Line, a ride on the Beijing subway costs ¥2 no matter where you're going or how many times you transfer. You'll find the subway stations have good English signs, and all train announcements are made in both English and Chinese. Hours of operation vary by line, but generally, trains run between 5:00 and 23:00 (see Beijing Subway Map on the back of pull-out map). To avoid getting up close and personal with a mob of strangers, avoid riding the train during the rush hours of 7:00-9:00 and 17:00-19:00.

All passengers will pass through a security checkpoint where purses or bags are put through a screening machine like at the airport. If you purchased an Yikatong, boarding the subway is easy. Just walk up to the ticket gate and press your card to the card reader. The gates will open and the fare will be deducted automatically. If you're buying fare cards as you go, you'll find a cluster of ticket vending machines that have an English option, but they only accept small bills and are frequently out of order. If that's the case, you can approach the customer service window and buy a ticket directly from the employee there.

Most of Beijing's top attractions are accessible via subway. See our list of attractions and subway stops in parenthesis below. As you'll see, it is fairly easy to organize a self-guided tour using the subway for transportation.

Line 1

Financial Street (Fuxingmen)
Tian'anmen Square (Tian'anmen East or Tian'anmen West)
Forbidden City (Tian'anmen East or Tian'anmen West)
National Museum (Tian'anmen East or Tian'anmen West)

Travel within Beijing Subway

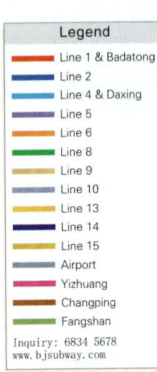

Legend
- Line 1 & Badatong
- Line 2
- Line 4 & Daxing
- Line 5
- Line 6
- Line 8
- Line 9
- Line 10
- Line 13
- Line 14
- Line 15
- Airport
- Yizhuang
- Changping
- Fangshan

Inquiry: 6834 5678
www.bjsubway.com

Line 1
Pingguoyuan		Sihui East	
First	05:10	First	05:05
Last	22:55	Last	23:15

Line 2 (Inner Ring)
Jishuitan	
First	05:03
Last	22:45

Line 2 (Outer Ring)
Xizhimen	
First	05:09
Last	22:59

Line 4
Gongyixiqiao		Anheqiao North	
First	05:10	First	05:00
Last	23:10	Last	22:45

Line 5
Tiantongyuan North		Songjiazhuang	
First	04:59	First	05:19
Last	22:47	Last	23:10

Line 6
Caofang		Haidian Wuluju	
First	05:15	First	05:23
Last	24:06	Last	23:16

Line 8
Zhuxinzhuang		Nanluoguxiang	
First	05:05	First	05:30
Last	22:05	Last	23:00

Line 9
NationalLibrary		Guogongzhuang	
First	05:59	First	05:20
Last	23:19	Last	22:40

Line 10
Bagou	
First	04:49
Last	22:35

Line 13
Xizhimen		Dongzhimen	
First	05:35	First	05:35
Last	22:42	Last	22:42

Line 14
Zhangguozhuang		Xiju	
First	05:30	First	05:45
Last	22:10	Last	22:10

Line 15
Wangjing West		Fengbo	
First	06:00	First	05:45
Last	22:55	Last	22:11

Beijing Subway

Batong Line			
Sihui		Tuqiao	
First	06:00	First	05:20
Last	23:22	Last	22:42

Changping Line			
Nanshao		Xi'erqi	
First	06:00	First	05:50
Last	22:35	Last	23:05

Daxing Line			
Xingong		Tiangongyuan	
First	05:54	First	05:30
Last	23:14	Last	22:38

Yizhuang Line			
Songjiazhuang		Ciqu	
First	06:00	First	05:23
Last	22:45	Last	22:08

Airport Express					
Dongzhimen		Terminal 3		Terminal 2	
First	06:00	First	06:21	First	06:35
Last	22:30	Last	22:51	Last	23:10

Fangshan Line			
Guogongzhuang		Suzhuang	
First	05:58	First	05:15
Last	23:00	Last	22:00

Transportation

043

Wangfujing (Wangfujing)
Silk Market (Yong'anli)
CCTV Building (Guomao)

Line 2

Drum and Bell Towers (Guloudajie)
Hutongs (Guloudajie)
Ritan Park (Jianguomen)
Chairman Mao Memorial Hall (Qianmen)
Beijing South Church (Xuanwumen)
Beijing Railway Station (Beijing Railway Station)

Line 4

Summer Palace (Beigongmen)
Old Summer Palace (Yuanmingyuan)
Beijing Zoo and Aquarium (Beijing Zoo)
Zoo Market (Beijing Zoo)
Peking University (East Gate of Peking University)

Line 5

Yonghegong Lama Temple (Yonghegong Lama Temple)
Confucian Temple (Yonghegong Lama Temple)
Ditan Park (Yonghegong Lama Temple)
Temple of Heaven (Tiantan Dongmen)
Hongqiao Pearl Market (Tiantan Dongmen)

Line 6

Nanluogu Xiang (Nanluogu Xiang)
Houhai (Beihai North)
Beihai Park (Beihai North)

Line 8

Bird's Nest (Olympic Green or Olympic Sports Center)
Water Cube (Olympic Green or Olympic Sports Center)
Shichahai (Shichahai)
Nanluogu Xiang (Nanluogu Xiang)

Line 10

Panjiayuan (Panjiayuan)

Bus

Beijing's buses can be daunting, even to locals. The extensive system of over 800 routes delivers about 5 billion rides per year. Many visitors avoid the bus system, either because the subway meets all of their needs or because the bus is too intimidating. Most Beijing city maps indicate the bus routes with a red or blue line and a dot on the line indicating a stop. Note that stops tend to be almost a kilometer apart. If you have your destination available in Chinese characters, the driver or your fellow passengers may be able to tell you when your stop is approaching. You certainly can't beat the price – ¥0.4 with your Yikatong.

Here are some bus routes that might be appealing to visitors.

Bus 1 and **double-decker bus 1**: From Beijing Railway Station East at Tian'anmen Square to the Military Museum
Bus 2: From Qianmen Dajie to Dongdan and Yonghegong Lama Temple
Double-decker bus 4: From Beijing Zoo to Qianmen
Bus 5: From Deshengmen on the Second Ring Road, past Forbidden City and Tian'anmen to Qianmen
Bus 300: Circles the Third Ring Road
Bus 332: From the Beijing Zoo to Beijing University and the Summer Palace

Taxi

Taxis may be a luxury in many big cities, but in Beijing, they're relatively inexpensive. Of course, there is the hidden cost of sitting in a horrific traffic jam, but for non-subway accessible destinations and when you just need a break from the crowds, cabs are a good option. Again, as discussed earlier, have your destination written out in Chinese characters for the best chance of communicating with your driver.

Taxis charge a starting fee of ¥13 and an additional ¥2.3/km after the first 3 km (1.8 mi). An average non-rush hour trip through the city costs around ¥20-30, and a cross-town journey about ¥50 (for example, from the city center to the north side of the Fourth Ring Road). There is a ¥1 gas surcharge on all trips over 3 km; the notice about the surcharge is posted inside the taxi. Note that this surcharge is not displayed on the meter, so if the meter says ¥18 the price is ¥19.

If the taxi driver "forgets" to start the taxi meter, remind him by politely saying *qǐng dǎbiǎo* ("please start the meter"). If that fails, simply point at the meter, they'll probably get the point. Once you arrive at your destination, it's not a bad idea to ask for a receipt by saying *fāpiào*, or by gesturing to the meter and making a writing motion. The receipt has the cab's number and other details, which will come in handy later if you're getting reimbursed or if you want to make a complaint. Furthermore, if you forget something in the taxi, you'll have a much better chance of getting it back with these details.

Bicycle

Biking is often the fastest way from point A to point B in Beijing, with the added bonus that you get to experience the texture and detail of neighborhoods in a way that's not possible from a subway tunnel. We highly recommend that you experience Beijing on a bike for at least one day.

Your hotel or hostel will probably rent bikes themselves, or know of someone who does. In big tourist areas like Houhai, you'll find bikes available for rent along the hutongs for ¥20 or ¥30 per hour. Perhaps your cheapest and best longer-term option is to use Beijing's public bikeshare program. With your passport, your Yikatong, and ¥400 for a deposit, you can go to one of the following offices to activate the bikeshare program on your card: Dongzhimen (东直门) Line 2 Exit A, Tiantan Dongmen (天坛东门) Line 5 Exit A2, Chaoyangmen (朝阳门) Line 2 Exit A, 100 m (328) ft north of the intersection of Xindong Lu (新东路), and Gongti Beilu (工体北路), 250 m (820 ft) east of the intersection of Nongzhanguan Beilu (农展馆北路) and Chaoyang Gongyuan Lu (朝阳公园路). It may sound like a hassle, but once you're set up, you'll have access to 20,000 bicycles in 500 locations, around town. There's a smart-phone app you can download at **www.beijingbikeshare.com** to see where the bikes are located. Your first hour of biking is free, then ¥1 per hour for a maximum of ¥10 per day. If a bike is not returned within 3 days, ¥20 will be deducted every day from your deposit.

If you're in Beijing for a long visit, you might even choose to buy a bike. Inexpensive models can be had for about ¥150 (about US$25), and it'll save you the trouble of renting. When it's time to go, you can sell it or give it away.

A good sturdy bike lock is a key accessory for successful biking in Beijing, especially if you're renting, in which case a stolen bike means a lost deposit.

On Foot

Beijing is a massive city, and what looks like a short walk on a map can take hours, not to mention that Beijing's smog, traffic and crowded sidewalks don't always make for a leisurely stroll. For certain neighborhoods and attractions, however, like Houhai Lake or the hutongs, it makes sense to attack on foot. For the most part you're better off saving your energy for exploring the attractions once you arrive.

Train & Bullet Train

Train Types

The level of comfort and speed of China's trains varies a lot depending on which route you buy. The high-speed trains that have been introduced to certain routes are very nice and new – with their smooth, silent rides, many people prefer them to flying. Each train is identified with a letter and number, here's what the letters mean:

G – Gāo Tiě (高铁): Ultra High-Speed Train
C – Chéngjì Lièchē (城际列车): Intercity High-Speed Train
D – Dòng Chē (动车): High-Speed Train
Z – Zhí Dá (直达): Direct Train
T – Tè Kuài (特快): Express Train
K – Kuài Chē (快车): Fast Train

Ticket Types

For all seat types, smoking is prohibited (except between cars, where the smokers gather). Lights generally go out around 22:00. In terms of amenities, they're pretty much limited to a hot-water dispenser and a very basic bathroom.

Soft Sleeper (Ruǎn Wò; 软卧)

The most expensive and most comfortable

option, soft sleeper tickets get you a bunk in an air-conditioned compartment with three other people. There's a door that can be closed for extra privacy and noise reduction. Tickets for upper berths are slightly cheaper than lower berths.

Hard Sleeper (Yìng Wò; 硬卧)

For about half the price of a soft sleeper, you can get the most popular ticket type: a bunk in a big doorless air-conditioned compartment. The bunks are stacked in threes and slightly less plush than a soft sleeper, but the more social atmosphere and cheaper price make up for it.

Seats (Yìng Zuò; 硬 座 – Hard Seat; Ruǎn Zuò; 软座 – Soft Seat)

Depending on the train you take, there may be several classes of seats offered, with the nicest having TVs, outlets, and two-across seating. So-called "hard seats" are the least desirable, not necessarily because the seat is hard but because the crowding, noise, and less-than-clean surroundings make for a hard trip if you're going far. If tickets have sold out, you may have the option of a Standing Ticket (Zhàn Piào; 站票).

Buying Train Tickets

Train travel is extremely popular in China. Most tickets can be booked 20 days in advance of your date of departure. For long journeys, sleeper tickets will sell out before seats. Only cash is accepted and you must show your passport at the time of purchase. Busy periods like Chinese New Year (January or February, lasting about half a month), May Day (May 1, lasting five to seven days) and National Day (October 1, usually lasting one week) set off an all-out free-for-all when it comes to buying tickets, and booking a train then can be downright impossible.

Ticket Counters

You can buy tickets directly at the train station ticket counters for no additional charge (but buying a round-trip ticket or buying a ticket for trains departing from other train stations costs an extra ¥5). The clerks may speak a small amount of English, but don't count on it – have a few phrases prepared or have your destination written in Chinese characters.

Ticket Agents

There are authorized train ticket agents throughout town selling tickets for a ¥5 service charge. Again, if you don't speak Chinese, have your destination written out. See their signage with the Chinese characters "火车票代售点"(Huǒchēpiào Dàishòudiǎn).

In addition, most hotels have a business center to book train or flight tickets for customers, charging ¥5 for their service.

Online

You can book online at **www.chinatripadvisor. com** or www.china-train-ticket.com, but be warned that these sites charge a hefty commission that could almost double the price of your ticket. If you're headed to Hong Kong, note that you can order tickets online for face value at **www.mtr.com.hk**.

Beijing Stations

Beijing Railway Station (Běijīng Huǒchēzhàn; 北京火车站) – Easily accessible via the Beijing Railway Station stop on subway Line 2, this is the station for slow trains and trains heading northeast. Prices in the table are for a hard sleeper ticket unless otherwise indicated.

Beijing West Railway Station (Běijīng Xīzhàn; 北京西站) – This massive station mostly accommodates fast Z trains and it's connected to the subway by the Beijing West Railway Station on Line 9. Fares in the table on the next page are for soft-sleeper tickets unless otherwise indicated.

Beijing South Railway Station (Běijīng Nánzhàn; 北京南站) – Connected to the subway via the Beijing South Railway Station stop on Line 4. This sleek glass station specializes in very high-speed bullet trains.

Beijing North Railway Station (Běijīng Běizhàn; 北京北站) – Just north of Xizhimen Station on Line 2, this much smaller station hosts trains that may be of interest to travelers (see the table on pg 48).

Pangda Travel (Pángdà Lǚyóu; 庞大旅游)

Pangda Travel is the first budget airline booking hub for travelers and expats in the Middle Kingdom. While other companies are Chinese owned businesses that target locals, Pangda Travel is a Canadian owned enterprise that knows and understands the needs of foreigners traveling in China. With excellent service, English speaking staff and extremely low prices, Pangda Travel is the preferred agent foreigners turn to when booking domestic and international flights.

Phone: (010) 8590 3026; 400 030 7900
Address: Suite 502, Block B, World City, 6 Jinhui Lu, Chaoyang District (朝阳区金汇路6号世界城B座502)
Email: pangdatravel@hotmail.com

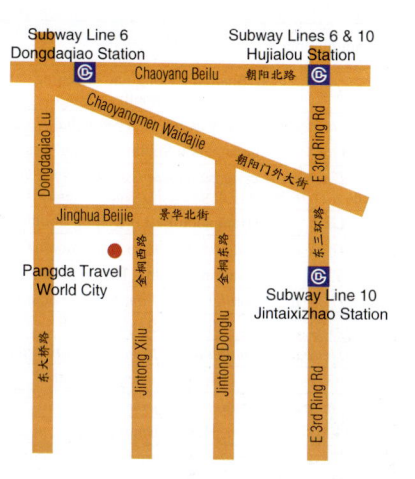

Getting In & Out

By Plane

Departure – Arrival	Frequency	Duration	Price
Guangzhou – Beijing	30 flights daily	3 hr 10 min	¥1,700
Shenzhen – Beijing	35 flights daily	about 3 hr	¥1,750
Haikou – Beijing	15 flights daily	3 hr 20 min	¥2,250
Chongqing – Beijing	31 flights daily	2 hr 30 min	¥1,560
Kunming – Beijing	15 flights daily	about 3 hr	¥1,810
Guiyang – Beijing	21 flights daily	2 hr 40 min	¥1,980
Guiling – Beijing	7 flights daily	about 3 hr	¥1,790
Nanning – Beijing	9 flights daily	3 hr 10 min	¥2,050
Chengdu – Beijing	28 flights daily	2 hr 30 min	¥1,440
Harbin – Beijing	21 flights daily	about 2 hr	¥960
Shenyang – Beijing	22 flights daily	1 hr 30 min	¥770
Dalian – Beijing	19 flights daily	1 hr 20 min	¥710
Urumqi – Beijing	14 flights daily	3 hr 25 min	¥2,410
Hohhot – Beijing	13 flights daily	1 hr 20 min	¥550
Xining – Beijing	6 flights daily	2 hr 20 min	¥1,450
Lanzhou – Beijing	12 flights daily	2 hr 10 min	¥1,340
Xi'an – Beijing	18 flights daily	1 hr 50 min	¥1,160
Changsha – Beijing	16 flights daily	2 hr 10 min	¥1,210
Nanchang – Beijing	9 flights daily	1 hr 50 min	¥1,300

Note: Prices listed above are full prices, but subject to an additional airport construction fee of ¥50 plus a fuel tax of ¥120. However, you can get 10-50% discount if you book the ticket at least one day early.

By Train

Train number	From – To	Departing – Arriving	Duration	Price
C2206	Tianjin – Beijing South	08:01 – 08:39	38 min	¥54.5

Note: There are nearly 100 bullet trains going from Tianjin to Beijing South daily: every 30 minutes from 6:40 to 22:45.

Train number	From – To	Departing – Arriving	Duration	Price
G2	Shanghai Hongqiao – Beijing South	09:00–13:48	4 hr 48 min	¥553
Note: There are 35 bullet trains from Shanghai Hongqiao (or Shanghai) to Beijing South daily.				
G66	Guangzhou South – Beijing West	10:00–18:00	8 hr 00 min	¥862
Note: There are 4 more bullet trains from Guangzhou South to Beijing West daily (08:28-18:21; 11:15-21:09; 12:10-21:45; 12:50-22:21), and 5 regular trains taking 20 to 30 hours.				
G32	Hangzhou East – Beijing South	08:30–13:28	4 hr 58 min	¥538.5
Note: There are 11 bullet trains from Hangzhou (or Hangzhou East) to Beijing South daily.				
G204	Nanjing South – Beijing South	07:37–12:15	4 hr 38 min	¥443.5
Note: There are 30 bullet trains from Nanjing South to Beijing South daily.				
G182	Ji'nan – Beijing South	07:15–09:19	2 hr 04 min	¥194.5
Note: There are 60 bullet trains from Jinan (or Jinan West) to Beijing South daily.				
D332	Qingdao – Beijing South	06:50–12:25	5 hr 35 min	¥249
Note: There are 10 bullet trains from Qingdao to Beijing South daily.				
G262	Hefei – Beijing South	07:30–11:45	4 hr 15 min	¥427.5
Note: There are 10 bullet trains from Hefei to Beijing South daily.				
G6706	Shijiazhuang – Beijing West	07:46–09:12	1 hr 25 min	¥128.5
Note: There are nearly 100 bullet trains from Shijiazhuang to Beijing West daily.				
G90	Zhengzhou East – Beijing West	09:00–11:30	2 hr 30 min	¥309
Note: There are 50 bullet trains from Zhengzhou East (or Zhengzhou) to Beijing West daily.				
G92	Taiyuan – Beijing West	08:30–11:00	2 hr 30 min	¥194
Note: There are 18 bullet trains from Taiyuan to Beijing West daily.				
G84	Changsha South – Beijing West	09:00–14:40	5 hr 40 min	¥649
Note: There are 15 bullet trains from Changsha South to Beijing West daily.				
G652	Xi'an North – Beijing West	07:50–13:17	5 hr 27 min	¥515.5
Note: There are 9 bullet trains from Xi'an North to Beijing West daily; there are 9 more regular trains taking 11 to 17 hours.				
G508	Wuhan – Beijing West	07:22–12:29	5 hr 07 min	¥520.5
Note: There are 28 bullet trains from Wuhan (or Hankou Wuhan, or Wuchang Wuhan) to Beijing West daily.				
D28	Harbin West – Beijing	06:50–14:55	8 hr 05 min	¥306.5
Note: There are 16 bullet trains from Harbin West to Beijing (or Beijing South) daily.				
D14	Shenyang North – Beijing	08:30–13:28	4 hr 58 min	¥206
Note: There are 30 bullet trains from Shenyang North (or Shenyang) to Beijing daily.				
D35/D38	Dalian North – Beijing	10:40–16:53	6 hr 13 min	¥261
Note: There are 7 bullet trains from Dalian North (or Dalian) to Beijing (or Beijing South) daily.				
D24	Changchun – Beijing	07:32–14:17	6 hr 45 min	¥267.5
Note: There are 8 bullet trains from Changchun (or Changchun West) to Beijing daily.				
G56	Fuzhou – Beijing South	08:00–18:36	10 hr 36 min	¥765
Z60/Z57	Fuzhou – Beijing West	16:55–12:58	20 hr 03 min	seat/sleeper: ¥251/¥456
T58	Chengdu – Beijing West	11:16–10:19	23 hr 03 min	seat/sleeper: ¥254.5/¥464.5
Note: There are 5 regular trains from Chengdu to Beijing West daily.				
Z68	Nanchang – Beijing West	20:12–07:38	11 hr 26 min	seat/sleeper: ¥173.5/¥317.5
Note: There are 5 regular trains from Nanchang to Beijing West (or Beijing) daily.				
T316	Hohhot – Beijing West	08:15–14:24	6 hr 09 min	seat/sleeper: ¥75/¥142
Note: There are 15 regular trains from Hohhot to Beijing (or Beijing West, or Beijing North) daily.				
T275/T278	Yinchuan – Beijing West	20:50–09:37	12 hr 47 min	seat/sleeper: ¥152.5/¥279.5
Note: There are 3 more regular trains from Yinchuan to Beijing (or Beijing West) daily (16:30 – 11:18; 17:42 – 09:41; 00:01 – 19:42).				

Top Attractions

pg 50 — The Great Wall

pg 62 — Forbidden City

pg 72 — Summer Palace

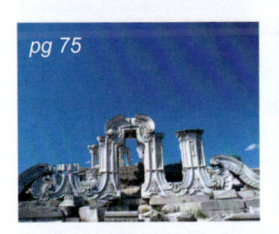

pg 75 — Old Summer Palace

pg 78 — Temple of Heaven

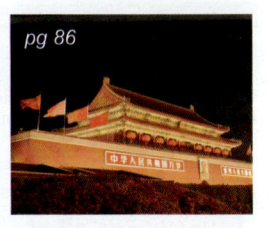

pg 86 — Tian'anmen Square

pg 98 — Shichahai Area

pg 107 — Beihai Park

pg 110 — Hutongs

pg 116 — Lama Temple

pg 123 — 798 Art District

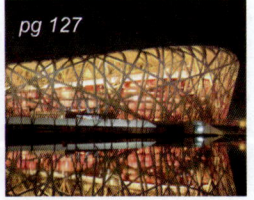

pg 127 — Olympic Legacies

The Great Wall

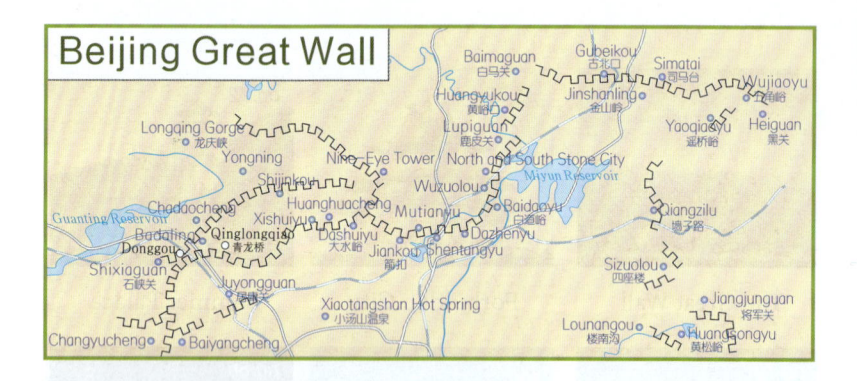

This section covers eight sections of the Great Wall: Badaling, Mutianyu, Huanghuacheng, Juyongguan, Simatai, Gubeikou, Jinshanling, and Jiankou.

The Great Wall of China is the single most iconic and legendary structure in all of Chinese history and is equally monumental as a stunning testament to the ingenuity and artisanship of the Chinese people. In a certain respect, the Great Wall is a misnomer, as it is actually a series of walls that has never actually been a contiguous single. The 2,000-year-old wall winds its way from the border of North Korea all the way to Lop Nur in the western province of Xinjiang. Snaking for a mind-boggling 8,852 km (5,500 mi) through numerous provinces and principalities, the wall is spectacular, and the most accessible regions sit just on the outskirts of Beijing.

Here we will cover eight of the most visited sections in Beijing. Each section has its own unique characteristics, from the rugged and untamed Jiankou route to the convenient but congested Badaling. The more touristy segments are superbly maintained and give the visitor a vivid impression of the ancient presence the wall exhibited two millennia ago. The rougher sections are more alluring to hardy adventure seekers; these often crumbling and overgrown portions provide some of the most breathtaking views on the wall, and their unrestored nature qualifies them as ultra-authentic.

Chinese name: 长城 (Chángchéng)
Length: 8,852 km (5,500 mi)
Construction Period: About 2,000 years; from the Warring States Period (476 BC-221 BC) to the Ming Dynasty (1368-1644).
Prices & hours: Both vary depending on the section you want to visit. Please see the vital info for each section.

History

Wall building was nothing new to the Chinese by the time of the Spring and Autumn Period, which ran from the 8th to the 5th centuries BCE. This period, and the subsequent Warring States period, saw the states of Qin, Wei, Zhao, Qi, Yan and Zhongshan all construct extensive fortifications to defend their individual borders. The walls were designed to withstand attacks from small arms such as swords and spears, and for this purpose they were just earth and gravel stamped between frames of wood.

The Warring States period came to a definitive halt with the establishment of the Qin Dynasty (221-207BC), as Qin Shihuang conquered all opposition and unified China in 221 BCE. With his imposition of centralized rule and efforts to discourage the resurgence of feudal lords, Qin had the wall sections that divided his empire along the former state borders reduced to rubble. With the strength of a unified empire at his back, he rerouted concerns and resources towards the raiding Xiongnu people from the north and ordered the construction of a new wall to connect the remaining fortifications along the empire's new northern frontier. The hugely cumbersome materials were not easy to transport, and the "ice road" technology of the Forbidden City had not yet been imagined. This meant that local resources were heavily relied upon, which in turn meant that in mountainous regions much of the wall was stone, while on the plains it was largely limited to rammed earth.

There are no surviving historical records indicating the exact length and course of the Qin Dynasty walls; erosion and wear have claimed most of them over the centuries, and very few sections remain today. The exact human cost of the construction is unknown, but some researchers have estimated that hundreds of thousands of workers died building the Qin wall over the course of ten years.

Heedful of their predecessor's earnest northern defense, the Han, Sui, and Northern Dynasties all repaired, rebuilt, or extended sections of the Great Wall at no small cost to their coffers or workers' lives. Besides a short section built by the Jin Dynasty during the 5th century in today's Mongolia, the wall received no more construction until the Ming Dynasty (1368-1644), some 1,000 years after.

Ironically, the massive wall that was kept up during the Jin Dynasty proved to be a spectacular failure against the might of Genghis Khan's Mongolia. Never truly being a contiguous wall, the Mongols inevitably identified the breaches, and it was through these gaps that Genghis Khan drove his armies to capture Beijing in 1225 and establish his Yuan Dynasty. The wall would see limited success over the years, with the most notable defensive stand coming at the end of the Ming Dynasty.

Ming Dynasty

The Great Wall proposal was thrown back on the table in the court of the Ming Dynasty during the 14th century. A long and drawn-out conflict with the Manchurian and Mongolian tribes was fatiguing the empire. Successive battles provided no upper hand, so the Ming court proposed the resurrection of a millennium-old strategy to keep the nomadic tribes out: a wall of epic proportions along the northern border of China. Wisely leaving the Mongol control established in the Ordos Desert unchallenged, the wall was constructed along the desert's southern perimeter.

Technologically contrasting with the earlier Qin fortifications, the Ming ramparts were far more stalwart and elaborate, with bricks and stone being used instead of rammed earth. Estimations of up to 25,000 watchtowers along the Ming wall give stunning testament to the grandiosity of the feat. Mongol raids were never far off, and the Ming emperors devoted heaps of resources to repair and reinforce the walls. Defending their capital of Beijing was a top priority, and it is largely because of the Ming emperors that the Beijing sections have been particularly well strengthened and maintained. In particular, Emperor Qi Jiguang, between 1567 and 1570, repaired and reinforced the wall, faced sections of the ram-earth wall with bricks, and constructed 1,200 watchtowers from Shanhaiguan Pass to Changping to warn of approaching Mongol raiders.

The end of the Ming Dynasty showcased the most adept stand of the Great Wall as a defensive bastion. On their approach to Beijing in 1644, the Manchus met with the Ming army at Shanhaiguan, where the wall connected with the sea in the east. The Manchus, who had already taken all of Liaodong (modern day Liaoning), could not penetrate the heavily reinforced pass and were prevented from entering the Chinese heartland. It was only through the traitorous Ming general Wu Sangui that the gates were opened and the Manchus allowed to overtake the Great Wall in 1644. They quickly seized Beijing and defeated both the rebel-founded Shun Dynasty and the remaining Ming resistance, establishing Qing Dynasty rule over all of China. With the Dynasty's annexation of Mongolia and, consequentially, a greatly expanded northern border, maintenance of the wall fell as quickly as the need for its protection.

Though the overall military effectiveness of the wall was often little more than mediocre, it did serve quite usefully as an ancient highway. Goods, equipment, and people could be transported very long distances over the rugged mountainous terrain. Traversing such terrain would have proven quite impossible without the wall, which is said to have the accommodation capacity for five galloping horses in certain sections. You can make your own discoveries when you visit one or many of the eight sections of the Beijing Great Wall.

Before You Go

The Great Wall has many areas to visit, and not all sections are the same. The restored sections provide their share of steep walking, but they are well maintained, beautifully crafted and quite safe. Badaling is the most touristy area of the wall, with Mutianyu holding a close second. Simatai, Jinshanling, and Huanghuacheng are partly-restored, and their commercialism tends to fall in the middle. The unrestored sections include Jiankou and Zhuangdaokou, among others. Hiking these can vary from challenging to downright dangerous. For each section we will provide you with an essential items list.

Most of the sections we list can be accessed

via public transport, and a few require a taxi for the last leg. Tours are readily available, but not all of them are desirable. Hotel or travel agency tours are not recommended as they tend to be highly commercialized and include unwanted and unnecessary frills and side trips. Hostel tours can be more reliable since they tend to cater to the adventurous Western mind, but they can be hit or miss. Below, we have provided a list of reputable non-hotel tour companies that we recommend, as well as a list of general essentials to bring on your Great Wall excursion. This list is not necessarily all-inclusive, so please check the "Hiking & Info" and "Packing & Additional Options" notes for your chosen section before you depart.

Our recommended tour companies:

Bike Beijing (phone: 133 8140 0738; website: www.bikebeijing.com)

Beijing Hikers (phone: 6432 2786; website: www.beijinghikers.com)

Bespoke Beijing (phone: 6400 0133; website: www.bespokebeijing.com)

Snap Adventures (phone: 400 188 SNAP; website: www.snapadventures.com)

Dandelion Hiking (phone: 156 5220 0950; website: www.chinahiking.cn)

Beijing Sideways (phone:139 1133 4947; website: www.beijingsideways.com)

Packing Essentials

Sunscreen – There are some places for shade on every section, but count on a lot of wall-walking, which means major sun exposure.

Water – Though touristy sections have water, it's quite expensive. Don't fork out the cash when you can bring your own.

Walking shoes – No matter what section you choose, expect some decent walking. Avoidable foot aches will detract from your experience.

Camera – Even if you are heading to Jiankou for a hardcore fitness adventure, you will be kicking yourself when you realize you'd love a picture of the unbelievable views but didn't pack a camera.

Badaling

Chinese name: 八达岭 (Bādálǐng)
Admission: ¥45 (Apr 1-Oct 31); ¥40 (Nov 1-Mar 31)
Hours: 6:30-19:00 (summer); 7:00-18:00 (winter)
Website: www.badaling.gov.cn (English option on top right corner)

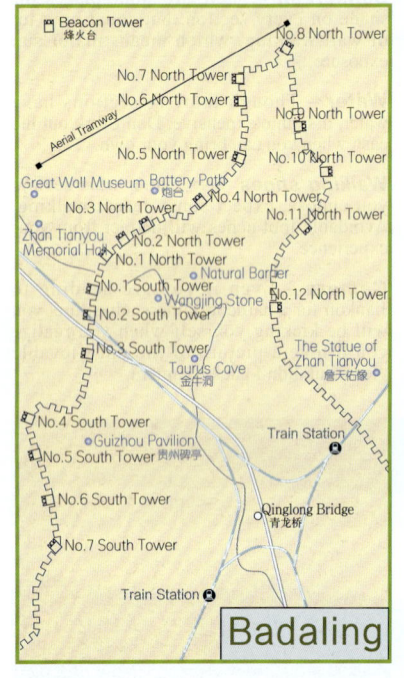

[Map of Badaling showing Beacon Tower, North Towers No.1-11, South Towers No.1-7, Great Wall Museum, Aerial Tramway, Zhan Tianyou Memorial Hall, Natural Barrier, Wangjing Stone, Taurus Cave, The Statue of Zhan Tianyou, Guizhou Pavilion, Qinglong Bridge, Train Stations]

The Great Wall amusement park of Badaling sure has a pretty wall – too bad you can't see it through all those tourists. OK, sometimes you can see the wall here quite well, but if you come to this most popular section on a summer weekend you can forget about seeing much of anything except people. Great Wall hiking elitism aside, for many people the convenience of this area is offset by the souvenir hawkers and the hordes of tourists that can at times make walking come to a standstill. The highest visitation day in Badaling's history saw 41,000 tourists.

While you digest that number remember that the section's most recent full renovation in the 1980s also makes historical authenticity pretty lackluster. Nevertheless, Badaling photos can be postcard worthy (again, if there aren't too many people), and its tourist facilities are top notch. Badaling is great for the leisurely visitor, those pressed for time, the disabled, or those who want to view the Wall in its most accurately restored form representing 14th century Ming bastions. Your best bet is to come on a weekday.

Hiking & Info

The steps can be quite large, and some short areas offer a steep descent, but Badaling is highly manageable, so walking this section is particularly well suited for those with physical impairments and/or small children. Keep in mind, however, that busy days can be so crowded that walking is no longer a convenient option, and pictures may be loaded with throngs of people.

Pack & Additional Options

Sunscreen, Water, Snacks, Camera

Cable car – ¥60 one way, ¥80 round trip

Transport

Taxi – ¥400 to ¥700 round trip.

Bus – Badaling-bound buses all depart from the north side of **Deshengmen** (德胜门) gateway. From Jishuitan (积水潭) subway station on Line 2, head east for 500 m (1,640 ft). Listed below are bus schedules:

887 – ¥12; 1 hour; 6:00 to 17:00; arrives at Badaling east car park
919 – ¥12; 1.5 hours; 6:00 to 18:30; arrives at Badaling west car park
880 – ¥12; 1.5 hours; 7:00 to 17:00; arrives at Badaling west car park

Tour Bus – Catch a tour bus at the Beijing Hub of Tourist Dispatch (Běijīng Lǚyóu Jísàn Zhōngxīn; 北京旅游集散中心; phone: 010 835 31111; website: www.bjlyjszx.com/english/index_1.htm), located south of Tian'anmen Square. Prices include return ticket and Badaling entry ticket.

Line A – ¥160; includes lunch and a trip to the Ming Tombs; departs 6:30 to 10:30 (Apr 1-Oct 15), 7:00 to 10:30 (Oct 16-Mar 31); this is a 9 hour trip
Line B – ¥190; includes lunch and a trip to the Summer Palace; departs at 9:30
Line C – ¥120; departs 6:30 to 11:00 (Apr 1-Oct 15), 9:00 to 10:30 (Oct 16-Mar 31)

Train – Beijing North Station next to Xizhimen subway station (line 2, 4 and 13) is your departure hub for Badaling. Return trains set off from Badaling station, next to the west car park.

> Morning departures – 6:12; 7:58; 8:34; 9:02 and 10:57
> Afternoon returns – 13:02; 15:19; 15:52; 16:21; 17:33 and 19:55

Mutianyu

Chinese name: 慕田峪 (Mùtiányù)
Admission: ¥45 (Apr 1-Oct 31); ¥40 (Nov 1-Mar 31)
Hours: 6:30-19:00 (summer); 7:00-18:00 (winter)
Website: www.badaling.gov.cn (English option on top right corner)

Although Mutianyu comes in second for Great Wall tourist destinations, putting it on equal ground to Badaling in terms of visitation would be inaccurate. There is a noteworthy gap in the volume of tour groups that come to Mutianyu, so if you're looking for convenience marked with less hordes, this might be your place. This section has also been recently renovated (1986), and features a chairlift, a cable car, numerous tourist facilities, and an ever-popular toboggan slide. Mutianyu takes a bit longer to reach than Badaling, so most tours here tend to sidestep the off-putting side trips to jade markets and silk factories that are problematic elements on Badaling tours. Though there are good hikes and the crowds are much more manageable than Badaling, Mutianyu can still get somewhat congested, especially from spring to mid-autumn.

Hiking & Info

Mutianyu is possibly the best of the wall sections to bring a family. Recent renovations have made it very photogenic and it is quite easy to hike and maneuver. Furthermore, souvenirs can be found (bargaining is highly advised) for those who want something from the wall, but the hawkers generally keep to the lower areas, so you can enjoy the scenery without being accosted. Finally, the presence of a cable car and toboggan slide can ease hiking time going up and down to various parts of this section.

Because Mutianyu is only 3 km (2 mi) long, trips to this area do not require much packing. Restaurants and fruit stands sit at the bottom, so food is available, though overpriced.

There is also accommodation at Mutianyu if you want to stay the night before or after a hike. **The Great Wall Villa** offers a more luxurious stay, while the **farmhouses** are scenic, charming, and have a rustic authenticity. They are equipped with a dining service and even – get this – karaoke!

Pack & Additional Options

Sunscreen, Water, Snacks, Camera

Charlift – ¥50 one way

Cable car – ¥60 one way; ¥80 round trip; children half-price

Toboggan slide – ¥60 adult; ¥50 child

Fuguihong Farmhouse (Fùguìhóng Nóngjiāyuàn; 富贵宏农家院; phone: 010 6068 1116) – ¥40 ordinary room; ¥50 standard room; ¥60 heated brick bed

Bao Sheng Ren Jia Farmhouse (Bǎoshēng Rénjiā Nóngjiāyuàn; 宝生人家农家院; phone: 010 6068 2120; 133 6626 8828) – ¥50-80 standard room; ¥100-120 luxury room; ¥60 heated brick bed

Great Wall Villa (Chángchéng Shānzhuāng; 长城山庄; phone: 010 6162 6395) – ¥180 standard room; there is a Finnish sauna here

Transport

Taxi – ¥500 to ¥600 round trip.

Bus – **Dongzhimen Wai** (东直门外) bus stop seasonally runs bus 867 to Mutianyu twice a day from March 15 to November 15 only, otherwise you will need a tour or the alternate bus option.

867 departing – ¥16, 2.5 hours, 7:00 and 8:30
867 returning – ¥16, 14:00 and 16:00

The other local bus option requires some extra steps, but is a nice little adventure for those so inclined. From **Dongzhimen Transport Hub** (东直门交通枢纽) which is right at Dongzhimen Subway Station, you will need to take bus 916 快 (快 is "*kuai*," or fast) to Huairou, exiting at the Mingzhu Guangchang (明珠广场) stop. Take your first right and grab one of the minivans waiting to take passengers up to the wall for ¥15 (30 mins).

916 快 departing to Huairou – ¥12, 1 hour, 6:30 to 19:30
916 快 returning from Huairou – ¥12, all day to 19:00

If you miss the last minivan coming home, grab a taxi to Huairou before 19:00. If you get to Huairou but miss the last bus, grab a taxi to the northernmost subway station on Line 15: Houshayu (后沙峪). You can subway it back from there.

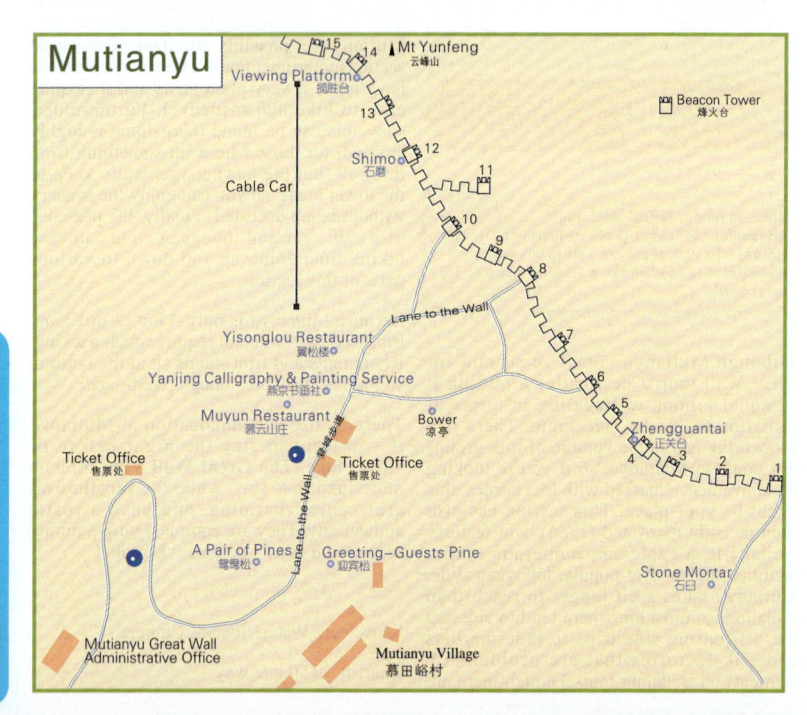

Juyongguan

Chinese name: 居庸关 (Jūyōngguān)
Admission: ¥45 (Apr 1-Oct 31); ¥40 (Nov 1-Mar 31)
Hours: 8:30–17:00
Website: www.juyongguan.com (English option on top right corner)

Juyongguan is more of a large fortress than a wall. Actually it's both – but mostly a fortress. It was fully restored in 1992 and 2000, so it is essentially a modern creation, albeit a pretty one. For authentic wall seekers Juyongguan will disappoint, but for others, the views at Juyongguan are breathtaking; perhaps the most amazing of any restored section. As early as the Jin Dynasty (1115 – 1234), it was known as one of the eight most beautiful scenic spots of Beijing, and in 1987 the renowned pass was listed in the World Heritage Directory.

The wall at Juyongguan slides right down to the parking lot, meaning there is no chairlift, and it is easily accessible from Beijing. The hiking along the wall can be steep, but the full, modern restoration means it is not rugged or technical. As long as you can climb stairs, Juyongguan will provide no unmanageable challenges.

Hiking & Info

The pass is circular with a perimeter of about 4 km (2.5 mi) and actually consists of two passes: Nan Kou to the north and Badaling to the south. If you are not in the mood to be annoyed we advise you to avoid heading in the Badaling direction, which is loaded with souvenir hawkers. Like all hawkers at the major tourist destinations, they can be quite persistent, so move quickly through them.

Attention, language dorks! Near the center of Juyongguan you will find a marble structure known as **Cloud Terrace**, or Yuntai. This beautiful stone tab is a rare survivor from the Yuan Dynasty and was built in 1365. Among its exquisite carvings is a Dharani Sutra in six different languages: Chinese, Mongolian, Sanskrit, Tangut, Tibetan, and Uighur. There are also temples and a giant water gate, all built in the ancient Ming style.

You can find plenty of restaurants at Juyongguan, the largest and most apparent being the not so aptly named **Juyongguan Pass Great Wall Old Inn**.

Pack & Additional Options

Sunscreen, Water, Snacks (recommended but not essential), Camera

Juyongguan Pass Great Wall Old Inn (Jūyōngguān Chángchéng Gǔ Kèzhàn; 居庸关长城古客栈; phone: 010 6977 8888; rooms start at ¥298). This luxury hotel features a 200-person dining room, swimming pool, Western breakfast, satellite TV, bowling, and a plethora of other amenities.

Transport

Taxi – ¥400 to ¥700 round trip

Bus – From the **Deshengmen** (德胜门) **Transportation Hub** you can catch a couple of buses to Juyongguan Great Wall. There are many buses that will take you to Deshengmen, but a more convenient option may be to take subway Line 2 to Jishuitan (积水潭) and walk east about 450 m (1,476 ft). From Deshengmen Station either grab the 880 or the 919 bus and take it to Nankouhuandao Bei Station (南口环岛北站). Next, hop on the Changping (昌平) 68 bus and take it to the terminal stop. Note: the number 68 bus has the Changping characters, so look for this on the placard: 昌平68.

880 – ¥6, 1.5 hours, 7:00 to 19:30
919 – ¥6, 1.5 hours, 6:00 to 18:30

昌平 68 – about ¥12

Tour bus – There are four different tour buses that make morning trips to the Juyongguan Great Wall area; you should be able to find one that is relatively close to your area.

> Tour bus 1 – Northeast part of Jianlou in Qianmen; departs 6:00-10:00
>
> Tour bus 2 – Beijing Railway Station; departs 6:00-10:00
>
> Tour bus 3 – Dongda Bridge; departs 6:00-10:00
>
> Tour bus 4 – Beijing Zoo; departs 6:30-10:00

Train – Trains to Juyongguan depart from **Beijing North Railway Station** (北京北站), which is located near Xizhimen Subway Station, and let off at Juyongguan Station. Please note each train's morning departure time and afternoon return time from Juyongguan.

> 7173 – 9:10 depart; 15:00 return
> L671 – 7:18 depart; 14:29 return
> L673 – 7:56 depart; 15:03 return
> L675 – 8:50 depart; 14:09 return

Huanghuacheng

Chinese name: 黄花城 (Huánghuāchéng)
Admission: ¥34
Hours: 8:00-17:00 (weekdays); 7:30-17:30 (weekends)
Website: www.huanghuacheng.com (English option on top right corner)

Less remote than the other partially restored sections of the Great Wall and less touristy than other areas in the Beijing vicinity, Huanghuacheng mixes the ancient with relative convenience. Huanghuacheng is closer to the city than Mutianyu, and straddles a small reservoir, yet it is strangely devoid of crowds (most likely because this area has undergone only partial restoration). The authentic Ming battlements are well preserved, and the area offers spectacular views without the peddlers of other sections. Those who are up for good hikes on some seriously steep inclines, but are not so tempted by the vertical climbs at Jiankou, may find Huanghuacheng to be the perfect half-day destination.

Hiking & Info

The partially restored Huanghuacheng makes for some excellent hikes through its relatively well-preserved ramparts and watchtowers.

The road towards the wall here has a left and a right option. The right option has a mighty incline; get ready for some exhilarating hiking. The left option moves toward the non-wild section near Zhuangdaokou village. The far better option is to go right and have a good hike from the dam, then scramble up the metal ladder at the second beacon tower. The ladder puts you on the wall, and you can hike east from here to Jiankou and Mutianyu. Keep your head up and pay attention, the wall will get very steep at points, and the worn stones can be slippery.

There are many places to eat around here, as long as you like fish. If you don't like fish you'd better bring some food. You can also choose to stay and eat at **Tenglong Fandian**, a lodge and restaurant just off the main road up to the wall. Some people like to get here and then stay overnight in order to tackle a big hike in the morning.

Pack & Additional Options

Sunscreen, Water, Lunch, Camera, Hiking or climbing shoes with good grip

Tenglong Restaurant (Ténglóng Fàndiàn; 腾龙饭店; phone: 010 6165 1929; 134 3955 5602) – meals ¥15-35, rooms with shared shared bathroom ¥50, private rooms ¥80

Transport

Taxi – about ¥500 to ¥600 round trip

Bus – The journey to Huanghuacheng requires an easy bus transfer, so heads up. Start from **Dongzhimen Transport Hub** and take bus 916 快 to the Nanhuayuan Sanqu (南花园三区) stop at Huairou. Follow that road about 250 m (820 ft) and cross the next block to get to the Nanhuayuan Siqu (南花园四区) bus stop. The bus from here has no number, look above the front windshield for a sign that reads, "怀柔 - 黄花城." The meaning is "Huairou to Huanghuacheng." The bus runs once an hour, so your other option is to do like Mutianyu and grab a minivan from Huairou for ¥10.

> 916 快 departing to Huairou – ¥12; 1 hour; 6:30 to 19:30
> 916 快 returning from Huairou – ¥12; all day to 19:00
> 怀柔 - 黄花城 – ¥8, 1 hour; all day until 18:00

Simatai

Chinese name: 司马台 (Sīmǎtái)

Simatai is one of the more rugged parts of the partially restored sections of the Great Wall, though some of the authentic characteristics – crumbly watchtowers and hundred-year-old bricks – may soon be a thing of the past. Simatai has grown vastly in popularity, and it was closed at the time of research for extensive renovation, with no exact date for completion. Though the historical authenticity of Simatai may be lost in restoration, the wonderful beauty of the scenery will still be worth a visit. Check back in future guides for updated information.

Gubeikou

Chinese name: 古北口 (Gǔběikǒu)
Admission: ¥25
Hours: 9:00-16:00

Gubeikou is one of the longest sections of the Great Wall near Beijing and, after Jiankou, is the most isolated section. Gubeikou has a western section that is in its original, unrestored condition and an eastern section that has been fully restored. There has been no commercial development of Gubeikou and there are no shops, toilets or other tourist facilities. You may need to squat in the bushes!

Gubeikou doesn't have the crowds of Badaling or Mutianyu and it's not dangerous or difficult to hike like Jiankou. This makes Gubeikou an excellent section of the Great Wall to visit if you want a bit of adventure but aren't into cracking your head open. Hit Gubeikou for an excellent view of the old and the new; the contrast of the east and west sections is a unique sight.

Hiking & Info

The wall at Gubeikou does not follow any steep cliffs or ridges and all the important steps are fairly intact, so walking it is not dangerous or too difficult. There are some sections with steep drops, but crossing these can be done safely. The eastern section is restored and very similar in condition to Mutianyu. Avoid the difficult western section unless you are a fit and experienced hiker.

The beginning of the western section is in such crumbly condition that the wall is not visible at all and there are only the brittle remains of two watchtowers. The condition of the wall at the beginning is so bad that much of the trail is beside the wall because the actual wall itself is either in ruins or is just piles of brick and rubble. As you head east the conditions improve, and certain areas of the wall (and several watchtowers) are almost complete.

If you want to stay overnight you have two options: **Gubeikou Hexi Village** (Gǔběikǒu Héxīcūn; 古北口河西村) or **Gubeikou Town Folk Village** (Gǔběikǒu Zhèn Mínsú Dùjiàcūn; 古北口镇民俗度假村). They offer local cuisine, and guests can participate in local activities, including fishing, dancing, cards and Mahjong.

Pack & Additional Options

Sunscreen, Water, Snacks, Camera, Toilet paper

Gubeikou Hexi Village – about ¥60 per person, per day

Gubeikou Town Folk Village – about ¥60 per person, per day

Transport

Taxi – ¥700 to ¥1,000 round trip

Bus – Hop on the subway to **Dongzhimen Station** (Line 13, 10) and leave through Exit B. Dongzhimen Wai long distance bus station is a short walk to the northeast. From here catch the 980 or the 980 快 bus to the village of Miyun and hop off in the center of the town. From here you can either catch another large public bus to Gubeikou township or one of several minibuses (¥10).

980 – ¥15; 1.5 hours; all day until 19:00 (last one from Miyun)

Jinshanling

Chinese name: 金山岭 (Jīnshānlǐng)
Admission: ¥65 (Mar 16-Nov 15); ¥55 (Nov 16-Mar 15)
Hours: 8:00-17:00

Jinshanling lies between the other two partially restored sections that neighbor the small outlying town of Gubeikou. This section of wall is the starting point for a well respected hike that goes from here to Simatai. The invigorating 7 km (4 mi) journey twists through inspiringly remote mountains, and the three to four hour hike can be heart-poundingly steep at times, especially where some of the stairs have collapsed. If you're in decent shape you'll manage just fine. The arid landscape seems to fit accordingly with the watchtowers that display a notable range of preservation.

Hiking & Info

Though Simatai is closed for renovations for an indefinite amount of time, you should consider the 7 km (4 mi) adventure. Bringing water is a must, as hucksters up here know their customers well and they will scour a high price out of the inevitably thirsty hikers. Packing your lunch is highly recommended as well since the hike takes three to four hours; you don't want to be halfway through with a gnawing hunger and no food. Make a left when you reach the wall and you're off to Simatai. There is a cable car as well if you feel the urge to save some energy.

If you don't want to bring your own lunch, fuel up at the farming courtyards near the west gate. They have local food and lodgings if you want to stay the night before or after you tackle the wall. The east gate, about 2 km (1 mi) from the west gate, offers a café with an English menu.

Pack & Additional Options

Sunscreen, Water, Lunch, Camera, Good hiking or walking shoes

Cable car – ¥30 one way, ¥50 round trip

Farming courtyards – ¥30 or so for a meal, ¥80-100 for a room

Transport

Taxi – ¥900 to ¥1,000 round trip fare

Bus – There are two bus options to get to Jinshanling, one of them includes a short taxi ride.

1. Start from **Sihui Long Distance Bus Station** (四惠长途汽车站), slightly southeast of Sihui Subway Station on Line 1. Take the bus that goes to Chengde (承德) but tell the driver you want to get off at Jinshanling (if you just say Jinshanling he will know what you mean). This means you will not ride the whole way to Chengde, but you will still need to pay the full fare. The bus will drop you on the highway about 1 km (less than 1 mi) from the Jinshanling east gate. Return to where you were dropped off on the main highway around mid-evening to flag a return bus.

> Chengde bus – ¥85; 2.5 hours; leaves every 20 minutes

2. Grab bus 980 from **Dongzhimen Transport Hub** to Miyun and then take a

taxi to Jinshanling.

980 – ¥15; 1.5 hours; all day until 19:00 (last one from Miyun)

Tour bus – **Dongzhimen Wai Bus Station** has one daily tour bus: Jīnshānlǐng Chángchéng Lǚyóu Bānchē Zhuānxiàn (金山岭长城旅游班车专线).

Jinshanling Changcheng Luyou Banche Zhuanxian – ¥120; 2 hours; 8:00 depart; 15:00 return

Jiankou

Chinese name: 箭扣 (Jiànkòu)
Admission: ¥20
Hours: 7:00-17:00

Hardcore wall-hikers lace up those boots, Jiankou is by far the wildest and most insanely remote section of the Great Wall. The panoramic views are amazing, the unrestored and overgrown wall is kickass, and many places are dangerous as hell – this hike is not for the inexperienced.

Hiking & Info

Jiankou is totally unrestored and should never be attempted in inclement weather. Traversing this wall at times encounters near-vertical inclines, and some areas can be truly dangerous. It is not unheard of to face a crumbled staircase that beckons with six meters of vertical bouldering, and unprepared hikers have been seriously injured. The isolation means that any fall requiring medical attention may not be satisfied for hours. Solid shoes with excellent grip and a clear, confident head are essential. You are also highly advised not to hike Jiankou alone; traveling with a friend will ensure that someone is there to help if you need it. This being said, experienced and fit hikers should not be discouraged from taking advantage of the fantastic hiking and camping opportunities at Jiankou when the weather is agreeable. Being aware of the risks and rewards will ensure an awesome experience at Jiankou.

From the ticket office, head immediately left to Xizhazi village and take the first path. The steep path is the perfect warm-up before hitting the wall. There are farming courtyards to eat at here, but bringing your own lunch is highly recommended. They do not speak any English, but they are always quite happy to meet foreigners.

Pack & Additional Options

Sunscreen, Water, Lunch, Camera, Good hiking or walking shoes

Farming courtyards – ¥30 or so for a meal

Transport

Taxi – ¥500 to ¥700 round trip

Bus – The bus to Jiankou is definitely part of the Jiankou adventure. From **Dongzhimen Transport Hub** take the 916 快 to the Mingzhu Guanchang bus stop at Huairou. Here you will need to haggle for a taxi to take you to Xizhazi Village (Xīzhāzi Cūn). Don't pay more than ¥130. From Xizhazi village it's an hour walk to the wall through a relaxing pine forest.

916 快 – ¥12, 1 hour, 6:30 to 19:30
Taxi to Xizhazi Cun – ¥100 – ¥130 one way, 1 hour

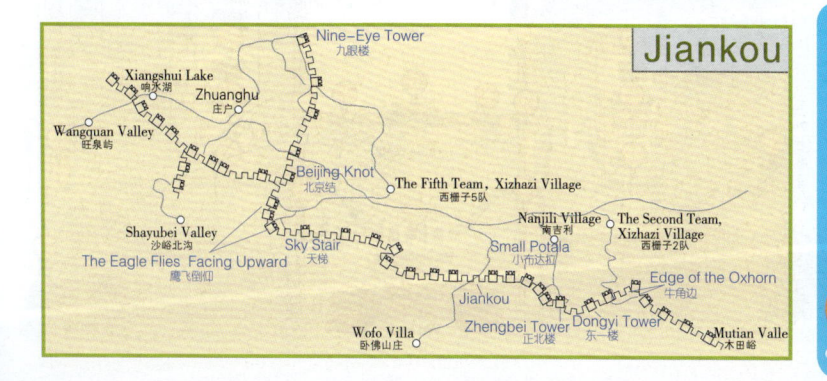

The Forbidden City

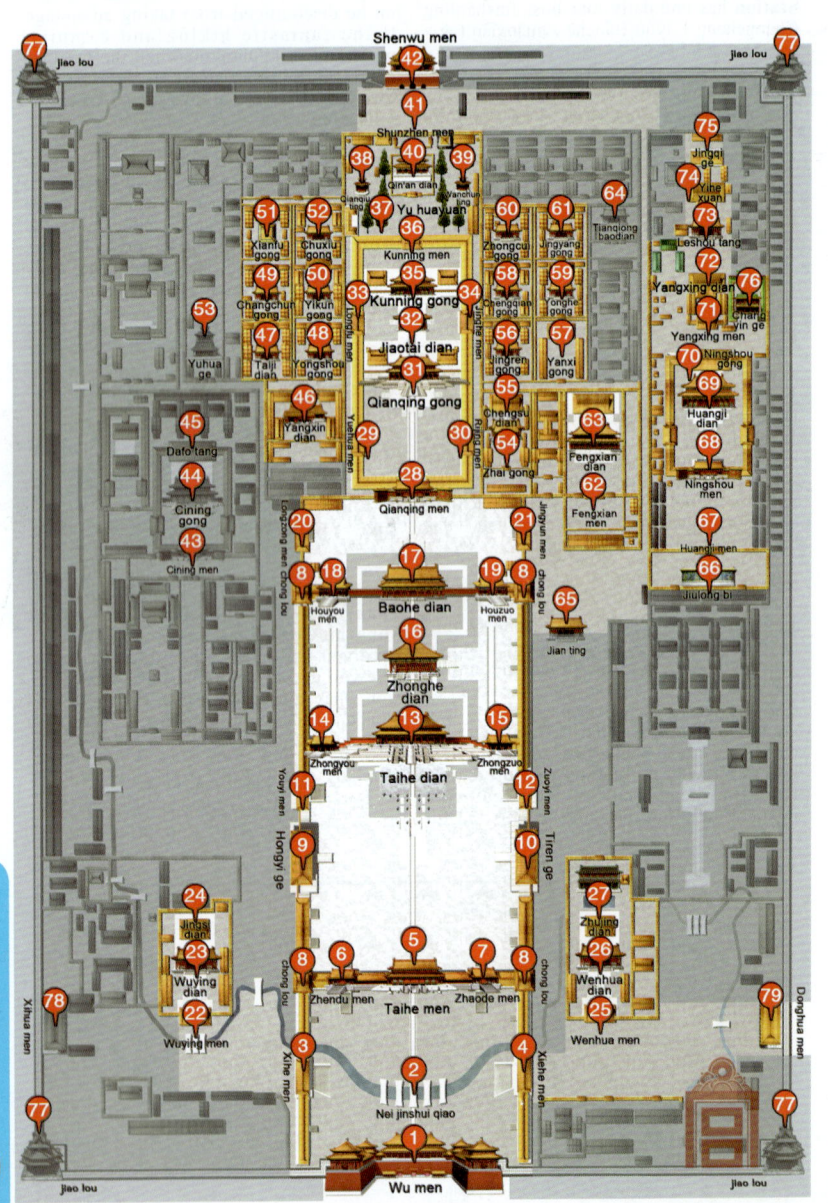

Chinese name: 故宫 (Gù Gōng)
Admission: ¥60 (Apr-Oct); ¥40 (Nov-Mar). For entrance to the Treasure Gallery (Zhenbao Guan, where the Stone Drum Gallery is located) and to the Hall of Clocks (Zhongbiao Guan), additional ¥10 tickets are necessary.
Hours: 8:30-17:00 (it might open early at 8:00 and close early at 16:30, depending on the season); closed Mon
Website: www.dpm.org.cn (English available)
Address: 4 Jingshan Qianjie (景山前街4号)
Transport:
Subway – Line 1, Tian'anmen East or Tian'anmen West Station, then walk north to The Forbidden City.
Taxi – Point this sentence out your driver if your Chinese will not suffice: 我想要去故宫。
If you cannot find the entrance please find some one and point to this sentence: 请问故宫正门怎么走。
Access: The Palace Museum adopts a south-north, one-way visiting system. The entrance is the Meridian Gate (Wu Men, the south gate) and the exit is the Gate of Divine Prowess (Shenwu Men, the north gate).

1. The Meridian Gate (Wǔ Mén; 午门)
2. Inner Golden Water Bridges (Nèi Jīnshuǐ Qiáo; 内金水桥)
3. Gate of Glorious Harmony (Xīhé Mén; 熙和门)
4. Gate of Mutual Harmony (Xiéhé Mén; 协和门)
5. Gate of Supreme Harmony (Tàihé Mén; 太和门)
6. Gate of Correct Conduct (Zhēndù Mén; 贞度门)
7. Gate of Manifest Virtue (Zhāodé Mén; 昭德门)
8. The Loft Pavilion (Chóng Lóu; 崇楼)
9. Belvedere of Spreading Righteousness (Hóngyì Gé; 弘义阁)
10. Belvedere of Embodying Benevolence (Tǐrén Gé; 体仁阁)
11. Right-wing Gate (Yòuyì Mén; 右翼门)
12. Left-wing Gate (Zuǒyì Mén; 左翼门)
13. Hall of Supreme Harmony (Tàihé Diàn; 太和殿)
14. Middle Right Gate (Zhōngyòu Mén; 中右门)
15. Middle Left Gate (Zhōngzuǒ Mén; 中左门)
16. Hall of Central Harmony (Zhōnghé Diàn; 中和殿)
17. Hall of Preserving Harmony (Bǎohé Diàn; 保和殿)
18. Rear Right Gate (Hòuyòu Mén; 后右门)
19. Rear Left Gate (Hòuzuǒ Mén; 后左门)
20. Gate of Thriving Imperial Clan (Lóngzōng Mén; 隆宗门)
21. Gate of Good Fortune (Jǐngyùn Mén; 景运门)
22. Gate of Martial Valor (Wǔyīng Mén; 武英门)
23. Hall of Martial Valor (Wǔyīng Diàn; 武英殿)
24. Hall of Respectful Thoughts (Jìngsī Diàn; 敬思殿)
25. Gate of Literary Brilliance (Wénhuá Mén; 文华门)
26. Hall of Literary Brilliance (Wénhuá Diàn; 文华殿)
27. Hall of Observing Sincerity and Esteem (Zhǔjìng Diàn; 主敬殿)
28. Gate of Heavenly Purity (Qiánqīng Mén; 乾清门)
29. Gate of Lunar Essence (Yuèhuá Mén; 月华门)
30. Gate of Solar Essence (Rìjīng Mén; 日精门)
31. Palace of Heavenly Purity (Qiánqīng Gōng; 乾清宫)
32. Hall of Union (Jiāotài Diàn; 交泰殿)
33. Gate of Flourishing Blessings (Lóngfú Mén; 隆福门)
34. Gate of Auspicious Harmony (Jǐnghé Mén; 景和门)
35. Palace of Earthly Tranquility (Kūnníng Gōng; 坤宁宫)
36. Gate of Earthly Tranquility (Kūnníng Mén; 坤宁门)
37. The Imperial Garden (Yù Huāyuán; 御花园)
38. Pavilion of One Thousand Autumns (Qiānqiū Tíng; 千秋亭)
39. Pavilion of Myriad Springtimes (Wànchūn Tíng; 万春亭)
40. Hall of Imperial Peace (Qīn'ān Diàn; 钦安殿)
41. Gate of Loyal Obedience (Shùnzhēn Mén; 顺贞门)
42. Gate of Divine Prowess (Shénwǔ Mén; 神武门)
43. Gate of Compassion and Tranquility (Cíníng Mén; 慈宁门)
44. Palace of Compassion and Tranquility (Cíníng Gōng; 慈宁宫)
45. Grand Hall for Worshipping Buddha (Dàfó Táng; 大佛堂)
46. Hall of Mental Cultivation (Yǎngxīn Diàn; 养心殿)
47. Hall of the Supreme Principle (Tàijí Diàn; 太极殿)
48. Palace of Eternal Longevity (Yǒngshòu Gōng; 永寿宫)
49. Palace of Eternal Spring (Chángchūn Gōng; 长春宫)
50. Palace of Earthly Honor (Yìkūn Gōng; 翊坤宫)
51. Palace of Universal Happiness (Xiánfú Gōng; 咸福宫)
52. Palace of Gathered Elegance (Chǔxiù Gōng; 储秀宫)
53. Belvedere of Raining Flowers (Yǔhuá Gé; 雨花阁)
54. Hall for Abstinence (Zhāi Gōng; 斋宫)
55. Hall of Sincere Solemnity (Chéngsù Diàn; 诚肃殿)
56. Palace of Great Benevolence (Jǐngrén Gōng; 景仁宫)
57. Palace of Prolonging Happiness (Yánxǐ Gōng; 延禧宫)
58. Palace of Celestial Favor (Chéngqián Gōng; 承乾宫)
59. Gate of Eternal Harmony (Yǒnghé Gōng; 永和宫)
60. Palace of Accumulated Purity (Zhōngcuì Gōng; 钟粹宫)
61. Palace of Great Brilliance (Jǐngyáng Gōng; 景阳宫)
62. Gate of Hall for Ancestral Worship (Fèngxiān Mén; 奉先门)
63. Hall for Ancestral Worship (Fèngxiān Diàn; 奉先殿)
64. Numinous Firmament Treasure Hall (Tiānqióng Bǎodiàn; 天穹宝殿)
65. Archery Pavilion (Jiàn Tíng; 箭亭)
66. Nine-dragon Screen (Jiǔlóng Bì; 九龙壁)
67. Gate of Imperial Supremacy (Huángjí Mén; 皇极门)
68. Gate of Tranquil Longevity (Níngshòu Mén; 宁寿门)
69. Hall of Imperial Supremacy (Huángjí Diàn; 皇极殿)
70. Palace of Tranquil Longevity (Níngshòu Gōng; 宁寿宫)
71. Gate of Spiritual Cultivation (Yǎngxìng Mén; 养性门)
72. Hall of Spiritual Cultivation (Yǎngxìng Diàn; 养性殿)
73. Hall of Joyful Longevity (Lèshòu táng; 乐寿堂)
74. Bower of Well-nourished Harmony (Yíhé Xuān; 颐和轩)
75. Belvedere of Auspicious Fortune (Jǐngqí Gé; 景祺阁)
76. Belvedere of Pleasant Sounds (Chàngyīn Gé; 畅音阁)
77. The Corner Tower (Jiǎo Lóu; 角楼)
78. West Prosperity Gate (Xīhuá Mén; 西华门)
79. East Prosperity Gate (Dōnghuá Mén; 东华门)

Nearly rivaling the iconic status of the Great Wall, the Forbidden City sits at the nucleus of Beijing, and for centuries was the heartbeat of China. The massive collection of over 8,700 rooms is one of the most historic sites in old Beijing and is a perfect example of classical Ming architecture. Also known as the Imperial Palace or the Purple Forbidden City, it was declared a **UNESCO World Heritage Site** in 1987 and is regularly maintained and restored to preserve its historical grandeur. The monument hosts an average of 40,000 visitors per day (with the all time highest day clocking more than 182,000 people), so get here early to beat the crowds. Honestly, though, you still won't beat them...

The Forbidden City is an absolute must see for any Beijing traveler – period. Like countless other hallowed Chinese monuments, the Imperial Palace is built along strict geometric functions that have a divinely significant connection with the cardinal directions and heaven and earth. What does all that mean? It means the city was built in a shape and direction to maximize energy flow and please the cosmos. Prepare to be blown away by the huge centrally aligned ceremonial halls, but don't forget about the charming courtyards, pagodas and museums on the peripheral edges. Brush up on the history that follows, and remember that the secret imperial life here only became public less than a century ago.

Before You Go

Though there are restaurants and cafes inside the Forbidden City complex, prices for water and other essentials will be considerably higher than outside. "Exorbitant" is a good word for it. The palace includes plenty of walking, so bringing your own fruit, snacks, and water is highly recommended to keep you hydrated and energized as you explore. Savvy travelers will raise an eyebrow at the posh Chinese women who wear heels and cocktail dresses on their visit; do we even need to tell you this is a bad idea? Finally, while the large courtyards will leave you captivated, they will also leave you exposed to the sun on beautiful days. Giving your skin a good slather of sunscreen before departing will save you from an unwanted sunburn souvenir.

Info & Cautions

Guides

Buzzing like bees around many top sights in China are would-be tour guides. They can be pests. Some may have excellent English, but you will pay a pretty penny for their services. Give no expressions or signs of interest if you don't want to be hounded. Maps are available inside the Meridian Gate, but you have a Panda Guides map in your hand! Automatic audio guides are available in 30 languages. Those who prefer a guided tour are advised to choose these options instead of a pricey personal guide.

Tickets

The first large gate you approach (the one with the giant portrait of Mao) is the Gate of Heavenly Peace. Passing under this gate is free and is the access point to the city. However, do not make the mistake of some guests and buy a ticket for the tower at this gate if you want to enter the Forbidden City. You must first pass under the Gate of Heavenly Peace and Mao's enormous picture and walk north towards the Meridian Gate. To your left and right sides there will be quick-moving lines where tickets to the inner complex can be purchased.

Taxis

Exiting from the north gate (the exit gate) pours guests into a land of aggressive rickshaw and black taxi drivers hustling people into taking a ride. Don't do it. You might be tired after a big day, but don't let your fatigue lull you into a sketchy situation where dubious drivers could haggle a price only to jack it up or add a zero upon arrival; it is not uncommon. Though most locals who may witness the fraud will sympathize with you, they will wisely refrain from getting involved. Instead, walk a few minutes from the exit to find a city-sanctioned taxi that operates by meter.

Scammers

Please see our section Hot Topics (pg 312) for information on scammers and black taxis.

Others

The inner Forbidden City has ATMs, toilets, restaurants, cafes and shops. Smoking is not permitted anywhere on the grounds, and is one of the few places in the city where the ban is well enforced. Wheelchairs and pushchairs are free to rent, however they require a deposit of ¥500 and ¥300 respectively, so prepare the cash if you need one.

History

The site of the current Forbidden City began its imperial career in the mid-14th century. Back then, Beijing was called Dadu, the Great Capital, under Kublai Khan's ruling Yuan Dynasty, and it was palace-crazy Kublai who built the first one at this site. When the Yuan collapsed and the Ming Dynasty stepped up to the plate they moved the capital to Nanjing and torched the Mongolian palaces. It was the third Ming emperor, Yongle, who moved the capital back to Beijing in 1403 and ordered the construction of the Forbidden City palace on the rubble of Kublai Khan's old place. From 1406 to 1420, the bold emperor commissioned legions of artisans and laborers – by many accounts more than a million – for the insane amount of work required to build the palace complex. Massive stones were carted in from around the Beijing countryside, and they were so heavy that the winter road was covered with water along the way so that the horse-drawn carts could slide the stones along a road of ice.

Occupying his divine palace in 1421, Yongle was the first of 24 emperors (14 of them Ming, 10 Qing) to reside in the city. The pampered emperors were regarded as the "Sons of Heaven" and employed tens of thousands of servants to tend to their every need, which sometimes included hours of kneeling in front of the Son of Heaven as he lectured. The mystery surrounding the happenings within the elite community was so intense the city might as well have been built inside a giant glass bottle, preferably with air-holes. The bizarre spectacle included droves of gossipy eunuchs and conspiring concubines who from time to time made their own grab for power. Emperors spent most of their lives in indulgent self-confinement, and venturing out of the city was done only when absolutely necessary. It was a good thing for the commoners, too, since the penalty for viewing the emperor (deliberately or not) was instant death.

This royal resort spanned two dynasties and finally came to a screeching halt in 1911. The insanity of the revolution had begun, and as the last mandates of the Manchu Qing Dynasty exited the palace, the mysteries behind the walls came with them. Puyi, the last Manchu emperor, was allowed to live with his court in the rear areas of the palace until 1924 when, just to stick it to him, the revolutionaries renamed the palace "Former Palace" (Gù Gōng; 故宫) and opened it to the public.

Today, nearly all of the wooden buildings are post 18th century structures. Carted in from southwestern China, the beautiful wood was well-known to be a tinder box, and foresighted emperors had 308 very cool copper cauldrons (of which 231 remain) tactically placed throughout the city as fire-preventative measures. Each massive pot weighs an impressive 1,696 kg (3,731 lbs) and has a diameter of 1.6 m (5.5 ft). To further increase fire safety, the Imperial Library's roof was tiled in black, the Chinese elemental color of water. Thought to have more than just a symbolic presence, the black paint was hoped to act like a roof drenched in water. It didn't. In spite of such "state-of-the-art" fire safety measures, a handful of blazes ravaged the city throughout its 500-year history, usually started by a strong wind and an unfastened lantern, a fireworks display, or a cunning servant who could see a nice payday through repairs. While several other particularly flammable buildings were also roofed in black tiles, the remaining were done in a brilliant yellow, the color of the imperial family. At one point 75 wells delivered water around the premises – 30 of which remain today – and an advanced drainage system addressed Beijing's spring rains.

An occupation of the city and several lootings brought trying times to the palace during the 19th and 20th centuries. The Anglo-French forces stomped their way into the city for an extended stay during the Second Opium War of 1860, and the Japanese and Chiang Kai-shek's Nationalist Party both looted the palace in the 1940s. While many of the relics that were carted off to Taiwan were later returned, a great deal of them still occupy the National Palace Museum in Taipei. Even so, the breathtaking beauty of the Forbidden City remains, with the restored buildings painstakingly crafted to their exact pre-1911 conditions, and many mini-museums displaying ancient artifacts and clothing of China's imperial past.

Layout

The Forbidden City is huge. The entire complex covers a staggering 720,000 sq m (7,800,000 sq ft), and holds over 980 buildings and over 8,700 rooms. A 52 m (170 ft) wide moat circles the walls, which are made of 12 million limestone bricks that were cemented together with glutinous rice and egg whites. The main ceremonial halls all sit on a centrally aligned, north to south axis, and face south to accept vitalizing *yang* energy, and to ward off troublesome *yin* energy from the north (including Gobi Desert dust storms and barbarians). This layout follows Chinese geomancy, the art of divination through the placement of objects in a geometric space.

Main Courtyard

Meridian Gate (Wǔ Mén; 午门)

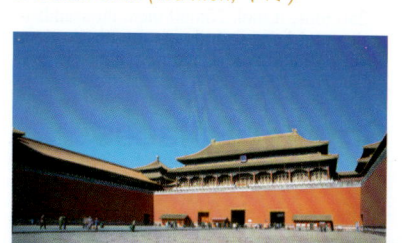

Towering over the Forbidden City's southern ambit at nearly 40 m (124 ft), the Meridian Gate is the complex's largest gate and only entrance. Check out the five towers and their flying phoenix carvings, which give the gate its alternate name, **Five-Phoenix Tower** (Wǔfèng Lóu; 五凤楼). At each end of the central tower great bells and drums are kept. Used as signals of the emperor's departure back then, the bells were rung when he swung left to the Temple of Heaven, while the drums were struck to announce his walk to the **Ancestral Temple** (Workers' Cultural Palace) to the right.

Hall of Literary Brilliance (Wénhuá Diàn; 文华殿)

When you first enter the courtyard from the Meridian Gate you can veer off to the right and cross through the **Gate of Mutual Harmony** (Xiéhé Mén; 协和门) to find the **Hall of Literary Brilliance**. This little I-shaped complex is where you'll find the great **Ceramics Gallery** with over 400 pottery relics in the front and the **Hall of Observing Sincerity and Esteem** (Zhǔjìng Diàn; 主敬殿) in the back. A Ming Dynasty creation, the Hall of Literary Brilliance served as the main hall of the prince.

Hall of Martial Valor (Wǔyīng Diàn; 武英殿)

Accross the courtyard from the Hall of Literary Brilliance and through the western Gate of Glorious Harmony (Xīhé Mén; 熙和门), the Hall of **Martial Valor** is worth a few minutes of your time as well. Also an I-shaped design, in the back you can "get respectful" in the Hall of Respectful Thoughts (Jìngsī Diàn; 敬思殿). More importantly this area features a solid **Calligraphy and Painting Gallery** that displays rare works of the Jin, Tang, Song and Yuan Dynasties, as well as many masterpieces of the Ming and Qing Dynasties.

Gate of Supreme Harmony (Tàihé Mén; 太和门)

Towering over the northern extreme of the Outer Court, the Gate of Supreme Harmony is guarded on either side by two bronze lions; the male has his paw on a sphere and represents the global power of the emperor, while the female caresses a cub and symbolizes a fruitful imperial family. This beautiful gate leads to the massive **Outer Court** on its north side, but before you head through don't miss the awesome engraved stele in the center of the gate's front stairway. The emperor was carried over this giant stone slab in a sedan chair by his immediate servants, and anyone else who tried had their head lopped off. On your way to Taihe Men you'll cross the five **Golden River Bridges** (Jīnshuǐ Qiáo; 金水桥), beautiful marble bridges that span the Golden River (Jīnshuǐ Hé; 金水河).

Three Great Halls

Hall of Supreme Harmony (Tàihé Diàn; 太和殿)

Mounted on a great marble terrace at the head of a 30,000 sq m (322,917 sq ft) courtyard, the Hall of Supreme Harmony is the largest of the Three Great Halls. Built in 1406 and painstakingly restored in the

17th century, the 35 m (115 ft) tall hall was a grand symbol of imperial power and was the highest structure in the Ming and Qing empires. Audiences of over 100,000 chubby eunuchs, robe-clad servants, and self-assured officials gathered for birthdays, coronations, and military appointments in the massive courtyard, whose lack of trees was to ensure that nothing stood higher than the emperor as he perched on the hall's lofty marble balcony. A total of 72 pillars in six rows support the roof, and it is considered the largest timber framework in China.

Hall of Central Harmony (Zhōnghé Diàn; 中和殿)

The smallest of the Three Great Halls, the Hall of Central Harmony marks the center-point of the Forbidden City. Serving as the emperor's rehearsal and meeting headquarters, it was here that he would use the hall's harmonizing energy to practice speeches, receive dignitaries, and prepare for his ritualistic journey to the Temple of Heaven (pg 79).

Hall of Preserving Harmony (Bǎohé Diàn; 保和殿)

Standing at the northern end of the three-tiered marble terrace shared by the Three Great Halls, the Hall of Preserving Harmony is similar in style but slightly smaller than the southern Hall of Supreme Harmony. The original 1420 construction was lost in a 1625 fire but quickly rebuilt the same year. Originally functioning as a sort of changing station for the Ming Emperors, it was here that they donned their ritual garments prior to the coronation of an empress or crown prince. The Qing Dynasty later refit the building as a banquet hall where the emperor would entertain his bride and her family, as well as provincial governors, Mongol princes, and civil and military officials. Thundering its way up the central stairway on the back side of the hall is the **marble imperial carriageway**, a 16.5 m- (54 ft)-long by 3 m- (10 ft)-wide stone relief of nine dragons dancing with pearls. The emperor would take a little servant-powered sedan-chair ride up this giant stone, much like the one outside the Gate of Supreme Harmony. Weighing in at 250 tons, it took 20,000 men, thousands of mules and horses, and two months to drag, push, pull and wedge the massive stele over the ice road to the city.

Smaller Palaces

Gate of Heavenly Purity (Qiánqīng Mén; 乾清门)

Also named the Gate of Celestial Purity, the Gate of Heavenly Purity divides the Inner Court and the Outer Court and serves as the main entrance to the imperial household inside the Inner Court. Two bronze lions guard this entrance to the most private of imperial spheres. Note that the flopped-over, closed ears on these lions differ from all the others in the Forbidden City, reminding discontent concubines and gossipy court ladies that heads would literally roll if their ears perked up too close to this area of official affairs.

Palace of Heavenly Purity (Qiánqīng Gōng; 乾清宫)

The largest structure in the Inner Court, the Palace of Heavenly Purity is a smaller reproduction of the Hall of Supreme Harmony and even features mini versions of the hall's furniture. Initially, the palace served as living quarters for all the Ming and two Qing emperors, as well as a private retreat for official meetings. Signing documents and interviewing ministers and envoys were all part of the fun, and the palace eventually evolved to hold banquets. Emperor Qianlong (1735-1796) twice courted the nation's male 60-somethings here with the "Banquet for a Thousand Seniors."

Hall of Union (Jiāotài Diàn; 交泰殿)

The Hall of Union is considered the unifying

hall of the Inner Court. Contained within the square building are the **25 Imperial Seals** of the Qing Dynasty. It also includes the Forbidden City's two official timekeepers: the **clepsydra**, a water clock from 1745, and a mechanical clock from 1797.

Palace of Earthly Tranquility (Kūnníng Gōng; 坤宁宫)

Site of grand Spring Festival celebrations, the Palace of Earthly Tranquility was originally the Ming Dynasty's imperial living quarters, and later became the nuptial chambers for the emperors and empresses of the Qing Dynasty. The two east side rooms, known as the East Warmth Chamber, were the bridal suite for the emperor and empress. Painted on the wall and on hanging lamps were the Chinese characters of "double happiness" (囍). Side rooms were designated for sacrificial rituals, which were held twice a day during Manchurian rule.

Hall of Spiritual Cultivation (Yǎngxīng Diàn; 养心殿)

The Hall of Spiritual Cultivation is on the west side of the Palace of Heavenly Purity. Originally designed as a temporary residence for emperors, its importance grew greatly when Emperor Yongzheng, the third Qing Dynasty (1644 – 1912) emperor, made this his living quarters. Beginning with Yongzheng to the end of the Qing Dynasty, eight emperors lived in this beautiful hall, which is fronted by the **Gate of Spiritual Cultivation** (Yǎngxìng Mén; 养性门). The yard out front displays a building that was once the room for on-duty eunuchs, but today it sells cheap trinkets. Don't miss the rare **jade screen wall** that's intricately carved with eight delicate dragons and faces the front gate.

Palace of Gathered Elegance (Chǔxiù Gōng; 储秀宫)

One of the Six Western Palaces in the Inner Court, Chuxiugong was the living residence of concubines during the Ming and Qing Dynasties. In 1852, the Empress Dowager Cixi lived here when she gave birth to Emperor Tongzhi. Initially, Cixi lived in the Palace of Eternal Spring (Chángchūn Gōng; 长春宫) and later moved to Chuxiugong in celebration of her 50th birthday. Check out the garden, which boasts a wall that is essentially a giant birthday card with inscriptions from officials wishing Cixi well on her Golden Jubilee.

Imperial Garden & Others

Imperial Garden (Yù Huāyuán; 御花园)

Located outside of the Gate of Terrestrial Tranquility, the resplendent imperial garden is peppered with several charming little pavilions and one very large incense burner; it would probably be relaxing if there weren't so many people here all the time. It was constructed during the Ming Dynasty in 1417, and its rectangular shape covers approximately 12,000 sq m (129,167 sq ft). This was a private retreat for the imperial family and is a typical example of Chinese imperial garden landscaping. There are around twenty structures in all, each of a different style. Keep an eye out for the **Gate of Divine Prowess** (Shénwǔ Mén; 神武门) and the **Gate of Loyal Obedience** (Shùnzhēn Mén; 顺贞门), where elephant statues awkwardly break their legs to kowtow before the emperor.

The Forbidden City palace complex is littered with plenty of interesting side tidbits. Play "I-spy" and see how many of these objects you can spot:

- fire-preventative copper and brass cauldrons
- palace protecting guardian lions
- water draining dragon-head spouts
- roof guardians on the upturned corners of the building eaves

- incense breathing bronze turtles
- masterful sundials that dot the complex grounds

Jingshan Park

What do you do with that 46 m (151 ft) high pile of dirt left over from building the Forbidden City moat? Build a park with it and call it Jingshan Park (Jǐngshān Gōngyuán; 景山公园). Sitting just outside the northern gate of the Forbidden City on the centerline of Beijing, Jingshan Park is one of the coolest artificial hills you'll ever come across and one of the best parks in the city. It was built by Emperor Yongle, and you've got to hand it to the guy, he sure knows how to make a big pile of dirt feel special. Jingshan consists of five individual peaks, which are each capped with an elegant pavilion. The highest elevated point in the city, Jingshan's main peak provides an unmatched panoramic view of the Forbidden City and the surrounding hutongs. In its dynastic heyday, this park was used for officials looking to kick back, and now it's your turn. The five peaks of Jingshan draw the approximate historical axis of central old Beijing.

Sample Itineraries

The Forbidden City is massive, and choosing where to go can be a bit daunting. To help smooth your decision, we have provided three sample itineraries, depending on your time, that reference to our numbered map (pg 62).

Two-hour tour: 1→5→9→11→13→16→17→28→31→32→35→37→42

Half-day tour: 1→25-27→5→13→16→17→62→63→31→32→35→46→52→36→39→40→42

Full-day tour: 1→22-24→25→27→13→16→17→31→32→35→46→51→60→54→63→62→66-75→42

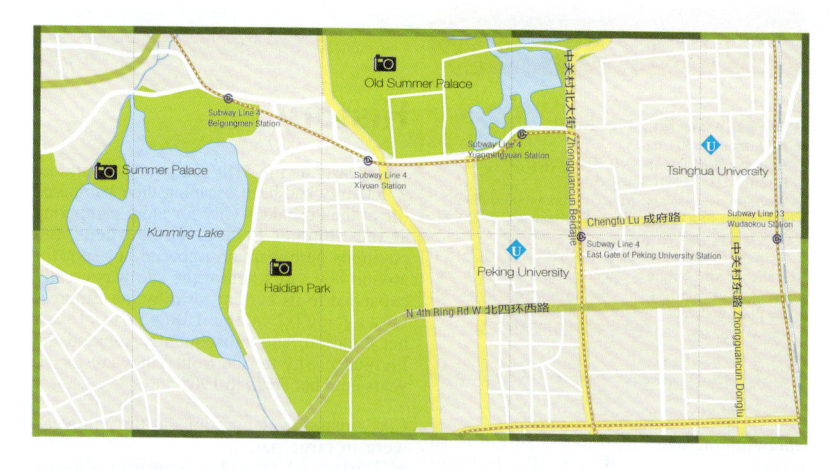

Summer Palaces & University Area

This section includes the descriptions and details of four areas: the Summer Palace, the Old Summer Palace, Tsinghua University and Peking University.

With the preserved architecture of a fading China, stunning artwork, a scattering of ancient temples, quaint bridges and lovely pavilions dotting a splendid lake, the Summer Palace is one of Beijing's most impressive attractions. Just to the northeast, the ruins of the Old Summer Palace once held a glorious melange of Eastern and Western architecture, but today the ruins attest to the sad breakdown of 19th century Sino-European relations and offer a haunting glimpse of history.

Summer Palace

Chinese name: 颐和园 (Yíhéyuán)
Admission: ¥30 (Apr-Oct); ¥20 (Nov-Mar)
Hours: 6:30-20:00 (Apr-Oct), 7:00-17:00 (Nov 1-Mar 31)
Phone: 6288 1144 (Chinese only)
Website: www.summerpalace-china.com (in Chinese)
Address: 19 Xinjiangmenmen Lu, Haidian District (海淀区新建宫门路19号)
Transport: Subway – Line 4, Beigongmen (北宫门) Station, Exit D, walk a couple minutes until you see the north gate on your left side. If you need help finding the place and your Chinese will not suffice, point this sentence out to a local. 请问去颐和园正门怎么走?

Sprawling across a luxurious 3 sq km (1 sq mi) of northwestern Beijing, the brilliant imperial escape of the Summer Palace (or Yiheyuan in Chinese) is an absolutely essential visit during any trip to China's capital. The architecture and landscaping of the former imperial playground are genius in their design and execution, with opulent temples, quaint pavilions, luxurious gardens, magnificent corridors and countless other marvels arranged around the splendor of **Kunming Lake**. A **UNESCO World Heritage Site**, the Summer Palace is the largest and best-preserved imperial garden in China, and hundreds of thousands of visitors come here each year (the busiest day ever saw 130,000 visitors).

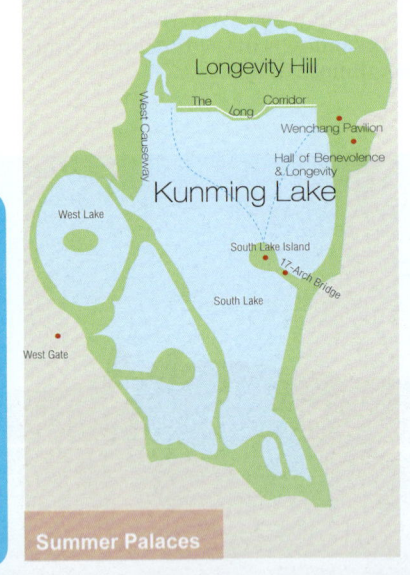

History

As early as the 11th century, the imperial family had been escaping their pampered life at the Forbidden City for more pampering at the Summer Palace. The gardens and pavilions here were an imperial hot spot for around 800 years before the site was greatly expanded to its current form by the Empress Dowager Cixi in the 1880s. Cixi loved her creation, and subsequently vacated the Forbidden City to rule from Yiheyuan for 20 years until her death in 1908.

Cixi's massive elaborations at the Yiheyuan were in large part a response to the 1860 pillaging of the Old Summer Palace (Yuanmingyuan) by the Anglo-French forces during the Opium Wars. Her expansive work at the new site was again struck by the remorseless Eight Nation Alliance in 1900 in the wake of the Boxer Rebellion. The determined Dowager reputedly diverted 30 million taels (a tael is about 38 grams) of silver meant for the navy to rebuild the palace once more. Six years later, the first Sino-Japanese War began and the Chinese navy for some reason found themselves too underfunded to win.

The Summer Palace was opened to the public in 1924 and later survived the Cultural Revolution thanks to Premier Zhou Enlai. Many relics continue to sit abroad in foreign museums, poignant reminders of imperialist piracy, but the palace is still a rocking testament to China's historical architecture.

Layout

Hall of Benevolence and Longevity (Rénshòu Diàn; 仁寿殿)

On the east side of Kunming Lake sits the main building of the palace complex, the Hall of Benevolence and Longevity. Inside is a hardwood throne, used by Cixi for important administrative meetings. The front courtyard is laid with several bronze animals.

Longevity Hill (Wànshòu Shān; 万寿山)

Emperor Qianlong conceived the manmade Longevity Hill as a gift to his mother on her 60th birthday – probably the most impressive pile of dirt you could give anyone for their birthday present. Coincidentally, the hill presents a 60 m (197 ft) incline and is littered with Buddhist temples and pavilions. As you mount the stairs, stop off at the serene **Buddhist Fragrance Pavilion** (Fóxiāng Gé ; 佛香阁) and the wonderful **Cloud Dispersing Hall** (Páiyún Diàn; 排云殿). At the top of the hill sits the beautiful **Sea of Wisdom Temple** (Zhìhuì Hǎi; 智慧海). The temple's three levels of upturned eaves are an awesome sight, almost as awesome as the view of Beijing (on clear days of course) from its top. Inside you can check out a sea of glazed tiles with little Buddha portraits on them.

Kunming Lake (Kūnmíng Hú; 昆明湖)

Extending across three quarters of the Yiheyuan parkland, Kunming Lake has a different personality for each season (and by each season we mostly mean winter and summer). In the winter, it is unbeatable for ice-skating, so head over and join the Chinese completely ignoring all the "Don't Walk On The Ice" signs. Summer invites the blooming of great round lotus leaves and their flowers, which blanket the lake in a sea of green and pink. Among the temples and pavilions, the summer character of Kunming Lake's field of lotuses is a sublime sight.

Take a walk around the lake to see some of the magnificent buildings that dot the shores. Opposite Longevity Hill's north shore, the **Dragon King Temple** (Lóngwáng Miào; 龙王庙) sits on the South Lake Island, where royalty came to pray to a statue of the Dragon King for rain. Don't miss the **Marble Boat**; it's made of wood, which is funny, but not a joke. The boat was built in 1755 from wood and then painted to look like marble.

Getting on the lake is easy. Vendors can equip you with skates in the winter, and boats are available in the form of paddleboats (4-6 people; ¥60 per hour, ¥300 deposit) or electric powered (¥100 per hour, ¥400 deposit) in the warm months.

Top Attractions

073

The Long Corridor (Cháng Láng; 长廊)

The Long Corridor is basically an extended hallway with a roof and open sides that shielded the emperor from the elements as he walked along the base of Longevity Hill. It's also one of the most beautiful and elaborate hallways you'll ever see, and it will remind you how *rough* life was for the emperors who had to walk down it every singe day during the summer. What a drag. It extends 728 m (2,388 ft) along the southern bank of the hill, running parallel to the northern shore of Kunming Lake. The sides open up to the fantastic scenery outside, while the ceiling bears 14,000 intricately painted scenes from Chinese history and legends, as well as classic Chinese literary excerpts, such as *Journey to the West* and *Dream of the Red Chamber*. This is one of the best parts of the area – don't miss it.

West Causeway (Xī Dī; 西堤)

Many tourists at Yiheyuan begin their journey by swinging east towards the Hall of Benevolence and Longevity. Avoid the crowds by taking the West Causeway instead, where you can take a stroll through a nice grove of mulberry and willow trees. Along this less beaten counterclockwise lap of Kunming Lake you will encounter two ancient bridges: the **Jade Belt Bridge** (Yùdài Qiáo; 玉带桥), built by Qianlong in the 18th century, and the **17 Arch Bridge** (Shíqīkǒng Qiáo; 十七孔桥) which leads over to South Lake Island.

Wenchang Pavilion (Wénchāng Gé; 文昌阁)

The Wenchang Pavillion (aka the Flourishing Culture Pavilion), sits just south of the Hall of Longevity and Benevolence. Housed within is the **Wenchang Gallery**, which is thoroughly worth a visit. Here you can find most of the remaining artifacts and relics that weren't looted by the allied powers. Among them are samples of Cixi's calligraphy, some pretty bronze and jade pieces, and beautiful Chinese porcelain.

Old Summer Palace

Chinese name: 圆明园 (Yuánmíngyuán)
Admission: ¥10 (automatic audio guides are available: ¥40 with a deposit of ¥100)
Hours: 7:00-19:30 (Jan-Mar & Nov-Dec); 7:00-20:30 (Apr, Sep & Oct); 7:00-19:00 (May-Aug)
Website: www.yuanmingyuanpark.com (in Chinese)
Phone: 6262 8501 (Chinese only)
Address: 28 Qinghua Xilu. Haidian District (海淀区清华西路 28 号)
Transport: Subway – Line 4, Yuanmingyuan (圆明园) Station, Exit B. If you arrive at the subway station and need help finding the place point this sentence out to a local. 请问去圆明园正门怎么走?

To the northeast of the Summer Palace, the remains of Yuanmingyuan, or the Old Summer Palace, stand as a dark reminder of the tumultuous two years of the Second Opium War (1858-60). Built with both Eastern and Western influences, it is mostly Baroque-style Italian and French masonry that scatters the ruins today. Head on over to enjoy some sunshine, paddle around in a boat, and see what happened when a bunch of angry white guys got their feelings hurt when the Chinese didn't want their opium anymore. Many locals like to take advantage of the park for picnics, an excellent idea. Remember, going early is a good way to beat the crowds – the busiest day ever tipped the scales with 70,000 tourists.

History

Construction of the Old Summer Palace began in 1707, and the site endured many years of expansion and restoration by the time of its last maintenance during the reign of the Qianlong Emperor (1736-1795). Originally intended as a "small" gift for the future Yongzheng Emperor (whose plush life included residence at the Lama Temple; pg 116), the palace was later retrofitted with European architectural styling during Qianlong's time due to the emperor's love affair with European palace and fountain designs. Qianlong commissioned such Western contemporaries as the Jesuit missionaries Guiseppe Castiglione, from Genoa, and French-born Michael Benoît. The latter is responsible for a water clock at Yuanmingyuan that combines Chinese philosophical tradition and European architecture.

The irony of Benoît's symbiotic creation, and truly that of much of the palace, was illustrated tragically during the Second Opium War. China's vast overestimation of its power turned titanic when the court attempted to expel the excess of exploitative foreign merchants who were shamelessly cashing in on the populace's opium addiction (largely instigated by the merchants). The Europeans saw the imperial court as xenophobic, and supposedly in the interest of "sparing the common people," the Old Imperial Palace was indiscriminately burned and looted. The traditional wooden buildings of the palace were utterly destroyed, and the remaining European stone structures have slowly dissolved over time from lack of restoration funds and local peasants plucking the stone to build homes.

Layout

The once exclusive playground for emperors and royalty is now a public park, visited and picnicked by locals in need of a day out. It is a popular, albeit less known, destination for tourists as well, who often come for a paddle on **Fuhai Lake** (Fú Hǎi; 福海). As with Kunming Lake at the Summer Palace, Fu Hai offers winter ice skating and summer water sports. To the east, in the **Palace Buildings Scenic Area** (Xīyánglóu Jǐngqū; 西洋楼景区), the popular **Eternal Spring Garden** (Chángchūn Yuán; 长春园) is scattered with the beautiful but melancholic remnants of the temple buildings (now essentially a rock garden of crumbling, post-Renaissance European marble masonry). Here you can find the work of Giuseppe Castiglione and Michael Benoît.

Better preserved artifacts can be found at the **Great Fountain Ruins** (Dàshuǐfǎ Yízhǐ; 大水法遗址) from 1759, and the **Guānshuǐfǎ** (观水法) at its opposite, sporting European carvings of guns, swords, military emblems and other pictorial saber rattling. From there, swing west to the **Hǎiyàntáng** (海晏堂) **Reservoir** and catch the water clock, designed in part by Benoît. It was previously characterized by 12 bronze humanoids crowned with animal heads that spat water in a 12-hour sequence. The heads have now been picked and looted, and Beijing is attempting to retrieve them from their current foreign homes. Recently, four have been secured and can be seen at the **Poly Art Museum** (Bǎolì Yìshù Bówùguǎn; 保利艺术博物馆; 9/F New Poly Plaza, 1 Chaoyangmen Beidajie – 朝阳门北大街1号新保利大厦9层; phone: 6500 8117; website: www.polyculture.com.cn). The **Garden of Yellow Flowers** (Huánghuā Zhèn; 黄花阵), an adept rendition of a flower maze, is also in the area.

University Area

The area around the Summer Palaces is also home to the campuses of Tsinghua University and Peking (Beijing) University. Tsinghua, specializing in science and engineering, is the best in the country, while the arts and literature school of PU is a close second. Seeing the campuses can be a fun alternative trip if you like academia, but they are definitely not must sees.

Tsinghua University

Chinese name: 清华大学 (Qīnghuá Dàxué)
Admission: FREE
Hours: 24 hours
Website: www.tsinghua.edu.cn/publish/then/index.html
Address: The campus at Tsinghua is large and therefore has no exact address. The main gate of the school (the east gate) is the beginning of Zhongguancun Donglu. The school is a well known city landmark, so people in the area will know exactly where to point you if you get lost.
Transport: Subway – Line 13, Wudaokou (五道口) Station, Exit A, walk 400 m west down Chengfu Lu, turn right onto Zhongguancun Donglu, walk 400 m

Covering a huge 400 hectares (989 acres), Tsinghua University was founded in 1911 on the site of Xichun Garden (later changed to Tsinghua Garden), an attached imperial garden of the Old Summer Palace. Named Tsinghua Xuetang (清华学堂) and funded with part of the Boxer indemnity, the school was a Western-style preparatory institution for government sponsored students sent to study in the United States. Although Tsinghua University has a comprehensive university degree program, its main focuses are science and engineering. Prominent alumni produced by Tsinghua include current President Xi Jinping (习近平), former President Hu Jintao (胡锦涛), former Prime Minister Zhu Rongji, and Nobel Prize (physics) winners Yang and Li. The student body totals more than 31,000, of which 17,000 are graduate students. There are plenty of foreigners as well, with 3,450 international students from 112 countries, in particular South Korea, the USA, Germany, Japan, and France.

Peking University

Chinese name: 北京大学 (Běijīng Dàxué)
Admission: FREE
Hours: 24 hours
Website: www.english.pku.edu.cn
Address: 5 Yiheyuan Lu, Haidian District (海淀区颐和园路5号)
Transport: Subway – Line 4, East Gate of Peking University (北京大学东门) Station, Exit A

Built in 1898 and originally named the Imperial University of Peking (京师大学堂), Peking University was the first national university of the country as well as the first university in modern China, marking the beginning of the modernization of China's higher education. The university acts in a way as the political barometer of China: among its stormy 20th century creations were the May 4th Movement and the New Culture Movement of 1919, which precipitated the rise of communism in China. Specializing in art and literature, the university has produced such alumni as current Chinese Prime Minister Li Keqiang (李克强).

Stop by to check out the bronze statues and commemorations on campus, including one dedicated to Cai Yuanpei (蔡元培, 1868-1940), former president of the university and inspiration for the May 4th movement.

With 29,880 students and 15,419 graduate students, Peking University is only slightly beaten by Tsinghua University in terms of headcount. A decent international population calls Peking University home as well, with 2,326 foreign students from 80 countries hitting the books. Mao Zedong was once a librarian here, and the famous revolutionary Li Dazhao and renowned writer Lu Xun had working stints on campus too. The latter two have residences in Beijing open for public viewing.

Temple of Heaven & the Prayer Altars

This section features the Temple of Heaven, the Earth Altar, the Moon Altar, the Sun Altar and the Altar of Agriculture.

The stunning prayer complex at the Temple of Heaven is one of Beijing's most unbeatable sights, and it is actually part of a larger five altar system that is precisely organized around the Forbidden City. The Temple of Heaven is actually called the Altar of Heaven (Tiantan) in Chinese and rests on the southern compass point. It is contrasted in the north by the Earth Altar (Ditan). With similar *feng shui* principles as those governing the Forbidden City, Tiantan's southern location puts it in prime position to receive positive *yang* energy from the sun (and heaven). Similarly, Ditan in the north assumes the nagative *yin* energy associated with the Earth. To the east and west sit the Sun Altar (Ritan) and the Moon Altar, respectively, while the southwest holds the Altar of Agriculture (Xiannongtan). None of the other altars compare to the Temple of Heaven, but they are set in lovely parks and their history of imperial sacrificial ceremonies makes them worth a trip if you have the time.

Temple of Heaven

Chinese name: 天坛 (Tiāntán)
Website: en.tiantanpark.com
Hours: 8:00-17:30 (Mar 1-Jun 30); 8:00-18:00 (Jul 1-Oct 31); 8:00-17:00 (Nov 1-Feb 28/29)
Admission: ¥15 for entrance, ¥35 for through ticket (Apr 1-Oct 31); ¥10 for entrance, ¥30 for through ticket (Nov 1-Mar 31).
Automatic guide ¥40 with a deposit of ¥100.
Address: 1 Tiantan Lu, Dongcheng District (东城区天坛路甲1号)
Transport: Subway – Line 5, Tiantan Dongmen Station, Exit A

Spellbinding in their conception and execution, the geometrically divine altars and halls built within Temple of Heaven Park are utterly transcendent. The complex is a masterpiece of Ming architectural design and valiantly demonstrates the significance of cosmology in China's dynastic history. More of a set of juxtaposed altars than a temple, they are divided into two sections: north and south. The northern group is laid out on a semi-circle – a circle represents heaven in traditional Chinese thought – and revolves around the peerless Hall of Prayer for Good Harvests. The southern group sits in a large square, and as such is a representation of the ancient Chinese impression of earth.

Since the 3rd century BCE, Chinese emperors were considered the Sons of Heaven, and for centuries they came to these hallowed altars to perform esoteric rituals, prayers and sacrificial offerings; a multi-day ceremony to atone for the sins of the nation and bring about good harvests. The symbolism of the magnificent complex is incredible to contemplate: a one-of-a-kind combination of shapes, colors, and even sounds built specifically to influence the cosmos.

Another great reason to hit up Tiantan (as if you needed one) is the huge 276 hectare (682

acre) park that surrounds the altars. A daily local hangout, it is one of the best places in the city to find Beijingers dancing, singing, playing cards or just getting down.

Before You Go

Expect a good half-day at the Temple of Heaven. It's one of Beijing's more captivating sights, so it's very unlikely that you'll be leaving early. There are snacks and drinks sold inside, but they are generally overpriced junk food. Bringing your own snacks can be worthwhile, but packing a lunch is not necessary. Unless you are on a tight budget, the neighborhood offers eateries as well. Good shoes are important, and packing water will prevent you from paying big markups inside.

Info & Cautions

There are two ticket types when entering the Temple of Heaven park: one gives you basic access to the park but not the buildings (¥15), but you can upgrade this ticket from the inside if you need. The other is a through-ticket that gives access to everything (¥35). If it is your first time visiting, don't fool around with the basic access ticket. We guarantee you will be dropping the extra ¥20 once you enter the parks and see the altars and halls looming in the background, so save yourself some time and buy the full ticket from the get-go. The all-access tickets have stubs that are torn off for each the northern and southern altars, so get your fill before moving on, as there is no reentry after the stub is torn.

History

It is not surprising that the Temple of Heaven was built at the same time as the Forbidden City, from 1406 to 1420, considering their ceremonial and cosmological relation (the Forbidden City is the central point of the altar system). The Ming Emperor Yongle oversaw the construction of the two mighty projects, built during the same 14 year period. The relatively close proximity of the two complexes was intentional, as each winter solstice the emperor would march to the Temple in a grand regal procession to commence several days of ritual and veneration to the ancestral dead and the cosmos. When the first lunar calendar month reached its middle, the emperor would again make a visit, expanding on his earlier reverence. It was the Emperor Jiajing who, in 1530, bestowed Tiantan with its current name and built the corresponding altars of the Earth, Sun, and Moon to the north, east, and west. The last dynasty-era renovations of the temple were made by the Qing Emperor Qianlong in the 18th century.

Like many unfortunate masterpieces of its time, the Temple of Heaven was occupied and ransacked by the Anglo-French alliance during the Second Opium War (1858-60), and again by the Eight Nation Alliance during the 1900 Boxer Rebellion. The large desecration of the temple's buildings increased even further when countless artifacts and relics were pirated from the complex, many of which remain abroad in museums and collections.

The last ceremonial procession entered Tiantan in 1914 when Yuan Shikai (袁世凯), then President of the Republic of China, performed a Ming prayer ceremony at the temple as part of an epically failed effort to have himself declared Emperor of China. In 1918 the Temple was turned into a park and for the first time opened to the public. About 80 years later it was inscribed as a **UNESCO World Heritage Site**.

Layout

The ancient Chinese belief that the Earth is square and heaven is round is dually reflected in the masterful design of the Temple of Heaven. First, the major altars and halls are circular in design and mounted inside great square yards. Second, and perhaps more ceremoniously significant, the design of the altar complex integrates two distinct cordons of walls: a southern section that is square, capped by a semi-circular northern level. The imperial approach to the temple proceeded via the southern Zhaoheng Gate (Zhāohēng Mén; 昭亨门); as the emperor proceeded from the squared south to the circular north, it geomantically symbolized his ascent into heaven.

The presentation of the major sights below will put you on course to follow the emperor, but you may enter the altar complex through any one of four gates, each located at one of the cardinal directions. Outside of these gates is the Temple of Heaven park area. There is a very nice forest of ancient trees covering a large area of the park, but their unnatural and systematic placement is a little bit odd. Keep an eye out for cypress trees dating back hundreds of years.

Circular Mound Altar (Yuán Qiū; 圜丘)

Odd numbers were considered heavenly in early Chinese thought, and being that nine is the largest single digit odd number, it is the name of the game at the artfully masoned Circular Mound Altar. Originally built in 1530 and again in 1740, the altar is cut from white marble, stands 5 m (16.5 ft) high and rests on a three-tiered terrace of nine rings each. It is said that each tier corresponds to a layer in a three echeloned universe: the upper symbolizing heaven, the middle as earth, and the bottom nine-ringed tier representing humanity. Count the stairs and balustrades and you will notice their nonuple (multiples of nine) presentations as well. Speaking from the center of the top terrace will reflect the speaker's voice among the balustrades and increase the volume at which it is heard. Apparently, even the powerful voice of the imperial Sons of Heaven needed an extra push to reach the cosmos.

Echo Wall (Huíyīn Bì; 回音壁)

A stone's throw north of the Circular Mound Altar is the Imperial Vault of Heaven, surrounded by the curious Echo Wall. A solid 65 m (213 ft) in diameter, the Echo Wall has an interesting acoustic quality: it can transport a mere murmur from one side to the other, retaining the volume of the original utterance. Grab a friend and be wowed as you converse at normal volume from 65 m apart. Unconcerned chattering tour groups or self-centered loudmouths on cellphones can make the Echo Wall frustrating at times, but it has been known to work during busy times, so give it a go. In front of the Vault of Heaven you can find the **Triple-Echo Stones** (Sānyīn Shí; 三音石). Supposedly, if you clap or shout from one of the three stones, it will be echoed a number of times corresponding to the stone you are standing on (that's once from the first, twice from the second, etc).

Imperial Vault of Heaven (Huáng Qióngyǔ; 皇穹宇)

The Imperial Vault of Heaven served as a clothes-changing chamber where the emperor would don his ceremonial robes. It also housed the arcane spirit tablets of his ancestors and it was said their spirits resided in the tablets during the ceremony. The vault is the same age as the neighboring Circular Mound Altar and sits on the same meridian line as the elder Hall of Prayer for Good Harvests. Behind the Vault of Heaven rests the Grandfather Tree or **Nine-Dragon Tree**, a 500-year-old juniper with grizzled knots and intertwining branches, said to represent nine dragons. From here the emperor works his way up the gradual incline of the **Vermillion Steps Bridge** (Dānbì Qiáo; 丹陛桥) – a 360 m (1,181 ft) long raised walkway – to the Hall of Prayer for Good Harvests.

Hall of Prayer for Good Harvests (Qínián Diàn; 祈年殿)

The Temple of Heaven's flagship structure, the Hall of Prayer for Good Harvests is so brilliantly enthralling it could singlehandedly make your trip to Tiantan worthwhile. Sitting majestically atop a three-tiered marble terrace and boasting a tremendous triple-gabled roof, the 38 m- (128 ft)-high hall is made entirely of wood and, stunningly, without a single nail or drop of cement. It is supported by 28 wood pillars. The central four pillars are known as the Dragon Fountain Pillars. They sit on compass points and symbolize the four seasons, while the next row of 12 pillars represents the months of the year, and the outer ring of 12 represents a day in twelve segments. The roof, with its three umbrella-style eaves, is carpeted with 50,000 blue tiles – blue represents heaven in the Chinese color schema – and is crowned with a golden bulb. Glance inside to see the painstakingly intricate patterning on the coffered ceiling, which surrounds a royal dragon motif.

The golden tip that adorns the towering structure has caught more than just the attention of the awestricken. In 1889 it was struck by lightning, and the ensuing blaze reduced the original 15th century building to cinders. It was at this time that the grand wooden pillars were carted in to rebuild the structure, taking great pains to remain faithful to every detail of the original Ming design. For allowing such an abominable event to happen, the heads of 32 "guilty" court officials rolled off the guillotine.

Others Buildings

As you peruse the complex, don't forget to grab a peek at the other interesting structures dotted about. The **Long Corridor** (Cháng Láng; 长 廊) is in the park grounds (not the cordoned temple area) and will greet guests who approach from the east entrance (or those that leave through there). It is unmistakably marked by Chinese pursuing an array of leisurely activities; such as playing cards and Chinese chess, singing Peking Opera, jamming traditional instruments, and dancing.

Near the Hall of Prayer for Good Harvests, the green glazed tiles of the **Animal Killing Pavilion** (Zǎishēng Tíng; 宰牲亭) are hard to miss. Good on its name, it was the happening spot where sacrificial oxen, sheep or other animals were brought to meet their maker. Peek in the **Divine Music Administration** (Shényuè Shǔ; 神乐署), to the west of the Hall of Prayer for Good Harvests to see where sacrificial music was rehearsed. Nearby, the **Palace of Abstinence** (Zhāi Gōng; 斋 宫) was the emperor's fasting quarters, and to the north you will find the flower embedded **Double Rings Longevity Pavilion** (Shuānghuán Tíng; 双环亭).

The Park

Don't miss the locals using the exercise equipment, quiet pathways, and danceable plazas in this park. The exercise equipment looks like something from an overgrown preschool, and the dancing you will find here ranges from bumping pop to bordering-on-perverse tangos. It's all a wonderful sight. There are also over 4,000 ancient cypress trees in the park, some of which are 800-years-old.

The Earth Altar

Chinese name: 地坛 (Dìtán)
Hours: 6:00-21:00
Admission: ¥2
Address: 2 Andingmen Waijie. Dongcheng District (东城区安定门外大街2号)
Transport: Subway – Line 2 or Line 4, Yonghegong Lama Temple Station, Exit A

Just north of the incense-laden Lama Temple is the Earth Altar, or Ditan. Lesser in stature than the mighty Temple of Heaven, it is still of great importance and merit in the Chinese cosmological psyche. The terraced altar platform is the main building attraction. It covers a grand 18,000 sq m (193,750 sq ft) and its great open space and red and yellow tiled walls and gates are more reminiscent of the Forbidden City than its counterpart at Tiantan. Less renovated surrounding structures dot the exterior and put off a rustic mystique that attests to their powerful ancient statuses. As was the case with the Temple of Heaven, ritual was common here until the end of the Qing Dynasty at the turn of the 20th century, and today, the large park and altar platform get regular attention from the locals, who participate in a grand, week-long festival here every year during the Chinese New Year.

History

Signifying their relation, the altar at Ditan, also called Fāngzé Tán (方泽坛), was built in conjunction with the Circular Mound Altar of the Temple of Heaven in 1530. Ditan's square shape is just another reminder that the ancient Chinese believed the Earth was square. It was at Fangzetan that celestial slaughters of animals were carried out in fashions and on dates coordinating with those at Tiantan. Prior to the sacrifices, emperors had to make sacrifices of their own, and fasting took place inside a triple-palace complex known as the Fasting Palace. Said to mimic another earth altar at the top of Zhongshan Mountain in the old capital of Nanjing, Fangzetan underwent large-scale renovations under the Qing Emperor Qianlong (1735-1796), which included a great enlargement of the park. The park was opened to the public in 1986, and since then there has been a large festival held every January.

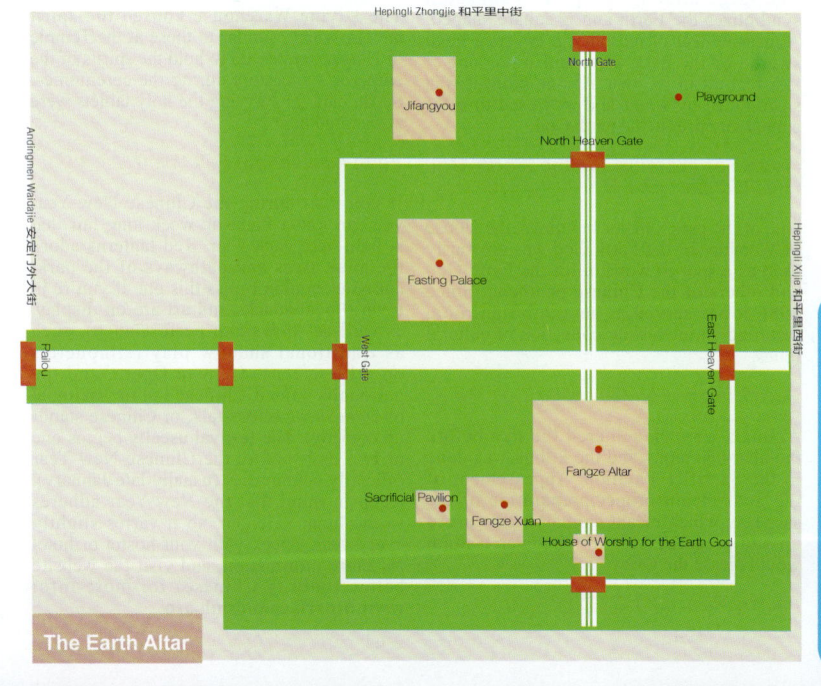

Layout

At 42.5 hectares (103 acres), Ditan is not as grand as Tiantan, but is still quite formidable as the second largest of the temple parks. The park is lovely and full of beautiful trees and gardens, and it's certainly worth a visit if you're in the area.

Fangze Altar (Fāngzé Tán; 方泽坛)

The large altar in the park, Fangzetan symbolizes the Earth and is square shaped. A massive feat of masonry, it covers a huge swathe of the park area, and traversing it is a feat all in its own. At one point it was surrounded by water and was used to offer animal sacrifices to the Earth God.

House of Worship for the Earth God (Huángqí Shì; 皇祇室)

One of the park's major buildings, the House of Worship for the Earth God was obviously used as a spot of worship for the Earth God and others of the Chinese pantheon. Since 1986 it has served as an exhibition room featuring an interesting collection of cultural relics.

Sacrificial Pavilion (Zǎishēng Tíng; 宰牲亭)

Animals were slaughtered the day before the altar ceremony and the killing was done in the Sacrifice Pavilion. Appeasement of the gods meant proper preparation of the sacrifice, which meant animals were carved up and prepared here in whatever fashion would please the gods.

Fasting Palace (Zhāi Gōng; 斋宫)

Actually consisting of three palatial buildings, the Fasting Palace was originally built in 1530, and then rebuilt 200 years later. Emperors were in charge of bringing good omens to their people, and any plights that befell the land were placed squarely on their head; this could lead to dethroning. To prevent losing his all-important power, the emperor would make his own sacrifice with a fast that could last for days.

Divine Warehouse (Shén Kù; 神库)

The Divine Warehouse housed the spirit tablets, which, similar to those at the Temple of Heaven, were said to hold the spirits of the emperor's ancestors during the ceremonies. Sedan cars for carrying the holy tablets were also stored here.

Earth Altar Temple Fair (Miào Huì; 庙会)

If you visit during the Chinese New Year you can join a fantastic week-long fair that is held here each year. Red lanterns adorn the altar, trees and pathways of the park, and you shouldn't miss this one if you're in town. Local snacks and art are on display, as well as shows and performances, such as traditional shadow play (silhouettes on a lit screen), Sichuan Opera, and the nationally famed Chinese comic dialogue of *xiangsheng* (cross-talk, or Chinese stand-up comedy). The festival usually begins one or two days before the Chinese New Year officially commences (usually late January). Keep in mind that the New Year adheres to the lunar calendar, so it varies slightly every year. Check with your hostel or hotel for more information, and visit the website below (only in Chinese) for more info: **www.dtpark.com/dtmh.asp**.

The Other Altars

Altar of the Sun

Chinese name: 日坛 (Rìtán)
Hours: 6:00-21:00 (winter); 6:00-22:00 (summer)
Admission: FREE
Address: 6 Ritan Beilu, Chaoyang District (朝阳区日坛北路6号)
Transport: Bus – 639, Ritan Gongyuan Stop (日坛公园站)

Altar of the Moon

Chinese name: 月坛 (Yuètán)
Hours: 6:00-21:00
Admission: ¥1
Address: 6 Yuetan Beijie, Xicheng District (西城区月坛北街甲6号)
Transport: Bus – 13, 15, 19, 42, 56, 623, Yuetan Gongyuan Stop (月坛公园站)

Altar of Agriculture

Chinese name: 先农坛 (Xiānnóngtán)
Admission: FREE
Address: 21 Dongjing Lu, Xicheng District (西城区东经路21号)
Transport: Walk 5 minutes east from the Temple of Heaven's south gate.

The corresponding east and west compass points are marked with the Sun Altar, (Ritan), and the Moon Altar (Yuetan). All four altars, Ditan, Ritan, Yuetan, and the Circular Mound Altar at Tiantan were built conjunctively in the 16th century. Witness to sacrificial rituals on specific intervals throughout the year, their correlation to each other is a further testament to the fundamental importance of cosmology and geomancy in the historical psyche of the Chinese. Like Ditan, Yuetan and Ritan are gracefully located in their own relaxing parks.

Due west of the Temple of Heaven and southwest of the Forbidden City, the Altar of Agriculture was used to appease the gods for good harvest. The altar proper shares the park with Jufu Hall, which was included in the 1998 and 2000 World Monuments Watch to discourage its imminent collapse. The inclusion successfully encouraged a large restoration project, and the site is now protected by the national government.

Tian'anmen Square & Surrounding Area

This section includes Tian'anmen Square, Tian'anmen Tower, the Monument to the People's Heroes, the Great Hall of the People, the Chairman Mao Mausoleum and the National Museum of China.

Tian'anmen Square is certainly an iconic part of Beijing, and it's definitely worth a trip to this famous plaza to see its austere surrounding structures, which are a mighty testament to the Soviet influence that perched atop the shoulders of 20th century Chinese communism. Paved with a myriad of stones on the footprint of a now-vanished extension of the old Forbidden City (then known as the Thousand Foot Corridor), Tian'anmen Square is a relatively young national emblem, yet one steeped in historical significance. The square has seen numerous mass gatherings, one in particular resulting in near riots at the death of Premier Zhou Enlai in 1976, and those who were globally cognitive in the late 1980s will find the plaza to be a poignant reminder of one of China's most infamous events. Around the area are a series of monolithic buildings harkening back to China's red days of communism, among which you can find a fantastic museum, the opulent home of Politburo meetings, and the final resting place of Mao Zedong.

Tian'anmen Square

Chinese name: 天安门广场 (Tiān'ānmén Guǎngchǎng)
Admission: FREE
Hours: 5:00-22:00
Transport:
Subway – Line 1, Tian'anmen East (天安门东) or Tian'anmen West (天安门西) Station, walk 5 minutes
Taxi – Point this sentence out to the driver if your Chinese will not suffice: 我想要去天安门广场。

Today, Tian'anmen Square is a proverbial Mecca for many Chinese. To this day it serves as a pilgrimage for those journeying to the political heart of the nation, with the embalmed body of Mao Zedong as an emotive relic of near godly status. The vast expanse of stone and statues is stringently monitored with uniformed and plain-clothed guards and closed circuit cameras, reminding visitors to refrain from religious or political demonstrations or any unseemly behavior. Despite the dour security, Tian'anmen Square gives off a certain humanism, where friendly travelers, families and lovers peacefully gather to kick up their feet. Strolling along the busy yet serene patchwork of stones, or finding a place to people-watch, can be as nice as a walk in the park.

Before You Go

Tian'anmen Square itself can be a very relaxing place to lounge and stretch a leg, despite the security and crowds. The plaza does not necessarily require a long visit or thorough prep, but visiting one or more of the surrounding museums or monuments can easily take a full day, so make an itinerary before you go. Bringing water or snacks is always a good idea, but be aware that bags are not allowed in the Mao Memorial Hall or the Great Hall of the People. There is a place to deposit your bags on-site, so bringing them can still be worthwhile if you expect a long day out. Finally, any meaningful visit will include plenty of walking, so you better make sure those boots were made for walkin'!

Info & Cautions

Security, scammers, and harassment from map touting salespeople can really bother some people. Our suggestion is to count these things as part of the experience, prepare yourself for them, and smile at the idea that your adventurous spirit can be nurtured as you learn to field such inevitable challenges in a positive way.

Top Attractions

Security

Security is tight around Tian'anmen Square, and though it can feel overbearing, it shouldn't affect you if you don't intend to make trouble. Bags may be checked and guards will be present, but you won't find anything that you haven't experienced at other high profile or politically sensitive areas in the world. It goes without saying that political or religious demonstrations are big no-no's, so keep the controversy at home. Unseemly behavior will be promptly visited by Segway-mounted guards, and a visa may be revoked. Meandering guests and lounging visitors, though, can expect a hassle free day.

Scams

Scammers take their business to this huge tourist destination. Please see page 312 in the Hot Topics section for more information on scams and how to avoid them.

Map Sellers

Map sellers troll Tian'anmen Square. Unless you actually want a map, they can be annoying. Snubbing can be effective for some of them, others may require a stern rebuff. Try your best to chuckle to yourself at their futile determination, and don't let them detract from your enjoyment.

History

While the site of Tian'anmen Square has a history as old as the Ming Dynasty, the plaza itself is only about 70 years old. In fact, the Forbidden City was at one time even more mammoth and commanding than it is today, and its front entrance expanded assertively into the space that is now Tian'anmen Square. The Tian'anmen Gate of the Forbidden City, facing the square from across Dongchang'an Jie, was built in 1415 during the Ming Dynasty, and it was the northernmost point of a massively jutting section of the Imperial City (Forbidden City) and was then known as the Thousand Foot Corridor (Qiānbù Láng; 千步廊).

The center of modern Tian'anmen Square was graced by the Great Ming Gate (Dàmíng Mén; 大明门), the southern gate to the Imperial City, which was fittingly renamed Great Qing Gate (Dàqīng Mén; 大清门) by the successive Manchurian Qing Dynasty, and finally the Gate of China (Zhōnghuá Mén; 中华门) during the short-lived Republic of China. The gate was unique in that it was purely a ceremonial gateway and was flanked by the now-lost Chang'an Left Gate and Chang'an Right Gate. Together, these three gates created a T shape that hugely extended the imperial grounds, with the left and right gates sitting slightly north from the ceremonial gatehouse. The Great Ming Gate sported three upturned arches, complimented by three watchtowers, and guarded by two stone lions. For an idea of what this magnificent gate would have looked like, make a journey to the Ming Tombs (pg 138), which have ceremonial gateways erected in a similar style. The gate was only opened when the emperor passed through, and to avoid unnecessary executions of the common "rabble" (who were immediately executed upon viewing of the emperor), commoners were warned of the imperial approach with a system of bells and drums.

In characteristic fashion of the time, the feudalistic Gate of China was demolished in 1949 to make room for a grand enlargement of the stoic Tian'anmen Square. November 1958 made way for a major expansion of the grand plaza, which was completed after only 11 months, in August 1959. This followed Mao Zedong's vision of making the square the largest and most spectacular in the world and it was intended to hold over 500,000 people. In that process, a large number of old residential buildings and other historical structures were sadly demolished in order to cater to the square as a massive metaphor for the enormity of Mao's Communist Party. In stark relief, the socialist modernist obelisk – the Monument to the People's Heroes – stands at the center of the grand plaza. The peripheries are authoritatively marked by the Great Hall of the People and the National Museum of China, part of the sternly Stalinistic Ten Great Buildings that were constructed from 1958-59 to commemorate the ten-year anniversary of the People's Republic of China.

Layout

Tian'anmen square is spread over a north-south axis, and is flanked by monolithic buildings that look like they fell out of the Iron Curtain. The Gate of Heavenly Peace (aka Tian'anmen Tower) marks the northern end of the square and sits across the main road. To the south lies the Front Gate (Qián Mén; 前门), which can be ascended and provides a wonderful view of the square and the surrounding areas. The plaza's north is fittingly framed by the Chairman Mao Memorial Hall (Máozhǔxí Jì'niàntáng; 毛主席纪念堂), which houses the embalmed remains of the late communist leader who conceived the idea of Tian'anmen Square.

The site has long been a place of *feng shui* design that pays homage to Chinese traditions of cosmic geometrical design, and Tian'anmen Square continues to evidence the same practices that governed the layout of the Forbidden City. As you move around the square, keep in mind that you are standing at the symbolic center of the Chinese universe.

Tian'anmen Tower

Chinese name: 天安门城楼 (Tiān'ānmén Chénglóu)
Admission: ¥15
Hours: 9:00-16:30
Transport: Same as Tian'anmen Square

Tian'anmen Tower, also known as the Gate of Heavenly Peace, faces the square from the northern side of the main road (Chang'an Jie) and has a spectacular view of the square and the Soviet-style "wedding cake buildings" that surround it. It was from this iconic vantage point that Mao historically proclaimed the People's Republic of China on 1 October, 1949. Jumping further back in history, the majestic gatehouse was used to promulgate the coronation of a new emperor during its dynastic days. Only imperial family members or aristocrats were allowed to enter the tower until 1912, when the Qing Dynasty came to an abrupt end in the face of revolutionary zeal. Massive military parades are still viewed from this tower by China's modern political elite.

The beautifully imposing tower hangs a 1.5-ton portrait of Mao just below his historical standing-point of the October 1st declaration, which is sandwiched by two giant placards. The left one reads "Long Live the People's Republic of China" (Zhōnghuá Rénmín Gònghéguó Wànsuì; 中华人民共和国万岁), while the right one reads "Long Live the Great Unity of the World's Peoples" (Shìjiè Rénmín Dàtuánjié Wànsuì; 世界人民大团结万岁). Head up the tower to view the 60 giant wooden beams, the intricate paintwork and a photographic history inside.

Free to pass under in transit to the Forbidden City, the tower will set you back ¥15 to climb up for a view. Tickets can be purchased on the north side of the tower.

Flag-Raising Ceremony

Every morning a regiment of PLA soldiers in flawless perfection goosestep their way across the main road (Dongchang'an Jie) at precisely 108 steps per minute. Traffic is halted for the event, as thousands of people often come to see the soldiers cross the street in unflinching order to raise the Five Star Red Flag of the Chinese Nation. Seeing the Guard of Honor raise the emblazoned flag is great fun, and considered a must by many Beijing tourists. You must get there by sunrise, which during the summer is before 6:00.

Monument to the People's Heros

Chinese name: 人民英雄纪念碑 (Rénmín Yīngxióng Jì'niànbēi)
Admission: FREE
Hours: 5:00-22:00

Standing at 38 m (125 ft), this lofty obelisk is the centerpiece of Tian'anmen Square. Completed in 1958, the stone pillar is made from granite that was lugged from the Shandong city of Qingdao, and its base delivers bas-relief sculptures of major revolutionary and patriotic events (e.g. Lin Zexu destroying British opium in Humen). Here you can also find engraved calligraphy from the Party's key players Zhou Enlai and Mao himself. Mao's particular etching reads "The People's Heros live in Eternal Glory" (Rénmín Yīngxióng Yǒngchuí Búxiǔ; 人民英雄永垂不朽). Swing by at night to see the monument bathed in a pretty sea of light.

Great Hall of the People

Chinese name: 人民大会堂 (Rénmín Dàhuìtáng)
Admission: ¥30
Hours: 9:00-14:00 (Jan-Mar & Dec); 8:15-15:00 (Apr-Jun); 7:30-16:00 (Jul-Aug); 8:30-15:00 (Sep-Nov)

The ironically named Great Hall of the People lies on the western side of the square, and it's the site of the China National People's Congress meetings and other political and diplomatic activities. Its monolithic size and menacing presence befit the imperious political cadre, which lines the streets with black limos when the NPC takes session here. Less a breathtaking construction and more a pompous display of power and wealth, it is fitting that the Great Hall of the People is the monument gracing the back of the ¥100 bank note, the largest currency note in China. Political history buffs will find interest in the Great Hall as host to Margaret Thatcher's infamous 1982 stair-tripping incident, Mikhail Gorbachev's protest-laden 1989 visit, and Richard Nixon's historic 1972 banquet.

Greeted by 12 marble posts through which you can make your ingress, the inside of the hall is composed of 29 uninspired conference rooms named for provincial regions and a host of bedecked halls and auditoriums. Further down, the **Central Hall** gloats as an ostentatious symbol of government wealth, laid out with a plush marble floor and embellished with crystal lamps that glint among the ceiling's embroidery. Don't miss the **Great Auditorium**, which has been witness to a history of party speeches and government bustle, and can simultaneously seat a stunning 10,000 representatives. Grab a peak at the auditorium's ceiling, which is lavishly decorated with a galaxy of lights and a centralized great red star encircled by an ocean of rippling patterns (said to represent the people).

Chairman Mao Memorial Hall

Chinese name: 毛主席纪念堂 (Máozhǔxí Jì'niàntáng)
Admission: FREE
Hours: 8:00-12:00; closed Mon

On the site of the vanished Gate of China sits the resting place of the Chinese Communist Party's nominal founder, Mao Zedong. The squat Stalinistic mausoleum was erected in urgency after Mao's passing in September of 1976 in the center of Tian'anmen Square, and is interestingly placed on Beijing's north-south axis of symmetry. It is divided into three halls, and the corpse of Mao is viewable in a crystal coffin.

Reverence of Mao Zedong is alive and well throughout the Chinese nation; the abundance of flowers and tears that surround his mummified remains lend a striking reminder of his place within much of the national psyche. It is not just Tian'anmen Tower or the Mao Memorial Hall that displays such arresting respect, living rooms and bell towers across the great expanse of Communist China continue to pay homage in the form of portraits and effigies.

In light of the intense approbation that you will find in the Mao Memorial Hall, take care to hold a dignified presence, and remove your hat upon entry. The statue of the "Great Helmsman" is venerated with flowers, and if you want to hand over the dough, you too can lay one for ¥3. In the following room lies the embalmed corpse of the late party leader, folded in an antiquated hammer and sickle red flag. Stern guards earnestly move the crowds through to the final room where the reverent spectacle is abruptly cheapened with an ocean of campy Mao memorabilia.

Passports are a must here – you cannot get in without them, and bags need to be stowed at the building that lies to the east of the mausoleum. Cross the road from Tian'anmen Square to find the bag storage.

National Museum of China

Chinese name: 国家博物馆 (Guójiā Bówùguǎn)
Admission: FREE
Hours: 9:00-17:00 (last admission at 16:00); closed Mon
Website: www.chnmuseum.cn (English available)

Flanking the square to the east is China's championed National Museum. Unequalled throughout the nation, the National Museum of China was first opened in 2003, but it underwent years of renovation until it was reopened in 2011. The current building is a combination of two museums: the **Chinese History Museum** (Zhōngguó Lìshǐ Bówùguǎn; 中国历史博物馆) and the **Chinese Revolutionary Museum** (Zhōngguó Gémìng Bówùguǎn; 中国革命博物馆). The superb exhibits are unmatched and fantastically displayed, and you should absolutely not miss the **Ancient China** (Galleries N20-N25, S15-S18, S20) exhibit on the basement floor. Prehistoric China up to the recently departed Qing Dynasty are magnificently represented with countless artifacts under thoughtfully implemented soft lighting and spacious viewing areas. The journey of Chinese civilization follows a 1.7 million year voyage here, one that is quite spectacular.

Other not-to-be-missed exhibitions include those in the **Bronze Art and Buddhist Sculpture** galleries (Central Hall 2), **Ancient Chinese Jades** (Gallery S13), and the top-floor **Ancient Chinese Money** display (Gallery S11). The museum is spacious and sweeping, so be prepared for a dazzlingly lengthy stay. When fatigue inevitably strikes, swing down to the main floor for a break in the café. Passports are required for entry.

The Tale of Tian'anmen Tower

There are few places in China that have seen as much as Tian'anmen Tower has during the last 600 years. Part of this is the fact that unfortunately many of China's incredible buildings from past millennia simply have not lived long enough to tell their story today. But there's something much more profound about what Tian'anmen Tower has to tell us. Though the first 500 years of its life saw the rise and fall of two of China's most prolific and influential dynasties (the Ming and the Qing), it is perhaps more the changes and events that transpired at Tian'anmen in the 20th century that make the tower's story so remarkable.

Tian'anmen, which means Gate of Heavenly Peace, was first constructed in 1417 by Emperor Yongle during the Ming Dynasty, a period that is considered by many to be one of China's golden ages. Yongle's gate was built in the *pai fang* tradition, meaning it was essentially a set of ornate pillars topped with multi-tiered roofs, and was much more of a gateway than it is today. In 1457 the *pai fang* gateway was burnt to cinders by a bolt of lightning, and the 1465 reconstruction reintroduced Tian'anmen in the tower design seen today. The first major event that Tian'anmen witnessed was the fall of the Ming Dynasty, culminating in the second destruction of the gate at the hands of rebel leader Li Zicheng in 1644. When the Qing Dynasty took power that same year, they ordered the tower rebuilt and, upon its completion in 1651, it was given its present name.

Originally the name of Yongle's gateway was Cheng Tianmen, or Gate of Accepting Heavenly Mandate. By itself, however, the word *cheng* means "connection between past and present," and there is nothing that can describe Tian'anmen Tower as it stands today better than that. Tian'anmen is the literal gateway to the Forbidden City and very much a figurative gateway to the past. A revolution that saw the end of 2,000 years of dynastic rule, the birth of a new socialist Chinese nation that has stormed its way onto the global stage, and even deadly protests – all happened in their most powerful moments right under the gaze of Tian'anmen. The tower has become such a commanding national symbol that in 1970 Premier Zhou Enlai ordered its entire reconstruction in secret (covered in tarps and scaffolding, the project was officially called a "renovation") because the 300-year-old tower was falling apart from such heavy use in the 1950s and '60s. Zhou knew all too well that the loss of the tower that was the epicenter of the Chinese universe would have been the loss of the legendary tale of modern China, and an irreparable blow to the nation.

And without further ado, the Tale of Tian'anmen Tower as told through some really sweet pictures.

Obviously we can't bring you any pictures from Tian'anmen as it was during its initial 15th century construction, nor can we show pictures of the events that happened in 1644, but we can give you this artist representation of Tian'anmen before the 20th century.

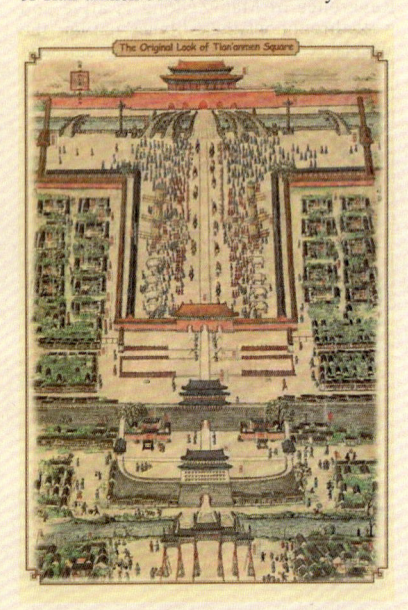

What you see in the back – or at the top rather – of the picture is Tian'anmen Tower. Notice how there are more towers and gates than there should be in the south. That's because the Forbidden City was once part of the Imperial City, which extended out into what is now Tian'anmen Square. This long area was called the Thousand Foot Corridor, and it ran to the gate below, called Qianmen (the Front Gate). Today, the Qianmen area is a reproduction of the boisterous local market that originally sat out front of the Imperial City.

Dynastic Days: The Final Years of the Qing Dynasty

It doesn't get much more old-timey than this *(above)*; Tian'anmen as it was in 1906 during the waning years of the Qing Dynasty. This was during the reign of the Empress Dowager Cixi.

Out with Puyi, in with the public.

Puyi abdicated in 1912, but he was allowed to live in the back of the Forbidden City until 1924, when he headed to Tianjin. This picture *(above)* is Tian'anmen Tower in 1928, just four years after Puyi was kicked out and the Forbidden City was opened to the public.

Somewhere inside Puyi, the last emperor of China, lives out his final days in the Forbidden City

A bit of a clearer image than the Qing Dynasty era, this picture *(above)* dates to 1917, the time when two warlords, General Zhang Xun, and a short-term president, Yuan Sikai, made their own grabs for imperial power. At the end of his five-year presidential run in 1916, Yuan declared himself the emperor and then died the following year.

In fact, the Imperial Government was officially deposed in 1911, so during this time there were a handful of leaders taking up the position of president as the government transitioned. However, it was the May 4th Movement in 1919, a string of student protests against the ineffective government, that seemed to define the decade and ushered in the chaos to come.

Revolution: The End of Dynastic China

Students from several Beijing universities (including Peking U and Tsinghua U) protest the government in front of Tian'anmen Tower in May 4, 1919

The Republic of China

Bet you thought the whole giant Big Brother portrait on Tian'anmen Tower began with Mao Zedong, didn't you? Nope. During the brief period of the Kuomintang, (aka the Republic of China), President Chiang Kai-shek had his own portrait hung out front. That's him up there in 1945 *(above)*.

As you may know, the Republic of China did not last long. There was a brutal civil war going on between Chiang's Kuomintang forces and Mao's communist PLA – the People's Liberation Army.

Revolution: The Chinese Communist Party Takes Control

On January 31, 1949 the PLA marched into Beijing (which was called Beiping at the time) and declared the city "liberated." The establishment of the CCP as the de facto ruling party in China is still to this day referred to as "liberation," which is often used as a reference of time (i.e. before liberation and after liberation). This picture below is from February 12; Mao's portrait and those of his generals and associates were hung in celebration of the "liberation." The words below his portrait read (from right to left in traditional Chinese): "Celebration of the liberation of Beiping."

For those who don't realize it, we'll tell you: this picture *(above)* is incredible. This is October 1, 1949, the day that Mao Zedong stood on top of Tian'anmen Tower and announced the founding of the People's Republic of China. Approximately 100,000 people attended the announcement in Tian'anmen Square, and millions more listened in from across the nation.

This is easily one of the most defining moments in modern Chinese history *(below)*.

Mao declares the founding of the PRC on October 1, 1949

Here *(above)*, Mao makes an announcement from atop Tian'anmen Tower sometime in 1954. Just five years after the PRC's founding, he held absolute power over the nation, and his personality cult began to grow. He would make endless announcements and despotic army inspections from the tower in his 28-year reign.

A perfect example of this can be seen in this picture *(below)*. In 1966, Mao received the Red Guard here at the base of Tian'anmen Tower to give them encouragement on their course to becoming full-fledged members of the PLA. Holding up Mao's Little Red Book (a book of his propagandist sayings and reflections) in utter adoration, the men in this picture are a remarkable testament to the cult around Mao and his personality.

Those who could shake his hand tried to never wash theirs again...

This picture *(above)* is from April 5, 1970. Tian'anmen Tower had witnessed the birth of a new and drastically different China. Notice how the theme of red goes right down to the paint on the bus, and how the people in the foreground are decked out in drab communist green.

The first staggering death of 1976 was Zhou Enlai, who died on January 8. His death saw thousands of mourners fill Tian'anmen Square *(left)*. Both pictures are from the days after his death, and the signs held by the people in the right picture read "The Prime Minister for the People, the People love the Prime Minister" (Zǒnglǐ Wèi Rénmín, Rénmín Ài Zǒnglǐ).

It was later that year that a second death dealt a further blow to the emotions of the nation, and the people struggled to regain their poise with the death of Mao.

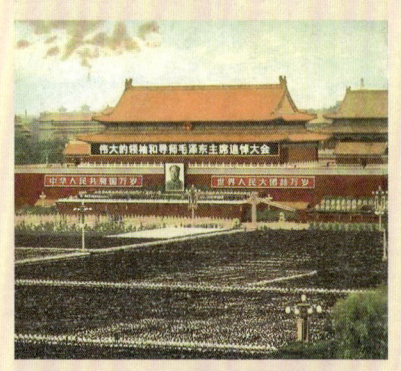

It's hard to put into words a picture like this *(above)*, which shows mourners in Tian'anmen Square and out front of Tian'anmen Tower upon Mao's death on September 9, 1976. It is said more than one million people gathered and the ground was wet from tears.

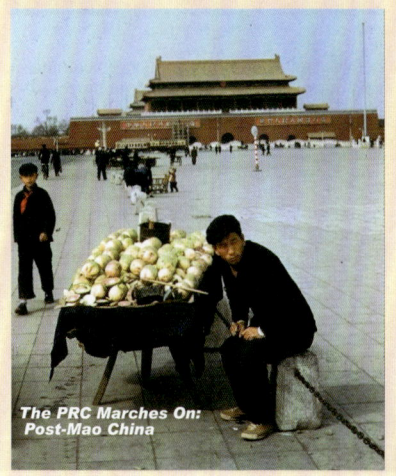

Some who have commented on this man *(above)* selling turnips in Tian'anmen Square in 1979 have called him the "Greatest Vendor Ever." Not only was such free street-side selling illegal (it was commonplace in pre-communist China) without a permit, but it is outright impossible and unthinkable to do so in today's ultra-secure Tian'anmen Square.

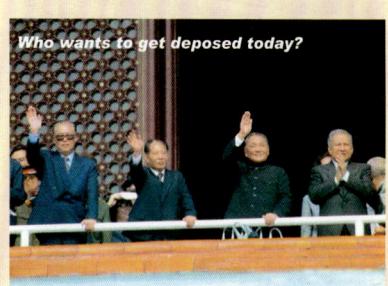

How do you gain great power after being fired? There are many politicians in Chinese history you could ask, but one of the best would be Deng Xiaoping, pictured here second from the right. After being ousted from party politics in the Cultural Revolution, he gradually snuck back in, and from the position of Vice-Chairman of the Military Commission he wielded de facto power from 1978 to 1992. This pic *(above)* is from 1984. To his left are Hu Yaobang and Zhao Ziyang, the Prime Minister and Vice Prime Minister, respectively (they were fired by Deng years later). Both were pro-democracy, and it was Hu's death in 1989 that lead to student demonstrations in Tian'anmen Square.

At the 35th anniversary of the founding of the PRC, Deng Xiaoping began a tradition of army inspection from a car driving out of Tian'anmen Tower *(left)* and down Chang'an Dajie *(right)* on October 1, 1984. Until this, inspections had only been from tower-top.

Jiang Zeming continues the tradition with the 50th anniversary on 1999 (below)

The 50th anniversary festivities continue (October 1, 1999)

Above you see former President Hu Jintao at the 60th anniversary on October 1, 2009

But, it hasn't all been military saber-rattling and authoritarian announcements that have dominated Tian'anmen Tower's vision. When it was announced that Beijing had won the bid for the 2008 Olympic Games in 2000, a massive celebration was held at Tian'anmen Square *(below)*. You can see Tian'anmen Tower in the background.

Indeed, the games were a game-changer for modern China. And though much of the age of progress that the games seemed to herald for the nation seems to have fallen by the wayside, there is no denying that the games put China in a world spotlight like never

The giant portrait of Mao is the largest hand painted portrait in Asia. It is 6 m (19.5 ft) tall by 4.6 m (15 ft) wide and weighs 1.5 tons; hence the cranes being used to replace the portrait at night in the below picture

before, and many of the influences coming in and out of the Middle Kingdom since 2008 have certainly changed the nation for the better.

The Mao portrait still sits atop Tian'anmen Tower, a reminder of the stunning and remarkable changes that have gripped the Chinese nation during the 20th century, much of which was witnessed right in front of this gatehouse. China and the PRC have moved boldly into the 21st century, and it is very hard to speculate what lies in store for the future of the nation, but you can be sure that the next couple of decades will likely bring events just as fascinating and monumental as the last 100 years. Keep your eyes on the tower!

Tian'anmen Tower has undergone great changes since its 15th century inception. The following page has a few then-and-now pictures from several Chinese, taken at the same spots in front of the tower as children and again on the 50th anniversary of the PRC in 2009.

Tian'anmen Tower at night

Four siblings in 1970 (left) and in 2009 (right)

A woman in 1982 (right) and in 2009 (left)

Shichahai Area

This section includes the Shichahai (aka Houhai) Lakes; Shichahai Bar Street; the Drum and Bell Towers; the former residences of Prince Gong, Song Qingling, Guo Moruo and Mei Lanfang; Nanluogu Xiang Hutong; and Yandai Xiejie (Tobacco Pipe Byway).

An old stomping ground for Manchu princes and Qing Dynasty officials, the Shichahai area today remains one of the most attractive and active parts of Beijing. Also known as Houhai, Shichahai can be translated as the "Sea of the Ten Buddhist Temples" and includes three lakes: Houhai (Back Lake), Qianhai (Front Lake), and Xihai (West Lake). Two of the lakes, Houhai and Qianhai, are connected, and their intersection is spanned by Yinding Bridge. Summer brings swimmers, Dragon Boat races and paddleboats, and winter freezes the lakes and invites ice-skaters to come break some bones on the frozen water. The whole area is essentially a giant outdoor playground, and in summer the action hits full throttle as everyone, from posh socialites to sunbaked farmers, finds a reason to answer Shichahai's call.

Making a visit to Beijing's Great Lakes is practically essential these days. Just about anyone can find something they like in the tranquil parks, paths, and hutongs that make Houhai their home. This is where Beijingers come to let their hair down, so make a trip over and catch local seniors and youngsters alike fishing, playing mahjong, flying kites or just chatting it up. The lakes are ideal for lazy bike riding too, and you can even catch a glimpse of people taking a swim in the filthy water. They even ice dip in the dead of winter! Bars, restaurants, and cafes line the shores of the lakes at the connection of Houhai and Qianhai, and summer nights erupt with good-natured youth out to take in some drinks – or a whole lot of drinks.

The bars around Houhai can be a bit tacky, and doormen are persistent in pushing their establishment to the wandering drinkers. But many of them can also be fun (and wildly overpriced). You can find plenty of live music here (as long as you're cool with the solo-guy-with-guitar-and-microphone setup that is painfully overplayed here) and there are also bars offering some decent rock and reggae performers. If you're not into cookie-cutter bars and formulaic music (you're not alone), then duck down one of the hutongs that surround the Houhai area. Some of the best little bars and cafes are tucked away just around the hutong corner.

Before You Go

The Shichahai area is huge. Good walking shoes are very important, but the wide availability of restaurants and shops means that you won't need to pack a bag unless you personally don't want to spend the money for outside meals and water. Sunscreen is always advised on sunny days, though Houhai provides plenty of shade. We suggest you skip the pack and just chill out in one of Beijing's most relaxing areas.

Info & Cautions

Scammers tend to stick to Tian'anmen and the Great Wall, and rickshaws in this area are generally much more dependable than at the Forbidden City; just make sure you come to a clear agreement first. Fake alcohol (see Scams on pg 312) can be a problem here. If you suspect something is afoul, find a new place to drink.

History

History around Houhai is abundant and diverse. Home to many generations of Manchurian Princes, Qing officials and affluent 20th century political bigwigs, Houhai's mini-museums and preserved *siheyuan* (traditional courtyard homes) still sport reminders of the area's dynastic past. Because Houhai is a large area, check the details that follow for more information on the historical sites and exhibitions.

Hutongs & Touring

The areas and hutongs around Houhai are excellent for mini-tours and self-tours. There are many ways to get around that can reduce foot travel. Bikes can be rented for ¥10 per hour, rickshaws will cruise you around the area for about ¥100 per person, and rowboats and paddleboats are available to bobble around the lakes for about ¥60-100 per hour (groups of four).

Shichahai Bar Street

Chinese name: 什刹海酒吧一条街 (Shíchàhǎi Jiǔba Yītiáojiē)
Transport:
Subway – Line 8, Shichahai.
Taxi – If you are centrally located expect to pay less than ¥30. If your Chinese will not suffice, show this sentence to the driver: 我想要去后海

The Sea of the Ten Buddhist Temples, or Shichahai, has a colorful nightlife scene along two main bar streets. The thoroughfare of **Lotus Lane** is the most happening spot, while the intersection of Qianhai and Houhai at **Yinding Bridge** packs quite a raucous crowd as well. Just about any night of the week you can find plenty of energy, loads of drink specials and live music.

Drum & Bell Towers

Chinese name: 鼓楼 (Gǔ Lóu), 钟楼 (Zhōng Lóu)
Admission: ¥20 (Drum Tower); ¥15 (Bell Tower)
Hours: 9:00-17:00
Transport: Subway – Line 2 or Line 8, get off at Gulou Dajie (鼓楼大街) Station, Exit E, then walk south for about 100 m (328 ft)

Drum Tower

Born in the Mongolian Yuan Dynasty under Kublai Khan, the Drum Tower was built in 1272 and stood at the northernmost point of the Yuan capital Dadu (Beijing's name under Mongol rule). The evolving Mongolian city eventually overtook the north enough that the two towers finally, and more fittingly, graced the capital's core. At that time the Drum Tower was blandly known as the Tower of Orderly Administration (Qizhenglou), and like nearly every other ancient wooden structure in Beijing, burnt to the ground in the 15th century. Ming Dynasty Emperor Yongle rebuilt the tower just east of the original site, which was highly renovated in 1800 under the Qing Emperor Jiaqing (this is what you see today, but much of the original Ming structure remains intact).

Back in Yongle's day there were 24 drums kept inside the beautiful red tower. Every evening at 19:00 the night hours were rung in and the city gates closed with 13 strikes on the drums. The drums were beaten again every two hours throughout the night in order to help guards track the time (and disturb all the sleeping local residents). The last drumbeat was at 5:00 in the morning, which marked the time that officials were to be present and kneeling in front of the Forbidden City's Hall of Supreme Harmony. Today, replicated renditions of the old Ming drum sessions can be seen at the Tower if you stop by at the right time. Don't forget to check out the only surviving one of the Ming drums – the **Night Watchman's Drum** (the drum is not as exciting as the name, but it's still very cool).

Performance Times: 9:30, 10:30, 11:30, 13:30, 14:30, 15:30 and 16:30.

Bell Tower

The Bell Tower was a Yuan Dynasty creation that was erected with the Drum Tower in 1272. A 15th century fire also cleared this tower for an updated version, which was built in the 1440s, but the structure you see now was put up in 1745. The current Bell Tower is less radiant than its drum counterpart, but its gigantic 63-ton iron bell is worth a visit. The hutong views from the top are notably better than the Drum Tower.

In conjunction with the rhythms of the Drum Tower, the Bell Tower also served as a timekeeper for the Yuan, Ming, and Qing Dynasties. After the 5:00 drums struck their last morning beat, the enormous iron bell was gonged two hours later to mark the official start of the day. As the city grew, the audible range of the iron bell proved too slight, so an even bigger bronze bell, which had a staggering 20 km (12 mi) range, replaced the iron one. That monster bronze bell has sadly vanished, but the iron bell still rests in the unrestored interior and is a must see before it falls through the floor.

Nanluogu Xiang

Chinese name: 南锣鼓巷 (Nánluógǔ Xiàng)
Transport: Subway – Lines 6 or 8, get off at Nanluogu Xiang Station

Houhai's surrounding areas are busting with hutongs, and their alluring secrets and buried gems can make for some of the most rewarding Beijing experiences. Nanluogu Xiang, at one time a quiet little ramshackle of a hutong, has exploded in the last decade and a half to become one of the most dynamic and energetic hutongs in the city (it all started by the opening of **Passby Bar** in 1999). Nanluogu Xiang was built in the Mongolian Yuan Dynasty, and those 800 years of history by themselves are reason enough for you to immediately start preparing your visit.

The main alley runs north-south from Gulou Dongdajie to Di'anmen Dongdajie, and from it offshoot numerous smaller alleys that are equally worth exploring. Hipster girls can pop in the quirky shop **Petal** for an array of colorful clothes, kitschy trinkets, and fine handmade items. Beer connoisseurs and drunks cannot miss **Great Leap Brewing** (pg 245), concealed east of the main alley on Doujiao Hutong and serving up original draft brews from honeyed Banana Wheats to biting IPAs. Borrow a book at **Treehouse Café**, brush up on local bands with a CD from **Tan**, or grab a latte and test your painting skills on the canvas at **Viva Coffee Bar**.

Yandai Xiejie

Chinese name: 烟袋斜街 (Yāndài Xiéjiē)
Transport: Subway – Line 8, Shichahai (什刹海) Station, walk north along Di'anmen Waidajie (地安门外大街) for about 100 m (328 ft); this popular hutong is on your left side.

Marking another of Beijing's traditional hutong alleyways is Tobacco Pipe Byway – one of the oldest hutongs in the city (though it's a bit commercialized now since its 2007 redevelopment). Lying to the east of Shichahai Bar Street, the busy hutong was originally named Drum Tower Byway from its Yuan Dynasty inception and kept the designation for 700 years to the end of the Qing Dynasty. Its current name came about when Shuang Shengtai, one of the numerous tobacco shops lining the street, placed a 1.5 m- (5 ft)-tall wooden tobacco pipe out front of the store placard. Soon the masses began calling the whole street after this landmark.

Tobacco shops can still be found on Tobacco Pipe Byway, but the more intoxicating haunts for non-smokers include more than 20 cafes and bars, and enough Indian clothes, Miao accoutrements and Tibetan apparel to equip you and your extended family for generations to come. Keep an eye out too for Lijiang crafts, Shaanxi pottery, and the ubiquitous Chairman Mao kitsch. Don't forget to grab a bite of some of the more unique food in the area, including medieval-like roast legs of lamb (烤羊腿), surprisingly tasty donkey meat (驴肉), Taiwanese omelets, and other snacks.

Prince Gong's Mansion

Chinese name: 恭王府 (Gōngwáng Fǔ)
Admission: ¥40
Hours: 7:30-18:30 (Mar 16-Nov 15; last admission at 16:40); 8:00-18:30 (Nov 16-Mar 15; last admission at 16:10)
Address: 17 Qianhai Xijie, Shichahai (什刹海前海西街17号)
Transport: Subway – Line 6, get off at Beihai North (北海北) Station, Exit B, walk northwest along Longtoujing Jie (龙头井街) for about 200 m (656 ft)

Embedded in a hutong just west of Yinding Bridge is one of Beijing's largest private residential compounds and the world's largest extant courtyard. For more information concerning this site, please see page 140.

Former Residence of Song Qingling

Chinese name: 宋庆龄故居 (Sòngqìnglíng Gùjū)
Hours: 9:00-17:30 (Apr-Oct); 9:00-16:30 (Nov-Mar)
Admission: ¥20
Website: www.sql.org.cn (in Chinese)
Phone: 6404 4205
Address: 46 Houhai Beiyan, Xicheng District (西城区后海北沿 46 号)
Transport: Subway – Line 8, Shichahai (什刹海) Station, Exit A2, walk west until you come to Qianhai Dongyan (前海东沿); then walk north along Qianhai Dongyan until you arrive at Yinding Bridge (银锭桥) where the name of the road changes to Houhai Beiyan (后海北沿); next walk about 200 m (656 ft) and you'll arrive at the residence

Within striking distance of Prince Gong's Mansion is the reverentially preserved home of the esteemed Madam Song Qingling. The late wife of the founder of the Republic of China, Sun Yat-sen, Qingling lived the later years of her life in this abode nestled in a delightful garden on the northern end of Houhai. The house previously belonged to Prince Chun, the father of the famous last emperor of China, Puyi. The home itself is comfortably decorated with period furniture, pictures, clothing, books and other bric-a-brac. The real gem here is the guest room to the side, which delivers a detailed mini-museum on her compelling life: her coddled upbringing in one of Shanghai's most prominent families, her marriage to Sun Yat-sen, her political life and even the car given to her by Joseph Stalin.

The Story of the Songs

Charlie Song — Ni Kwei-tseng

Ailing Song — H H Kung   Qingling Song — Sun Yat-sen   TV (Tse-Ven) Song   Meiling Song — Chiang Kai-shek

It was to the dismay of her father, Charlie Song (Sòng Yàorú; 宋耀如), that Qingling (Sòng Qìnglíng; 宋庆龄) married his close friend, Sun Yat-sen (Sūn Zhōngshān; 孙中山), who was 30 years her elder. One of the most prominent and politically influential families in the history of modern China, the Songs included three daughters and a son (actually three sons, but Tse-Ven is the only well-known one) raised under the wealth of father Charlie, who became a rich businessman after obtaining a Methodist education in the United States. Qingling's sister's Ailing (Sòng Ǎilíng; 宋霭龄) and Meiling (Sòng Měilíng; 宋美龄) are known to the Chinese to have loved money and power, but only Qingling truly loved China. She was the only Song to live in China after 1949, and it is said that she used her wealth to donate trucks, ambulances and uniforms to the military in Shanghai during the devastating Sino-Japanese War of 1937.

Beyond Qingling and Sun Yat-sen, the political arms of the Songs ran deep. Ailing – said to be the first Chinese girl to own a bicycle – married H H Kung (Kǒng Xiángxī; 孔祥熙), a wealthy descendant of Confucius, head of the Bank of China, and later the finance minister of the Republic of China. Meiling likewise married Chiang Kai-shek (Jiǎng Jièshí; 蒋介石), the head of the Kuomintang (Nationalist Party of China) and later president of the Republic of China. She fled with Chiang to Taiwan when the Nationalists were overrun by Mao's communist forces.

Charlie's cherished son, TV (Tse-Ven) Song (Sòng Zǐwén; 宋子文), captured his share of the spotlight as well. Educated in economics at Harvard University, TV worked briefly at the International Banking Corporation in New York before returning to China to become one of the most prolific Chinese men of the 20th century. Under the Nationalist government of brothers-in-law Chiang Kai-shek and Sun Yat-sen, TV served in a succession of financial offices – where he successfully balanced the budget as Finance Minister – before becoming unsettled by Chiang's appeasement of the Japanese during the war. During his frank and unyielding negotiations with Joseph Stalin, Tse-Ven cited his connections with the American military to get Stalin to recognize the Republic of China as the legitimate government of China and to negotiate an oral treaty to end Soviet occupation of Chinese Manchuria. The wealthiest Chinese man of his generation, he retreated to New York when the Nationalists were driven from China, where he lived until his death at 79.

Former Residence of Guo Moruo

Chinese name: 郭沫若故居 (Guōmòruò Gùjū)
Hours: 9:00-16:30, closed Mon
Admission: ¥20
Address: 18 Qianhai Xijie (前海西街 18 号), west next to Prince Gong's Mansion.
Transport: Subway – Line 6, Beihai North (北海北) Station, Exit B, walk east for 20 m (65.5 ft), turn left onto Qianhai Xijie and walk north about 60 m (197 ft)

In his day Guo Moruo (1892-1978) was a revered writer who rose to fame after studying at Kyushu Imperial University in Japan. Today, the Sichuan-born author's works are considered a bit stuffy, but his period home is worth a visit if you want to get a feel for cozy old Chinese courtyards. Guo was influential in the rise of Chinese communism, and his familial wealth is evident in the stylish home's polished floors, elegant period furniture and the posh courtyard in which it's all set.

Former Residence of Mei Lanfang

Chinese name: 梅兰芳故居 (Méilánfāng Gùjū)
Hours: 9:00-16:00; closed Mon
Admission: ¥10
Website: www.meilanfang.com.cn (in Chinese)
Phone: 8322 3598
Address: 9 Huguosi Jie, Xicheng District (西城区护国寺街 9 号)
Transport: Subway – Line 6, Beihai North (北海北) Station, Exit A, walk west for 60 m (197 ft), turn right onto Deshengmen Neidajie (德胜门内大街) and walk north about 60 m (197 ft)

The popularization of Peking Opera in the West is owed almost entirely to the man who is considered by many to be the greatest opera singer of the 20th century: Mei Lanfang. The man best known for his smooth perfectly timed poise nearly always played a woman, and he is even said to have influenced Charlie Chaplin. Opera devotees make yearly pilgrimages to this traditional courtyard house, which has been preserved as a mini-museum. Inside you can find costumes, pictures of Mei in his famous female costume, opera programs and video presentations of his distinguished performances.

Follow the Panda! Beijing Bike Tour

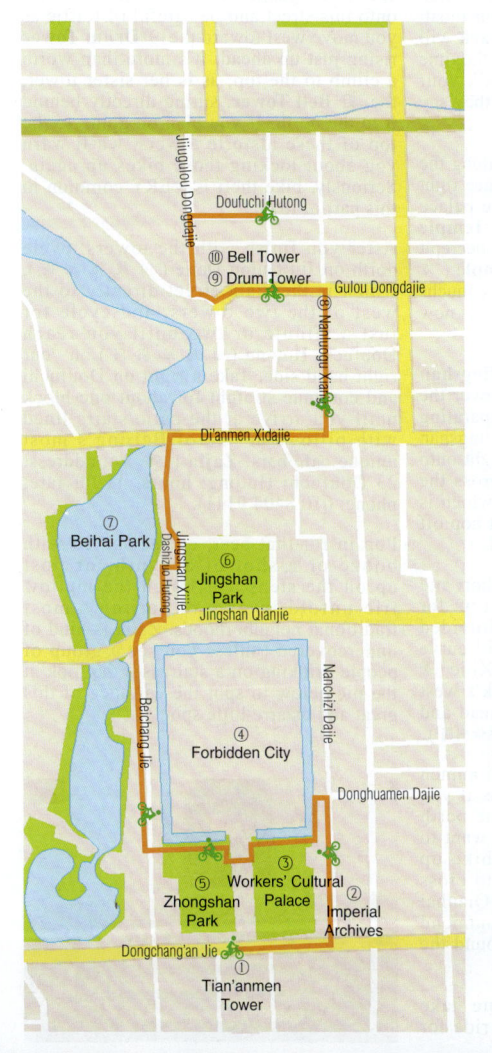

There are tons of ways to zip around Beijing, but few are better than from the top of a bicycle seat. It certainly helps that the vast majority of the city is flat as a pancake; the only worry you really face on a bike are cars… and their fumes. Nonetheless, clear summer weekdays when most people are busy at work offer the best chance to cruise the city relatively unhindered, and you'll quickly find that the hutongs are ideal for a mellow bike tour.

The ride that we have set up for you here is a fairly common one, and the red hutong signs along the way (written in pinyin and characters) make following along a breeze. While this is one of our favorite little cruises, the city abounds with plenty more. In fact, several of our top itineraries are perfect for a bike ride, so grab your Panda Guides map and let your legs pedal you through the city.

The ride gets going from out front of ① **Tian'anmen Tower**, and you'll cruise east down Dongchang'an Jie (东长安街) just a hair until you reach Nanchizi Dajie (南池子大街). Take a left and head north.

As you head up this road keep an eye out for the ② **Imperial Archives** on the right and then the ③ **Workers' Cultural Palace** on the left. Both of them have a solemn royal flare fit for their vicinity to the Forbidden City, and from inside the latter the roof of the Supreme Temple pokes its head out.

As you approach the ④ **Forbidden City** on the left keep a lookout for Donghuamen Dajie (东华门大街), where you will turn left for a tour around the moat, for which you'll need to quickly veer left again onto the road between the moat and the walls. Here you'll have some superb views of Old Beijing.

From here, it gets a bit more adventurous after you pass through Quezuo Men (阙左门), which leads you right through the masses of people waiting to pass through the Meridian Gate (午门) into the Forbidden City. After you cross the mobs, the gate on the other side of the square is Queyou Men (阙右门) and your call back onto your moat/wall bike path. ⑤ **Zhongshan Park** will be to your left. Be warned, most of the time security guards will make you walk your bike through this section, so do as they say to avoid any complications.

Following the road north puts you along the wall on Beichang Jie (北长街). Glance right to the buildings that tower over the palace walls to see the formidable **Fuyou Temple** (福佑寺), and look to the left for the decrepit remains of **Wanshou Xinglong Temple** (万寿兴隆寺). Once home to imperial eunuchs displaced after the end of Qing rule, it's now little more than a residential area.

Soon you'll see the lofty hill of ⑥ **Jingshan Park** emerging on your right side over the tail end of the palace complex. Separating the Forbidden City and the park is Jingshan Qianjie (景山前街). Swerve right onto Jingshan Qianjie and prepare to cross the road to the first hutong you see – which is Dashizuo Hutong (大石作胡同) – but hop off the bike and walk it across the street.

The alley of Dashizuo Hutong is short and sweet and fairly unremarkable except for the fact that some of this area provided stone for the Forbidden City; it will curve right and spit you out on Jingshan Xijie (景山西街), just outside Jingshan Park's west gate. Take this road north to its head and continue onto Gongjian Hutong (恭俭胡同).

Gongjian Hutong lets out onto Di'anmen Xidajie (地安门西大街). From here, if you swing left (west), you'll reach the north gate of ⑦ **Beihai Park**. If you want to have a walk around, lock that bike up and go for it. Another option is to cross Di'anmen Xidajie to tour around Qianhai and Houhai. However, we'd recommend reserving a whole day to cycle around the lakes since there's a lot to be seen.

Continuing with the outlined route, take a right on Di'anmen Xidajie and ride for several minutes until you reach Nanluogu Xiang Metro Station. That's your signal to get off your bike, walk it across the road, and take a nice stroll north along the wildly popular ⑧ **Nanluogu Xiang** (南锣鼓巷). Along this street there are dozens of places to park and have a snack or coffee, but don't wait too long because there's another destination coming up (plus you can always come back). You are allowed to bike on this road, but there may be so many people that it's impossible.

Nanluogu Xiang eventually hits the busy Gulou Dongdajie (鼓楼东大街); swing left onto this street and be careful of traffic as you move west toward the ⑨ **Drum Tower** rising just up ahead. It's more than worth a climb to the top, as is her sister tower, the ⑩ **Bell Tower**, sitting directly behind it to the north. If you plan on going to the top of these historic towers, we'll warn you about locking those bikes up again. Seriously, bike theft is VERY common in this part of town.

After you finish with the towers, cycle north on Jiu Gulou Dajie (旧鼓楼大街), which is the main street directly to the west of the two towers, and cycle for just a minute or two until you reach Doufuchi Hutong (豆腐池胡同) on your right hand side. Take a right on Doufuchi and continue straight for about one block until you arrive at the patio/stairs lined with pillows at one of Beijing's most unique café/bars: **Zajia** (杂家 ; address: 23 Doufuchi Hutong; hours: 11:00–late; phone: 010 8404 9141).

Pop in for that beer, coffee spiked with booze or a shot of absynth, or post up on the steps and watch the mellow life unfold in one of Beijing's most traditional neighborhoods. Zajia is kind of undercovered (unless you see a group of people drinking on a staircase), so look at the pic below to spot the entrance of this great and bizarre little spot.

Beihai Park

The remarkable history of Beihai Park as an imperial playground puts the world-class gardens on the same playing field as the Summer Palace. A millennium ago, Kublai Khan built his palace here, and the site has since been expanded, upgraded and improved by various dynastic rulers. The beautiful temples, pavilions, and palatial structures that surround the glorious centerpiece of Beihai Lake are a masterpiece of gardening technique, quintessential in their display of the superb architectural skill of traditional Chinese garden art. Few who visit can deny its peerless mystique, and today the park is an inner city oasis, combining slick historical sights with laid back recreational activities.

> **Chinese name:** 北海公园 (Běihǎi Gōngyuán)
> **Admission:** ¥10 (Apr-Oct); ¥5 (Nov-Mar)
> **Through Ticket:** ¥20 (Apr-Oct); ¥15 (Nov-Mar)
> **Hours:** 6:30-20:00 (Jan-Mar, Nov-Dec); 6:30-21:00 (Apr-May, Sep-Oct); 6:30-22:00 (Jun-Aug)
> **Phone:** 6403 3225
> **Address:** 1 Wenjin Jie (文津街1号)
> **Website:** www.beihaipark.com.cn/en
> **Transport:**
> **Subway** – Line 6, Beihai North Station, Exit D
> If you need help finding the place and your Chinese will not suffice, point this sentence out to a local: 请问到北海公园正门怎么走?

History

The origins of Beihai have a much longer history than that of the park itself. A Qin Dynasty (221-206 BCE) legend tells of an enclave of gods residing in the three mythical eastern mountains of Penglai, Yingzhou, and Fangzhang who possessed an elixir that could give eternal life to mere mortals. When Qin Shihuang failed to find the gods or their magic potion, he instead piled up three mounds of earth and dug a lake, attempting to mimic the energy of the fabled mountains. Qin set a trend that would continue throughout Chinese history, and 1,000 years later the Liao Dynasty built its own version of the triple-mound combination at Beihai in 916 CE.

Kublai Khan came storming through China's gates in the 13th century to establish the Yuan Dynasty (1271-1368) and built his palace (the Round City) at Beihai garden. Successive Ming and Qing emperors subsequently enlarged the area and added to the regal grandeur over a millennium. These days, a great deal of what characterizes the park are 18th century restorations or reconstructions from the Qing emperor Qianlong. The park was first opened to the public in 1925.

Before You Go

Beihai includes a lot of walking, so hopefully you brought some good shoes. If not, buy a cheap pair and learn a lesson for next time. Beihai is also a great place for a picnic on nice days, so packing a lunch is an excellent idea. There is plenty of shade, but sunscreen is always recommended. Don't forget to bring water as well – there are places to buy, but it's better if you don't have to go tromping around for a drink stand.

Info & Cautions

Entering the park requires the purchase of a ticket. There is a simple park ticket for ¥10 and a through ticket for ¥20. It's a better idea to just purchase the through ticket, which will get you into all the major temples and pavilions. The subway will take you to the north gate, but be aware that if you tour to the south of Beihai and then plan to enter Houhai (just to the north) later on, you will have to march your way back to the north.

Layout

Beihai Park extends across a grand 68 hectares (168 acres), about half of which is taken up by the lake. The lake is divided in two: Beihai proper in the north (which connects with Shichahai), and the beautiful Central Southern Lake (Zhongnanhai) to the south. Around both lakes a collection of good sights are scattered, including pavilions, temples, restaurants and the footprints of old palaces and imperial relics.

Jade Islet

Jade Islet (Qióng Dǎo; 琼 岛) has the most impressive scenery in the park, and it was built out of a giant pile of dirt. Romantic, isn't it? It's true, this verdently shrubbed island on the southeastern corner of the lake was made from the mound of mud scooped out to make Beihai Lake – but it is one of the prettiest mud piles you'll ever see. It also has some of the best history in the park, so get moving.

The ascent up the Jade Islet hill starts with a 600-year-old bridge that leads over to the **Temple of Eternal Peace** (Yǒng'ān Sì; 永安寺), an impressive Buddhist temple introduced by the **Hall of the Wheel of Law** (Fǎlún Diàn; 法轮殿), which contains numerous bodhisattvas and *luohans*. Up the twisting steps of the man-made hill, the **White Dagoba**, originally built in 1651 in homage to the visit of the fifth Dalai Lama, dominates the skyline of Jade Island. It was the unfortunate victim of an earthquake on two separate occasions – the first in 1679 and again in 1731 – but was quickly rebuilt after each of the disasters. Here you can hire paddle boats to roam the lake (¥80 per hour, ¥200 deposit).

The Northern Shore

Opposite Jade Island, the Northern Shore features many Ming era pavilions, halls and the excellent temple of the **Western Paradise Hall** (Xītiān Fànjìng; 西天梵境). Similar to Lama Temple, and every other Buddhist temple out there, it features its own **Hall of Heavenly Kings**. Inside, the fierce visages and expressions of the Four Heavenly Kings stand guard around the Maitreya Buddha. Also check out the temple's **Dacizhenru Hall** (Dàcízhēnrú Diàn; 大慈真如殿) for a collection of various Buddha statues.

On the northwest side of the shore you'll find the **Five Dragon Pavilion** (Wǔlóng Tíng; 五龙亭), a set of Ming period structures that zig zag and weave to a final double-eaved pavilion that forms the head of a slithering dragon when seen from above. More Buddhist lore can be found to the west at the **Tower of Ten Thousand Buddhas**, which unfortunately lost many of its relics to European looters in 1900 during the Boxer Rebellion. Don't forget as well to head to the **Miniature Western Pavilion** (Xiǎo Xītiān; 小西天), which was built in 1770 and is the largest pavilion in China, and the colorful **Nine Dragon Screen** (Jiǔlóng Bì; 九龙壁), a 5 m- (16 ft)-high and 27 m- (88 ft)-long glazed tile spirit wall emblazoned with nine ferocious dragons.

Round Town

This large round jade structure is the remnants of Kublai Khan's palace, built here in 1265. Within Round Town (Tuán Chéng; 团城) you can also find the **Receiving Light Hall** (Chéngguāng Diàn; 承光殿), housing a 1.5 m- (5 ft)-tall white jade statue of Buddha with inlaid jewels and apparently a lot of light.

At the time of research, this area was sadly closed. Please check future editions or the official Beihai website to see if renovations have been finished (www.beihaipark.com.cn/en).

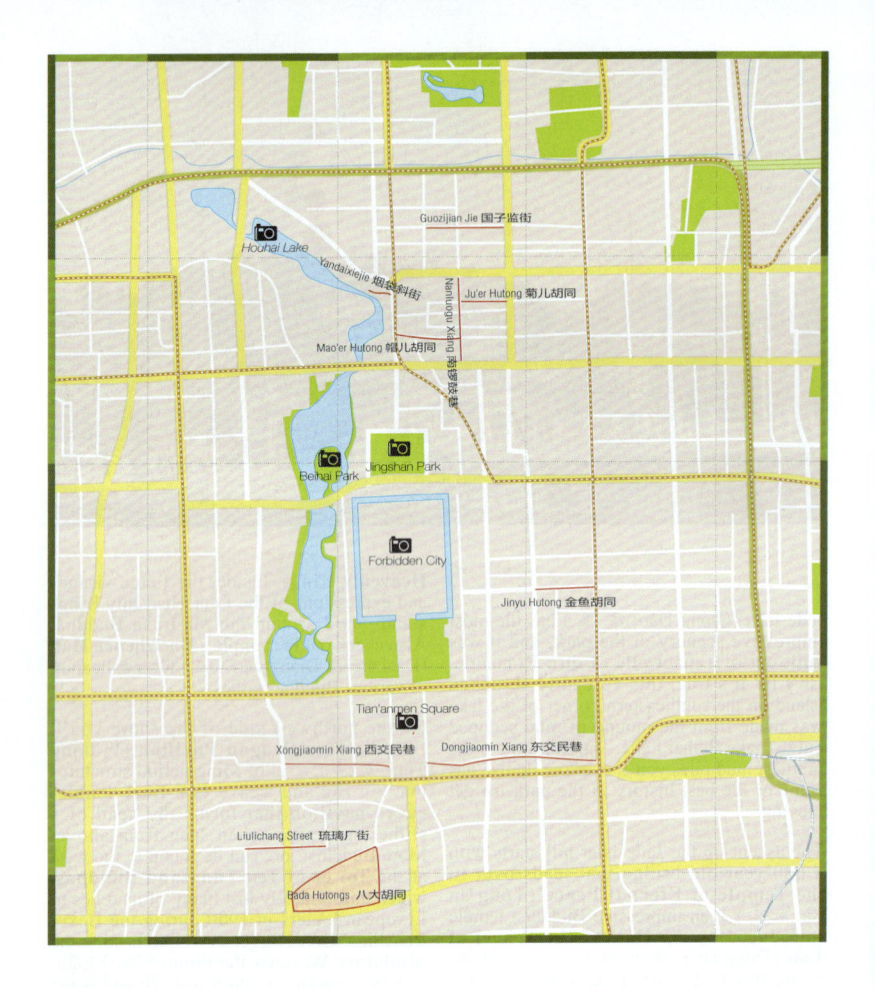

Hutongs
Hútóng 胡同

In contrast to the court life and elite culture represented by the Forbidden City, Summer Palace and the Temple of Heaven, the hutongs capture the culture of the everyday folk who make Beijing what it is. These residential neighborhoods still form the heart of Old Beijing and are not to be missed.

Hutongs in Old China

Hutongs are a type of narrow street or alley, most commonly associated with Beijing, that are formed by lines of *sìhéyuàn* – traditional residences of four-sided houses built around a courtyard. Many neighborhoods came about when several *siheyuan* were built in an area, together forming a series of alleys.

During China's dynastic period, emperors planned the city of Beijing and arranged the residential areas according to the social classes of the Zhou Dynasty (1027 – 256 BCE). This system was still in use when the term hutong (a word which is actually Mongolian in origin and means "town") first appeared during the Yuan Dynasty (1271-1368).

During the Ming Dynasty (1368-1644), the center of Beijing was the Forbidden City, which was surrounded by the concentric circles of the Inner City and Outer City, which were in turn cordoned by Beijing's sadly vanished old city walls. Citizens of higher social status were permitted to live closer to the center of the circles (i.e. aristocrats lived just to the east and west of the imperial palace). The large *siheyuan* of these high-ranking officials and wealthy merchants often featured beautifully carved and painted roof beams and carefully landscaped gardens, and the hutongs they formed were orderly and lined by spacious homes. Further from the palace, and to its north and south, were the commoners, merchants, artisans, and laborers. Their *siheyuan* were far smaller in scale and simpler in design and decoration, and the hutongs were narrower.

Following traditional Chinese *feng shui* design, nearly all *siheyuan* had their main buildings and gates facing south to accept vitalizing *yang* energy, and for this reason a majority of hutongs ran from east to west. Between the main hutongs, many tiny lanes ran north and south for convenient inter-hutong travel.

Historically, a hutong was also used as the lowest level of administrative division within a city in ancient China. One example of this was the *páifāng* (牌 坊) system, where the largest division within a city was a *fāng* (坊), equivalent to a current day precinct. Each *fang* was enclosed by walls or fences, and the gates of these enclosures were shut and guarded every night, somewhat like a modern gated community. Each *fang* was further divided into several *pái* (牌), which is equivalent to a current day unincorporated community or neighborhood. Each *pai* in turn contained an area that included several hutongs.

As the ancient Chinese urban administrative division system gave way to population and household divisions instead of geographical divisions, the hutongs were no longer used as the lowest level of administrative geographical division and were replaced with other approaches.

Decline of the Hutongs

At the turn of the 20th century, the Qing court was disintegrating and China's dynastic era was coming to an end. The traditional arrangement of hutongs was also affected. Many new hutongs, built haphazardly with no apparent plan, began to appear on the outskirts of the old city, while the old ones lost their former neat appearance. The social stratification of the residents also began to evaporate, reflecting the collapse of the feudal system.

During China's Republican period from 1912 to 1949, society was in a state of rapid deterioration from the fall of the Qing Dynasty, a bloody civil war and foreign invasions. Beijing crumbled and the conditions of the hutongs worsened. *Siheyuan* that were previously owned and occupied by single families were subdivided and shared by many households, with additions built with whatever materials were available tacked on as needed. The 978 hutongs listed in Qing Dynasty records swelled to 1,330 by 1949.

Following the founding of the People's Republic of China in 1949, many of the old hutongs of Beijing disappeared, replaced by wide boulevards and high rises. Many residents left the lanes where their families lived for generations for apartments with modern amenities. In Xicheng District, for example, nearly 200 hutongs out of the 820 it held in 1949 have disappeared.

Since the mid-20th century, the number of Beijing hutongs has dropped dramatically as developers demolish them to make way for new roads and buildings. More recently, some hutongs have been designated as protected areas in an attempt to preserve this aspect of Chinese cultural history.

The older neighborhoods that survive today offer a glimpse of life in the capital city as it has been for generations. Many hutongs, some several hundred years old in the vicinity of the Bell Tower, Drum Tower and Shichahai Lake, still remain, but many more have been lost forever.

Names of Hutongs

The naming of different hutong lanes has a very interesting history. In ancient times, hutong names were passed by local word of mouth. There were no signposts, and it was not until the Ming and Qing Dynasties that the age-old names slowly began to be posted on signage. Generally speaking, the naming methods can be categorized into four main kinds.

Locality

Many hutongs were named for their location, or a local landmark or business:

• City gates: Inner Xizhimen Hutong is located in the Xizhimen Nei (Inner Xizhimen) neighborhood, which is on the inside of Xizhimen Gate, a gate on the former city wall.

• Markets and businesses: Yangshi Hutong (Yangshi literally means "sheep market") and Yizi Hutong (a local term for soap is *yizi*) were named for the commodities traded by their local businesses.

• Local features: Liushu Hutong (Willow Hutong) was originally named "Liushu Jing Hutong," which literally meant "Willow Tree Well Hutong" because it marked a local well and its willow tree.

People

Some hutongs were named after people, such as Mengduan Hutong, which commemorated Meng Duan, a Beijing mayor during the Ming Dynasty who lived in this hutong.

Attributes

Many hutongs were given a name based on certain attributes. Jiudaowan Hutong, literally meaning Nine Turns Hutong, breaks the traditional mold of a straight hutong and was named for its 19 snaking curves.

Others were given an auspicious name, with words that carry generic positive attributes, such as Xiqing Hutong (Xiqing means "happy" and "lucky").

Directional

Hutongs sharing a name or longer hutongs divided into sections are often identified by direction. For example, there are three Hongmen Hutongs, or Red Gate Hutongs. They are comprised of the West Hongmen Hutong, the East Hongmen Hutong, and South Hongmen Hutong. Sadly, all three Hongmen Hutongs were destroyed in 2011.

Beijing's Top 10 Hutongs

The following are the ten most famous hutongs in Beijing (listed in alphabetical order).

Bada Hutongs (Bādà Hútóng 八大胡同): Red Light District of Old Beijing

During the Qing Dynasty, the Bada Hutongs were notorious as the city's biggest red light district, housing more than 2,000 brothels. The structure of each brothel varied, and all were different from ordinary houses. After 1949, many brothels were turned into hotels and/or residences.

First emerging in the 18th century outside the city gates, Bada Hutong is part of a location name of eight hutongs situated in close proximity to each other. Bada Hutong consists of Hanjia Hutong, Shitou Hutong, Shaanxi Xiang, Wangguanfu, Yanzhi Hutong, Baishun Hutong, Zhujia Hutong and Lishaomao Hutong. Today, much of the area has been demolished and rebuilt, but you can still feel some of the color of old Beijing.

Dōngjiāomín Xiàng (东交民巷): The Longest Hutong in Beijing

Located in Dongcheng District, Dongjiaomin Xiang Hutong starts from Tian'anmen Donglu in the west and stretches nearly 3 km (2 mi) to Chongwenmen Neidajie (崇文门内大街) in the east.

Dongjiaomin Xiang came into being in the late 13th century when Marco Polo visited China. Called Beijing's "Embassy Row" in the early 20th century, Dongjiaomin Xiang was a district where foreign legations were located before the establishment of the PRC, and served as Beijing's diplomatic center for over 700 years. After the establishment of the People's Republic of China, the area continued to further serve as an embassy zone, and many new diplomatic buildings were constructed.

Guozijian Street (Guózǐjiān: 国子监): Beijing's Famous Scholarly Hutong

Tranquility, relaxation and the scent of incense: this is Guozijian Street, a place where antiquity flirts with the avant-garde, and past meets present. Housing the Confucian Temple in the east and the Imperial College in the west, the street gradually took shape some 700 years ago.

Guozijian connects to the **Yonghegong Lama Temple** in the east, where perfumed sandalwood from the incense shops on the street fills the air with a tantric aroma. Gradually, the scent of ancient books takes over as one explores further down the street and towards the **Confucian Temple** and **Imperial College**. See page 116 for these sites.

Outside the Confucian Temple, where sacrifices to Confucius were made during the Yuan, Ming and Qing Dynasties (1271-1911), aged cypress trees guard the gate. On each side of the gate stands a huge marble stele inscribed in Mandarin and Mongolian that orders all horse riders, even the emperor, to dismount.

Beside the Confucian Temple is the Imperial College, the highest educational institution during the Yuan, Ming and Qing Dynasties, and once the greatest aspiration of ancient Chinese scholars.

Jīnyú Hútóng (金鱼胡同): The Most Modern Hutong in Beijing

Situated at the Dongcheng District, Jinyu Hutong connects Dongdan Beidajie in the east with Wangfujing Dajie in the west. Lying next to the commercial area of Wangfujing, the hutong neighbors big brand hotels and large shopping centers.

The **Jixiang Theater** is one of the most famous spots in Jinyu Hutong. It was built as a tea house at the north gate of the old Dong'an market in 1906 and is considered a symbol of the Beijing Opera.

After eating Wangfujing's street food, Jinyu Hutong can be an ideal conclusion to your neighborhood cruise.

Jú'ér Hútóng (菊儿胡同): Historic Centipede Lane

Hugged by Jiaodaokou Nandajie to the east and Nanluogu Xiang to the west, the 400 m (1,312 ft) Ju'er Hutong, like many other lanes around this area, dates back to the Yuan Dynasty. Because this hutong is narrow and long like a centipede, Ju'er is also called Centipede Lane.

During the Qing Dynasty, this was the gathering place of the Xiang Huang bannermen, an upper class brigade of the eight banners commanded by the emperor. Another historical claim to fame, the buildings at numbers 3, 5 and 7 of Ju'er once held the former home of Rong Lu, a provincial governor, minister of war, and right-hand man of Empress Dowager Cixi during the late Qing Dynasty.

Liulichang Street (Liúlíchǎng Jiē; 琉璃厂街): The Most Cultured Hutong in Beijing

Located outside the Heping Gate in Xuanwu District, the long history of Liuchang Street dates back to the early Liao Dynasty (916 – 1125), when it was a village called Haiwang. The street's name literally translated as "Beijing Colored Glaze Factory Street," suggesting its role throughout the history of Beijing's glazed-tile roofed buildings. In the Yuan and Ming Dynasties, a colored glaze factory was set up here, and later, in the early Qing Dynasty, antique dealers brought their business to the street. The factory is now long gone, but its name has endured to this day.

Great changes have taken place in this old street since the end of dynastic days. In 1980, the street was renovated to house 54 of China's time-honored brands, such as **Rongbao Zhai**, a house of precious calligraphy and paintings; the **China Book Store**, where visitors can buy reproductions of Chinese ancient books; and **Baogu Zhai**, an art-junkie hotspot with countless famous artistic works and elegant embroideries.

Mào'ér Hútóng （帽儿胡同）: The Hutong of Relics

Mao'er Hutong is an interesting place because of its location. Hidden in plain sight and in close proximity to well-known places, there are four spots on this alleyway identified as cultural relics, and each one is so fervently protected that none have been officially opened to the public.

Mao'er Hutong is generally translated as Hat or Hat Maker Lane. The area dates from the Ming Dynasty when it was named after the Wenchang Gong, a Taoist temple honoring the spirit belonging to the sixth of China's 28 constellations. The current name came into usage during the succeeding Qing Dynasty.

The hutong runs west to east from Di'anmen Waidajie to Nanluogu Xiang in the Jiaodaokou sub-district. To find it, go to Shichahai Metro Station, Exit C, and walk south toward Di'anmen Waidajie for less than five minutes. It will be on your left.

Nánluógǔ Xiàng （南锣鼓巷）: Beijing's Most Popular Hutong

The old lane of Nanluogu Xiang is renowned for its long history, culture, specialty stores, and distinctive foods. It runs for a solid 768 m (2,519 ft) and is joined at the north end by Gulou Dongdajie and Di'anmen Dongdajie in the south end. There are eight parallel hutongs on each side of the old lane, and together they form part of the original 25 historic hutongs.

This hutong has been designated by the Beijing government as a historical site for the preservation of Chinese cultural heritage. It's a worthy attempt to save it from the fate of many other old Beijing traditional hutong neighborhoods, which have been pulled down in recent years.

Nanluogu Xiang and the surrounding east-west hutongs are a favorite spot for local hipsters, musicians, artists, and tourists, as there are many stores, restaurants and cultural experiences to be discovered. For more on this attraction, flip to page 101.

Xījiāomín Xiàng （西交民巷）: The Original Financial Street

Xijiaomin Xiang is the west section of Jiaomin Xiang (Jiaomin Lane), which ran uninterrupted through Dongjiaomin Xiang before the construction of Tian'anmen Square.

While Dongjiaomin Xiang was the old Qing Dynasty embassy district and famous for its diplomatic functions, it was Xijiaomin Xiang that played the more important role as a banking district. Many international and domestic banks chose Xijiaomin Xiang as the site for their headquarters – like an old-timey Chinese Wall Street. Today, most of the banks are gone, but at the east exit of Xijiaomin Xiang there is a money museum and the first branch of the Bank of China, founded over 100 years ago.

Yāndàixié Jiē （烟袋斜街）: One of the Oldest Streets in Beijing

Yandaixie Jie (Tobacco Pipe Byway) is one of the most famous hutongs in Beijing. It measures 232 m (761 ft) from end to end, connecting Di'anmen Waidajie at the east end and joining Xiaoshibei and Ya'er Hutong on the west end.

During the Qing Dynasty, this street was called Drum Tower Byway because it ran at an angle just outside the Drum Tower. Opium was a hot commodity at the time, and the increasing demand for pipes encouraged the opening of many pipe shops on the street. The shops all sported their version of a particular symbol – a wooden tobacco pipe with a black stem and a golden bowl. It wasn't until the shop Shuang Shengtai placed a 1.5 m- (5 ft)-tall wooden tobacco pipe out front of the store to attract the lion's share of clientele that customers began using the current name of Tobacco Pipe Byway.

Today, the hutong has mushroomed to include many different kinds of bars, tea and coffee houses, and souvenir shops. At night, the streets are ablaze with lights, adding a power surge of explosive energy to an already electrifying street. See page 102 for more on this hutong.

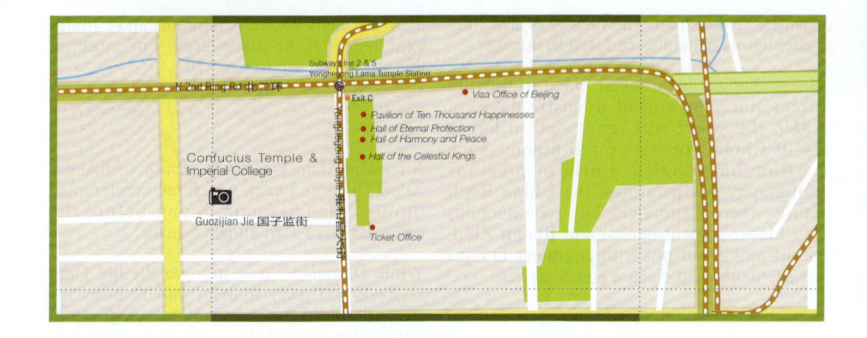

Lama Temple Area

This section includes the Lama Temple, the Confucian Temple and the Imperial College.

Lama Temple is the foremost Tibetan Buddhist temple outside the snowy ranges of Tibet. Enough cannot be said about the rich work of the beautiful archways, ceilings, glazed tiles, golden statues, Chinese lions, and tapestries (just to name a few) that flourish within the temple and its five radiant halls. Incense rules the day at Lama temple, so make sure your nose is ready, because nearly everyone, from praying monks to devout civilians, can be seen prostrating (bowing or kneeling in prayer) to the many different manifestations of Buddha with offerings of burning incense. It goes without saying that Lama Temple is a great place for a relaxing stroll, and you shouldn't forget to check out the revolving prayer wheels and the Mongolian, Manchu, Tibetan, and Chinese writings that decorate the hall boards.

Practically within arm's reach of Lama Temple are the Confucian Temple and the Imperial College. Set among a shady, tranquil hutong, the temple and the college area give the peaceful vibe of Lama a run for its money. The vicinity is so close to Lama Temple – literally across the street and down the block – that you're probably losing big karma points if you don't go.

Lama Temple

Chinese name: 雍和宫 (Yōnghé Gōng)
Admission: ¥25
Hours: 9:00-16:00 (Nov-Mar); 9:00-16:30 (Apr-Oct)
Website: www.yonghegong.cn (in Chinese)
Phone: 6404 4499
Address: 20 Yonghegong Dajie (雍和宫大街 20 号)
Transport: Subway – Line 2, get off at Lama Temple Station, Exit C, then walk south about 100 m (328 ft) to the entrance

Before You Go

See our sample itineraries on page 296 for great suggestions. You won't need to bring much, as there are plenty of restaurants and shops in the hutongs nearby (especially in the up and coming **Wudaoying Hutong** (五道营胡同) in between Andingmen and Lama Temple Metro Stations). Some can be a bit pricey, but the quality is high and the atmosphere is heavenly. Plenty of Buddhist and Confucian jewelry, statuettes, and other trinkets can be bought in the area, so if you need to splurge on some spiritual knick knacks you might want to bring a bag.

Info & Cautions

The biggest thing you'll need to worry about around the Lama Temple area are the incense hawkers outside. They are very pushy, and if you touch the incense they will insist you buy. It's wildly overpriced, even if you haggle. Unless you're a devout Buddhist or just dying to get some incense and pray, you'd better just sidestep them. Other than that, this holy land is pretty peaceful and you don't have to worry about too many other annoyances.

Buddhism in China

The introduction of Buddhism to China is difficult to pinpoint. The earliest reports of the religion, including one from the Buddhist Encyclopedia, claim that the Buddhist monk Li Fang arrived with 17 others in Xi'an in 217 BCE. The earliest historical evidence, however, places Chinese worshipers of Buddha around the Yangze River in 67 BCE. It most likely arrived, like countless other ideas that entered China, via the Silk Road, and the large majority of early Buddhist influence in China came from neighboring India. Today, the Mahayana school of Buddhism holds the most prevalence in Chinese Buddhist adherence.

Early Chinese esoteric beliefs were largely Taoist or Confucian philosophies. Buddhist principles, like its monastic system and aversion to social affairs, tended to conflict with long-standing Chinese principles at the time, such as the importance of family and social responsibility. However, Buddhism's meditative tradition was often equated to Taoists, who found its inner cultivation of wisdom appealing, while Confucians found common ground in the religion's emphasis on ritual and morality. Early Indian translators drew on this common ground and created medium systems of introductory Buddhism in order to adapt native Buddhist tenets into Taoist ideology.

Buddhism hit its peak during the Tang Dynasty (618-907) when several emperors officially supported the religion. Tang Empress Wu Zetian was the Dynasty's last stringent adherent, and her abdication in 705 precipitated a sudden growth in anti-Buddhist sentiments. Many equated the foreign nature of the religion to barbarism, since the Buddha spoke a foreign tongue, wore exotic clothes, and seemed detached from the familial structure that was at the core of Chinese life. Feelings of its draining and alien energy were made more palpable by huge numbers of tax-exempt monasteries, hundreds of thousands of monks and nuns making no tangible contribution to society, and the large amounts of precious metals used to create statues. Upon his coronation, Emperor Wuzong, a man heavily influenced by Taoists (who competed with Buddhism for attention), waged a war of oppression against the foreign import, destroying more than 40,000 temples and 4,600 monasteries, displacing 240,000 nuns and monks.

As evidence of the resilience of the Buddhist devout, ten Chinese schools of Buddhism grew from the rubble of Wuzong's destruction, two of which remain influential today: Chan (Meditation or Zen Buddhism) and Amitabha (Pure Land, a form of Mahayana Buddhism).

Around the 7th and 8th centuries CE, Buddhism made its way to Tibet. Called Lamaism, the Tibetan form of Buddhism incorporated their indigenous Bon religion and its elements of shamanism and animism. Consequentially, the aptly named Lama Temple is named for the shamanistic form of Tibetan Buddhism that graces its halls.

Buddhist Tenets and Customs: Graceful Traveling at Lama Temple

Buddhist temples, like many hallowed spiritual sites, have customs and adherences pertaining to their traditions. Lama Temple is understood as a tourist destination, and tourists are not necessarily expected to follow customs. However, attempting to respect a few guidelines during your visit to Lama Temple will earn the respect and appreciation of those around you. These are just guidelines, and you shouldn't worry too much about being stringent; you won't be scolded or scoffed at for forgetting anything.

Remove Your Hat: Not a strict rule, but removing your hat is a courteous gesture.

General Respect: Those around you may not always show a dignified side, but you can show common respect by turning off mobile phones, removing headphones, not shouting, avoiding inappropriate conversation and not smoking or chewing gum.

Respect the Buddha Statues: It should go without saying: do not sit near or climb on a Buddha statue or the raised platform. Seriously, we can't believe we have to say this one, but you'd be surprised.

Avoid Conspicuous Pointing: Pointing at things or people around the temple can be a bit uncouth. To indicate something, it's better to use your right hand with the palm facing upwards. When sitting, avoid pointing your feet at a monk or image of Buddha.

Stand vs Sit: If you happen to be sitting in the worship area when monks or nuns enter, standing will show respect. Wait until they have finished their prostrations before sitting again.

Prostrating: Prostration is not required, but those who wish to make a wish or prayer to Buddha should place their knees on the cushion, feet facing away from the statue, and bow three times.

No Inside Photography: Photography is not permitted inside the halls, but you are free to click away outside in the courtyards.

Interacting With Buddhist Monks

Monks are generally very kind and have a high regard for life. Do not worry about being strict around them – they do not expect it – but knowing a bit about them can enrich your experience.

Eating: Monks do not eat after noon; be mindful about eating or snacking around them.

Body Language: If a monk is sitting, show respect by sitting before starting a conversation. Try to avoid pointing your feet at any Buddhist while sitting.

Right Hand Only: Only use your right hand when giving or receiving something from a monk.

Greeting A Monk: The traditional greeting for a monk is to place the hands together in a prayer-like gesture and give a slight bow.

Entering and Exiting: Entering a building with your left foot first and exiting by leading with your right foot symbolically represents a whole.

Donations: If you enjoyed your visit, giving a little extra cash is certainly appreciated. A typical donation is ¥10-100 (US$2-15). You can find metal donation boxes throughout the complex

History

Ground was broken for Lama Temple in 1694 as a fancy residence for court eunuchs. A creation of the reigning Qing Dynasty, it caught the eye of Prince Yin Zhen, who settled in to make it his court and residence. Upon his ascension to the throne to become the Yongzheng Emperor in 1722, half the complex was converted into a lamasery, a monastery for monks of Tibetan Buddhism (or lamas). Upon Yongzheng's death in 1735, his coffin was placed in the building and Qianlong took the throne.

Qianlong took it upon himself to give the temple imperial status, which meant replacing all of the temple's turquois tiles with the imperial color of yellow. Soon after, in 1744, the temple gained full-fledged status as a lamasery, and Tibetan and Mongolian monks flooded its grounds. Qianlong had recently quelled an uprising in Tibet, and he saw Lama Temple as an opportunity to implement a new administrative system over the Tibetan Buddhists. Two golden vases were employed for the system; one was kept in Lhasa's legendary Jokhang Temple to determine the reincarnation of the Dalai Lama, the other kept in Lama Temple for selecting the Panchen Lama. If it sounds dubious, it was.

Lama Temple only survived the Cultural Revolution thanks to the foresight and swift hand of Zhou Enlai. It was opened to the public in 1981, and to this day it operates vibrantly as a place of worship for countless pilgrims and worshippers, many of whom make grand journeys to pay their respects.

Layout

The Lama Temple accords with Chinese *feng shui* design and is situated along a 480 m- (1,575 ft)-long north-south central axis. The main gate, Yonghe Gate, is at the southern end of this axis. Five main halls dot the axis and are separated by courtyards: the Hall of the Celestial Kings or Devaraja Hall (Tiānwáng Diàn; 天王殿), the Hall of Harmony and Peace (Yōnghégōng Dàdiàn; 雍和宫大殿), the Hall of Eternal Protection (Yǒngyòu Diàn; 永佑殿), the Hall of the Wheel of the Dharma (Fǎlún Diàn; 法轮殿), and the happiest place on earth, the Pavilion of Ten Thousand Happinesses (Wànfú Gé; 万福阁). It's way happier than Disneyland.

The Hall of the Celestial Kings

The first hall you will enter via Yonghe Gate is the Hall of the Celestial Kings. The southernmost of the main halls, it served originally as the main entrance to the monastery. In the center of the hall stands a statue of the Maitreya, the prophesized future Buddha. Around the sides of the Maitreya, the four Celestial Kings stand as guardians, so don't mess around unless you want a lesson in celestial butt-kicking!

The Hall of Harmony & Peace

The amazing Hall of Harmony and Peace is the main hall of the temple. It houses three gilded bronze statues of the Buddhas of the Three Ages: in the center sits the **Gautama Buddha** (Buddha of the Present), and he's flanked to the right by the **Kasyapa Matanga** (Buddha of the Past) and the **Maitreya Buddha** (Buddha of the Future) to the left. Along the sides of the hall you can find the statues of the 18 arhats chilling in a state of nirvana. Known in Chinese as *luóhàn*, these immortals were said to be undefeatable in hand combat and were the inspiration for the Buddhist kung fu style known as Luohan Fist (Luóhàn Quán; 罗汉拳), a staple of Shaolin Kung Fu.

The Hall of Eternal Protection

Opposite the courtyard from Yonghe Dian, the Hall of Eternal Protection contains the Buddhas of longevity and medicine. Worshipers prostrate to these Buddhist deities in hopes of health for friends and family. When Emperor Yongzheng resided in the monastery as prince, this hall served as his living quarters and is where his coffin was placed after his death.

For a little chuckle, head to the **East Side**

Hall (Dōngpèi Diàn; 东配殿) to see the cool cobalt-blue Buddhas who share the shade with a lizard-like Buddha. Note the cloth draped over him. The covering makes it a little hard to make out, but if you look closely you can see a woman with the lizard having sex. It's said that back in the day the dragon-like forms of the deity came down to earth and coupled with human females, producing half-god offspring – sort of like a Buddhist Hercules.

The Hall of the Wheel of Dharma

In the middle of the Hall of the Wheel of Dharma stands the 6 m- (20 ft)-high statue of the smiling Tsong Khapa (1357-1419), the founder of the Yellow Hat sect of Buddhism, appropriately clad in yellow. Behind Tsong Khapa is a miniature sandalwood mountain, surrounded by 500 *luohan* figures made of gold, silver, iron, copper, and tin, and all wearing a different expression. The throne is where the Dalai Lama sat when he taught in the monastery.

Pavilion of Ten Thousand Happinesses

The final hall is marked by an amazing 25 m- (80 ft)-tall carving of the Maitreya Buddha. It is said to be carved from a single piece of white sandalwood and it is awesome! This ultra-impressive Tibetan form of Maitreya, clothed in yellow satin, is a big (or should we say tall?) reminder of the wholly Tibetan nature of the Buddhism practiced at Lama Temple.

The three story Wanfu Pavilion is linked by an overhead walkway to the **Yansui Pavilion** (Yánsuí Gé; 延绥阁), where you can check out a beautiful giant lotus flower with revolving petals. Also worth a view behind Wanfu Pavilion is the **Suicheng Hall** (Suíchéng Diàn; 绥成殿), featuring the Green Tara and White Tara.

Confucian Temple & Imperial College

Chinese name: 孔庙 (Kǒng Miào); 国子监 (Guózǐ Jiān)
Admission: ¥30
Hours: 9:00-17:00
Website: www.kmgzj.com/en/index.aspx
Phone: 8401 1977
Address: 13 Guizijian Jie (国子监街13号)
Transport: The Confucian Temple is just a short walk down Guozijian Jie from the Lama Temple.

The Confucian Temple is noticeably lacking in worshipers, attesting to the withered status of the moral philosophy that once underpinned traditional Chinese society. It's not completely empty though, as most of the time you can find it full of domestic tourists working on a new philosophy: loud cell-phone talking. The temple is one of the largest in China outside of Confucius' birthplace in Qufu, Shandong Province, and though Confucian thought has seen a conscious resurgence since the 1980s, no one seems to be rushing in to recite the 13 Confucian classics carved on the **198 Stone Tablets** in the temple's rear building. They are an impressive sight and worth a visit, however.

In the main courtyard, the names of the 51,624 candidates who passed the civil service exam are also inscribed on a little forest of steles. The exam included flawless recitation of the classics over a period of three straight days, all while locked inside a 1.5 sq m (5 sq ft) cubicle. They neighbor the **Gate of the First Teacher** (Xiānshī Mén; 先师门).

Taking it slow at the Confucian Temple is actually easier than at Lama Temple, mostly because there are less people, and the neighborhood proudly delivers some of Beijing's last remaining *páilóu* (牌楼), or decorated archways. Swing out to the hutong outside to check out the relaxing cafes, restaurants and shops. In the cool hutong shade you will also find local residents getting a little crazy with spirited games of chess and cards. Often groups of more than a dozen local friends will crowd around these games and feverishly give their own two cents (literally) – they gamble on almost every game.

Be sure as well to see the Imperial College that sits next door to the temple. Also known as Guózǐjiān (国子监), it has around 700 years of history and was the highest educational institution and educational administering post during the three dynasties of the Yuan, Ming, and Qing. Guozijian was originally built in the Yuan Dynasty in 1306 and underwent major renovations during the reign of the Ming Yongle Emperor. Students of this college – who were known as *Jiānshēng* (监生) – mostly studied the Confucian classics. Keep an eye out for paintings of them kneeling in the courtyard in the thousands while the emperor explained the classics (notice the boredom on their faces). Today, the Imperial Academy displays fine Confucian architecture and opens a fascinating window into the strict life under Confucian tutelage.

Tourists who have visa issues should take note of the visa administrative office located in this area (see map on pg 116; address and vital info below.

Division of Exit and Entry Administration of Beijing Public Security Bureau (Běijīngshì Gōng'ānjú Chūrùjìng Guǎnlǐchù; 北京市公安局出入境管理处）

Address: 2 Andingmen Dongdajie, Dongcheng District (东城区安定门东大街 2 号)
Phone: 8402 0101
Office hours: 8:30-16:30 (Mon-Sat)
Website: www.bjgaj.gov.cn/eng/index.jsp

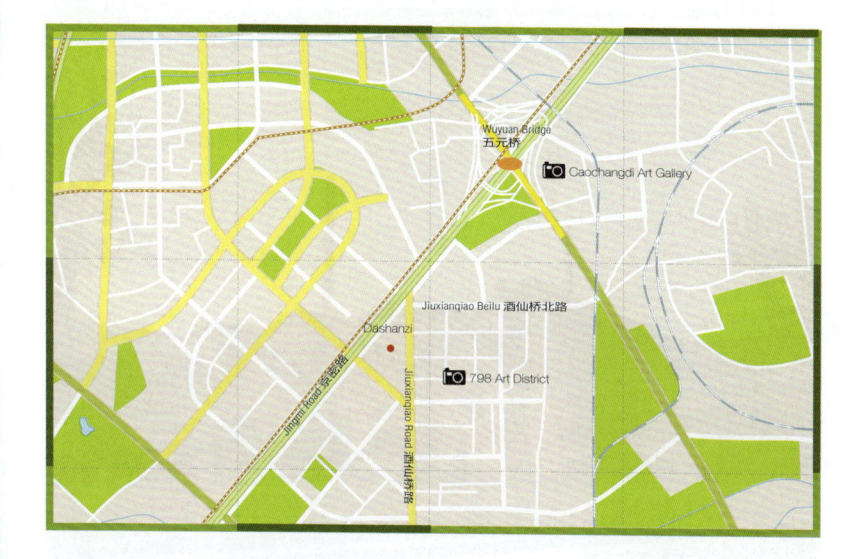

798 Art District

Chinese name: 798 艺术区 (Qījiǔbā Yìshùqū)
Admission: FREE
Hours: Most galleries open between 10:00 and 11:00 and close around 18:00 (the best time to visit is early afternoon)
Website: www.798art.org (in Chinese); for English we recommend www.798district.com
Transportation:
Subway – Dongzhimen Station, Exit C, then take bus 909
Bus – 909, get off at Dashanzi Lukou Nan (大山子路口南), look for the large red 798 signs (20:30 last bus)

Set amongst the post-industrial chic of swooping arches and soaring chimneys, the 798 Art District promotes its artistic spin on "ironic-effect" by housing Beijing's leading modern art galleries in vacated Bauhaus-style factories. Also known as Dàshānzi (大山子) Art District, it plays host to some of the Chinese art world's most prominent and well established artists, such as the politically fractious Ai Wei Wei, as well as international acts and up-and-comers. The district nearly became defunct in 2007, but prominent artists, architects and curators rallied to convince landlords Seven Star Realty of the area's lucrative potential. Today, the district thrives with a nascent café culture, avant-garde exhibitions and creative performances.

Info & Cautions

Dashanzi is large, so you'll need good walking shoes (avoid the heels). Some galleries are closed on Mondays (such as BTAP) so that they can open on the weekends. There's plenty of food and drink in the area, and it's a great part of the experience, so we also suggest you set aside some money for an overpriced meal in a trendy café.

History

Factory 798, for which the art district is named, was originally part of a larger project known as Joint Factory 718. By 1951, industrial expansion in China was railroading through the nation, helped in great part by the Soviet Union. However, the People's Liberation Army was in dire need of modern electronics components, and the Soviets' full docket of industrial projects urged the Chinese to turn to the East Germans. A vast 640,000 sq m (6.9 million sq ft) of Dashanzi, then a fringe patch of Beijing's low-lying farmland, was chosen. In their form-follows-function tradition, the German architectural designers drew up plans for their Bauhaus-style factories, which featured saw-toothed ceiling arches and giant indoor spaces designed to allow maximum natural light. Despite numerous disputes between notoriously obstinate Soviet, German, and Chinese experts, the factory complex opened in 1957 in a grandiose display of communist brotherhood.

The factory complex boasted considerable social benefits to its workers, who were the highest paid in Beijing and had access to a plethora of amenities and facilities, including fully furnished rooms for their families, diverse social and sporting events, several athletics teams, a team of German stunt-motorcycles, an orchestra, literary clubs, and a state-of-the-art hospital. Morale was kept high with frequent training sessions, German-Chinese personnel exchanges, "model-worker" award systems and celebrity VIP visits. The ostensible model of social progress that was Dashanzi Joint Factory 718 evidenced the government's militaristic priorities and manifested equally as a propaganda tool, gilding the plight of the proletariat, the vast majority of whom were mired in poverty.

Eventually, Deng Xiaoping's reforms that began in the late 1970s put a limited lifespan on the factory complex, and by the early '90s the majority of the factories were in disuse and 60% of the workers laid off. A major retooling of the factories' managerial remnants resulted in the creation of the Seven Star Huadian Science and Technology Group, which was charged with finding tenants for the derelict buildings. The timing was perfect for Beijing's displaced contemporary artists, whose avant-garde art was severely frowned upon by the government, leaving most artists in far-flung regions of the city. In 1995, Beijing's Central Academy of Fine Arts took up Factory 706 as a workspace, and five years later the Dean of the Department of Sculptures relocated his personal studio to the area, laying the groundwork for the artistic influx that followed. Soon after, Timezone 8 Art Books, run by the Texan Robert Bernell, snatched up a former canteen location, and its fashion designer helped more artists through the rental process.

The real catalyst for the area came later in 2001 when Tabata Yukihito, curator of the voguish Tokyo Gallery, founded Beijing Tokyo Art Projects (BTAP) in Factory 798's spacious central hall. Beijing Afloat, BTAP's opening exhibition, attracted an audience of 1,000 visitors and catapulted the eponymous factory into a mainstream infatuation. Over the next decade, increasingly notable exhibitions, rising-stars and controversial performances created a thriving bohemian culture.

The explosive popularity of Dashanzi allowed the area to overcome a near eviction in 2005, and the area received a major renovation in 2009, including repaved roads and another incursion of new galleries. Today, international exhibits continue to flow through, and major names, such as the outspoken Ai Wei Wei and the inveterate Huang Rui, exemplify the lucrative so-called Bobo class – or Bohemian-Bourgeoisie – that is now a household name among the youth of China.

(To clarify, Bobo is basically a Chinese Yuppie, also known as Chuppie.)

Major Galleries

There are dozens of galleries to visit at the 798 Art District, even though the area is named after just one factory. Major galleries include **BTAP**, the district's flagship exhibition hall (closed on Mondays); **UCCA**, which is technically not a gallery but has several halls, ¥15 film screenings, and an artsy-fartsy little shop; **798 Space Gallery**, mostly used for fashion shows (check out the unique Bauhaus ceiling, rare now even in Germany); **798 Photo Gallery**, housing one-of-a-kind photography from owner Chen Guangjun; and **Pace Beijing**, a cavernous space with some excellent exhibitions. Take a walk around the area and discover small galleries, cafes, and other hidden gems.

Cǎochángdì (草场地)

An offshoot of Dashanzi Art District, the galleries located at Caochangdi are 3 km (2 mi) northeast, and can also be reached by bus 909; exit the bus at the Caochangdi Stop. This is where Ai Wei Wei's self-designed (and trendsetting) home can be found.

Sòngzhuāng (宋庄) Art District

For information on Beijing's other galleries at Songzhuang, please see page 192 in the Other Attractions section.

Beijing Tokyo Art Projects (BTAP) (Běijīng Dōngjīng Yishù Gōngchéng; 北京东京艺术工程)

As one of the first international galleries in 798, BTAP hosts a continuous stream of great exhibitions, including artists from Japan and beyond.

> Hours: 10:00-18:30 (Tue-Sun)
> Address: 4 Jiuxianqiao Lu, 798 Art District (朝阳区酒仙桥路4号)
> Phone: 8457 3245
> Website: www.tokyo-gallery.com

798 Space (Qījiǔbā Shítài Kōngjiān; 798时态空间)

798 Space is the namesake of the 798 area and a factory space that once produced weapons. Now you can catch an occasional exhibit in between high couture product launches that draw crowds at night.

> Hours: 11:00-21:00 (daily)
> Address: 4 Jiuxianqiao Lu, 798 Art District (朝阳区酒仙桥路4号)
> Phone: 6438 4862; 6437 6248
> Website: www.798space.com

798 Photo Gallery (Bǎinián Yinxiàng Shèyǐng Huàláng; 百年印象摄影画廊)

798 Photo Gallery is the best place in Beijing to find a wide selection of ethnographic and artistic photographic editions, as well as monthly rotating shows of Chinese and international photographers.

> Hours: 10:00-18:00 (daily)
> Address: 4 Jiuxianqiao Lu, 798 Art District (朝阳区酒仙桥路4号)
> Phone: 6438 1784; 6437 5284
> Website: www.798photogallery.cn

Pace Beijing Galleries

With excellent exhibitions sets inside several halls, the large Pace Beijing is one of the district's highlights.

> Hours: 11:00-19:00 (Tue-Sun)
> Address: 2 Jiuxianqiao Lu, 798 Art District (朝阳区酒仙桥路2号)
> Phone: 5978 9781
> Website: www.pacebeijing.com

Ullens Center for Contemporary Art (UCCA) (Yóulúnsī Dāngdài Yishù Zhōngxīn; 尤伦斯当代艺术中心)

UCCA earned 45th place in "The World's 50 Greatest Galleries" by *The Times* in May 2013. *The Times* comments, "The 798 Art District is set amid decommissioned military factories and now, with its boutiques, galleries, and cafes and shops, bears comparison to SoHo in New York. In 2007, a year before the Beijing Olympics, Belgian arts patrons Guy and Myriam Ullens opened the UCCA, offering a platform to artists from China. One of the largest contemporary art spaces in the country, this not-for-profit center has hosted more than 60 exhibitions."

> Hours: 10:00-19:00 (Tue-Sun)
> Address: 4 Jiuxianqiao Lu, 798 Art District (朝阳区酒仙桥路4号)
> Phone: 5780 0200
> Website: www.ucca.org.cn
> Admission: ¥ 15 (adults); FREE on Thu. FREE for students and children under 1.3 m (4.2 ft)

Olympic Legacies

This section includes the National Stadium (Bird's Nest), the National Aquatics Center (Water Cube), Olympic Forest Park, and information on the effects of the 2008 Olympic Games on the city of Beijing.

The second most watched games in Olympic history was one of the most galvanizing events to hit Beijing since the founding of the People's Republic in 1949, but the legacy left from the successful Olympiad has proven to be a mixed bag. With many reports placing the cost of the games at around US$44 billion, the games that auspiciously began on 8/8/08 continue to be far and away the most expensive ever (until the Sochi Winter games in 2014), and cemented China's bold 21st century ambitions for gold on the global podium. In the wake of the games, however, uncertainties abound for the iconic venues of the long-gone Olympiad, as well as the venturesome age of progress that it heralded.

Green Olympics

In its bid to win the 2008 games, Beijing unveiled unprecedented plans to clean up its air and introduce great recycling systems; a widely touted Green Olympics that was set to present the city as a model of environmental protection. While the moving of high-pollution factories to outside the city limits, the banning of coal burning within the Fourth Ring Road, and the restriction of private vehicles by license plate all delivered great success for the games, such success was marred by a quick return to normalcy in the Games' wake. A staggering 4 million cars cruised Beijing's roads in 2009, marking a two-fold increase in two years, and largely reducing the concept of "blue-sky days" to rhetoric. With more than 5.2 million on the road in 2013, the government has stepped up campaigns to reduce air pollution in the last few years, but the glorious green of the environment in August 2008 has yet to see any permanence.

Transportation

No doubt the most enduring legacy of Beijing's faded summer Olympics, the public transit system saw vast upgrades that have hardly slowed in 2014. With the addition of three subway lines in 2008 to accommodate the enormous influx of visitors, the now-16-line system has since seen consistent improvement in order to move the 8 million passengers per day that are expected to fill 20 lines in 2015. Beijing Capital Airport's magnificent Terminal 3 was also superbly outfitted for the games. By welcoming more than 75 million passengers a year, it is the second largest terminal in the world (surpassed only by Dubai International's T3). Trains got a bump-up as well, with the state-of-the-art South Station highlighted by the world's fastest conventional trains, rocketing through Tianjin and on to Shanghai at breakneck top speeds of 350 km/h (220 mp/h).

Shaping Up

Clearly inspired by the extravaganza produced by their homeland, Chinese athletes tipped the podiums with 51 gold medals, the most of the games, and boasted a not-too-shabby 100 total medals. Fitness took a new priority among the locals, and lucky August 8 (8 is a lucky number in Chinese numerology) hit official status as a day to promote sporty endeavors among the athletic layperson. Beijinger's these days show a characteristic increase in exercise – the mountains play host to great numbers of hikers forgoing the chairlift – but Chinese youth still trail a good many of the world's others in physical activity. Intense pressure from school leaves many with little time, and flocks of computer addicts who fill the internet cafes are surely not helping.

A Controversial Mix of Culture

Many who are familiar with Beijing's recent history are aware of the controversial demolition of historical neighborhoods in the last 40 years. More than 800 years of heritage lie in many of its hutong alleyways, and the building of the city's Olympic venues in the 2000s saw many ancient blocks lost forever to 21st century architectural aspirations. While traditionalist protesters – locals and foreign alike – certainly held a point, it's hard to imagine how a 3,000-year-old city like Beijing could have constructed modern venues without losing some of its historical relics and sites. Though much of Beijing's historical cultural heritage areas are now under state protection, many hutongs continue to fall tragically under the wrath of the wrecking ball.

Olympic Venues

National Stadium

Chinese name: 国家体育场 (Guójiā Tǐyùchǎng)
Admission: ¥50
Hours: 9:00-18:00 (Mar-Oct); 9:00-17:30 (Nov-Feb)
Website: www.n-s.cn/en
Transport:
Subway – Line 8, Olympic Green (奥林匹克公园), Exit E, walk west to the stadium

The exposed lattice structure of the 2008 Olympics' most iconic venue may be one of the more innovative stadiums ever built, but the so-called Bird's Nest (Niǎo Cháo; 鸟巢) holds its intrigue for a dwindling number of tourists every year. It was designed by famed Swiss architects Herzog and de Meuron, with input from China's own Ai Wei Wei (who eventually distanced himself from the games). The unbelievable price tag for the stadium topped out at US$423 million, and what has now become an epithet for China's month of glory remains largely dormant, hosting but a handful of sporting and musical events since August '08. Swinging down and viewing the stadium can be a treat, but if you want to enter it will cost you ¥50. Plans for shopping malls and theme parks are in the works, but until then the US$15 million a year maintenance bill will continue to eat up tax payers' cash.

National Aquatics Center

Chinese name: 国家游泳中心 (Guójiā Yóuyǒng Zhōngxīn)
Admission: ¥30
Hours: 9:00-21:00
Website: www.n-s.cn/en
Transport: same as National Stadium

Resembling a box of bubble wrap, the Water Cube (Shuǐ Lìfāng; 水立方), as it's colloquially known, is layered with plastic bubbles to provide strength and concentrate natural light and heat, reducing energy requirements. The Cube now houses the

Happy Magic Water Park (¥200 adult, ¥150 kids), a fun place with crazy slides and goofy wave pools. The Cube seems to get more regular use than its steel-trussed neighbor, and it was here that Michael Phelps set an Olympic Record for most gold medals in a single Olympics with eight.

Olympic Forest Park

Chinese name: 奥林匹克森林公园 (Àolínpǐkè Sēnlín Gōngyuán)
Admission: FREE
Hours: 6:00-20:00
Website: www.bopac.gov.cn/english
Transport: Subway – Line 8, South Gate of Forest Park (森林公园南门站)

A bird aviary and a lovely garden mark the north and south of Forest Park. It saw hockey, tennis, and archery in the 2008 games, and is now visited by locals and tourists alike. Strolling the park is free, and bikes and electric scooters are available for rent.

Other Attractions

- Famous Residences..................pg 132
- Ancient Observatory...................pg 136
- Marco Polo Bridge (Lugou Bridge) ...pg 137
- Ming Tombs ....pg 138
- Peking Man Site..........................pg 139
- Prince Gong's Mansion................pg 140
- Badachu Park............................pg 141
- Big Bell Temple ....pg 142
- Five Pagoda Temple ....pg 143
- Hongluo Temple.........................pg 144
- Ordination Terrace Temple...........pg 145
- Ox Street Mosque ....pg 146
- Pool & Mulberry Tree Temple ....pg 147
- Temple of Azure Clouds ....pg 148
- Temple of Cloud Dwelling.............pg 149
- Temple of Great Awakening...........pg 150
- Temple of the Recumbent Buddha...pg 151
- Temple of Vast Succour................pg 152
- White Cloud Temple.....................pg 153
- White Dagoba Temple ....pg 154
- Beijing Aquarium........................pg 155
- Beijing Capital Museum ....pg 156
- Beijing Museum of Natural History..pg 157
- Beijing Planetarium....................pg 158
- Beijing Wildlife Park....................pg 159
- Beijing World Park.....................pg 160
- Beijing Zoo...............................pg 161
- CCTV Building...........................pg 162
- China Aviation Museum...............pg 163
- China Red Sandalwood Museum......pg 164
- Chinese Ethnic Culture Park..........pg 165
- Grand View Garden ....pg 166
- Happy Valley Amusement Park.......pg 167
- Military Museum ....pg 168
- Workers' Cultural Palace..............pg 169
- Beijing Botanical Garden ....pg 170
- Chaoyang Park..........................pg 171
- Fragrant Hills Park.....................pg 172
- Jingdong Grand Canyon...............pg 173
- Longqing Gorge ....pg 174
- Longtan Lake Park.....................pg 175
- Phoenix Hill Nature Park..............pg 176
- Purple Bamboo Garden ....pg 177
- Stone Flower Cave.....................pg 178
- Taoranting Park........................pg 179
- Ten Ferries...............................pg 180
- Tuanjiehu Park ....pg 181
- Western Hills National Forest Park...pg 182
- Yuyuantan Park.........................pg 183
- Zhongshan Park........................pg 184
- Beijing Acrobatics Shows.............pg 185
- Beijing Opera Theaters................pg 186
- Laoshe Teahouse ....pg 187
- Legend of Kungfu Show...............pg 188
- National Art Museum..................pg 189
- National Center for Performing Arts pg 190
- North Putuo Film & TV City...........pg 191
- Songzhuang Art Village ....pg 192

Famous Residences

Former Residence of Lu Xun

Chinese name: 鲁迅故居 (Lǔxùn Gùjū)
Admission: ¥5
Hours: 9:00-15:30; closed Mon
Recommended time for visit: 1 hour
Address: 19 Gongmenkou, 2nd Alley, Fuchengmen Neidajie, Xicheng District（西城区阜成门内宫门口二条19号）
Transport: Subway – Line 2, Fuchengmen（阜成门）Station, Exit B, walk straight ahead to Fuchengmen Neibeijie（阜成门内北街）; the residence will be on the left

One of the most important Chinese writers of the 20th century, Lu Xun was born in Shanghai in 1936 and is widely considered to be the leading figure of modern Chinese literature. His breakout 1918 short story entitled "A Madman's Diary" (Kuángrén Rìjì; 狂人日记) was a scathing criticism of outdated Chinese traditions and feudalism, which he said were "gnawing at Chinese like cannibalism." The work was highly influential in the May Fourth Movement and helped to cement his status as a leftist revolutionary. He spent 14 years in Beijing, passing the last two of them in this charming courtyard house that can be found just west of Fucheng Gate (Fùchéng Mén; 阜成门).

The simple house is adorned with a garden of colorful flowers and is very well preserved. There are two buildings on the site: a northern three-roomed home and a smaller southern one. The larger of the two holds Xu's mother's room, his wife's room and an elegant dining room with period furniture and general bric-a-brac from their day. The quainter one is Lu Xun's bedroom and study. If you're not terribly blown away by these two somewhat inert buildings, move to the small museum of Xun to the east. It offers a bit more flavor, housing his personal effects, writing samples and preserved relics.

Other Attractions

Former Residence of Li Dazhao

Chinese name: 李大钊故居 (Lǐdàzhāo Gùjū)
Admission: ¥10
Hours: 9:00-16:00 (Wed-Sun)
Address: 24 Wenhua Hutong, Xicheng District (西城区文华胡同 24 号院)
Transport: Subway – Line 1, Fuxingmen (复兴门) Station. Walk east 400 m (1,312 ft) and turn right at Naoshikou Dajie (闹市口大街). Then walk straight 150 m (492 ft) and turn left onto Wenchang Hutong (文昌胡同). Next walk 30 m (98 ft) and turn right onto Naoshikou Zhongjie (闹市口中街). From here walk 70 m (230 ft), and turn left onto Wenhua Hutong (文华胡同), then walk 180 m (590 ft), and you'll arrive at the residence.

The old residence of the former Marxist intellectual Li Dazhao is located about 2 km (1 mi) southwest of Nanhai in Xicheng District and is one of the few former residences in Beijing that is not in its original condition. The house was picked apart, rearranged and looted by local residents for years until 2007 when the government shelled out the funds to ship the residents to a new area.

The large-scale renovation that ensued has left a mere 30% of the original structure, and it is uncertain how many of the relics, furniture and other personal effects are forgeries. Still, its worth a visit if you're in the neighborhood. The home features a good deal of information about Li's life, including his role in the founding of the Chinese Communist Party and his seven other residences within the city.

Former Residence of Qi Baishi

Chinese name: 齐白石故居 (Qíbáishí Gùjū)
Admission: ¥5
Hours: 8:00-17:00
Recommended time for visit: 1 hour
Address: 13 Kuache Hutong, Xicheng District (西城区跨车胡同 13 号)
Transport: Subway – Line 4, Lingjing Hutong (灵境胡同) Station, Exit D, walk 800 m (2,624 ft) west along Picai Hutong (辟才胡同)

"The rich man of three hundred stones" was the self-given moniker of Qi Baishi, one of the most famous Chinese artists of the 20th century. A peasant turned painter, Qi had no formal training in art but managed to master a great deal of techniques, including watercolor, calligraphy and seal carving (for which his nickname is given). His ambrosial watercolor paintings are noted for their whimsical (often playful) style, and their value has seen an unbelievable return in recent years. One painting titled "Eagle Standing on Pine Tree" sold for US$65.5 million at an auction in 2011 – too bad the old genius wasn't around to see the payoff. His traditional courtyard home is located in Xicheng District, near the Peking Youth Hostel. Inside the courtyard there is a statue of the late artist, and the inside of his home has many of his watercolor scrolls on display (though they are reproductions), as well as a short video on his life and work.

Former Residence of Lao She

Chinese name: 老舍故居 (Lǎoshě Gùjū)
Admission: FREE
Hours: 9:00-16:00; closed Mon
Address: 19 Fengfu Hutong, Dongcheng District(东城区丰富胡同 19 号)
Transport:
Subway – Line 5, Dengshikou (灯市口) Station, Exit A, walk 500 m (1,640 ft) west along Dengshikou Dajie (灯市口大街), then turn onto Dengshikou Xijie (灯市口西街) and walk 200 m (656 ft)

The great novelist and dramatist, Lao She credited the nationalistic May Fourth Movement of 1919 as the inspirational energy that allowed him to become a writer. His best known novel, *Rickshaw Boy*, considered a classic of Chinese literature, became a US best-seller in 1945 and was adapted into a film in 1982. Other works, such as the tragic story "Crescent Moon," or his play *Teahouse*, were noted for their colorful use of the Beijing dialect. The home lies about 200 m (656 ft) east of the Forbidden City in Fengfu Hutong, and it's easy to find (unlike some of the others...). The house features well preserved period furniture, clothes, a library, and many of Lao's manuscripts. Captions are all in Chinese, but short guides on his life are available for purchase with English translations.

Former Residence of Mao Dun

Chinese name: 茅盾故居 (Máodùn Gùjū)
Admission: ¥5
Hours: 9:00-16:00; closed Mon
Address: 13 Houyuan'ensi Hutong, Dongcheng District (东城区后圆恩寺胡同 13 号)
Transport: Subway – Line 6, Nanluoguxiang (南锣鼓巷) Station, Exit B, walk to the end of Nanluogu Xiang, turn right at Houyuan'ensi Hutong (后圆恩寺胡同), then walk east 130 m (426 ft)

Shen Dehong (沈 德 鸿) adopted the pen name Mao Dun – meaning contradiction in Mandarin – to express his sentiments about the political climate of China in the 1920s. A caring friend changed the first character to another of the same pronunciation, but with the new meaning of "thatched," protecting Mao Dun from certain political persecution. A novelist, journalist, and cultural critic, he helped found the Literary Study Society in 1920, and joined the League of Left Wing Writers the following year. His initial hesitation towards the caustic political energy of the time eventually folded, and he later found himself deeply immersed in the political world of the communists. His home is located in the Houyuan'ensi Hutong, southeast of the Drum and Bell Towers, and it dually serves as a museum about the writer.

Ancient Observatory

Chinese name: 北京古观象台 (Běijīng Gǔguānxiàngtái)
Admission: ¥10
Hours: 9:00-17:00; closed Mon
Recommended time for visit: 1 hour
Address: 2 Dongbiaobei Hutong, Dongcheng District (东城区建国门东裱褙胡同２号)
Transport: Subway – Line 1 or Line 2, Jianguomen (建国门) Station, Exit C, walk to the southeast corner of Jianguomen Bridge

Do you love stars, planets and wacky machines? If so, then you should probably hightail it down to the Beijing Ancient Observatory, which displays a fascinating 500-year history from atop one of the only remaining sections of the Ming era (1368-1644) city wall.

The pre-telescopic observatory was built in 1442 when the Yongle Emperor (who had just completed the Forbidden City and the Temple of Heaven) was apparently ready to build some other cool toys and ordered the return of astronomical equipment from the former capital in Nanjing. Most of those instruments were Jin Dynasty constructs from 1227, but the crazy gizmos on display now are actually from the 17th and 18th centuries. Many were brought in by the Jesuit Ferdinand Verbiest, who was put in charge of the observatory in the mid-1600s.

If you've heard of an **armillary sphere** then you'll probably be pumped to know that this observatory has three – that's right three – armillary spheres. If you have no idea what an armillary sphere is (they were used to determine the coordinates of celestial bodies) then you've got even more reason to get down to the Ancient Observatory and check out this bizarre equipment. There are even two **altazimuths** (you might want to use Wikipedia for this term) that are actually pretty fun to look at.

A small museum just off the courtyard has a further collection of eccentric instruments and a detailed history of astronomy in China.

Marco Polo Bridge

Chinese name: 卢沟桥 (Lúgōu Qiáo)
Admission: ¥20
Hours: 7:00-19:00 (Apr-Oct); 8:00-17:00 (Nov-Mar)
Recommended time for visit: 30 minutes
Address: Yongding River, Fengtai District (丰台区永定河)
Transport:
Subway – Line 1, Wukesong (五棵松) Station, Exit D1; next take bus 624 to Kangzhan Diaosu Yuan (抗战雕塑园) Station
Bus – 952, 310, 313, 452, 624, 661, 715, 971, 329, 843, 983, 77, 662, 693, 978, 309, 301, 339, 459, 458 to Kangzhan Diaosu Yuan (抗战雕塑园) Stop

Marco Polo has a bridge in China? Nope. But he did write about Lugou Bridge in a book, and now all the hip people are calling it Marco Polo Bridge. About 15 km (9 mi) south of Tian'anmen Square, the marvelous bridge is an architectural masterpiece: one massive piece of solid granite that stretches an eye-popping 266.5 m (874 ft) across the Yongding River.

Atop the bridge's 281 support pillars, hundreds of stone **lion guardians** are perched. Each lion statue has more lions crawling from shoulders, paws, bellies, and any other place you might be able to hide a lion on another lion. Supposedly, several attempts have been made to count the lions, but each attempt turned up a different total – their final tally was somewhere between 482 and 496.

The original bridge was built by the Jin in 1192, and then rebuilt during the Qing Dynasty in 1698. Most of the lions date from the Ming or Qing Dynasties, but if you look you can find rare statues from the Yuan and Jin times as well. Don't forget to check out the impressive white **marble steles** at either end of the bridge. One documents Emperor Kangxi's 17th century reconstruction, and the other is emblazoned with Emperor Qianlong's engraved calligraphic reflection: "Morning over Lugou." There are four pretty ornamental columns next to the steles.

Other Attractions

137

Ming Tombs

Chinese names: 明十三陵 (Míng Shísānlíng); 长陵 (Cháng Líng); 定陵 (Dìng Líng); 昭陵 (Zhāo Líng); 神道 (Shén Dào)
Admission: Changling Tomb – ¥45 (Apr-Oct), ¥30 (Nov-Mar); Dingling Tomb – ¥60 (Apr-Oct), ¥40 (Nov-Mar); Zhaoling Tomb – ¥30 (Apr-Oct), ¥20 (Nov-Mar); Sacred Way – ¥30 (Apr-Oct), ¥20 (Nov-Mar)
Hours: 8:00-17:00
Recommended time for visit: 2 hours
Website: www.sun-park.com (in Chinese)
Address: Changping District (昌平区)
Transport: Bus – Special tourist Bus 872 runs directly from Deshengmen (德胜门) to Dingling and Changling every 30 minutes from 7:30-19:00

This massive complex of imperial burial chambers set 50 km (31 mi) northeast of Beijing is the final resting place for 13 of the 16 Ming Emperors and is one of the top day trips for any Beijing visitor. A **UNESCO World Heritage Site**, the complex rests at the foot of Tianshou Mountain (天寿山) and is scattered with a series of 15th century tombs, each one itself a great complex that rears up to a grand burial mound. Only three tombs are open to the public (one has been fully excavated), but what you do see is gripping enough to make you drool with excitement at what treasures must be waiting in the rest of the burial chambers.

The 7 km (94 mi) approach to the tombs follows the **Sacred Way**, which begins with the beautiful triple archway known as the **Great Palace Gate** (Dà Gōngmén; 大宫门). From here you will continue to pass through the **Stele Pavilion** (Shí Páifāng; 石牌坊), an imposing structure guarded by 12 stone animals and officials, along with the largest stele in China. Notice the vibrant colors of the **Great Red Gate** (Dà Hóngmén; 大红门) as you move towards the end of Sacred Way upon Changling Tomb.

The largest and best preserved of the burial sites, **Changling Tomb** is the final resting place of the Yongle (永乐) Emperor, one of Ming's most productive emperors. Yongle's body is here, as are those of his wife and 16 of his concubines, entombed to keep him sensually satiated in the afterlife. The tomb has a basic imperial layout, with a main gate and the first of a series of courtyards leading to the main hall. Stroll a bit further and you will find the **Soul Tower** (Míng Lóu; 明楼), and beyond that the burial mound.

At one time containing the body of Emperor Wanli (万历; 1572-1620) and his wife and concubines, **Dingling Tomb** and the bodies it contained, along with many priceless artifacts, were burned during the turbulent 1960s. Many treasures were also damaged from being stored in an unsealed room that leaked water, but the ones that remain are impressive, and it is the only tomb in the complex where you can climb in for a look. Check out the explanation on display of how archaeologists made their way in using directions on a stone tablet (probably with the *Indian Jones* theme song playing in the background). There is also a small museum at Dingling.

The **Zhaoling Tomb** is the smallest of the tombs, but it is also worth a visit. This is where Emperor Zhu Zaihou (朱载垕) is buried with his three empresses. This less visited tomb is more tranquil than the others, and it's a good way to kick it with some imperial ghosts without the crowds.

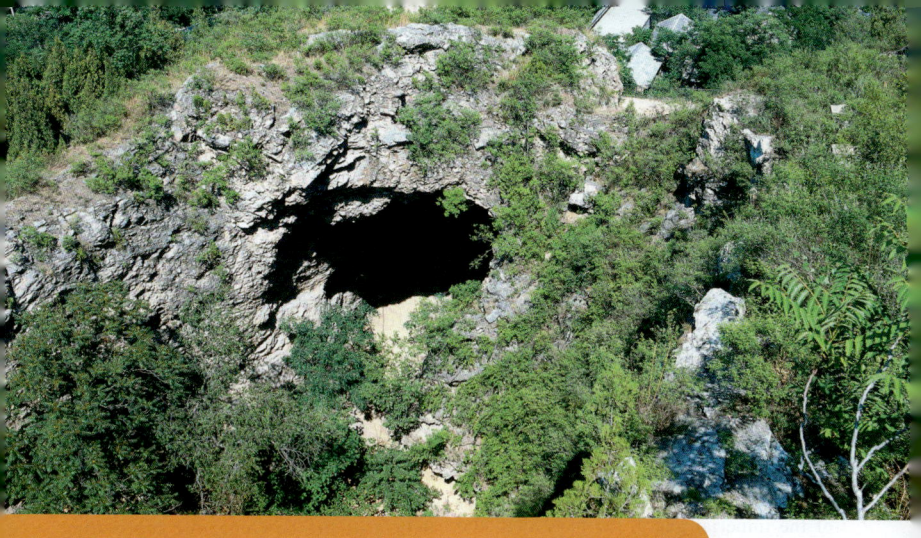

Peking Man Site at Zhoukoudian

Chinese name: 周口店北京人遗址 (Zhōukǒudiàn Běijīngrén Yízhǐ)
Admission: ¥30
Hours: 8:30-16:00 (Nov-Mar); 8:30-16:30 (Apr-Oct)
Recommended time for visit: 1 hour to visit, prepare for 1.5 hours travel from the city center by bus.
Website: www.zkd.cn/IBS (in Chinese)
Address: 1 Zhoukoudian Dajie, Fangshan District (房山区周口店大街1号)
Transport:
Bus -
1. Bus 917 from Tianqiao (天 桥) Bus Stop to Zhoukoucun Lukou (周口村路口), then change to Fangshan (房山) bus 38 to Yuanren Yizhi (猿人遗址)
2. Bus 616 from the south square of West Railway Station to Liangxiang Ximen (良 乡 西 门), then change to Fangshan bus 38 to Yuanren Yizhi

Taxi – ¥160 from city center, 1.5 hours

In the 1920s some very exciting bones were unearthed at the limestone caves of Dragon Bone Hill, southwest of Beijing – but they were not dragon bones. They were human bones, and the fact that two decades of digging here produced 200 human fossils from the Middle Pleistocene era (some 770,000 – 230,000 years ago) is still a pretty amazing discovery. In all, the fossils comprise of around 40 individuals, and there is an onsite museum with more than 3,000 relics from prehistoric Chinese cave-dwelling people.

Peking Man Site was named a **UNESCO World Heritage Site** in 1987. The artifacts on display, some from nearly 1 million years ago, showcase outstanding historical preservation from what is one of the cradles of Chinese civilization. (That being said, those who are not particularly interested in relics from ancient peoples and anthropological reconstructions of fossilized human remains may want to skip this one.) There are eight archeological sites that can be visited from a sometimes narrow and steeply-stepped pathway. Each cave is well maintained and surprisingly clean, and statued depictions of the life of Peking Man put on a cheesy, albeit entertaining, performance. The descriptions can be a bit lackluster, but the hike is refreshing and the history is unmatched.

Peking Man is 57 km (35 mi) from Beijing's center, and we recommend hiring a taxi or a driver for your visit to reduce transit time.

Ruins of Pekingman Zhoukoudian

Prince Gong's Mansion

Chinese name: 恭王府 (Gōngwáng Fǔ)
Admission: ¥40
Hours: 7:30-18:30 (Mar 16-Nov 15; last admission at 16:40); 8:00-18:30 (Nov 16-Mar 15; last admission at 16:10)
Address: 17 Qianhai Xijie, Shichahai (什刹海前海西街17号)
Transport: Subway – Line 6, get off at Beihai North (北海北) Station, Exit B, walk northwest along Longtoujing Jie (龙头井街) for about 200 m (656 ft)

Prince Gong's Mansion was constructed around the year 1777 and was originally the private residence of Heshen. A member of the imperial guard, the handsome and intelligent 25-year-old Heshen came to the attention of the Qing Dynasty Emperor Qianlong (1736-1796), and Heshen's manipulative ways and cunning mind quickly earned him promotions to positions normally occupied by the most experienced officials, including those controlling finance and the appointment of civil servants. Through his unscrupulous methods he acquired a great deal of wealth, but the aging Qianlong did nothing to curb Heshen's corruption. Heshen's judgement day finally came when the succeeding Emperor Jiaqing (1796-1820) had Heshen executed and confiscated his 800 million silver ounce-valued property. After passing it to Prince Qing in 1799, the mansion eventually made its way to Prince Gong, for whom it is known today.

Embedded in a hutong just west of Yinding Bridge, it is one of Beijing's largest private residential compounds and the world's largest extant courtyard. Often called the Palace of Prince Gong, the captivating retreat spans 5.7 hectares (14 acres). Among its lush gardens, rockeries, pools, pavilions and intricate gateways, guests can find Beijing's only preserved Qing Dynasty theater, the **Qing Dynasty Opera House**, where guests are served tea by women wearing traditional costumes of the era. Performances include the China Conservatory of Music and Peking Opera.

Badachu Park

Chinese name: 八大处公园 (Bādàchù Gōngyuán)
Admission: ¥10
Hours: 6:00-20:00 (Apr 16-Aug 31)
  6:00-19:30 (Sept 1-Nov 15)
  6:00-19:00 (Nov 16-Apr 15)
Recommended time for visit: 2 hours
Website: www.badachu.com.cn (in Chinese)
Address: South foot of Western Hills Scenic Area, Shijingshan District (石景山区西山风景区南麓)
Transport:
Subway – Line 1, Pingguoyuan (苹果园) Station, northeast exit. Find the Pingguoyuan Ditie Beimen (苹果园地铁北门) Stop and take bus 972 to Badachu Stop.
Bus – 958, 347, 972, 389, 598 to Badachu (八大处) or Badachu Middle School (八大处中学) Stops.

Literally meaning the "Eight Great Sites," the Badachu is a series of famous Buddhist temples and nunneries sitting at the outskirts of western Beijing on the Shijingshan (Western Scenic Hills) District. Ancient and beautiful, the temples provide a refreshing contrast to the grandiosity of many of Beijing's more colossal shrines. The Badachu has been renovated into a park – it includes the three beautifully landscaped hills of Cuiwei (翠微山), Pingpo (平坡山), and Lushi (卢师山) – across which the temples are scattered. Strolling between the eight sights is quite manageable, and the sanctuaries are enshrined in a park grounds that serves essentially as an ancient arboretum. Some of the rare trees are over 600 years old, with twisted roots entrenched deep in the soil.

Every autumn the park sees a sharp rise in its already formidable popularity when the leaves change to their fall reds and yellows, overwhelming the park with resplendent scenery. Many tourists take this chance in autumn to climb the hills in the crisp air to catch a glimpse of the breathtaking views of the city. A cable car is also in service for those who need it.

All the sights here are worth a visit, and we encourage you to stroll at your leisure. Of particular note are the stupa and golden fish pond (full of brocade carp) at Lingguang Temple, the 18 arhats (or *luohan*) of the Hall of Mahavira carved 800 years ago by Yuan Dynasty sculptor Liu Yuan (刘元), and the steles at Xiangjie Temple with inscriptions from emperors Kangxi, Qianlong and Jiaqing.

Nearby sights

Western Hills (pg 182) – 2 km (1 mi) west

Badachu Eight Temples

The Temple of Eternal Peace – Changan Temple (Cháng'ān Sì; 长安寺)
The Temple of Divine Light – Lingguang Temple (Língguāng Sì; 灵光寺)
The Nunnery of Three Hills – Sanshan Nunnery (Sānshān Ān; 三山庵)
The Temple of Great Mercy – Dabei Temple (Dàbēi Sì; 大悲寺)
The Nunnery of Dragon Spring – Longquan Nunnery (Lóngquán Ān; 龙泉庵)
The Temple of the Fragrant World – Xiangjie Temple (Xiāngjiè Sì; 香界寺)
The Cave of the Precious Pearl – Baozhu Cave (Bǎozhū Dòng; 宝珠洞)
The Temple of Thorough Transformation – Zhengguo Temple (Zhèngguǒ Sì; 正果寺)

Big Bell Temple

Chinese name: 大钟寺 (Dàzhōng Sì)
Admission: ¥20
Hours: 9:00-16:30; closed Mon
Recommended time for visit: 1 hour
Website: www.dazhongsi.org (in Chinese)
Address: 31A Beisanhuan Xilu, Haidian District (海淀区北三环西路甲31号)
Transport:
Subway – Line 13, Dazhongsi (大钟寺) Station, Exit A (northwest exit), walk north 150 m (492 ft) to the 3rd Ring Rd. Walk along the south side of the road 400 m (1,312 ft), then cross to the north side of the road. At the traffic light you will see the outer wall of the temple.
Bus – 300 (快外), 323 (快), 87, 88, 361, 422, 425, 604, 617, 658, 695, 718, 967, 特8外, Yuntong (运通) 101 or Yuntong 201, get off at Dazhongsi (大钟寺) Stop

Big Bell Temple is about– you guessed it – bells! In particular, it is about the mighty 46.5-ton bell that rocks the hutongs of Beijing on the eve of every Spring Festival with its resounding "gong!" Bells are auspicious items in Chinese divination (fortune telling), and the Big Bell Temple continues a 300-year tradition of bringing good omens to the main events of the year by making a lot of noise.

The temple was built in 1733 and has several buildings. Laid out around the main Big Bell Tower are the Bell and Drum Towers(Zhōnggǔ Lóu; 钟鼓楼), **the Scripture Collecting Pavilion (**Cángjīng Lóu; 藏经楼), the **Mountain Gate (**Shān Mén; 山门) and several other towering structures. A construction of the late Qing Dynasty, its original name of Juesheng Si was changed ten years later when the giant bell was carted into the temple. The cumbersome item was a nightmare to transport, so a channel was dug and filled with water and the bell was slid along when the water froze in the winter. The same technique was used for the massive stone steles inside the Forbidden City.

Also known as the Yongle Big Bell, it was named after Ming Dynasty Emperor Yongle, who commissioned the temple as part of his three grand projects when he relocated the capital to Beijing in the early 15th century, which also included the Forbidden City and the Temple of Heaven. Check out the bell's chunky 3.5 m (11 ft) diameter, where Buddhist mantras of 227,000 characters are skillfully and meticulously inscribed.

It is said that after the bell made its epic journey across the ice road to the temple in the 18th century, a great mound of dirt was piled under the tower's interior in order to hoist the enormous object to the top of the archway.

Super into bells? (That's why you're here, right?) Then get ready for a bell bonanza at the temple's **Ancient Bell Museum**, displaying hundreds of cultural artifacts, including a diverse collection of bells from ancient China and around the world. With decent descriptions and captions, the museum is sure to impress. Replicas of the bell relics displayed here can be purchased if you've just got to have one for a special occasion.

Five Pagoda Temple

Chinese name: 五塔寺 (Wǔtǎ Sì)
Admission: ¥20
Hours: 9: 00-16:30; closed Mon
Recommended time for visit: 1 hour
Address: North of Beijing Zoo, Haidian District (海淀区西直门外动物园北)
Transport:
Subway – Line 4, National Library (国家图书馆) Station, Exit C, walk eastward along Wutasi Lu (五塔寺路) for 500 m (1,649 ft)

The unique Five Pagoda Temple (also known as Zhenjue Temple) is a Buddhist temple in the style of the Indian Vajrasana Pagoda, or the Diamond Throne Pagoda. Including one in Inner Mongolia, China has five Buddhist shrines based on the Vajrasana design, and Zhenjue Temple of Beijing – or the Temple of the Righteous Awakening – is the country's oldest.

How righteous is it? Sitting on an impressive rustic square throne, four powerful pagodas dot the corners of the 8 m- (25 ft)-tall foundation, with the tallest 13-story one crowning the center. The bluestone foundation is six stories, with the upper five levels narrowly eaved and emblazoned with exquisite pictorials of Buddhas, shrines, bas-reliefs of Buddhist objects, and arcane Sanskrit texts. Don't forget to get up close and personal with the pagodas, too. Carved with their own Bodhi trees and delicately engraved Buddhas and sutras, they drive home the righteousness of Zhenjue. Its architecture is a fantastic combination of Indian and Chinese design (including the Chinese art of glazed tiled roofs) and is one of the more standout Buddhist temples in the city.

It is still uncertain as to how the Diamond Throne Vajrasana design entered China, but one tradition says it snuck in during the reign of the Ming Emperor Yongle in the 15th century. Perhaps less of a "sneaking in" and more of a straight bribe, the temple was built by Yongle in 1473 after an Indian monk supposedly "presented" him with five golden Buddha statues and a draft of the Vajrasana design. The temple has undergone numerous renovations in its lifetime, keeping the 500-year history of the temple faithfully preserved. If you can work it in, this temple is a must see.

There is also a small Art Museum of Stone Carvings on the premises, offering visitors a look at an excellent collection of over 2,000 pieces of ancient Buddhist stone artwork.

Nearby sights

Beijing Zoo and Aquarium (pg 161) – 800 m (2,624 ft) east

Hongluo Temple

> **Chinese name:** 红螺寺 (Hóngluó Sì)
> **Admission:** ¥54
> **Hours:** 8:00-18:00
> **Recommended time for visit:** half a day
> **Address:** Hongluo Mountain, Qihu Town, Huairou District (怀柔区雁栖湖镇红螺山)
> **Transport: Bus** – 867 or 936 branch line from Dongzhimen (东直门) Bus Station to Hongluosi (红螺寺) Stop

Perfect for those day trips to the Great Wall's Mutianyu, the Honglou Temple (literally meaning the "Red Shells Temple") is 57 km (35.5 mi) to the north of Beijing and sits 20 minutes from Mutianyu Great Wall. Embraced by some of the most striking natural scenery in the city, the typical Buddhist temple is beautiful, but the main draws here are the unique and sometimes downright bizarre natural wonders that dwell in the enormous pine forest. The watery **Imperial Bamboo Forest** (Yùzhú Lín; 御竹林) hosts plenty of bamboo, the 1,000-year-old androgynous **Duo Ginkgoes** (Cíxióng Yínxìng; 雌雄银杏) will give you a lesson in longevity, and the **Wisterias Wreathing Pine** (Zǐténg Jìsōng; 紫藤寄松) is a giant pine tree ensared in creeping Chinese wisterias.

Said to be one of the main disseminators of Mahayana (Pure Land) Buddhism, the main sect of Buddhism in China, the 1,000-year-old Red Shells Temple is extremely significant in Chinese Buddhist culture and history and is the premier Buddhist Temple in Northern China. A fantastically prosaic Chinglish saying goes: "In the south, Putuo Temple is primarily recommended, while in the north, Hongluo Temple is especially valued." Don't expect monks on your visit, as the temple is less a spiritual center these days than an offbeat mountain retreat.

If you know anything about Chinese *feng shui* you won't be surprised to find out Honglou Temple sits on a north-south axis facing south, since nearly every other Buddhist temple in Beijing is exactly the same. You'll find ubiquitous Buddhist halls and statues here, such as Devajara Hall (Tiānwáng Diàn; 天王殿) and its Heavenly Kings and Maitreya Buddha, but an even better idea is to cruise over to check out the **Hall of the Thousand Armed Goddess** (Qiānshǒu Guānyīn Diàn; 千手观音殿) in the east and the western **Damo Hall** (Dámó Diàn; 达摩殿). They offer something a little out of the ordinary as far as Buddhist temples go. In particular, Damo (known as Boddhidharma in India) was the founder of Zen Buddhism, and the originator of the physical training that began Shaolin Kung Fu. Step outside to Damo Hall's courtyard to find the 1,000-year old Duo Gingkoes.

Mahavira Hall (Dàxióng Bǎodiàn; 大雄宝殿) is not a bad sight either. Here you can pray for some vitality to Sakyamuni, the Buddha of medicine, and check out the 18 arhats surrounding him. Exit this hall to find the Wisterias Wreathing Pine.

Do not forget as well to catch the **500 Arhat Statues** (Wǔbǎi Luóhàn Yuán; 五百罗汉园) that cover 20 hectares (50 acres) of the ancient pine forest. They surround the laughing Maitreya Buddha and were designed in proportion to living humans, unlike many other arhats adorning Beijing's temples, and each one casts a different visage. The mountain also features a popular toboggan slide (¥50 round trip).

Fall colors are unbeatable here, making September to October a particularly ideal time for a mountain assault. There is also an excellent temple fair sometime around the beginning of January (depending on the lunar calendar).

Ordination Altar Temple

Chinese name: 戒台寺 (Jiètái Sì)
Admission: ¥45
Hours: 8:30-17:30
Recommended time for visit: 1-2 hours
Address: Ma'an Mountain, Yongding Town, Mentougou District (门头沟区永定镇马鞍山)
Transport : Subway – Line 1, Pingguoyuan (苹果园) Station, Exit D; then take bus 948 for 17 stops to Jietaisi (戒台寺) Stop. The bus runs every one hour from 6:50 to 17:35, the whole journey takes about 45 minutes.

When the monk Fajun (法均) built the terrace at Jietai Si during the Liao Dynasty (916-1125), the Emperor commended his work by bestowing upon the eminent holy man his personal Yùzhì Jièběn (御制戒本), a Buddhist sutra that was hand copied by the emperor himself. The sacred text was so hallowed that it singlehandedly recognized Fajun as the chief of the Lu sect of Buddhism, and to this day Jietai Si is considered the highest Lu Buddhism institution in China. The temple itself was originally built during the Sui Dynasty (582-618) and rebuilt later during the Tang Dynasty (618-907), making it one of the oldest in Beijing, and its 3.5 m- (8.5 ft)- high bluestone-terraced tower gloats as the largest extant Buddhist ordination altar in China. True to its name, it is here that monks and nuns are officially ordained, 32 km (20 mi) from the city center.

Besides the ordination altar, located inside the **Grand Hall of Ordination** (Jiètán Dàdiàn; 戒坛大殿), the rest of the temple features several halls that are pervasive in nearly all other Buddhist Temples in Beijing. The **Hall of Heavenly Kings** (Tiānwáng Diàn; 天王殿) houses the Maitreya Buddha and the Four Kings, the **Mahavira Hall** (Dàxióng Bǎodiàn; 大雄宝殿) displays three Buddha statues, and the less ubiquitous **Hall of a Thousand Buddhas** (Qiānfó Gé; 千佛阁) unfortunately sits in ruins. Just inside the main gate hall, you can catch a glimpse of a tablet with an inscribed calligraphic passage from the Qing Emperor Kangxi (1661-1722).

The garden work outside does much to beautify the temple, and the five famous pines (Jiètái Wǔsōng; 戒台五松) – each of whom have their own personality – as well as the 1,000 lilac trees, spice up a visit that can be a bit redundant for those who have seen their share of Buddhist temples. When the lilacs bloom between April and May, the fragrant aroma is commemorated with a lilac festival. Grab a look at the **Peony Yard** (Mǔdān Yuàn; 牡丹院), featuring peony trees planted by Prince Gong (1833-1898), and one said to have been planted by the Kangxi Emperor.

During the Dragon Boat Festival (held in early June, depending on the lunar calendar) Jietai Si holds a fair. Visitors can eat zòngzi (粽子; sweet sticky rice wrapped in leaves), wear scented sachet pouches, and pray in ceremonies. The Chinese New Year is heralded here with a great bell-tolling.

Ox Street Mosque

Chinese name: 牛街礼拜寺 (Niújiē Lǐbài Sì)
Admission: ¥10
Hours: 8:00-16:00
Recommended time for visit: 1 hour
Address: 88 Niujie Zhonglu, Xicheng District (西城区牛街中路88号)
Transport:
Subway – Line 2, Changchunjie (长椿街) Station, Exit C1, walk about 1.5 km (less than 1 mi) south
Bus – 10, 48, 88, 213 or 717, Niujie Libaisi (牛街礼拜寺) Stop

The Ox Street Mosque is a fascinating combination of Chinese traditional wooden palace design and Islamic holy décor. The premier mosque of the capital city has hosted thousands of Islamic worshipers over the course of 1,000 years and is the largest and oldest of Beijing's 80-some mosques. Unfortunately for non-Muslim tourists, entrance into the Prayer Hall is not allowed, and thus the most eye-catching section of the mosque is largely non-viewable. Admission is cheap, however, and it is worth a trip if you're in the area.

The Mosque at Ox Street was built in 996 CE, and has been renovated and expanded to keep the historic building from dying of old age. In contrast to south-facing Chinese holy buildings, the mosque faces Mecca in the Muslim holy land. The Arab-style decorations feature no human or animal figures, which are taboo in the Islamic tradition, but instead a series of relief sculptures along the large wall of the front gate. Most of the sculptures depict happiness and fortune, and the 40 m (132 ft) wall is touched with a great marble pedestal. Inside the gate, the hexagonal **Watching Moon Tower** (Wàngyuè Lóu; 望月楼) was so named for the imams who perched here to view the moon in order to properly mandate fasting times. The two-story tower is 10 m- (33 ft)-tall and capped with a golden glazed roof. Follow the paths alongside the tower to the **Prayer Hall** (Lǐbài Diàn; 礼拜殿), where non-Muslims sadly will miss the flower paintings and glass beads inside, but can check out the Koran poems that adorn the exterior. Language geeks will delight in the poems written in the Arabic script of Al-Kufi, a rare sight in China.

Shaded in a dense thicket of cypress trees to the southeast of the Prayer Hall are the black brick graves. Their 1,000-year-old epigraphs are still quite readable and lend greatly to the study of Islamic history in China.

Pool & Mulberry Tree Temple

Chinese name: 潭柘寺 (Tánzhè Sì)
Admission: ¥55; ¥100 (Zen & Martial Art performance)
Hours: 8:00-16:30
Recommended time for visit: 1-2 hours
Website: www.tanzhesi.cn (in Chinese)
Address: Tanzhesi Town, Mentougou District (门头沟区潭柘寺镇)
Transport: Subway & Bus – Line 1, Pingguoyuan (苹果园) Station, transfer to bus 931 at the bus station on the west side and get off at the final stop, Tanzhesi (潭柘寺) (29 stops in total). The bus runs every hour from 6:50 to 17:35, and the whole journey takes about 1.5 hours (a taxi may be a better idea).

The oldest Buddhist temple in Beijing has around 1,700 years of history and a mighty claim to fame as the site of the ordination of Kublai Khan's daughter into the Buddhist nunnery. Constructed sometime during the Jin Dynasty (265 CE-316 CE), the aged temple has seen its share of renovations and reconstructions, meaning that most of the current buildings are Ming or Qing creations, but Jin and Yuan Dynasty (1271-1368) pagodas can still be found. The temple is located 40 km (25 mi) from the city center in the lush and rugged Western Hills, and in the characteristic fashion of Chinese *feng shui*, it faces the energizing *yang* energy of the south. It has gone through many names in its impressive lifetime, and its current appellation was given by laypeople describing of the Dragon Pool and mulberry trees on the temple grounds.

Spanning an impressive 2,500 sq m (26,910 sq ft), the Pool and Mulberry Tree Temple is methodically arranged, with the main halls all focused along the central axis, courtyards to the east, and various altars out west. **Mahavira Hall** (Dàxióng Bǎodiàn; 大雄宝殿), with beautiful yellow glazed tiles and glazed-green adornments on the double-eaved roof, is the main hall and features statues of Mahavira and his students, as well as a fascinating 2 m (6 ft) diameter bronze pot that was used to cook for the monks and nuns of the temple. At one time there were three pots, and this grand cauldron was the smallest of them, believe it or not. Tree huggers should get a load of the **Emperor Trees** (Dìwáng Shù; 帝王树), a pair of ancient gingkoes in Mahavira's backyard. The 30 m- (98 ft)-tall one to the east is over 1,000 years old. Emperor Qianlong gave the trees their name during his visit, and it was said (during the Qing Dynasty) that whenever a new emperor was crowned a new branch would sprout.

Beyond Mahavira Hall is the **Vairochana Pavilion** (Pílú Gé; 毗卢阁), a two-story building with carved brickwork. Check out the dragons playing with pearls and the phoenixes in peonies carved on the ridge adornments. Traditionally, dragons represented male energy and phoenixes female, which generally meant dragons were positioned on top. Those at Tanzhe are flipped, however, and legend has it this was done in honor (or maybe fear) of the Empress Dowager Cixi when she reconstructed the pavilion. Swing out to the east for a glance at the wooden-framed, marble-floored **Floating Cups Pavilion** (Liúbēi Tíng; 流杯亭) and west to **Avalokitsesvara Hall** (Guānyīn Diàn; 观音殿). The latter is where Kublai Khan's newly ordained daughter – princess Miaoyan – prayed so intensely to Bodhisattva she left knee grooves on the stone displayed inside. You can also check out a very cool deep green stone **fish sculpture**, made from a meteorite that contained bronze (hence the green color).

The temple also holds a Zen and martial arts (¥100) performance throughout the day.

Other Attractions

Temple of Azure Clouds

Chinese name: 碧云寺 (Biyún Sì)
Admission: ¥10 (visitors also need to buy the ¥10 entrance ticket for Fragrant Hills Park (pg 172) to get into the temple)
Hours: 8:00-16:30
Recommended time for visit: 1 hour
Address: North gate of Fragrant Hills Park, Haidian District (海淀区香山公园内)
Transport: Bus – 563, 318, 714, 698, 331, 360, 696, 630 to Xiangshan (香山) Stop

Just north of the beautiful Fragrant Hills Park is the calming Temple of Azure Clouds. It was first built in the Yuan Dynasty, but underwent reconstructions during the Ming and Qing Dynasties. The temple does offer some surprises, such as the fact that the temple is fronted by the **Gate of Azure Clouds**, which is guarded by two stone lions and flanked by two Buddhist guards that were carved during Ming rule. The temple is Buddhist, so get ready for the obligatory Buddhist statues and likenesses, including the Four Heavenly Kings, Maitreya, Sakyamuni and the arhats. The arhats are vivid, colorful, and definitely worth a view, especially if you like 500 of them all wearing a different expression. Check them out, as well as the other statues in the **Five Hundred Arhats Hall** (Luóhàn Táng; 罗汉堂) on the west side.

Perhaps the most famous site at Biyun Temple is the **Sun Yat-sen Memorial Hall** (Sūnzhōngshān Jì'niàntáng; 孙中山纪念堂) in the center of the complex. The building pays homage to the late President of the Republic of China with photos, handwriting, books and a statue of the revolutionary leader. His crystal coffin, gifted to China in 1925 by the USSR, is on display, though it's really only for face value as Sun himself is currently entombed in Nanjing. Calligraphy by his wife, Song Qingling (whose former residence can be seen in the city; pg 103) can be viewed here as well.

Before you leave the Temple of Azure Clouds or Fragrant Hills Park, be sure to freshen up your visit by heading over to the **Vajra Throne Tower** (Jīngāng Bǎozuò Tǎ: 金刚宝座塔) on the West Hill (Xī Shān; 西山). It is one of the most strikingly beautiful structures at the temple, having been built in the Indian Vajrasana (diamond throne) design, and is the highest building in the complex at 35 m (115 ft). Superb views of Beijing are waiting for you from the top of the tower.

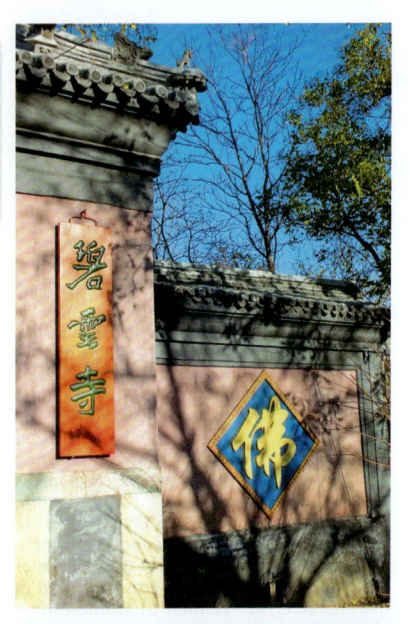

Nearby sights

Beijing Botanical Gardens (pg 170) – 1 km (less than 1 mi) west

Temple of Cloud Dwelling

Chinese name: 云居寺 (Yúnjū Sì)
Admission: ¥40
Hours: 8:30-17:00 (summer); 8:00-16:30 (winter)
Recommended time for visit: 1 hours
Website: www.bjyjs.org (in Chinese)
Address: At the foot of Baidai Mountain, Fangshan District (房山区白带山下)
Transport:
Bus –
1. Take bus 917 from Tianqiao (天桥) Long Distance Bus Station to Liangxiang Ximen (良乡西门), then change to Fangshan (房山) buses 12, 19 or 31 to Yunjusi (云居寺) Stop
2. Take bus 832 to Liangxiang Tiyuchang (良乡体育场), and then transfer to the local Fangshan bus 12 and get off at Yunjusi Stop

Secluded a good 70 km (43 mi) southwest of the city center in Beijing's Fangshan District, Yunju Temple holds some of the best preserved Buddhist relics, sutras and lore of any Buddhist temple in Beijing. The shrine was originally built in 605, but was ransacked in the 1930s at the hands of the Japanese during the Sino-Japanese War. Make sure to put on your "I Heart Sutras" hat, because Yunju Temple holds 100,000 sutra tablets on wood and stone, covering over 1,000 years of Buddhist culture. The holy site is still a highly active spiritual center, where visitors can get hands-on with Buddhist culture and activities.

The monk Jingwan, supposedly in hopes of preserving his work from Taoist reprisal during a period of spiritual debate, began carving sutras on a stone tablet circa 616 CE. Over the course of 1,000 years his students continued the work, eventually engraving a total of 14,278 stone tablets, which they hid in the **Shijing Mountain Grotto** (Shíjīng Shān Cángjīng Dòng; 石经山藏经洞) outside the temple. A whopping 10,082 of them are on display through a glass closet. In addition to the impressive stone tablets, 77,000 wooden tablets are inscribed with Long Zang (Dragon Tripitakas) as well. As long as you're not squeamish, you should have a look at the paper sutras too – some of the most sacred were inked by the famed monk Bhiksu Zu Hui with the blood of his tongue. Take a walk to Leiyin Grotto to see over 1,000 carvings of Buddha.

In addition to Yunju's abundance of sutras and relics, guests may participate in traditional grain crushing on a Chinese millstone, and have a go at old school sutra printing. Those visiting in May or June should keep an ear out for an annual fair held at the temple in honor of Sakyamuni Buddha's birthday.

Temple of Great Awakening

Chinese name: 大觉寺 (Dàjué Sì)
Admission: ¥20 (on Wed, FREE for the first 200 visitors)
Hours: 8:00-17:00
Recommended time for visit: 1-2 hours
Website: www.dajuetemple.com (in Chinese)
Address: Southern slope of Yangtai Mountain, Sujiatuo Town, Haidian District (海淀区苏家坨镇阳台山麓)
Transport: Bus – 633 to Dajueji Stop

Also known as the Temple of Enlightenment, Dajue Temple sits 35 km (22 mi) from Beijing's center and has a relatively unique design since it faces east instead of south like every other Chinese *feng shui* design. It is said that the Liao people – who founded the temple in 1068 and worshiped the sun – built the temple facing east to honor the solar body upon its morning rise. The original name of the temple was Clear Water Temple (Qīngshuǐ Sì; 清水寺) because of an immaculate stream that ran through the grounds. These days the water's cleanliness may be a bit more dubious than it was 1,000 years ago, but the creek is still a fine sight, and the natural scenery here is nothing to scoff at. Nearly 400 years after its Liao founding, the ever-constructive Ming rebuilt the temple in the 15th century.

To the west of the Hall of Heavenly Kings (Tiānwáng Diàn; 天王殿) in the middle section of the temple is the **Gongde Pond** (Gōngdé Chí; 功德池), or the Fish-Setting-Free Pond. Take a look at the stone animal fountains that spit water into the pool. These statues boast a lifespan of nearly 1,000 years and are flanked to the north by a grand cypress tree entwined by a set of vines. The main hall is the **Sakyamuni Hall** (Dàxióng Bǎodiàn; 大雄宝殿) – the second hall of the middle section – which is a great place to see the calligraphy of dead emperors. When you get inside, look at the ceiling to find a stone tablet inscribed by Emperor Qianlong. The sides of the hall also have plaques inscribed by Empress Dowager Cixi.

Search around the exterior of Sakyamuni Hall to find the **King of Ginkgoes**, a 25 m-(82 ft)-tall, 900-year-old ginkgo tree. Over at the **Hall of Great Compassion** (Dàbēi Tán; 大悲坛) sits the temple's oldest relic – a Liao Dynasty stone tablet from 1086. If the King of gingkoes didn't satisfy your insatiable tree craving then check out Beijing's tallest magnolia tree in the **Siyi Hall** (Sìyí Táng; 四宜堂; also known as the South Magnolia Hall). The tree is 10 m (33 ft) tall, 300 years old and produces fist-sized white flowers in April. A magnolia festival is held here when the tree is in bloom.

Temple of the Recumbent Buddha

Chinese name: 卧佛寺 (Wòfó Sì)
Admission: ¥5 (must pay admission to Botanical Gardens first)
Hours: 8:30-16:00
Recommended time for visit: 1 hour
Address: Wofosi Lu, north foot of Xishan, Haidian District (海淀区西山北侧卧佛寺路)
Transport: Bus – 331, 505, 563, 696 to Wofo Si (卧佛寺) Stop

What's better than a giant 54 ton effigy of Buddha? A giant 54 ton effigy of Buddha reclining as he enters nirvana! And that's exactly what you'll find at Wofo Si: a sprawling 5 m (16.5 ft) statue of Sakyamuni Buddha that is said to have "enslaved 7,000 people" in its creation. If the idea of thousands of slave laborers seems very un-Buddhist to you, we couldn't agree more, but the statue is still a fine sight, especially since the temple sits inside the excellent scenery of the Beijing Botanical Gardens.

The statue was built in 1321 and is the oldest structure on the temple grounds. Everything else was originally built in the 7th century, but Ming reconstructions mean that what you see now is quintessentially Ming. Twelve other Buddhas that surround Sakyamuni are said to be taking instructions from the newly enlightened deity. Hopefully they're not learning how to enslave 7,000 people.

The rest of the temple grounds feature their own versions of prevalent Buddhist temple structures, such as the Hall of the Heavenly Kings (Tiānwáng Diàn; 天王殿) and the Three Buddhas Hall (Sānshìfó Diàn; 三世佛殿). The latter hall has been used for sacrifices, and one of the 18 arhats inside wears the clothing of a lowly mortal (arhats have achieved enlightenment and thus wear celestial clothes). Supposedly, this statue represents Emperor Qianlong. In front of the three Buddhas in the same hall is an ancient tree that was transplanted from distant India. Grab a look at the bamboo garden and the giant peony garden to the west of the temple buildings as well.

Nearby sights

Beijing Botanical Gardens (pg 170)– this temple is inside of the Botanical Gardens
Temple of Azure Clouds (pg 148) – 1 km (0.5 mi) east

Temple of Vast Succor

Chinese name: 广济寺 (Guǎngjì Sì)
Admission: FREE
Hours: 7:00-16:30
Recommended time for visit: 1-2 hours
Address: 25 Fuchengmen Neidajie., Xicheng District (西城区阜成门内大街25号)
Transport:
Subway – Line 4, Xisi (西四) Station, Exit A (northwest exit), walk northwest
Bus – 623, 685, 42, 102, 13, 604 or 603 to Xisi Lukou Xi (西四路口西) Stop

Pay a visit to the Temple of Vast Succor to learn a little about the temple's impressive 900-year history and you'll also learn the less impressive fact that the original Jin Dynasty (1115-1234) buildings were destroyed in a fire…three separate times. The current buildings are all Ming, and their 400-year old glazed-tile roofs and eaved edges are still a very handsome sight.

Greeted by the magnificent triple-arched doors of the main gate, you'll be equally impressed by the giant commemorative stele that sits out front. Head inside the gate to check out the roof-mounted **Wheel of Dharma** (Fǎ Lún; 法轮), or Wheel of Law, that spins out sweet justice from the top of the Hall of Heavenly Kings (Tiānwáng Diàn; 天王殿), and don't miss the large **bronze vessel** out front of Mahavira Hall (Dàxióng Bǎodiàn; 大雄宝殿). This giant pot is etched with the eight Buddhist treasures: the wheel, the shell, the spiral, the umbrella, the flower, the vase, the fish, and the knot. Notice that many of them are circular in nature, symbolic of the symmetrical patterns and cycles of the universe. Step inside Mahavira Hall to view the 18 arhat statues and be wowed by the brilliant 10 m- (33 ft)- wide **fresco painting** of Buddha expounding doctrine on the wall behind them. Fu Wen, an honored painter of the Qing Dynasty, created the work using only his fingers. It is the largest extant fresco in China and one of the most impressive finger paintings ever made– way better than a kindergartener's.

Last but not least, check out the Sutra Hall, holding over 100,000 sutras. The most revered of them are from the Song and Ming Dynasties and are inked with blood. Gross!

White Cloud Temple

Chinese name: 白云观 (Báiyún Guàn)
Admission: ¥10
Hours: 8:30-16:00
Recommended time for visit: 1 hour
Address: Baiyunguan Jie, Xicheng District (西城区白云观街)
Transport: Bus – 45, 80, 717, 319, 26, get off at Baiyunguan (白云观) Stop.

White Cloud Temple was founded in 739 CE and has since served as one of the most important Taoist facilities outside of the famed Wudang Mountain. Many renovations and expansions have kept the temple alive over its 1,300-year lifespan, and the current architecture is mostly Ming (1368-1644) and Qing (1644-1912). Though operations shut down briefly when the communists took over in 1949, the temple today is a highly active spiritual center, whirring with white-robed, topknot-haired priests and housing the Chinese Daoist Association headquarters.

The *feng shui* design of White Cloud sits on a north-south axis facing south. An excellent triple-arched gateway greets visitors with vibrant blues and greens, as well as delicate engravings of flowers, clouds and cranes (a very special animal in Taoist martial arts). Keep an eye out for the **relief monkey** that peeks from a hidden nook beside the middle archway. The monkey is thought to be an incarnation of a deity, and touching it supposedly brings good luck. There are a total of three engraved monkeys within the temple grounds, and you can join the other visitors striving to touch all three in order to have a wish granted.

Yuhuang Hall (Yùhuáng Diàn; 玉皇殿) is the first of the main halls on the central axis and it houses a statue of one of Taoism's principal deities, the Jade Emperor, as well as some good looking Ming Dynasty wall murals. **Qiuzu Hall** (Qiūzǔ Diàn; 邱祖殿) was originally built in 1228 on the site of Qui Chuji's grave as a shrine to Qui, the late patriarch of the temple's Quanzhen school of Taoism. Grab a peek at the small gallery of Taoist works and writings inside. The last of the main halls, **Sanqing Hall** (Sānqīng Sìyù Diàn; 三清四御殿; Hall of the Three Pure Ones) features the robust statues of the Three Pure Ones, eyebrow-heavy and piercing-clad Taoist Immortals who cast fierce visages.

The temple also holds ordinations and festivals, so keep your ear to the ground. Every year around March a grand birthday party honors Qui Chuji, engulfing the grounds in an assembly of artisans, street performers, martial arts acts, and a potpourri of traders and snacks.

White Dagoba Temple

Chinese name: 白塔寺 (Báitǎ Sì)
Admission: ¥20 (FREE for the first 200 visitors on Wed)
Hours: 9:00-16:30
Recommended time for visit: 1 hour
Address: Fuchengmen Neidajie, Xicheng District (西城区阜成门内大街)
Transport:
Subway – Line 4, Xisi (西四) Station, walk west
Line 2, Fuchengmen (阜成门) Station, walk east
Bus – 685, 612, 101, 202, 623, 7, 47, 42, 102, 103, 13, 211, 409, 603, 604, or 614 to Baitasi (白塔寺) Stop

It was Kublai Khan who commissioned the construction of the White Dagoba (a dagoba is a kind of stupa) in the 1270s, and it was Kublai who was sent to the afterlife in style with a sacrificial ceremony here upon his death in 1294. Completed in 1279, the dagoba was comissioned by Khan as a gesture to the Tibetans, who resisted his consolidation of their western areas (it seems little has changed in 800 years).

Originally, the temple grounds around the giant stupa covered an enormous 160,000 sq m (1.7 million sq ft); the breadth was so large that the locals coined it the "Golden City and Jade Dagoba." To plan the layout of the surrounding temple buildings, the emperor reportedly fired four arrows in each direction from the top of the tower. When a fire in 1368 reduced everything except the dagoba to cinders, the ever-capable Ming Dynasty rebuilt the complex to its more modest current span of 13,000 sq m (139,931 sq ft), shocking the world with their bold design plans that didn't include bows and arrows. The dagoba itself underwent large-scale repairs in 1976 when the Tangshan Earthquake damaged some of the temple's priceless relics and nearly toppled the stupa.

Mounted on a triple-layered Sumeru pedestal-style platform, the White Dagoba is amazing. The "inverted alms-bowl" shape of the body supports a towering 13-tiered limestone steeple and is capped with a dangly canopy of wood and pounded bronze. The superstructure is built with bricks and coated with a beaming layer of limestone, while the canopy hangs a massive set of twinkly wind chimes and is topped with another bronze stupa. That's right, a stupa on a stupa. You know you want to see this.

Nepalese architect Araniko originally designed the extraordinary dagoba, along with several temples on Mount Wutai in southwestern Shanxi Province. Look for a statue of the cone cap-wearing designer inside the temple complex. This is one of two White Dagobas in Beijing (the other sits atop Jade Island at Beihai Park) and is the oldest Tibetan dagoba in the city.

Beijing Aquarium

Chinese name: 北京海洋馆 (Běijīng Hǎiyángguǎn)
Admission: ¥130 per person (Beijing Zoo and Panda Hall are included in Aquarium ticket).
Hours: 9:00-17:30 (Apr-Oct); 10:00-16:30 (Nov-Mar)
Recommended time for visit: 1-2 hours
Website: www.bj-sea.com (in Chinese)
Address: Near the north gate of Beijing Zoo (动物园北门内)
Transport: Subway – Line 4, Dongwuyuan (动物园) Station, Exit A

The Beijing Aquarium is actually part of the Beijing Zoo (pg 161) and by many standards is by far the best part of the fairly dubious zoo. It is the largest and most state-of-the-art aquarium in China, and it usually delivers a standout show. Well maintained, clean, and featuring a good variety of sea life, it can be a strong choice for those traveling with children. The conch shaped building is comprised of six exhibition halls: **Rainforest Wonder** (Yǔlín Qíguān; 雨林奇观), with over 100 species of rainforest and freshwater fish in an Amazonian habitat; **Shark Hall** (Shāyú Guǎn; 鲨鱼馆), displaying plenty of interest for the shark lover (including great whites); **Whale and Dolphin Bay** (Jīngtún Wān; 鲸豚湾), showcasing a fine display of marine mammals; **Seabed Travel** (Hǎidǐ Huányóu; 海底环游), an enthralling and well executed underwater glass tunnel that gives you a mollusk's eye view of sea life (sharks here as well); the oddly named **Feel Pool** (Chùmō Chí; 触摸池), giving you a chance to touch some of the more sensitive sea life (such as starfish and turtles); and **Ocean Theater** (Hǎiyáng Jùyuàn; 海洋剧院), featuring the brainier mammals (i.e. sea lions and dolphins) in lively shows set against a less-than-campy Hawaiian backdrop. Admission to the Beijing Zoo and Panda Hall is included in the Aquarium admission.

Other Attractions

Beijing Capital Museum

Chinese name: 首都博物馆 (Shǒudū Bówùguǎn)
Admission: FREE, but visitors need to book the ticket at least a day in advance. (English reservation website: www.capitalmuseum.org.cn/en/reservation.htm)
Hours: 9:00-17:00; closed Mon
Recommended time for visit: 2-3 hour
Website: www.capitalmuseum.org.cn/en (in English)
Address: 16 Fuxingmen Waidajie, Xicheng District (西城区复兴门外大街 16 号)
Transport: Subway – Line 1, Muxidi (木樨地) Station, southeast exit, walk 200 m (656 ft) to the museum

The state-of-the-art Capital Museum matches its compelling exterior design with equally engrossing and well displayed galleries of magnificent relics unearthed from Beijing and around Asia. The museum was first built in 1981, but moved to its present location in 2006 when the Confucian Temple proved too dainty for its expanding collection. Only a fraction of the more than 200,000 relics are on display, but it's still possible to pass several hours here and only glimpse a portion of the brilliance. Included in the viewable collections are hypnotic ancient Buddhist statues, sumptuous Chinese porcelain, and beautiful jade carvings and statues. The museum also pays particular attention to the city of Beijing with a chronological history, an exhibition of Peking Opera relics, and a display of Beijing Folk Customs.

This is one of China's best museums, it's definitely worth a visit.

Nearby sights

White Cloud Temple (pg 153) – 700 m (2,296 ft) southwest

Beijing Museum of Natural History

Chinese name: 北京自然博物馆 (Běijīng Zìrán Bówùguǎn)
Admission: FREE (but visitors need to book a ticket at least one day in advance)
Booking: 6702 4431; 6702 0733
Hours: 9:00-17:00; closed Mon
Recommended time for visit: 2 hours
Website: www.bmnh.org.cn (English available)
Address: 126 Tianqiao Nandajie, Dongcheng District (东城区天桥南大街126号)
Transport: Bus – 2, 6, 7, 15, 17, 20, 34, 35, 36, 59, 110, 120, 707, 729, 742, 743, 744, 803, 819, 822, 826, 859, 105, 106 to Tianqiao (天桥) Stop

The staunch brickwork of the Beijing Natural History Museum presents a world of fossils, insects and overworked natural theories throughout China's non-human prehistory. A vast spread of scientific media is covered within the walls, with everything from paleontology and anthropology to botany and zoology, making this 1959 creation the first and most comprehensive of its kind in China.

The first of the large permanent exhibits is the formidable **Gallery of Ancient Reptiles and Dinosaurs** (Gǔ Páxíng Dòngwù Tīng; 古爬行动物厅). Here you can learn about the dinosaurs of the Chinese subcontinent and how to combine Latin and Chinese to make goofy scientific fossil names. Check out the *Lufengosauras huenei young*, the first dinosaur fossil discovered by Chinese scientists, and don't miss the hulking skeleton of the largest sauropod fossil in China, the *Mamenchisauras jingyanensis*.

Warm blooded distant cousins can be found in the prolific **Gallery of Ancient Mammals** (Gǔ Bǔrǔ Dòngwù Tīng; 古哺乳动物厅), ranked second in the world, along with the most complete stegadon (a giant prehistoric elephant) skeleton in the world: the *Stegadon zdanskyi*. Entomologists can get their fill of six legged creepers at the Insect World, part of the large **Gallery of Animals** (Dòngwù Zhǎntīng; 动物展厅). Darwinists and those with a taste for evolutionary posits are encouraged to tour the **comprehensive Origin of Life Gallery** (Shēngmìng Qǐyuán Zhǎntīng; 生命起源展厅).

Apart from the permanent exhibitions, a number of temporary exhibits flow through the museum several times a year. There is also a very popular 4D theater, featuring six different educational films, 3D glasses, and raucous chair movements.

Nearby sights

Temple of Heaven (pg 78) – 200 m (656 ft) east
Temple of Agriculture (pg 85) – 800 m (2,624) west

Beijing Planetarium

Chinese name: 北京天文馆 (Běijīng Tiānwén Guǎn)
Admission: ¥10
Hours: 9:30-15:30 (Wed-Fri); 9:30-16:30 (weekends); closed Mon & Tue.
Recommended time for visit: 1-2 hours
Website: www.bjp.org.cn/en
Address: 138 Xizhimen Waidajie, Xicheng District (西城区西直门外大街138号)
Transport: Subway – Line 4, Beijing Zoo (动物园) Station, Exit D, walk west for about 200 m (656 ft)

The Beijing Planetarium is good for a short visit with the kids, but don't expect any groundbreaking astronomical revelations. The biggest reason for this is that the vast majority of the information here is captioned only in Chinese. Two buildings comprise the complex: Building A features the Celestial Theater and east/west exhibition halls; Building B houses several more exhibition halls, the Digital Space Theater (Yǔzhòu Jùchǎng; 宇宙剧场), and the 3D and 4D Theaters. Most of the worthwhile exhibits can be seen on the ground floor of Building B, which is generally divided into sections of the solar system and, while some are not bad, there is no English and non-Chinese speakers will fall short of comprehension.

Upstairs are the theaters, whose showings can be hit or miss as far as entertainment value goes, but again there's no English. The 3D shows are generally better than the 4D shows, which can be more of an experiment in how much prodding and poking your back can take from the 4D "effects" than anything else. Kids often get a kick out of the 3D shows and the neighboring interactivity of the Game Zone media consoles, but they can also lose interest quickly due to the lack of English. Building A has more comprehensive English captions and legends, however it occupies a much smaller area and is sometimes host to seemingly irrelevant art exhibitions.

Tickets are sold in an office separate from the entrance, towards the left as you approach. Admission to the exhibition halls is an easy ¥10 per head, with children under 1.2 m (3 ft 9 in) free, but does not include the cinematic experiences, which cost around ¥40.

Nearby sights

Beijing Zoo and Aquarium (pg 161) – across Xizhimen Waidajie, 500 m (1,640 ft) east
Five Pagoda Temple (pg 143) – 860 m (2,821 ft) north

Beijing Wildlife Park

Chinese name: 北京野生动物园 (Běijīng Yěshēng Dòngwùyuán)
Admission: ¥80
Hours: 8:30-17:00
Recommended time for visit: half a day, but 1.5 hours from the city center by car.
Website: www.bjwildlifepark.com (in Chinese)
Address: Donghulin, Yufa Town, Daxing District (大兴区榆垡镇)
Transport:
Bus – 943 or 828 to Donghulin (东胡林) bus station, then walk 500 m (1,640 ft) to the east
Taxi – ¥150 from city center, 1.5 hours

If you have kids who are dying for some animal encounters and the Beijing Zoo just won't cut it, you may consider the 50 km (31 mi) long trek north to the Beijing Wildlife Park. There is a zoo-like area with animals in less dismal pens than at the city zoo, but their care and management is hardly better and possibly worse at times.

A safari ride is available through a large sectioned park area, and you can fork over the extra ¥10 for a more open mesh cage on the back of a pickup. Animal viewing is rushed here, with the drivers seeming to care more about being leader of the pack, while the in-coach guides offer little as far as passenger support. You need to dish out more money for veggies to feed the animals, but there is so little time to feed them before moving on that you may as well eat the produce yourself. (On second thought, don't do that...).

Be prepared as well to be carted along destinations that will entice your kids with kiddie rides or photo ops with snakes, which will require you to throw out more cash. The park is there for the animal lover to try, but don't set your sights too high – you're probably better off spending your money lobbying for better conditions at the Beijing Zoo.

Beijing World Park

Chinese name: 世界公园 (Shìjiè Gōngyuán)
Admission: ¥100 (Apr 20-Oct 31); ¥65 (Nov 1-Apr 19)
Hours: 8:00-16:30
Recommended time for visit: half a day
Address: 158 Fengbao Lu, Huaxiang, Fengtai District (丰台区花乡丰葆路 158 号)
Transport: Bus – 969, 959, 967, 981, 840, 913, 451, 477, 692, 480 to Shijie Gongyuan (世界公园) Stop

It is hard to imagine that many world travelers would be interested in a large theme park built entirely of models of the world's great sights, but this massive tourist trap in Beijing's southwestern Fengtai District pulls in an estimated 1.5 million visitors a year. Seriously.

Somewhere between Las Vegas without the smut and Epcot with less tact (believe it or not), Beijing World Park sounds all the tacky tourist-trap warning bells at once: over-priced entrance fee, zero history or authenticity, souvenir hawkers and a gratuitous display of campy models built for nothing else but cheesy photo ops. That being said, for those on a long stay in Beijing and in need of something very atypical and with smaller crowds, or those with a good sense of humor who enjoy overpriced kitsch, gag photos and the spectacle of Chinese wedding photos taken in tasteless locales, Beijing World Park will deliver. Around 50 countries and regions are represented in 109 fairly detailed models at the gaudy theme park, and there are performances and cultural demonstrations by actual expats who take the "performing monkey" archetype to the next level. Good for a laugh if you have ¥100 to blow or for the expats who have seen it all, but we wouldn't recommend it for short stays.

Beijing Zoo

Chinese name: 北京动物园 (Běijīng Dòngwùyuán)
Admission: Excluding the Panda House – ¥15 (Apr-Oct); ¥10 (Nov-Mar); including the Panda House – ¥20 (Apr-Oct); ¥15 (Nov-Mar)
Hours: 7:30-17:00 (Nov-Mar); 7:30-18:00 (Apr-Oct)
Recommended time for visit: 2-3 hours
Website: www.beijingzoo.com (in Chinese)
Address: 137 Xizhimen Waidajie, Xicheng District (西城区西直门外大街137号)
Transport: Subway – Line 4, Beijing Zoo (动物园) Station, Exit A, look for the south gate (point out the Chinese name to a local if you need help)

The 90-year history of the Beijing Zoo is showcased in its relaxing, well landscaped trees and gardens, reminding visitors that the area is a former imperial garden. It can be a great place for a relaxing stroll around the willowy lakes and shaded pathways, and will certainly top the list of those traveling with children. The zoo was the first of its kind in China, and though it doesn't quite stand up to the lush retreat in Shanghai, it does house over 450 different species of animals, including American bison, kangaroos and African animals. The 16 exhibition halls and areas are fairly diverse, but the meager pens and lackluster living conditions of the animals is a major deterrent for many. The Panda House does pick up the slack a bit, with large and clean living areas for China's prized mascots, though visitor reviews of this area are often mixed. Easily the best-kept and most conscientiously planned part of the Beijing Zoo is the high quality aquarium (pg 155). Buying a ticket for the Beijing Aquarium will grant admission to the Zoo and the Panda Hall.

Nearby sights

Beijing Planetarium (pg 158) – across Xizhimen Waidajie, 500 m (1,640 ft) east
Five Pagoda Temple (pg 143) – 800 m (2,624 ft) north

CCTV Building

Chinese name: 央视大楼 (Yāngshì Dàlóu)
Admission: Not open for tourists
Address: East 3rd Ring Middle Rd, Chaoyang District (朝阳区东三环中路)
Transport: Subway – Line 10, Jintaixizhao (金台夕照) Station, Exit C

What Beijingers banteringly refer to as Dàkùchǎ (大裤衩), or "Big Underpants," the unmistakable building of the CCTV (China Central Television) headquarters is comprised of two towers connected by a seemingly impossible overhang that together looks like a squatting pair of pants. The building is an architectural marvel, built by Dutch architects Rem Koolhaas and Ole Scheeren from the Rotterdam based OMA. The overhang – the gravity-defying buttocks of the pants – utilizes a unique architectural technique where two separate buildings with cantilever overhangs connect together, supported by a loop base of six horizontal and vertical sections. For those not into architecture, it's a fancy way to connect two buildings that look like they should fall over without them actually falling over (yet). Rem Koolhaas and Scheeren's one-of-a-kind creation is occasionally the butt of some jokes, but it is no doubt one of the most noteworthy and impressive buildings in Beijing's skyline.

"Ass" if the tushy-shaped building wasn't "fanny" enough, the building was the site of a February 2008 fire famously started by CCTV's own stray fireworks during Lantern Festival. China Central News coverage completely ignored the blaze, which severely damaged the Beijing Mandarin Hotel, reducing the visitor center and a theater to ashes. When the Big Underpants escaped unscathed, Chinese netizens quickly remarked on how the biggest news story of the night was left untouched by the broadcasters who lit the fire. What a "bum"-mer.

China Aviation Museum

Chinese name: 航空博物馆 (Hángkōng Bówùguǎn)
Admission: ¥20 for the Cavern Exhibition Hall and ¥20 for the Integrated Hall
Hours: 8:30-17:30; closed Mon
Recommended time for visit: 1-2 hours to visit, 1.5 hours from the city center by bus.
Website: www.chn-am.com (in Chinese)
Address: Foot of Xiaotang Mountain, Changping District (昌平区小汤山下)
Transport:
Bus – 945 or 643 to Hangkong Bowuguan (航空博物馆) Stop
Taxi – ¥150 from city center, 1.5 hours

Out in Beijing's northeastern Changping District, the Chinese Aviation Museum is best tackled by military buffs, gear heads or those with a penchant for marching around giant yards of technology. The complex is massive, and if you are not particularly interested in aviation technology or rocket mounted explosive devices, you may find exploring this sprawling zone a bit trying.

Formerly part of Shahe Airbase, the museum greets visitors with a white, single-seat light fighter, appearing to be in flight, mounted on a cloud-white pillar. To the south of the entrance is the massive **Cavern Exhibition Hall** (Dòngkù Zhǎntīng; 洞库展厅), a daunting 20,000 sq m (215,275 sq ft) former bunker displaying military aircraft and high-altitude fighters, including those from China, the former Soviet Union, Japan, and a plethora of Western countries. North of the entrance is the **Open Air Exhibition Area**, featuring more fighters, important figure transports, helicopters, and cargo transportation crafts. The **Integrated Hall** (Zōnghé Zhǎnguǎn; 综合展馆), as the name implies, integrates civilian, military and archaic aviation technology and is the most diverse area in the complex – "diverse" being used very loosely here. More than 200 pieces of aviation relics are on display, and there are activities, such as air steam gun firing and a flight simulator.

The Cavern Hall and Integrated Hall are ¥20 each, and some of the smaller aircraft, such as the Orbis flying hospital airplane or Mao's airplane, are an extra ¥5 to enter.

Other Attractions

163

China Red Sandalwood Museum

Chinese name: 中国紫檀博物馆 (Zhōngguó Zǐtán Bówùguǎn)
Admission: ¥50
Hours: 9: 00-17: 00; closed Mon
Recommended time for visit: 1-2 hours
Website: www.redsandalwood.com (in Chinese)
Address: 23 Jianguo Lu, Chaoyang District (朝阳区建国路23号)
Transport: Subway – Batong Line, Gaobeidian (高碑店) Station, Exit A, walk 400 m west

The Red Sandalwood Museum has on display over 1,000 pieces of exquisite wood carvings, furniture, sculptures and wood paintings in an equally beautiful 25,000 sq m (296,097 sq ft) building. Most of the furniture pieces are modern creations, but that does little to diminish the stunning poise of the 3 m- (10 ft)-tall scale **model of the Forbidden City tower** or the awesome 320 dragons (all in a different pose) from Shanxi's Longquan Temple. Nearly all of the hand crafted pieces are made from the rare and perfectly hard red sandalwood, but there are also breathtaking pieces of rich Bengalese ebony and tropical mahogany. Also on display are fantastic models of the Beijing quadrangles and the Feiyun building in Shanxi Province. If the pieces themselves are not impressive enough for you, keep in mind that every piece in the massive collection was done without a single nail or screw.

Owned by the famous Chen Lihua (陈丽华), the China Red Sandalwood Museum strikes a second claim to fame through its association to Mrs Chen, who once was the wealthiest woman in Mainland China. Chen was in the national spotlight on many occasions, once being labeled somewhat eccentric for her marriage to Chinese actor Chi Zhongrui (迟重瑞), who is 11 years her junior (it is very rare for women to marry a man so much younger in China). Chi is one of the most famous actors in China, having played the role of Tang Monk (唐僧) in the wildly popular TV series "Journey to the West" (西游记). If you're up for it, pay a visit to Chen's Beijing club, the **Chang'an Club** (长安俱乐部), one of the top four clubs in the city. Chen, who now lives in Hong Kong, runs the club with her son from her previous marriage (before Chi).

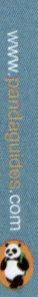

Chinese Ethnic Culture Park

Chinese name: 中华民族园 (Zhōnghuá Mínzú Yuán)
Admission: ¥90 (Through Ticket); ¥60 (South Park), ¥60 (North Park)
Hours: 8:30-18:00
Recommended time for visit: 2 hours
Website: www.emuseum.org.cn/en
Address: 1 Minzuyuan Lu, Chaoyang District (朝阳区民族园路1号)
Transport:
Subway -
1. Line 8, Olympic Sports Center Station (奥体中心), Exit D
2. Line 10, Beitucheng (北土城) Station, Exit A (northwest exit)

China is home to a wonderful variety of 56 different ethnic groups, and if you don't have time to travel the country experiencing each of them, you can head to Ethnic Culture Park to see 40 of them partitioned off in their own little "habitats." The park's original English translation for its name read "Racist Park," and though their error was pointed out and quickly changed, it can be hard to shake the exploitative nature of the park, let alone its propaganda. A bit like a human zoo, the park is sectioned off into ethnic pods where the different cultures present authentic indigenous representatives, all of whom are dressed in their native clothing. You can catch colorful singing and dancing performances, festivals, arts and crafts and an array of other semi-educational activities. Several ethnic groups grow traditional crops, such as paddy rice or buckwheat, and each day Tibetan lamas from the Tar Monastery of Qinghai chant Buddhist sutras. When here, make sure to try the Tibetan Zang people's butter tea and don't forget to look at some of the more than 100,000 authentic cultural relics on display. The best time for a visit is between April and November since the winter weather is too cold for the park's mostly outdoor activities.

Nearby sights

National Aquatics Center (pg 129) – 500 m (1,640 ft) north

Just a few of the festivals & activities

1. Tibetan Shoton Festival (藏族)
2. The New-rice Festival of the Va (佤族)
3. The Sowing Festival of the Va (佤族)
4. The Sanduo Festival of the Naxi (纳西族)
5. The Munao Singing Festival of the Jingpo (景颇族)
6. The Water-splashing Festival of the Dai (傣族)
7. The Huaer Fair of the Tu (土族)
8. The Sheba Festival of Tujia (土家族)
9. The Knife-shaft Festival of Miao (苗族)
10. The Horse Milk Festival (蒙古族)
11. The Pepper Festival of the Salar (撒拉族)
12. Raoshanlin Singing Festival of the Bai (白族)
13. The Fashion Show of the Yi (彝族)

Grand View Garden

Chinese name: 大观园 (Dàguān Yuán)
Admission: ¥40; ¥70 (night show)
Hours: 7:30-16:30
Recommended time for visit: 2 hours
Address: 88 Nancaiyuan Jie, Xicheng District (西城区南菜园街88号)
Transport:
Bus -
1. 53, 59, 63, 84, 122, 458, 474, 717 to Daguanyuan (大观园) Stop
2. 56 or 423 to Daguanyuan Ximen (大观园西门) Stop.

The fairyland garden of the famous Cáo Xuěqín (曹雪芹) novel, *Dream of the Red Chamber* (Hónglóu Mèng; 红楼梦) was faithfully recreated in 1989 for CCTV's television adaptation of the book. Blending a combination of natural scenery and manmade features into a rather harmonious whole, the large 13 hectare (32 acre) garden features more than 40 scenic spots, and many of the book's and Jia family members' chambers are represented. If you loved Cao Xueqin's prolix novel then you'll probably explode when you see this place. If you didn't flip over the wordy classic you might still appreciate the classical architectural style of the pavilions, palatial buildings, courtyards, rockery fountains and nunnery. There are even animals here.

Catch a glimpse into the ancient culture of China in which *Dream of the Red Chamber* is set with a visit to the garden's relatively lavish **Beijing Red Mansion Culture and Art Museum**. Displays on the cultural period of *Red Chamber* can be found here, as well as performances depicting life during the time of the Jia family. The garden also features the Grand View Garden Restaurant, a high-end establishment with very tasty dishes.

Happy Valley Amusement Park

Chinese name: 欢乐谷 (Huānlè Gǔ)
Admission: ¥200
Hours: 9:00-18:30 (night show: 18:30-22:00)
Recommended time for visit: half a day.
Website: bj.happyvalley.cn (in Chinese)
Phone: 6738 3333
Address: Southeast corner of Sifang Bridge, East 4th Ring Rd, Chaoyang District (朝阳区东四环四方桥东南角)
Transport:
Subway – Line 1, Dawanglu (大望路) Station, Exit A, cross to the north side of Dawang Qiao (大望桥) and take bus 31 to Houfengqiao Nan (厚俸桥南) Stop, then walk 10 minutes to the park
Bus – 31 or 41 to Houfengqiao Nan Stop

Get your buzz on with the fast-paced, twisting, turning, speeding, jerking, all around adrenaline pumping rides that fill this American-style amusement park in southeastern Beijing. With six themed parks, such as the ancient Greek Aegean Harbor and the Central American Lost Maya, and covering an area of 560,000 sq m (6 million sq ft), the dizzying reminiscence of Disney or Six Flags that is found at Happy Valley is well suited for extreme families with extreme children. Many of the roller coasters are on par with some of the most famous in the West, and though the different themed areas are ludicrous and artificial, if you need a mindless day of childishness or a high-speed rush, this is your place. Be aware that although the lines often move quickly, they can be so long that a trip on the weekends is often not worth your time. Height restrictions are also strictly enforced, so if you've got a little one in your group you may be limited to kiddy rides.

October and November, as well as March and April, see some high winds, and coasters will be closed if the park's management feels the weather is too harsh. April to October has great weather for the park, but also the most crowds. The park hosts many festivals that are complete with riotous performances on a large, well-outfitted stage. Everything in Happy Valley is captioned in English, and maps are available inside.

Nearby sights

Panjiayuan Antique Market (pg 256) – 4 km (2.5 mi) west

Military Museum

Chinese name: 中国人民革命军事博物馆 (Zhōngguó Rénmín Gémìng Jūnshì Bówùguǎn)
Admission: FREE (passport required to enter)
Hours: 8:30 – 17:30; closed Mon
Recommended time for visit: 2 hours
Website: eng.jb.mil.cn
Address: 9 Fuxing Lu, Haidian District (海淀区复兴路9号)
Transport: Subway – Line 1, Military Museum (军事博物馆) Station

An armor-plated, bullet-tipped campaign through the communist wars of past, present, and future (you didn't know the CCP can see the future?) awaits those willing to storm their way down to the Military Museum of the People's Revolution. Constructed in 1959 as a tenth anniversary commemoration of the founding of the People's Republic, the Soviet-style behemoth is topped with the starred Guild Badge of the Chinese Army and greets guests with a bronze gate fashioned out of magazine cartridges. Intense.

Inside, the cavernous **Hall of Weapons** on the first floor briefs guests on a massive array of – you got it – weapons; including small arms, artillery weapons, tanks, APCs, missiles and others that have been either used by the Chinese Army or bought or confiscated from foreign armies. Vehicles for the Chinese space program are also on display in this main hall.

There are nine halls in all, each of them bristling with all manner of weaponry, fighter jets and armored vehicles, as well as swords, armor and 5,000 years of Chinese military history in the **Hall of Ancient Wars**. For a particularly revolutionary blitz of communist wars, make your ingress to the **Hall of the Agrarian Revolutionary War**, featuring an eyebrow-raising version of the wars against the feudal land system from 1927-1937, and the **Hall of the War to Resist US Aggression and Aid Korea**, full of Red rhetoric on the Korean War from 1951-1953. This hall is very similar to the same museum in North Korea.

The museum is closed on Mondays. Passports are required for entry. There is a limit of 30,000 guests per day, so those that are set on a visit should plan to get here early.

Workers' Cultural Palace

Chinese name: 劳动人民文化宫 (Láodòng Rénmín Wénhuàgōng)
Admission: ¥2
Hours: 6:00-22:00 (Jun-Oct); 6:30-21:00 (Nov-May)
Recommended time for visit: 1-2 hours
Website: www.bjwhg.com.cn (English available)
Address: East of Tian'anmen, Dongcheng District (东城区天安门东侧)
Transport: Subway – Line 1, Tian'anmen East (天安门东) Station

The Workers' Cultural Palace was originally known by the slightly more imaginative name of the Royal Ancestral Temple (Tài Miào; 太庙) and is one of the best less-traveled destinations in the city. Considered an offshoot of the original Forbidden City, the sacrificial grounds turned park is an excellent alternative for those turned off by the crowds, craziness, or sheer size of the Forbidden City. And at a cool ¥2 entrance fee, what more could you ask for?

Back in the day, the Royal Ancestral Temple was used for sacrifices to the ancestors of the emperor. This was done under the yellow-tiled roof of the **Hall of Ancestral Worship** (also known by its even more exciting name: the Front Hall), which has a plaque above the entryway that reads in Mandarin and Manchu. Behind the Front Hall is the **Resting Hall** (or Middle Hall), decorated with beds, pillows, chairs, desks, and other daily house-wares for ancestors to use in heaven. Apparently, the biggest joke on the Chinese dead is that this stuff is unavailable in the afterlife. The biggest joke on travelers is that the Resting Hall was not open to visitors at the time of this book's research.

Nonetheless, you can check out the **Halberd Gate** (Jǐ Mén; 戟门) on the third wall, which is the only significant relic in the palace that has not been altered or restored, and you should also swing by the seven **single-arched stone bridges** spanning the placid Golden River (Jīnshuǐ Hé; 金水河). Finally, if you've always dreamed of playing tennis in some ancient Chinese palace (who hasn't?) then this is your chance! The onsite **tennis court** (¥20 per hour) allows guests to brush up on their backhand in the shadow of the Forbidden City.

Nearby sights

Tian'anmen Square (pg 86) – less than 1 km west
National Museum (pg 86) – at Tian'anmen Square
Great Hall of the People (pg 86) – at Tian'anmen Square

Beijing Botanical Gardens

Chinese name: 北京植物园 (Běijīng Zhíwùyuán)
Admission: ¥10
Hours: 6:00-20:00 (summer); 7:30-17:00 (winter)
Recommended time for visit: 3 hours to visit; 1 hour travel time from the city center by bus.
Website: en.beijingbg.com (in English)
Address: Wofosi Lu, Xiangshan, Haidian District (海淀区香山卧佛寺路)
Transport:
Subway & Bus –
 1. Line 2 or Line 13, Xizhimen (西直门) Station, Exit D, transfer to bus 563, get off at Beijing Zhiwuyuan Namen (北京植物园南门) Stop
 2. Line 4, Beigongmen (北宫门) Station, transfer to bus 331, 696 or 563, get off at Beijing Zhiwuyuan Namen (北京植物园南门) Stop

Taxi – ¥90 from city center, about 1 hour

Beating the socks off the Beijing Zoo and the Wild Animal Park, the Beijing Botanical Gardens is superbly maintained and bursting at the seams with beauty during its springtime blossom. Planted at the base of the scenic Western Hills 22 km (14 mi) from the city center, it is positioned perfectly for a visit following a safari at Fragrant Hills Park, which lies a short kilometer to the southwest.

In 1956 the Botanical Gardens was audaciously conceived to include around 4 million sq m of space. That didn't quite work out. Today, its more realistic size of 2 million sq m (21,500,00 sq ft) is still no small feat, so head on down to pass a few relaxing hours walking among the shady trees, bamboo thickets, pines, orchids and lilacs of the most extensive plant collection in China (over 6,000 species of plants). It really is a sublime experience.

The gardens are also home to the largest display greenhouse in Asia: the 9,800 sq m (105,486 sq ft) **Botanical Gardens Conservatory**, which displays four different ecosystem galleries and boasts 3,100 varieties of plants. Particular standouts of the conservatory are the Tropical Rainforest Area and the Desert Plains. Visit the Gardens between April and October for the most excellent stretch of the blossoming season.

Inside the Botanical Gardens grounds is the **Temple of the Recumbent Buddha** (pg 151), which shows off a massive statue of Sakyamuni Buddha kicking back just before reaching nirvana. Out east of the gardens you can find the **Cao Xueqin Memorial**, dedicated to the man who penned *Dream of the Red Chamber* and *The Story of Stone*; the former is considered far and wide as one of the Four Great Chinese Novels.

Nearby sights

Temple of Azure Clouds (pg 148) – 1 km (0.6 mi) west
Fragrant Hills Park (pg 172) – 1 km (0.6 mi) southwest

Chaoyang Park

Chinese name: 朝阳公园 (Cháoyáng Gōngyuán)
Admission: ¥5
Hours: 6:00-22:00 (Mar 15-Nov 14); 6:00-21:00 (Nov 15-Mar 14)
Recommended time for visit: 1 hour
Website: www.sun-park.com (in Chinese)
Address: 1 Chaoyang Gongyuan Nanlu, Chaoyang District (朝阳区朝阳公园南路1号)
Transport: Subway – Line 10, Tuanjiehu (团结湖) Station, Exit C, walk 20 minutes to the south gate of Chaoyang Lake

Beijing's largest park (3 km X 1.5 km; 1.7 mi X 1 mi) caters strongly to the recreational bug inside the thousands of tourists who visit each day. Though the majority of the land is lush green space, more than 20 play areas await those looking for a less history-oriented day out. You can cause a ruckus on the roller coaster in the park's fairgrounds or dive into one of several large open-air swimming pools. Spiking in the western perimeter is the reconstructed 2008 Olympics beach volleyball venue, which now serves as a **bathing beach** and swimming area for 3,000 visitors a day (don't drink the water). You can also relax at the wooden pavilions, sculptures and large open meadow at **Binshui Island** (Bīnshuǐ Zhīzhōu, 滨水之洲) on the edge of **Lotus Lake** (Liánhuā Hú; 莲花湖).

In summertime, check out the **Art Square**, which features fine art sculptures and yodel-worthy Austrian landscapes.

If you're hankering for some upscale shopping, head to the Blue Harbor in the northwest and join the shoppers around the **Solana Shopping Center** (Lánsè Gǎngwān; 蓝色港湾; pg 260). Just across Chaoyang Lu from Solana you can find a litter of swanky international restaurants, cafes and bars.

April to October is a great time for a flower-filled visit, but those who visit Beijing in the fall should look out for the **Pop Music Festival**, which dances its way into Chaoyang Park every September. Many other festivals and exhibitions are held here, so keep your ear to the ground for those that might be coming up during your visit. The festival during Chinese New Year (late January or February) always shows visitors a good time. Bikes and boats are available for rent to cruise around the large park grounds and lakes.

Nearby sights

Sanlitun Bar Street (pg 243) – 2 km (1 mi) west

Fragrant Hills Park

Chinese name: 香山公园 (Xiāngshān Gōngyuán)
Admission: ¥10 (Apr 1-Nov 15); ¥5 (Nov 16-Mar 31); ¥50 for cable car ticket
Hours: 6:00-18:30 (Apr 1-June 30); 6:00-19:00 (July 1-Aug 31); 6:00-18:30 (Sept 1-Nov 15); 6:00-18:00 (Nov 16-Mar 31)
Recommended time for visit: half a day; prepare for 1 hour travel from the city center by car.
Website: www.xiangshanpark.com/en
Address: 40 Maimai Jie, Haidian District (海淀区买卖街40号)
Transport:
Subway – Line 4, Beigongmen (北宫门) Station, Exit A, transfer to bus 331 or 696 to Xiangshan (香山) Stop
Bus – 563, 318, 714, 698, 331, 360, 696, 630 to Xiangshan Stop
Taxi – ¥90 from city center, 1 hour

Like the Summer Palace and the Western Hills, Fragrant Hills Park was also an old imperial summer retreat. In fact, Fragrant Hills Park is the main entrance to the Western Hills, so planning a day to see the park and then hiking the mountains is a solid move.

We highly recommend taking the blood-pumping hike up to the top of the park's **Incense Burner Hill**, which is crowned by two giant stones that resemble incense burners. Here you can enjoy sweeping panoramic views of the rolling mountains and the city to the east, and there is also a cable car (¥50 one way; ¥100 round trip) if your legs aren't up to the task. Legions of locals scramble to the top in autumn to enjoy the changing leaves, which explode across the mountainsides in great patches of red, orange and gold. If you come in the fall you may want to join them. The flower gardens around the base of the hill are outstanding in summer.

Before or after hiking to the top, get a load of the fantastic Yuan Dynasty creation – the **Temple of Azure Clouds** (pg 148), located just inside the front entrance. The area also includes the **Sun Yat-sen Memorial Hall** and the magnificent Indian designed **Vajra Throne Pagoda**. Just to the southwest of the Temple of Azure Clouds is the **Temple of Brilliance**, a Tibetan-style hall with a beautiful neighboring glazed-tile pagoda. It's brilliant.

Keep in mind that the neighborhood leading up to Fragrant Hills Park is saturated with bargain snacks, cheap restaurants, and – most importantly – cold beer. Few things are better after a sweaty summer hike than a cold beer.

Nearby sights

Botanical Gardens (pg 170) – 1.5 km (1 mi) northeast
Summer Palace (pg 71) – 5 km (3 mi) east

Jingdong Grand Canyon

Chinese name: 京东大峡谷 (Jīngdōng Dàxiágǔ)
Admission: ¥78
Hours: 7:30-17:00
Recommended time for visit: 1 day to visit; around 2 hours by car from city center.
Address: Yuzishan Village, Shandongzhuang Town, Pinggu District (平谷区山东庄镇鱼子山村)
Transport:
Bus – 918 at Dongzhimen Bus Station (meaning Dongzhimen Traffic Hub, not Dongzhimen City Bus Station) to Pinggu Bus Station (¥10, 2 hours), then take local bus 平 12 to the canyon. This local bus leaves every half an hour from 7:00 to 17:30
Taxi – ¥300 from city center, about 2 hours

The perilous peaks and plunging waterfalls at Jingdong Grand Canyon provide some spectacular natural scenery outside a city consumed with development and modernity. At 85 km (53 mi) from downtown, the canyon is a trek-and-a-half (there is a place to stay overnight), and the remoteness is evidenced by the picturesque green hills and remarkably clear water that characterize the area. Climb onto the precariously suspended plank roads above the **Five Dragon Pond** (Wǔlóng Tán; 五龙潭) for an excellent view of their deep green and blue colors.

The selling point of Jingdong Grand Canyon, however, is **Tongtian Gorge** (Tōngtiān Xiá; 通天峡) – a jutting rock wall seemingly smote by the gods, with a spectacular chasm of sheer drops and fantastic views. There are tons of excellent hiking paths around the area, so get your fill.

Those who prefer to save their feet from soreness can use the aerial cable car, which runs 1,000 m (3,281 ft) from end to end, and provides nerve-wrackingly high views of the area. If the thrill of the cable car is not enough, a harebrained **high wire** is available for psychos to climb on and terrify the rest of the visitors. You must wear a safety harness, though.

Boats are available for rent on **Dragon Door Lake** (Lóngmén Hú; 龙门湖), and you can pull your pant legs up and wade in as well. From July to October the gorge hosts a harvest celebration, allowing basket toting visitors to hand pick their own apricots, apples, pears and hawthorns.

The **Holiday Village** provides a comfortable place for guests to stay, which is almost a must, considering the long voyage it takes to arrive in Jingdong.

Longqing Gorge

Chinese name: 龙庆峡 (Lóngqìng Xiá)
Admission: ¥40
Hours: 9:00- 17:00
Recommended time for visit: 1 day; around 2 hours by train or 2-3 hours by car from the city.
Website: www.longqingxia.cn (in Chinese)
Address: Northeast of Yanqing County (延庆县东北处)
Transport:
Bus – 919 from Deshengmen (德 胜 门) to Yanqing County, then change to bus 875; first bus 5:30, last bus 18:00
Train – S2 from Beijing North Station to Yanqing Station, then change to bus 875 or grab a taxi for about ¥40
Taxi – ¥300 from city center, 2-3 hours

If there were a Chinese *Lord of the Rings* the directors would probably film some of it here. The natural beauty of Longqing Gorge is top rated in China, and certainly one of the best natural scenic spots around Beijing.

The Longqing dam first appears upon entering the area as the mountains retreat into a towering canyon filled with monolithic rocks piercing the sky and an immaculate river basin below. Few rivers in China are so pristine, the surface acts as a natural mirror, perfectly reflecting the lush cliff sides and the crisp blue sky above.

Keep your eye out for the garish green and yellow dragon that zigzags up the bluff-side. It's pretty hideous – you can't miss it. It does hide an even more unsightly escalator, but we're still not sure why a mountainside needs an escalator in the first place. From the top of the dragon you can take a tourist boat back down the river for ¥100, with fantastic views from the canyon floor. The boat drops you off at a jetty, and from here you can take a steep hike up stone steps to **Illusion Pavilion** for even more awesome views of the river below. You can also rent a three-person paddleboat at the jetty for ¥50. If the hike or the bluffs don't get your blood running, there is **bungee jumping** and a **zip line** across the river.

Wintertime makes way for an awesome ice festival at the gorge, which showcases dozens of colorfully lit ice sculptures set against the backdrop of the canyon and frozen waterfalls. If you come to Beijing in winter this should be a top consideration, especially if you have kids.

There are restaurants and drink stalls just outside the entrance. Taxis from Beijing are convenient, but the 83 km (53 mi) journey is expensive and can take a long time; your best bet is to grab the S2 train from Beijing North Station (¥6; about 100 minutes; 16 trains daily from 6:00 to 22:36) and then swing a 20 minute taxi from Yanqing station. The last train back is 21:18. Visiting Longqing Gorge is totally rad, but the long trek may be a bit ambitious for some.

Longtanhu Park

Chinese name: 龙潭湖公园 (Lóngtánhú Gōngyuán)
Admission: ¥2
Hours: 6:00-21:00
Recommended time for visit: 1 hour
Address: 8 Longtan Lu, Dongcheng District（东城区龙潭路8号）
Transport:
Bus -
1. 8, 12, 561 to Longtanhu Stop.
2. 6, 8, 12, 60, 116, 352, 650, 684, 958 to Longtan Gongyuan Stop

More than just a local park, Longtanhu Park (or Dragon Pool Park), just east of the Temple of Heaven, is one of the better-kept secrets of downtown Beijing. With its main attraction being the large willow-fringed boating lake, marked by charming covered bridges and pavilion-nestled islands, Dragon Pool Park offers an excellent leafy retreat without the crowds that can plague bigger parks like Jingshan or Beihai. This park is mostly sought by locals, and catching them mid-tai chi session or any of their other endearingly funny morning exercises (like walking backwards and clapping) is a treat all on its own.

The scenery in the park may fall a bit short of the larger attractions, but the lilies, shady trees, and fragrant blossom of flowers in the spring is nothing to scoff at. Also, be sure to swing out to the northeast of the park, where the greenery rears up to a refreshing watery cascade.

You may not be in the market for a new pet bird – understandable – but you should still headover to the park's large outdoor bird market. You'll spot a flock of beautiful birds chirping about, some of them being taught to speak by their owners. Bring the kids down to see them and then tire them out at the small carnival area, replete with kiddie rides, cheap toys, and a bouncy castle.

Can you find the black dragon statue hidden somewhere along the path that snakes through the park? It's actually not hidden, but it is cool and makes for a great reason to cruise the grounds. Explore to find your own little nooks and crannies, and there's even a bungee rig for those who have completely lost it.

Drop by during Chinese New Year for a great temple fair, with loads of snack stalls, singing, dancing and general festival mayhem. The Dragon Boat Festival (usually around early June) hosts Dragon Boat Races on the lake. Ask your hotel or hostel staff if it's going on during your trip. You can hire your own paddleboats or electric boats on normal days for ¥40 per hour and ¥80 per hour, respectively, with a ¥200 deposit. These are four-seaters, but six-seaters are available for ¥120 per hour with a ¥400 deposit.

Phoenix Hill Nature Park

Chinese name: 凤凰岭 (Fènghuáng Lǐng)
Admission: ¥25
Hours: 6:00-18:00 (summer); 6:30-17:30 (winter)
Recommended time for visit: half a day; about 1 hour travel from the city center by car.
Website: www.bjfhl.com/EN
Address: 19 Fenghuangling Lu, Sujiatuo Town, Haidian District (海淀区苏家坨镇凤凰岭路19号)
Transport:
Bus – 346 to the terminal
Taxi – ¥160 about 1 hour from the city center

Essentially a state park, the enormous 15 sq km (6 sq mi) Phoenix Hill Nature Park offers some of the most extensive non-Great Wall hiking in the metro area. You will be mystified by the dozens of once-secluded Buddhist, Taoist, and Confucian sites here that are said to cultivate health and longevity. Set an easy 30 km (18 mi) from the city center, the park is almost as swift to get to as the Summer Palace, and is an excellent alternative to some of the more distant natural scenery, like Longqing Gorge. Lush greenery, limpid water, and clean air characterize this well-conserved ecological area, which is sometimes called "The Lung of Beijing" for its comparatively high air quality.

There are more than 40 scenic spots along Phoenix Hill's three main routes, of which the **north route** has the highest concentration. Along this path you can find lofty bluffs at the Physiognomy of Sea Cliffs, as well as the Buddhist Geyi Nunnery (Gēyī Ān; 揅衣庵), Shangfang Temple (Shàngfāng Sì; 上方寺), Linglong Pagoda (Línglóng Tǎ; 玲珑塔), several hermetic caves, Almighty Fountain (Shén Quán; 神泉), the Taoist-named Yijing Pond (Yíjìng Tán; 怡境潭), and the Golden Dragon Pool (Jīnlóng Quán; 金龙泉).

Follow the **middle route** for a series of four Buddhist and Taoist caves that together make up the largest and most complete health preservation cave group in China. Up this way as well is the Shadow Pavilion (Yǐnliáng Tíng; 荫凉亭), where legend says Taoist Immortals once sat in riveting games of chess.

Shoot out to the **south road** for a visit to the picturesque Che'erying Village (Chē'ěrying Cūn; 车耳营村), full of Beijing folk customs, arts and trades for sale, and delicious local bites and drinks.

Purple Bamboo Garden

Chinese name: 紫竹院公园 (Zǐzhúyuàn Gōngyuán)
Admission: FREE
Hours: 6:00-21:00 (summer); 6:00-20:00 (winter)
Recommended time for visit: 1 hour
Website: www.zizhuyuangongyuan.com/index_en.aspx
Address: 35 Zhongguancun Nandajie, Haidian District (海淀区中关村南大街 35 号)
Transport: Bus – 114, 334, 347, 362, 482, 534, 714, 689, 87, 360, 118, 211, 206, 77, 588 to Zizhuyuan Nanmen (紫竹院南门) Stop

If you're crazy for bamboo, then your head might be knocked right off at the 48 hectare (118.5 acre) Purple Bamboo Garden, where everything from bridges, tables and buildings are composed of and revolve around bamboo. The willowy retreat was once a low-lying wetland (where the Tonghui River flowed) that was excavated by the Yuan Dynasty mathematician and astronomer Guō Shǒujìng (郭守敬). Guo probably didn't see in the stars that the area would be dredged in 1949, with the dirt scooped out for the lakes used to form several small hills on the eastern shores. The garden is now a sanctuary for bamboo lovers of all walks, and cultivates nearly 50 different species of the tall grass shoots.

The three lotus-dotted lakes, pavilion capped islets, and foggy rolling hills are all connected by a system of bridges and corridors, creating an otherworldly feel. The man-made gardens are an excellent example of Chinese landscape design, but the fairy tale atmosphere can feel a bit overstretched at times, with scattered pavilions and corridors holding steadfast to the bamboo theme. Still, the serenity is striking, and the two islands at Blue Lotus Islet and Moon Islet are highly worth a tour.

The latter of the two mounts an elegant two-story pavilion teetering on the waterside – views of the lilied lake from here are superbly vivid. Swing down to the south side of Blue Lotus Islet as well to check out Bayixuan Pavilion, considered by many to be the most scenic spot in the park. There is also an art museum in the park featuring – you guessed it – bamboo!

The best months for scenery are May to September.

Stone Flower Cave

Chinese name: 石花洞 (Shíhuā Dòng)
Admission: ¥70
Hours: 8:00-17:00
Recommended time for visit: several hours; 1.5 hours travel from the city center by car.
Website: www.shihuacave.cn (in Chinese)
Address: Nancheying Village, Hebei Town, Fangshan District (房山区河北镇南车营村)
Transport:
Tourist Bus – From Xuanwumen (Tourism Hub) a bus is available on weekends and holidays from Apr to Oct. Also available on weekends and holidays from early Jun to early Oct is a shuttle bus that leaves every day at 9:00 from Pingguoyuan (苹果园) Station on subway Line 1 and returns at 14:00. A single bus trip costs ¥10.
Bus -
1. 832 from Tianqiao (天 桥) Long Distance Bus Station to Liangxiang Beiguan (良乡北关) Stop, then take bus 833 to Shihuadong Daokou (石花洞道口) Stop; then change to Fangshan (房山) bus 43 to Shihuadong Stop, or hire a local mini van to the cave from Fangshan
2. 836 from Tianqiao Bus Station to Liangxiang Ximen (良乡西门) Stop, change to Fangshan Bus 43 and get off at Shihuadong Stop

Taxi – ¥170 from city center, 1.5 hours

Less popular these days than a decade ago, Stone Flower Cave is a karst cave formation out in the Beijing boondocks. The interior is a bit spooky: eerie stalactites and stalagmites have taken millennia to inch toward the opposing surfaces, while the haunting drip-drop of water steadily echoes through the deep black of the cave.

Karst formations are a dissolution of soluble rock (water has made big holes in the rock), making this particular cave a combination of seven distinct layers, of which three are viewable to the public (sadly the seventh layer subterranean river is not open to visitors). One of the largest caves in China, the first layer is 300 m (984 ft) long and has countless corridors and branch caves. Visitors are guided along by iron railed stairs and spooky lighting.

Check out the **Silver Fox Cave** on the second level, a 1,000 m (3,281 ft) cave with dozens of strange and bewitching sights, including the **Yuènǎi Shí** (月奶石), or milk-white stone, and the **silver fox stone**, upon which crystal deposits look like hundreds of hairs. Flowers can also be found growing in the upper level, a very impressive feat considering the minimal sunlight that penetrates the cave.

The adventurous can take a local bus to the cave, but the more practical route is just to hire a taxi for around ¥150-170.

Taoranting Park

Chinese name: 陶然亭公园 (Táoránting Gōngyuán)
Admission: ¥2
Hours: 6:00-21:00
Recommended time for visit: 1 hours
Website: www.trtpark.com (English option)
Address: 19 Taiping Jie, Xicheng District (西城区太平街19号)
Transport: **Subway** – Line 4, Taoranting (陶 然 亭) Station, Exit C, walk east 650 m (2,132 ft) to the north gate

In Mandarin, Taoranting Park means Joyful Park. So if you've got a Glummy Gus in your group, consider bringing them. If the lush gardens, arboreal byways, multi-eaved pavilions and mini golf course of Joyful Park don't boost their mood, then ditch them and go play in Taoranting's Water Wonderland water park or the Deer Gardens.

In China's days of yore, when Beihai, the Summer Palace and Fragrant Hills Park (among others) were strictly reserved for the too-good-for-everyone-else imperial family, Taoranting was buzzing with Beijing's literati writing, reciting and pounding wine with the local bourgeoisie. In the words of Tang Dynasty poet Bái Jūyì (白 居 易), "Wait till the chrysanthemums are yellow and home-made wine is ripe, [I'll] drink with you [at Taoranting] and be carefree." (Gèngdài júhuáng jiāniàng shú, yǔjūn yīzuì yī Táorán; 更待菊黄家酿熟, 与君一醉一陶然)

These days, people-watching at the garden park is still great fun. Besides practicing tai chi or keeping fit in other ways, locals can be found chatting and playing instruments or Mahjong, often with a raucous slur on their lips and a glass of *baijiu* (Chinese liquor) in hand.

Taoranting's pavilions join those in the cities of Hangzhou, Changsha and Chuzhou as the **Four Famous Historical Pavilions of China**. The park itself houses 36 total pavilions, ten of which are replicas of famous ones from around the Middle Kingdom.

Ten Ferries Scenic Area

Chinese name: 十渡 (Shí Dù)
Admission: Separate admission fees are applied at many of the attractions: Green Wave Resort (¥70), Isolated Stronghold (¥80), Bungee Jumping (¥200), Juma River Drift (¥80), Langya (The Wolf's Teeth) River Drift (¥80), East Lake Port (¥50), West Lake Port (¥32)
Hours: 8:00-18:00
Recommended time for visit: 1 day to visit; 2-3 hours travel from the city center by car
Website: www.shidu.com (in Chinese)
Address: Shidu Town, Fangshan District (房山区十渡镇)
Transport:
Subway – Fangshan Line, Suzhuang (苏 庄) Station, then take bus 917 to Shidu.
Bus – Board bus 836 at Tianqiao (天 桥) Stop or Guang'anmen (广安门) Stop and get off at Shidu. The bus departs from Tianqiao every hour from 6:00 to 17:00.
Train – 6437 leaves from Beijing West Railway Station at 17:45 and arrives at Ten Ferries Station at 20:05 (¥6.5; 2.5 hours); train 6438 returns at 9:58 and gets to West Railway Station at 12:27
Taxi – ¥300 from city center, 2-3 hours

If you're up for a solid adventure to some unbeatable natural scenery, then you might consider the two hour, 54 km (33.5 mi) trip out to the prehistoric karsts of the Ten Ferries Scenic Area. Cutting through the craggy, forested countryside, the valley of the meandering Juma River is an awesome sight as it thunders with enormous, pinnacle-shaped bluffs, relaxing riverside shoals, and ancient caves. It is sure to knock the socks off anyone with a pair of eyes, so be sure to bring extra socks.

Covering an enormous 300 sq km (116 sq mi) and encompassing 21 villages, Shidu is essentially a national park. The name comes from the ten river crossings that dot the Juma – travelers had to cross each one while traveling from the town of Zhangfang to Shidu – and each one is itself a tourist spot with its own entrance and activity prices, as well as local scenic attractions, hiking trails, and other crazy activities.

The assortment of outdoorsy recreation at Ten Ferries is hard to beat in China, and they range from horseback riding to hang-gliding and bamboo kayaking. For a taste of the boundless scenery and enjoyable diversions unique to each of the ten ferry crossings, check out our by-no-means-all-inclusive list here.

Ferry One: Stone Gate Cliffs (Shí Mén; 石门)

Ferry Two: Open river shoal, Five Fingers Mountain (Wǔzhǐ Shān; 五指山), Great Sword Fissure, 1.6 billion-year-old Fairy Habitat Cave

Ferry Three: Southern Grand Canyon, Muke Fortress

Ferry Four: Bathing Beach

Ferry Five: Fairy Peak Valley, horseback riding, tour boats

Ferry Six: Swimming and beaches, Great Wave Resort (water resort), barbeque, yachts

Ferry Seven: Isolated Stronghold, geological demonstrations

Ferry Eight: River Park, Stalagmites Hill, Looking Buddha Temple, bungee jumping

Ferry Nine: Hotels, the water coaster, hang-gliding, kayaking, Biying Water Playground

Ferry Ten: Luoquan Lake, the Tashan Fairy Pool, the Stone Gate, Dragon Mountain, Tiger Mountain

Transportation Tips

Please notice that there are three bus 836's: The first bus 836 goes to Dahanju (大 韩 继), the second bus 836 goes to Zhangfang (张 坊) and the third goes to Shidu (十 渡). Make sure you take the third one. There is a signboard on the left side of the bus' windshield that says "Shidu" in Chinese (十渡).

The Shidu bus 836 runs hourly from 6:00 to 17:00. The 836 from Shidu back to Beijing runs hourly from 7:00 to 17:00. The trip takes over 2 hours.

Board bus 836 on Beiwei Lu (北纬路). Beiwei Lu is an east–west street with its east end starting from Tianqiao Nandajie (天桥南大街), across from the Beijing Museum of Natural History. From here, walk about 400 m (1,312 ft) west and you will find the stop (it has iron railings) where you will board bus 836.

Tuanjiehu Park

Chinese name: 团结湖公园 (Tuánjiéhú Gōngyuán)
Admission: FREE
Hours: 7:00 – 22:00
Recommended time for visit: 1 hour
Website: bj.happyvalley.cn (in Chinese)
Address: 16 Tuanjiehu Nanli, Chaoyang District（朝阳区团结湖南里16号）
Transport: Subway – Line 10, Tuanjiehu（团结湖）Station

Tuanjiehu is a great local park, and those who have a long stay in Beijing or need some less touristy family activities can find plenty of quality R&R time here. The park itself is well maintained and the entire flora is lush and vibrant. Bring the kids or a date to the **roller skating rink**, or wander over to the **beach** for some water-park action, complete with a wave pool, a play ship and water slides. People-watching is unique here and borders on the line of sociological experiment at the unofficial **sunbathing area** (across from entrance) – muscular men in skimpy trunks and tattooed tanning women put on a smirk-inducing display of modern China. Families can catch some more wholesome fun around the lounging pool, while swimmers can get in some laps at the lap pool (though if your hotel has one it may be a better option than this one). Those looking for traditional beach action can smack the ball around at the volleyball court, though it's certainly seen better days. Good *kao rou* (roast meat) can be found here and there are free lockers.

Other Attractions

Western Hills National Forest Park

Chinese name: 西山公园 (Xīshān Gōngyuán)
Admission: ¥10
Hours: 7:00-18:00 (Mar 15-Nov 15); 8:00-17:00 (Nov 16-Mar 14)
Recommended time for visit: 3-4 hours
Website: www.kmxishan.com (in Chinese)
Address: 6 Hanhe Lu, Xiangshan Mountain, Haidian District (海淀区旱河路6号)
Transport: Bus – 505, 318, 360 Express, 714, 698, 360, 630 to Nanhetan (南河滩) Stop, walk west 200 m (656 ft)

Engulfed in a sea of maple, oaks and ancient cypress trees, the Western Hills National Forest Park bears an alluring taste of Beijing's natural beauty without costing half a day in travel. The park is rich with natural and historical points of interest, and cliffs, caves, river gorges and hot springs, as well as temples, historic homes, secluded retreats and ancient ruins, await the hike-hungry. The hills are perfect for those jaded with the clamor of the inner city, and the close vicinity of the Beijing Botanical Gardens (pg 170) and the Temple of Azure Clouds (pg 148) makes them a solid contender for a fulfilling daytrip.

Seasonality is a big feature of the 60 sq km (23 sq mi) national park: fragrant peach and apricot trees burst into bloom during the spring, great splashes of red and orange maple leaves saturate the autumn hillsides, and a sweeping blanket of snow quiets the park in the winter. Summer days here can be sultry, but the sweet smell of an ocean of awakening floral life is dually refreshing under the shady forest canopy. Over 250 species of plants sprout, stretch and climb through the park, and bird watchers can pull out their binoculars to spy the 50 species of birds chirping from tree to tree. There are also wild animals about, so keep your eyes peeled.

The very popular Fragrant Hills Park (pg 172) is situated at the base of the Western Hills, and for many it acts as the gateway to these arboreal mountains.

Yuyuantan Park

Chinese name: 玉渊潭公园 (Yùyuāntán Gōngyuán)
Admission: ¥2
Hours: 6:30-19:00 (Dec-Mar); 6:00-20:30 (Apr-May & Sep-Nov)
Recommended time for visit: 2 hours
Website: www.yytpark.com (in Chinese)
Address: 10 Xisanhuan Zhonglu, Haidian District (海淀区西三环中路10号)
Transport:
Bus -
1. To the East Gate: 114, 717 to Yuyuantan Dongmen (玉渊潭东门) Stop
2. To the West Gate: 394, 374, 323, 368 to Yuyuantan Ximen (玉渊潭西门) Stop
3. To the South Gate: 32, 78, 414, 65 to Yuyuantan Nanmen (玉渊潭南门) Stop

Squeezed in between the Diaoyutai State Guesthouse and the needle-rific China Central Radio and Television Tower, Yuyuantan Park blends colorful floral scenery with an urban backdrop in one of the city's most popular springtime havens. The sizeable park spans 2 km (1 mi) from east to west, and 61 of its 137 hectares are water. Wildly popular in late March and early April, Yuyuantan hosts an annual **Cherry Blosom Festival** (Yīnghuā Jiē; 樱花节), showing off the 3,000 cherry trees in the northwest of the park that have been skillfully cultivated from the original 180 gifted by Japan in 1973. The festival sees a bundle of traders and snacks peddling their treats, and the energy is high among the cool spring air and soft white flowers. Metasequoia trees and bamboo are in season here even when the cherries are not, particularly in the high season of June to August.

Lying in the east is the **Luichun Garden** (Liúchūn Yuán; 留春园). Luichun means "perpetual spring" and refers to the forsythias, magnolias, roses and crab-apples as they bloom one after another over several weeks during spring. Stretched across several meters in the south of the garden is a screen wall dotted in charming porcelain paintings. The jumbo island of **Zhongshan** (Zhōngshān Dǎo; 中山岛) in the southwest is long and thin, and you can climb the small hill that straddles the lakes for some sweeping views of **Bayi Lake** (Bāyī Hú; 八一湖) and **West Lake** (Xī Hú; 西湖) from the crowning double-upturned eave pagoda. Check out the old men fishing on the banks of **Yinshui Lake** (Yǐnshuǐ Hú; 引水湖) in the northeast and foster your hoary wisdom at the **Ancient Pine Forest** that abuts the south gate, full of Qing Dynasty pines from over 100 years ago.

Nearby sights

Military Museum (pg 168)- 1.5 km (1 mi) west

Other Attractions

Zhongshan Park

Chinese name: 中山公园 (Zhōngshān Gōngyuán)
Admission: ¥5
Hours: 6:00-22:00
Recommended time for visit: 1 hour
Website: www.zhongshan-park.cn (in Chinese)
Address: 4 Zhonghua Lu, Dongcheng District (东城区中华路4号)
Transport: Subway- Line 1, Tian'anmen West, Exit B, walk east for 5 minutes to the South Gate

Zhongshan Park is one of over 40 parks throughout China commemorating Sun Zhongshan, the alternate name of the Republic of China's founder, Sun Yat-sen. Situated just on the southwest corner of the Forbidden City, the park's pleasant views of the Forbidden City's cool water moat and lofty battlements are a great way to get you ready for a visit beforehand, or deliver contemplative reflection after a day in the mighty imperial complex. The park shelters one of the ever-capable Emperor Yongle's altars, the **Altar of Land and Grain** (Shèjì Tán; 社稷坛), which is symmetrically opposite the Ancestral Temple (Workers' Cultural Palace; pg 169) and was the sacrificial site for gifts to the land and harvest deities. Various wooden halls and pavilions scatter the park, including the Forbidden City Concert Hall in the east and a beautiful greenhouse, which displays fresh flowers year-round (the 39 varieties of tulips here were a gift from the Princess of Holland in 1977). Make your strike on the Forbidden City through the park's northeast exit, which spits you out at the Meridian Gate, or bear south to reach Tian'anmen Square. Hitting the park from June to September delivers outstanding blooming foliage.

Nearby sights

National Center for the Performing Arts – 700 m (2,296 ft) southwest

Beijing Acrobatics

A head-spinning mix of gymnastics, magic, juggling, martial arts and tricks (like a dozen people building a human pyramid on a free-standing ladder), Chinese acrobatics has existed for almost 3,000 years. It spread along the Silk Road and became a form of popular entertainment, eventually fading a bit except in rural areas. Acrobatics got a boost from the Cultural Revolution, when it was proclaimed a respectable "proletarian" art form. The style is over-the-top and kitschy, but the feats are so impressive you won't mind.

There are several places in Beijing to check out a Chinese acrobatics show.

Chaoyang Theater (Cháoyáng Jùchǎng; 朝阳剧场)

Everyone from local Chinese to the International Olympic Committee has taken in a show at this 3,000 sq m (32,291 sq ft) theater, including some 3 million foreigners. Conveniently located in the CBD, this is probably the biggest and best well-known acrobatics show in the city. The lobby is lined with souvenir stalls, and if you're not in a hurry, wait until after the show begins to get a discount. Tickets cost ¥180, though you may be able to get a better deal if you arrange through your hotel or hostel.

Time: 17:15 and 19:15 nightly; show lasts 1.5 hours
Location: 36 Dongsanhuan Beilu (朝阳区东三环北路36号). On the east 3rd Ring Road, take subway Line 10 to Hujialou (呼家楼) Station, Exit C1. The theater is 20 m (65.5 ft) south.
Phone: 135 5252 7373
Email: beijingguide@hotmail.com
Website: www.chaoyangtheatre.com

Tiandi Theater (Tiāndì Jùchǎng; 天地剧场)

The Chinese Acrobatics Troupe performs out of the Tiandi Theater, where routines like pole-climbing and extreme bike-riding are very popular among audiences; it's a great mix of inherited traditional antics and new innovations.

Time: 19:15 nightly
Location: 10 Dongzhimen Nandajie (东城区东直门南大街10号) Take subway Line 2 to Dongsishitiao (东四十条), Exit B. Tiandi is 100 m (328 ft) north of the Poly Theater (Bǎolì Jùyuàn; 保利剧院).
Phone: 135 5252 7373
Email: beijingguide@hotmail.com
Website: www.tianditheatre.com

Tianqiao Acrobatic Theater (Tiānqiáo Zájì Jùchǎng; 天桥杂技剧场)

This newly-remodeled theater, known as the oldest base of acrobatics in Beijing, once hosted the emperors of the Ming and Qing Dynasties. The official Beijing Acrobatic Troupe began here, and its legacy of offbeat contortions and tricks with an emphasis on high-wire action lives on. For an entertaining show with a dose of history, come to Tianqiao.

Time: 17:30 and 19:30 nightly; show lasts 1.5 hours
Location: 95 Tianqiao Shichang Lu, Xicheng District (西城区北纬路东口天桥市场95号). Near the west gate of Temple of Heaven.
Phone: 135 5252 7373
Email: beijingguide@hotmail.com
Website: www.tianqiaoacrobatictheater.com

Beijing Opera

It may resemble Western opera in the sense that it features high-pitched singing and a sometimes-incomprehensible plot, but Beijing Opera is truly an art form unto itself. Amazingly enough, it's only one of China's 350 or so regional operatic styles. The highly stylized performances are usually based on historical or mythological themes and draw on China's symbolic relationships with color to enhance the drama (red means loyalty, yellow is fierceness, blue for cruelty, and white for evil).

Beijing Opera features finely and strictly differentiated character types. Female roles are generally known as *dan* and male roles as *sheng*, while male clowns are called *chou* and depicted by a patch of white on the face. Male characters who are frank and open-minded but rough, or those who are crafty and dangerous, are known as *jing* or *hualian*. Each role has style and personality rules of its own and it's a lot of fun trying to decipher the storyline.

Beijing Opera is definitely worth seeing while you're in town. Here's where you can catch a show:

Huguang Guild Hall (Húguǎng Huìguǎn; 湖广会馆)

First built in 1807, this restored theater also has a small opera museum (only in Chinese) where you can see picture and costumes of famous performers from the past. Sip tea while you watch a performance in the same space that many legendary Beijing Opera stars once occupied.

Times: 19:30 nightly
Tickets: ¥180-380
Location: 3 Hufang Lu (西城区虎坊路3号). Take subway Line 2 to Hepingmen (和平门) and walk south 20 minutes.
Phone: 135 5252 7373
Email: beijingguide@hotmail.com
Website: www.huguangguildhall.com

Liyuan Theater (Líyuán Jùchǎng; 梨园剧场)

Located inside the Qianmen Hotel, this is the best-known Beijing Opera theater in town. The audience can not only witness an authentic performance, they can watch actors put on their makeup, take pictures with them, and even try on costumes. The theater uses English subtitles to help the audience stay on top of the plot.

Times: 19:30 – 20:50 nightly
Tickets: ¥70-180
Location: 1/F, Qianmen Jianguo Hotel, 175 Yong'an Lu (永安路175号前门建国饭店内)
Phone: 135 5252 7373
Email: beijingshows@gmail.com
Website: www.liyuantheatre.cn

National Center for the Performing Arts (Guójiā Dàjùyuàn; 国家大剧院)

This giant egg-shaped dome near Tian'anmen Square is a show in and of itself. There's a 2,000-seat opera hall with top-of-the-line acoustics and lighting, plus an English subtitle screen. See more on page 190.

Times: 19:30 nightly
Tickets: ¥150 and up
Location: 2 Xichang'an Jie, just west of Tian'anmen Square

Laoshe Teahouse

Named for the famous Chinese novelist Lǎo Shě (老舍) and his masterpiece drama "Teahouse" (Cháguǎn; 茶馆), this small spot near Qianmen is a perfect place to encounter Beijing Opera and a number of other Chinese folk arts, like martial arts, face-changing, shadow play, and crosstalk (xiàngshēng; 相声): a form of Chinese standup comedy. Have a seat and join the more than 2 million visitors who have already soaked up the atmosphere of old Beijing in this comprehensive setting. Various teas and authentic Beijing desserts are also available.

The show (7:50 – 21:20 daily, ¥180-380, 3/F, Big West Hall) includes Hand Shadow Play, Folk Dance, Face Changing, Acrobatics, Magic Tricks, the Comic Dialogue Show and Chinese Martial Arts. Other shows include Shadow Puppetry (14:00 – 18:00, Mon – Fri, Free, 1/F) and Beijing Opera (15:00 – 16:10, Sat & Sun, ¥30-90).

Location: Bldg 3, Zhengyang Market (正阳市场), Qianmen Xidajie (前门西大街), Xicheng District
Website: www.laosheteahouse.com (in Chinese)

The Legend of Kung Fu

The Chinese martial art of kung fu (gōngfu; 功夫) has its roots some 4,000 years ago in self-defense, and hunting and military training. Over time, kung fu has evolved to become a holistic system of health maintenance and cultivation. The influence kung fu principles like centeredness, balance, focus and strength have had on Chinese society is evident throughout writings and film, not to mention the reputation that kung fu has developed in the West as a highly honed art form.

A nightly show put on at the **Red Theater** (Hóng Jùchǎng; 红剧场) gives visitors an engrossing dramatization of the principles of kung fu, mixed with traditional Chinese arts, modern dance and acrobatics. The Legend of Kung Fu follows a young boy pursuing his dream of becoming a kung fu master – he makes great strides, but faces temptation by a beautiful young woman. How he strays from the path of enlightenment and eventually returns is up to you to find out. The Red Theater uses truly modern stage design, sound and lighting to create a dramatic night of entertainment. Though the actors do not talk, a screen displays English subtitles to keep the audience informed of the plot.

Time: 17:15–18:20, 19:30–20:50
Ticket Prices: ¥180/280/380/680
Location: 44 Xingfu Dajie (幸福大街44号). Take subway line 5 to Tiantandongmen (天坛东门) and walk from Exit B to Tiyuguan Lu (体育馆路). Turn left at Xingfu Dajie and see the theater on your right-hand side.
Phone: 138 1069 4544
Email: beijingtour86@gmail.com
Website: www.redtheatre-kungfu.com

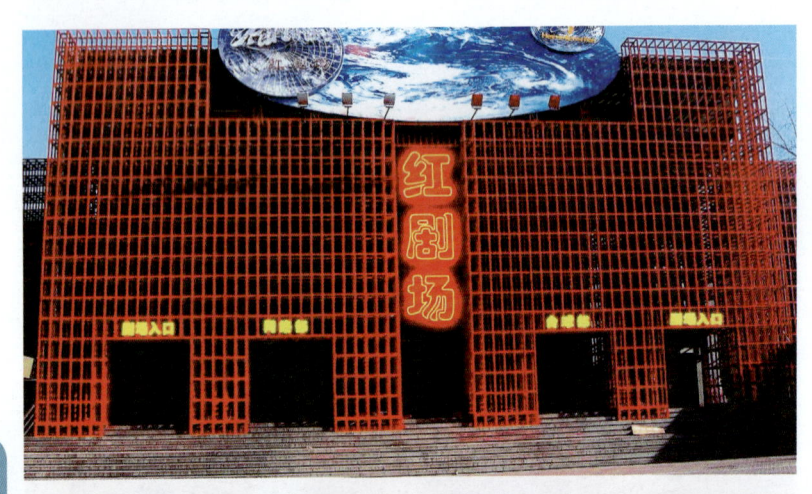

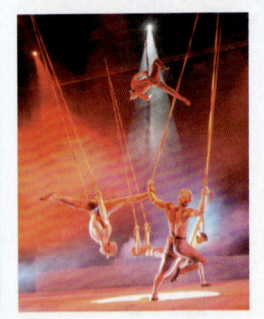

National Art Museum

Chinese name: 中国美术馆 (Zhōngguó Měishùguǎn)
Admission: FREE
Hours: 9:00-17:00 (last admission at 16:00)
Recommended time for visit: 1-2 hours
Website: www.namoc.org/en
Address: 1 Wusi Dajie, Dongcheng District (东城区五四大街一号)
Transport:
Bus –
1. 614, 202, 103, 211, 111 to the National Art Museum (美术馆) Stop
2. 685, 101, 420, 109, 112, 609 to National Art Museum East (美术馆东) Stop
3. 201, 104, 108 to National Art Museum North (美术馆北) Stop.

Built in 1962, the National Art Museum is host to more than 100,000 diverse artistic works from all over China, as well as around 1,000 pieces from well known foreign artists. In particular, it features traditional Chinese paintings, oil paintings, print, sculptures, traditional picture stories, caricatures, watercolors, pottery and an assortment of cultural costumes.

The museum's more traditionalist approach, even in its modern art, differs stylistically from the more experimental avant-garde 798 Art District. The interior of the museum is upscale, with excellent eye-level displays, prudent soft lighting and posh decorations, and at times it's reminiscent of a Manhattan installation. Some of China's most famous artists of the last 200 years have fantastic collections on display here, including over 200 from the shrewd and vivid natural landscapes of Ren Bonian (任伯年, 1840-1895). Qi Baishi (齐白石; 1864-1957), one of the most talented watercolorists in modern history, whose former home (pg 134) can be visited in Beijing, has a masterful collection of 337 works here. Be sure to catch his stunningly delicate paintings, such as the famous "Shrimp" from 1947, and the fantastic album *Flowers and Insects*.

Other Attractions

National Center for the Performing Arts

Chinese name: 国家大剧院 (Guójiā Dàjùyuàn)
Admission: ¥30
Hours: 9:00-17:00; closed Mondays
Recommended time for visit: half an hour (if not watching performances)
Website: www.chncpa.org/ens
Address: 2 Xichang'an Jie, Xicheng District (西城区西长安街2号)
Transport:
Subway – Line 1, Tian'anmen West (天安门西) Station, Exit C. There is an underground passageway directly to the theater.
Bus -
1. 99, 90, 52, 1, 10, 728, 22, 205, 5 to Tian'anmen West (天安门西) Stop
2. 5 to Nanchangjie (南长街) Stop
3. 10, 22 to Shibei Hutong (石碑胡同) Stop

French Architect Paul Andreu's ultra-modern design for the National Center for the Performing Arts in Beijing was certainly not lacking in controversy. Standing just west of the communist monolith Great Hall of the People, the NCPA, as it juxtaposes with its Soviet surroundings, is a symbolic testament to the progress that Beijing has made in the last half century. With modernists praising its innovativeness and traditionalists scorning its sci-fi visage, the strikingly futuristic dome resembles a kind of half glass airplane hangar or moon base, and some have pejoratively referred to it as a giant egg. Paul Andreu is well known for dome-like structures (such as the Osaka Maritime Museum that he designed), but the Performing Arts Center in Beijing is one of his greatest and most state-of-the-art creations. Featuring more than 18,000 titanium plates melding halfway down the silo-esque building with sheets of ultra white glass, the radiant bubble has excellent natural lighting, which illuminates a great interior area of green space and an artificial lake. Below the surface, underground corridors delve nearly ten stories below the earth.

There are three main performing venues, seducing patricians and high-society to their refined and discriminating performances. Belting away within the **Opera House** are a host of operas, from Peking Opera to the traveling Qinqiang folk opera of southwestern Shaanxi Province, to dance dramas and large scale shows. The **Concert Hall** hosts high-class performances from symphonies and Chinese traditional music performances. Don't miss the fantastic pipe organ in this hall, sporting 6,500 pipes and 94 stops, it is the largest in Asia. The **Theater** hosts smaller operas, traditional Chinese stage plays, and national songs.

North Putuo Film & TV City

Chinese name: 北普陀影视城 (Běipǔtuó Yǐngshìchéng)
Admission: ¥36
Hours: 10:00-22:00
Recommended time for visit: 2 hours
Address: Nangong Village, Yinghai Town, Daxing District (大兴区瀛海镇南宫村)
Transport:
Bus -
1. 953, 341, 526, 926 from Yongdingmen to Beiputuo Yingshicheng (北普陀影视城)
2. 497, 526, 679, 652, 665, 978, 678, 300, 300 Express from Muxiyuan Qiao (木樨园桥) to the film city

Those who are interested in the blossoming Chinese film industry can take a trip to this film studio/tourist destination in Yinghai Town, south of Beijing. The glitzy history of Beijing's film and television industry is on display, as well as several studio locations, a set for the 1980s television adaptation of *Dream of the Red Chamber*, and some lovely natural beauty. In total, there are more than 50 sights and 20 scenic areas, and the charming but modest Arhat Hill and Bei Putuo Islet offer a bit of diversity to the large 20 hectare (50 acre) complex. The replica ancient town is built in the ancient Ming and Qing Dynasty style and can be an enjoyable mosey for an ancient fantasy daydream. There are activities and performances as well, including the "Martial Arts on the Bridge" performance and painting and calligraphy in the Painting and Calligraphy Hall.

Songzhuang Art Village

Chinese name: 宋庄艺术区 (Sòngzhuāng Yìshùqū)
Admission: FREE
Hours: 9:00-17:00
Recommended time for visit: 2-3 hours
Website: www.chinasongzhuang.cn (in Chinese)
Address: Xiaobao Village, Songzhuang Town, Tongzhou District (通州区宋庄镇小堡村)
Transport:
Bus – 808, 809 to Songzhuang Meishuguan (宋庄美术馆)
Taxi – ¥100 from city center, 30 minutes

Far away from the mainstream, Songzhuang Art Village is in many ways what the more famous 798 Art District was half a decade ago. While 798 has become increasingly commercialized, with high-end luxury cars lining the streets and critics scolding the scene for being more about money and fame than art, Songzhuang Art Village has a far more noticeable appetite for expression. Set in the east Beijing suburbs of Tongzhou District, the village features artists' homes and gardens designed to express their individual inner personality. Some are as much works of art as the pieces sold in their studios.

Songzhuang has also begun building its own claim to fame, but sans the kitschy cafes and ostentatiousness of its more profit-oriented neighbor. Most of the artists live entirely off the sale of their art, and many works are sold directly to the international art market and are often favored by museums and collectors. This self-formed artistic community has converged from all over China with the desire to fuel the Chinese modern art movement and thrive off of their creations.

Perusing the small studios and bedecked farmhouses at Songzhuang, the air seems to buzz with passion and emotion so palpable you wonder if it's about to burst. Deep conceptual meaning and dutiful representation of the conflicting combinations of tradition and modernization synergize with the raw emotions of these artists' works, producing a scope of stunning modern art and a deeply supportive community unlike anything else in China.

Sleeping

Location should be your first consideration when selecting a place to stay. Most of the sites (and almost all of the "old Beijing" vibe) are located within the Second Ring Road, so unless you have a convincing reason to be elsewhere, we recommend that you stay in this area. Trying to save money by staying in the outskirts of the city is likely to backfire in the form of wasted time, and it won't likely be much cheaper, anyway. That being said, we have recommended hotels in several different areas of the city so you can have a choice.

Why should I stay in . . .

Dongcheng District? This is the area to take advantage of the traditional hutong atmosphere along with fantastic dining and nightlife. It's also probably the most walkable district with the most public transportation options. Forbidden City, Tian'anmen Square, Lama Temple and Temple of Heaven are located in this district.

Chaoyang District? If having Western amenities and dining options is important to you, consider staying here – it's the most expat-geared area in Beijing. Many embassies, the popular Chaoyang Park, the 798 Art District, the CCTV Tower, the World Trade Center, the Bird's Nest and the Water Cube are also located in this district.

Xicheng District? Beijing's Financial Street is located here. This district covers a lot of ground on the west and north side of the city, mostly within the Second Ring Road, so depending on your location, you'll still be relatively central. Beihai Park and Houhai are located in this district.

Haidian District? If you want to be close to Beijing's university area or if you want proximity to the Zhongguancun business and technology hub, this is the neighborhood for you. It's far from most tourist sites except the Summer Palace and Old Summer Palace.

What can I expect from Chinese hotels?

Beijing is not really known for its hotels, and unless you're paying Western prices, you should anticipate more hiccups than you would at comparable properties in the US or Europe. To travelers familiar with reliable mid-priced hotel chains in the West, Chinese mid-range hotels can seem dim and dingy.

Non-smoking rules may be ignored, and the beds are likely to be much harder than you're used to. You may be surprised to find out that the hotel's English-speaking staff actually only know a few words, that five on-site restaurants may turn out to be two, and the pool that looked so good in the brochure may be closed for renovation. For the most part, Beijing's hotels are perfectly nice places to lay your head, but everything changes rapidly in Beijing, and that applies to hotels as well.

Mid-range hotels are the most unpredictable category in Beijing, as many of them see fewer foreigners than the hostels or high-end hotels in town. In fact, until recently, Beijing's Public Security Bureau had the power to decide which hotels were allowed to accept foreigners, so many properties are relatively new at this. (Though the PSB no longer technically has jurisdiction, it's not unheard of for foreigners to be turned away at the cheapest Chinese hotels – or for Chinese visitors to get the cold shoulder at hotels catering to Westerners.)

Are hotel prices negotiable?

They may be. At the cheapest hostels in town, you probably won't be able to push the price any lower than it already is. But everywhere else, a 10%-50% discount is easily obtainable, either by asking the front desk or by doing your research online and finding what discount sites (we particularly like **agoda.com**) are offering. However, if you can't score a deal online, remember to look for our blue discount ribbons listed next to our recommended hotels and hostels. Just show up to the front desk, show them your Panda Guides guidebook, and start saving.

Express Hotels

If you're just looking for a place to crash and like the reliability of a hotel chain, choose one of Beijing's "express hotels," which have popped up all over the city. Hanting Express is essentially a Chinese Holiday Inn, and the others aren't much different. A clean, basic single room usually costs between ¥200-350 – that's the low end of mid-range in Beijing. Most of these places have English websites, or you can use the following well-regarded sites to make a reservation.

Ctrip (Xiéchéng; 携程 *)*
Toll-free: 400 619 9999
Website: english.ctrip.com

Elong (Yìlóng; 艺龙 *)*
Toll-free: 400 617 1717
Website: www.elong.net

List of express chain hotels in Beijing:

Green Tree Inn (Gélínháotài Kuàijié Jiǔdiàn; 格林豪泰快捷酒店 *)*
Phone: 400 699 8998
Website: www.998.com/eng

Home Inn (Rújiā Kuàijié Jiǔdiàn; 如家快捷酒店 *)*
Phone: 400 820 3333
Website: www.homeinns.com
(English option on top right corner)

Hanting Express (Hàntíng Kuàijié Jiǔdiàn; 汉庭快捷酒店 *)*
Phone: 400 812 1121
Website: ir.htinns.com

Pod Inn (Bùdīng Kuàijié Jiǔdiàn; 布丁快捷酒店 *)*
Phone: 400 880 2802
Website: en.podinns.com

7 Days Inn (Qītiān Kuàijié Jiǔdiàn 七天快捷酒店 *)*
Phone: 400 874 0087
Website: en.7daysinn.cn (in Chinese)

> *Panda Tips*
>
> • Whether you book directly with the hotel or through a third-party site, make sure you have confirmation in writing when you arrive to check in.
>
> • Ask your hotel concierge or front desk staff for a local map if possible; and ask the staff to fill out the Emergency Card (see pg 39).
>
> • English is generally spoken much better at youth hostels than at mid-range or pricier hotels.
>
> • Most hostels and hotels can help you with ticketing – train tickets, plane tickets, tickets to local shows and performances – for a small commission.
>
> • The recommendations below are not comprehensive – if you want to explore further options in Beijing, hit the internet. Two websites that are excellent for hostels in particular are **www.hostels.com** and **www.hostelworld.com**.

Dongcheng District

Budget

Beijing City Central Youth Hostel (Běijīng Chéngshì Qīngnián Jiǔdiàn; 北京城市青年酒店 *)*

This mega-hostel with more than 200 rooms is the largest in Beijing. Adjacent to the Beijing Railway Station, it's perfectly positioned for hopping on Line 2 of the subway. A ¥15 per person breakfast buffet will help you get full and on the road quickly, and there's also wifi, a library, coffee bar, pool tables, DVD collection, ATM, post office and other amenities you'd expect in a big hostel (there's even karaoke). It's hectic and not always spotless, but it's conveniently located and straightforward enough. Four and eight bunk dormitories, singles, and doubles available. Dorms from ¥56, ¥135 and up for private rooms.

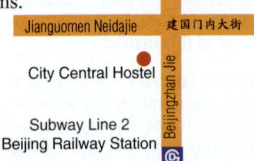

Surroundings: Beijing Railway Station, Tian'anmen Square, the Forbidden City, Wangfujing shopping street

Address: 1 Beijingzhan Qianjie (北京站前街1号)
Phone: 8511 5050

Dragon King Hostel (Lìsìlù Qīngnián Lǚshè; 力四路青年旅舍)

We could say the same ole stuff about this hostel: clean, friendly staff, wifi… yawn. Where this place really sets itself apart is its daily happy hour with free Chinese rice wine! How's that to bring the customers pouring in? It's also very close to a metro station and lies in a neighborhood scattered with plenty of good restaurants in case you don't fill up on the hostel's delicious dumpling parties. Dorms start at ¥80.

Address: 78 Dongsi Jiutiao, Dongcheng District (东四九条78号)
Phone: 8403 6146
Website: www.dragonkinghostel.com
Email: dragonkinghostel@yahoo.com

Home Hostel (Fùshān Guójì Qīngnián Lǚshè; 富山国际青年旅舍)

One FREE beer

Home is close to Nanluogu Xiang – a bustling street full of cafes, bars and shops. The hostel offers spartan rooms (though some guests have claimed that they are a little bunker-like) and it's just a short stroll down the hutong to Houhai and the other imperial lakes for paddleboats, people-watching and drinking. Many excellent and inexpensive restaurants are nearby, from Japanese to cheeseburgers. It's just a short walk to Nanluogu Xiang Metro Station on Line 6 or Gulou Dajie on Line 2. Eight-bed dorms from ¥60 and private rooms from ¥160.

Surroundings: Houhai, Nanluogu Xiang, Drum Tower, Imperial Academy Street and Lama Temple.

Address: 21 Cheniandian Hutong (车辇店胡同21号)
Phone: 6405 7111

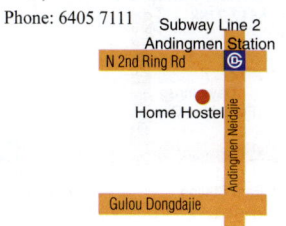

Lucky Family Hostel (Xiángjiā Dàyuàn; 祥家大院)

One FREE beer

This charming new spot is located on a quiet, shady hutong three minutes from subway Line 5. The free breakfast, common-area wifi, and lounge with a big-screen TV and library are enough to recommend it, but what really makes Lucky Family stand out is the staff, who are unusually warm, helpful, and proactive. For a laid-back, inexpensive stay in the heart of Beijing, this is a great choice.

Surroundings: Guijie (Ghost Street) and Lama Temple

Address: 12 Xinsi Hutong, Dongsi Shi'er Tiao (东四十二条辛寺胡同12号)
Phone: 8403 9929

Mid-range

Tianrui Hotel (Běijīng Tiānruì Jiǔdiàn; 北京天瑞酒店)

¥20 OFF

A quiet, airy, clean hotel with very spacious rooms and an in-house noodle shop, but the staff here have limited English. A moment's walk from the Dengshikou station on Line 5. ¥330 and up.

Surroundings: Tian'anmen Square, Forbidden City, Wangfujing Street

Address: 15 Baishu Hutong (柏树胡同15号)
Phone: 6526 6699

Days Inn Forbidden City Beijing (Běijīng Xiāngjiāng Dàisī Jiǔdiàn; 北京香江戴斯酒店)

This consistently well-reviewed mid-range hotel is tidy, if a little tired. It manages to capture some of the courtyard flavor while offering a pretty standard mid-range hotel experience. It's a guidebook's throw away from the Forbidden City and other central city attractions, including the shopping Mecca of Wangfujing. All rooms are equipped with desks, high-speed network access, large-screen LCD TVs, satellite TV channels and so on. A 15-minute walk to Wangfujing or Tian'anmen East subway station on Line 1. ¥360 and up.

Surroundings: Tian'anmen Square, Forbidden City, People's Congress Hall, Dongfang Square

Address: 1 Nanwanzi Hutong, Nanheyan Dajie (南河沿大街南湾子胡同1号)
Phone: 6512 7788

King Parkview Hotel Beijing (Běijīng Huáyù Bīn'guǎn; 北京华育宾馆)

One FREE drink at 2/F coffee shop

This (relatively) hidden gem on a back alley opened at the end of 2008. Its quiet and pleasant confines incorporate relics from Princess Hejia's mansion, the Imperial University of Emperor Qianlong, and other local antiquities. Just north of the Forbidden City, it's perfectly positioned for access to Jingshan Park and a short walk to the Dongsi subway station on Line 5. Rooms start at ¥380.

Surroundings: Forbidden City, Beihai Park, Tian'anmen Square, Wangfujing, Shichahai Bar Street, Imperial Palace Wall Relics Park

Address: 55 Shatan Houjie (沙滩后街55号)
Phone: 5165 2988; 5875 7888

Pentahotel Beijing (Bèi'ěrtè Jiǔdiàn; 贝尔特酒店)

With an unusually clean and swanky atmosphere for a mid-range Chinese hotel, this hip spot is just a two-minute walk to Chongwenmen subway station (Lines 2 and 5). It offers a gym, indoor swimming pool, and sauna, and the Pentalounge is a café/deli/noodle bar that gets rave reviews. They'll rent bikes and send you out into the city with a "Pentafun bike map" that shows you easy routes to explore top attractions and little-known gems that you can only discover on two wheels. ¥480 and up.

Surroundings: Tian'anmen Square, Temple of Heaven, Pearl Market, Tiantan Park, Qianmen.

Address: 3-18 Chongwenmen Waidajie (崇文门外大街3-18号)
Phone: 6708 1188
Website: www.pentahotels.com

Splurge

Orchid Hotel

One FREE drink

Co-owned by a Canadian and a Tibetan, this newly-opened hutong hotel is a perfect blend of Old Beijing and new luxury. The rooms, arranged around a central courtyard, are decorated in a pleasantly minimalist style, with deluxe amenities like under-floor heating and eco-friendly bath products. Some rooms have terraces or balconies overlooking the hutong roofs in every direction. The lobby has a great bar with an excellent wine and cheese option, and each room has a fresh fruit basket refilled daily. Some of the rooms even come with a free local cell phone for use during your trip. Tucked away on Baochao Hutong in the hip Gulou area. Rooms start at ¥700.

Surroundings: Drum and Bell Tower, Houhai, Lama Temple

Address: 65 Baochao Hutong (鼓楼东大街宝钞胡同65号)
Phone: 8404 4818
Website: www.theorchidbeijing.com

Hotel Cote Cour Beijing (Běijīng Yǎnyuè Jiǔdiàn; 北京演乐酒店)

Simple in terms of amenities, but with top-notch East-meets-West minimalist design, this romantic hutong hotel boasts a magnolia courtyard, making for a serene atmosphere in the summer months. Rent bikes for ¥50 a day and explore some of the most charming hutongs in Beijing nearby. A 15-minute walk from Dengshikou Station on Line 5. ¥1,068 and up.

Surroundings: Forbidden City, Beihai Park, hutongs

Address: 70 Yanyue Hutong (演乐胡同 70 号)
Phone: 6523 7981

Sheraton Beijing Dongcheng Hotel (Běijīng Jīnyú Xǐláidēng Jiǔdiàn; 北京金隅喜来登酒店)

This well-appointed Western-style hotel, managed by the Starwood Group, features Chinese, Japanese, and Italian dining under one roof, plus a heated pool, fitness center, spa and a lobby bar. No hard Chinese beds here – their trademark Sheraton Sweet Sleeper mattress is heavenly at the end of a long day. ¥1,100 and up.

Surroundings: China Science and Technology Museum, Lama Temple

Address: 36 Beisanhuan Donglu (北三环东路 36 号)
Phone: 5798 8888

Regent Beijing (Běijīng Lìjīng Jiǔdiàn; 北京丽晶酒店)

There are many outstanding reviews for this five-star hotel, which bills itself as a tranquil and luxurious retreat just off of Wangfujing shopping street. There are stunning views of Beijing on the upper floors, floor-to-ceiling windows and marble bathrooms throughout. The fitness center, pool, hot tub and spa offering massages and beauty treatments are superb, and there's also a children's playground and game room for travelers with families. Starting rate is ¥1,200.

Surroundings: Dong Hua Men Night Market, Silk Street Market, China Museum of History and Tian'anmen Square.

Address: 99 Jinbao Jie (金宝街 99 号)
Phone: 8522 1888

Hilton Beijing Wangfujing (Běijīng Wángfǔjǐng Xī'ěrdùn Jiǔdiàn; 北京王府井希尔顿酒店)

The enthusiastic management of this hotel has really made it a great experience for visitors to Beijing. The sophisticated Zen-like atmosphere is a welcome oasis, while a range of activities for little ones (including cooking classes and aquarium visits) means the whole family will be happy. For an extra splurge, don't miss the decadent buffet, which features everything from world-class sushi to a five-foot chocolate fountain. It's a 20-minute walk to the Forbidden City, and ten minutes to Dengshikou Station on Line 5. ¥1,300 and up.

Surroundings: Wangfujing, Forbidden City

Address: 8 Wangfujing Dongjie, Dongcheng District (王府井大街 8 号)
Phone: 58128888

Chaoyang District

Budget

Xinghelou Hotel (Xīnghélóu Bīn'guǎn; 星河楼宾馆)

This hotel is a 20-minute walk from the Dongzhimen Transportation Hub, where you can catch Line 2, Line 13, the Airport Express, and any number of buses. Simple rooms include free broadband internet, satellite TV, and good showers. There's a Hubei restaurant and breakfast buffet at Jiutouniao restaurant in the same building. Nothing memorable, but good basic amenities and value. ¥180 and up.

Surroundings: Sanlitun area

Address: 15 Zuojiazhuang (左家庄15号)
Phone: 6468 1133

Huatong Youth Hostel (Huátōng Guójì Qīngnián Lǚshè; 华通国际青年旅舍)

Smack in the heart of the Sanlitun bar and nightlife district, this hostel is not a good choice for quiet nights in. But if you're looking for an upbeat, international atmosphere with wifi, a library, movies, bike rental, laundry, airport transfer, pool tables, foosball and even an electric guitar, consider this spot. There's a free dumpling party every Friday and a hot-pot get together on Wednesdays. Dorms ¥60, private rooms from ¥120.

Address: 1 Chunxiu Lu (春秀路1号)
Phone: 5190 9288

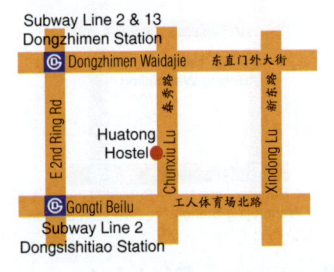

Beijing Lanting Youth Hostel (Běijīng Lántíng Guójì Qīngnián Lǚshè; 北京蓝亭国际青年旅舍)

This traditional courtyard hostel has internet, aircon, safety boxes, bike rental, a ticket office, a guest kitchen, bar and recreation area. Discounted rates for dorms from ¥45, doubles from ¥246.

Address: 17 Sanqu, Anhuaxili, Anhualu (安华路安华西里三区17号)
Phone: 6425 8738

Discovery Youth Hostel (Běijīng Yǒujiā Guójì Qīngnián Lǚshè; 北京有家国际青年旅舍)

¥10 OFF

Located in the CBD and with free internet, safety boxes, fridges, laundry facilities and AC. Discounted rates for dorms/doubles without bath ¥55/¥128.

Address: Bldg 10, Jintaili, Jintai Lu (金台路金台里10号楼)
Phone: 65976597

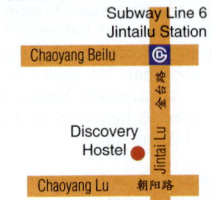

Zhaolong Youth Hostel (Zhàolóng Qīngnián Lǚshè; 兆龙青年旅舍)

10% OFF

Attached to the Zhaolong Hotel, this neat, air-conditioned property is perfectly positioned at the edge of Sanlitun, three minutes south of the Tuanjiehu subway station on Line 10. Don't expect much in terms of atmosphere or service, but the location can't be beat. ¥120 and up.

Address: 2 Gongti Beilu (工体北路2号)
Phone: 6597 2666

Eastern Inn (Běijīng Yìyǔ Liánsuǒ Jiǔdiàn; 北京逸羽连锁酒店）

A 10-minute walk from the newly-opened Dongdaqiao Station on Line 6, this very basic and "blah" hotel is nevertheless an easy-on-the-wallet option if you're determined to stay in Sanlitun. It's situated in a more homey and low-key corner of the neighborhood, but near the very popular Q Bar if you're into upscale cocktails. ¥180 and up.

Address: 6 Baijiazhuang Lu（白家庄路6号）
Phone: 6508 6611

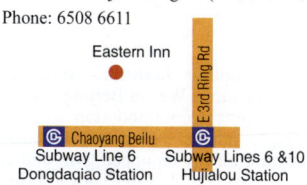

Mid-range

Saint Angel Hotel (Shèngtiānshǐ Jiǔdiàn; 圣天使酒店）

This quirky hotel with self-professed "European flair" features a Chinese restaurant, karaoke bar, beauty salon, game room, sauna, laundry service, tour assistance, limousine rentals, babysitting service, meeting rooms, a business center and off-street parking. If that wasn't enough, it's also steps away from the International Trading Center, New CCTV Tower, Sanlitun and Embassy Row – convenient but out-of-the-way enough to avoid the hustle and bustle of Sanlitun. ¥300 and up.

Surroundings: New CCTV Tower, Sanlitun, Embassy Row

Address: 10-4th Ln, Xiangjun Beili, Hujialou（呼家楼向军北里4巷10号）
Phone: 5190 8833; 6591 9988
Website: en.stsjd.com/zzsts.html

Great Hotel Beijing (Běijīng Guìguó Jiǔdiàn; 北京贵国酒店）

What's in a name? This straightforward hotel earns high marks from guests for its smooth customer service and consistent rooms with good attention to detail. Both Chinese and Western cuisine are available in the in-house restaurant. Very convenient for guests traveling to the China International Exhibition Center, and a ten-minute walk to Sanyuanqiao Station on Line 10 and the Airport Express. ¥360 and up.

Surroundings: Yansha Shopping Center, Guomen Mansion, International Exhibition Center

Address: 1 Zuojiazhuang（左家庄1号）
Phone: 8451 3388; 8451 5259

King Wing Hot Spring International Hotel (Jīngruì Dàshà; 京瑞大厦）

Rougher around the edges than it once was, this hotel still offers the unique feature of a hot spring 1,600 m (5,249 ft) underground that feeds into the bathtub in every guest room. It boasts a range of facilities, including an outdoor pool, spa, fitness center, wifi and free parking. It's a ten-minute walk to Panjiayuan Station on Line 10 and there are four restaurants onsite. Rooms start at ¥400.

Surroundings: Beijing Curio City, World Park, World Trade Center, Temple of Heaven

Address: 17 Dongsanhuan Nanlu（东三环南路17号）
Phone: 6766 8866
Website: www.kingwing.com.cn/en/reservation.html

Chang'an Grand Hotel (Cháng'ān Dàfàndiàn; 长安大饭店）

Boasting an impressive gilded lobby with decent rooms, this big and spacious hotel is near the southeast corner of the Third Ring Road. Perfect for antique lovers, it's adjacent to Beijing's Antique City and the Panjiayuan Flea Market. A walk to Panjiayuan stop on Line 10 is just five minutes. ¥500 and up.

Surroundings: Panjiayuan Flea Market, Capital Library

Address: 27 Huaweili (华威里27号)
Phone: 6773 1234

Website: www.changangrandhotel.com/en

Splurge

Kuntai Royal Hotel (Kūntài Jiāhuá Jiǔdiàn; 昆泰嘉华酒店)

This hotel is nondescript on the outside but packs a punch on the inside, with heavily decorated and dramatically lit common spaces. It's conveniently located near Chaoyang Station, and just a short hop to Sanlitun and Chaoyang Park. ¥720 and up.

Surroundings: Sanlitun Bar Street, Chaoyang Park

Address: 12B Chaoyangmen Waidajie (朝阳门外大街乙12号)
Phone: 5828 5588
Website: www.kuntairoyalhotel.com

Hotel Kunlun (Kūnlún Fàndiàn; 昆仑饭店)

On the banks of Beijing's Liangma River, this 29-floor hotel looks a little dated and '80s on the outside, but it's elegant and comfortable inside. There are 12 different restaurants and bars located throughout, and recent renovations were completed to incorporate *feng shui* elements into the modern décor. Only a 20-minute drive from Beijing Capital Airport and a five-minute walk from Liangmaqiao subway station on Line 10, it's a nice location that's still close to most of the central city. ¥800 and up.

Surroundings: Lufthansa Shopping City, Guomao commercial area

Address: 2 Xinyuan Nanlu (新源南路2号)
Phone: 6590 3388
Website: www.hotelkunlun.com

The Westin Beijing Chaoyang

Set in the popular Sanlitun entertainment area, the luxurious Westin Beijing Chaoyang offers spacious accommodation with floor-to-ceiling windows. The property boasts an indoor pool, a fully equipped gym and eight dining choices. The Westin Chaoyang Beijing is a ten-minute walk from Liangmaqiao Subway Station and a ten-minute drive from Beijing Railway Station. It is a 25-minute drive from Beijing Capital International Airport. ¥1,400 and up.

Address: 7 Dongsanhuan Beilu, Chaoyang District (朝阳区东三环北路7号)
Phone: 5922 8888

Crowne Plaza Beijing Chaoyang U-Town (Běijīng Cháoyáng Yōutáng Huángguàn Jiàrì Jiǔdiàn; 北京朝阳悠唐皇冠假日酒店)

Spotless, relatively new, spacious, and comfortable, this pricier hotel adjoins the popular U-Town Lifestyle Center and Shopping Mall. Light wood bathrooms and rich jewel tones in the rooms give a feeling of luxury and relaxation. It's adjacent to the Ministry of Foreign Affairs, Embassy area, Sanlitun Bar Street and the Silk Market, plus only a five-minute walk from Chaoyangmen Station and a 30 minute drive from Beijing Capital Airport. Nothing too unique, but a reliably top-notch Western-style hotel to say the least. ¥900 and up.

Surroundings: Silk Market, Sanlitun Bar Street, Ministry of Foreign Affairs

Address: 3 Sanfeng Beili (三丰北里3号)
Phone: 5909 6688

Opposite House (Yúshě Jiǔdiàn; 瑜舍酒店)

This boutique luxury hotel in the heart of Sanlitun's nightlife and shopping area offers avant-garde design and world-class service: it was named one of the best new hotels in the world when it opened in 2008. If you want your accommodation to be as unique and memorable as the rest of your trip, Opposite House might fit the bill. A 20-minute walk to Tuanjiehu station on Line 10. Rooms begin at ¥2,100.

Surroundings: Sanlitun Bar Street, embassies, Chaoyang Park

Address: The Village, Bldg 1, 11 Sanlitun Lu (三里屯路11号院1号楼)
Phone: 6417 6688

Xicheng District

Budget

Beijing Drum Tower Youth Hostel (Běijīng Gǔyùn Qīngnián Lǚshè; 北京鼓韵青年旅舍)

This 40-room hostel has a roof terrace with views of the Drum and Bell tower – a perfect place to relax and watch the bustle of the neighborhood unfold. This hostel boasts free wifi and a capable tour office to help you make travel arrangements, and it's also close to good bars and restaurants (including the Box and McDonald's incase you need a burger fix). It's conveniently located by Line 2, and you can choose from dorms starting at ¥60 or private rooms starting at ¥130.

Surroundings: Drum and Bell Tower, Shichahai, Nanluogu Xiang

Address: 51 Jiugulou Dajie, Xicheng District (西城区旧鼓楼大街51号)
Phone: 8401 6565

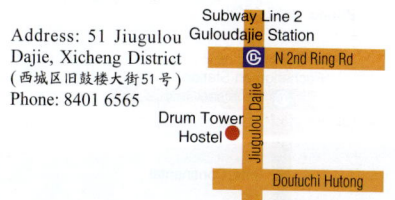

Beijing Lotus Hostel (Běijīng Liánshè; 北京莲舍)

This hostel is located in a traditional courtyard with a nice old Beijing touch. There's a cool common area for meeting other people, but the toilets and showers are not great. Free internet, bike rentals, pool table, safety boxes and laundry facilities are available. There's also a restaurant and bar for good eating and cheap drinking. Discounted rates for dorms from ¥40, doubles from ¥160.

Address: 29 Beiqitiao, Xisi (西四北七条29号)
Phone: 6612 8341

Aoxiangge Hotel (Àoxiānggé Bīnguǎn; 奥香阁宾馆)

This totally serviceable hotel advertises itself as being near the Beijing Traffic Management Bureau, to give you an idea of the "excitement" of the surroundings. But really, it's a reliable, decent place to stay if you need to be on the west side of town, and as a bonus, it's near the Mei Lanfang Grand Theater, home to nightly Beijing Opera performances. A five-minute walk to Chegongzhuang Station on Line 6, 24-hour hot water, free broadband internet access and a business center. ¥160 and up.

Surroundings: Beijing Exposition Center, Beijing Zoo, Capital Stadium, China Foreign Affairs University

Address: 26B Zhanlan Lu (展览馆路乙26号)
Phone: 6831 3399
Website: www.aoxianggehotel.com

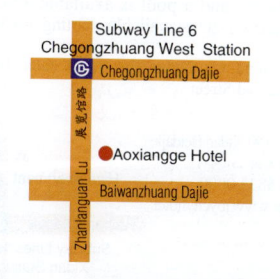

Mid-range

Bamboo Garden Hotel (Zhúyuán Bīn'guǎn; 竹园宾馆)

10% OFF

The Bamboo Garden Hotel is a classical Chinese courtyard in a quiet lane west of the Drum Tower. Some rooms have no views, and there are the usual headaches of a Chinese hotel, like weak hot water and dim lighting, but there's a bit of atmosphere here, and it's a great home base for exploring the hutong neighborhoods. A five-minute walk to Gulou Dajie station with access to Lines 2 and 8. Breakfast is available for ¥60 per person and rooms go for ¥460 and up.

Surroundings: Drum Tower, Forbidden City, Tian'anmen Square, Houhai

Address: 24 Xiaoshiqiao Lane, Jiugulou Dajie (旧鼓楼大街小石桥 24 号)
Phone: 5852 0088
Website: www.bbgh.com.cn/english

Hwa Apartment Hotel (Dàyuèchéng Jiǔdiàn; 大悦城酒店)

If you're traveling with kids or settling in for a longer stay, consider this apartment hotel, which offers rooms with separate bedrooms and lounges for more privacy and breathing room. Each room has a kitchen equipped with basic cooking supplies if you're interested in self-catering. It's not the most exciting neighborhood in town, but it's a mere five-minute walk to the Xidan subway station on Line 1, which can whisk you to Tian'anmen Square and other sights in minutes. It's located immediately adjacent to Joy City shopping mall, one of Beijing's biggest and newest, and a pool is available. One and two-bedroom suites available, starting at ¥560.

Surroundings: Xidan Business Center, Beijing Financial Street

Address: 130 Xidan Beidajie (西单北大街 131 号)
Phone: 5833 0000
Website: www.joycityhotel.com/en

Spring Garden Courtyard Hotel (Běijīng Chūnqiūyuán Sìhéyuàn Bīn'guǎn; 北京春秋园四合院宾馆)

10% OFF (15% OFF for laundry)

This basic, peaceful courtyard hotel goes a step beyond just offering traditional Chinese architecture – it includes a pictorial history of China in every room. Each room also features an emperor from China's past and gives you a taste of the dynasty in which he lived. ¥660 and up.

Surroundings: Xidan Shopping Center, Summer Palace, Beihai Park

Address: 11 Xisi Beiliutiao Hutong, Xisibei Dajie (西四北六条 11 号)
Phone: 6653 2900

Splurge

InterContinental Beijing Financial Street (Zhōujì Jiǔdiàn; 洲际酒店)

The Intercontinental is what you picture when you think of a swanky hotel. The staff is extremely helpful and attentive, giving it a personal touch, and with 25 floors of luxurious rooms, a steak restaurant that some call the best in Asia, heated swimming pool, sauna, massage and spa center, coffee shop, business center, and more, and you'll be happy to come back here at the end of a long day. Each room is equipped with high-speed internet access, a satellite TV, a mini-bar, a refrigerator, a coffee maker and in-room safes. It's just a short walk to Fuchengmen Station on Line 2. ¥1,400 and up.

Surroundings: Financial Street, Parkson Center, Seasons Place shopping mall

Address: 11 Jinrong Jie (金融街 11 号)
Phone: 5852 5888

Presidential Plaza (Guóbīn Jiǔdiàn; 国宾酒店)

All the rooms are equipped with modern facilities, including wifi and satellite TVs. In addition, there's a nice range of restaurants and bars: the coffee bar in the garden offers a buffet of international tastes and cuisine ranging from Cantonese, Shanghai, Sichuan and regional Chinese dishes. There are also exercise facilities, yoga courses, a swimming pool, sauna, hot tub, steam bath, and Chinese therapeutic massage parlor. ¥750 and up.

Surroundings: Beijing Exhibition Hall, Beijing Zoo

Address: 9 Fuchengmen Waidajie (阜成门外大街9号)
Phone: 5858 5588
Website: www.presidentialplazahotelbeijing.cn

Haidian District

Budget

PekingUni International Hostel (Běijīng Wèimíng Guójì Qīngnián Lǚshè; 北京未名国际青年旅舍)

Located in the university district, this hostel is ideal for international students moving into their new dorms. Singles and doubles with en-suite bathrooms are available, and dormitories with shared bathrooms are also an option (unfortunately the shared bathrooms are a little grimy and the hostel desperately needs a make-over). On the up side, there's also a large variety of restaurants and loud student bars in the area, making it a good place to meet new friends. The hostel is near Wudaokou (五道口) Station (Line 13). Dorms start at ¥60, privates from ¥200.

Surroundings: Beijing Language and Culture University, Tsinghua University, Peking University, Summer Palace, Old Summer Palace

Address: 150 Chengfu Lu, Haidian District (城府路150号)
Phone: 6254 9667

Mid-range

Songlu Shengfang Holiday Hotel (Sōnglù Shèngfāng Jiàrì Fàndiàn; 松麓圣方假日饭店)

A quick 15 minutes from Beijing's bustling West Railway Station, this decent three-star hotel has respectable furnishings, air-conditioning, cable TV, minibars and clean bathrooms. Rooms start at ¥256.

Address: 8 Tianchun Lu, Haidian District (海淀区田村路8号)
Phone: 8863 7878

Xinxing Hotel (Běijīng Xīnxīng Bīn'guǎn; 北京新兴宾馆)

This business hotel by the Third Ring Road mostly caters to Chinese tourists and businessmen, but the friendly staff – which speaks almost no English – will do their best to give you a comfortable stay. There is free internet access, but you will need to make sure you specifically ask for a room that provides it. There is Chinese breakfast on the second floor until 9:00 and a swimming pool in the building on the side.

Address: 17 Xisanhuan Zhonglu (西三环中路17号)
Phone: 8823 6688

Splurge

Beijing Friendship Hotel (Běijīng Yǒuyì Bīn'guǎn; 北京友谊宾馆)

Originally built to house Soviet experts and scientists who came to build up China's infrastructure in the 1960s and '70s, this massive and unique hotel features freestanding buildings arranged around a central garden area. The rooms themselves are standard, but you'll enjoy relaxing with a cold beer and some lamb kebabs on the outdoor patio and wandering the beautifully landscaped grounds; a nice change of pace from the grit and bustle of Beijing. It's a short walk to Lines 13 and 10 at the Zhichunli subway stop, and the State Administration of Foreign Experts Affairs has an office inside in case you have any visa issues. ¥500 and up.

Surroundings: Peking University, Tsinghua University, the Summer Palace

Address: 1 Zhongguancun Nandajie (中关村南大街 1 号)
Phone: 6849 8888
Website: www.bjfriendshiphotel.com/siteen

Jade Palace Hotel (Cuìgōng Fàndiàn; 翠宫饭店)

This huge hotel is well-suited for business travelers looking for proximity to the Zhongguancun tech hub. With 9,000 sq m (96,875 sq ft) of meeting rooms and office area, it's also home to a huge pool, massage center, beauty salon, karaoke bar, and the usual slate of in-room amenities. If you're hungry, there are several restaurants serving Guangzhou cuisine, Huaiyang cuisine, Japanese food, Russian food, and more. Right next door to the Zhichunli subway stop on Line 10. ¥620 and up.

Surroundings: Summer Palace, Fragrant Hills Park, Beijing University

Address: 76 Zhichun Lu, Haidian District (海淀区知春路 76 号)
Phone: 6262 8888

Website: www.jadepalace.com.cn/en/index.html

Shangri-La Hotel, Beijing (Běijīng Xiānggélǐlā Fàndiàn; 北京香格里拉饭店)

This gorgeous hotel is a blend of sleek marble and traditional Chinese architecture – dotted with koi ponds, waterfalls and floor-to-ceiling windows. There are some great onsite restaurants, and its out-of-the-way location is balanced by its tranquil vibe and attention to detail. Guests rave about the high-level customer service. ¥1,500 and up.

Surroundings: Technology Park, the State Guest House, Summer Palace

Address: 29 Zizhuyuan Lu (紫竹院路 29 号)
Phone: 6841 2211

Crowne Plaza Beijing Zhongguancun (Běijīng Zhōngguāncūn Huángguānjiàri Jiǔdiàn; 北京中关村皇冠假日酒店)

Rooms have internet access, but for a bonus there's an onsite business center, fitness center, swimming pool and sauna. The Chinese and Western restaurants are superb, though the service is OK at best. The location is nothing to call home about either, but the metro is within walking distance. Doubles start at ¥1,826, but discounted rates can go as low as ¥772. Breakfast is ¥170, but included in more expensive rooms.

Address: 106 Zhichun Lu (知春路 106)
Phone: 5993 8888

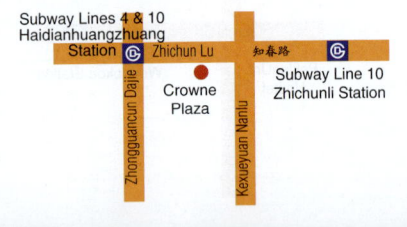

Eating

Eating in China

China has been perfecting the art of gastronomy for thousands of years, and its cuisine has been greatly influenced by foreign invaders, ethnic minorities and even the emperor's own palate. This makes it quite difficult to classify what Chinese food is due to its diversity and the sheer size of distinct culinary styles. In fact, if you travel extensively around China, one of the first things you'll notice is the change in food culture, ingredients and preparation from one town to another.

When considering "Chinese food," many Westerners may think of things like fortune cookies, chop suey and General Tso's Chicken – all of which are not actually authentic Chinese dishes. The Chinese food found in Western countries is mostly influenced by the southern school of Chinese cooking since the area around Guangdong is where the majority of Chinese immigrants came from, but their original recipes were greatly modified to meet Western tastes. That means you shouldn't expect to find too many of your favorites from home here. However, there are a few mainstream Chinese dishes – like sweet and sour pork, kung pao chicken, spring rolls, fried rice, dumplings, won ton soup, Peking Duck and stir fried noodles – that you may recognize.

The Chinese love nothing more than a good meal, so it should be no surprise that one of the greatest pleasures in traveling around China is eating. And with hundreds, if not thousands, of types of diverse meals, there's always something new to try. But before plunging in head first, check out **www.appetiteforchina.com** for more about the local eating culture and **www.beijingboyce.com** for the latest news on Beijing drinking spots. We also highly recommend you read these 15 very important tips on the next page to keep you from "losing face" at a Chinese restaurant.

Panda Restaurant Tips

1. Chinese restaurants will not have forks and knifes, only chopsticks. If you don't know how to use two twigs to pick up food, then you better start learning (see How to Use Chopsticks on pg 242). For soup, some establishments may provide an oriental style spoon; if not drink it straight from the bowl.

2. Don't expect any English to be spoken by the staff or written on the menu (though some menus do have English, or at least "Chinglish"). The good news is picture menus are quite common.

3. If you ask for napkins, you'll get a roll of toilet paper or some tissues.

4. You'll most likely never see ice cubes here, and if you want a cold beer or drink, you must specify that you want it cold (bīng de; 冰的) or else it'll come room temperature.

5. When nature calls and you need to use the bathroom, be prepared to squat, and don't expect the bathroom to be up to Western standards of cleanliness.

6. When you sit down at youR table, the waiter will hover over you like a vulture, waiting for you to make a decision. Don't feel pressured; just take your time because this is normal. If you absolutely need some space say, "I'll call you" (Wǒ huì jiào nǐ; 我会叫你).

7. Although no smoking signs are everywhere and it's technically illegal to smoke indoors here, hardly anyone abides. If you want to smoke, light up. If not, you must unfortunately hold your breath.

8. No one tips unless you're at a very fancy restaurant or hotel. When you try to leave money on the table, they will chase you down the road to return your cash. When you try paying extra as a tip, they will think you don't know how to count.

9. If you don't eat meat, try telling the waiter, "I'm a vegetarian"(Wǒ chī sù de; 我吃素的). That being said, they'll still probably throw some bits of bacon fat into your veggie dish just because the concept of vegetarianism just hasn't caught on yet, despite centuries of Buddhist influence. Meat was a luxury during the Cultural Revolution, so many Chinese today still don't understand why some people refuse to eat it.

10. When Chinese people go out to eat, it's common for one person to order all the food. Several dishes are ordered and shared by all, with everyone picking food from the various platters presented. Usually the host (the one who ordered) will pay. It's OK to split the bill with your friends, but if a Chinese friend or host insists on paying, let them.

11. There are hardly any table manners in China, so forget what mom told you and put your elbows on the table, spit chicken bones on the floor or table, and even let out a belch if you fancy. No one will raise an eyebrow (this is different at very formal or business meetings).

12. Desserts aren't common in China. Locals prefer to eat a little bit of fruit after dinner instead of a chocolate mousse cake.

13. The drinking culture is very different in China. If you order a bottle of beer, it will come with a few small glasses, which you should fill for everyone. Cheers by saying "dry glass" (gànbēi; 干杯) and take a healthy drink. The glass is often drained in one shot, but not always. If you're really adventurous, try substituting báijiǔ (白 酒) for beer, which is 120 proof distilled Chinese alcohol with a paint thinner aroma. Drink at your own risk.

14. If you're sitting down and a complete stranger comes to sit at your table to eat, don't be scared. This is a country of 1.4 billion people and seats are limited.

15. Last but not least, try to be as open minded as possible. There's a vast cultural difference between the East and West, so if you thought you ordered something correctly by pointing at pictures, there's still a chance that you will get something completely different. Roll with the punches, laugh it off, and put it in the "good stories to tell people back home" box.

Eating

207

Keep in mind that the 15 aforementioned rules apply to your average Chinese restaurant and not a five-star Michelin establishment frequented by President Xi. To find out how Beijing's top dogs match up with other Asian cities, visit the Daily Meal's list of Asia's 101 Best Restaurants at www.thedailymeal.com and be prepared to be amazed by how many are in Beijing. For more on domestic dining, here is some useful info concerning the six basic categories of restaurants found in China:

Luxury – If the restaurant is in a major luxury hotel or is internationally ranked, chances are your dining experience will fit into this category. While the quality, service and environment are excellent, the downside is you'll be lacking a true local experience since they tend to be Westernized or altered to meet foreign preferences.

High end – Restaurants on this end of the spectrum can be found in fancy modern complexes or in remodeled ancient buildings. While the food, hygiene and classical ambience are superb, places such as these are known for having inflated prices to attract businessmen on company credit cards who are looking to impress clients. Furthermore, you're not going to get a true taste of China.

Middle level – Restaurants such as these are easily identifiable by their cloth table coverings and printed calligraphy portraits on the walls. These places attract a variety of social classes, and everything, from the hygiene to the price can vary from place to place. Nonetheless, the majority provide tasty meals, a comfortable ambiance and a good spread of the local population.

Food courts – Nowadays, China has an obsession with gigantic shopping malls. Mix that and their obsession with eating and you get loud, boisterous, crowded food courts. Food court restaurants usually fit into the category of Chinese fast food since they provide quick, decent food at a fair price. With a big emphasis on veggie dishes and grains, Chinese fast food is still far healthier than Western fast food. Expect your dining experience to be at least equal to and usually better than Western fast food, depending on the establishment.

Cheap restaurants – These restaurants were made for the working man, and you can expect cheap prices and zero table manners. Though the hygiene isn't grade A, you will find some of China's most traditional meals here, which can be surprisingly tasty. These places can be found on just about every block.

Street food – Don't be deceived by the name – street food is not only extremely cheap; the atmosphere is alive with locals shouting *gānbēi!* as they down shots of *báijiǔ*. It's also the best place to sample the most traditional (and often tastiest) food and experience local culture at its best. In other words, your visit to China will not be complete unless you have street food at least once.

Beijing Food

Though China actually recognizes eight regional schools of cooking, there are four major cooking styles that we will address here. The North is represented by the hearty food of Beijing, the East is characterized by the sweets of Shanghai, the South (or Cantonese) is embodied by Guangdong/Hong Kong's fresh seafood, and the Western school of Sichuan is known for mouth numbing spice. To make things more complicated, there are literally dozens of other branches that derive from these four main pillars, usually coming from the ethnic minorities, Han people in other provinces or a combination of both.

To break it down, we'll first start with Beijing cuisine. Beijing has been the capital of China for centuries and has therefore been influenced by various styles. Its origins derive from the Emperor's Kitchen (meals cooked for the emperor inside the Forbidden City), because of the fact that emperors would gather the best cooks from around the country to partake in an ancient "Top Chef" competition. The winners stayed to become the emperor's chef while the losers… well, let's just say there was no consolation prize. The earliest versions of Peking Duck were recorded on the emperor's menu during the Yuan Dynasty (1271-1368), but it wasn't until the mid-20th century that the dish finally became a national icon among the commoners.

Since the emperor's chefs had roots from various corners of the kingdom, it's difficult to know which dishes originated from Beijing. Today, several ingredients, like dark soy paste, sesame oil, scallions and fermented tofu see particularly frequent use in Beijing cooking, and the city tends to use less rice than other regions because the climate isn't suitable for the crop. Beijingers are also known for using different methods of frying, eating lots of meat, and snacking on small eats throughout the day.

While in Beijing, there are several famous dishes that you should consider trying:

Peking Duck (Běijīng Kǎoyā; 北京烤鸭)

You might have tried a version of Peking Duck at your local Chinese restaurant back home, but nothing compares to the original from its hometown. Ducks are rubbed with salt and vinegar, inflated with air, hung up to roast over an open fire and then dried. Next, they're sliced into thin, succulent pieces right at your table by a trained expert and placed inside a thin pancake with a delicious fermented bean paste, scallions and cucumbers. There are a number of specialty roast duck establishments throughout Beijing, so check out our listings on **pages 217 and 219** for a reference.

Beijing Hot Pot (Běijīng Huǒguō; 北京火锅)

Hot pot was first introduced to Beijing during the Mongolian occupation in the 14th century, but it was mutton hot pot (shuàn yángròu; 涮羊肉) that became a city-wide icon under the Manchu run Qing Dynasty during the 18th century. This is how it works: First, you drop thin slices of raw mutton and veggies like cabbage, potatoes, yams, tofu and mushrooms into a boiling broth in the middle of your table. When they're ready take the cooked ingredients out, dip them in a sesame sauce and enjoy! For unbeatable mutton hot pot, take a seat at **Donglaishun Hot Pot** (Dōngláishùn Huǒguō; 东来顺火锅), where they've been serving up the city's finest for 100 years.

Mung Bean Milk (Dòujiāng; 豆浆)

For a traditional Beijing breakfast, try mung bean milk with a hot crispy-on-the-outside, soft-in-the-middle stick of **fried dough**

(yóutiáo; 油条). Though you may be hesitant to try it at first, remember that mung bean milk is quite similar to soy milk and is a very healthy breakfast option (minus the fried stick of dough) that's packed with fiber, protein and Vitamin C.

Fried Sauce Noodle (Zhájiàng Miàn; 炸酱面)

This is another regional favorite. It's simple ingredients are noodles, marinated pork cubes and a dark, heavy soy sauce, all stir fried together in a wok. There are so many of these restaurants in Beijing that you might end up eating it without even looking for it.

Stewed Pork Liver (Chǎo Gān; 炒肝)

You may be turned off by the name, but you'll never know if stewed pork liver is your new favorite dish if you never give it a try. The liver comes in a thick, brown gelatin stew with a few other vegetables thrown in, and many locals also like to eat steamed buns stuffed with meats or vegetables (bāozi; 包子) along with this dish.

Rolling Donkey (Lǘdǎgǔn; 驴打滚)

The name Rolling Donkey does not reflect what you actually get with this dish. It's not really donkey meat (although donkey meat is rather popular in Beijing and you can find it in many restaurants, just look for 驴肉 – lǘròu), but rather a sweet, vegetarian pastry made of sticky rice and fried bean flower that's stuffed with red bean paste. The ingredients are then rolled together, cut into individual pieces and tossed around in brown soy bean flower. The final product resembles a donkey rolling in dirt. If a rolling donkey doesn't sound appetizing, try a **sweet ear** (táng ěrduo; 糖耳朵), which isn't actually an animal part either, but rather a small white cake made of flour and sugar.

Wheaten Cake Boiled in Meat Broth (Lǔzhǔ Huǒshāo; 卤煮火烧)

This is another strange one, but we wouldn't mention it if it weren't good, so trust us on this one. Dating back to the Qing Dynasty (1644-1911) and similar to a goulash or gumbo, this dish has cuts of wheaten bread, tofu, pork chops, chitterlings and pork lung all pilled together in one large bowl. The ingredients are then mixed together with garlic, chili oil, vinegar and chives in a dense broth. This dish is big, and you usually need several people to help finish it off.

Tánghúlú (糖葫芦)

Also referred to as *bīngtáng húlú* (冰糖葫芦), this typical Beijing snack is found all over the city and is adored by locals. If you're tired of the city's thick and salty meals and need to satisfy your sweet tooth, just look for the bamboo skewers of bright red, green, orange and yellow crystallized bulbs protruding out from the street vendors' carts. Tanghulu is made from pieces of fruit (usually cherry tomatoes, strawberries, mandarin oranges, blueberries, pineapples, grapes, banana and kiwi) dipped into a sugary syrup paste and left to dry, harden and crystallize. Sweet and crunchy on the outside, fruity and chewy in the inside – what's not to like?

Tripe (Dǔ; 肚)

Pig tripe is perhaps the most popular intestinal dish you'll find around the capital city, but lamb tripe is also common, while beef tripe is best served as a snack with beer. In fact, sticking to the Chinese philosophy of using every part of the animal, pig tripe is actually considered a delicacy in China, and you can find it prepared in many forms (stewed, fried, tossed with noodles, etc) depending on the restaurant you visit. A type of sausage called *guànchǎng* (灌肠) is another tripe dish that's stuffed with minced meat, herbs and spices.

Fried Pancakes (Dàlián Huǒshāo; 褡裢火烧)

These are quite tasty and very cheap. Dalian Huoshao are basically just flat wheaten pancakes filled with pork, lamb, cabbage, green onions and other vegetables. You can also get a vegetarian option if you wish. The pancake is lightly fried so it's crispy on the outside and warm in the inside. This is also one of the favorites of the expat community in Beijing.

Snack Streets

If you're looking to rub elbows with the locals, get a true Chinese experience, eat the most traditional food in town, save money and have a casual laugh with friends over a few drinks, then street food is right up your alley.

With that in mind, not all snack streets and their street food are created equal. Some, like Wangfujing or Ghost Street, are highly tourist-oriented, and the food is quite pricey (especially at Wangfujing). You will not meet too many locals here, but you will meet a ton of domestic tourists. Others, like Jiumen Snack Street, are more down the traditional lane. But while all of the streets mentioned below are great fun and worth a visit, your best bet for cheap, local-style street food is to march the neighborhoods where locals live and look for carts frying up noodles and roasting meat next to lucite tables and wobbly stools.

Wangfujing Snack Street (Wángfǔjīng Xiǎochījiē; 王府井小吃街*)*

Perhaps the weirdest street food hangout in all of Beijing, Wangfujing is a must. This place is world famous for serving exotic delicacies such as scorpions, starfish, grasshoppers, insects, deep fried bugs, sea horses, an array of "animal parts" and other creepy crawling critters. You can also find meat kebabs and candied fruits in case the items listed don't get your chops watering, or just come down and watch the brave sample bizarre bites from a distance.

> Address: Wangfujing Street, Dongcheng District (东城区王府井)
> Transport: Take subway Line 1 to Wangfujing Station, Exit A

Donghuamen Night Market (Dōnghuámén Měishífāng Yèshì; 东华门美食坊夜市*)*

This is another popular food alley that lies directly north of Wanfujing Snack Street near the eastern gate of the Forbidden City. They too have delights like deep fried crickets, lizards, silk worms and "particular" sheep body parts, but they also have a selection of things like spring rolls, dumplings and crab cakes for the less adventurous. For some reason, it's a little more expensive than its sister night market in Wangfujing, so make sure to stop by the ATM before going.

> Address: Dong'anmen Dajie, Wangfujing Street, Dongcheng District, east of Nanheyan Dajie (东城区王府井东安门大街、南河沿大街东)
> Transport: Take buse 2, 82, get off at Donghuamen (东华门) Stop; or walk west 100 m (328 ft) from Wangfujing

Ghost Street (Guǐ Jiē; 簋街*)*

Ghost Street was the first and is the most famous snack street in Beijing. You can find almost anything here, but the locals recommend the hot and spicy crawfish (málà xiǎolóngxiā; 麻辣小龙虾). It's also open until the wee hours of dawn for those with the midnight munchies, and there's a plethora of sit-down restaurants ranging from cheap to expensive in the surrounding area.

> Address: Dongzhimen Neidajie, Dongcheng District (东城区东直门内大街)
> Transport: Take bus 106, 124 or 807 to Beixinqiao; or take the subway Line 5 to Beixinqiao or subway Line 2 to Dongzhimen

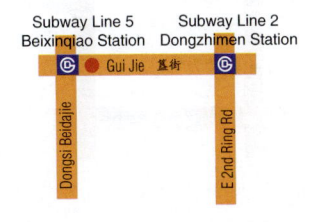

Jiumen Snack Street (Shíchāhǎi Jiǔmén Xiǎochījiē; 什刹海九门小吃街*)*

The "Nine Gates" Snack Street is cool because it's tucked away in a narrow hutong and claims to have over 200 traditional

Beijing specialties. It's also probably the best place to find Beijing's sweetest treats. The entire alley is under the same management, so you must purchase a street food debit card beforehand and swipe it at each stall.

Address: 1 Xiaoyou Hutong, Shichahai, Xicheng District (西城区什剎海孝友胡同1号)
Transport: Take bus 55, 800, 44, 380, 27 or 409 to Deshengmen Stop

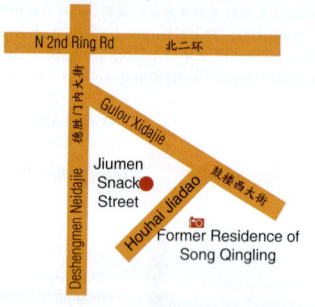

Niujie Muslim Snack Street (Niú Jiē; 牛街)

Located right near the Ox Street Mosque – Beijing's largest and oldest mosque – this unique night market specializes in famous street food from China's ethnic minorities. More than 20 distinct type of Muslim and non-Muslim ethnicities reside in the area, though the most prominent are those from the Islamic Hui minority. You'll definitely find some interesting and delicious food around here, so come hungry and with a sense of adventure.

Address: Around Guang'anmen Neidajie & Niujie, Xicheng District (西城区广安门)
Transport: Take bus 5, 6, 10, 38, 48, 109, 626 or 717 and get off at Niujie Stop.

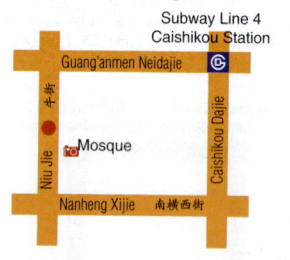

Fucheng Street (Fùchéng Lù; 阜成路)

Fucheng Street is the upscale version of the stereotypical, grungy China's street food alley. The majority of the clients who come to this 3 km- (2 mi)-long strip are predominately businessmen or government officials, and most of the restaurants specialize in outer provincial flavors, especially those from the spice belt of Sichuan, Chongqing and Hunan. There are also some good Cantonese seafood stalls if you want to mix it up.

Address: It is located between Hangtian Bridge (航天桥) and Dinghui Bridge (定慧桥) in Haidian District

Lucky Street (Hǎoyùn Jiē; 好运街)

Lucky Street is an upscale business district that combines restaurants, bars, cafes, exclusive clubs and brand name shops. Some of the restaurants specialize in imported Maine lobster, Italian pasta, Indian curry and Japanese teppanyaki. If you're in the mood for foreign flavors then Lucky Street is worth a shot, but you'll still be able to find some hot pot and other regional Chinese restaurants just in case you change your mind once you arrive.

Website: www.luckystreet.cn/indexe.htm
Address:1 Chaoyang Gongyuan Lu, Chaoyang District (朝阳区朝阳公园路1号)
Transport: Take bus 402, 413, 418, 419, 420, 503, 621, 659, 677, 682, 688, 701, 909, 955, 985, get off at Anjialou (安家楼) Stop, walk east about 200 m (656 ft), on your right you'll see the Lucky Street sign which is the north part of Chaoyang Gongyuan Lu (朝阳公园路).

Regional Chinese

Beijing cuisine (Jīngcài; 京菜) is a pillar of Chinese cuisine and is a solid representation of northern Chinese food. The area's weather greatly influences its eating habits, so many of the traditional dishes are hearty enough to help the locals tromp through the freezing winter months. You will find more bread-based dishes and larger platters of meat and root vegetables like potatoes in many of the capital's favorites. Some of Beijing's most famous meals include Peking Duck, northern style hot pot, thick dumplings and meat skewers (just look for the character 串 if you need a quick kebab).

Sichuan cuisine (Chuāncài; 川菜), from the southwestern province of Sichuan, is one of the most recognized styles of Chinese cooking, and is famed for its fiery spice. The people of Sichuan are known to load their dishes up with red chilies and mouth numbing peppercorns – a combination that will leave your lips blazing for days. Some of Sichuan's most famous meals are hot pot (which is spicier than the Mongolian influenced northern hot pot), *mápó dòufǔ* (麻婆豆腐; spicy bean curd) and kung pao chicken (gōngbǎo jīdīng; 宫保鸡丁; spicy chicken cubes with red peppers and peanuts). If you think you can handle the heat, check out page 226 for Beijing's spiciest Sichuan restaurants.

Cantonese cuisine (Yuècài; 粤菜) is eaten by the people of Hong Kong and Guangdong Province. The Cantonese kitchen is full of fresh seafood due to its proximity to the coast, and they also use various sweet and sour sauces. Perhaps the most famous meal to come out of Canton is dim sum, a brunch that has become an international favorite. The small dishes of dim sum include jasmine tea, congee, seafood dumplings, sticky rice wrapped in a bamboo leaf, crunchy spring rolls and much more. For dim sum and other Cantonese favorites, visit page 219.

Shanghai cuisine (Hùcài; 沪菜), another one of China's famous coastal cuisines, is generally a little sweeter than other Chinese dishes and uses plenty of fish, eels, shrimp and other seafood. Shanghai is well-known for its hairy crab (máo xiè; 毛蟹), crab roe dumplings, *xiǎolóngbāo* meat dumplings, various bok choy dishes and braised clay pot meat soups. If you're heading to Shanghai make sure to check out the Panda Guides *Shanghai* book for the city's best restaurants, otherwise you can refer to page 225 for Beijing's favorite Shanghai eateries.

Xinjiang cuisine from the Uighurs – a predominately Muslim minority with Turkish roots – may not be a traditional pillar of the Chinese kitchen, but it is distinguished throughout the country. Its ingredients have ties to many foreign regions, particularly the Middle East its lamb kebabs, flat breads and sugary sweets; Central Asia's oily pilaf rice dishes, meat pies (*samsas*) and mu.. dishes; and inner China with its wheat noodles, veggie salads and hearty stews. For Uighur dining options in Beijing, see page 227.

Because China's Han ethnicity comprises more than 90% of the population, it can be hard to see the diversity within the homogeneity. In fact, the Chinese government officially recognizes 55 ethnic minorities (such as Mongolian, Uighur, Tibetan, Yi, Miao and Hui), while other officially unrecognized groups (like the Tuvan) make up the small remainder of the Chinese people's heritage. Every single one of China's plethora of ethnicities is represented in Beijing, and that means that sampling China's unbelievable range of culinary styles is almost too easy in this wonderful city. A great part of many people's adventures in Beijing include hitting up as many diverse eateries as possible, so flip through our listings to see which ones make your stomach growl.

International Cuisine

Don't forget that Beijing is also a major player in global affairs and has attractsed citizens from all over the world. Finding mouthwatering international meals is a piece of cake in Beijing. From East Asian delicacies out of Japan and Korea to an array of Indian, Pakistani, Turkish, Thai, Vietnamese, Mongolian, Malaysian and other Asian styles, eating Asian (pg 231) in Beijing is not just about eating Chinese.

There's also a very large European population in Beijing, many of whom have come to show off their home country's culinary magic. You can find French, German, Mediterranean, English, Irish, Italian, Portuguese, Spanish, Russian and other European favorites all over town. Some of these also have great drink specials and happy hours with imported wines, beers and vodkas. Check **out page 235** for Beijing's best.

Beijing even has a big slice of down-home American options as well, and we're not just talking about fast food. Real American burgers, steaks, milk shakes, hot dogs and onion rings are just some of the fare you can find from the USA (pg 229). Fusions and upscale options make an appearance too, so don't be shy.

Latinos know how to mix good music, drinks and food for a festive eating experience. If you're hungry and in good spirits, Beijing

...b options from some of the ...n America. The city is teeming ...n *churrasco*, cheesy Mexican ...ff margaritas done so well, you'll ... for more. Go to page 235 for our

There are even several good places to grub for those looking to experience regional African cooking at its best. Most of the good African restaurants (pg 229) specialize in either sub-Saharan staples or northern/Moroccan specialties, and they're also fun places to scope out a bit of African culture, art and music while in the Middle Kingdom.

Apart from regional delicacies representing countries and continents from around the world, there are numerous specialty restaurants around the city. Dessert stores focusing on sweets, pies, cakes, ice cream, cookies and other sugary snacks are plentiful. Other specialty restaurants we've included have vegetarian dining, organic food, fusions, contemporary cuisine, BBQ, delivery and fresh seafood houses as well.

Beijing's Top 20 Restaurants

Pricing guide per person (excluding drinks):

$$$ More than ¥250 (US$40)
$$ ¥100 to ¥250 (US$15-40)
$ Less than ¥100 (US$15)

$$$ Maison Boulud (Lǔgōng Fǎguó Cāntīng; 鲁宫法国餐厅)

This is the Beijing branch of New York celebrity chef Daniel Boulud's Maison Boulud. In case you were worried about overdosing on too much Chinese food, Boulud comes to the rescue with some of the finest French-inspired recipes to be found in all of Asia. The weekend brunch is particularly enthralling, especially since the signature DB Burger – a medium rare Wagyu pattie topped with truffles, short ribs and all the trimmings, and served with a cup of fries – is to-die-for. Complimentary deserts are also served at the end of every meal.

Address: 23 Qianmen Dongdajie (前门东大街23号)
Phone: 6559 9200

$ Baoyuan Dumplings (Bǎoyuán Jiǎoziwū; 宝源饺子屋)

This modest, no-frills dumpling house with brash décor attracts everyone from the bourgeoisie to the proletariat. Patrons customize their own dumplings with multicolored vegetable-dyed wrappers and choose their preferred meat stuffing.

Address: 6 Maizidian Jie, Chaoyang District (麦子店街6号楼北侧)
Phone: 6586 4967

$ Three Guizhou Men (Sānge Guìzhōurén; 三个贵州人) `10% OFF`

This restaurant was (not surprisingly) opened by three men from Guizhou Province. Customers will experience an assortment of flavors and textures from inimitable dishes, like the "beef on fire" served over a bed of charcoal and chili. Open late night, this one attracts a large crowd of Sanlitun clubbers.

Address: 39 Dongsanhuan Zhonglu, Chaoyang District (朝阳区东三环中路39号)
Phone: 5869 0598

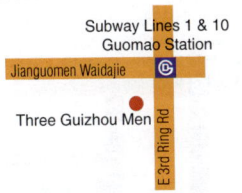

$$ Mercante

Without question the best Italian food in Beijing, Mercante's dishes don't require you to spend a fortune to enjoy them. This non pretentious hutong restaurant stays modest with agreeable pricing, a very nice wine list and imported ingredients

Address: 4 Fangzhuanchang Hutong, Dongcheng District (东城区方砖厂胡同4号)
Phone: 8402 5098

$ Haidiliao Hot Pot (Hǎidǐlāo Huǒguō; 海底捞火锅) `PANDA PICK`

This traditional Sichuan hot pot restaurant has branches all across the Middle Kingdom. With an immense selection of various raw meats, veggies and seafood ready to be cooked right at your table in a roaring pot of fiery, bubbly broth, you'll quickly understand why the Chinese have a small obsession with this place.

Address: 2A Baijiazhuang Lu, Chaoyang District (朝阳区白家庄路甲2号, 八十中学西侧)
Phone: 6595 2982; 6595 0079

$$$ The Courtyard by Brian McKenna (Sì Hé Xuān; 四合轩)

British chef Brian Mckenna features a fusion of European classics and Asian ingredients, and the magnificent view of the Forbidden City adds to its sophistication. Try the 12 course tasting menu to sample McKenna's ingenuity.

Address: 95 Donghuamen Dajie, East Gate of The Forbidden City (东华门大街95号)
Phone: 6526 8883
Website: www.bmktc.com

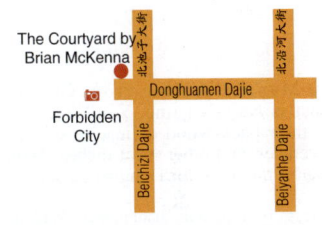

$ Crescent Moon Muslim Restaurant (Wānwānde Yuèliàng; 弯弯的月亮) `One FREE snack or dessert`

This budget eatery hosts some of the city's most bona fide Chinese Muslim specialties, including Uighur delicacies from China's northwestern province of Xinjiang. Succulent lamb kebabs, stuffed naan, pomegranate wine and hookahs are just some of the fun.

Address: 16 Dongsi Liutiao, near Chaoyangmen Beixiaojie (东城区东四六条16号)
Phone: 6400 5281

$$ Lei Garden (Lì Yuàn; 利苑)

For the best dim sum this side of the Yangtze, come to Lei Garden for a brunch of luscious Cantonese classics like steamed shrimp dumplings, stir-fried oysters, lobster clay pot and *boazi* bread dumplings.

Location One

Address: 3/F, Jinbao Tower, 89 Jinbao Jie (金宝街89号金宝大厦三层)
Phone: 8522 1212

Location Two

Address: C2-C3, Tower C, World Trade Center, 6 Jianguomen Waidajie, Chaoyang District (朝阳区建国门外大街甲6号中环世贸中心C座C2-C3)
Phone: 8567 0138

$$ Nàjiā Xiǎoguǎn (那家小馆)

Hearty Manchu cuisine from China's northeast is Najia's game. You'll want to sample their back-wood delicacies of wild game, venison and other meat dishes. Najia Xiaoguan is *the* place for Dongbei cuisine.

Address: 10 Yong'anli, Jianguomen Waidajie, south of Xinhua Insurance Bldg (朝阳区建国门外永安里10号)
Phone: 6567 3663; 6568 6553

$ Noodle Loft (Miàn Kù; 面酷)

One FREE cold dish

The most casual option on our list serves up a hearty working man's feast of noodles topped with grade-A ingredients. Chefs hand make the noodles right in the middle of the store, and the loud murals on the wall add to the already vibrant atmosphere.

Address: 2/F, Fuma Mansion, 33 Guangshun Beidajie (朝阳区广顺北大街33号福码大厦2楼)
Phone: 8472 4700; 8472 2339

$ Mr Shi's Dumplings (Lǎoshí Jiǎoziguǎn; 老石饺子馆) PANDA PICK

Mr Shi's is a laid back, no nonsense establishment with some of the most unique and delectable dumplings you've ever tasted. It's a must to order at least one portion of the fried, crunchy and cheesey three-sided fried dumplings (sān miàn jiǎo; 三面饺) and dunk them in their hit garlic-vinegar-chili sauce.

Address: 74 Baochao Hutong, Gulou Dongdajie, near Nanluogu Xiang (鼓楼东大街宝钞胡同74号)
Phone: 8405 0399

$$ Southern Barbarian (Nán Mánzi; 南蛮子)

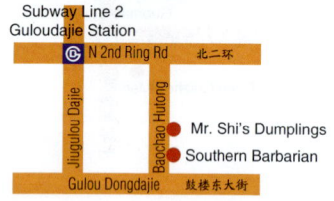

Owner Feng Jianwen brings the southern flavors of his home province of Yunnan to the streets of Beijing with specialties such as *guòqiáo miàn* (across the bridge noodles): a steaming bowl of chicken or beef broth and all your veggies, noodles and meats on the side for you to toss in. The décor is lined with photographs from some of China's best artists.

Address: 107 Baochao Hutong, Dongcheng District (鼓楼东大街宝钞胡同107号)
Phone: 8408 3372;
Website: www.southernbarbarian.com

$$ Hatsune Sushi (Yīnquán Rìběn Liàolǐ; 隐泉日本料理)

This long time local favorite rolls the best sushi in town and tops it off with a wonderful selection of name brand sake and craft beers. Be sure to try their signature California Rolls and some of their non-sushi main courses. The casual atmosphere welcomes all walks of life and prices are surprisingly sensible.

Address: 2/F, Tower C, Heqiao Mansion, 8A Guanghua Donglu (朝阳区光华东路甲8号和乔大厦C座2楼)
Phone: 6581 3939

$$ Da Dong (Dàdǒng Kǎoyā; 大董烤鸭)

This massive dining complex is inhabited by 300 chefs serving up more than 200 dishes, such as table-side cooked filet mignon and fresh lobster. Despite the diverse menu, critics rave about head chef Dong Zhenxiang's lean and crisp Peking roast duck, the house's smash hit.

Address: 1/F & 2/F, Nanxincang International Plaza, 22A Dongsishitiao (东城区东四十条甲22号南新仓国际大厦1-2楼)
Phone: 5169 0329

$$ Susu (Sūsū Huì; 苏苏会)

A comfy courtyard house in the hutongs hidden away from the hustle and bustle of the capital, Susu is a master of deception with its Beijing appearance. It actually specializes in Vietnamese cuisine, including make-your-own spring rolls, *banh mi* and grilled fish.

Address: 10 Qianliang Hutong Xixiang (东城区钱粮胡同西巷10号)
Phone: 8400 2699
Website: www.susubeijing.com

$$$ Quánjùdé (全聚德) **PANDA PICK**

This fancy restaurant is a time honored cornerstone of the city's world famous Peking roast duck. VIPs from Fidel Castro to Richard Nixon have eaten here, and these days it has become quite the tourist hot spot, so make a reservation to avoid the long wait. There is more than one location of this restaurant in town, including one on Wangfujing Street.

Address: 8 Guangqumen Waidajie, Chaoyang District; west of Shuangjing Qiao (朝阳区朝阳区广渠门外大街8号，双井桥西南角)
Phone: 5861 2288

Wangfujing Location

Address: 9 Shuaifuyuan Hutong, Wangfujing Street, Dongcheng District (东城区王府井大街帅府园胡同9号)
Phone: 6525 3310

$$$ Capital M

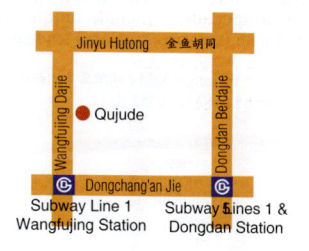

Living up to its cousins "M at the Fringe" in Hong Kong and "M on the Bund" in Shanghai, Capital M presents a phenomenal view of the Forbidden City and Tian'anmen Square along with a changing seasonal menu of modern European cuisine.

Address: 3/F, 2 Qianmen Dajie (东城区前门大街2号3楼)
Phone: 6702 2727
Website: www.m-restaurantgroup.com

$$$ Temple Restaurant Bar (TRB)

One of the city's hottest restaurants at the time of research, TRB is housed in the former Tibetan temple of Zhizhusi. This culinary holy experience is highlighted with delights such as lobster and pâté on toast, grilled pigeon, and a lavish wine list.

Address: Songzhusi Temple, 23 Shatan Beijie
(东城区沙滩北街23号萬祝寺)
Phone: 8400 2232

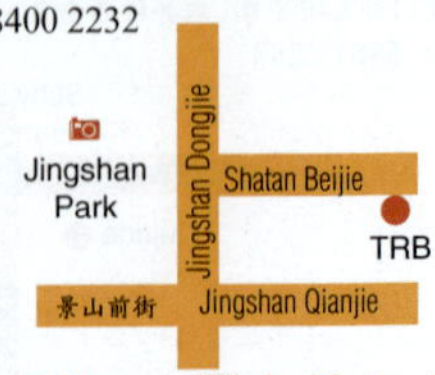

$$$ Green T House (Zǐyún Xuān; 紫云轩)

One FREE ice cream or green tea

Trendy, slick, modern and fashionable, Green T House attracts the city's upper echelon with its excellent selection of exotic teas and an ultra-modern refurbished interior. Apart from tea, their specialties include unique dishes cooked with (surprise, surprise) tea leaves.

Address: 6 Gongti Xilu (朝阳区工体西路6号)
Phone: 6552 8310; 6552 8311

$$$ Duck de Chine (Quányājì; 全鸭季)

One of the best places in town to get Beijing's most popular meal, Duck de Chine is located in an old communist factory that has been renovated into a conventional Beijing courtyard house. Duck de Chine puts a French twist on this time-honored feast, and it also boasts other French inspired duck dishes, champagne and a great wine selection.

Address: 1949 The Hidden City, Courtyard 4, Gongti Beilu (工体北路4号院1949内)
Phone: 6501 8881

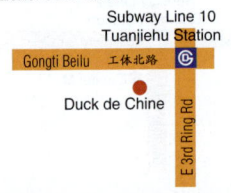

Chinese Regional

Pricing guide per person (excluding drinks):

$$$ More than ¥125 (US$20)
$$ ¥50 – ¥125 (US$8-20)
$ Less than ¥50 (US$8)

Anhui

$ Huīshāng Gùlǐ (徽商故里)

A traditional getaway tailored for the locals of Anhui, at Huishang, stinky fish, smelly tofu, flat bread tortilla wraps, tripe soup and pickled vegetables are just some of the many fetid yet tasty items you'll find on the wall menu.

Address: 2 Chaoyangmen Nanxiaojie (near the intersection of Chaoyangmen Neidajie), Dongcheng District (东城区朝阳门南小街2号)
Phone: 5864 2222

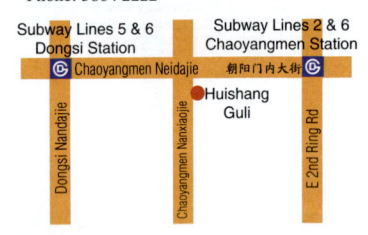

Beijing

$$ 61 Leg of Lamb (Liùshíyīhàoyuàn Tànkǎo Yángtuǐ; 六十一号院碳烤羊腿)

Chow down on a gigantic roasted leg of lamb on a spit. 61's hutong locale makes for an exuberant dinner while the locals hack away at chunks of meat and down shots of *baijiu*. Come with a group if you're looking to get the leg of lamb, but if not there are other items for smaller parties.

Address: 61 Fangjia Hutong, Dongcheng District (东城区方家胡同61号)
Phone: 139 0133 3774

$$$ Donglaishun Hot Pot (Dōngláishùn Huǒguō; 东来顺火锅) **PANDA PICK**

One of the city's most popular hot pot hotspots, this place is always packed, so getting here early is a good idea. Boiled in a large copper pot with an inverted funnel shape over hot charcoals, the broth here is said to be Beijing's best. Order your food as a set meal (which includes a lot of dishes) or go a la carte, but if you come in the summer try to avoid the private rooms, which can sometimes get suffocatingly hot.

> Address: 12 Xinyuanxili Zhongjie, Chaoyang District (朝阳区新源西里中街12号)
> Phone: 6467 3707; 6460 0671

$$$ Beijing Private Restaurant (Běijígé Sījiā Càiguǎn; 北极阁私家菜馆)

A luxurious setting in a revamped hutong courtyard hotel and styled with glowing red lanterns, dim lighting and wooden fixtures, this one has pricey menu that specializes in imperial Beijing cuisine, so you'll wine and dine like it's 1369.

> Address: 24 Beijige Santiao Hutong, Dongdan Beidajie, Dongcheng District (东城区东单北大街北极阁三条胡同24号)
> Phone: 6522 8288

$ Hǎiwǎnjū (海碗居)

A noodle connoisseur's paradise, Haiwanju boasts many noodles, but its two principal types are the main staples: guòshuǐ (过水) is served at a lower temperature and the warmer guōtiāo (锅挑) is perfect for a cold winter day.

> Address: 36 Songyu Nanli, Chaoyang District
> 朝阳区松榆南里36号
> Phone: 8731 3518

$$$ Jiuhuashan Roast Duck (Jiǔhuāshān Kǎoyā; 九花山烤鸭)

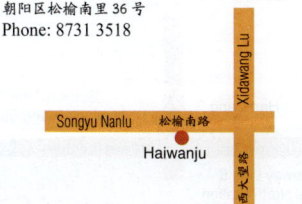

This is another famous roast duck establishment, but apart from their succulent Peking-style bird, the restaurant serves up interesting side platters of duck dumplings, duck feet and duck liver.

> Address: 1/F, Ziyu Hotel, 55 Zenguang Lu, Haidian District (海淀区增光路55号紫玉饭店1-2楼)
> Phone: 6848 3481

Cantonese

$$$ 8th Cantonese Mansion (Yuècài Jiǔjiā; 粤菜酒家)

Who needs to be on the coast to enjoy great seafood when you have a tank as big as the Pacific? For the freshest in fashionable Cantonese dining, this mansion with a marvelous interior design surprises even the staunchest of critiques.

> Address: Chaoyang Park West Gate, inside the No 8 Apartments, Chaoyang District (朝阳区朝阳公园西门八号公馆内)
> Phone: 6508 9999

$$ Beijingers' Restaurant (Běijīngrén Dàjiǔlóu; 北京人大酒楼) **PANDA PICK**

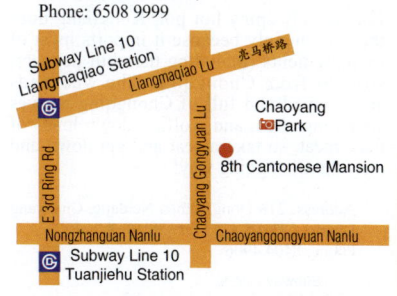

A fine, mid-range Cantonese restaurant with seafood recipes inspired from China's south coast, Beijingers' great family atmosphere, reasonable prices and grand Canton-themed decorations will make anyone smile.

Address: 6 Erqi Juchang Lu, Yuetan Nanjie, Xicheng District (西城区月坛南街二七剧场路甲6号)
Phone: 6802 2636

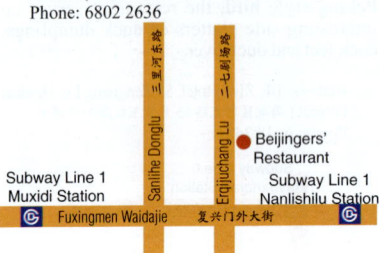

Dongbei

$ Bazhen Dumpling (Bāzhēn Jiǎozi; 八珍饺子) **10% OFF**

Cheap and to the point, Bazhen Jiaozi has awesome dumplings. Order a bunch of their *guotie* (pot stickers) – long, skinny and crispy pan-seared dumplings.

Address: 42 Jiugulou Dajie, Dongcheng District, Andingmen (东城区旧鼓楼大街42号)
Phone: 6202 9030

$$ Xīlóng Cháodiǎn (西龙潮点)

Standard dim sum and Hong Kong delights with an upbeat atmosphere; what more could you ask for?

Address: S6-32, 3/F, Bldg 6, Sanlitun Village South, 19 Sanlitun Lu, Chaoyang District (朝阳区三里屯路19号三里屯Village南区3号楼S6-32单元)

$ Wàngshùngé (旺顺阁)

Wangshunge has all the Manchurian and Dongbei specialties available, even the region's specialty of fish head soup served with bread (yútóu pàobǐng; 鱼头泡饼).

Address: 2A Xinzhong Jie, Dongzhimen Waidajie, Dongcheng District (东城区东直门外大街新中街甲2号)
Phone: 5120 3232

Chongqing

$$ Kongliang Hotpot (Chóngqìng Kǒngliàng Huǒguō; 重庆孔亮火锅)

For fiercely spicy hot pot, Kongliang does the trick mainly because it imports most of its ingredients (including the chili peppers) straight from Chongqing. The weekends are jammed and full of Chongqing natives slamming shots and wolfing down loads of fiery meat, so take a seat and get down and dirty the Chongqing way!

Address: 218 Dongzhimen Neidajie, Chaoyang District (朝阳区东直门内大街218号)
Phone: 8404 4906

Fujian/Hakka

$$ Shichahai Hakka Restaurant (Shíchàhǎi Kèjiācài; 什刹海客家菜)

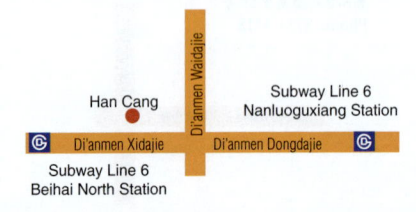

This is a great place for Fujian style seafood and earthy Hakka dishes. The outside presents a marvelous view of Qianhai Lake from the second story terrace, while the inside the walls are plastered with tattered Chinese calligraphy scrolls. The paper-wrapped fish (zhǐbāoyú; 纸包鱼) is remarkable.

> Address: 12 Qianhai Nanyan, opposite North Gate of Beihai Park, Xicheng District (西城区前海南沿12号，北海公园北门对面)
> Phone: 6403 2606; 6403 2616

$ Kejiayuan Restraurant (Kèjiāyuán; 客家园)

The oldest Hakka café in all of Beijing has all this ethnic minority's greatest bites, including signature duck dishes and the popular "three cup chicken" (sānbēijī; 三杯鸡).

> Address: 2-2 Tuanjiehu Beilu, Chaoyang District; southeast corner of Changhong Qiao, a few doors south of Da Dong (朝阳区团结湖北路甲2-2号，长虹桥东南角)

$ Wuyishan Farmland (Wǔyíshān Nóngjiācài; 武夷山农家菜)

Located in the heart of Beijing's Little Fujian on Maliandao Tea Street – hidden amongst dozens of other Fujian cafes and tea houses – sits this faithful Fujian establishment. The owner specializes in fowl, so be like the cool kids and order the duck or the wild goose and wash it all down with some delicious Fujian tea. Afterwards, take a stroll around the neighborhood to see what other Fujian delights you can find.

> Address: Maliandao Hutong, Xicheng District; enter from Maliandao Lu and walk about 300 m (985 ft) (西城区马连道胡同)
> Phone: 131 2669 6251

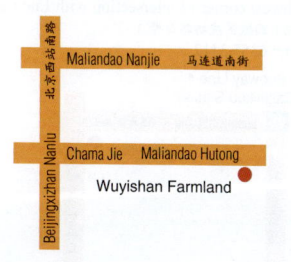

Guangxi

$$ Guǎngfúyuán (广福缘餐厅)

For the most authentic Guangxi restaurant in town, make a pit stop here at the Guangxi Autonomous Region Office. The pork ribs could pass for a miracle and the chef should be canonized.

> Address: Guangxi Autonomous Region Office, 6 Shuanghua Yuan Nanli, Chaoyang District; opposite intersection of Baiziwan Lu (朝阳区朝阳区东三环中路双花园南里6号)
> Phone: 6776 0911 ext 700

Guizhou

$$ Gui Sour Soup Fish (Èrguì Suāntāngyú; 2贵酸汤鱼)

This small eatery gets big props for Southeast Asian tastiness, specializing in a sweet and sour fish soup (suāntāng yú; 酸汤鱼) that's similar to *tom yum*. Make sure to try their homemade Guizhou wines.

> Address: Block 1, Ganluyuan Nanli, Qingnian Lu, Chaoyang District; near the Gome Electrical Appliances Store (朝阳区朝阳区青年路甘露园南里一区1号楼，近国美电器)
> Phone: 8575 1765

$ Courtyard 28 (Èrshíbāhàoyuàn Sījiācài; 28号院私家菜) **10% OFF**

Located in a hutong around the Lama Temple, this trendy restaurant has all the best from China's southwest along with large draft beers to wash it all down. Try the crispy finned fish.

> Address: South of 1 Xilou Hutong, Dongcheng

District (东城区戏楼胡同一号南侧)
Phone: 8401 6788

Jiangsu/Huaiyang

$ *Huáiyángfǔ* (淮扬府)

Savor the flavor of Jiangsu Province's legendary Huaiyang cuisine, which is considered one of China's Eight Culinary Traditions. Free range chickens and country ham dot the menu, and the stir fried prawns and lion's head crab-flavored meatballs are outstanding.

Address: 198 Andingmen Waidajie, Dongcheng District (东城区安定门外大街 198 号)
Phone: 6426 5858; 6426 5959

$ *Wúmíngjū* (无名居)

Literally meaning "No Name House," the prosaic title is overshadowed by the restaurant's sweet and tangy flavors from Jiangsu's ever colorful palate. Their fish dishes are excellent, and they find a good balance between Huaiyang cuisine and other dishes from all corners of Jiangsu.

Address: 32 Zaoying Beili, Maizidian Jie, Chaoyang District (朝阳区麦子店街枣营北里32号)
Phone: 6502 1568

Hebei

$ *Fatty Wang (Wángpàngzi Lǘròu Huǒshāo;* 王胖子驴肉火烧) **PANDA PICK**

If you wish to eat ass in Beijing, this is the place to be. This renowned chain specializes in donkey meat; especially their famed donkey burger. The toasted flat bread sandwich with thin slices of donkey meat and diced green peppers may not seem appetizing at first, but trust us on this one, it's delicious! They also have other donkey dishes like donkey hot pot, but most people come for the burgers.

Address: 80 Gulou Xidajie, Xicheng District (西城区鼓楼西大街 80 号)
Phone: 8402 3077

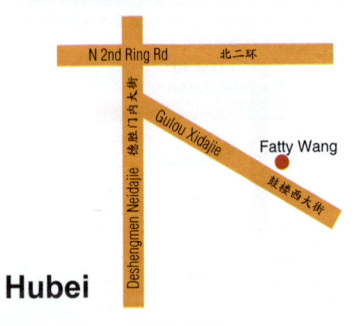

Hubei

$ *Chǔwǎnyuán* (楚畹园)

For large portions, mammoth hunks of meat, and enough carbs to keep you rolling for a week, swing by Chu Wan Yuan for a Hubei farmer's feast. This tavern-like atmosphere and the crunched seating can be a little nerve wracking for the claustrophobic, but after a bite of their *hànzhēnglú yā* (汗蒸炉鸭; Hubei's rebuttal to Peking Duck) or the *sānxiān dòupí* (三鲜豆皮; a pork and mushroom sandwich that's served on the street in Hubei) you'll either be coming back for more or be on the next train out to Hubei.

Address: 3 Hufang Lu, Xicheng District; southwest corner of intersection with Luomashi Dajie (西城区虎坊路 3 号)
Phone: 6355 3112

Hunan

$ Càixiānggēn (菜香根酒楼)

With branches all over the city, this popular café cooks up the spiciest eats from Xiang (aka Hunan) cuisine. It's very casual and always packed with heavy-drinking, hard-hitting Hunan men and their *làmèi* girlfriends.

> Address: 9 Yuetan Nanjie, Xicheng District (西城区月坛南街 9 号)
> Phone: 6802 1707

$$$ Mao's Restaurant (Máojiā Fàndiàn; 毛家饭店) **PANDA PICK**

For the best of Xiang cooking, including many of Mao Zedong's favorites (remember that Mao was originally from Hunan), Mao's has it all. Sample the Chairman's favorite red cooked pork (hóngshāo ròu; 红烧肉), and salute the commander with the dozens of portraits of him plastered on the wall. Note that many Mao specialty restaurants across the country jack their prices up solely because many will pay more for his name scribbled on the menu.

> Address: D409, 4/F, Wangjing Cadenza Mall, 16 Guangshun Beidajie, Chaoyang District (朝阳区广顺北大街 16 号华彩国际中心 4 楼 D409 号)
> Phone: 5981 4118

Jiangxi

$$ Poyanghu Restaurant (Póyánghú Dàjiǔlóu; 鄱阳湖大酒楼)

This superb restaurant offers Jiangxi cooking at its finest and most authentic. Among the specialties of Jiangxi are their slow-cooked soups, which are called *wǎguàn tāng* (瓦罐汤) for the clay pots in which they are simmered for hours at a time. Try the Tianmu bamboo and old duck soup (tiānmùsǔn lǎoyātāng; 天目笋老鸭汤), the spicy *yānsǔn chǎolàròu* (烟笋炒腊肉 ; smoked bamboo shoots stir-fried with pork), village-style wild garlic shoots (xiāngcūn yějiàotóu; 乡村野藠头) or the water-boiled smoked bamboo (shuǐzhǔ yānsǔn; 水煮烟笋).

> Address: 3A Wanshousi Lu (万寿寺路甲 3 号院)
> Phone: 6204 4830

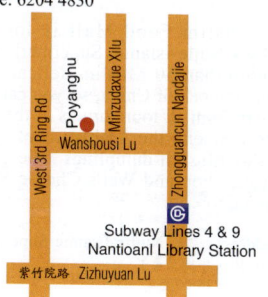

Muslim

$ Báikuí Lǎohào (白魁老号)

Founded in 1780, Baikui Laohao is celebrated for its spice braised mutton soup, which has passed the test of time and is still adored today.

> Address: 158 Jiaodaokou Nandajie, Dongcheng District (东城区交道口南大街 158 号)
> Tel: 6404 0967

$$ Dàshùntáng (大顺堂)

A Muslim restaurant specializing in halal cuisine from China's Hui minority, Dashuntang is where many local Hui hold their wedding banquets, so you might get invited to partake in the ceremony if you stumble in on the right day.

> Address: 1/F, Bldg 5, Fayuansi Xili, Xicheng District (西城区法源寺西里 5 号楼 1 层)
> Phone: 6353 0644

all around Xibei, this no-frills, down to earth restaurant gets the job done. Their homemade yoghurt served in a ceramic vase goes great with their flame-broiled kebabs.

Address: 48 Dongsanhuan Nanlu, Chaoyang District (朝阳区东三环南路 48 号北人泽洋大厦)
Phone: 5962 7288

$$$ *Niujie Muslim Food Mall (Niújiē Qīngzhēn Chāoshì Měishíchéng;* 牛街清真超市美食城 *)*

This Muslim Food Mall is located in Beijing's Nujie Islamic Supermarket. There are more than 50 Muslim delicacies from various regions of China, so you can sample a variety from all four corners of the country. We recommend the Arabian beef cake and the juicy Muslim dumplings. The glutinous rice cake shop and Wei's Cheese Store are excellent, too.

Address : 2/F, Niujie Islamic Supermarket, 5 Niu Jie (牛街 5 号).
Phone: 8355 7354

Northwestern (aka Xibei) (Ningxia, Qinghai & Gansu)

$$ *Lanzhou Hotel Restaurant (Lánzhōu Bīn'guǎn Cāntīng;* 兰州宾馆餐厅 *)*

For Gansu specialties and plenty of Lanzhou noodles, roasted lamb kebabs and sweet desserts, this hotel restaurant is as genuine as it gets, though the inside is as brash as the Hexi Corridor.

Address: Bldg 5, 58 Xizhimen Waidajie, Xicheng Distric; inside the Jinghui Jiayuan complex (西城区西直门北大街 58 号院金晖嘉园小区 5 号楼)
Phone: 8229 1133 ext 108

$ *Xibei Youmiancun Restaurant (Xībèi Yóumiàn Cūn;* 西贝莜面村 *)*

With a variety of samplers and courses from

$$ *Feitian Restaurant (Fēitiān Dàshà Cāntīng;* 飞天大厦餐厅 *)*

Established by the Gansu Provincial Government, Feitian brings the best from Gansu's diverse kitchen, with may Hui dishes. If you don't know what to order, a classic bowl of beef noodles made with hand-pulled, Lanzhou-style noodles never fails.

Address: 3/F, Feitian Mansion, 5 Guangqumen Wainanjie, Dongcheng District (东城区广渠门外南街 5 号飞天大厦 3 层)
Phone: 6777 8000 ext 8323

Shandong

$$ *Tàifēnglóu (* 泰丰楼 *)*

This joint is no doubt the tastiest Shandong restaurant in town. The stir fried tripe is otherworldly, and there are some other rare dishes from the province's cookbook that are hard to find anywhere else outside of Shandong.

> Address: 2 Qianmen Xidajie, Xicheng District (西城区前门西大街 2 号)
> Phone: 6301 0153; 6302 3174

Shanghai

$ *Hujiang Xiangmanlou (Hùjiāng Xiāngmǎnlóu;* 沪江香满楼 *)*

Cooking up delicious Shanghai street food in a well decorated arena with a garden like atmosphere, Hujiang Xiangmanlou is a very pleasant dining experience.

> Address: 34A Dongsishitiao, Dongcheng District (东城区东四十条甲 34 号)
> Phone: 6403 1368

Din Tai Fung (Dīngtàifēng; 鼎泰丰 *)*

PANDA PICK

The bright and contemporary design of this long-awaited restaurant is a perfect compliment to the succulent and delicate dishes served up from China's renowed Zhejiang, Shanghai and Jiangsu food circles (even though the restaurant is from Taiwan). Besides their excellent steamed dumplings and deadly-delicious red bean desserts, this place is famous for serving up some of the absolute best *xiaolongbao* in the country.

> Address: 24 Xinyuan Xili Zhongjie, Liangmaqiao, Chaoyang District (朝阳区新源西里中街 24 号)
> Phone: 6462 4502

Shaanxi & Shanxi

$ *Pàomóguǎn (*泡馍馆*)*

The interior of Paomoguan is refurbished to resemble an old Shaanxi country house and has small wooden stools for seating. Many patrons order *mó* (a type of unleavened bread) to accompany a bowl of sweet and sour dumpling soup, but their most popular dish is the *paomo*, a lamb stew with bits of *mo* shredded up into the mix and delicious pickled garlic on the side.

> Address: 53 Chaonei Nanxiaojie, Dongcheng District (东城区朝内南小街 53 号)
> Phone: 6525 4639

$$ *Shitang Restaurant (Shítáng Cānguǎn;* 食唐餐馆 *)*

This restaurant is a Shaanxi landmark that focuses on Muslim cuisine from the province. Try the thick and hearty mutton noodle stew.

> Address: 907, Section 9, Jinsong, Guangming Qiao, East 2nd Ring Rd, Chaoyang District (朝阳区东二环光明桥辅路劲松 9 区 907 号)
> Phone: 6776 9193

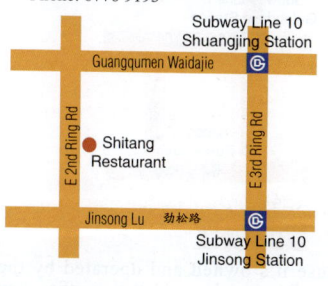

Sichuan

$$ *Bāguó Bùyī* (巴国布衣)

Baguo Buyi has grown a bit touristy because of its popular Sichuan face changing performances and Sichuan opera, but that does little to take away from the mouth-numbing dishes that you'll find here. They also have an unconventional cold turtle dish that locals rave about. The interior is designed in a traditional Sichuan architectural style, with intricate wooden designs in an open-air environment.

Address: 68 Xizhimen Nanxiaojie, Xicheng District (西城区西直门南小街68号)
Phone: 6615 2230

$ *Baochao Restaurant (Bǎochāo Fàndiàn;* 宝钞饭店)

This place has a homey vibe with an amicable staff, and the prices are a bargain. There's enough spice in the food to catch the roof of your mouth on fire, Baochao's non-pretentious hutong locale makes it a wonderful place for a relaxed gathering spot for friends, families and couples.

Address: 107 Baochao Hutong, Xicheng District (西城区西城区宝钞胡同107号)
Phone: 6401 5822

$$ *Chuan Ban (Chuānbàn Cān tīng;* 川办餐厅) **PANDA PICK**

Because it's owned and operated by the Sichuan Provincial representation office, you know the quality and authenticity of Chuan Ban will be top of the line. That being said, out of all the other restaurants operated by provincial representation offices, this one takes the cake for being the best (in our humble opinion). Definitely order a platter of the kung pao frog (gōngbǎo niúwā; 宫保牛蛙) and bacon fried in chili. They also have a nice selection of Sichuan *baijiu* if you're looking to kick the party up a notch.

Address: 5 Gongyuan Toutiao, Jianguomen Neidajie, Dongcheng District (东城区建国门内贡院头条5号)
Phone: 6512 2277 ext 6101

$$ *Chuanchengyuan (Chuānchéngyuán Málà Xiāngguō;* 川成元麻辣香锅)

At Chuan Cheng Yuan you'll find plenty of Sichuan's favorites, albeit a Westernized version of them. This might be a good option if your belly can't handle the unbearable spice found at some of the other more standard Sichuan places.

Address: B1, Guorui Shopping Center, 18 Chongwenmen Waidajie, Dongcheng District (东城区崇文门外大街18号国瑞购物中心B1楼)
Phone: 6714 7859

Taiwan

$$ *Golden Spoon Taiwanese Food (Jīntāngshí Sīfángcài;* 金汤匙私房菜)

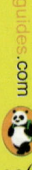

For an elegant taste from across the straights at a price that won't have you drowning in debt, the Golden Spoon offers outstanding meals in a classy milieu for a pleasant dining experience. Do yourself a favor by getting the tofu cooked with shrimp and baby back ribs.

Address: 5/F, South Place, The Place, 9 Guanghua Lu, Chaoyang District (朝阳区光华路9号世贸天阶南街5层)
Phone: 6587 1472; 5905 1789

Tibetan

$$ Makye Ame (Mǎjí'āmǐ; 玛吉阿米)

A restaurant made famous for its Tibetan singing and dancing, Makye Ame's food is also high quality and the Lhasa-inspired décor provides a charming faux-getaway.

Address: 11A Xiushui Nanjie, Jianguomenwai, Chaoyang District (朝阳区建国门外秀水南街甲11号)
Phone: 6506 9616

$$$ Qomolangma (Zhūmùlángmǎ; 珠穆郎玛)

With its location in the hotel at the Tibet Provincial office, you would expect to find more traditional flavors at Qomolangma, but the palate here is rather subdued to meet the taste of foreigners. Qomoloangma (which is the name for Mt Everest in Tibetan) has cultural shows on the weeknights and reservations are recommended. The elegant, walled compound in the middle of a rustic hutong neighborhood makes you feel like you're in the marvelous Potala Palace.

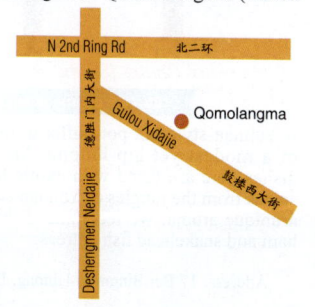

Address: 149 Gulou Xidajie, Xicheng District; inside Tibet Provincial office (西城区鼓楼西大街149号西藏驻京办事处)
Phone: 6401 8822 ext 2828

Xinjiang

$$ Afunti (Āfántí; 阿凡提)

Despite being a bit touristy due to the stellar Uighur house band, Afunti is still an entertaining venue with a decent menu. Come for the food, stay for the hookah and Islamic geometric patterns.

Address: 17 Ritan Beilu (日坛北路17号)
Phone: 6527 2288, 6525 1071

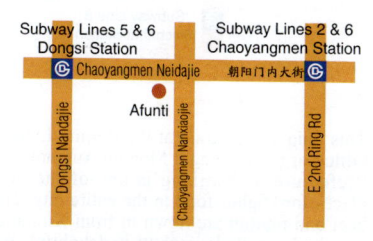

$ Kashgar Restaurant (Kāshí Fànzhuāng; 喀什饭庄) **PANDA PICK**

With genuine taste with spices straight from the bazaars of Kashgar and art and music from China's remote Northwest, Kashgar Restaurant's lamb kebabs, hand pulled noodles and naan are so good that some believe they are being served in Jannah (Islamic paradise).

Address: 60 Pen'er Hutong, Xicheng District (西城区盆儿胡同60号)
Phone: 6355 7618

$ Wangdelou Muslim Restaurant (Wàngdélóu Qīngzhēn Cāntīng; 望德楼清真餐厅)

This old-school diner caters particularly to the city's Muslim ethnic minorities, meaning that dishes like the mutton soups with chunks of bread are made strictly to the Xinjiang style and are among the most delicious in the city. All of the fried dishes are also superb. The only complaint is that service moves slower than a 1st century Silk Road caravan.

Address: 26 Di'anmen Waidajie, Xicheng District (地安门外大街 26 号)
Phone: 6402 2589

$ Muslim Food Fare (Jīnsītè Cāntīng; 金丝特餐厅)

This unique restaurant at the Beijing Liaison Office of the Bayangol Mongol Autonomous Prefecture of Xinjiang is one of the best places for Uighur food in the entire city. The beef and mutton are flown in from Xinjiang, and the homemade yoghurt is delightful. We suggest the mutton grill served with naan bread and Xinjiang pilaf rice.

Address : 2 Zaojun Miao, Haidian District (皂君庙 2 号新疆巴州驻京办事处内)
Phone: 6211 1856

Yunnan

$$ Aimo Town (Āiméng Xiǎozhèn; 埃蒙小镇)

This chill hutong eatery has a host of appetizing platters from the various ethnic minorities of Yunnan Province. The fish and meat dishes here are both marvelous, but remember to order a plate (or two or three) of crisp mint leaves that are chewed in between bites for a palate cleanser.

Address: Bldg G, 46 Fangjia Hutong, Dongcheng District (东城区方家胡同 46 号艺术园区 G 座)
Phone: 6400 1725

$$$ Dali Courtyard (Dàlǐ Yuànzi; 大里院子)

Fine dining with an elegant feel and sophisticated ambiance can be found on the outdoor patio of Dali Courtyard. It's a romantic setting during the warmer days and when it's illuminated with smooth lighting, exquisite floral displays and on-the-ground cushion seating. We have no recommendations for you since the set menu is decided by the chef in advance, so take a seat, admire the scenery and enjoy the element of surprise.

Address: 67 Xiaojingchang Hutong, Gulou Dongdajie, Dongcheng District (东城区鼓楼东大街小经厂胡同 67 号)
Phone: 8404 1430

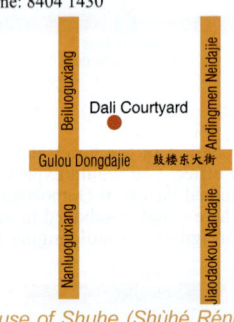

$$ House of Shuhe (Shùhé Rénjiā; 束河人家)

10% OFF afternoon tea & snacks

A Yunnan-style hot pot buffet in the middle of a modest yet hip hutong. Most of the dishes here are fused with exotic herbs and spices from the jungles of Yunnan and put off a unique aroma. We recommend the country ham and snakehead fish entrees.

Address: 17 Bei Bingmasi Hutong, Dongcheng

District (东城区北兵马司胡同17号)
Phone: 5721 8898

Zhejiang

$$ Fēngsāo Zhèrén (风骚浙人)

Situated in a renovated courtyard for an elegant and comfortable setting, Fengsao brings the delights of mellow Zhejiang to Beijing. Try the Hangzhou delicacy known as beggars chicken (jiàohuā jī; 叫花鸡) and get a glass of their homemade brandy: *huángjiǔ* (黄酒).

Address: 35-37 Jinbao Jie (at the east end), Dongcheng District (东城区金宝街35-37号 金宝街东口)
Phone: 6527 7877

International

Pricing Guide (excluding drinks):

$$$ More than ¥250 (US$40)
$$ ¥100 – ¥250 (US$15-40)
$ Less than ¥100 (US$15)

AFRICAN

$$ Casablanca (Kǎsàbùlánkǎ; 卡萨布兰卡)

This above-average traditional Moroccan restaurant has an even better wine list, and the organic falafels, lamb tagine and grilled lamb sausages here are highly recommended.

Address: 14 Xihai Nanyan (西海南沿14号)
Phone: 6613 1929

$$$ Pinotage South African Restaurant and Wine Bar

A plentiful selection of well-priced South African wines, along with traditional national dishes like lamb tomato "bredie," make Beijing's first South African restaurant quite stylish.

Address: Unit 2-105, Bldg 2, Sanlitun Soho, 8 Gongti Beilu, Chaoyang District (朝阳区工体北路8号三里屯 Soho2号商场2-105室)
Phone: 5785 3538; 5785 3539

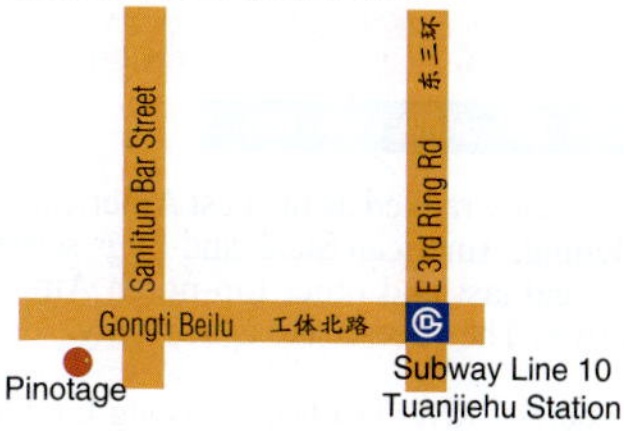

$ Turay's Africa House (Túruì de Fēizhōu Zhījiā; 图瑞的非洲之家)

A distinctive place to try West Africa's best. Ask the waiters at Turay's for their favorite recommendations in case you don't know where to begin, and enjoy the art and drum beats of Africa while you wait.

Address: 2/F, Unit 5, 39 Xingfu Er'cun, Chaoyang District (朝阳区幸福二村39号首开广场5号单元2层)
Phone: 8444 4169

AMERICAN

$ The Box — 10% OFF (drinks excluded)

The best burgers in all of China (no lie) can be found at this hip hutong joint. The owner Paca serves up massive, innovative burgers and even allows the winner of the Box's annual hamburger eating contest (held at the beginning of August if you're interested) to create their own unique sandwich to be featured on the menu. The recently remodeled interior and cool music make the Box a real hit amongst locals and expats.

Address: 5 Qianmachang Hutong, Jiugulou Dajie (旧鼓楼大街前马厂胡同5号)
Phone: 6401 3293
Subway Line 2 Guloudajie Station

$ American Steak and Eggs (Xǐláizhōng Běiměi Xīcāntīng; 喜来中北美西餐厅)

10% OFF (drinks excluded)

Consistently ranked as the best American diner in Beijing, American Steak and Eggs serves all day breakfast and other top-notch American favorites. The cheesecake is heavenly.

Address: River Garden, 7 Yuyang Lu, Shunyi (榆阳路7号，顺义裕京花园会所)
Phone: 8046 6648; 6592 8088; 186 0005 4094

$$ Chef Too (Měixīxī Cāntīng; 美西西餐厅)

With some of the juiciest steaks in town, this simple American restaurant serves up only the freshest cuts of beef and also has a quality deli.

Address: Opposite the West gate of Chaoyang Park, Chaoyang District (朝阳区朝阳公园西门对面)
Phone: 6591 8676

$$ Tim's Texas Bar-B-Q

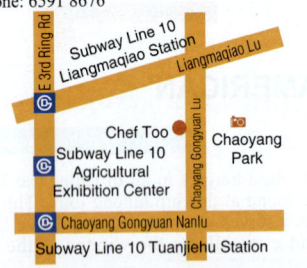

You'll feel like you're truly in Texas with the Dixie Chicks blasting through the speakers, waitresses clunking around in cowboy boots, and A&M banners covering every patch of the walls. The BBQ grill passes the test if you're craving ribs, brisket and sausage, and they even have some Tex-Mex and southern soul food like chicken fried steak.

Address: 14 Dongdaqiao Lu (2 Silk Street), Chaoyang District (朝阳区东大桥路14号秀水2号院)
Phone: 6591 9161
Website: www.timsbarbq.com

$$$ The CUT Steak and Seafood Grill (Rèn Bāfáng Cāntīng; 刃扒房餐厅)

With superb service, elegant décor, excellent presentation, world class steaks and a renowned selection of wines, this upscale steak house located in the Fairmont Beijing Hotel is the perfect setting for a fine dining experience.

Address: Fairmont Beijing Hotel, 8 Yong'an Dongli, Jianguomen Waidajie, Chaoyang District (朝阳区建国门外大街永安东里8号华彬费尔蒙酒店)
Phone: 8507 3617

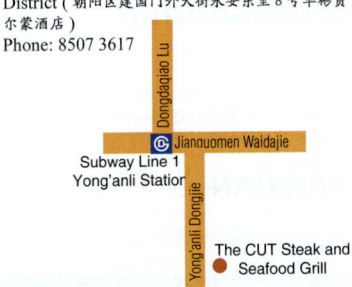

$ Nola's Café

One FREE coffee or tea; 50% OFF some drinks

Gumbo, po'boys and etouffee make every day Mardi Gras in this Crescent City Cajun diner. (Actually, stop by during Fat Tuesday for a *fais do-do*, king cake and an all-you-can-eat feast.) The lunch buffet is good and you can be sure the spice will be "kicked up a notch." *Laissez les bons temps rouler!*

Address: 11A Xiushui Nanjie, Chaoyang District (朝阳区秀水南街11号)
Phone: 8563 6215

$$ Blue Frog (Lán Wā; 蓝蛙)

It's not hard these days to find good burgers and other American-style bun-and-pattie based food in Beijing, and to make your search even easier, you can just head over to Blue Frog – Beijing's slice of a long-favored Shanghai chain. It's hard to beat their flagship "Blue Frog Burger," even back in the US, but while you munch on some char-broiled awesomeness consider that their 16:00 to 20:00 (four hours long!) daily happy hour has buy-one-get-one drink specials. With Mexican and Italian options as well, this hamburger-heaven is one addicting toad.

Address: 167, 1/F, Indigo, 18 Jiuxianqiao Lu, Chaoyang District (朝阳区颐堤港店酒仙桥路18号1层167号); located in the Dashanzi/798 Art District (大山子艺术区)
Phone: 8426 0017

Sanlitun Location

Address: 4-3-1, 3/F, S4 Tower, in Taikoo Li, 19 Sanlitun Lu, Chaoyang District (朝阳区三里屯路19号太古里E4号楼3F4-3-1号)
Phone: 6417 4030

ASIAN

Indian

$$ *Ganges Indian Restaurant (Hénghé Yìndù Cāntīng;* 恒河印度餐厅)

The best place for Indian food in town, Ganges' curries are delectable, and it's essential to throw in some of their garlic naan bread for good measure. The Bollywood music is cool, though it can be a bit too loud at times. They have four locations: Dongzhimen, Chaoyang CBD, Lido and Haidian. Visit their website for more info.

Address: Suite 202, 2/F, Bldg 1, Shimao Department Store, 13 Gongti Beilu, Chaoyang District (朝阳区工体北路13号世贸百货1号楼2层202)
Phone: 6416 0181
Website: www.ganges-restaurant.com

$$ *Khajuraho (Kèjiǔlāhuò Yìndù Cāntīng;* 克久拉霍印度餐厅)

A Westernized Indian restaurant with a chic interior, Khajuraho cooks up a Goa coconut prawn curry that gets outstanding reviews, and everyone can agree on sticking around for dessert after a wonderful meal.

Address: Unit 1122-1-2, Sanlitun Soho, Gongti Beilu, Chaoyang District (朝阳区工体北路三里屯Soho1122-1-2室)
Phone: 8527 0464

Indonesian/Malaysian

$ *Cocolol* 我爱南洋菜 *(Wǒ'ài Nányángcài;* 我爱南洋菜)

An unfussy set with a lighthearted approach, low prices, neat Southeast Asian memorabilia and, most importantly, lots of flavor, Cocolo is an Indonesian dream. Dishes like *perkedel* and the Indonesian fried noodles are the best, but they also have other treats from greater South and Southeast Asia, like samosas and curries.

Address: 2 Xiushui, 14 Dongdaqiao Lu, Chaoyang District (朝阳区东大桥路14号院秀水2号)
Phone: 6500 5860

Japanese

$$ Ajitoku (Wèidé Rìběn Liàolǐ; 味德日本料理)

A small restaurant specializing in model Japanese dishes like braised ox tongue, sashimi and roasted eel, Ajitoku rocks.

Address: Bldg C, B113, Raycom Infotech Park, 2 Kexueyuan Nanlu, Zhongguancun, Haidian District (海淀区科学院南路2号融科资讯中心C座地下一层)
Phone: 8286 1993

$$ Bāwèifāng (八味坊)

This Japanese themed steak and grill fires up quality cuts of imported meat all while keeping the costs at bay.

Address: Chaoyang Park West Gate, inside the No 8 Apartments, Chaoyang District (朝阳区朝阳公园西门八号公馆内)
Phone: 6500 5555

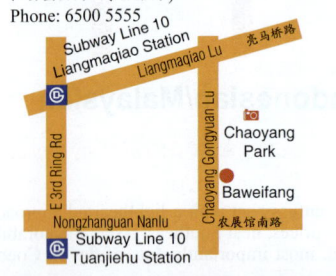

$ Edomea Sushi (Jiānghùqián Shòusī; 江户前寿司)

One of the favorites of the city's Japanese expat community, Edomea has extraordinarily fresh seafood and presents only the best of the country's most authentic sushi and sashimi dishes. We recommend trying whatever they have listed as their daily special; it just came off the boat that day. There's a nice catalog of good sake as well.

Address: Room 0925, Bldg 9, Jianwai Soho, 39 Dongsanhuan Zhonglu, Chaoyang District (朝阳区东三环中路39号建外Soho 9号楼0925)
Phone: 5869 8112

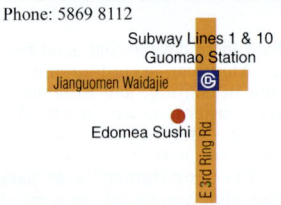

$ Fish Mama (Yújiàng Liàolǐ; 鱼匠料理)

Excellent presentation and service together with fresh seafood and delectable "Japanese comfort" food like oden, tempura and sushi make this one our favorite Japanese establishments. The inside is fashioned with traditional wooden furniture, but by far the best part of it all is the array of outrageous presentation schemes. Go in person to find out yourself!

Address: 4/F, Shimao Department Store, 13 Gongti Beilu, Chaoyang District (朝阳区工体北路13号世茂百货4楼)
Phone: 8400 4685

Korean

$$ Běnjiā Hánguó Liàolǐ (本家韩国料理)

For phenomenal Korean BBQ, this is the

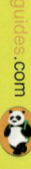

place to be. This well-known chain has branches in other Chinese cities and is renowned for its marinated beef and *bulgogi*, and you can rest that assured there's plenty of kimchi and pickled veggie appetizers to go around.

Address: S7, CLASS 13, Guangze Lu, Chaoyang District (朝阳区望京广泽路CLASS13号S7)
Phone: 8473 0101

$$$ Gaon Korean Restaurant (Gāo'ēn; 高恩)

A dimly lit, upscale dining establishment with a ritzy glare and imported products from Korea, Gaon has set dinner menus available for a hefty price, but come in for lunch for equally great specials at half the cost.

Address: 5/F, East Tower, LG Twin Towers, 12B Jianguomen Waidajie, Chaoyang District (朝阳区建国门外大街乙12号双子座大厦东塔5层)
Phone: 5120 8899

$ Oh Jook Hun (Wūzhú Xuān; 乌竹轩)

This cozy and modest place with a wide variety of genuine cuisine from the Korean Peninsula has a generous list of Korean beer, soju and wine, and there are even some tasty sweets.

Address: 1 Haoyun Jie, Chaoyang District (朝阳区朝阳公园路好运街1号)
Phone: 5867 0230

Middle Eastern

$$ 1001 Nights (Yīqiānyīyè Cāntīng; 一千一夜餐厅)

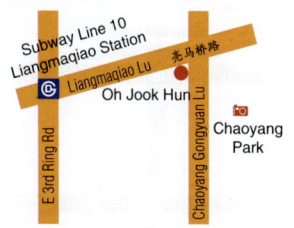

1001 Nights isn't your ordinary restaurant. This entertainment complex boasts a glamorous display of Middle Eastern architecture, art and music, along with belly dancing in the evenings (warning: you may be targeted to dance on stage with them). Apart from the stellar shows, the food is appetizing; the Middle Eastern expat community of Beijing swears the kebabs are as good as the ones back home.

Address: North side of Solana Mall, 6 Chaoyang Gongyuan Lu, Chaoyang District (朝阳区朝阳公园路6号SOLANA内)
Phone: 5905 6316

$ Biteapitta (Bādā Bǐng; 吧嗒饼)

This budget eatery has oily yet delicious Westernized Middle Eastern pitas and other snacks. Though they specialize in pitas, the falafel is also outstanding.

Address: 1/F, Tongli Studio, 43 Sanlitun Beijie, Chaoyang District (三里屯北街43号同里大厦1楼)
Phone: 6467 2961

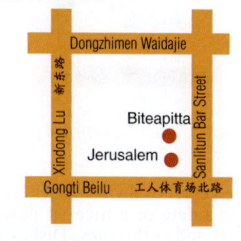

Mongolian

$$$ Ordos Restaurant (Áobāohuì; 敖包会)

A massive compound the size of the old Mongolian empire with off-the-wall shows and performances, Aobaohui will blast you away with music, dancing and reenactments of weddings, all while the waiters swish around in traditional Mongolian *buryats*. Apart from its flamboyant recitals, Aobaohui is known for serving up massive racks of ribs, sheep legs and even an entire roasted cow for a whopping ¥29,999!

Address: 30 Zhongguancun Nandajie, Haidian

District (海淀区中关村南大街30号)
Phone: 6216 8176

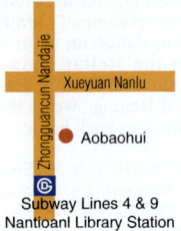

Thai

$ Serve the People (Wéirénmín Fúwù ; 为人民服务)

Smack dab in the middle of Sanlitun's bar street is Nam Nam, a solid Vietnamese restaurant serving the whole shebang: pho, fried spring rolls, grilled fish and high octane Vietnamese iced coffee. It's a wonderful place to grub before or after hitting up the area's bar strip.

Address: 1 Xiwu Jie, Sanlitun (北京朝阳区三里屯西五街1号)
Phone: 6468 6053

$$ Laburnum Thai Restaurant (Jīnliànhuā Cānyǐn; 金链花餐饮)

A romantic yet relaxed vibe makes Laburnum perfect for a date or a nice sit down meal with friends and colleagues. Dishes include the crisp and tender fried crab curry (though it's a bit messy) and the grilled turbot that comes with a complementary glass of wine.

Address: West Gate of Workers' Stadium, Gongti Xilu, Chaoyang District (朝阳区工体西路工人体育场西门)
Phone: 6652 9999

$$$ Lan Na Thai (Lánnà Tài; 兰纳泰)

This upscale Thai restaurant is marked by unprecedented presentation and service, factors that make it difficult to begin your meal when all the dishes are absolute masterpieces of artistic zeal. The quality of the food matches the appearance, so be prepared to pay for what you get.

Address: 26 Dongcaoyuan, Gongti Nanlu, Chaoyang District (朝阳区工体南路东草园26号)
Phone: 6551 6788

Vietnamese

$ 4 Corners (Sìjiǎo Cāntīng; 四角餐厅)

PANDA PICK

Cozy and casual and nestled between the gorgeous lakes of Houhai and Qianhai, this zesty Vietnamese café is run by owner, head chef and TV personality Jun Trinh, who says that he wants his artsy venue to be all about "food, drinks, art and people." There are regular cultural events and live music, and if you're feeling adventurous, go for Trinh's favorite: the hot and sour fish head soup. It's a little hard to find, unfortunately.

Address: 27 Dashibei Hutong, Xicheng District, near west end of Yandai Xiejie (西城区大石碑胡同27号，烟袋斜街西口附近)
Phone: 6401 7797

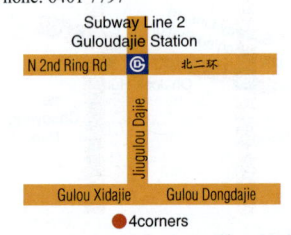

$$$ Asia Bistro

Asia Bistro's location in the JW Marriot Hotel already makes it worthy, but the Sunday ¥388/288 Thai and Vietnamese brunch buffet with free flowing champagne and beer is the best way to end your busy weekend. Brunch runs from 11:30-15:00.

> Address: 1/F, JW Marriott Hotel, 83 Jianguo Lu, China Central Place, Chaoyang District (朝阳区建国路83号JW万豪酒店)
> Phone: 5908 8511

LATIN AMERICAN

Brazilian

$$$ Alameda

Alameda is a steak restaurant (non-*rodizio*, steaks are prepared and served by order) with a Brazilian attitude. The *feijoada* here is outstanding and they also offer a "rapido" lunch special for a good bargain.

> Address: Sanlitun Beijie, Chaoyang District; beside the Nali Mall (朝阳区三里屯北街)
> Phone: 6417 8084; 6413 1939

$$ Brazilian Barbeque Gauchos (Kǎwūxiù Bāxī Kǎoròu; 卡乌秀巴西烤肉) ▶ PANDA PICK

For a carnivorous Brazilian feast, turn your cards up on green and let the waiters spoil you with roasted cuts of pork, beef, chicken, lamb and any other meats you can sink your teeth into. The locale is superb: right in the middle of Chaoyang Park under the trees by the lake. Come in the warmer months to grab a seat outside when the place is packed and animated the Brazilian way.

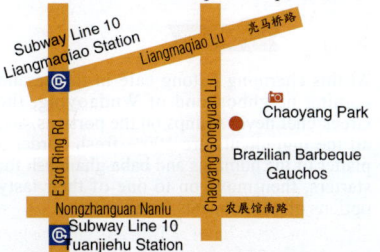

> Address: Gate 3, inside Chaoyang Park, 20 Chaoyang Gongyuan Xilu, Chaoyang District (朝阳区朝阳公园西路20号.朝阳公园3号门内)
> Phone: 8595 2661

Mexican

$ Avocado Tree (Yóulíshù; 油梨树)

A sloppy, budget Mexican restaurant that's admired amongst Wudaokou's university students, Avocado Tree and its burritos are by far the best in town, and the service is speedy and attentive.

> Address: 310 Pinnacle Plaza, Shunyi District (顺义区顺一天竺房地产开发区荣祥广场)
> Phone: 186 0010 8613

$$ Q Mex

Besides the phenomenal guacamole and a nice terrace for the warmer months, the tequila selection at Q Mex is unreal, helping to turn this popular hangout more into a bar than a sit down restaurant. But if you're hungry the menu is certainly adequate, and for the record, the churros are heaven on Earth.

> Address: Gongti Beilu, Courtyard 4, near The Bookworm and d lounge, under Kro's Nest (工体北路4号院)
> Phone: 6585 3828

EUROPEAN

French

$$ Bleu Marine (Lèxiào; 乐笑)

This delightful French restaurant has

imported wines and great steak frites served on a wooden board with a heart healthy salad. The red lanterns and Chinese ornaments may fool you into believing it's not really French, but after your first bite you'll surely be shouting "Mon dieu!"

> Address: 5 Guanghua Xili, Chaoyang District, 100 m (328 ft) north of the Silk Market（朝阳区光华西里5号，秀水往北100米左右）
> Phone: 6500 6704

$ Crepanini (Kěbǎinínì; 可百尼尼)

The two Francophile Brits who opened Crepanini captured "le vrai essence" of France with their scrumptious crepes, the best of which (in our opinion) is the Riviera. Any dessert crepe smothered with molten chocolate wins our approval as well.

> Address: Unit A110, 1/F, Nali Patio, 81 Sanlitun Lu, Chaoyang District（朝阳区三里屯路81号那里花园1层酒吧街对面）
> Phone: 5208 6093
> Website: www.crepanini.com

German

$$ German Food Center (Déguó Shípǐndiàn; 德国食品店)

More of a German gourmet specialties meat and cheese shop than a sit-down restaurant, German Food Center functions like a deli, and you can order a sandwich or gyro and take a seat in this shop situated in a German expat neighborhood. Stock up and bring some goods home or to one of the city's many parks for a picnic.

> Address: 105 Binduyuan Mansion, 15 Zaoying Beili, Maizidian, 800 m (2,624 ft) east of Nongzhanguan Beilu（朝阳区麦子店枣营北里15号宾都苑公寓105号（长城饭店南侧，农展馆北路往东走800米路北）
> Phone: 6591 9370

$$ Café Konstanz (Dénán Miànbāofáng; 德南面包房)

Café Konstanz is where to head for beer, sauerkraut, mashed potatoes, sausages, and the best schnitzel in the capital. Afterwards, head downstairs to the South German Bakery for desserts, apple strudel and great pastries.

> Address: 27 Haoyun Jie, 1 Chaoyang Gongyuan Lu, Chaoyang District（朝阳区朝阳公园路1号好运街27号）
> Phone: 5867 0201

$$ Paulaner Brauhaus (Pǔlānà Píjiǔfāng Cāntīng; 普拉那啤酒坊餐厅)

Situated in the Kempinski Hotel, this smart, casual micro-brewery and traditional German restaurant is a great place for business or to grab some beers with friends when the live band performs on the weekends. The outdoor courtyard patio packs a good crowd during the summer when locals and expats come to enjoy a handcrafted brew under the sun.

> Address: Kempinski Hotel Beijing Lufthansa Center, 50 Liangmaqiao Lu（朝阳区亮马桥路50号）
> Phone: 6465 3388 ext 4211

Greek

$ Argo **PANDA PICK**

At this charming hutong café in the up and coming neighborhood of Wudaoying, the Greek chef never skimps on the portions, and all the ingredients are 100% fresh. Order a platter of the hummus and baba ghanoush for starters, then move on to one of their tasty options of grilled meats for an entrée.

Address: 59 Wudaoying Hutong, Dongcheng District; 100 m (328 ft) west of Vineyard Café (东城区五道营胡同59号)
Phone: 8403 9748

```
Subway Line 2            Subway Lines 2 & 5
Andingmen Station        Yonghegong Lama Temple
          Ⓒ   N 2nd Ring Rd   Ⓒ
  Andingmen Neidajie                  Yonghegong Dajie
                  ● Argo
              Wudaoying Hutong
```

$ Greek Delicacy (Xīlà Měiwèi; 希腊美味)

For a quick fix of tzatziki-doused gyros and feta loaded salads, look no further than Greek Delicacy. The low prices and generous portions here make this place a great deal.

Address: Solana Lifestyle Shopping Park, 6 Chaoyang Gongyuan Lu, Chaoyang District (朝阳区朝阳公园路6号蓝色港湾国际商区)
Phone: 5905 6380

```
   Subway Line 10
   Liangmaqiao Station      亮马桥路
         Ⓒ  Liangmaqiao Lu
                              ● Greek
                                Delicacy
  E 3rd Ring Rd    Chaoyang Gongyuan Lu
                              🏛 Chaoyang
                                 Park
```

Italian

$$$ Alla Osteria (Yìshàng Yìdàlì Cāntīng; 意尚意大利餐厅)

Alla Osteria's upscale fine Italian dining has all the favorites from the old country: pastas, pizzas and imported thick cuts of meat and ham. Alla Osteria places heavy emphasis on its wine, and there's even a spacious wine cellar with seating. If that's too cool for you, try the outdoor terrace on a sunny day.

Address: Room 1112, Soho Shangdu, 8 Dongdaqiao Lu, Chaoyang District (朝阳区东大桥路8号Soho尚都1112号)
Phone: 5900 3112

```
              Ⓒ Chaoyang Beilu
   Dongdaqiao Lu  Subway Line 6
                  Dongdaqiao Station
              Jinghua Beijie
              ● Alla Osteria
```

$ Bittersweet Café (Bàtáng Kāfēi; 半糖咖啡)

A budget option for quick and delicious Italian meals, this one's pizzas are amongst the best in town, and the cappuccinos are quality. The tranquil vibe at this snug café attracts a lot of singles with laptops and pairs enjoying a laid-back conversation.

Address: 12 Xinyuanxili, Chaoyang District (朝阳区新源西里东街12号)

```
   Xindong Lu           新东路
                                Xinyuan Nanlu
       ● Bittersweet Café
                        Xindong Lu
```

Portuguese

$$ Camoes (Jiǎméishì Púcāntīng; 贾梅士葡餐厅)

Camoes is a very nice Portuguese seafood restaurant that won't strain your wallet. The grilled bacalhau is the house specialty, and there is even a business three-course lunch set that comes with your choice of coffee or tea.

Address: Legendale Hotel, 90-92 JinbaoJie, Dongcheng District (东城区金宝街90-92号励均达酒店)
Phone: 8511 3388

```
         Ⓒ Subway Line 5
           Dengshikou Station
   Dongdan Beidajie
           Jinbao Jie    金宝街
                      ● Camoes
           东单北大街
```

$$ Macau Taste (Àomén Wèidào; 澳门味道)

If you can't make it to the Vegas of Asia, then swing by Macau Taste for a taste of Macau. The former Portuguese colony's kitchen combines elements from the empire's African, American, India and Asian colonies, but has a fine touch of finite European preparation. The Macau-style sandwiches are recommended, and they even have Cantonese dim sum and noodle dishes.

Eating

237

Address: L-15A, Sanlitun Village South, 19 Sanlitun Lu, Chaoyang District (朝阳区三里屯路19号三里屯 Village 南区 L-15A)
Phone: 6415 1399

$$$ Vasco's (Wànsīgé Xīcāntīng; 万斯阁西餐厅)

This classy buffet in the Hilton Hotel is more international than traditional Portuguese (e.g. Japanese sushi and Maine lobster), but there are a few fish dishes from the cookbooks of old Lisboa. Vasco's highlight is the Sunday Champagne brunch.

Address: 5/F, Hilton Beijing Wangfujing, 8 Wangfujing Dongjie, Dongcheng District (东城区王府井东街8号希尔顿北京王府井酒店5层)
Phone: 5812 8888

Russian

$$ Traktirr Pushkin (Bǐdébǎo É Cāntīng; 彼得堡俄餐厅)

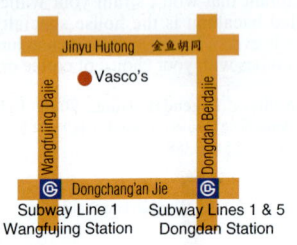

PANDA PICK

Regularly voted as the best Russian Restaurant in Beijing, this middle-upscale dining establishment serves the best from Russia with borscht and caviar, and it even has Ukrainian platters like the delicious Chicken Kiev. The vodka menu is superb and they also have imported Russian beers and kvas.

Address: 5-15 Dongzhimen Neidajie (东直门内大街5-15号)
Phone: 8407 8158

Spanish

$$$ Agua

At Agua, upscale fine dining marches to the rhythm of Spain. The inside looks like a refined 1950s European café with wooden floors, high ceilings and waiters dressed in all black, but its formality doesn't make it conceited by any means. There are Spanish dishes like paella, as well as other meals with influences from continental Europe, but we recommend one of their incredible seafood based main courses.

Address: 4/F, Nali Patio, 81 Sanlitun Lu, Chaoyang District (朝阳区三里屯路81号那里花园4层)
Phone: 5208 6188; 5208 6198

$$ Carmen (Kǎmén Xībānyá Cāntīng; 卡门西班牙餐厅)

PANDA PICK

A high spirited place with live flamenco guitar, Spanish architecture, tapas, sangria and wine, Carmen's tapas menu is extensive and has all the well-known items like *chorizo*, *boquerones*, imported cheeses, prosciutto, *empanadillas*, *tortilla de patata*, *croquetas* and mixed olive plates. Its location in the trendy Nali Patio in Sanlitun brings in a lot of expat party-goers who always brighten the already upbeat mood.

Address: 81 Sanlitun Lu, Chaoyang District (朝阳区三里屯路81号)
Phone: 6417 8038

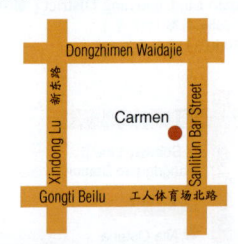

Other

Bakeries & Desserts

$ A Sugar Bowl Cafes and Teahouse (Gélóu Tiánpǐn; 阁楼甜品)

A small café near the lakes with a lovely atmosphere and even better Vietnamese coffee. This place can get a bit touristy in the summer, making it a better place to hunker down during winter.

Address: 12 Di'anmen Xidajie, Dongcheng District (东城区地安门西大街12号)
Phone: 6402 5798

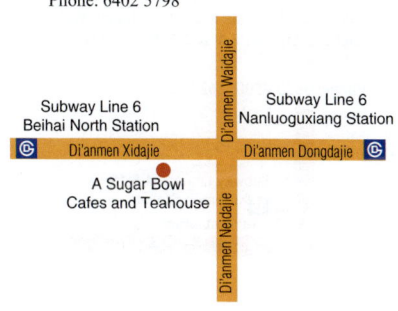

$ Snowball (Sīnuòbǎo Zhēnzhū Bīng qílín; 斯诺宝珍珠冰淇淋)

Snowball specializes in ice cream, desserts and ice cream pellets; come here and reconnect with your inner child.

Address: CC06, B-1 Oriental Plaza, Dongcheng District (东城区王府井东方广场地铁层CC06)

$ Two Guys and a Pie (Gēmen'ér Bǐng; 哥们儿饼)

From the sweet and tangy to the meaty and greasy, these two Aussie owners have just about every kind of pie. Most of their orders are take-away, but there are a few seats if you want to stick around. FYI, the meat pies are the perfect remedy for a hangover.

Address: 32 Sanlitun Nan, Chaoyang District, behind Yashow Market, across from Friend Bar (朝阳区三里屯南32号，雅秀后边朋友酒吧对面)
Phone: 138 0106 9721

Delivery

$$ Hutong Pizza (Hútóng Pīsà; 胡同比萨)

PANDA PICK

Pizza in a hutong? Now you're talking! This is by far our favorite pizza joint in all of Beijing. The square pizzas come in portions large enough to satisfy the Yeti and the sides of fried calamari, French fries and fresh garden salads are equally delicious. The ambiance is also pretty chill. As mentioned, it's located down a small hutong right around the Houhai Lakes (making it a bit hard to find), and you'll have to cross a small foot bridge over a koi pond inside the restaurant to get from your table to the toilets. The best part about Hutong Pizza is that they deliver to your hotel or hostel, but if you're enjoying a homemade brew at Great Leap's hutong location and crave some gub, give Hutong Pizza a ring and the staff at Great Leap will let you eat it in the pub. We recommend the Three Cheese Carnivore Carnival, the Shrimp Pesto and the Duck Confit pizza.

Address: 9 Yindingqiao Hutong, Xicheng District (西城区银锭桥胡同9号)
Phone: 8322 8916

$ Bang! Bang! Pizza

Man's nirvana is often pizza, beer and televised sports; luckily for you women you can keep him at home with this restaurant's punctual delivery.

Address: Room 103, Bldg 24, Hopson International Park, Shuanghuayuan Nanli, Area 3, Shuangjing, Chaoyang District (朝阳区双井双花园南里3区合生国际花园24号楼103单元)
Phone: 8776 4533; 136 0100 0343
Website: www.bangbangpizza.net

$ Annie's

PANDA PICK

This award winning Italian restaurant has extraordinary pastas, soups, salads, risottos and desserts, and it also has a large seating area for a great dining experience. It's also worth mentioning that they have a wonderfully priced wine list with top brand names, and they can deliver right to your door as well. Get the Prosciutto di Parma pizza – you won't be disappointed.

Address: West Gate of Chaoyang Park (朝阳公园西门南侧)
Phone: 6591 1931
Website: www.annies.com.cn

$ Flo Prestige (Fúlóu; 福楼)

A French restaurant with take-out service. The handmade canapés are recommended.

Address: 18 Xiaoyun Lu (霄云路18号)
Phone: 6595 5135

Themed

$$ Toilet Restaurant (Biànsuǒ Cāntīng; 便所餐厅)

If you've got a bold stomach, a taste for gross adventures and a 5-year-old's sense of humor, you might want to plop down at Beijing's Toilet Restaurant. Everything from the real toilets you sit on to their Winnie the Pooh covers, the turd-shaped ice cream and squidgy dishes like "poo funny mud" (mashed potatoes), served in mini toilets and urinals, pay a steaming tribute to John Harrington. If you've had trouble reading through this without gagging then this one is not for you.

Address: 5/F, Kaide Mall, 1 Xizhimen Waidajie, Xicheng District (西城区西直门外大街1号凯德商场五层)
Phone: 5623 4500; 5623 4503

$$$ Chengfu Courtyard (Chéngfǔ Yàn; 程府宴)

You know a place is legit when the grandson of Mao's personal chef runs the show. The mightily popular Chengfu Courtyard serves imperial cuisine and some of the Chairman's favorites on a fixed set menu, so it's best to come in a group. Reservations required.

Address: 38 Nanchang Jie, Dongcheng District (东城区南长街38号)
Phone: 6606 9936

$ East is Red (Hóngsè Jīngdiǎn; 红色经典)

PANDA PICK

Packed with action and nightly song and dance performances, East is Red (named for the derelict song of the same name) will make you feel like it's 1968 with all the socialist propaganda. For a fun evening and above average cooking, East is Red will "reeducate" you with a good time.

> Address: 66 Xiangshan Lu, Haidian District, north of Qinglong Qiao (海淀区香山路青龙桥北上坡66号)
> Phone: 6574 8289; 6574 8290

Vegetarian/Organic

$ Ban Ruo (Bānruò Sùshí; 般若素食)

Traditional Buddhist vegetarian meals can be found here, including soy kebabs and other imitation meat products. The interior is skillfully decorated with religious art and architecture for a Zen-like atmosphere.

> Address: 33 Gulou Dongjie, Changping District (昌平区鼓楼东街33号)
> Phone: 6970 0208; 8971 8400

$ Elaine's Vegetarian Restaurant and Bar (Sùxīn Xiǎozhù; 素心小筑)

Elaine's focuses on imitation meat dishes, and they do a pretty good job at duplicating the real thing. They also offer other quintessential veggie trays like salads and soups.

> Address: Walk 800 m (2,624 ft) along the banks of Luoma Lake, 100 m (328 ft) north of Luoma Roundabout, Houshayu, Shunyi District (顺义区后沙峪镇罗马环岛向北100米左转，沿罗马湖畔800米)
> Phone: 8048 5088; 8048 5566

$ The Veggie Table (Chīsù de; 吃素的)

PANDA PICK

With great vegetarian items ranging from burgers and pizzas to soups and falafels, the Veggie Table knows how to please herbivores. Get the Mixed Meze Platter for your choice of five spreads served with pita bread, and take pleasure in the comfortable setting lined with couches, exotic plants, and photos of China's ethnic minorities.

> Address: 19 Wudaoying Hutong, Dongcheng District (东城区五道营胡同19号)
> Phone: 6446 2073

How to Use Chopsticks

Don't know how to use chopsticks? Then you better learn quickly because you won't find too many forks and knives around here, and we guarantee no one will know how to tie the rubber bands at the end like they do at your local Chinese eatery. Like anything, you won't learn in a day, but while you're here you really have no other choice. So let's get started!

1.

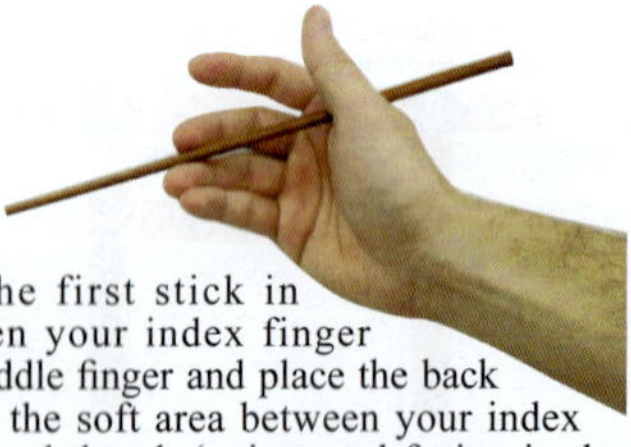

Rest the first stick in between your index finger and middle finger and place the back end on the soft area between your index finger and thumb (pointy end facing in the same directions of your fingers). This is your anchor stick and it should not move while eating.

2.

Grasp the second stick with your index finger and thumb tips. This is the stick that moves, and you can position it by simply twisting your thumb and index finger. You can brace it on your middle finger for better control. Make sure both pointy ends are facing the same direction.

3.

To pick up food, place the bite in between the two pointy edges and tighten up using the stick in between your index and thumb tips.

4.

Note that many meals in China will be served with a bowl of rice. It is acceptable to place bites of food on top of the rice, so bring the bowl close to your mouth with your left hand and use your chopsticks to shovel the rice and food into your mouth. Using chopsticks as a shovel is easier and it's perfectly acceptable in Chinese table etiquette.

5.

Another common misconception is that stabbing the food with your chopsticks like a fork is unacceptable. This is perfectly fine and no one will laugh at your amateur skills. Chinese people do this all the time, especially with hard to eat foods that are slippery, slimy or simply just too large to pick up the old-fashioned way.

6.

Last but not least, practice. After a few meals you'll be on your way to expertise!

Drinking & Nightlife

Over the past decade Western bars, pubs, clubs and lounges have sprouted up in Beijing like bamboo after a spring rain. Most drinking holes are packed with expats, but many local Beijingers – especially from the younger generation – are showing up, while the older generation still prefers to drink *baijiu* on the streets and play cards with their friends. In fact it's quite common to be invited for a shot with the old timers when strolling through the hutongs, but beware, they may drink you under the table!

KTV (or karaoke) is China's favorite form of entertainment since everyone from kids to adults enjoys singing cheesy pop songs. It is worth noting that some establishments are a little sleazy and may ask if you want a woman to "sing" with you, but most are respectable, especially the ones we've listed.

Live music can be found all throughout the city: protest punk rock, blues, jazz, country, electronic, hip-hop, trance... just about any musical taste can be satisfied in Beijing's live music venues.

The city is even seeing an increase in the acceptance of homosexuality, as **gay bars** begin to find their own niche in the drinking scene, while a few non-gay bars host their own gay nights. It's still not what one would call progressive, but Beijing's LGBT scene has certainly made strides since the Cultural Revolution (when homosexuality was listed as a psychological disorder).

Night clubs are becoming more popular as China's youth born during the years of Reform and Openness grow up. There are discos with cutting edge styles found all over the city, but most of them lay around Wudaokou and south of Worker's Stadium.

Beijing wouldn't be a Chinese city unless it had at least one **bar street**. Basically, a bar street is exactly what it sounds like – a strip of several bars all crammed side by side into one street. These are good places if you're looking to bar hop, and there's always some good street food nearby for snacks. Here are the best bar streets in Beijing:

Sanlitun Bar Street (Sānlǐtún Jiǔbājiē; 三里屯酒吧街)

Located right in the middle of Beijing's largest expatriate community, this used to be the best bar street in the city. Nowadays it's a little shady on the edges and you may be asked for a "massage" or a "lady friend" every ten steps. Nonetheless, the area is going through a revival as some new places join the show. **Nali Patio** (Nàlǐ Huāyuán; 那里花园), for example, has a small cluster of bars and cafes that cater to expats, and the area south of **Workers' Stadium Stadium** (Gōngrén Tǐyùchǎng; 工人体育场) is a big clubbing district for new China's rebellious youth.

Houhai Bar Street (Hòuhǎi Jiǔbajiē; 后海酒吧街)

This bar strip is a lot tamer than many of the others, but it's starting to beep louder on the tourist radar due to the gorgeous scenery of the surrounding lakes. The good news is that this is making the quality of the bars much better, but the bad news is its also inflating prices. Most of the bars have top decks with an enchanting view of old Beijing, and you should keep in mind that to the east of Houhai is the Drum Tower, which also has plenty of small hutong bars branching out from its roots.

Nánluógǔ Xiàng (南锣鼓巷)

The favorite bar street for Beijing's hipsters, Nanluogu Xiang and the area around it is perhaps the best drinking spot if you're looking for cheap drinks, live music, artsy décor and people wearing lens-less glasses. Boutique bars are scattered throughout the hutongs, so they can be a little hard to find, but discovering them is half the fun and they're worth the hunt, especially since many offer creative menus (often with international dishes) and phenomenal (stiff) drink specials.

Chaoyang Park (Cháoyáng Gōngyuán; 朝阳公园)

Located at the west gate of Chaoyang Park, this area caters to an affluent crowd with happy hours and easy music. With European-style architecture, fountains and cuisine, it's not necessarily the place to be if you're craving a wild night out on the town, but it's ideal for a drink made just right after a long day of work. Saying that, this is Beijing and anything goes, so it's not completely uncommon to see a few suit and ties shaking their booties here every once in a while. Another bar strip in the area is **Lucky Street**, which can be hit or miss, depending on whether you're lucky or not.

Wǔdàokǒu (五道口)

Situated smack in the heart of the city's university district, this is the number one party area for Beijing's diligent, hard-working students. And just like any other university bar strip in the world, it's a little grungy, sporting dirt-cheap drinks, strong shots, deafening music and late night raves. Wudaokou won't let you down, but it will give you a horrendous hangover.

Bars & Pubs

Drink Pricing Guide

$$$ Drinks from ¥30 (US$5)
$$ Drinks from ¥20 (US$3.5)
$ Drinks from ¥10 (US$1.5)

$ Heaven Supermarket   PANDA PICK

We could say that Heaven Supermarket resembles a supermarket with a huge selection of just about anything and everything you'd ever want to drink and eat, except for the fact that it straight up is a real supermarket!

Don't let that discourage you, though, it's actually a superb place to sit, with a warm wood interior, and there's a fresh outdoor patio in the summer. Here, the hardest part is choosing from a seemingly endless variety of alcoholic decisions. Buy yourself a bottle of imported beer or bottle(s) of liquor, then add a leaning tower of nachos to the party and get smashed. (Open daily 11:00-late)

Address:15 Xindong Lu, Chaoyang District（朝阳区新东路15号）
Phone: 6415 6513

$$ Great Leap Brewing   PANDA PICK

This American-owned establishment is the best micro-brewery in all of Beijing. It's tucked away in a narrow hutong and has a wide range of hand-crafted brews. We personally recommend the tingly Honey Ma that's infused with Sichuan peppercorns. They also just opened a new branch that has the same great beer along with American bistro cuisine (the cheeseburger is to die for) in Sanlitun. (Open Tue-Thu 17:00-22:30; Fri 17:00-23:00; Sat 14:00-23:00; Sun 14:00-22:00; closed Mon)

Address: 6 Doujiao Hutong, Xicheng District（西城区豆角胡同6号）. See map below
Phone: 5717 1399

Sanlitun Address: 12 Xinzhongjie, Chaoyang District（朝阳区新中街乙12号）No map
Phone: 6416 6887
Website: www.greatleapbrewing.com

$$ Cuju   One FREE Rum

Cuju is a small hutong bar that packs a big punch. This place is unique because there's always a sports game on the flat screens, while the Moroccan owner Badr presents some incredible snacks from his home country. There's a different drink/food special every day and the "ice-cold" rum shots are awesome. This is the place for NFL just in case you were wondering. (Open 18:00-late; closed Tue; Xiguan Hutong is accessible from Dongsi Beidajie)

Address: 28 Xiguan Hutong, Dongcheng District（东城区细管胡同28号）
Phone: 6407 9782
Website: www.cujubeijing.com

$ El Nido/Bar No. 59

With over 100 types of imported and domestic beers, El Nido is Beijing's beer haven. Get here early since this small nest has limited seating. There's a homey self-service policy where you can pick your favorites right out of the fridge, and an outdoor film projector on top of some old, dusty books for movies screenings. (Open daily 16:00-late; Fangjia Hutong is accessible from Andingmen Neidajie)

Address: 59 Fangjia Hutong, Dongcheng District（东城区方家胡同59号）
Phone: 8402 9495; 8403 5004

$$ Mao Mao Chong

Creative and unpretentious, this chill place has good homemade art, better cocktails and great gourmet pizzas. An extensive international selection of beers and wines is also available. (Open Sun, Wed & Thu 19:00-00:00; Fri-Sat 19:00-1:00; closed Mon & Tue)

Address: 12 Banchang Hutong, Dongcheng District (东城区板厂胡同)
Phone: 138 1035 1522; 6405 5718
Website: www.maomaochongbeijing.com

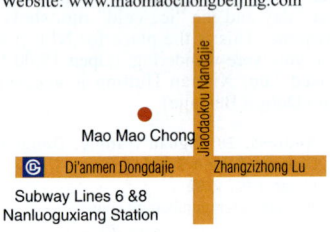

$ Ball House (Bōlóu Jiǔba; 波楼酒吧)

Pool (¥30/hr), table football (free) and a pleasant view are the perks of this popular bar. Though often crowded, there are plenty of private booths away from the noise. (Open daily 14:00-3:00)

Address: 40 Zhonglouwan Hutong, Dongcheng District (东城区钟楼湾胡同40号)
Phone: 6407 4051

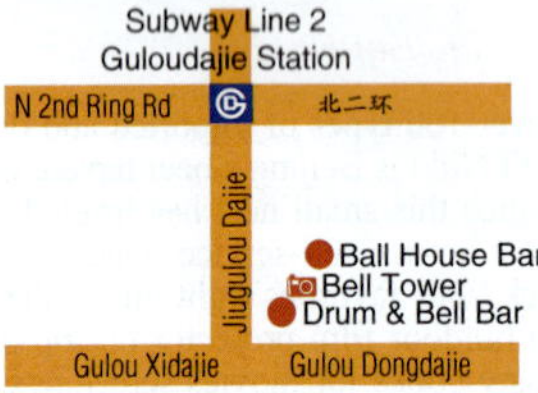

$ Drum & Bell (Jiǎoxià Kāfēiguǎn; 脚下咖啡馆)

This bar between the Drum and Bell tower has a wonderful roof top terrace overlooking the charming hutongs below. It's also a great place to relax and enjoy a lazy beer while people watching, and the pizzas aren't bad either. (Open daily 13:00-2:00; see map above for location)

Address: 41 Zhonglouwan Hutong, Dongcheng District (东城区钟楼湾胡同41号)
Phone: 8403 3600

$$ The Tree (Yǐnbì de Shù; 隐蔽的树)

A big expat hangout with imported Belgian beers, a midnight happy hour and thin crust pizzas, the Tree ain't screwing around. For another option try **Nearby the Tree** (www.nearbythetree.com), which is "nearby" and owned by the same management, but has cheaper ¥10 draft beers. (Open Mon-Sat 11:00-late; Sun 13:00-late)

Address: 12 Sanlitun Nanjie, Chaoyang District (朝阳区三里屯南街12号)
Phone: 6509 3642
Website: www.treebeijing.com.cn

$ Modernista PANDA PICK

One of the newest bars to hit the Beijing party block, Modernista has the feel of a 1950s European café and showcases film screenings, DJs and live bands on the weekends. The masses get a little tipsy during the 00:00-2:00 ¥10 shot happy hour and often push the tables out of the way to dance. Don't shy away from the absinthe, either. (Tue-Sun 12:00-2:00, Baochao Hutong is accessible from Gulou Dongdajie)

Address: 44 Baochao Hutong, Dongcheng District (东城区宝钞胡同44号)
Phone: 136 9142 5744

$$ Paddy O'Shea's

A typical Irish pub with European football (soccer), rugby, Gaelic sports and of course Guinness. There's also a decent menu with pub favorites and exceptional service, so your glass will never run dry. (Open daily 10:00-late)

Address: 28 Dongzhimen Waidajie, Chaoyang District (朝阳区东直门外大街28号)
Phone: 6415 6389
Website: www.paddyosheas.com

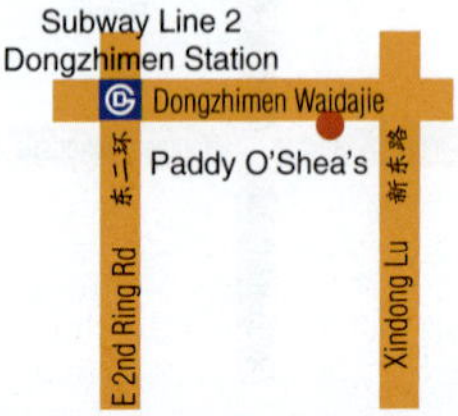

$$ First Floor (Yīlóu; 壹楼)

A fine pub with pints of beer and ten different types of delicious burgers, First Floor ramps it up with outdoor seating in the warmer months, but if it's too crowded you can head upstairs to its uniquely named sister bar **Second Floor**. (Sun-Thu 10:00-2:00; Fri-Sat 10:00-4:00)

Address: 1/F, Tongli Studios, Sanlitun Back Street, Chaoyang District (朝阳区三里屯后街, 同里, 1层)
Phone: 6413 0587
Website: www.floorbeijing.com

$ Wudaokou Beer Garden

If you walk just west of the Wudaokou metro station during the warmer months you'll spot several outdoor patios offering ¥10 draft beers. The beer gardens are usually packed with thirsty students, and there are also some tasty street snacks. Wudaokou's infamous bars and clubs are a bottle's throw away in case you want to keep the party going. (Open daily only during the warmer months from late afternoon to late)

Address: Chengfu Lu, Haidian District (海淀区成府路), west of the Wudaokou subway station

$$ Zájiā (杂家) **PANDA PICK**

Voted as one of Beijing's "Most Unusual Bars," Zajia must be seen to know why. The dark interior is loaded with mid-20th century appliances such as typewriters and radios, and all the couches came straight out of the 60s. Music from the Doors rolling through the ground level, a second story loft that's reachable by ladder, stairs out front doubling as a patio, and the absinthe shots will all make you trip (in more ways than one). If you need to sober up, just order one of their delicious and strong coffees, or step out into the hutong for a local snack.

Address: Hong'en Daoist Temple, 23 Doufuchi Hutong, Jiugulou Dajie, Dongcheng District (东城区旧鼓楼大街豆腐池胡同23号洪恩观前殿)
Phone: 8404 9141

$$ Amilal

Amilal is perhaps the city's best kept secret, and a few loyal regulars want to keep it that way. There are some quality scotches, whiskeys, imported beers and Andean wines, while Kazakh/Mongolian bands occasionally twist things up for a unique ambiance. (Open daily 13:00-late)

Address: 48 Shoubi Hutong, Dongcheng District (东城区寿比胡同48号)
Phone: 8404 1416

$$ Mai Bar (Mài; 麦)

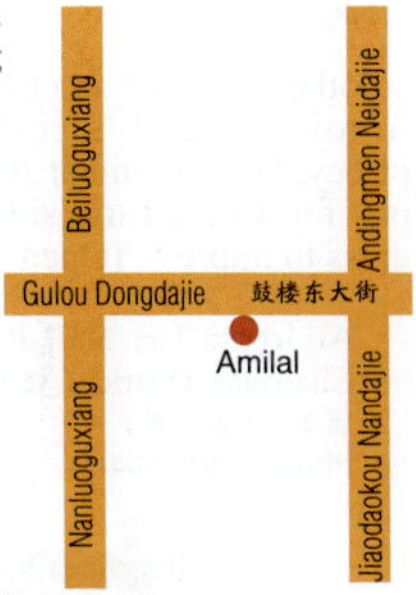

A cozy drinking hole with a slick interior and wonderful whisky selection, Mai Bar may be small and a bit hard to find, but then again what underground Beijing hipster hutong bar isn't? (Open daily 17:00-midnight)

Address: 40 Beiluogu Xiang, Dongcheng District (东城区北锣鼓巷40号)
Phone: 138 1125 2641; 6406 1871

Cocktail Bars

$$ *Yin (Yĭn;* 饮*)* PANDA PICK

With a hot tub, a gripping view of the Forbidden City, a Thursday happy hour from 16:00-22:00, and a DJ on the weekends, Yin does it all. The drinks are expensive, but they do have a generous selection of cocktails, wines, beers and champagnes. Located on the top floor of the Emperor Hotel. (Open 19:00-late daily)

> Address: 33 Qihelou Dajie, (Emperor Hotel rooftop) Dongcheng District (东城区骑河楼街33号皇家驿站)
> Phone: 6526 5566 ext 6651
> Website: www.theemperor.com.cn

$$$ *Apothecary (Jiŭshù;* 酒术 *)*

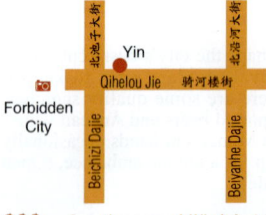

Apothecary may be one of the nicest places in town to grab a cocktail, so drinks are pricey, but remember that you get what you pay for. Come early since it fills up fast and dress to impress. (Open Tue-Sun 18:00-late)

> Address: 3/F, Nali Patio, 81 Sanlitun Lu, Chaoyang District (朝阳区三里屯电路81号那里花园3层 D302 室)
> Phone: 5208 6040

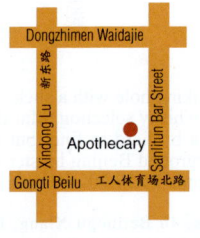

$$$ *Atmosphere*

This classy establishment is Beijing's highest bar, located on the 80th story of the city's tallest building. The view isn't for the acrophobic, but the Cuban cigars always have a way of smoking the fear out. (Open Noon-2:00 Sun-Thur; 12:00-4:00 Fri-Sat)

> Address: 80/F, China World Summit Wing, 1 Jianguomen Waidajie, Chaoyang District (朝阳区建国门外大街1号北京国贸大酒店80层)
> Phone: 6505 2299

$$ *d lounge* PANDA PICK

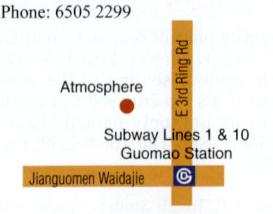

This art-gallery-by-day, lounge-by-night mainly attracts an artsy crowd that enjoys wavy electronic music. The furnishings resemble an old Soviet warehouse and there's no sign except for a simple "d." (Open daily 20:00-late)

> Address: Courtyard 4, Gongti Beilu, Chaoyang District (朝阳区工体北路4号院)
> Phone: 6593 7710

$$$ *Ichikura (Yīzàng Jiŭba;* 一藏酒吧 *)*

This high-end Japanese bar is for the whisky connoisseur looking for a sophisticated drink. The ingredients, service and presentation are superb, with a special attention to detail. (Open daily 18:00-1:30)

> Address: 36 Dongsanhuan Beilu (entrance at south side of Chaoyang Theater), Chaoyang District (朝阳区东三环北路36号)
> Phone: 6507 1107

Clubs

$$ *Propaganda* PANDA PICK

The Holy Grail for the city's university

students, Propaganda offers cheap drinks, blaring hip-hop and late night booty grinding. This dark and smokey basement has the reputation of being a great place to meet new people and pick up a few numbers. (Open daily 20:00-4:00, no cover charge)

Address: First and Basement floors, East Gate of Huaqing Jiayuan, Wudaokou, Haidian District (海淀区五道口华清嘉园东门向北1层及地下)
Phone: 8289 3991

$$ Mix

A rocking neon club with international DJ appearances, dance music and a sweaty dance floor, Mix is where you want to be, especially if you're under 25 years of age... or look 25 years old. Cover varies but is usually around ¥50 (Open daily 20:00-6:00)

Address: Inside the Workers Stadium North Gate, Chaoyang District (朝阳区工体北门内)
Phone: 6530 2889
Website: www.clubmixchina.com

$$$ Chocolate

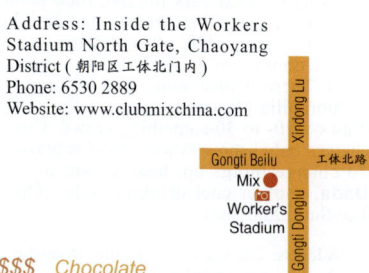

Why go to Russia when you can go to Chocolate? Situated in the heart of Beijing's Russian District around Ritan Park, many Russian tourists and expats flock to this spot for drinks and, of course, top of the line vodka. (Open daily until late)

Address: 19 Ritan Beilu, Ritan, Chaoyang District (朝阳区日坛北路19号)
Phone: 8561 3988

$ Vics

There's free entry on Mondays and Tuesdays, ladies drink for free before midnight on Wednesdays, and it's always rowdy on the weekends. Vic's is a pick up joint and the walls are lined with mirrors, which makes walking around while inebriated tough, but if that's your style then you'll love Vics! Cover charge depends on DJ but is usually ¥50. (Open daily 20:30-late)

Address: Inside Workers Stadium North Gate, Chaoyang District (朝阳区工体北门内)
Phone: 5293 0333
Website: www.vics.com.cn

$$ GT Banana

GT is the mother of all clubs done the Chinese way – big, loud and with three stories of madness – each level blasting different styles of music. There are also karaoke rooms, mini-skirt dancers and DJs on the weekend. Cover charge is usually ¥30. (Open Mon-Fri 20:30-4:30; Sat-Sun 20:30-5:30)

Address: 1/F, 22 Jianguomen Waidajie, Chaoyang District (朝阳区建外大街22号赛特饭店1层)
Phone: 6528 3636

Gay & Lesbian

$$ Destination

The first and best clubbing destination for Beijing's (mostly male) gay community, Destination is always action packed, and on weekends it's full of wild dancing, flashy light shows and pride music. Cover charge is usually ¥60. (Sun-Thu 20:00-2:00; Fri-Sat 20:00-late)

Address: 7 Gongti Xilu, Chaoyang District (朝阳区工体西路7号)
Phone: 6552 8180
Website: www.bjdestination.com

$$ The Boat (Chuánba; 船吧)

This club is actually a boat floating in the Liangma River. Upstairs is a bar, and downstairs is the dance floor, and all the staff wear cute sailor uniforms. Thursdays are gay nights while Fridays and Saturdays still bring in a few from the LGBT communities. (Sun 20:00-00:00; Mon-Thu 20:00-3:00; Fri & Sat 20:00-5:00)

Address: 8 Liangmahe Nanlu, Chaoyang District (朝阳区亮马河南路8号)
Phone: 6467 6877

KTV

$$ Tango KTV (Tángguǒ; 糖果)

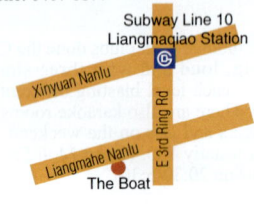

To show off your singing skills, give Tango KTV a try. A room of five or six people costs around ¥180 per hour, not including food and drinks. (Open 24/7)

Address 1: Ditan Park (地坛公园), South Gate of Ditan Park (next to Jin Ding Xuan restaurant), Dongcheng District (东城区地坛公园南门)
Phone: 6425 5677; 6428 2288
Website: www.clubtango.cn

Address 2: Sanlitun (三里屯), Gongti Xilu (beneath Gongti 100 bowling alley), Chaoyang District (朝阳区工体西路工体100保龄球馆下面)
Phone: 6551 9988

$$ Melody KTV (Màilèdí; 麦乐迪)

Though Melody is a little classier and more expensive than Tango, dress is still casual (as it is at most KTV parlors). A five- or six-person room is around ¥200 per hour not including food and drink. (Open 10:00-6:00).

Address 1: Shuangjing / Dongsihuan (双井东四环), Next to Viva Shopping Mall, Fuli Cheng, 61 Dongsanhuan Zhonglu, Shuangjing, Chaoyang District (朝阳区东三环中路61号,近富力广场)
Phone: 5903 7188

Address 2: Zhongguancun (中关村), Opposite The Central University of Nationalities, 24 Zhongguancun Nandajie, Haidian District (海淀区中关村南大街24号,中央民族大学对面)
Phone: 6218 9088

Address 3: Chaoyangmenwai (朝阳门外), Opposite of Landao Shopping Center, 77 Chaoyangmen Waidajie, Chaoyang District (朝阳区朝阳门外大街77号,蓝岛对面)
Phone: 6551 0808

Music Venues

$$ Temple PANDA PICK

Well known and easy to find, Temple is one of the city's best bars for live rock bands and DJs. When things get going some hit the dance floor, while others lay low at the long wooden tables with drinks close at hand. There is also some cool motorcycle memorabilia plastered on the walls, and it draws a 20- to 30-something crowd. Cover charges only happen when a band is playing. To change things up, head downstairs to **Dada**, another cool drinking hole. (Open Tue-Sun 17:00-late)

Address: 206 Gulou Dongdajie, Dongcheng District (东城区鼓楼东大街206号)
Phone: 131 6107 0713
Website: www.templebarlivehouse.com

$$ 2 Kolegas (Liǎnggè Hǎopéngyǒu; 两个好朋友)

This grungy concert venue with a huge outdoor lawn is a landmark of Beijing's ever popular music scene. Live music here comes in every genre, from metal to folk, so check their website to see which tunes are rocking that weekend. (Open daily 21:00-late, cover charge is usually ¥30)

>   Address: 21 Liangmaqiao Lu, in the drive-in movie theatre park, Chaoyang District (朝阳区亮马桥路21号，汽车电影院内)
>   Phone: 6436 8998
>   Website: www.2kolegas.com

$$ MAO Live House (Guāngmáng; 光芒)

With a monstrous sound system that will blow you off the third story of this complex, MAO Live House is a bit cleaner and well-organized than some of Beijing's other alternative music houses. Cover charge depends on band.

>   Address: 111 Gulou Dongdajie, Gulou, Dongcheng District (东城区鼓楼东大街111号)
>   Phone: 133 6612 1459; 6402 5080
>   Website: www.maolive.com

$$ Yugong Yishan (Yúgōng Yíshān; 愚公移山)

You name it – blues, hip-hop, death metal, electronic, acoustic, folk and jazz – you can find it here. There are even film screenings and some trippy psychedelic light shows. Cover charge depends on band.

>   Address: 3-2 Zhangzizhong Lu, Dongcheng District (东城区张自忠路3-2号段祺瑞执政府旧址西院)
>   Phone: 6404 2711
>   Website: www.yugongyishan.com

$$ 13 Club

Metal-head heaven. This dungeon-like cave with ear-crushing speakers and cement walls is reserved mainly for ska, punk and heavy metal shows. Cover charge depends on band. (Open daily 20:00-2:00)

>   Address: 161 Lanqiying, Chengfu Lu, Wudaokou, Haidian District (海淀区五道口蓝旗营161号成府路)
>   Phone: 8261 9267

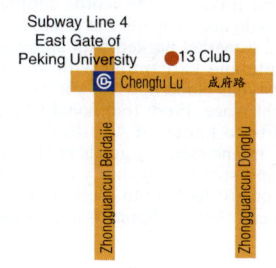

Shopping

For some travelers, the words shopping and fun do not compute. But if the idea of wandering a market packed with aggressive salespeople and bargaining with all your might gets your blood flowing, you've come to the right place. From traditional Chinese handicrafts to knockoff "Abibas" shoes, there's an insane range of goods in Beijing's markets and stores. Whether you're a true collector or just looking to score some cool souvenirs and clothes, Beijing is a great place to be.

The adage "if it seems too good to be true, it is" definitely applies to shopping in Beijing. The quality of fakes has become so good that even New York's Metropolitan Museum may have been duped: while they stand behind an exceptionally rare silk scroll they acquired in 2007, some experts have questioned its authenticity. By some estimates, bogus antiques and art constitute as much as 80% of the value of goods for sale in Hong Kong, and most of them originate in Mainland China.

Export of genuine antiques dating before 1911 is not allowed without special government approval, but a special wax seal signifies special permission. Many of these items can be found at government stores, and a certificate is also given to allow legal export. Buying antique porcelain without the seal or proper paperwork can be risky. It could be a fake, or it could be real and obtained by dubious methods, but either way it does not have the proper documentation and could be confiscated upon departure from China.

As long as you're not dead set on getting the real thing, you can have a lot of fun shopping in Beijing. Read on for tips on what to buy, where to go and how to get the best deal.

What can I buy in Beijing?

What can't you buy in Beijing is more like it! The key is to narrow down what you're interested in while keeping in mind what you're willing to carry or ship back. (The extra empty bag we recommend in our Getting Prepared section will come in handy if you hit the markets). Silk, ceramics, pearls, jade, embroidery, carpets, furniture, paintings, calligraphy, tea, tea sets and jewelry are all widely available (in widely varying quality) in Beijing markets. In addition to these "classic" crafts, many travelers are interested in clothing and shoes, Mao-era propaganda posters and cheap pirated DVDs of international TV shows and movies.

When it comes to clothing and shoes, you may find yourself out of luck if your size is especially large (for shoes, above size 11 for guys and size 9 for ladies). See the chart to convert your American shoe size to its Chinese equivalent (it's very similar to European sizes). Trying on clothes isn't common either, as there's often nowhere to do it in a crowded market. Some sellers will let you try something on over your clothes or, if you really push them, they'll let you try it on in the bathroom.

Women's sizes

US	5	5.5	6	6.5	7	7.5	8	8.5	9	9.5	10	10.5	12
China	35.5	36	37	37.5	38	39	39.5	40	41	41.5	42	43	44.5

Men's sizes

US	7.5	8	8.5	9	9.5	10	10.5	11	11.5	12	12.5	13	13.5	14
China	-	42	42	43	43.5	44	44.5	45	45.5	46	46.5	47	47.5	48.5

SHOPPING TIPS ▶

1. If you're not used to bargaining, you might not know when to do it and when to pay the sticker price. Here's where you should bargain really hard: public markets, souvenir stands and really anywhere that doesn't have marked prices (especially the Pearl Market [pg 258] and the Silk Market [pg 255]). In restaurants, shopping centers, grocery stores, 7-11s, etc, prices are fixed.

2. If you don't get excited about bargaining, there's a low-energy strategy that can be equally effective. Act like you're bored, in a hurry, or not that interested. Refuse to say a price, no matter how much the seller asks you to. After you've worn them down, just walk away and they'll probably chase you down with an offer. If that's not your style, try hard-ball bargaining (see next page).

3. If an item doesn't have a price tag, just know that you're probably going to end up paying more than a Chinese person would – their assumption is that foreigners have more money than locals. If you hate the idea of getting "ripped off" by paying foreigner prices, avoid buying anything that doesn't have a stated price. Another sure sign that you're probably paying too much is that the seller speaks very good English. The likeliest reason for this is that they cater exclusively to foreigners and have built up their skill in order to sweet talk more money out of you. It doesn't have to stop you from buying – maybe that pack of postcards is really worth ¥60 to you – but just know you're not getting the best deal.

4. Don't assume something is a good deal just because it's cheaper than it would be in your home country. It might still be marked up significantly from the real value. Also consider quality: is getting a pair of jeans for $10 really a bargain if they fall apart the first time you wear them?

5. If a seller seems annoyed that you're bargaining really hard, don't be deterred. They're not upset with you personally, they're upset that they won't get a huge profit off of you.

How to bargain

The best strategy for paving your way to a good deal is to arm yourself with information in advance. If there's something in particular that you want, go online and do some research on the hallmarks of authentic goods so that you can knowledgably inspect what's for sale. There are relatively simple tests that even non-experts can use to get an idea of the quality of pearls, jade, silk, and other typical Beijing items.

Other than knowing what you're getting into, the most important factor in successful bargaining is your attitude. Go into it with a smile and a sense of humor. If you're shy, get over the idea that you're being rude or pushy. It's all a game and everyone knows it. Even if a seller starts trying to appeal to you with statements like, "You're making me lose money!" or "I guess my family won't eat tonight," know that they are never going to sell something at a loss. Most of the vendors you'll encounter deal with foreigners all the time and speak good enough English to conduct the transaction – though you'll usually go back and forth with your offers by punching them into a calculator, so there's no confusion. The calculator is also used to prevent other customers from knowing what kind of prices they give to each person. Oftentimes, it's actually better for your bargain to use the calculator, since they won't likely give you a lower price if you blurt it out for everyone around to hear.

The general strategy practiced by bargaining ninjas is this:

1) Look at the item and decide how much you're willing to pay for it. Keep that number in mind throughout the process and don't go over, no matter how much the seller stresses you out!

2) When the seller asks you what you're willing to pay, avoid offering a specific number right away. Try to stall and dramatically inspect the item, pointing out any flaws or signs of low quality.

3) When it's time to name your price, DO NOT start with how much you're willing to pay. Offer 1/3 of it and slowly work your way up. So, if a pair of shoes is worth ¥100 to you, start at ¥30 and go up in small increments.

4) If the seller refuses to go low enough, just say thank you and walk away. Nine times out of ten they'll chase you down and make a better offer. And if they don't, you've avoided overpaying.

Here's an example of a successful bargaining transaction:

YOU: (Admiring a wool sweater, thinking you'd pay ¥200)

SELLER: How much you pay?

YOU: I'm not sure... it seems low-quality...

SELLER: No, it is very high-quality, very nice... how much you pay?

YOU: How about 70?

SELLER: Ha! No way. 400, final offer.

YOU: 75.

SELLER: 350.

YOU: (With a smile on your face) 80.

SELLER: 80? I lose money! Final price 280.

YOU: (Walking away) No, thanks...

SELLER: OK, OK, 250!

YOU: 100.

SELLER: 220.

YOU: 110.

SELLER: 200, final price!

YOU: I'll take it.

You did it! Of course you'll never know how much that ¥200 sweater was actually worth, but if you payed what you wanted to pay, you've done alright for yourself.

Here are some rough price targets you can aim for when the bargaining gets started.

T-shirts: ¥20-25

Running shoes: ¥50-80

Dress shoes: ¥80-100

"Timberland" boots: ¥120

Belts: ¥20

Ties: ¥10

Custom shirts: ¥80

Custom suits: ¥600-800

Jeans: ¥80

Jackets: ¥100-150

Baby clothes: ¥20-40

Beijing Shopping Map

Where can I shop in Beijing?

Silk Street (Xiùshuǐ Jiē; 秀水街)

With over 1,000 retailers, Silk Street is now regarded as a symbol of Beijing right along with the Great Wall and roast duck.. The original Silk Street has been rebuilt and now has seven stories of shopping, not to mention a number of restaurants and coffee shops. There's also a traditional Chinese pharmacy and a Silk Museum where you can learn about the ancient Chinese art of silk before you make your purchases. In addition to the usual wide selection of clothing, shoes, and gadgets, there are a number of well-respected brands selling antiques, silk, porcelain, Chinese paintings and calligraphy, jade, and more. If that's not enough, you can also get a manicure or a massage on the premises. Xiushui Jie is truly a Beijing classic, and if you're into shopping, it's not to be missed.

Hours: 9:30 – 21:00
Transport: Yong'anli Station (永安里站) on

Line 1 has direct tunnel to the basement of Silk Street via Exit A

Panjiayuan Antique Market (Pānjiāyuán Gǔwán Shìchǎng; 潘家园古玩市场)

With 48,309 sq m (520,000 sq ft) of floor space, Panjiayuan is the biggest, cheapest, and most popular market for second-hand goods and antiques in Beijing. Antique lovers could spend a whole day inspecting calligraphy, Chinese paintings, ivory carvings, traditional instruments, porcelain, jade, furniture and more. There's also an especially good collection of propaganda posters from the Cultural Revolution era, although you should note that most of the wares are reproductions, not authentic antiques. Use caution when making a purchase and make sure to check the authenticity. Stalls here tend to be of three types: special stores with high-quality, high-price goods; individual shops where the good and the bad and the real and the fake are mixed together; and low-quality inexpensive stalls. Come on the weekends when the street stalls open up, but stores inside the market are open every day.

Hours: 8:30–16:30 (Mon–Fri); 4:30–16:30 (Sat & Sun)
Location: Panjiayuan Lu South, Chaoyang District
Transport: Subway – Line 10, Panjiayuan Station (潘家园站)

Yashow Market (Yǎxiù Shìchǎng; 雅秀市场)

Also known as Yaxiu, this four-story market is packed with bargains. The selection is unbeatable, but be prepared to bargain hard as the sellers here are very accustomed to tourists and won't hesitate to hustle you. Everything from fake jeans, bags, and shoes to handicrafts and custom-tailored traditional Chinese clothing is available if you have the patience to comb through all the stalls. Yashow is located right next to the high-end Sanlitun Village mall, if you're interested in a range of shopping experiences.

Hours: 9:30 – 21:00 daily

Location: 58 Gongti Beilu, Sanlitun, Chaoyang District
Transport: Subway – Line 10, Tuanjiehu (团结湖) Station, walk west 20 minutes along Gongti Beilu (工体北路) following the signs pointing to Yashow

Nánluógǔ Xiàng (南锣鼓巷)

This pedestrian street is mostly cafes, bars, and restaurants, but there are quite a few hip shops in the mix as well. **Plastered T-shirts** at 61 Nanluogu Xiang offers shirts, mugs, and more with retro Beijing designs, while **The Pottery Workshop** at #23 has many lovely tea sets and larger pieces that make memorable souvenirs. **Grifted** at #32 is a great place to pick up a goofy Mao Zedong doll. Other stores offer everything from boutique women's apparel and designer postcards to bumper stickers. Warning: it can be extremely crowded on the weekends!

Hours: Vary by store, but for shopping, between 10:00 and 19:00 is best
Location: Nanluogu Xiang, south of Gulou Dong Dajie
Transport: Subway – Line 6, Nanluoguxiang Station (南锣鼓巷), Exit A; this exit is right at the southern end of Nanluogu Xiang

Wángfǔjǐng (王府井) Shopping Street

This 800 m- (2,624 ft)-long pedestrian street is the first modern-style commercial street in Beijing, with aspirations to rank

among New York's Fifth Avenue or Ginza in Tokyo. Anchored by large upscale shopping malls, Wangfujing also features plenty of stores selling clothes, tea, shoes, souvenirs, books, hats and more. There's also a foreign language bookstore, a street full of authentic Beijing snacks, and restaurants serving everything from McDonald's to Peking Duck. At the northern end of the walk is the huge St Joseph's Cathedral, a Catholic church built centuries ago by Portuguese Jesuits. The cathedral itself is open only for mass, but its courtyard is a great spot to enjoy a cold drink and take a load off after some intense shopping.

> Hours: Vary, but generally 10:00 – 22:00
> Location: Central Beijing at the intersection of Wangfujing Street and Chang'an Dajie
> Transport: Subway – Line 1, Wangfujing Station, Exit A

Xīdān (西单)

Some locals say that the Silk Market is for foreigners and Xidan is for Beijingers. This massive shopping zone is located west of Tian'anmen Square, mirroring the location of Wangfujing on the east of the square. While Wangfujing offers more expensive international brands, Xidan has an eclectic and inexpensive array of just about everything. The Xidan Department Store has clothes, shoes and accessories, as well as dried and fresh food in strange shapes and flavors. The underground mall **77th Street** overflows with creativity and energy in the form of bizarre knick-knacks, jewelry, lamps, magic tricks and novelty items, and there are also stuffed toy vendors with oversized teddy bears (possibly bigger than you) for ¥210. The **Xidan Books Building** has plenty of English language classics, cookbooks, coffee table books – you name it! The 13-story **Joy City** mall boasts over 100,000 sq m (107,639 sq ft) of retail space and the largest cinema in the country.

> Hours: Vary, but genera
> Transport: Subway – Line

Dàshílar (大栅栏)

This ancient pedestrian street has more than 580 years of history – the prosperous classes of the ancient capital used to visit the businesses here. Today, it is famous for all kinds of stores with an antique flavor. Every day there are more than 150,000 visitors who come to appreciate the old Beijing vibe. Much of the ancient architecture is preserved and many famous old shops and time-honored brands of old Beijing still provide high-quality products. There's also something a little unique – **Liùbìjū** (六 必 居), a pickle shop that was first opened in the Ming Dynasty. Its name refers to the six daily necessities according to an old Chinese saying: fuel, rice, oil, salt, soy sauce and vinegar.

> Hours: Generally 8:00 – 20:00
> Location: Outside the Qianmen Gate, south of Tian'anmen Square
> Transport: Subway – Line 2, Qianmen (前门) Station

Tianyi Market (Tiānyì Pīfā Shìchǎng; 天意批发市场)

one of the smaller markets, but it's ... miss thanks to the crazy collection ...animal statues that adorn the building. Its location near popular tourist spots Houhai, Gulou, and Nanluogu Xiang make it a convenient stop. More classic than trendy, Tinayi offers everything from household items, electronics and stationery to clothing, shoes, and purses.

Hours: 7:00 – 18:00
Location: 158 Di'anmen Waidajie, Xicheng District (西城区地安门外大街158号).
Transport: Subway – Line 6, Nanluoguxiang Station, Exit A, walk west on Di'anmen Dajie for about 500 m (1,640 ft) and turn right on Dianmenwai Dajie, walk 50 m (164 ft) north until you see Tianyi's trademark animal façade; another location at 259 Fuchengmen Waidajie (西城区阜成门外大街259号) with plenty more local shops

Zoo Market (Dòngwùyuán Pīfā Shìchǎng; 动物园批发市场)

The Zoo Market is actually a group of seven wholesale markets that together represent the largest distribution center in northern China. In most of the stalls, prices are as low as ¥10-60 for shirts, tops, jeans, pants, skirts and more. Jewelry should set you back about ¥15-20. Come prepared to bargain hard and spend a few hours wandering around. When you're bargained out, there are plenty of fast food chains to grab a seat and a bite, including Western and Chinese options.

Hours: 9:00 – 17:00
Location: Across the street from the Beijing Zoo, Xizhimen Waidajie (西直门外大街)
Transport: Subway – Line 4, Beijing Zoo Station, Exit D

Hongqiao Pearl Market (Hóngqiáo Zhēnzhū Shìchǎng; 红桥珍珠市场)

Don't let the name fool you – there's much more than just pearls here. Another four-story market with bags, shoes, clothes, silk, tea, toys, souvenirs, and of course, pearls and jewelry. Convenient if you're also visiting the Temple of Heaven – it's located just east of the east gate.

Hours: 8:30 – 19:00
Location: 36 Tiantan Donglu, Dongcheng District, opposite east gate of Temple of Heaven (东城区天坛东路36号)
Transport: Subway – Line 5, Tiantandongmen (天坛东门), Exit A1 or A2, walk slightly north up Tiantan Lu until you see Hongqiao

Maliandao Tea Market (Mǎliándào Cháyè Shìchǎng; 马连道茶叶市场)

Drinking and learning about tea can be a great way to deepen your cultural experience of Beijing. To the south of Beijing West Railway Station, this four-story market can take your learning even further as you immerse yourself in the strong scent of tea and an ocean of traditional tea sets. In addition to what's for sale, there are exhibits on the third and fourth floors on the history and development of tea in China.

Hours: 9:00 – 19:00
Location: 11 Maliandao Jie, Guang'anmenwai, Xicheng District (西城区广安门外马连道街11号)
Transport: Take a taxi or bus 46, 89, 414, 27 to Maliandao Hutong

Liulichang Cultural Street (Liúlíchǎng Wénhuàjiē; 琉璃厂文化街)

Liulichang is a district in downtown Beijing known for a group of traditional stone dwellings that sell crafts and antiques. A mix of state-run and privately owned shops, this area also features some traditional teahouses and wine stores. Liulichang was said to be a favorite gathering place for scholars, painters, and calligraphers during the Ming and Qing Dynasties. It's been renovated since then, but the charming and more low-key aspects remain. Like all Beijing shopping experiences, you shouldn't expect authenticity.

> Hours: 9:00 – 18:00
> Location: Hepingmen, Xicheng District
> Transport: Subway – Line 2, Hepingmen Station (和平门站), Exit D1 or D2, walk south for 500 m (1,640 ft)

Beijing Antique City (Běijīng Gǔwánchéng; 北京古玩城)

Beijing Antique City is one of the largest antique distributors in Asia, covering more than 2 hectares (5.5 acres). Bronzeware, furniture, carpets, clocks, jewelry, and just about anything else you can think of are available for your perusal here. If you're visiting during one of Beijing Antique City's festivals (Folk Culture Festival in January, Auction Week in May, or Exhibition Fair in October), there's even more reason to stop by. Antique City also hosts a number of experts who can give appraisals and offer antique lovers some guidance on the history and quality of Chinese antiques. This location is only 300 m (984 ft) south of Panjiayuan Flea Market, so hardcore shoppers can easily choose to visit both.

> Hours: 10:00 – 19:00
> Location: 300 m (984 ft) south of Panjiayuan Flea Market, Huawei Bridge (华威桥), southeast corner of the 3rd Ring Road
> Transport: Subway – Line 10, Panjiayuan Station (潘家园站)

Guanyuan Pet Market (Guānyuán Chǒngwù Shìchǎng; 官园宠物市场)

Unless you want to import a new family pet, this market is probably more for the experience than for real shopping. Turtles, fish, parrots, rabbits, cats, mice, lizards, dogs, and even crickets are for sale – and the shopkeepers tend to be very welcoming and relaxed even if you're not looking to buy. See locals teaching their birds to talk and try to figure out why old Beijing men keep crickets in their shirt pockes. A fun side trip, especially if you're traveling with children.

> Hours: 9:00 – 17:00
> Location: 1/F, Guangyuan Plaza, Zizhuyuan Lu, Haidian District (广源大厦一层)
> Transport: Subway – Line 9, National Library Station (国家图书馆站), cut through Zizhuyuan Park (紫竹院公园) to the Guangyuan Mansion building where the market is located

Zhōngguāncūn (中关村)

This huge electronics market offers a wide range of products from mobile phones and cameras to computers and computer games. The "market" is really a whole neighborhood of malls and buildings, including Dinghao Electronics Market, Taipingyang Digital Market, Zhongguancun Plaza Shopping Mall, and others. Expect to encounter a maze of shops, and don't expect these goods to be much cheaper than they would be in your home country.

Hours: 9:00 – 21:00
Location: Zhongguancun Dajie, Haidian Distict
Tranportation: Subway – Line 4, Zhongguancun Station (中关村站)

Solana (Lánsè Gǎngwān; 蓝色港湾)

This upscale "lifestyle shopping park" claims to offer a beautiful European-style respite from the not-so-natural landscape of Beijing. Home to more than 1,000 international brands and many plush bars and restaurants, bargaining is off the table in these high-end stores, and you should expect to pay as much or more for familiar brands as you would back home.

Hours: 11:00–21:30 (Mon – Thu); 11:00–22:00 (Fri–Sun)
Location: 6 Chaoyang Gongyuan Lu (朝阳公园路6号)
Transport: Subway – Line 10, Liangmaqiao Station (亮马桥站), Exit B, walk east down Liangmaqiao Lu (亮马桥路) until you hit the second traffic light, turn right (south) down Chaoyang Gongyuan Lu and you'll see Solana

The Place (Shìmào Tiānjiē; 世贸天阶)

Two luxury mall buildings surround an enormous LCD screen that forms the ceiling of an outdoor patio area. Part mall, part office building, part art exhibit, The Place is not as boring as its name. Expect high-end international brands and boutique shopping.

Hours: 10:00–22:00
Location: 9 Guanghua Lu – near the Silk Market (朝阳区光华路甲9号)
Transport: Subway – Line 1, Yong'anli (永安里), Exit B, walk north along Dongdaqiao Lu (东大桥路), after the first intersection you will see the Place on your right

Sanlitun Village

This eye-catching modern complex has a north and south section, both teeming with popular clothing brands like Uniqlo, Esprit, and Mango, plus an Apple Store and Adidas' flagship China store. More than 30 restaurants and a multiplex cinema are also on the premises.

Hours: 10:00 – 22:00
Location: Sanlitun Lu, Sanlitun
Transport: Subway – Line 10, Tuanjiehu (团结湖), walk west one long block along Gongti Beilu (工体北路) following the signs for the Village

Buying English Books in Beijing

The Bookworm

This bookstore, café, and event space is more than just a place to buy books – it's a touchstone of the expat community in Beijing. Novels, non-fiction and just about anything else can be found. Though the selection is rather small, it's well-curated, and the Western food is worth a trip on its own.

> Address: Courtyard 4, Nan Sanlitun Lu (北京市朝阳区南三里屯路4号楼)
> Phone: 6586 9507
> Email: books@beijingbookworm.com
> Website: www. beijingbookworm.com

The Bookworm also has branches in **Suzhou** (77 Gunxiufang, Shiquan Lu, Suzhou; phone: 0312 3269 8547; website: www.suzhoubookworm.com) and **Chengdu** (2-7 Yulie Donglu, 28 Renmin Nanlu; phone: 028 8552 0177; website: chengdubookworm.com).

Page One

Offering fiction, non-fiction, and reference books in English, this bookstore is probably the closest thing Beijing has to a Barnes & Noble. They offer everything from cookbooks to maps to novels. Three locations:

> Sanlitun Village South, 19 Sanlitun Lu, S2, 1-2/F, Chaoyang District (朝阳区三里屯路19号三里屯 Village 南区2楼1-2层); phone: 6417 6626

> China World Mall, 3B201, 2/B, China World Trade Center Phase 3 (国贸商城三期地下二层 3B201); phone: 8535 1055

> Indigo Mall, 18 Jiuxianqiao Lu, Chaoyang District (酒仙桥路18号); phone: 8426 0408

Beijing's *Top 10* Souvenirs

While you can buy just about everything in China, your friends from home might appreciate something more traditional than a stack of pirated DVDs (which will also present a problem at customs). If you're struggling with ideas, here are the top 10 best souvenirs from Beijing:

Silk

China is the birthplace of silk. In fact, traders from around the globe have been traversing the Silk Road since the Han Dynasty (206 BCE-220 CE) just to get their hands on it. Luckily, today you can simply purchase authentic silk products like a *qípáo* (旗袍; a long Chinese dress), scarves, sheets and other garments without trekking thousands of kilometers.

Tea

The history of Chinese tea dates back millennia, and there are five basic categories of the drink: black tea, brick tea, scented tea, green tea and oolong tea. You can find specialized tea stores that sell quality brands at a high price or cheaper ones at any local supermarket. Another good gift idea that goes well with tea is a tea pot, tea cups or a tea set, which provides a matching pot with cups.

Embroideries & Brocades

The Middle Kingdom is known to have some of the finest embroideries and decorative brocades around. Though embroideries and brocades were considered luxurious and very expensive dynasties ago, nowadays they're quite common and cheap. You can even have the artist customize designs on clothes, slippers, robes, silk and other items to make wonderful, personalized presents.

Calligraphy

Chinese is perhaps the world's most unique written language. With a deep history and aesthetic appeal, it's no wonder the calligraphy of Chinese characters has become so popular. Every dynasty painted with different styles of calligraphy, and characters are also commonly found on sculptures and paintings. Other similar gifts are calligraphy stationary items like brushes, brush holders, ink pots, scrolls and customized stamps with your Chinese name carved into them.

Porcelain

It's no coincidence that porcelain is also known as "china" or "fine china," since the Middle Kingdom invented this delicate art. Porcelain, along with silk, was another valuable commodity heavily sought by traders on the Silk Road, and it's still an international favorite in contemporary times. A variety of objects like vases and bowls can be found with this characteristically shiny, translucent porcelain surface, so be sure to keep your eye out for them while shopping.

Cloisonné

This ancient technique is used to decorate metallic sculptures. Popular cloisonné (jǐngtàilán; 景泰蓝) crafts like animal statues, bowls, plates and tea cups are embellished with glass, jewels, gold wire, rubies and jade, then heated to extreme temperatures to make the colors come alive. Cloisonné objects are easily recognizable by their bright, vibrant colors, so you can't miss them at souvenir shops.

Chinese Medicine

A unique souvenir that also possesses health benefits is traditional Chinese medicine. There are countless types of medicines that are used to treat a variety of illnesses, while some are merely used to keep you young and healthy. Chinese medicine is found just about everywhere in this country, from supermarkets to specialized shops to pharmacies.

Lacquer

Lacquer is an early art that is characterized by the glossy finish on wooden objects. It has been widely used by countless cultures, including Japan and the Middle East, but Chinese lacquer is still considered to be among the most elegant. There are various styles of lacquer that have evolved over the years, and many types of lacquer-ware are can be found all over Beijing.

Jade

Jade has a history of more than 4,000 years and it symbolizes power, beauty and immortality in Chinese culture. There are different types of jade stone that derive from different Chinese provinces, but you'll be able to find every kind in Beijing. You can buy individually-crafted jade figures used for decorations, jade jewelry or other types of jade products at just about any popular market.

Foods & Liquors

Good gifts come from the heart, but the best gifts go to the stomach! To give your loved ones a taste of China, purchase some specialty foods like meat jerky, candy or spices. Spirits and high-grade *baijiu* are also good options. In fact, when many Chinese travel to different provinces they often buy specialty foods and drinks from that region as souvenirs, and they always bring some as a gift when they visit someone's home. Plus if your family and friends don't like your gift, you can always drink it or eat it yourself!

Distractions

Just because your trip to Beijing may be once-in-a-lifetime, doesn't mean you have to suffer through traditional sightseeing and hit all the top attractions if you don't want to. Many travelers start to burn out as the temples and museums and parks blend together in a haze of traditional architecture and signs announcing the exact square meterage of every site. Here are some surprising and engaging distractions in Beijing – add a few of them to your itinerary and watch your experience of the city take on a whole new dimension.

Massage

With all the walking and luggage-hauling you've been doing (not to mention jet lag), a massage is just what you need to restore your body and energize you to charge ahead through your itinerary. Luckily, Beijing is home to hundreds of quality massage centers, and you're going to like the price.

Bodhi Therapeutic Retreat is a favorite of expats in Beijing. For ¥188, Bodhi offers a foot reflexology session that amounts to 80 minutes of attentive, expert foot massage, with a head, neck, and shoulder massage thrown in, too. The real kicker is the free, unlimited drinks and snacks ranging from green tea and smoothies to dumplings and peanut butter toast. Group treatment rooms allow the whole family to enjoy at the same time. Plunk down in the muted, serene surroundings for a price you could never match back home. There's a Chinese body massage (also ¥188) and a wide variety of other treatments, including facials.

> Address: 17 Gongti Beilu (工体北路17号) opposite Workers' Stadium
> Phone: 6417 9595; 6413 0226
> Operating hours: 11:00 – 00:30
> Website: www.bodhi.com.cn

Blind Massages are pretty popular in Beijing. It might seem odd to visitors, but many blind people in China train to become expert massage therapists, and they are renowned for their supposedly enhanced sensitivity. Blind massage parlors dot the city on practically every street, and while most of them are totally legit, some are a little sketchy. We recommend **Aibosen Blindman Massage** (Àibósēn Mángrén Ànmóyuàn; 爱博森盲人按摩院), where ¥88 gets you a 50-minute body massage or a 70-minute foot massage. It's open from 10:00 – 1:00 daily, and offers a selection of free snacks and juices to accompany your treatment. The surroundings aren't luxurious, but they're clean and relaxing. The staff doesn't speak English, but they're well accustomed to foreigners.

> Address: 11 Liufang Beili, Chaoyang District (柳芳北里11号)
> Phone: 6465 2044; 6466 1247
> Address: 2/F, Donghua Hotel, 32 Dengshikou Xijie (灯市口西街32号东华饭店二楼)
> Phone: 6525 7532 ext 3201
> Transport: Subway – Line 13, Liufang Stop

Cooking Classes

Delicious Chinese food doesn't have to go away when you go home. Attend one of these very well-run cooking classes to try your hand at Chinese cuisine and learn some tips to help you recreate the taste of your trip long after it's over.

Black Sesame Kitchen offers cooking classes every Tuesday, Thursday or Saturday from 10:00 – 1:00 in an atmospheric hutong location off of popular Nanluogu Xiang. ¥300 per person gets you three hours of cooking excitement, from learning how to use Chinese knives and woks to preparing ingredients and putting together a dish. Black Sesame offers a multitude of courses, from Imperial Chinese dishes to home-style dumplings, and snacks from Sichuan to Beijing. If you're traveling with a group, they can arrange a private lesson, and for an extra fee they'll throw in a market tour and teach you how to select the best ingredients. Check their website for the courses available during your stay. Closed on Mondays.

> Address: 3 Heizhima Hutong (黑芝麻胡同3号, inside Nanluogu Xiang), Dongcheng District.
> Email: reservations@blacksesamekitchen.com
> Phone: 136 9147 4408
> Website: www.blacksesamekitchen.com
> Transport: Subway – Line 6, Nanluoguxiang Station

The Hutong is a popular teaching kitchen focusing on fresh, local, seasonal ingredients that make tasty, wholesome meals from scratch. Their charming facility is located, as the name suggests, in an old hutong. Their skilled chefs try to tell a story with every dish and examine Chinese culture through the lens of its cuisine. ¥250 per person gains you access to classes including Yunnan Cuisine, Hand-pulled Noodles, Dim Sum Delicacies and more. Scope out their website for a schedule and more details, and make sure to see if chef Johana is cooking that day for an extra delicious experience.

> Address: 1 Jiudaowan Zhongxiang (东城区九道湾中巷1号)
> Email: info@thehutong.com
> Phone: 159 0104 6127
> Website: www.thehutongkitchen.com
> Transport: Subway – Line 5, Beixinqiao Station

Hiking, Biking & Camping

Beijing Hikers is always a good one. The rural outskirts of Beijing provide the setting for the friendly, well-organized hikes led by Beijing Hikers. Since 2001, they've been taking travelers and expats to locations they'd never find on their own: secluded sections of the Great Wall, natural hot springs, and picturesque mountain valleys. Each hike begins with a meetup at a central location where you'll load into buses and head for the hills. Beijing Hikers include transportation, snacks, meals, water, and guides in their fee, which is usually about ¥400 per person per hike. Check out their website, where hikes are described in detail and with great information on their level of difficulty. **www.beijinghikers.com**

A cycling tour with Bike Beijing is a great way to experience the city that was long known as a place where bikes outnumbered cars. While that's less true today, a bike is still one of the best ways to cover ground in this big, flat city. Bike Beijing offers tours to accommodate every possible interest, from the hutongs to the mountains bordering the Great Wall, and tours range from half-days to weeks. Bike Beijing will hook you up with like-new bikes, helmets, and an English-speaking guide to lead you through the city, providing information and stories along the way. They get rave reviews from travelers, who love the opportunity to get up close and personal with the city in a way that riding around in a tour bus doesn't allow. Half-days start at around US$40 per person, but the price goes down as your group gets larger. **www.bikebeijing.com**

Beijing Sideways is a unique company that offers unforgettable tours of Beijing using motorcycles with sidecars to zip you around the city quickly and in style. From two-hour highlight tours to multi-day overnight journeys to the Great Wall where you stay in a cozy, hidden guesthouse, their eccentric and enthusiastic guides will unveil spots that even locals don't know. Prices, photos, and tour options at **www.beijingsideways.com**.

Camping on the Great Wall is awesome, so if spending the night in an abandoned guard tower on the Great Wall sounds kick ass, you're in luck. Camping on the Great Wall is technically not allowed, but that hasn't stopped a number of companies from pitching tents. Starting at around US$150 per person, these tours tend to include transportation, equipment, food, and guides. See their sites for details on destination, price, and schedule. Dandelion Hikers **www.chinahiking.cn**; Wild Great Wall Adventure Tours **www.wildgreatwall.com**; and The Great Wall Adventure Club **www.greatwalladventure.com** are the three best.

Strange Museums

Forget about museums you've visited in the past – these two surely offer something you've never seen before, whether it's ancient sex toys or poems dedicated to fruit.

Eunuch Museum (Huàngguān Wénhuà Chénlièguǎn; 宦官文化陈列馆) – The imperial eunuch Tian Yi is honored at this alternately creepy and informative museum. The pleasant grounds include a small museum area that documents the daily life of eunuchs back in the day, while displays outline the castration process and showcase some old mummies and ancient sex toys. If that's not enough, you also have the option of visiting the scary underground tombs. The displays are all in Chinese, but the rather graphic nature of the content makes itself pretty clear.

> Hours: 9:00 - 16:00
> Admission: ¥8
> Address: 80 Moshikou Dajie (石景山区模式口大街80号)
> Phone: (010) 8872 4148

Watermelon Museum (Xīguā Bówùguǎn; 西瓜博物馆) – This epically large museum is completely devoted to watermelons, housing more than 600 specimens and 900 illustrations of the fruit. From the history of watermelons in China to the technology used for growing them, this museum has got it covered. There's also a collection of Chinese poems and paintings offering tribute to the fruit. A second hall takes it to the next level by discussing the watermelon's role worldwide, including such goofy features as a list of the top professional watermelon farmers around the world. The weirdly futuristic décor is a contrast to the humble subject matter, and we're pretty sure you'll never see another museum like it.

> Address: Remotely located at the Huangcun County Culture Center, South of the Panggezhuang Zhen State Bldg in Daxing District
> Hours: 10:00 – 15:30 daily
> Entrance fee: ¥20 (¥10 for students)
> Transport: Public transportation not an option – you need to hire a cab (大兴区庞各庄镇政府南)

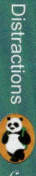

Side Trips from Beijing

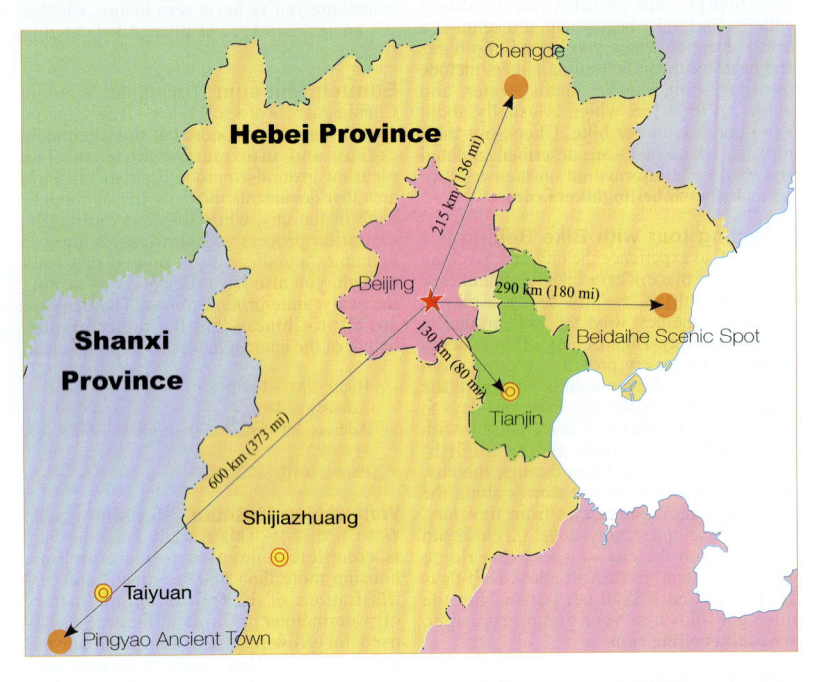

Map labels:
- Chengde
- Hebei Province
- 215 km (136 mi)
- Beijing
- 290 km (180 mi)
- Beidaihe Scenic Spot
- Shanxi Province
- 130 km (80 mi)
- Tianjin
- 600 km (373 mi)
- Shijiazhuang
- Taiyuan
- Pingyao Ancient Town

A week or two jaunt in Beijing will bring the average adventurer enough palaces and temples to keep them pious and pomp for a lifetime. While seeing the historical structures and parks of the city is a head-spinning romp that is absolutely unbeatable, there are times when you need an intermission from the show. One of the best ways to keep yourself and your trip fresh is to make an excursion to one of the alluring retreats on Beijing's peripheries. Packed with hotels and cool attractions, these offbeat interludes are worthy of a day or overnight visit. So pack up your gear and put on your gung ho shoes, it's time for a vacation from your vacation.

Tiānjīn 天津

Tianjin is an amalgamation. Swaggering in the sea spray of the largest man made port in China are a collection of European villas styled after the great powers of the old world, and their exotic flavor stands as a smug reminder of the contentious force of 19th century imperialism. The thousands of chateauxs are certainly beautiful, and their contrast with the neighboring Qing Dynasty (1644-1912) style architecture of Jinmen Guli Street makes for a charming juxtaposition. At the same time, however, this nexus of East and West also gives way to stark reminders of China's own unscrupulous papering over of heritage, where most "Qing" buildings on Jinmen Guli or Hotel Street are just face-value reproductions. Still, Tianjin is often called an "architectural museum" for its party bag of structural design, and the magic of the sprightly food streets, shopping zones and exotic neighborhoods is hardly diminished along these vibrant cultural jungle gyms. Set against the backdrop of the Pacific Ocean and the Haihe River, and boasting one-of-a-kind temples, sculptures, and a broad palate of Chinese cuisine, Tianjin is a feast for the eyes and a party for the mouth.

Attractions

Jīnmén Gùlǐ (津门故里)

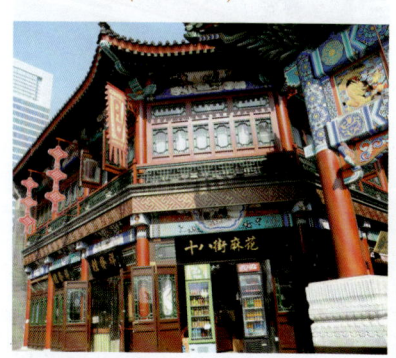

Jinmen Guli, the alternate name for Tianjin's Ancient Cultural Street (Gǔwénhuà Jiē; 古文化街), is full of amusement for your first night out, as long as you don't fixate upon the gilded nature of the "ancient" buildings. It's good for a lighthearted stroll, and you can find plenty of antiques, jade (be careful of fakeries) and colorful kites to feed your

Chinese shopping bug. Keep an eye out here for the famous **mud sculptures**, hand crafted clay folk art holding to a tradition dated from the Neolithic Period.

There are some other interesting sites around the Old Town as well. **Tianhou Temple** (Tiānhòu Gōng; 天后宫 ; 80 Guwenhua Jie – 古文化街80号 ; FREE) is dedicated to the Taoist goddess of the sea, Matzu. Nearby, the **Drum Tower** (Gǔ Lóu; 鼓楼 ; FREE) is a fine sight in the middle of town, and the **Museum of Opera** (Tiānjīnshì Xìjù Bówùguǎn; 天津市戏剧博物馆 ; ¥10), built at the turn of the 20th century, hosts a fine collection on Peking Opera. There is also a handsome **Confucian Temple** (Wén Miào; 文庙 ; ¥30).

For a more modern twist of Tianjin, walk north 1.5 km (less than 1 mi) along the Hai River to the **Tianjin Eye** (Tiānjīn Yǎn; 天津眼 ; child/adult ¥35/70; 9:00-21:00) – a massive Ferris wheel – for an eye-in-the-sky view of the megalopolis.

Transport: 1, 605, 610, 619, 632, 641, 646, 670, 671, 804, 908, 954, get off at Dongbeijiao (东北角) Stop

Nanshi Food Street

Chinese name: 南市食品街 (Nánshì Shípǐn Jiē)
Transport: Bus – 606, 611, 634, 642, 645, 651, 672, 675, 801, 806, 824, 829, 846, 878, 954, 962, get off at Nanshi Shipinjie Stop

Culinary adventurers will want to make several trips to southern Tianjin for the Food Street in the city's Nanshi Commercial District (Nánshì Shāngyèqū; 南市商业区). Seven out of China's eight classic cuisines make an appearance in over 50 restaurants that will engulf you in an ocean of tasty aromas. Get prices before you order, many are not listed.

Dule Temple

Chinese name: 独乐寺 (Dúlè Sì)
Admission: ¥40
Hours: 8:00-17:30
Recommended time for visit: 1 hour
Phone: (022) 2914 2904
Address: 41 Wuding Jie, Ji County (蓟县城内武定街41号)
Transport: Bus – 531 to Dulesi Stop

If you're not templed-out from the plethora in Beijing, strike out north of the city to peak at the 1,000-year-old Dule Temple, holding the oldest multi-storied wooden pavilion in China and the eleven faces of the 16 m- (52 ft)-tall clay statue of Guanyin (观音 ; the female bodhisattva of compassion).

Dagu Fort

Chinese name: 大沽炮台 (Dàgū Pàotái)
Admission: ¥30
Hours: 8:30-16:30
Recommended time for visit: 1 hour
Address: 1 Dongpaotai Lu (东炮台路1号)
Transport: Bus – 116 to Fudi Tonggoujian (福迪砼构件) Stop

Head 60 km (37 mi) southwest from the city center, where the edifices of the 19th century Dagu Fort bristle with replica and antique weaponry, and chafe with reminders of the battlement's ineffectiveness against foreign invaders. There is an eclectic mix of exhibits, and the fort has been tastefully restored.

In the City

If a voyage out of town is not in the cards, take a breezy stroll through the lush trees, flowers and parks of the cozy **City Beltway** (Zhōnghuán Cǎiliàn; 中环彩练), the Cupid's Arrow through the heart of Tianjin. Couples, musicians, and energetic 80-somethings fill the pathways with character and add to the refreshing aura of the scenery. The nine islands and three lakes of the city's local misnomer, **Water Park** (Shuǐshàng Gōngyuán; 水上公园) – which is a park with some streams, not a water park – are sprinkled with relaxing pathways and pagodas to cool the steam off your brow after a zesty Sichuan-style lunch. Don't forget to stroll along the skyscrapers and traditional architecture that surround the **Haihe River** (Hǎi Hé; 海河), too.

Most importantly, however, is the old **Foreign Concession**. This area that was handed over to foreign powers by the Qing government in the 19th century houses some outstanding European Gothic and Renaissance-style architecture. The best way to find it is to make your way to the **Five Avenues** (Wǔdàdào; 五大道) and explore from there.

Sleeping

Tianjin has plenty of hotels and hostels that can likely suit your needs. For the sake of simplicity we have recommended two of our favorites, but feel free to shop around.

Orange Hotel (Júzi Jiǔdiàn; 桔子酒店)

This modish hotel sports very nice rooms and a handsome interior. The clientele is mostly young professionals and it sits cozily next to the river. Bikes can be rented here, with the first two hours for free. Rooms start at ¥238.

> Address: 7 Xing'an Lu, Nankai District (南开区兴安路7号)
> Phone: (022) 2734 8333; 400 819 0099

Tangla Hotel Tianjin (Tánglāyǎxiù Jiǔdiàn; 唐拉雅秀酒店)

One of the fanciest places in China, and certainly the fanciest in Tianjin, Tangla (formerly Raffles Tianjin) is a seductive penthouse-style hotel which lures high-end clients with its elegant chandelier-decked lobby and immaculate rooms. Rooms start at ¥798.

> Address: 219 Nanjing Lu, Heping District (和平区南京路219号)
> Phone: (022) 2321 5888

Getting In & Out

Trains from Beijing to Tianjin depart throughout the day. High speed bullet trains will cost you around ¥55-65 for second and first class, respectively, and last about 30-45 minutes. Bullet trains all depart from Beijing South Railway Station. These train numbers begin with C, D, or G (such as C2109). The cheaper route is to hop on a regular train from Beijing Station or Beijing West Station, which will run you ¥18-25 for a seat and takes 1.5-2 hours. These train numbers either start with a T or a K, or have no letter prefix on the number (such as 4419).

Píngyáo 平遥

The two pronged effect of Pingyao's status as the former "Wall Street of China" has produced a time-capsule of a tourist destination, with 800-year-old buildings embraced in the loving care of the old city wall and a peak season tourist rush that smashes the ancient daydream like a piggy bank. The famed Jin Businessmen (Jìn Shāng; 晋商) of Pingyao's Shanxi Province cultivated a thriving merchant class here for hundreds of years, encouraging the growth and protection of China's now best wholly preserved ancient town.

Little has been forgotten since the merchants' days of yore: a drift through the inner city requires you to buy a ticket to visit the ancient sights, while vendors and shops hustle their own pretty penny within the walls. Still, it's hard to say no to an entire town that passed **UNESCO**'s impressive World Heritage requirements in 1997, and you'll be thrilled by the sight of antiqued manors, red lantern-lit ancient alleyways, archaic banks and a bounty of genuine character that whirls within the lovely old town.

Attractions

Nandajie (南大街)

The main drag of Pingyao's inner city, **Nandajie** (or Ming-Qing Street) can get jam-packed with flag toting tour groups clad in homogenous yellow T-shirts, but when the flurry begins to swell, you can swing out to the side streets for plenty of authentic charm without all the hubbub. Your best bet is to hit the souvenir shopping of Nandajie in the morning or evening to avoid the groups, and then make the rounds through the rest of the old city sights by day.

City Wall (Chéngqiáng; 城墙)

A great start to your day may be a quick circuit of the City Wall for a giant's view of the inner city's fantastic Ming and Qing architecture. The wall was originally built in 1370 and is nicked with 72 watchtowers, each written with a passage from Sun-Tzu's *The Art of War*. Apart from a southern section that collapsed and was subsequently restored in 2004, the historic wall is all original.

Risheng Chang Exchange Shop Museum (Rìshēngchāng Piàohào Bówùguǎn; 日升昌票号博物馆)

The Risheng Chang Exchange Shop should be on your first day's docket as well. The father of China's financial powerhouse (the Bank of China), it was here that Pingyao's propensity for profit blossomed and broke the ground for China's modern banking institutions. Now a museum, the shop was originally an 18th century dye house that eventually exploded into China's first draft bank in 1823. The museum has nearly 100 rooms, including offices, living quarters, and several old cheques.

Temples

If you need a little spirituality you can get folksy at the **Temple of the City God** (Chénghuáng Miào; 城隍庙) and the **Confucian Temple** (Wén Miào; 文庙) on Chenghuangmiao Jie (城隍庙街), all of which offer excellent glimpses into the history of local life.

The oldest surviving building of Pingyao, **Dacheng Hall** (Dàchéng Diàn; 大成殿), is located within the Confucian Temple, which in its heyday saw hosts of civil servant hopefuls lining up for the grueling imperial examinations.

County Government Office (Yámén Guānshè; 衙门官舍)

Feel the justice at the County Government Office on Yamen Jie (衙门街), where you can get a look at 18th century Chinese courtrooms. It's even complete with an old-timey prison.

Old City Neighborhoods

Make sure to wander the old neighborhoods throughout the ancient city, where you may get a little green with envy at the old Ming-style grand residences and courtyards. This is a great place to find the quintessential China of your childhood daydreams, where red lanterns hang off ancient upturned eaves, all set against the backdrop of a fairy-tale city wall. A "joint-sight ticket" includes Nandajie, the City Wall, the County Government Office, and the Temple of the City God. This can be a bit ambitious for some, so if you're not feeling a mad museum-dash you can pick and choose your attractions.

Outside the City

If you spend two days in Pingyao, day number two may be good for a daytrip, where you can mix and match from two prominent temples and a triplet of old merchant family compounds dotted around the Pingyao countryside.

One solid combination is to first head 40 km (25 mi) north of the old city to take in the mighty **Qiao Compound** (Qiáojiā Dàyuàn; 乔家大院), whose unique Northern China architectural style was built during Qianlong's (1735-1796) reign, and was the home of eminent 18th century capitalist Qiáo Zhìyōng (乔致庸). Next, cruise back towards the city, stopping off 12 km (7.5 mi) northeast for a wander among the 1,000-year-old wooden walls of **Zhenguo Temple** (Zhènguó Sì; 镇国寺).

Combo number two is to strike southwest instead, first hitting the amazing architectural encampment at the **Wang Compound** (Wángjiā Dàyuàn; 王家大院), 35 km (22 mi) southwest of Pingyao and brimming with outstanding Qing Dynasty villas and statues. On your way back, make a pit-stop 6 km (3.5 mi) from town for a gape at the 2,000 vividly painted sculptures of the Yuan, Ming, and Qing Dynasties at **Shuanglin Monastery** (Shuānglín Sì; 双林寺); some are nearly 1,000 years old. An incense stick's throw northeast of Shuanglin is the **Cao Compound** (Cáojiā Dàyuàn; 曹家大院), a remarkable assortment of seven homes mounted on four noble courtyards and boasting a history of 400 years.

Sleeping

Pingyao has a head-spinning variety of hotel options. You can shop around the snack streets and commercial areas without declaring bankruptcy, so jump in and find your own adventure. A great place to start is **Nandajie**.

Harmony Guesthouse (Héyìchāng Kèzhàn; 和义昌客栈)

The rooms at Harmony Guesthouse are built over two beautifully preserved courtyards in a fantastic 300-year-old Qing building. The majority of the rooms come with traditional stone *kàng* (炕) beds (with padding on top, of course), wooden bed-top tea tables and wonderful wooden inlaid windows. Dorms are available, as well as bike rental (¥10 per day), laundry (¥10 per kg), internet, wifi and train station pickup. Singles start at ¥80.

> Address: 165 Nandajie (平遥南大街165号)
> Phone: (0354) 568 4952

Cui Chenghai Hotel (Cuìchénghǎi Kèzhàn;)

A more upscale option compared with Harmony Guesthouse or other hostels in the area, Cui Chenghai Hotel offers more elegantly furnished rooms surrounding three lovely Ming Dynasty courtyards. The cheaper rooms are furnished in a more modern building off to the side and are a bit lacking in charm, but still a very nice, classic stay. Singles start at ¥162.

> Address: 178 Nandajie (平遥南大街178号)
> Phone: (0354) 577 7888

Getting In & Out

There are no high-speed trains to Pingyao, so you'll be looking at a 12-14 hour overnight journey on a regular or a K train (K603, 1163, 2602/2603) departing from Beijing Railway Station. We highly advise you to get a bed, which are available in a hard sleeper or soft sleeper. This does not describe the firmness of the mattress: hard sleepers are six-bed open partitioned chambers and soft sleepers come in four-bed private rooms with a door. Hard beds range from ¥150-186 per bed and soft beds go for ¥240-301 per bed. If you're broke and bold you can consider a seat for ¥82-98 per ticket, but it will be at a long trip on a hard plastic bench smothered by local farmers and crying babies.

Běidàihé 北戴河

Beidaihe is the perfect spot for the city-jaded. With a great combination of heart-pounding hikes and salty seaside views, this kitschy beach resort is one of the more refreshing of the Beijing side trip destinations. A damp monsoon climate makes the area ideal for year-round travel (though May to October is best), and its soft pebbled sand is the ideal place to lay out and catch a blistering sun burn. These days, Beidaihe has gained its own calling as a proverbial "Summer Palace," as the local government puts some luxury and swank on its bureaucratic business when it fills the beach resort in the summer – many of the nation's policies are discussed by top national officials on holiday at this summer haven. Besides the abundance of local snacks, holiday villages, swimming spots, and seafood, kicking back at the seaside parks and beaches in the cool ocean breeze is essential R&R at Beidaihe.

The 24 Scenic Spots (Èrshísì Jǐng; 二十四景)

Known by the locals as the 24 Scenic Spots, endless activities and historic sights await you in Beidaihe. You will want to spend at least two days enjoying the ocean sunrise at the top of Yingjiao Pavilion (Yīngjiǎo Tíng; 鹰角亭) or Wanghai Pavilion (Wànghǎi Tíng; 望海亭) in **Dove Nest Park** (Dēziwō Gōngyuán; 鸽子窝公园), or do the trapeze and go river drifting at **Jifa Agricultural Sightseeing Garden** (Jífā Nóngyè Guānguāngyuán; 集发农业观光园). Grab your trunks and make a splash at the more than 30 bathing areas of **Bohai Bay**, or catch the magical views of Eagle Corner Pavilion and Lotus Flower Rock Park. If you didn't get enough Great Wall in Bejing, Beidaihe is home to the **Shanhaiguan Great Wall** (Shānhǎi Guān Chángchéng; 山海关长城), the site of the battle that collapsed the Ming Dynasty. Make sure to book hotels early if you're coming out in summer. Check with your hostel or hotel for more information on the boundless activities at this lovely beach resort.

Getting In & Out

There are 23 trains that run daily to Beidaihe, all departing from Beijing Railway Station. The fastest ones will begin with a D, such as the D11. These generally take about 2 hours and cost around ¥80. Mid-speed trains begin with T, such as T47, and will run about 2.5 hours and cost about ¥87. The slowest trains are the K trains, and they take between four and five hours and go for ¥40-50.

> Once you have arrived at Beidaihe, hop aboard bus 34 to cruise around to all the major scenic spots in the area.

Sleeping

Beidaihe is littered with hotels and places to stay. Here are a couple of our recommendations, but it is by no means an exhaustive list.

Beidaihe International Club (Běidàihé Guójì Jùlèbù; 北戴河国际俱乐部)

Beidaihe International Club is located on Binhai Lu. The rooms are modern and elegant and range all the way from singles to suites. Most are well outfitted with a telephone, bar, refrigerator and safe-deposit box. A true high end resort hotel, you can get in games of bowling and buff up at the gym, as well as do some sharking in the billiards hall. There is also a KTV (karaoke) room. As you might have already imagined, this luxury hotel will punch a hole in your wallet.

Address: 50 Binhai Dadao (北戴河滨海大道50号)
Phone: (0335) 418 1777

Beidaihe Zhangyanxia Hostel (Zhāngyànxiá Jiātíng Lǚguǎn; 张艳霞家庭旅馆)

A great little hostel off of Liuzhuang North, BZH has clean and well maintained rooms, and the staff is friendly and works to please. Bikes can be rented for cruising around Beidaihe's beachy beltways, and the prices won't cost you an arm and a leg.

Address: 10-8 Liuzhuang Beili (北戴河区刘庄北里8排10号)
Phone: 139 3354 8778

Beidaihe: China's Smoke Filled Room

It seems that all over the world the taste for government power and politics goes hand in hand with a taste for money and luxurious comfort. Politicians love to take their planning and meetings to some of the most comfortable places in the world – on tax payer dollars of course – and China is a sterling example of this iffy practice. So where does Beijing's political coterie like to go for their luxurious work away from work now that the Summer Palace is open to the public? Beidaihe of course.

One US diplomat described the meetings between China's political elite every July at the Beidaihe beach resort as "China's smoke-filled room." In fact, the strategies and devices planned at the whisper-soft meetings in Beidaihe are so secret, it's rare that they ever get even a slip-of-the-tongue from the state media. Not that it's surprising that the state does not let the state-run media speak of super secret state meetings, but that just goes to show how hush hush everything is.

Despite the secrecy, Beidaihe as a CCP summer meeting hotspot is hardly a secret to the Chinese. Mao himself – who was certainly a lover of comfort and luxury – had his own summer resort here, and the later members of the Party have kept up his tradition of summer luxury under the umbrella of state planning. From Mao's influence a number of workers' sanatoriums sprang up in the area during the 1950s, as well as a large "Friendship Guesthouse" meant to house the Soviet "older brothers" of the 1930s and 40s.

One of the most infamous events of Red China occurred here in 1971. On September 13, Lin Biao, a marshal and field commander for the PLA who was at one time set to succeed Mao, fled his villa at Beidaihe in what appeared to be a failed coup on Mao. He and his family boarded a plane that was destined for the Soviet Union, but they never made it. The plane "crashed" in Mongolia, killing all on board.

Chéngdé 承德

Not to be confused with the Sichuan capital city of Chengdu, the mountain resort city of Chengde boasts a powerful and impressive imperial history on par with Beijing. At the turn of the 18th century, the Kangxi Emperor became enamored with the verdant mountains and struck up a decision to build an imperial holiday playground here – a move largely done to escape Beijing's oppressive summer heat. The palace-away-from-the-palace that he began building here reached its completion 89 years later. From then on it became the seat of the imperial government and Manchu foreign affairs whenever the Qing emperors came here for holiday.

The "Avoiding-the-Heat Mountain Villa," as the imperial resort is known in Chinese, is not the only fantastic sight you can behold in cool Chengde. You can also get your fill of spirituality from a series of wonderful temples dotting the mountains around the imperial resort, including a not-so-small version of Lhasa's mighty Potala Palace. Summer is a great time to come and escape the rampant oven heat of Beijing, but you will be greeted by walls of tourists, and wintertime is frigid. Your best bet is an autumn visit, when you can avoid the crowds and the weather, and make it to see the colors that saturate the mountainsides.

Attractions

Imperial Mountain Resort

Chinese name: 避暑山庄 (Bìshǔ Shānzhuāng)
Admission: ¥120
Hours: 8:00-17:30
Recommended time for visit: half a day
Phone: (0314) 202 9771
Website: www.bishushanzhuang.com.cn/Language/shanzhuangeng
Address: 20 Lizhengmen Lu (丽正门路 20 号)
Transport: Bus – 5, 7, 11, 15 to Huoshenmiao (火神庙) Stop

If you want an idea of how insanely big the spectacular **UNESCO World Heritage** listed

Imperial Mountain Resort is then try these facts on for size: the 10 km (6 mi) defensive wall encloses the largest royal garden in China – which also includes eight lakes – and the whole complex covers an area of 5.5 sq km (2 sq mi), almost half of Chengde's entire urban area. Now that is one huge palace complex!

Construction on the palace began in 1703 under the illustrious Kangxi Emperor, who loved hunting and wanted to make this his personal hunting grounds. It was finally completed in 1792. The vast garden space was expertly designed to encompass a multiplicity of China's finest southern regions, embodying mountains, lakes, forests and cliffs, as well as northern Mongolian grasslands in an incredible system that together includes 72 specific scenic spots strewn throughout an arrangement of pagodas, halls and temples. This place really is incredible.

Eight Outer Temples (Wàibā Miào; 外八庙)

Hours: 8:00-17:30 for all temples

Scattered around the exterior of the Mountain Resort's northern and eastern walls, the Eight Outer Temples offer up a unique twist on the art of Chinese temple building. Owing to the fact that they were built for diplomatic reasons by the Kangxi Emperor, who was out to awe Tibetan and Mongolian tribes whom he hosted in Chengde, many of the temples purport a fancy foreign façade, while their interior is loyal to traditional Chinese designs. The Mongolians – like the Tibetans – were avid lamas (Tibetan Buddhists), so many of the temples will look Tibetan from the outside and have a distinctly Chinese flavor inside.

Just across the street from the Mountain Resort is the Taoist **Guandi Temple** (Guāndì Miào; 关帝庙; ¥20; 8:00-17:00); a great place to see Taoist priests in all their top-knotted glory. Check out the giant 1,000-armed statue of Guanyin at Chengde's only active Buddhist temple, **Puning Temple** (Pǔníng Sì; 普宁寺; ¥50). Down the road from Puning is **Putuozongcheng Temple** (Pǔtuózōngchéng Zhīmiào; 普陀宗乘之庙; ¥80), a replica of the renowned Potala Palace in Lhasa. Another replica is the **Temple of Sumeru, Happiness and Longevity** (Xūmífúshòu ZhīMiào; 须弥福寿之庙), which mimics Tibet's Tashilhunpo Monastery, home of the Panchen Lama. The last temple open to visitors is the **Pule Temple** (Pǔlè Sì; 普乐寺; ¥30). All of the remaining temples today where built between 1713 and 1780.

Sleeping

Chengde is not exactly budget friendly, and nearly all the cheap options are not allowed to accept foreigners. Good luck finding twins or singles for less than ¥300. Prices will always be higher during the weekend and astronomical during holidays (like National Day in the first week of October or the Spring Festival).

Ming's Dynasty Hostel (Míngcháo Guójì Chéngshì Qīngnián Jiǔdiàn; 明朝国际城市青年酒店)

The family-run Ming's is more than just the best budget option in town; it is the only budget option in Chengde. The atmosphere is warm and the friendly and attentive staff will bend over backwards to help guests, handing out free maps of the city and lots of good advice. Rooms are cozy and clean, and they can help book transportation for you. Five minutes to the right after you exit the train station.

Address: Huilong Plaza, Xin Juzhai, Chezhan Lu (车站路新居宅会龙大厦)
Phone: (0314) 761 0360; 136 4314 0882
Email: chengdehostel@live.com
Website: www.mingsdynastyhostel.com

Mountain Villa Hotel (Shānzhuāng Bīn'guǎn; 山庄宾馆)

On the plus side, the Mountain Villa Hotel has a ton of rooms, discounts of up to 50% in slow times, and is close to the Mountain Resort. The bad news is that the discounts come on top of already steep prices and the rooms are boring and spartan for the price you pay. Still, the rooms are actually an OK deal for a place as exorbitant as Chengde. Rooms start at ¥201.

Address: 11 Lizhengmen Dajie (丽正门大街11号)
Phone: (0314) 209 1188

Eating & Drinking

On **Shaanxiying Jie** (陕西营街) you can find a night market cooking up loads of scrumptious Shaanxi fare, including Muslim noodle dishes, roast meats (shāokǎo; 烧烤) and the always delicious *ròujiámó* (肉夹馍; pork or beef in a biscuit). Some bars can be found here as well. If you're in the mood for hot pot then head over to **Dongxing Lu** (东兴路).

Check the street south of the Mountain Resort – **Wulie Lu** (武烈路) – for local *pubang* deer meat clusters (Púbàng Lùròu; 蒲棒鹿肉; ¥4-5) and other local specialties. Wulie Lu has beer gardens in summer.

Daqinghua Dumplings (Dàqīnghuā Jiǎoziguǎn; 大清花饺子馆)

Calling Daqinghua the best dumpling house in Chendge sells this place short – it might be the best in all of Hebei. The *jiaozi* here come in a great variety of delicious meat and veggie styles and fit perfectly with the joint's warm pinewood interior. There are plenty of other dishes here as well, in case you're craving something else. They have a picture menu.

Address: 19 Lizheng Lu (丽正路19号, 避暑山庄对面)
Phone: (0314) 203 6111

Getting In & Out

Trains to Chengde are a four- to six-hour ride (seven trains daily) from Beijing, and your best bet is to get a K train (e.g. K7711), which means *kuai* (快) for "fast," in order to reduce time. Seats are ¥36-41, and though beds are available (hard sleeper: ¥82-95; soft sleeper: ¥125-141) it's not likely that you'll need one.

Several minibuses can get you between the train station and different locations around town. Minibus 1 goes to the East Bus Station, minibus 6 heads to the Eight Outer Temples, and minibus 5 heads to Lizhengmen Dajie. They all cost ¥1.

Travel Stories

My Travel Story
By Tony

In the summer of 2012 I decided it was time to check out the Middle Kingdom. A sprightly 23 year old at the time (I'm only 24 now and still quite sprightly), I had already done my share of excursions through South Africa, Australia and 12 countries of Europe, so taming the dragon in the Far East seemed like the next logical step. I had heard China could be elusive for some trying to get a visa, but I got started early; a good two months before my planned departure date, I had no problems getting set up. So, I set out in mid-June for a two week jaunt in the land of jade and silk – first stop: Beijing.

Day 1

The long flight to Beijing requires patience and plenty of leg stretching; free alcohol on international flights doesn't hurt either. The 13-hour flight gave me plenty of time to sleep, so I felt ready for action by the time we landed at 8:00. I made sure to do my research before going, or at least as much as I could, and I knew that I needed to bee-line around the taxi touts waiting outside the luggage claim area. I found many of them were being hustled out the door by a fulminating police officer, but the persistent drivers would do their best to trickle back in on the peripheral edges. It was quite an amusing sight.

The better bet to me seemed to hop on the subway, which was just ¥25 for the airport express, and then ¥2 more for the rest of the subway, instead of forking over ¥100-plus for a taxi. The ¥27 total took me to Xinjiekou on Line 4, and I then grabbed a ¥10 cab ride to my hostel. I dropped my stuff off at the office for safe keeping, and headed out the door around 10:00 to hit up Beijing's best seller: the Forbidden City.

The monolithic enormity of the Forbidden City had been totally lost on me from the pictures I had seen. I knew it was big, but not a hulking behemoth. A couple hours definitely sufficed, as it was impressive, but it got a little repetitive after a while. The architecture was unbelievable, and the side courtyards and little museums of ancient clothing and artwork were cool, but the giant halls and terraces can be a little homogenous. Still, it was beautiful; definitely a must for any Beijing trip.

From there I set out for some lunch and rented a bike from my hostel, which is right next to the awesome Houhai Lakes, and cycled around the water and hutongs with some hostel buddies I met at lunch. As the evening set in, we had some drinks and swapped stories at some raucous Houhai bars before biking back and turning in for the night.

Day 2

The sun rose on Day 2 and I could feel the Great Wall's call. I had slept well, and my body was begging for some good hiking action. I wasn't in the mood for crowds or a restored wall, so I went for the Jinshanling section, which ended up setting me back around ¥900 for a round trip driver. This section of the wall was quite peerless though, and the 7 km (4 mi) hike to the Simatai section was insanely beautiful and a formidable workout. The walk is fairly unrestored, which really hit the authentic sweet spot, and the mountainside views are world class.

After a long day of hiking I was tired to my bones, but I felt vivacious from the blood pumping through my veins, so I decided to take a little hutong tour and look for an American-style brewery that I had heard rumors about. Great Leap Brewing turned out to be just a hop, skip and a jump away from my hostel on the east side of the lake. A couple hostel buddies came with, and we made our ingress around 19:00 for a welter of tasty brews, ranging from hoppy pale ales and IPAs to dusty cinnamon beers and malty darks. It was a beer-drinker's dream, right in the ancient hutongs of Beijing, and we even ordered from Hutong Pizza straight to the brewery. The laughs and beer swilling went deep into the night, and eventually we happily stumbled our way back to the hostel.

Day 3

I was planning to visit a friend in Shanghai on Day 4, spend a few days there, and then come back to Beijing for the last few days of my trip. Even though I'd be back, I wanted to take in one of the more must-see Beijing sights before heading out of the city. On Day 3, the Summer Palace beckoned, and I knew I was in for something special. I hadn't slept quite as well as the first night, so getting up was a little rough, but I was excited, and my energy quickly returned with a hutong breakfast of delicious *jian bing* (egg and corn flour wraps) and a hostel coffee. I jumped on the subway, which took me to within a few hundred meters of the gate.

The Summer Palace was epic. I couldn't believe a complex like this existed, much less the fact that the Qing emperors spent their leisurely summers at such a regal playground. I spent a good couple hours wandering around the beautiful Kunming Lake before rambling up to the top of Longevity Hill. The day was super clear, but the crowds were quite annoying: Chinese tourists may take the cake these days in terms of self-absorption and general apathy for anyone but themselves. Still, some of them were nice, and the views were totally spectacular. I hadn't hired a boat yet in Beijing, and I decided Kunming Lake was the perfect chance. A ¥300 deposit later and I was cruising the lake on a paddleboat. It was fun, but one hour was good enough for me, and upon returning the boat I got my deposit back minus ¥60 for the hour. It was hard to leave the splendor of the Summer Palace, but the complete lack of decent food inside (except for crappy dumplings and instant noodles) put me off enough to head back for food and pack for Shanghai.

I grabbed a few new hostel buddies, and we wandered out around Nanluogu Xiang Hutong for some street food adventuring and cold street beers. The endless little cafes, bars and restaurants were far too tempting around the hutongs, and though we wanted to step into each one, we were able to keep it to a cool seven or so. The night wound down eventually, and I put my gear together for the train the following day, not ready to leave Beijing, but content in the fact that I would be back soon.

My Travel Story
By Teresa

When our daughter decided to spend a semester studying abroad in Beijing, we were thrilled – what a great opportunity for her to experience another culture and explore the world! But I have to admit, when she suggested that we all join her in China for the holidays, I was... less than excited. Eating dumplings in a hotel somewhere just didn't sound like Christmas to me. But I could not have been more wrong. It was such a blast. We'll be talking about our Christmas in Beijing for a long time – and the memories we made there will seriously last forever.

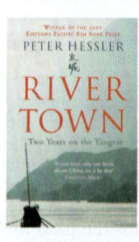

My husband and I set out from Chicago with our teenage son, who was so excited he barely slept at all on the flight, instead reading the book *River Town*, by Peter Hessler, the whole time. (Highly recommend, it's about a young American Peace Corps volunteer's experience in a small town in China during the 1990s; very funny and packed with observations we wouldn't have made on our own.) When we landed in Beijing around 17:00, we recognized the weather from home: freezing cold and overcast, with a few flakes of snow fluttering in the air. Maybe this would be a Christmas trip after all!

We were so jetlagged and out of sorts that we decided to crash at a hotel near the airport and get up early the next day to start sightseeing. We quickly learned that the Chinese prefer very hard beds! Not what we're used to, but honestly, we were so tired we could have slept standing up.

Day 1 of our trip officially began at sunrise, when we all woke up feeling surprisingly OK. It was a gorgeous winter day, with endless blue skies, perfect for some dramatic views at the Forbidden City. We loaded ourselves and our luggage into a cab and drove into downtown Beijing and the Orchid Hotel, where we'd made a reservation for the next few days. They were kind enough to let us store our stuff there while we were out and about all day. From the Orchid, we hopped into another cab, which after a short 10-minute drive deposited us at the front gate of the Forbidden City. We thought that the cold would cut down on the number of visitors that day, but boy were we wrong. Under the iconic portrait of Chairman Mao outside the gate, what seemed like thousands of people were milling around, taking pictures and preparing to go inside.

The Forbidden City did not disappoint. The colors were so vivid and the scale so enormous, and we loved learning little details like how the number of dragons on the roof of a temple indicated how important it was. If you don't mind shelling out 40 RMB (plus a 100 RMB deposit), I cannot recommend the audio tour highly enough. My teenage son loved the high-tech way it worked: you hold a sensor that detects your location in the tour, and it automatically plays the correct introduction to whatever you're looking at. Very well done. When the whipping winds became too much, we ducked into an indoor museum portion of the Palace. I never thought I would say this, but the collection of cabbages carved out of jade was actually really neat.

After about four hours we reached the end of the Forbidden City and crossed the street to Jingshan Park, where we climbed to the top of the hill inside – the highest point in Beijing! There were great photo opportunities, and the park was full of locals, so we got a good taste of day-to-day life in Beijing. At that point we were basically frozen solid and went back to our hotel to regain feeling in our fingers and toes. The staff at the Orchid recommended a Xinjiang-style restaurant just around the corner, and it really hit the spot. Lamb kebabs, grilled peppers, spicy tofu and tasty round bread sprinkled with sesame seeds. Full and sleepy, we retreated to the Orchid for a good night's rest.

The Orchid is hidden away on a traditional hutong called Baochao – you would never see it if you weren't looking for it. The rooms are all cozy and newly remodeled with a very eco-friendly minimalist vibe. We loved the wine and cheese in the lobby, and our son loved that every room came with an Apple TV and a wide selection of movies. From our balcony, we could look out over the snowy roofs of the neighboring houses. It really felt very peaceful.

On Day 2, our daughter had no classes, so she joined us for an adventure to the Great Wall. With her help and outstanding language skills, we scooted over to the Deshengmen bus terminal and hopped on a public bus to Badaling. I'm not sure we could have navigated the chaos without her! After an hour or so ride, we piled out of the bus and headed for the Wall. Thankfully, it was another clear day, so our uphill climb was rewarded with some amazing views. My son was peeking out of a window in one of the guard towers and imagining what it would be like to defend the Wall – it definitely got his action-movie instincts going! On the way down, we bought some boiled corn on the cob from a woman at a stand to keep us going. It always seemed like a summer food to me, but we saw it everywhere during our trip. Back on the bus and back to Baochao Hutong, we got a table at Mr Shi's Dumplings. Let me tell you, plate after plate of pork dumplings and cold beer was the perfect way to thaw out after a long day outdoors.

After our Wall excursion, we decided to keep Day 3 – Christmas Day – in the neighborhood. Using a map that the Orchid provided, we wound our way through the hutongs toward the Lama Temple. Honestly, just walking through the hutongs was fascinating. Very humble little homes are mixed in with gorgeous restored courtyard houses, and people pass by on all kinds of bikes, motorcycles, and cars. We could even smell what people were cooking! It was a very intimate and cool experience.

At Lama Temple, we saw the giant multi-story gold Buddha and watched people lighting incense and bowing at the various shrines. Then we walked a long block south to Gui Jie (Ghost Street), where our daughter introduced us to hot pot! We had never seen anything like it. Not only was it very warming and tasty, it was a lot of fun and we tried a few new foods, like lotus root and fish balls. From there, my daughter and son split off to go souvenir shopping on Nanluogu Xiang, a big touristy alley nearby. That left my husband and I alone to grab a relaxing afternoon coffee and catch up on the news on his iPad. We found a very European-feeling café called Café Zarah and hunkered down for a few hours with croissants, Nutella and espresso. I felt guilty for having such a Western afternoon while we were halfway around the world in China, but it was a much-needed break.

Around dinnertime we rendezvoused with the kids back at the hotel. We asked them how they wanted to spend their Christmas night and they said "out wandering the neighborhood some more." We ended up circling Houhai Lake, which was beautiful and quiet. The neon lights from all the bars and restaurants were almost like Christmas lights! And the best part, while we were out exploring, the kids saw a guy selling pirated DVDs and found a copy of *Elf*, our favorite Christmas movie! We stopped at a convenience store and bought a bunch of weird-looking Chinese snacks to try, and ended the night curled up in bed watching our movie. It was a very sweet and relaxing end to three jam-packed days in Beijing. For the mix of culture, food, and energy, I can't think of a better family vacation destination than this city.

My Travel Story
By Trey

In late 2008 I left Moscow and headed east on the Trans Mongolian Express towards a country that had fascinated me since childhood. After downing vodka shots with former Soviet air force pilots on the train, living in a *ger* for several weeks in Mongolia, and even getting mugged in the streets of Ulan Bator, I successfully crossed into the Middle Kingdom and arrived in Beijing in one piece (barely).

Standing there in the Beijing train station, I couldn't help noticing how different everything was. The flashing neon characters that somehow represented a written language, the smell of MSG flickering off street food woks, and the thousands of people brushing my shoulder in every direction caused a jolt of culture shock to electrify my soul. Sure, I was a bit nervous, but at the same time I was excited to be in a foreign environment so full of life.

I checked into a hostel that evening in the Sanlitun District and immediately hit the streets to explore the nightlife. It didn't take me long to enter a bar with a live rock band (typical in Beijing's thriving music scene), but before ordering a beer a group of Chinese invited me to their table. They taught me the words "*ganbei!*" (Mandarin for cheers) and continuously filled my glass with a mixture of chilled red tea and whisky. They even showed me traditional Chinese drinking games such as liar's dice and other games which I proved to be horrendous at. Nonetheless, we all had a good laugh and they welcomed me to their home country with open arms and recommended some good places to check out.

There are several places in Beijing that people will say, "If you didn't see [add attraction here], then you didn't see Beijing." Despite the cold temperatures, I hiked the Simatai section of the Great Wall and captured some of the most amazing photos I'd ever snapped in my life. I toured the Forbidden City and learned about the extensive history of the country's former imperial dynasties. I passed under the gigantic picture of Chairman Mao in Tian'anmen Square. I awed in amazement at the sheer beauty of the Summer Palace ,which is truly a marvelous work of art. I even visited 21st century China by taking a stroll around the Bird's Nest Stadium used for the Summer 2008 Olympic Games, and scoped out the jagged edges of the futuristic CCTV Tower in the Central Business District.

The list goes on, so much so that a week in the capital isn't nearly enough time to see everything, especially taking into consideration all the fun things that aren't international tourist icons. In retrospect, my favorite thing about Beijing was just seeing local life thrive as it has for centuries. The best attraction in my humble opinion is the hutongs: ancient residential neighborhoods that are mainly found around the center of the city inside the Second Ring Road. These houses have classical Chinese roots, are located in long, narrow alleyways, and even have communal toilets. As I paced the hutongs, I spotted old men bundled up in thick overcoats smoking tobacco, women hanging laundry on the clothesline, and miniature dogs barking out of each door. They're quiet and a bit eerie at times, but the hutongs are certainly a blast into China's ancient past.

Another memory that sticks out in my mind is the food. Beijing is not only the political capital of China, but also the cultural capital, meaning people from every Chinese province and every ethnic minority are represented. And with the way the Chinese cook coupled with the diverse ingredients found throughout this vast country, it should be no surprise that Beijing is a foodie's nirvana. Of course, I ate meat kebabs charbroiled on an open flame right off the street, just like a true Beijinger, but I also sampled a fiery Sichuan hot pot that left me sweating for days, filled up on Guangzhou dim sum for breakfast, and indulged in some typical Shanghai sweet snacks. I even went to some Uighur restaurants to taste the famous cuisine of the Muslims from the far northwestern province of Xinjiang, and tried yak meat for the first time at Tibetan restaurant. Beijing certainly has it all!

Seven days later my trip came to an end, so I decided to call the Chinese who welcomed me to their city my first night in town and thank them for all their wonderful advice. I told them about my trip, but they asked if I had eaten the strange food on Wangfujing Street. I hadn't, so they responded with, "Well, if you didn't see Wangfujing Street, then you didn't see Beijing." Two hours later I met up with them on the infamous street food alley to down some tasty treats such as sea horse, scorpion and starfish. I didn't even know you could eat a starfish! Some were good, others... well, not so good, but nonetheless it was a fitting end to my time in China's capital.

The next day on a plane back home, I realized something was missing. I couldn't get Beijing off my mind. There was just so much to do every second of the day and night; so much culture and so much weirdness that the thought of going home to reality seemed boring. In the end, that feeling never went away, and later I had found a job in Beijing, moved into a hutong with the locals, and today I continue to experience the ancient past, changing future and ever-mysterious present of China's most vibrant city: Beijing.

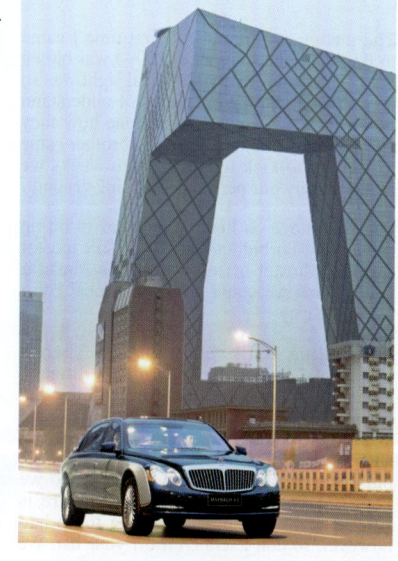

Beijing in Two Days
By Robert

Beijing is full of sights, sounds, smells, and plenty of tastes. Most of them are excellent, some are terrible and others are downright cringeworthy, but all are interesting. Just as Rome was not built in a day, Beijing cannot be experienced in a day. In fact, it can't really be (truly) experienced in a week or even two. From the glitzy to the gritty, everything that Beijing has to offer up is spread densely over the city, clinging to the sides of smoggy superhighways and cozied up in quaint little hutongs. To truly grasp everything that Beijing brings to the table, you could spend a lifetime and still come up short. But that's why a few days scratching the surface of Beijing is so extraordinary; it's touching the tip of the seemingly infinite iceberg that makes you ache so deeply for more. Just as life is about the journey and not the destination, a city like Beijing is more about the tease – the allure of what's to come, rather than what's already been discovered.

Day 1
Blown Away, Summer 2009

Temple of Heaven

The picture says it all. The first time I came to Beijing in the summer of 2009 I was blown out of the water. Every historical sight was so monumental and epic; I couldn't understand how such things existed, let alone how they were built by humans. Soon my brother came to Beijing to kick it, and for two weeks we made the city our personal stomping ground.

Our first move on his first day was to hit up the nearby Forbidden City. It wasn't too far from our hostel off of Wangfujing, but far enough that we could grab some local color along the way.

Wangfujing is all about tourists. There's plenty of Chinese, but few are Beijingers. The general haps on this boardwalk is who has money, and more importantly who can show it off by buying the most overpriced stuff. I'm not saying it's a bad thing per se, but I'm not into ¥60 beers or Gucci, so we kept our Wangfujing time short. There is some excellent people watching to be had however, so don't scratch it off your list. We saw five high heel-wearing women in a row trip over the same pothole while staring at a Tiger Woods ad – five in a row! It was like a circus act!

9:27
Walking Wangfujing

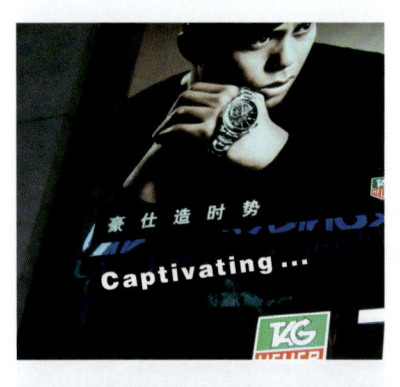

The Forbidden City awaited, and we were pumped, but a pit stop at Tian'anmen Square was definitely in the cards. So we cruised through the underpass and Brennan (my brother) got his first glance at Beijing's less-than-intimidating subway security guards.

The resemblance to the security guard is... well, not uncanny, but you get the idea

The day was a bit "foggy" – as the government loved to spin it then – and we hadn't even thought about purchasing some of the trendsetting "fog masks." I'm pretty sure we'd have looked a little too cool wearing them, and we didn't need any extra attention. The Soviet monolith that is the Great Hall of the People was beckoning us from its stony perch on the east of Tian'anmen, but we still had our eyes on the prize…

Tian'anmen Gate: Entrance to the Forbidden City

They're more afraid of you than you are of them

BLOWN AWAY!

Great Hall of the "People"

Travel Stories

The Forbidden City: it's huge, it's magnificent, it's a perfect display of Ming architectural perfection. Nothing screams "China!" like epic buildings with upturned-eave roofs and mind-blowing intricacies tapered into the overhangs. You can tell by my expression that it's almost too much to handle when you see it in person. I'll leave the rest of the Forbidden City for you to explore. This is just a taste – a little tease to show you just the tip of the iceberg.

Of course, no foreigner's visit to the Forbidden City is complete without the obligatory "excited-Chinese-seeing-foreigner photo op." In China, the two fingers are for victory.

Next it was time for a quick lunch to refuel before jetting off to the next sight.

Yes, we went for the "duck blood" soup. Not quite like the picture, though. While tasty, the texture was a bit gritty. We washed it down with the ever important ice-cold beers.

It was time for my personal favorite in Beijing: The Temple of Heaven (Tiantan). But first we had to jump on board the subway, which is always an adventure in its own right. Hordes of people fill certain stations even during the "slow" hours. The spectacle of Chinese either walking aimlessly while hurried others try to pass them, or the gratuitous shoving and line cutting, are all part of the show. As my brother and I conceded: don't despair, and don't get annoyed, cause there's little you can do. Just chuckle to yourself and enjoy the hilarity.

Hailing the subway with your thumb is not needed, though it does make for a decent action shot.

What people?

Get your exercise on

Words will always fall short of describing how stupefying Tiantan is to me. The architecture seems nothing short of miraculous when you consider that the Hall of Prayer for Good Harvest (pictured below with my bro) was built without a single nail, screw or glue! Nothing can truly capture the painstaking labor that went into these buildings. Though I tried with all my might to describe them in all their glory in Top Attractions, words are trite when compared to how amazing Tiantan is. Throw in the sounds of Tiantan's Echo Wall and the quirkiness of the surrounding parks, and you've got a recipe for legendary success.

It takes two to tango, and one to get fresh

19:48
Heading back

As the day continued, we were beginning to feel a little like this guy. No matter how excited you may be, enough walking will definitely catch up to you at some point. Later, we headed back to the hostel for some dinner, a couple beers and some solid sack time.

Day 2

Hitting the Hutong Crowds

The hutongs of Beijing need little introduction (especially because you've probably already read about them in this book). Day two of our peek into Beijing's first few layers brought us to the Lama Temple, the Confucian Temple and the hutongs that zigzag around them. The smell of incense from Lama is so strong around here that you can smell it for blocks. Either that or it was the smell of hippies.

Travel Stories

10:12 At Lama Temple (Yonghegong)

Lama is the home of lamas. Lamas are Tibetan Buddhists, so stop thinking of those weird Peruvian pack animals (llamas). If you want a little slice of Tibet while in Beijing, head down to Yonghegong and check out the Lhasa style architecture and the bald monks running around in saffron robes and sandals.

Keep your eye out for a bit of censored sensuality between the lizard man Buddha and his lucky lady.

Prude or proper?

Probably the best sight in Lama Temple is the 25 m- (80 ft)-tall statue of Buddha inside the Pavilion of Ten Thousand Happiness. I have a picture, but that wouldn't be as fun as you just going and seeing it for yourself. So go!

12:49 Wandering the Hutongs

Smoking is huge in China. But it's mostly limited to men… and apparently dogs. We caught this little guy wandering in the Lama Temple neighborhood, and he seemed quite at home among the Chinese chess players, chain smokers and loungers that electrified the hutong.

Let's get some flavor

Hutongs are known for their character; they are the vibrant nooks and crannies of Beijing. Do not – I repeat – do not leave Beijing without visiting them.

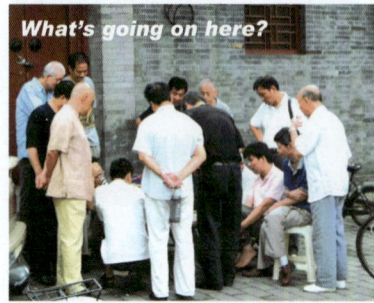

What's going on here?

Chinese chess, cards and Mahjong are the three staples of the Chinese gambling world, and games will often draw crowds of more than ten boisterous onlookers. Best places to catch them: parks and hutongs.

Chinese chess

Mahjong

Besides gaming and betting, the hutongs offer up a chance to see Beijingers doing what they do best: being themselves. The faces, leisure, and humor of the hutongs – not to mention their history – make them one of the most unique places in the world.

A typical goods delivery in Beijing.

Having a good hutong sit

Now that you've gotten a nibble, the rest of Beijing is yours to explore. The more you learn, the more you will want to seek. So let your hair down and dig into one of the most amazing up-and-coming cities in the world – Beijing.

A last word of advice: When you're in the hutongs of Beijing (or anywhere in the city really), the summers can get hot. Your best bet is to learn to beat the heat the local way, as my brother did here when he learned a new meaning to "bottoms up!"

Hot Topics

Sample Itineraries

Beijing is a dauntingly big city. Actually, monstrously enormous is probably a more fitting description. And besides its vast sprawl and endless amount of people, it's the head-spinning amount of rich history and culture of China's fascinating capital that makes tackling this town such a challenge. Fret not, because you bought this book for a helping hand, and we've got your back!

Let's be clear about one thing: no matter how long you stay in Beijing you will not be able to see it all. That is a good thing much more than it is a bad thing, as it means there's always something new to explore. It does, however, leave one big, glaring question: "What things in Beijing can I not miss?" The answer to that largely depends on what your tastes and preferences are, and though we certainly can't cover the countless types of people out there, we've tried our hardest to put together enough diverse sample itineraries to please the most finicky adherents out there. All of these day itineraries run along themes, and most of them try to incorporate sights and attractions in a certain area to make travel between them easy. Some of them may require a bit more travel around town, but all of them will provide you with all the daily necessities, including meals.

Remember that these are just suggestions. If you want to follow them to a tee and hit each sight exactly as we have planned, then great! If you just want to take a bit here and there and mix them up with your own ideas, start your day with one and see where it goes, or just run willy-nilly through them and go with the flow, go for it. All we hope is that our ideas help you to have an awesome trip in Beijing.

1. Beijing Bigshots

Tian'anmen Square → Qianmen Street → Chairman Mao Memorial Hall → Great Hall of the People → National Museum of China → Tian'anmen Tower → Forbidden City → Jingshan Park → Wangfujing Street

The Beijing Bigshots tour is all about the most famous, iconic sights within the city proper. Yes, the Great Wall is about as bigshot as you can get, but it's important and far away enough that it gets its own day. Our suggestion on this day is to start off early, really early, but we know that this idea is not for everyone. If rising at 4:30 is not for you (though you should really consider it) then this day works just fine starting out at your own pace. Everything is in the same vicinity, but this itinerary still has a lot of walking, so strap on your most comfortable shoes and consider packing some snacks.

Begin by rolling your sleepy butt out of bed around 4:30 or 5:00. You're going to **Tian'anmen Square** to see the **flag-raising ceremony**. The flag comes up with the sun – which in the summer is before 6:00 – so you really do need to get up this early. Daybreak varies by season, so check before you go to bed, because if you're not there before dawn you will miss it. It's only about 10 minutes long, but it's very much worth watching the PLA soldiers march perfectly down the street, and it will certainly be one of your more unique experiences in Beijing. Crowds will get very large, so consider getting here even earlier to avoid staring at the back of a bunch of heads.

When that's all wrapped up, march your way down south to **Qianmen Street** for some traditional Chinese breakfast. You should get there around 6:00 or 6:30, just in time for the first *bāozi* (包子 ; bread dumplings filled with meat or veggies), *yóutiáo* (油条 ; fried bread sticks akin to donuts without sugar or lard), *jiānbǐng* (煎饼 ; salty pancakes with egg and savory sauce), *xīfàn* (稀饭 ; millet porridge) and a selection of other stall food. If this doesn't sound good (we urge you to try it) then you can find some fast food around here.

Once you're powered up with breakfast it's time head back north to the **Chairman Mao Memorial Hall** (closed on Mondays) for a viewing of the embalmed PRC leader and plenty of crying Chinese and stern guards. Get there when it opens at 8:00 and you'll be done by around 9:00, at which time you're headed for a peek in the **Great Hall of the People** (just a peek, the tours are drab and you're better off using that time for the museum); then cross the square for a few hours in the standout **National Museum of China**.

Packing a lunch is a great idea so that you don't have to go out of your way to eat before crossing the street for your assault on the **Forbidden City** (closed on Monday). If not, you can swing around the hutongs on the east side to find restaurants. Cross Chang'an Jie, grab some pictures in front of **Tian'anmen Tower** and then head to the top to see what Mao saw when he declared the founding of the PRC in 1949. When your tower fun is done, move towards the Forbidden City and prepare for a mind blowing imperial tour. The exit of the Forbidden City is in the north and spits you out right in front of **Jingshan Park**, where you can take in some exquisite natural scenery as you mount the hill for outstanding views of the Forbidden City and surrounding hutongs. Hunger will be gnawing at your gut again by now (and you earned it with all that walking); this time you're heading east to **Wangfujing Street** for some weird snacks and street-side beers, or a Peking Duck dinner at **Quanjude Beijing Duck Restaurant** (pg 217).

2. The Great Wall & Dead Emperors

Great Wall (Badaling, Mutianyu or Huanghuacheng Sections) → Farmhouse lunch → Ming Tombs

Don't be deceived by the fact that there are only three destinations for this day. There is plenty of walking and by the end of the Ming Tombs you will be ready to head back and call it quits.

First, get out of bed at a decently early hour and power up on a hardy breakfast before you hit up the **Great Wall** (see the Great Wall listing on pg 50 for more info on the wall sections) for plenty of hiking in superb scenery and very cool history. We have mentioned these three sections specifically because they will put you in the best position to head to your next destination at the Ming Tombs. Before you head there, however, grab some lunch below the wall at one of the many **farming villages** that surround these sections. A cheap and tasty home-cooked meal and the most genuinely Chinese experience you may have in China await you in the home of these friendly locals.

Beijing's version of Luxor's Valley of the Kings, the 13 imperial graves at the **Ming Tombs** put on quite a stunning show amongst the verdant countryside scenery. Though only one of the excavated tombs is open for the public to fully enter, there are still plenty of relics, treasures and exceptionally intriguing history to be found around these ancient mausoleums. You'll find plenty of walking here too, so once you wrap up your time here and make the car or bus trip back to the city, it will probably be time for a relaxing dinner near your hotel or hostel before an early bedtime.

3. Cultural Kick Back

Temple of Heaven → Dashilar → Lao She Teahouse → Liulichang Culture Street → National Center for the Performing Arts

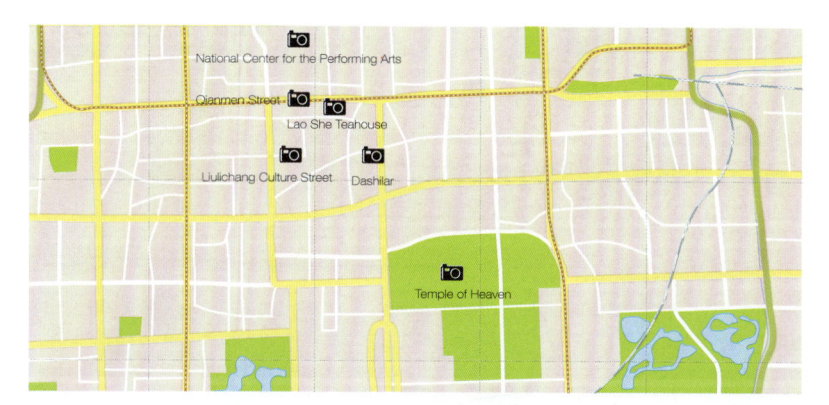

The Cultural Kick Back itinerary is all about one word: relaxation. This is the day to take it easy breezy and check out the worlds of Beijing's best ancient and modern folk culture.

Start out your day with a good breakfast and then make your move to the excellent **Temple of Heaven**. This is one of the city's must-sees for any Beijing traveler, and besides the incredible and beautiful architecture of the altars and halls, this area has a superb park where you can catch Beijingers chilling out with some of their favorite leisurely activities. Though any time of the day you can see them dancing, singing, playing cards and getting their exercise on, it's the mornings here that are the most special, littered with seniors doing tai chi and morning *qigong* activities. We suggest arriving at 8:00 to beat the crowds.

After a soothing stroll around the Temple of Heaven, it's time to move northwest to the **Dashilar** shopping area near Qianmen Street. Dashilar was Old Beijing's most prosperous area, and these days it keeps up tradition with a wide and comfortable walking mall filled with easy-going window shopping and delicious places to eat. After lunch, it's show time at the **Lao She Teahouse**, where your tea is served by women in traditional Qing Dynasty costumes, and you get to settle in for a number of fun and engrossing folk art shows on their handsome wooden stage. Beijing Opera, Sichuan Opera, kung fu, acrobatics, or the comedic stylings of *xiàngshēng* (相 声 ; cross talk, i.e. Chinese standup comedy) are all featured shows at Lao She, and any of them are more than worth a viewing. Once you're all hopped up on tea and riled from a rousing performance, swing out southwest for a different kind of shopping on **Luilichang Culture Street**, sparkling with all manner of antiques, traditional paintings, calligraphy, scrolls and plenty of other folk arts and crafts.

To close out the day, move north to **Qianmen Street** for some dinnertime grub before moseying over to the French designed **National Center for the Performing Arts** for an evening show that could range from domestic or international virtuoso musicians to ballets or opera pieces. If there are no tickets, or the "high culture" just isn't your cup of tea, the glistening egg shaped dome of the NCPA is certainly worth a stare and a few pictures.

4. Imperial Gardens

Peking University or Tsinghua University → Old Summer Palace or the Summer Palace → Beihai Park

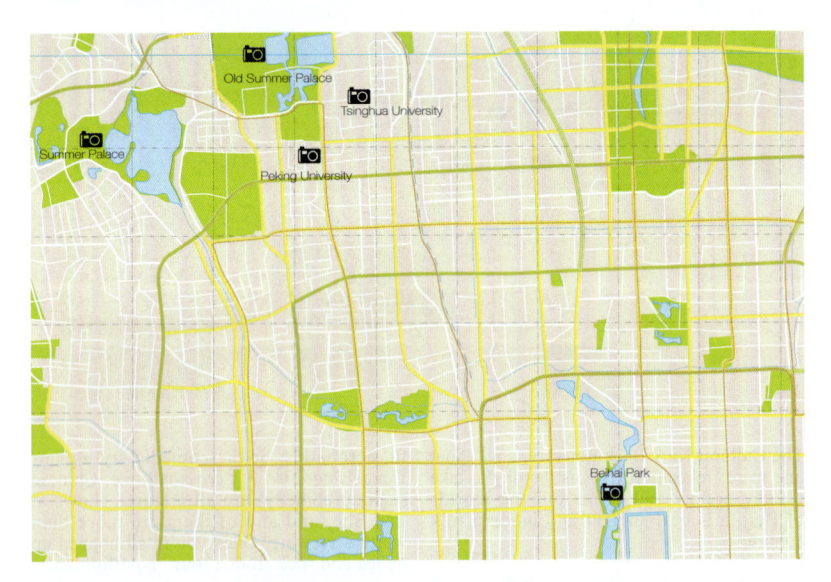

Our Imperial Gardens itinerary starts in the far northwest of the city and ends right in the center, giving you a taste of Beijing's finest ancient gardens, universities and old palaces. There's a lot to cover, so make sure you're well rested and ready to go for this one.

First start at **Peking University** or **Tsinghua University** to get a taste of China's best and brightest; these schools have produced many of China's modern leaders. Basically, Peking and Tsinghua are the country's equivalents to Harvard and MIT, and the campuses themselves are quite beautiful.

Also, due to the amount of foreign exchange students at these learning institutions, the university district of Wudaokou is filled with plenty of Korean, Japanese and Western eating options, boasting a cool international vibe. Use this to your advantage and grab some lunch at one of these restaurants and rest those feet, you still have much more walking to do.

After lunch, make it over to the **Old Summer Palace** ruins or the **Summer Palace** to bask in yet another old imperial summer resort. Both of these places are huge and will take half a day, so you really can't do both in a day unless you do nothing else. You could also skip out on touring the universities to fit both the Old Summer Palace and Summer Palace into one outing. If you only have time for one, choose the **UNESCO** worthy Summer Palace since its incredible temples and palace structures are still wonderfully preserved – it's one of the top sites of the city.

After that the day will be growing long and you can throw Kublai Khan's original royal retreat on to your evening plans with a stroll around the lake at beautiful **Beihai Park.** Take metro Line 6 to Beihai Park Station and start near the Jade Islet and work your way north to cap off your evening with drinks and dinner around the Qianhai and Houhai Lakes. Not only are the lakes gorgeous and jumping with action at night, ending here will put you right back in the middle of town and presumably closer to your hotel.

5. Olympic Gold

Olypmic Forest Park → Bird's Nest (National Stadium) → Water Cube (National Aquatics Center) → Chinese Ethnic Culture Park

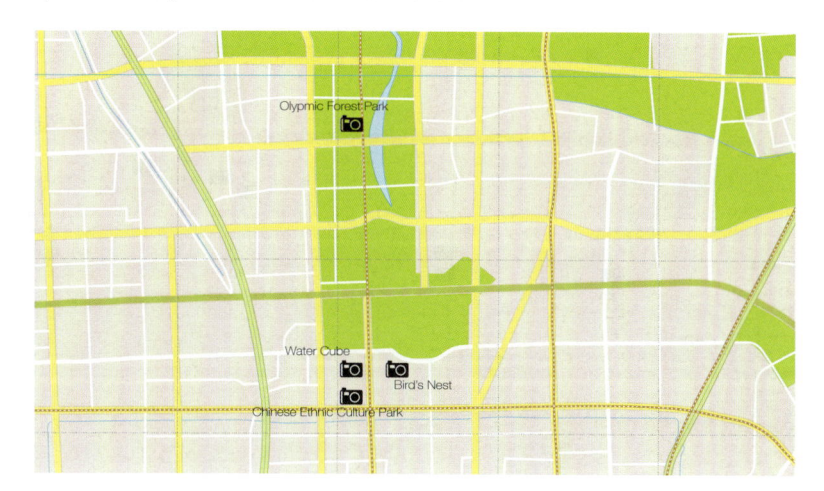

Remember when Beijing hosted the 2008 Olympic Games? The Chinese sure do, and you'll see reminders of China's first Olympiad of more than half a decade ago all over town, from liquor ads and subway videos to the front of milk boxes and baby formula containers. If you're still as excited about 2008 as the Chinese, then the Olympic Gold itinerary is most definitely for you! It's also good if you have kids (there's a wild water park in the Cube).

Fuel up on breakfast and then hop on subway Line 8 and get off at the South Gate of Forest Park Station. This is – that's right – the southern entrance to **Olympic Forest Park**, the massive man-made nature park built especially for the 2008 Olympics. There are tons of walking, jogging and biking paths here, so you might consider renting a bike from your guesthouse and taking a spin up here at one of the most peaceful parts of rowdy Beijing. The lakes here were designed for the rowing competitions during the games.

Move it on down to the **Bird's Nest** and the bubbly complexion of the **Water Cube**. Both structures are an impressive if somewhat audacious sight – don't forget that camera. They are even more impressive when they are all lit up at night, so if you've passed most of the morning here there are a few things you can do to pass the time until dark falls and they glimmer like galaxies.

One is to splash around in the Water Cube's excellent **water park**, featuring a typhoon of slides, rides and other activities to make you forget about how pruned your fingers are. Your other option is to scamper south to the nearby **Chinese Ethnic Culture Park** for an educational song and dance-o-rama through China's huge array of different ethnic minority groups, complete with a dazzling look at each of their clothing and dwelling styles. You could do both the water park and Ethnic Culture Park in one afternoon, but you might be pushing it.

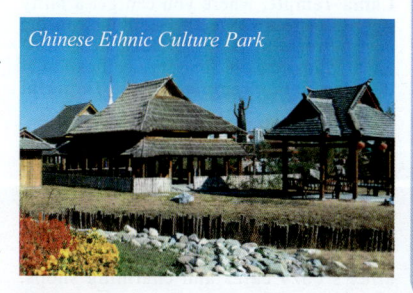

Chinese Ethnic Culture Park

6. Old Beijing & the Hutongs

Lama Temple → Confucian Temple → Imperial College → Nanluogu Xiang → Drum Tower → Bell Tower → Shichahai

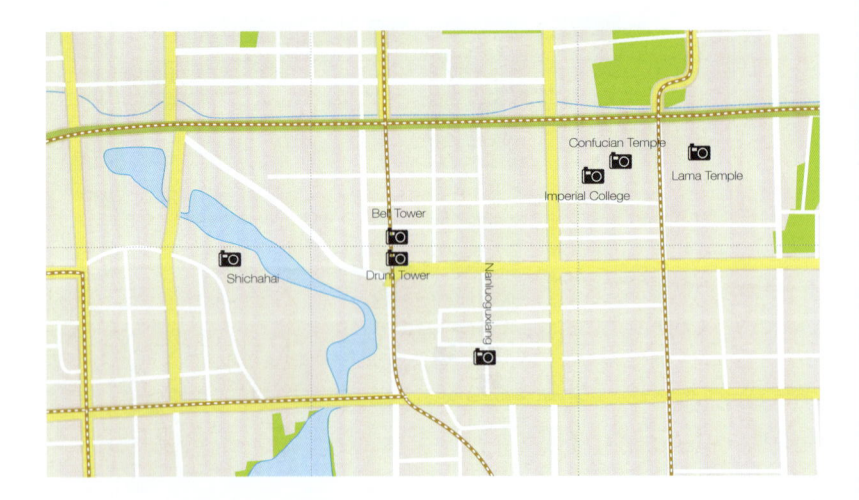

This is one of the Panda's favorites, but if you want to make the most of it you'd better rent a bike to reduce travel time from place to place. This will also allow you to roll smoothly around the lakes at Shichahai at the end of your day.

As the name suggests, this itinerary is right in the thick of Beijing's splendid **hutongs**. Try to leave yourself some time to get lost in the labyrinth of old alleys, houses, courtyards and villages to discover the true essence of Old Beijing.

Take the metro (Line 2 Yonghegong Lama Temple) or your bike to the **Yonghegong Lama Temple,** where you can get a fairly sizable taste of Tibetan Buddhism on the dusty streets of Beijing. Next, head west down Guozijian Jie for some edification at the **Confucian Temple** and the **Imperial College.**

After your spiritual morning, walk or bike south to Gulou Dongdajie and continue meandering to the west until you reach the lively but laid back ancient hutong of **Nanluogu Xiang** to peruse the arts, crafts, clothing and quirky souvenirs along the alley's cozy cafes and charming shops.

Take some time to explore some of the surrounding hutongs, and grab some lunch; there are plenty of great eating options.

There are also plenty of spots to get your grub on in the alleys outside of the **Drum Tower** and **Bell Tower**. To get to these two ancient towers originally built by the Mongols during the Yuan Dynasty, strike back north on Nanluogu Xiang to Gulou Dongdajie, then head west. The twin towers are right at the end of the road, you can't miss them

When you wrap things up here, it's time to bike over to the **Shichahai area,** an old court official stomping ground where you can ride your bike around the lake, go paddle boating and even swimming before hitting up the the bar street for a raucous night of drinks and bar hopping.

7. The Chaoyang Way

798 Art District and Caochangdi → Chaoyang Park → Solana → Embassy District → Sanlitun Village

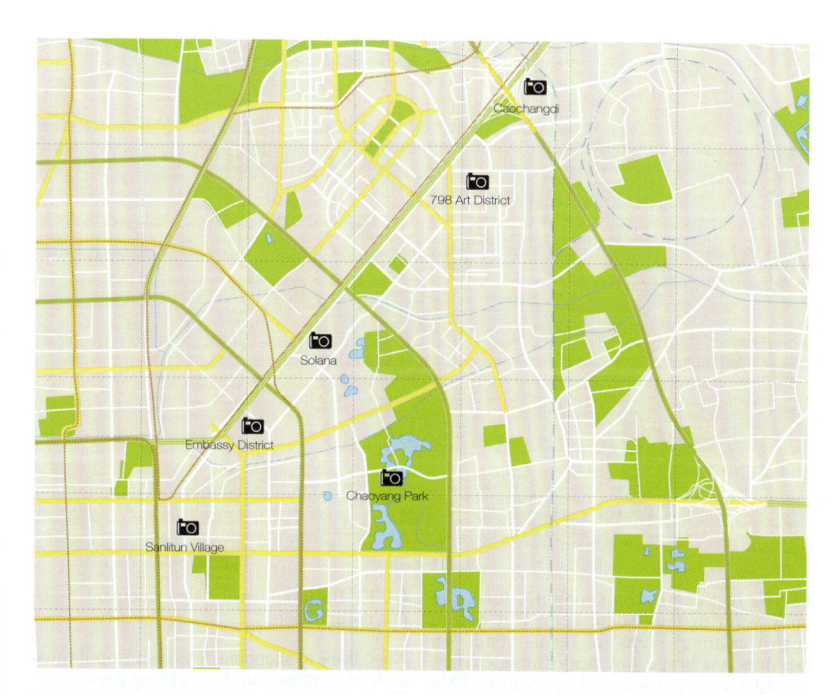

The culture of Chaoyang District is strikingly hip, and it's here that the avant-garde resides just north of the diplomats clubs. There's plenty of walking to be had at 798 and Caochangdi, but you'll likely be bussing or cabbing it between these areas. Do not choose this one on a Monday, most of 798's galleries will be closed.

After breakfast at your hostel or hotel, head on down to the modern art galleries at the **798 Art District** to catch them when they open around 9:00 or 10:00. If you're really an art geek you can also grab bus 909 (which will take you to get here) and continue north for quite a few more galleries at **Caochangdi**, 3 km (2 mi) north. Grab lunch and some coffee at one of any number of places at 798 before cruising down to **Chaoyang Park**. The Central Park of Beijing is gorgeous for a stroll, and it may be hard to leave once you discover there's a beach, walking trails and many lakes. However, pull yourself out of there because Chaoyang has much more to offer. Close by is the upscale shopping center at **Solana.** Grab some lunch here at one of the many al-fresco cafes and do some window shopping.

Next stop is the **Embassy District**, where the area around the cordoned diplomatic fortresses provides an intriguingly pleasant walk through one of the cleanest parts of the city. This may not seem like an attraction, but it really is quite cool, and it's on the way to your final stop of this itinerary, so why not?

Sanlitun Bar Street has quite the bad reputation for selling fake alcohol, having "lady bars," and jacking up their prices, but the bar strip directly behind the **Sanlitun Village** outdoor shopping mall is pretty fun, and there are lots of bars and clubs covering all styles and music. There are also some other drinking and dining options, so grab some dinner, then some drinks, and get ready to party the Chaoyang Way!

8. Shop Til Ya Drop

Yashow Market → Xiushui Street Silk Market → CCTV Building → Guomao → Panjiayuan Antique Street → Dashilar → Liulichang → Nanluogu Xiang

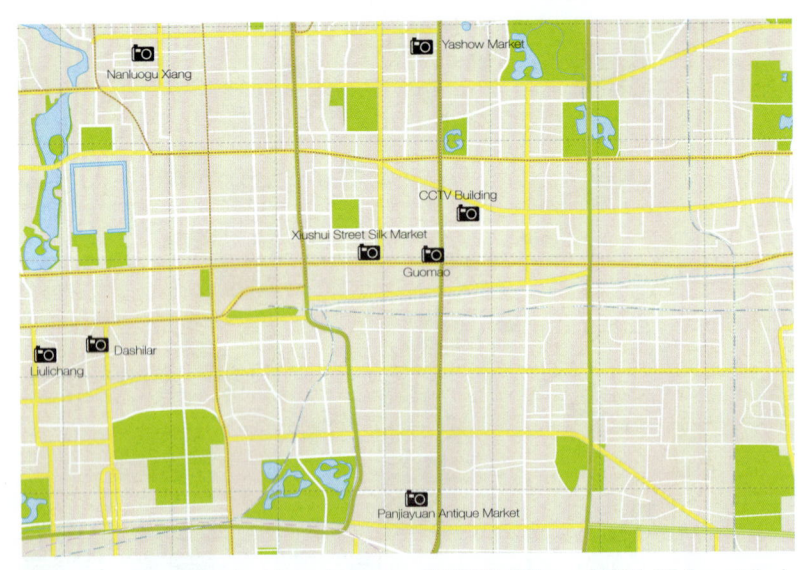

If you just can't stop shopping, then you may want to seek some help. But before a professional steps in, let us send you on one last binge to empty those coffers along Beijing's must-shop zones. This one is nothing but shopping, so if you fall somewhere in the "less insane for shopping" category then feel free to snatch up just a bit of this for one of your half days. The first five of these destinations before Nanluogu Xiang are all in the same part of Chaoyang District.

After breakfast, head straight over to the bargain shopping at **Yashow Market** in Sanlitun. Most, if not all things here are fakes, but you can round up a rodeo of screamingly good deals if you know how to haggle. Next, hit up one of the best shopping destinations in Beijing – the **Xiushui Street Silk Market** (south of Ritan Park), where deals are a dime a dozen. You can find literally everything here, but make sure to bargain like there's no tomorrow. After that, change it up and go the the **Guomao** Metro Station for a quick bite of Beijing's modern sites. The Beijing World Trade Center competes for status (one of them is the tallest in the city at 328 m [1,076 ft] tall), and the **CCTV Building** – aka "Big Underpants" – is just north of here.

Now, back to shopping. The next stop throws a bit of contrast into the shopping equation at **Panjiayuan Antique Market** (way south of Guomao, but both metro stations are on Line 10). This is the best place in the city for unique items and one-of-a-kind arts and crafts.

Grab a cab to the Qianmen area for mid- to upscale shopping at **Dashilar**, including the urban chic styles and excellent sales of the Japanese owned Uniqlo. Your next stop is the **Liulichang** area just west of Dashilar, where folk crafts mix with hip clothes and unique objects to round out a rowdy day of shopping.

Your inner shopper will need some food soon, so catch a cab west to the quirky and charactered hutong bargains north to **Nanluogu Xiang**, Beijing's most famous hutong. When you're finished, head north on Nanluogu Xiang, cross Gulou Dongdajie and continue north onto Beiluogu Xiang. There are many bars around here for a perfect way to end the evening.

9. The Foodie Adventure

Maliandao Tea Market → Ox Street Mosque → Shichahai → Ghost Street

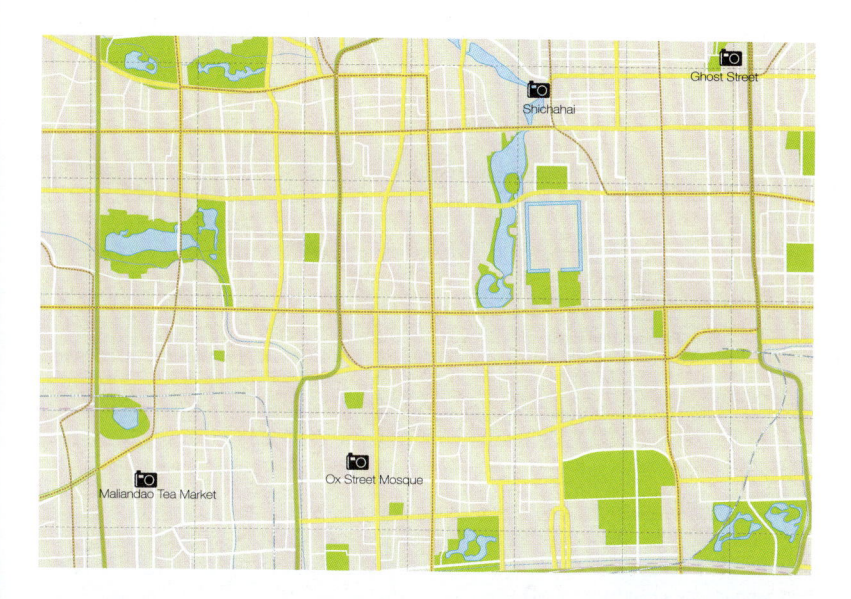

Why tour your way around Beijing when you can eat your way around the city? This tour was designed to give you a diverse taste of different foodie neighborhoods. They're far in distance, so consider taking taxis (unless you want to walk off some of those calories, of course).

First start at the fragrant **Maliandao Tea Market**, and while you indulge in China's most famous leafy drink to start a wonderful day of eating and drinking, think of a friend back home who would love a case of real Chinese tea. From here it's a straight shot east to the **Ox Street Mosque**. Grab some spicy and delicious Muslim food that's mostly influenced by the Hui Muslim ethnic minorities in this area, then give the beautiful mosque an hour of your attention.

From Ox Street take a crosstown taxi to **Shichahai** and wander around the lakes for some R&R. Since you just had a Muslim feast, chances are you won't be hungry, but snacks like deep fried squid, coconut milk, meat kebabs, cotton candy, Old Beijing yoghurt, and others are everywhere.

Lastly, stomp east past the Forbidden City to the boisterous eating alley of **Ghost Street** (Guǐ Jiē) – called so because the pronunciation of this *gui* sounds just like the word for "ghost" in Chinese. Down some dinner and beers under hundreds of brightly-lit red lanterns. If you're taking the metro, you can take Line 5 to Beixinqiao Station, but you could also walk it (30-45 minutes) from Shichahai. There are dozens of options to choose from on Ghost Street, but we recommend hot pot, specifically Kongliang Hotpot (pg 220).

Ghost Street

10. Beijing's Great Outdoors

Badachu Park → Fragrant Hills Park → Beijing Botanical Gardens

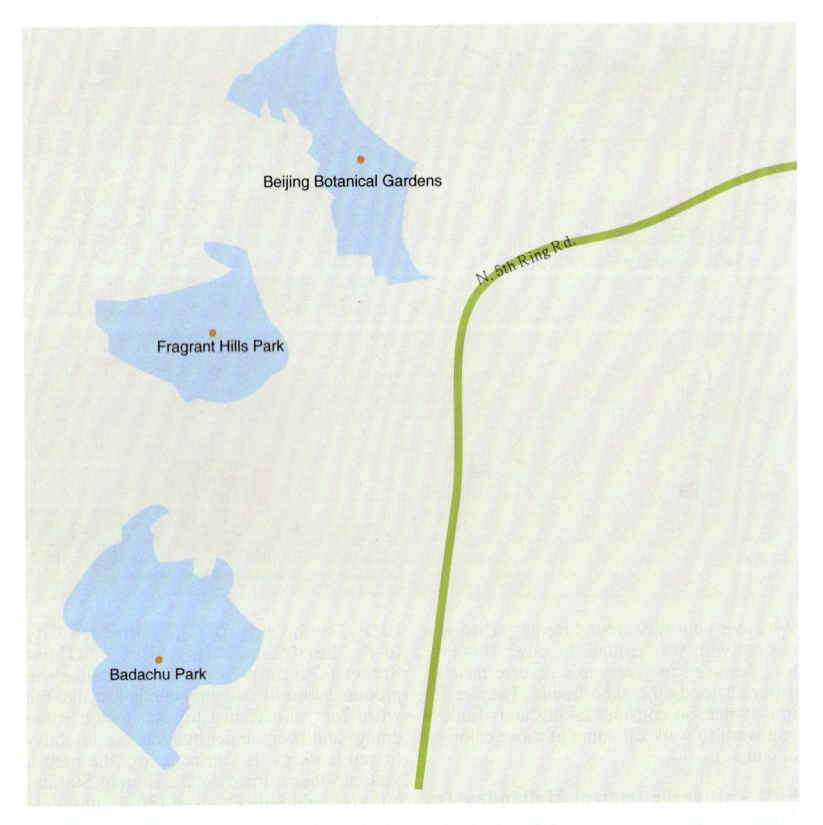

A plethora of temples (eight of them) built during various dynasties (Tang, Song, Yuan and Ming) await you in the far flung northwestern reaches of Beijing, as does a mountainous park that's stunning in the fall and one of the best botanical gardens you'll ever see.

The **Badachu** – meaning the "Eight Great Sights" – are in the same area as **Fragrant Hills Park**, making the first two a great pairing for an outdoorsy day in two of the city's most strikingly beautiful natural park areas. They open at 9:00, so grab some breakfast beforehand at the little village down below where the buses let you off. After you've discovered all eight of the temples at Badachu Park, head over to the Fragrant Hills to check out the fine flower gardens, Indian-inspired temples and a memorial to China's late president Sun Yat-sen.

Give the village a revisit for lunch before heading over to the massive 2 million sq m **Beijing Botanical Gardens**, which features over 6,000 species of plants in the Middle Kingdom's most extensive collection. You can also find the Temple of the Recumbent Buddha in here. Don't be surprised if you easily pass three peaceful hours here, by which time dinner will be calling you back into the city to reacquaint you with the steel jungle.

Air Pollution in Beijing

If your trip to Beijing was inspired by colorful photos of the Forbidden City on a blue-sky day, or by the chance to stand on the towers of the Great Wall and behold the green countryside as far as the eye can see, be prepared for the unfortunate reality of the Chinese capital: many days in Beijing don't look like that. In fact, if you're following the news, you've surely encountered some less appealing images of the city, like Beijingers sporting futuristic face masks commuting through thick smog and the sun hidden behind a grimy haze. Reports of Beijing's pollution problem swept the globe in 2013, as Beijing's air quality soared from bad to hazardous to levels beyond any existing index. Some expats and their families left the city for good, unwilling to reckon with the potentially harmful effects of the "Airpocalypse."

You don't have to be a long-term resident of Beijing to be concerned about air pollution. In February 2013, immediately following the January "Airpocalypse," the number of tourists passing through Chinese customs and immigration plummeted to 165,000 for the month, a decrease of 262,000 from the previous February and the lowest number of visitors for any month in the past three years.

Travelers on a tight schedule may fret over canceled flights when heavy smog cuts down visibility at Beijing International Airport, while travelers with children may worry about the impact of polluted air on their little ones' health. Pollution can have a real impact on your travel plans, but the air quality index doesn't have to make or break your trip. Below, we'll outline what you need to know about air pollution in Beijing, and what you can do to minimize its impact on your travel and your health.

What are the causes?

Beijing's toxic air is the product of a number of factors, with coal-burning industrial operations as the leading cause. Coal provides 80% of China's electricity, and much of the coal used here is a type that is particularly high in sulfur. Meanwhile, Beijing's surrounding provinces, like Inner Mongolia, Shandong and Hebei, are home to a wealth of coal mining operations, cement

White Pagoda during a clear day and polluted day. Do we even have to tell you which was taken during the polluted day?

and steel factories, and oil refiners that burn an estimated 350 million tons of coal every year.

Another factor is the soaring number of cars in the capital, which reached 5 million in 2012, up from 3.5 million in 2008. The impact of heavy traffic is made worse by the fact that China has been slow to adapt to international standards for fuel quality, resulting in much higher amounts of sulfur dioxide being released into the atmosphere by personal vehicles.

Geography and weather patterns influence the city's atmosphere as well. Since Beijing is surrounded by mountains to the west and northeast, pollution tends to become trapped in the low-lying city until wind direction changes and helps move bad air along. Generally speaking, north winds and west winds from heavily industrialized areas bring heavy smog, while east winds from the Pacific Ocean create immaculate days.

Seasonal factors occasionally compound these causes and add up to an even more polluted city. During the winter, coal use increases even further, as most central heating in northern China is powered by coal. In the spring, generally between March and May, sandstorms from the Gobi Desert sweep tons of dust into Beijing's atmosphere. Air quality readings even see a big spike during the Chinese New Year, when the sky fills with fireworks.

How is air quality measured?

There are two types of air pollution measured in Beijing: PM10 (particles less than 10 microns in diameter) and PM2.5 (particles less than 2.5 microns in diameter). The United States Embassy and the Beijing government each maintain equipment that provides hourly readings, and both publish their own air quality index that incorporates both PM2.5 and PM10 data. Their hourly readings are reported on a 1-500 scale. Depending on the source you're consulting, the same reading may be described differently, as you can see in the chart below.

The efforts to monitor pollution in Beijing have not been without controversy. Previously, the Chinese Ministry of Environmental Protection's index did not include data for the smaller PM2.5 pollutants. When it comes to air quality, smaller particles are considered more harmful because they are small enough to penetrate the lungs and enter the bloodstream. After public outcry and pressure, the MEP began including PM2.5 data in their measurements as of January of 2012. Even after that adjustment, observers

AQI Range	Chinese Ministry of Environmental Protection (MEP)	American Environmental Protection Agency (EPA)
0-50	Excellent	Good
51-100	Good	Moderate Unusually sensitive people should consider reducing prolonged or heavy exertion.
101-150	Lightly Polluted	Unhealthy for Sensitive Groups People with heart or lung disease, older adults, and children should reduce prolonged or heavy exertion.
151-200	Moderately Polluted	Unhealthy People with heart or lung disease, older adults, and children should avoid prolonged or heavy exertion; everyone else should reduce prolonged or heavy exertion.
201-300	Heavily Polluted	Very Unhealthy People with heart or lung disease, older adults, and children should avoid all physical activity outdoors. Everyone else should avoid prolonged or heavy exertion.
301-500	Severely Polluted	Hazardous Everyone should avoid all physical activity outdoors; people with heart or lung disease, older adults, and children should remain indoors and keep activity levels low.

have noted that the US Embassy readings are frequently higher than the Chinese readings, a discrepancy that has only made deciphering air quality more complicated. One possible explanation for the discrepancy is the fact that the US and Chinese pollution monitoring locations are located across the city from one another. The US measures PM2.5 levels from its embassy in eastern Beijing, near the heavily trafficked Third Ring Road, while the Beijing government releases measurements from a monitoring site in Xicheng District on the west side.

Despite the disagreement between different indexes, monitoring hourly air quality readings is a good way to take control and make plans based on the day's pollution levels.

What are the health effects?

Depending on the timing of your visit, you may be facing a string of hazardous air days or a week of beautiful blue skies. (Remember that Beijing isn't polluted every day.) If the air is polluted while you're in Beijing, take heart that the health effects of short-term exposure to polluted air are likely to be limited. On a heavily polluted day, it's possible to develop irritation of the eyes, nose, and throat, along with coughing, phlegm, chest tightness, and shortness of breath, or to simply feel sluggish and under the weather. Travelers with heart conditions should note that air pollution has been associated with an increased risk of heart attack and an increase in blood pressure.

To put the exposure risk into context, Beijing-based family doctor Richard Saint Cyr teamed up with a professor at Brigham Young University to study how the effects of breathing polluted air compare with the effects of smoking cigarettes. He concluded that "A day in Beijing is like smoking one sixth of a cigarette. More specifically, on an average day in Beijing, an average adult inhales a total of 1.8 mg of PM2.5 particles from air pollution, which is 1/6 of the average 12 mg of PM2.5 particles inhaled from an average cigarette" (www.myhealthbeijing.com). This comparison may be reassuring to some, or potentially alarming to travelers with children, the elderly, asthmatics, or those with heart conditions.

Travelers with children may be especially concerned about pollution, and research does seem to suggest that children are more vulnerable. For starters, children take in more air per unit of body weight at a given level of exertion than do adults. But children are considered more at risk mostly because their lungs are still developing. For girls, lungs finish developing at 18, while a boy's lungs mature by their early 20s. Luckily, the steps you can take to prevent exposure for children are the same as for adults (see below).

Travelers planning a long-term stay in Beijing face more intense, but still manageable, risks. Long-term exposure to polluted air is the number one cause of lung cancer, which is the leading cause of death in China. Cases of lung cancer in Beijing increased by 56% between 2000 and 2009. Extended exposure to pollutants is associated with depressed lung functions even in healthy people. Studies have tied premature births, birth defects, and low-weight babies to pollution. Overall, the World Health Organization estimated in 2007 that 656,000 Chinese were dying prematurely every year from health conditions caused by indoor and outdoor air pollution.

What can you do about it?

Short-term travelers

Time your visit wisely. Unfortunately, it's difficult if not impossible to forecast air quality in advance. However, certain seasons are reliably cleaner than others, so if you're serious about avoiding pollution, shoot to visit Beijing in spring or autumn. The weather is nicest then, anyway.

Check the web or download apps to monitor air quality. You can't make wise decisions about pollution unless you have information. (A sunny, nice-looking day in Beijing isn't always an indicator of great air quality either, so it's best to consult an official reading). Navigate to **www.aqicn.org** for real-time data from a number of locations in Beijing, or download one of the many Beijing air quality apps available for iPhones, Androids, and other smartphones (see pg 309). You'll find Beijing to be very wifi equipped, so check the air quality early and often during your visit. If you're interested in the Chinese Ministry of Environmental Protection data, you can find it at www.cnemc.cn (in Chinese).

Buy a face mask. Inexpensive pollution masks can be found at 7-11s and other chain convenience stores throughout the city, including expat-oriented grocery stores such as April Gourmet and Jenny Lou's. Simple cloth surgical-type masks will provide very limited protection, but for a short stay they're better than nothing. "N95" type masks are also widely available – search for an "N95" face mask online and you'll get a number of results. Purchasing these at home before you leave is wise, though again, they are available once you arrive. If you're looking for something a little more heavy-duty, try to purchase a mask in advance. One commonly recommended model is a Totobobo (**www.totobobo.com**), which filters PM10 and PM2.5 and can be easily adjusted to fit a child. On the high end, masks such as a 3M brand 8812 industrial facemask will remove more than 95% of pollutants.

Stay away from heavily-trafficked areas. Harmful pollution is concentrated around Beijing's busy roads and highways. When you're exploring the city on foot, choose to walk on smaller roads and streets (they tend to be a lot more interesting, anyway). If you're trying to maintain an exercise routine while on vacation, practice caution: never go running outside without checking the air quality first, and if you choose to run, again, avoid busy streets.

On a heavily polluted day, limit outdoor activity. You may get lucky and have beautiful weather during your stay in Beijing. If you don't, don't fight it. On heavily polluted days, plan indoor activities, like trying your hand at cooking classes, visiting one of the city's many excellent museums or seeing a Beijing Opera performance. Your lungs will thank you.

Long-term travelers

Invest in an air purifier or find accommodation that provides them. If you're going to be in Beijing long-term, make an effort to stay somewhere as pollutant-free as possible by keeping an air-purifier in your bedroom. You'll find a wide variety of models of all sizes and prices, but no matter which one you choose, it should have a HEPA filtration system and use activated carbon. IQ Air is the most reputable brand on the market, but can run as much as US$6,000, depending on room size.

Fill your home with green plants. Household plants are inexpensive and have been shown to purify air indoors.

Drink clean water and eat fruits and vegetables. If you can't avoid being exposed to pollution from the air, minimize your exposure from other sources. Beijing tap water contains heavy metals and other chemicals that can't be eliminated by boiling. Choose bottled water instead, and get it from a large reputable supplier. Help your body fight the harmful effects of pollution by eating plenty of fruits and vegetables, which contain antioxidants and enzymes that counteract pollution damage.

Food & Water Safety

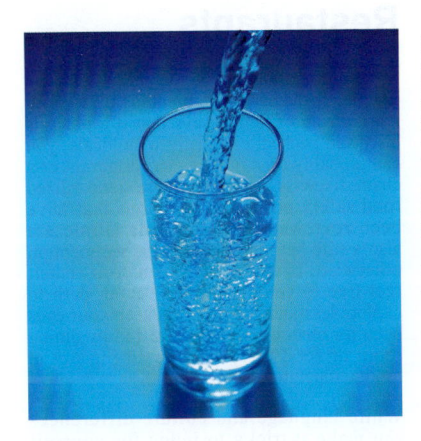

Water Safety

Unlike in most Western countries, the tap water in Beijing is undrinkable before it is boiled. In addition to pollution at and near the reservoirs that provide Beijing's water, the underground pipes that deliver water throughout the city are often in terrible repair, allowing groundwater, bacteria and other contaminants to seep into the supply. Many cases of "food poisoning" are actually the result of food being washed or prepared with contaminated water.

It's very important to avoid drinking tap water during your visit, but you shouldn't go thirsty, either. What are your options for staying healthy and hydrated in Beijing?

Boiled and bottled Water. Hotel rooms often feature an office-style water cooler which delivers both cool and hot purified water. Other hotels offer a water heater or thermos that you can use to boil water. In some cases, four- or five-star hotels may supply high-quality mineral water for free or for a minimal charge. If you're thirsty in a restaurant but don't want to pay sky-high prices for bottled water, ask for boiled water – kāishuǐ (开水).

Boiling water will prevent you from getting acutely sick, but your glass will still contain high concentrations of heavy metals and other chemicals. Your healthiest bet in Beijing is bottled water, which is ubiquitous and inexpensive. Several popular brands of bottled water, such as Wahaha (Wáhāhā; 娃 哈 哈), Nestle (Quècháo; 雀巢), Ice Dew (Bīnglù; 冰露 ; produced by Coca-Cola) and Nongfu Spring (Nóngfū Shānquán; 农 夫 山 泉), are available for purchase in many street stands, shops, supermarkets, restaurants and hotel stores for ¥1-2 per bottle. Check to be sure that the bottle was properly sealed before you drink it.

Other things to consider. Order your drinks without ice cubes; they could be made with tap water. Luckily, the Chinese prefer to drink warm or hot water, even on the hottest summer day, so you're unlikely to be served ice water.

Using a minimal amount of tap water is generally OK for brushing your teeth. Alcoholic drinks and drinks made with boiled water, like coffee or tea, are also safe to drink.

Food Safety

Forget about General Tso's chicken and fortune cookies. Thanks to the amazing diversity of Chinese cuisine, dining can be one of the most thrilling aspects of your time in Beijing. As with any international destination, however, you're probably worried about what is safe and what will make you sick, and how you'll be able to tell the difference. It doesn't help that China seems to be in the news every month with a new food safety scandal, from glow-in-the-dark pork and melamine-laced baby formula to exploding watermelons and fake eggs.

China undeniably lags behind much of the West when it comes to food safety regulation and enforcement. Why? China's enormous population means a massive number of companies are involved in producing food – ranging from small mom-and-pop operations to mega farms – which makes accountability and enforcement tough. And until the State Food and Drug Administration was created in early 2013, oversight was conducted by a haphazard list of different ministries and agencies. And, as a rapidly-growing, still-developing country, China finds itself in a similar position to the United States around the turn of the 20th century, when exposés like Upton Sinclair's book *The Jungle* revealed the horrific standards at meat-production plants, causing outcry over food safety standards.

Despite some high-profile scandals and room for improvement, eating in Beijing can be completely safe and fun with a little knowledge and preparation. Below, we'll outline some basic precautions and common-sense suggestions to keep an eye-opening culinary experience from becoming a painful one

Before You Leave

There are a few things you can do before you leave home that will pave the way for a safe eating experience in Beijing. It's not a bad idea to put together a mini-medical kit stocked with Immodium, Pepto Bismol, Tums, and other over-the-counter stomach aids. These medicines may be available in Beijing, but could be hard to find and expensive. Next, ask your doctor to prescribe an antibiotic such as Ciprofloxacin (Cipro) that is effective against traveler's diarrhea. In the event that you do eat something you regret, antibiotics can seriously cut down on the duration of your suffering. Also, consider bringing a supply of hand sanitizer. Soap and hand driers are relatively rare in Beijing public restrooms, and you'll be out in the streets encountering all kinds of new dirt. Keeping your hands clean will go a long way toward keeping you healthy. For vegetarian travelers or travelers with food allergies, consider learning how to express your special requirements in Mandarin (see the Mandarin Phrasebook on pg 336). Or, print out a small card that states your allergies in both English and Chinese – you can show this card to waiters and waitresses. Be aware that it can sometimes be difficult to tell when a dish contains meat or other ingredients you're trying to avoid, but most restaurants will be reasonably cooperative with special requests. Last but not least, be prepared to carry a small roll of toilet paper with you at all times. It's frequently not available, especially when you need it the most.

Restaurants

There are a number of factors to help you judge whether a restaurant is safe to visit. An old rule of thumb says that if a place is busy and packed, especially with locals, you can probably trust it. A bigger restaurant or a chain, likewise, may have more standardized food safety practices. Locations that have been reviewed in your Panda Guide are also a safe bet, unless of course we mention otherwise. If you're an adventurous eater, feel free to venture off the beaten path to explore less-known spots, but keep your eyes open for obvious red flags like a filthy dining room or food that has been sitting out at room temperature.

While language and culture differences can make it tricky to judge for yourself whether a restaurant seems clean, Beijing has made it easier for you by establishing a universal grading system for restaurants. You'll notice the signs hanging in many restaurant windows reading A, B or C with a corresponding smiley (or less-smiley) face. An A rating denotes good health and sanitary conditions, B stands for standard and C means basic. As of June 2013, ratings for all restaurants in Beijing, big or small, will be available online at www.bjhi.gov.cn, the official website of the Beijing Health Inspection Institute (unfortunately for some, it's in Chinese).

Once you've chosen a restaurant, there are things you can do to minimize your risk of food poisoning. If a dish arrives at your table and it seems undercooked, rotten or just slightly "off," trust your gut. Ask for a replacement or don't eat it.

Street Food

There's an amazing variety of snacks available on the street in Beijing, from meat kebabs to cookies. Street food can actually be some of the tastiest (though maybe not the cleanest) out there. Stand back and watch the vendor make the food for a few minutes if you want to get an idea of how it's handled. On many food streets you'll see lines of folks lining up for snacks pineapple or peppers you buy from a roadside stand will probably be just fine, and interacting with hawkers and vendors is definitely part of the Beijing experience. But if you're really concerned about food safety, the rule "bigger is better" applies when buying food on your own. That means that you're better off getting groceries at a big, well-known, usually foreign-based chain, like Tesco (UK), Carrefour (France), or Walmart (US). These stores have better-developed supply chains and more standardized food storage and food safety practices. Just use caution and common sense and wash your purchases very thoroughly with purified water.

– this is usually a sign that the stall has a good reputation. You may want to avoid meat snacks in the heat of summer and snacks that include anything raw, but dumplings, pancakes and fried anything are fair game.

Markets & Shops

If you're hoping to do some self-catering during your trip, keep in mind that not all markets and shops are created equal. In Beijing, you'll see small fruit and vegetable carts and mini-markets popping up anywhere and everywhere. Some of these will be more organized outdoor set-ups, while others may simply be a man standing next to a pile of vegetables on the sidewalk. Most likely, the

Toilets in Beijing

The Chinese toilet experience is one of the city's contradictions – amusing to some, horrifying to others. For starters, the Chinese are credited with inventing toilet paper way back in 1391 CE, when the Bureau of Imperial Supplies began producing 720,000 sheets of 6.5 m X 10 m (2 ft X 3 ft) sheets of toilet paper a year for use by emperors, but good luck finding a few squares in Beijing when you need them today! And although the high-end toilet market is booming, with 5% of toilets purchased in 2010 costing between US$150 and US$6,000, you'll see plenty of Chinese infants relieving themselves not in diapers but freely on the ground, through split pants designed exactly for this purpose.

So, you could say that Chinese bathroom culture is in transition. The good news is that toilets in China's major cities, Beijing included, have improved dramatically in recent years, and your experience will likely be just fine. Beijing is home to everything from glass-and-marble restrooms with fresh flowers and classical music piped in to grungy side-by-side squat toilets in public restrooms. Private plumbing is a relatively new phenomenon in Beijing, where in 1993, 70% of the population of Beijing still relied on public toilets. Today, about 20% use them. You'll certainly be part of that squatting 20% at least once during your trip, so read on to get the lowdown on toilets: where to find them, how to use them, and some expert tips for making the best of it.

How can I locate public toilets in Beijing?

Public toilets are more common in some neighborhoods than others. In hutong areas, you'll find one every few hundred steps, and airports, train stations, subway stations, hotels, shopping centers, chain restaurants like KFC or McDonalds, tourist attractions and grocery stores are likely to have them too. Feel free to walk confidently into these places and go right for the bathroom – most places are very permissive about non-customers using their facilities (there's a bit of foreigner privilege at play, too). Wherever you are, facilities will probably be marked with the Chinese characters 女 (nǚ for female) or 男 (nán for male). Learn to recognize these characters. If the location of the bathroom isn't obvious, you can ask *Xǐshǒujiān zài nǎli?* (洗手间在哪里 ?) which means "Where is the toilet?" If you'd rather rely on English, choose "toilet" instead of "restroom," "bathroom," or "washroom" – it's more likely to be understood.

Western-style toilets are becoming more and more common in public restrooms, and you'll sometimes see just one or two in a row of squat toilets. Keep your eyes peeled for a sign or a picture on one of the stall doors with a picture of a Western toilet.

What is a squat toilet and how do I use it?

A squat toilet looks more or less like the photo on this page. Stand with your back to the wall and place your feet on the grooved areas. Squat over the hole, doing your best to aim. Used toilet paper should always be placed in the small wastebasket to the side of the toilet to avoid backing up the plumbing and making an already-messy situation even worse. Squat toilets usually flush by pressing a button or foot pedal on the floor. That's all there is to it, really – it can be an intimidating process at first, but you'll get the hang of it.

Some public restrooms will have private stalls dividing the toilets, while others may have only waist-high dividers with no doors, or no partitions at all. Some toilets have splash guards to keep you and your pants legs from getting caught in the crossfire. Try to relax and take care of business as quickly as possible – eventually you'll be as accustomed as the locals and expats, who shrug and count their blessings when they find a decently clean place to pee.

Advanced toilet tips: how can I survive my Beijing bathroom experience?

Want to squat with the best of 'em? Here are some tips for ensuring a smooth squatty potty experience.

Never go anywhere without TP

The number one tip is to always, always carry a small supply of toilet paper with you. A bottle of hand sanitizer can't hurt, either.

Know the rules of lining up

Unlike Western countries, people tend to line up outside one specific stall rather than forming one big line and taking the next one that becomes available.

Hand off bags and purses to a friend before venturing in

There may not be hooks to hang a bag, and the floor might be covered in something you'd rather not carry around with you all day.

Ditto for phones and keys

It's better to approach the squat with nothing in your pockets – at least nothing that you don't want to fall down the black hole and never come back.

Roll up your pants

Public restrooms can be very wet –

sometimes because they're frequently mopped, and sometimes because they're not.

Get in the Chinese mindset

To the Chinese, it's Western-style toilets that are unsanitary, since everyone's bare butt touches the same seat. Think of your squatting experience as a new trend in hygiene. Or, consider that some studies suggest that squatting to use the bathroom is healthier than sitting, because sitting constricts some of the muscles used for evacuation. It's thought that sitting on the toilet is a factor in the higher rates of hernias, hemorrhoids, and gastroesophageal reflux disease (GERD) in the West.

There's no way I can use a squat toilet. What's my alternative?

You can use the bathroom before you leave your hotel in the morning and try to plan the rest of your pit-stops at places where you know there's likely to be a nice, clean bathroom (think international hotels or upscale restaurants and shopping malls). If you have a tour guide, ask him or her to suggest good opportunities to use the restroom throughout the day – they're usually very well-acquainted with the quality of the facilities in popular tourist areas.

Smart-phone Apps for Traveling Beijing

Technology is making traveling easier by the day. Not too long ago suitcases and backpacks alike would be jammed with maps, language dictionaries, books, reservation confirmations, plane/train tickets, cameras, video recorders and other travel necessities. Nowadays all you need is your smart-phone and Panda Guides guidebook or e-book, and you're set for the trip of a lifetime! For your convenience, we've made a list of the best smart-phone apps that will make your journey through the Middle Kingdom as hassle free as possible. Type the bold heading in the app store and your desired app will appear.

Weather, Date & Time

China Air Quality Index (FREE) – Due to the notorious clouds of smog covering the country, this app provides an up to date air quality index for every city in China. It's also a great way to avoid places with high levels of pollution.

The Weather Channel (FREE) – Though not limited to Chinese cities, it's still probably the most professional and accurate weather app available. It literally has everything you need to know about the weather conditions in every city in the world.

World Clock- Time Zones (FREE) – China technically only has one time zone (don't tell the people of Xinjiang that since they created their own unofficial individual time zone), but it's still beneficial for contacting those on other side of the globe.

Calendar Conversion (FREE) – With so many festivals in China, and with those like Spring Festival (aka Chinese New Year) greatly affecting transportation comfort and pricing, you'll definitely need to know which days local holidays fall on. Calendar Conversion does just that and can help you avoid hectic travel seasons throughout the year.

Currency & Unit Converter

Convert Free (FREE) – As straight forward as it comes, this one converts currency and every other international unit of measurement.

XE Currency (FREE) – XE is better than Convert Free if you're solely looking to convert currencies rather than other units of measurements. It has over 80 international currencies and gives an instant update with the shake of a phone.

Transportation

Metroman Beijing (FREE) – Metroman is a great tool to help you navigate the Beijing Metro with information, a map and connection routes for all stations.

Explore Beijing ($1.99) – This is another

Top 10 Most Used Apps in the World (Weixin/WeChat is the only Chinese app listed)

App	Percentage
Google Maps	54%
Facebook	44%
YouTube	35%
Google+	30%
Weixin / WeChat	27%
Twitter	22%
Skype	22%
Facebook Messenger	22%
Whatsapp	17%
Instagram	11%

great option for exploring Beijing's ever expanding metro. It sets itself apart from other Beijing metro guides since its "location services" tells you the closest metro stop to where you're standing just in case you're in a rush.

Metro China Subway ($2.99) – This one presents a complete guide with maps and other useful information for the largest subways in Mainland China (Beijing, Shanghai, Shenzhen, Guangzhou, Tianjin and Nanjing), Hong Kong and Taipei, Taiwan.

Drive Me To ($1.99) – This app is a virtual address book with all the major points of interest in Mainland China and Hong Kong. Upon selecting your destination, a polite request note with the address written in Chinese will appear on your screen to show your driver.

Driving in China ($1.99) – In case you're tired of using overcrowded public transportation, get a car, go your own way and be prepared to face massive traffic jams. This app quizzes and prepares you for the national Chinese driving test that's required for both locals and foreigners looking to obtain a driver's license.

Aibang Trains (Àibāng Lièchē; 爱 帮 列 车) **(FREE)** – Despite requiring an internet connection, Aibang is still useful for checking national train times, information regarding specific train routes and departing/arrival stations. It is even updated for the speedy new D trains (aka bullet trains) for those in a hurry.

Mandarin

Pleco Chinese Dictionary (FREE) – Pleco is perhaps the best Mandarin/English electronic dictionary out there. You can write in English or pinyin for a translation or upgrade some add-ons at a cost to get flashcards, a camera based optical Chinese character recognition device, full touch screen handwriting and other tech-savvy accessories.

HanZi Card ($5.99) – An electronic flashcard system coupled with a voice pronunciation feature for the top 3,000 most used words in the Chinese language. You can even personalize your list to narrow down your trouble words. This one is recommended for anyone serious about learning Mandarin.

Nemo Chinese Phrases (FREE) – Nemo is a user friendly app for the short-term traveler that has the 50 most used phrases in Mandarin. It's also compatible with English, pinyin, and Chinese characters, and has an audio voice device.

Waygo Chinese Translator (FREE) – In case you don't want to purchase a camera based character recognition device on Pleco, get Waygo's for free. Though it's mostly aimed towards menu vocab and simple phrases, it's still extremely useful. All you have to do is take a picture of the characters on your phone and Waygo will translate them instantly into English.

Google Translator (FREE) – Just like everything else Google makes, this is another popular app. Type English, pinyin or simply draw the character with your finger on the touch screen to get an instant translation. You can also use the voice translation function, which is fairly accurate.

Entertainment

China Travel Guide by Triposo (FREE) –

A complete travel guide for all major Chinese cities with the latest info concerning everything from nightlife, entertainment, hotels/hostels, leisure activities, tours, tourist attractions, restaurants/cafes, outdoor activities, parks and shopping. It also includes maps, pictures, recommendations, prices and operating hours.

World Travelpedia Nightlife ($5.99) – The app a party animal can't live without, this displays the hottest parties, nightclubs and bars from every major city in the world. There's even a map to show you the best spots closest to you in case you get drunk and lost from one club to another.

City Weekend (FREE) – This app lists all the popular listings such as bars, restaurants and other popular venues by category and area in the Beijing metropolitan zone. It also provides a map, directions, reviews and contact information of each place.

Beijing Locals Recommend (FREE) – Why read it when you can see it? This unique interactive guide has locals offering their best advice and tips on streaming video.

Beijing Guide (FREE) – This city guide by Vok Dams is another alternative to the other Beijing based city guides out there. It specializes in hotels, shopping, restaurants, nightlife, sightseeing, special events and other recommended sites throughout the capital. It also translates all addresses into Chinese for your convenience.

Communication & Social Media

QQ (FREE) – QQ is China's favorite instant messaging portal and is used by everyone from students to businessmen. In fact, you may hear the signature QQ *beep beep beep beep* for incoming messages hundreds of times a day while in China. It's fantastic for keeping in touch with local friends or meeting new ones.

WeChat/Weixin (FREE) – Another popular Chinese instant messaging program, WeChat (known as Weixin in Chinese) also allows you to send voice messages, share photos, meet new friends with the shake of the phone and meet random people with a "message in a bottle."

WhatsApp (FREE) – Though more popular in the West, WhatsApp is growing quickly in China and the rest of Asia. It's another great instrument for keeping in touch with those back home, chatting with your local friends and meeting new people.

Skype (FREE) – Skype is without a doubt one of the cheapest and easiest ways to contact loved ones far away. There's also a video chat so you can actually show them all the fun you're having.

News

China Daily News (FREE) – Stay informed with one of China's premier English news services. Here you can get the inside scoop on all the latest news happening across China.

Accommodation

Hostelworld (FREE) – Handy for booking hostels within and outside of China.

Booking.com (FREE) – Another accommodation app similar to Hostelworld, but focuses more on hotels than hostels.

History

Chinese History Timeline (FREE) – This one can help the confused traveler digesting 5,000 years of history make sense of all the dynasties and historic relics found all over the country.

Maps

iMaps+ for Google Maps ($1.99) – With Google's classic street view, road maps, GPS and directions, this is a wonderful gizmo to get you from point A to point B. However, it must be noted that Google is frequently "unavailable" in China.

百度地图 **(Bǎidù Dìtú) (FREE)** – This might be a better option for the traveler who can read Chinese. It's similar to Google Maps but with better walking, driving and public transportation directions.

Other

Sit or Squat (FREE) – A potential life saver, especially if you haven't learned how to say the most important travel phrase out there, "Where's the bathroom?" Sit or Squat shows you the closest public restrooms near your current location and, get this, even rates them on cleanliness. You've got to love technology!

Tudou (土豆) (FREE) – Sites like Youtube are blocked in China unless you have a VPN. If you don't use a proxy, try Tudou – the Chinese equivalent to Youtube – which has many Chinese and Western videos, movies and TV shows. It also has many of the viral videos seen on Youtube for those who can't live without them.

Scams

Though Beijing is probably one of the safest cities in the world, scammers can truly make a meal out of some of the top tourist sites. Buzzing like bees, they hover near places like the Forbidden City, Wangfujing Dajie and Tian'anmen Square looking for those unwitting and unaccustomed to their land. While they are pesky and persistent, for the most part they are nothing to fret about – just be aware and avoid them. This section describes the scams you will certainly encounter at some point if you plan to see the big attractions; with a quick read you will be well armed to deal with or avoid the cons.

Black Taxis

Taxis are ubiquitous in downtown Beijing. Update your knowledge on them first and stay alert.

The scam: What the Chinese call *hēichē* (黑车), or black taxis, troll the streets for gullible tourists to bite on their unlikely stories. These taxis will overcharge unaccustomed tourists, take detours or jack up the agreed price at the end of the trip.

How to avoid it: You should only take metered taxis. The most conspicuous of the *heiche* are the private taxis, civilian cars with (often) small red lights below the rear-view mirror. Such operations are usually accompanied by a man, or men, whose job is to accost travelers to jump in their cars. Do not take these cabs, plain and simple.

The first thing to be aware of when grabbing a cab is the placard on the top of the car. These are government sanctioned (official) taxis, and you should only hail them; no placard, no go. Taxi drivers are required by law to use their meter, so say *dǎbiǎo* (打表) to make them turn it on. Some official taxi drivers may have a story about their meter being broken or some other hoodwinking reason for why theirs is a set price. If this happens, forget that taxi; get out and get a new one.

Note: Capital Airport is crawling with these illegal private operations, and they are likely to be your first encounter in Beijing. Fervently deny them, and get in the official taxi lines. Don't let a long taxi line daunt you – they are fast moving.

Rickshaws

Rickshaws can be a fun and refreshing way to see an area, especially in the summer. But, keep in mind that rickshaws are for tourists, and those waiting outside hotels and touristy areas can be sketchy. Places like Houhai are much better for a rickshaw ride than Tian'anmen.

The scam: The shadier drivers will lurk outside the heavy tourist areas, but they can be found elsewhere in the city too. Rickshaws have no meters, so the price is agreed on (but not paid) ahead of time, and fraudulent drivers often call on the language barrier or some other excuse when they raise the price or add a zero at the end of the journey. Some have been said to switch drivers mid-journey and then ask for a payment for each driver. There are also reports of drivers taking passengers to small alleys and demanding large payments. This is essentially robbery.

How to avoid it: Be exceptionally clear about every aspect of the deal before getting in the car. If you want the rickshaw experience, you should carry a pen and a piece of paper and make them write the agreed-on price before you set off. Make sure the currency is clearly stated and written down as well; there is a big difference between ¥30 and $30. Low-ball price quotes (under ¥10) are often scams also – a quote of ¥3 can turn into ¥300. Remember, you'll never get anywhere for less than ¥10. You must also be very clear of stipulations such as duration and number of people. Some drivers have been known to agree to a price, say ¥70, only to stop halfway to the destination and inform the passengers that the price was per person for half an hour. If you feel something is afoot, or the driver is taking you somewhere you don't want to go, stand your ground, and feel free to show some anger.

Personal Account

My brother just got (nearly) ripped off by a rickshaw that was waiting outside his hotel near Tian'anmen Square. The driver asked for ¥30 at the start, and then about halfway through the ride they swapped drivers. The second driver kept saying "three money," obviously setting him up for a misunderstanding. Soon my brother was taken to a quiet alley and the driver then demanded ¥300 for each of the drivers (¥600 all together) for going about 300 meters. The man began to get aggressive in voice and manner, and my brother (who is strong and fit) returned the anger in kind. He says the driver was intimidated and began to back down when two fairly large Chinese came walking down the alley. That's when he pushed the driver aside and made a run for it out of the alley. He escaped intact and didn't pay a dime, but I've heard of others having no choice but to fork over the cash.

Taxi Drive-offs

Easy to avoid if you have a heads up, a new scam hitting the market is the drive-off.

The scam: China Daily covered two police reports where taxi drivers asked passengers to exit the car and help push the car (claimed to have a dead battery) or help to close the trunk. With the passengers removed from the car the drivers quickly hit the gas, in one instance making off with ¥16,500 ($2,700) and a laptop.

How to avoid it: Never exit a cab with your articles still inside. The obvious response to any driver who requests your assistance (before you have reached your destination and have all your belongings) is to give a firm "No!" Do not exit a vehicle without all your personal effects, and do not be afraid to firmly refuse an insistent driver. Eventually they will want to get on with life and will drop the issue. If you arrive at your destination and have removed all your possessions from the car, feel free to lend a hand to a friendly driver if he needs one.

Tea Houses

Many international youth hostels and large hotels are now warning of the Tea House scammers. They have become quite prolific around Wangfujing and the Tian'anmen area, but you have a chance to encounter them elsewhere too.

The scam: Nearly always encountered as well spoken locals or domestic or international tourists (one of our writers met one claiming to be from Mongolia), these friendly and charming crooks invite naïve and unaccustomed travelers to absurdly priced tea houses (with no labeled price) and proceed to foot the unfortunates with bills often exceeding US$100. Though the teahouse is the most prominent type of this scam, drinks, meals and coffees might also be offered. These scammers often prey on men by using pretty girls as their representatives.

How to avoid it: Be suspicious of any stranger on the street offering to take you somewhere. Obvious tourists (i.e. with an open guidebook, map, or a foreign face) are major bait for these scammers, so be on high alert at tourist hot spots like Tian'anmen. The key word in this scam is *stranger*. The friendly Chinese person you met having breakfast at your hostel that wants to share a day out with a new friend is one thing; the stranger that approaches you on the street to take you to a food or drink venue is totally different. Strangers who insist on choosing the venue raise another big red flag. Conversations started randomly by strangers offering to take you for food or drinks are almost always a scam. They can be persistent as well, offering to walk you to your destination. Quite simply, do not agree to go anywhere with strangers if it doesn't feel right.

Personal Account

I was down around Tian'anmen Square the other day, on a trip to Beijing from Europe, and this great looking woman struck up a conversation with me. I'm usually a very savvy traveler, but this woman was so good looking and so charming that I took the bait hard and accompanied her to a teahouse for, as she put it, just some conversation and drinks. The conversation was friendly, interesting and dynamic, and the time seemed to fly by.

Before I knew it, she was ordering, snacks, a fruit plate, and some whiskey for us (low quality whiskey by the taste, I had to keep putting coke in it). I didn't imagine fruit and nuts could be particularly pricey, but I joked with her anyway that I might be in trouble when the bill came, also informing her (truthfully) that I only had ¥200 on me. She assured me everything would be fine, so we indulged. The conversation began to turn to "hot fun" back at my hotel, which was exciting for a single guy, but her next suggestion of another friend suddenly made me realize I might be in some trouble. I decided it was time to pay up and move on and asked for the bill. They murmured some prices, such as the fruit plate for ¥130, and when I asked for a written bill they weren't so excited. Finally, I was given a written total... ¥6,300! My mind was blown, and I had a sinking feeling as I realized I had been completely scammed. I reminded her that I needed to go back to my hotel to get more cash, but she said she would accompany me. I also noticed a very large Chinese man who was apparently going to accompany us as well.

It was luck that one of those electric golf-cart police cars came by. The girl had a short discussion with the cops (who spoke no English but seemed to realize what was going on), and as things went a bit awry for her she tried to snatched the glasses off my head. I was able to block her (with a little bit of force), but the cops gave me a verbal scolding and made me get in the cart. They drove me several blocks away while the woman continued cursing, saying she would find me. A few blocks later the police gave me one word: "Out." I hopped out, shaken but none the poorer and much the wiser. I'm endlessly thankful, because I know that it could have been worse, a lot worse. Learn from my naïve mistake, don't get scammed by teahouse strangers.

Art Students

Very similar in nature to the Tea House scams, pesky "art students" patrol the big tourist spots, in particular Tain'anmen and Wangfujing, striking up friendly conversations with strolling tourists.

The scam: How many of them are actually art students remains uncertain, but what ensues is a trip to an overpriced art gallery where a high pressure buying situation can sour your mood quickly. Certain foreigners may enjoy the friendly chitchat, but keep in mind that if they feel they have hooked you, it will not be easy to get rid of them.

How to avoid it: Identify the situation and just say "No!" Avoiding this one is almost exactly the same as the teahouse scam above – strangers approaching you are big red flags. Our advice is to give them a friendly brush-off.

Personal Account

My first time in Beijing, I stayed near the Wangfujing area, a heavily trafficked tourist area. I was young, fresh-faced and ready for my first China adventure. With such a positive outlook and totally unaccustomed to Chinese culture, I was easy prey for the "art students" who begin their scams with charming pleasantries. As I walked down Wangfujing Street, ready to make my way to the Forbidden City, I was surprised to hear a friendly "Hello! Where are you from?" Two young, seemingly friendly and average Chinese (a guy and a girl) were strolling alongside me and had a look of unbridled interest in their eyes. We exchanged names and shot back-stories, and they even wrote my name for me in Chinese to put a little icing on the cake, so to speak.

As it turned out, they were art students and they had a fantastic exhibit just around the corner they wanted me to see. It seemed I had made a genuine connection with a local, and being so pumped on my first Chinese experience, I heartily agreed. The gallery was little more than a dim, gutted apartment room with several walls of painted Chinese scrolls depicting animals, rivers, flowers and plants; quintessentially Chinese scenes of nature. There was no denying their beauty, and I was fairly enchanted.

The charming couple proceeded to tell me about the meanings of each painting that I seemed to show an interest in. "So, which ones (notice the plural) do you want to buy?" They asked me. I did like several of the larger ones, so I picked out two and asked the price. ¥300 for each one. "*Yikes!*" I thought. It was turning out to be a pricey outing. I had little idea about what was a reasonable price, and by US standards 50 bucks for each seemed reasonable to me. But this was not enough for them.

With puppy dog eyes they informed me that I had only selected his paintings (which were obviously not painted by either of them) and none of hers. Knowing I had a girlfriend, they suggested a smaller one depicting two plants that traditionally signified love. It was a "mere" ¥150. I was starting to feel suckered, but I had already picked some out, so I reluctantly agreed. I didn't have enough money in hand, so the boy accompanied me to the ATM outside (obviously just keeping an eye on me) and I got my cash and made my purchase. They made sure to drive the scam home by exchanging emails with me as I left. Jerks.

I do really like the paintings I bought. They are beautiful and I still have them displayed. But, not only are they probably not very genuine, the experience itself was as fake as it gets. I have since realized that those scrolls should actually cost about ¥10 to ¥30 each, and though they are nice, it's the rip-off and the feeling of being a total sucker that sours the paintings. It could have been worse, and I chalked this one up to a very important learning experience.

Pickpocket

Theft on the surface may not seem like a scam, but those pickpockets who work in teams are akin to con artists.

The scam: In public areas it is not uncommon for partnered rogues to play the bump and cut combination. That is, one may distract you (ask a question, bump into you, ask for a photo op, etc) while another slits your bag or pocket with a razor and nimbly extracts your valuables.

How to avoid it: Keep your valuables as close to your body as possible and within your field of vision. The best way to guard against this is to keep your money and other valuables in a money belt under your shirt (or otherwise close to your body), and right where you can see them. Items that may not fit so close to your body should be kept inside a snug interior pocket of your bag, one that is hidden and inaccessible from the bag exterior. When riding public transportation, it is advisable to wear your bag on the front of your body where it can be easily seen.

Bag Snatching

This is not exactly a scam, and definitely not unique to China, but very pertinent.

The scam: Some tourists have become the unfortunate victims of the drive-by bag-snag, where a running thief snatches an unfastened, unattended or otherwise vulnerable bag at full sprint. Because the thief hits at full speed, the dazed victims are unprepared, and by the time it dawns on them what has happened, the quick bandit is long gone.

How to avoid it: Keep your bags away from the open. When dining or relaxing in public areas, always keep your bags close and away from the road – the backs of chairs or places adjacent to trafficked areas are especially vulnerable. Good spots to place your bag include the seats of chairs that are between you and the wall or on the floor (if it seems clean enough) between your legs.

Massage

It goes without saying that many massage parlors in Beijing double as brothels, or at least have a seedy side.

The scam: Unsuspecting patrons have found their relaxing massages taking sudden and unwelcomed erotic turns, and the embarrassed victims shell out for the extortionate bill in lieu of causing a scene.

How to avoid it: Only use massage parlors that are suggested by a reliable source or this guidebook. A good general rule to follow is avoiding massage parlors with tasteless red neon signs or those that staff only women. Your best bet is to check with your hostel or hotel for recommendations close to you; they can usually suggest something reputable.

Counterfeit Bills

One of the less common scams but one of the more difficult to spot, counterfeit cash in China is limited to ¥50 and ¥100 bank notes, and they are dealt out by dishonest taxi drivers and small shops. There are two ways you may be given a fake bill.

The scam (1): The scam is played out when you pay for your goods or transport with a ¥100 (or less often with a ¥50) note and the driver or shopkeeper "inspects" it, often outside your field of vision. They then inform you that the bill is fake, return it to you, and ask for another one. This may happen several times, and when you suspect something is amiss and check your bills later, you will realize that the bills they returned to you were switched out for fakes by their crafty hands. It is a sleight of hand parlor trick.

The scam (2): Sometimes the attempt to pass you a bogus bill occurs when the driver or shopkeeper tries to give you a large bill in change claiming they have no change. Maybe your cab fare was ¥60 and they try to give you a ¥50, using the "no change" excuse and even saying they'll give you a slight discount. What they are actually doing is passing you a fake note. If they truly don't have change, they will go to another shop and exchange for it.

How to avoid it: Pay attention to your large bills and watch the driver's and shopkeeper's hands very carefully. To beat this scam, first keep one thing in mind: banks are masters at screening for fake bills, which means that whether you exchanged for Chinese RMB at a bank back home or grabbed some from a Chinese ATM, you can be 100% sure that your bank issued 100s are not fake. When paying a suspicious taxi driver or shop owner with a large bill, watch their hands very carefully, and feel free to make a fuss if they try to examine the note out of sight, even if it's just behind the counter. The extra cautious will check the serial number on the bank note and write it down in view of the recipient to discourage any funny business. If they manage to pull one over on you, and you are close enough to your hotel, grab one of the staff to come out and get the driver's information.

Beggars

Beggars are not as bad in Beijing as in some second or third-tier cities, but you will likely encounter some, especially on the fringes of tourist areas.

The scam: Beijing has a phenomenon of the professional beggar. Though it's not unique to the city, one of its characteristics that is less common in the West is that many beggars make more money than white-collar office workers. Some statistics suggest that 85% of beggars in Beijing are not actually poor and beg professionally. If you give money to some of these people, they may hound you for more, or you may be subject to a train of beggars who quickly caught word of the generous foreigner. There are also those children who sadly beg for money and are almost 100% of the time kidnapped and forced by a crime syndicate to beg for money, which of course goes to the unscrupulous bosses.

How to avoid it: Don't give money to those you can't be sure are legitimate. Ignore them, plain and simple. Some may pester you for a bit, such as an old woman clutching a few small bills and making gracious gestures while murmuring *xièxiè* (thank you). Just ignore them. Looking through your phone or chatting with others is a good way to snub these panhandlers. Do not give money to child beggars; it only promotes their tragic situation, and the money you give them will not stay in their hands. If you really feel the urge to help them, give them some food to eat, then you know that what you gave truly went to them. However, if you do this you may be subject to a spree of children who heard of your generosity.

Note: Sometimes you will see those with shocking disfigurements, or those affected by terrible accidents (such as people who have obviously been severely burned or lost limbs). It can be heart wrenching (so be prepared), and many of these people actually cannot work to pay for large medical bills. They are far less likely to hound you, because their need is often genuine. If you feel the urge to give, these people are far more legitimate (and gracious) recipients.

KTV Scam

This one is not terribly common, but it is one that can really ruin what begins as a fun-filled, jovial night.

The scam: Usually happening to lone travelers, but can also happen to a couple friends or gullible groups, the scam usually begins when you meet a friendly Chinese man (who often gussies up the role to look like a businessman) while out to dinner. He invites you to eat with him and a couple of very pretty ladies who have just come to meet him. He's so friendly in fact, that he pays for the whole meal, yours included, and invites you to come sing some songs at the local KTV karaoke joint. Before you know it, the alcohol is flowing, dishes of fruit and snacks are being brought out, and you end up footed with an outrageous bill – often in the thousands of dollars – that you never imagined you'd suddenly be muscled into paying. Bad end to a great night.

How to avoid: Don't run off with strangers you meet. Your mother told you this one, didn't she? There are endless friendly and honest Beijingers who would love to be your friend, but it's very unlikely that these are the kind of people who invite random strangers out for a night of drinking and karaoke on their tab. Meeting friends at hostels is a different story, just be very wary of random people wanting to show you a high-priced good time.

Bar Tab Scam

Having some kicks out at the bars is for many an integral part of the traveling experience. Just remember that alcohol impairs your judgment and memory, and there are some places who may try to take advantage of you in your inebriated state.

The scam: You're having a good time drinking with some friends. The time is flying by and the beers are going down. The servers have a tab running for you, or maybe they suggest just leaving the bottle caps on the table to tally up when you are done. The problem is, you've been having too much fun to keep track, and they maybe even slyly snuck a few extra caps onto your table from departed patrons. When all is said and done, your tab is much higher than it should be, but you're in no position to argue now.

How to avoid: Pay for every drink as you order. Easy enough, right? It really is. You buy a beer, you pay for it. Get a round of shots, pay before the server leaves the table. By consistently paying each round there is no way they can throw on extras at the end, and you can easily stand your ground if they try to say otherwise.

Fake Alcohol

China has a problem with fake alcohol. Be aware of it and try to avoid it.

The Scam: A bar will use rubbing alcohol or some other potentially dangerous alcohol "substitutes" (like ethylene glycol) to refill or fill their alcohol containers. Sometimes this will be done by the distributor and then sold to bars looking to cut costs; fake alcohol is cheaper than the real deal.

How to avoid it: Taste your drinks carefully. This scam isn't so common that you need to be paranoid about having some drinks in Beijing, and there isn't any foolproof way to avoid it. The best things you can do are stick to alcohol brands you know well (i.e. know their taste and feel) and stop drinking anything that seems, tastes or feels amiss. Oftentimes you will notice that a drink, or especially a shot, just doesn't taste right and isn't making you feel the way you normally do. These are signs to find a new place to drink.

Restaurant Scams

There are two scams that you should watch out for in restaurants. They are not terribly common, but they do happen to domestic and international tourists, so be aware of them.

The scam (1): Many restaurants will keep separate English and Chinese menus. When a foreigner comes in, the owner will immediately provide them with an English menu, and while the prices may seem approximately equivalent to those in the West, in China they are steep, and actually much higher than those on the Chinese menu.

How to avoid it: This one may be a bit harder to avoid than others, but fortunately it's less common. The big red flag to look out for is if you are immediately greeted with an English menu. If this happens, request a Chinese menu. If they refuse you can be pretty sure they are up to something – choose a different place to eat. Also, if you order from the Chinese menu, be sure they do not try to charge inflated prices in the end; you should make a stink about it until they give you the original prices from the menu you ordered from.

The scam (2): One that happens to domestic tourists and foreigners alike, a restaurant will have two menus that look identical except one has significantly inflated prices. They first give you the menu with reasonable prices to order from, then when the bill comes at the end of the meal it's higher than it should be. When you protest, they bring out the menu with higher prices and try to make you out to be the fool.

How to avoid it: Beating this one is simple. Using a smart-phone or camera, simply take pictures of the items on the menu and their prices, and if they try to show you a different menu at the end, simply pull out your picture and you've got them red-handed.

Culture Shock for Travelers

Language Barrier

Travelers may be surprised to find that English isn't widely spoken in Beijing, despite the impression in the West that everyone in China is furiously studying it. That impression is true to some extent – English is a requirement of high school curriculums across the country – but most people learn just enough to pass the test and then rarely use it again. Tour guides, hotel staff, and others who work with tourists on a regular basis are likely exceptions.

Think about your own language skills in this context. Even if you studied Spanish in high school back in the day, if a Central American tourist approached you in your hometown speaking native-level *español*, you'd probably be pretty startled and might not have a clue what to say. Here are a few tips to ease the language barrier during your stay.

An English sign outside doesn't mean English is spoken inside. Around the time that Beijing hosted the Olympics in 2008, there was a huge push to increase English signage around town. As a result, many businesses, especially in downtown Beijing, have an English name or English on their signs. But don't expect to walk into "Smile Bakery" or "Convenient Store" and conduct your business in English; in all likelihood, no one inside will speak it. In more expat-centric areas like Sanlitun or Gulou, the staff might know basic words. Don't let this intimidate you, just be prepared to find alternate ways of expressing yourself. Which brings us to:

Don't be shy about gesturing. When ordering from a menu or buying things in a store, don't hesitate to simply point at what you want. No one will be offended. Likewise, don't be afraid to use your fingers to show how many you want. You might feel a little silly, but it's a language everyone can understand. That being said, before you head out on your trip, it can't hurt to:

Learn a little Chinese. Even if you only learn a few phrases and numbers, your effort will be recognized and appreciated. Your basic Mandarin may not always get your point across, but it will always earn a little goodwill from whoever you're interacting with. See page 336 for an overview of basic Mandarin.

Download some helpful language apps. If you have a smart-phone, there are a number of apps that you can use to ease the language barrier. Some apps simply provide Chinese phrases on your phone that you can point to when instructing a taxi driver, or alerting a waitress to your food allergies. Others have cool tools like the ability to trace a Chinese character on the screen with your finger and get an instant English translation. See page 309 for an overview of helpful apps.

Transportation

You may notice a different attitude toward transportation as soon as the wheels of your plane touch the ground in Beijing and Chinese passengers leap from their seats, grab their luggage, and make a mad dash for the exit.

When it comes to getting from point A to point B in China, sometimes it seems like the only rule is there are no rules. Read up on the following common Beijing situations and you'll feel less shocked when you arrive.

Traffic lights and pedestrian signals are pretty much ignored. Unlike in the West, where a green "walk" sign reliably means that it's safe to cross the street, in Beijing all bets are off. No matter the color of the light, there's bound to be a stream of vehicles – buses, trucks, vans, cars, motorcycles, bikes, electric scooters, and three-wheeled carts – coming at you from pretty much every direction. The only way to know when it's safe to cross is to wait, watch carefully, and follow the locals when they go – there's safety in numbers. Also note that the white striped "zebra crossings" that are supposed to indicate a safe place for pedestrians to cross mid-street are almost always completely ignored.

Flagging down a taxi can be tough. There are 66,000 taxis roaming the streets of Beijing, which seems like a lot, especially compared to New York's 15,000. But when many of Beijing's 20 million residents are looking for a cab at the same time – during rush hour, on the weekends, or during bad weather – taxis can become scarce. You may get angry and start to assume that drivers are refusing to pick you up because you're a foreigner. Keep your cool – catching a cab is frustrating for everyone, and you'll never really know why a cab passes you by. Even if you're lucky enough to get one, it's possible that the driver will refuse to take you where you want to go for any number of reasons: it's too close, it's too far, he's unsure of his ability to communicate with foreigners, he's going the other direction, he's about to end his shift, etc. Given Beijing's stubborn traffic and the efficiency of the subway system, it's really better not to rely on a taxi to get you where you want to go, especially if you're in a rush.

Honking! Honking! Honking! For drivers in Beijing, honking isn't a way of getting other drivers' attention so much as a reflex, a constant announcement that "Hey! I'm driving!" The constant beep of horns can be annoying, but you'll learn to tune it out after a few days.

The subway has a security checkpoint. Don't let it frighten you. If you're expecting an authoritarian Chinese government interrogation, you'll be pleasantly surprised. It can be jarring or annoying to have to put your bag through an X-ray scanner every time you board the subway, and it's not common in much of the West, but the checkpoint is quite simple and the security employees are usually friendly and laid-back.

Behavior

When you imagine Beijing, do you picture a super-crowded street with hordes of people fighting their way down the street en masse? If so, you might be pleasantly surprised by the elbow room in many parts of the city. But there are definitely different norms for public behavior here that you should be aware of.

Forget your "personal space" bubble. Maybe it's a natural consequence of growing up in a country with 1.4 billion people, or maybe it's China's emphasis on a communal society, with multiple generations often living under one roof. Whatever it is, it means you won't have nearly as much personal space as you're probably used to. On a crowded subway car, you can be pressed up against a stranger in a way that you wouldn't expect until after your third date. An elevator will be crammed with twice as many people as it could ever fit. People passing you in the street will brush up against you and not acknowledge it. Try to take it in stride.

Cutting in line – if there is a line at all – is common. You probably haven't thought about someone "skipping" you in line since kindergarten, but be prepared to battle it again during your visit. An orderly, formal line is something you probably won't encounter here. Assert yourself and don't be afraid to stand very close behind the people in front of you – what might seem like a respectable distance to you looks like an opening to someone else.

You're going to get a lot of curious looks and stares. Foreign tourists have become a common sight, but Beijing is still a very homogenous city, and anyone who looks "different" will be an object of curiosity.

Look out for spitballs. Expect to see people spitting on the ground, even indoors, in Beijing. Often it can transcend mere spitting, becoming an elaborate hacking and coughing routine that produces a phlegm wad the size of a golf ball. Heavy air pollution and high smoking rates may be partly to blame. Not everyone does it, but don't be shocked when you do see (and hear) it.

Casual littering is accepted. Despite garbage cans and anti-littering posters, you will see garbage on the street in Beijing. It can be surprising to see a grown man unwrap a Snickers bar and let the wrapper fall to the ground, but there's simply a different set of expectations. You may also notice the orange-clad sanitation workers with a broom and a dustpan scouring each block for trash – perhaps that explains why Beijingers seem so casual about littering. Don't add to the problem by joining in.

Regular conversation volume is much

louder. After a few hours in Beijing, you may start to wonder why everyone is yelling. It's not in your imagination. Former NBA superstar and Chinese native Yao Ming even coached his fellow countrymen that they should try to speak more softly to be good hosts during the Olympics. It's hard to say why shout-talking is so prevalent here, perhaps some people tend to speak up to demonstrate authority, make a point or simply show energy and friendliness.

Food & Eating

"They will eat everything that swims except a submarine, everything that flies except an airplane, and everything with four legs except a table." That's a famous saying about the people of Guangdong Province in southern China. Beijing doesn't have quite the same reputation for culinary adventurousness, but you're likely to encounter foods – or part of animals – being served here that would be totally alien in your culture. Think turtle soup, chicken feet, pig hooves, fish heads, and stinky tofu. Western culture is actually unique in its refusal to eat many animal parts, so either say a polite "no thank you" or give it a shot! 1.4 billion people can't be too wrong.

Chinese food in China isn't like Chinese food at home. If you come to Beijing expecting to feast on General Tso's Chicken, crab Rangoon, egg rolls, and fortune cookies, you're in for a letdown. None of these dishes are common here, they're mostly Americanized versions of Chinese food created by immigrants from southern China. There's a huge and delicious variety of real Chinese food waiting for you, though, so don't be disappointed.

Chinese restaurants can be crowded, noisy and smoky. Depending on where you eat during your trip, you may encounter restaurants that aren't exactly what you're used to in terms of ambience. Diners are often crowded around small tables and seated on stools, a TV might be blaring in the corner, people smoke heavily and ash their cigarettes on the floor, and shouting to get the waiter or waitress's attention is perfectly normal. None of these things mean the restaurant won't be delicious, in fact, it might be a good sign that you've found a popular local spot.

All my drinks are warm! The Chinese believe that drinking too many cold beverages is unhealthy and throws your body out of balance. You might be frustrated to find that everything you order, including soda, juice, water, and beer, arrives at your table room temperature, or in the case of water, steaming hot. Try to have a "when in Rome" attitude about this one. You shouldn't consume ice, anyway, since it's likely made from tap water.

You call this breakfast? The foods that Beijingers prefer for breakfast, from hot rice porridge and deep-fried dough to hot soymilk and fluffy meat dumplings, might not exactly scream "breakfast" to your Western tastes. Coffee is becoming more popular, but is not reflexively served with breakfast the way it is in other places. It can be had at cafes and coffee chains like Starbucks and Pacific Coffee, but it's relatively expensive here, usually costing upwards of ¥25 (about US$4).

Eating dogs and cats is acceptable in China. Well, yes, you may find dog and cat on the menu in China, but it's much more common in very rural areas and in the south, not in large metropolitan cities. Protests and public outcry have increased, however, and public opinion has started to turn against this custom, especially when it comes to cats. As a tourist in Beijing, you're unlikely to end up in any restaurants serving either. Again, it's basically unheard of in the West, but not totally uncommon in other areas of the world.

Out & About

The air is hazy and polluted. We've already mentioned this, but if the pollution is high during your trip, it can take your breath away. See our section on air pollution (pg 301) for more details on how to keep gray days from ruining your trip.

Smoking is very common and seems to be allowed everywhere. Smoking rates have fallen off in most Western countries, but in China over 50% of men are smokers. (The rate for women is much lower, as in most societies.) Not only are there more smokers, they seem to have free reign to smoke indoors, outdoors, in restaurants, offices, elevators, and hospitals – you name it. A "no smoking" sign on the wall is usually no indication that the air will be smoke-free.

Chinese people may take your photo, or even ask to take a photo with you. You might start to feel like a celebrity after a day walking around Beijing for the number of people who snap your picture. In some cases you may be asked to pose with a stranger. These people are usually motivated by harmless curiosity and may just want a picture of themselves hanging out with foreigners that they can use to impress their friends.

Salesmen and scammers can be very aggressive with tourists. Everyone from fake handbag sellers to rickshaw drivers sees a tourist as a potential money-making opportunity, so don't be surprised if you find yourself being constantly approached or followed by them in touristy areas. If you're not interested, just keep walking and don't make eye contact. A few choice Chinese words like *bú yaò* ("don't want") can be helpful too.

Many girls are carrying umbrellas, but it's a sunny day. Maintaining very white skin is considered desirable among Chinese women, so they take sun protection seriously. You'll see plenty of girls carrying frilly and cutely-decorated umbrellas to stay in the shade, and you might start to want one yourself if you're visiting Beijing in the height of summer.

It seems like everyone's face is buried in a smart-phone, whether they're walking, biking, riding the subway, or even driving. Personal computer ownership rates are much lower in China than in most Western countries, but most people in Beijing own some type of internet-enabled phone. When you consider that non-computer owners have to do all their email, gaming, and chatting on their phones, it makes more sense. On top of that, instant-message programs called QQ and

Wechat are massively popular in China, and many people remain logged in all day to keep in touch with friends. One study even showed that white-collar office workers in China spend an average of 6.72 hours a day on their phones. That may seem like a shocking number, but many people spend as much as three hours a day commuting back and forth to work – and unlike many subway systems elsewhere in the world, cell phones get reception even when you're underground – so you can see how the time begins to add up.

Others

***B**argaining is the rule when shopping at markets.* There are good deals to be had in Beijing on everything from DVDs to dresses, but you may have to bargain for them. Haggling might be unfamiliar to you and make you feel rude or cheap, but rest assured that it's expected here. See page 254 for tips on successful bargaining.

Websites like Facebook, The New York Times, Blogspot and YouTube are blocked in China. If you were expecting to keep in touch with family and friends on your Facebook account or your blog, you're out of luck. Many common websites are inaccessible in China thanks to what some call the "Great Firewall" put up by the Chinese government. The list of blocked sites is long and ever-changing. If it's very important to you, you can set up a VPN (Virtual Private Network) to get around the restrictions during your travels, but for most people it's most practical to just close the computer and go see more of the city.

Nobody wants to tell you "no." You might not notice this right away, but it's an aspect of Chinese culture that you should keep your eye out for, partly because it's fascinating and partly because it could save you a lot of headaches. Chinese people are often reluctant to tell someone "no" or deliver disappointing news, because to do so would mean a loss of "face" (see next page for more).

To the Chinese, directly denying a request means a loss of face, so they will often either fail to give any response at all or will try to subtly say no with a comment such as, "Well, that might not be very convenient." For example, if you ask a staff member at your hotel to help get you tickets for a certain performance and they repeatedly suggest other shows besides the one you requested, it may be because the one you wanted is sold out and they are trying to avoid telling you that they cannot help.

In Chinese culture the context of one's words – like actions, attitude, and body language – bear more weight than the actual words being spoken. For example, when asked a direct question by a Westerner, a Chinese person might say yes but act as if they have said no. This confusing communication is a red flag to alert the Westerner that the real answer is no but that they value your relationship and do not want to offend you. Westerners place far more emphasis on the literal meaning of spoken words and can become upset when we feel like we're being "lied to" or "given the run-around."

Etiquette & Taboo in Chinese Culture

When it comes to taboo and etiquette in China, there's good news and bad news for foreigners. The bad news is that China is a 5,000 year-old culture that has developed completely apart from Western civilization, so there are a lot of rules and habits that can be confusing and not at all intuitive to outsiders. But the good news is that with a little preparation, you can easily learn to make a good impression. Plus, the Chinese give foreigners (lǎowài; 老外) a lot of leeway when it comes to local customs and are unlikely to be offended if you break any rules.

When considering manners, it's important to note that "politeness" doesn't have the same implication that it does in the West. In Chinese, kèqì (客气) means polite, but to be kèqì is not necessarily a good thing. Kèqì implies that by being polite, you are hiding your true feelings and keeping a formal distance from others. As Chinese people become closer friends, they drop the kèqì to the extent that it's perfectly acceptable for good friends to make the most honest and critical remarks to each other. This is not considered rude; it's a sign of trust. If the people at the next table in the restaurant sound like they're having a huge fight, they're probably not. Losing one's temper in public would be shameful in China. Those people are just bantering, exchanging opinions, enjoying each other's company, and not being overly kèqì.

After a few days in Beijing, you might be thinking, "Chinese manners? What a joke! Some guy just cut me in line, everyone's yelling, and I can't even count how many have spit on the sidewalk right next to me!" The reality is that many Chinese apply a double standard when applying etiquette rules. They divide the world into two groups: people they know, and everyone else. They may practice impressive manners when it comes to their circle, but when dealing with strangers on the street, it's every man for himself. Take China's history. In a country that as recently as a generation ago was facing wars, famines, political repression, and countless other hardships, families survived by sticking together, which often meant being indifferent to the anonymous masses.

Below, we've outlined some basic etiquette rules. Apart from helping you put your best face forward, they offer interesting insights into Chinese culture.

Losing & Saving Face

The concept of face has been extremely important in Chinese culture for a very long time. Though it's quite difficult to translate, it basically means something along the lines of honor, prestige or reputation. So if you hear someone say "lose face" (diūliǎn; 丢脸), it means they lost honor or, in layman's terms, got embarrassed. On the other hand, saving face is what Chinese people do to avoid losing face or to keep from making a fool of themselves.

A boss can lose face when he makes a false statement in front of his subordinates, especially if one of his subordinates corrects him. However, this scenario is very unlikely since it's understood in the unwritten social contract never to correct your superior and just keep your mouth shut to ensure he or she doesn't lose face (unless of course it's a life or death situation). Indeed, if you make your boss lose face, you'll be in the hot seat!

One can also lose face if they lose their temper in public. If you see an open dispute, bystanders, cars and mopeds will stop immediately in their tracks to watch. After the quarrel is over, the ones involved will probably cover their face and run off to keep from losing face. You can also lose face if you get too drunk, trip while walking up the stairs, make a ridiculous comment or do something else humiliating.

In regards to saving face, if the Chinese side in a business negotiation no longer wishes to pursue the deal, they may not tell you. In an attempt to save their own face, they may become increasingly inflexible and hard-nosed, forcing you to be the one to break off negotiations. This way they can avoid any blame for the failure.

In another attempt to save face, the Chinese avoid saying "no" as much as possible and instead opt for nonchalant phrases such as "unfortunately it's not convenient" or " "that may cost a little too much money" or "give me some time to think about it." In this manner, both parties – the one making the invitation and the one declining the invitation – save face.

Remember, in the end the best way to behave in China is in a manner that allows you and the people around you both to never lose face.

Conversations

There are a number of conversation topics that are best avoided by foreigners in China. Listed below are some of the most serious:

· **Sino-Japanese relations** – The two countries have been fighting or at odds for much of the 20th century and are constantly walking on thin ice, so never compare the two neighbors.

· **The Three "T's"** – Taiwan, Tibet and the events that took place at Tian'anmen Square on June 4th, 1989. There's a lot of national sentiment that can be aroused by the first two, and frankly, many people don't know much about the Tian'anmen Square incident.

· **The Falun Gong** or religious and human rights in general.

· Anything negative about Chinese cleanliness or manners, or anything **comparing China negatively to another country.**

· **The Cultural Revolution**, or what someone's family went through during any of Mao's campaigns. Just like any country, there are liberals and conservatives, so it's best just to keep politics out of it because the conversation can get heated fast.

· Asking someone "How many children do you have?" There's still a **One Child Policy** for most Chinese, and calling attention to it could make for awkward small talk.

Greetings

· Punctuality is considered a virtue in China. Being on time shows respect for others.

· Always stand up or remain standing when being introduced.

· Handshaking is the most common form of greeting. Unlike what you may have heard, Chinese people usually don't bow when greeting someone. They also don't hug or kiss on the cheek when meeting someone for the first time.

· The oldest person is always greeted first as a sign of respect.

· Use family names and appropriate titles until specifically invited by your Chinese host or colleagues to use their given names.

· Chinese family names are placed first with the given name (which usually has one or two syllables) coming last. So in the Chinese name Chén Ruì, Chén is the family name and Ruì is the given name.

· Among more casual acquaintances, a common greeting is "Have you eaten?" (Nǐ chī le ma? 你吃了吗?).

· Do not overreact when asked personal questions regarding marital status, family, age, job or income. This is very common and is done to seek common ground, not to be nosy.

Body Language

· The Chinese dislike being touched by strangers. Do not touch, hug, lock arms, back slap or make any body contact.

· Clicking fingers or whistling is considered rude.

· Never put your feet on a desk or a chair. Never gesture or pass an object with your feet.

· To get the attention of a Chinese person, face the palm of your hand downward and move your fingers in a scratching motion. Never use your index finger to get anyone's attention.

· Sticking your pinkie up is an ugly gesture, so avoid doing it. They also know all about the middle finger, so don't flip the bird either.

Gifts

· In general, gifts or red envelopes filled with money are given at Chinese New Year, weddings, births, and birthdays.

· Bringing a gift is also a good idea when

you're invited to someone's home, and a small gift is expected when meeting a business acquaintance for the first time.

· Food and a nice basket of fruit make a great gift.

· Do not give scissors, knives or other sharp objects as they indicate that you want to cut off the relationship.

· Do not give clocks, handkerchiefs or straw sandals since they are associated with funerals and death.

· Do not wrap gifts in white, blue or black paper. Choose red, pink, or a colourful pattern.

· Never give gifts in groups of four since it's an unlucky number. It's better to give them in groups of eight since it's the luckiest number.

· Always present gifts with two hands.

· Gifts are usually not opened immediately in front of the giver – but if you're unsure, ask "Should I open it now?"

· The Chinese, especially older people, may try to refuse a gift several times before finally accepting it. Just smile and keep insisting that they accept it.

Visiting a Home

· Since Chinese people often live in small homes or apartments, many people prefer to entertain in public places rather than in their homes, especially when entertaining foreigners.

· If you are invited to their house, consider it a great honor. If you must turn down such an honor, explain the conflict in your schedule so that your actions are not taken as an insult and cause them to lose face.

· Arrive on time. Unlike in the West, when you're invited to a dinner party at 19:00, the food is likely to be on the table at 19:00 sharp.

· Remove your shoes before entering the house. Your host may offer you a pair of house slippers when you arrive – try to wear them, even if they don't fit perfectly.

· It's always polite to bring a small gift for the hostess or host.

Eating

· In China, there is no such thing as "going Dutch." If you are invited to dinner, your dinner will usually be paid for by the host. It's considered polite to offer to pay, but if you actually do pay, it will embarrass your host.

· Learn to use chopsticks, period.

· Wait to be told where to sit. The guest of honour will be given a seat facing the door.

· The host begins eating first, and the host offers the first toast.

· Be prepared to make a small toast for all occasions.

· The first toast normally occurs during or after the first course, not before. After the next course, the guest should reciprocate.

· It is not necessary to always drain your glass after a toast, although a host should encourage it.

· You should try everything that is offered to you.

· Never eat the last piece from the serving tray. Leave some food on your plate during each course of a meal to honor the generosity of your host. It is bad manners for a Chinese host not to keep refilling guests' plates or teacups.

· Be observant to other people's needs. If you want to pour yourself more tea, first ask if anyone else would like more. Serve them first, then fill your own cup.

· Do not be offended if a Chinese person makes slurping or belching sounds; it merely indicates that they are enjoying their food.

· Never leave your chopsticks stuck in a bowl of rice sticking upwards. Doing so wishes a bad curse on the proprietor since it resembles sticks of incense used at funerals and/or dead ancestors' shrines.

Business Etiquette

· As mentioned, punctuality is especially important in business. Being late is considered very rude and meetings always begin on time.

· Business cards are exchanged upon meeting. Business cards should be printed in English on one side and Chinese on the other. Make sure the Chinese side uses simplified characters and not traditional characters, which are used in Taiwan and Hong Kong. Also be sure to use two hands when handing out or receiving a business card.

- Be prepared for the possibility of long meetings and lengthy negotiations with many delays.

- The Chinese will enter a meeting with the highest-ranking person entering first. They will assume the first member of your group to enter the room is the leader of your delegation.

- Seating is very important at a meeting. The host sits to the left of the most important guest.

- There may be periods of silence at a business meeting. As uncomfortable as it may seem to you, do not feel the need to break the silence.

Numbers

Lucky Numbers

2 (èr; 二) is a good number since the Chinese often use it to amplify the meaning of positive feelings like double happiness.

The character and sound of 3 (sān; 三) is lucky because it looks and sounds like the word birth (shēng; 生).

6 (liù; 六) is pronounced the same as smooth (liù; 溜) and to flow (liú; 流), and is therefore considered good for business. Therefore, you will see the number 6 at many business functions, and 666, contrary to the West, is extremely lucky in China.

As in the West, 7 (qī; 七) is important, especially when dealing with relationships, because it's similar to the word together (qǐ; 起) and life (qì; 气).

8 (bā; 八) is by far the luckiest number because it sounds similar to fortune (fā; 发). Many people like to use 8 in their telephone number, when pricing items and the time/date of special events. (The Beijing Olympic Games began on 8-8-2008 at 8 seconds and 8 minutes past 8:00 pm local time. In 2003, Sichuan Airline acquired the phone number 028 8888 8888 at the cost of over 7 million RMB).

A good number to use for future relationships is 9 (jiǔ; 九) since it phonetically sounds like long lasting or time (iiǔ; 久). The pronunciation of the number 9 is also identical to the word for alcohol (jiǔ; 酒) so if you see a bar with 9 in its name, it probably represents booze and not that they wish to build a future relationship with you.

Unlucky Numbers

0 (líng; 零) is bad because it represents emptiness.

Therefore, when giving money the traditional way in red envelopes, it's best to give an amount that doesn't end with zero. For example, it'd be better to give ¥88 instead of ¥90 even though you'd be giving them extra money for two reasons: eight is a lucky number so it's better to use it as much as possible and 90 ends in zero which is unlucky.

4 (sì; 四) is the most unlucky number mainly because it sounds like the word death (sǐ; 死). It's best to avoid using the number four whenever logically possible and you won't see it in many elevators.

The number 4 is omitted in some Chinese buildings.

Internet & Phone Access

Internet Access

Hotels

Most mid-range and high-end hotels provide wired broadband internet access for guests with their own laptops, though there may be a daily fee (it tends to be more expensive in the fancier hotels). Many hotels and almost all hostels will have wireless internet free of charge, but sometimes it's only available in common areas like the lobby. In youth hostels you often find a PC or two in the lobby either for free or for a small hourly fee.

Wifi cafes

More and more people are choosing to travel with their laptops, and a café with wireless internet can be a good place to have a quick lunch and check your email. Beijing is full of Western-style cafes and bars that offer wifi, especially in popular expat zones like Gulou, Sanlitun and Wudaokou. You'll know you're on the right track when you see a small "wifi" sticker in the window or notice that many of the patrons are on their laptops.

Internet cafes

If you're not traveling with a computer, internet cafes are an easy way to get online. They might not be obvious at first, but once you keep an eye out for the characters 网吧 (wǎngbā, or internet café) you'll start seeing them all over town. (You can remember the characters easily because the wǎng looks like a net). These cafes can be dark and smoky, but they offer PCs for public use at a cheap rate of ¥3-6 per hour (US$0.5-1). The price may vary depending on when you visit, and they're often open 24 hours. You'll need to provide your passport before getting web access, and the café may hold on to it until you're ready to leave. Be aware that your visit may be monitored in one way or another. Your picture may be taken at the front desk before you're given a card with a user number and password that you use to log in. One caution: if you're hoping to be able to print something out, make copies, or burn a CD, internet cafes aren't your best option. They tend to cater to gamers and online-chatters and probably won't be set up to provide these services. Try a Kodak Express store instead, the chain is quite common throughout Beijing.

Censorship & VPNs (Virtual Private Networks)

No matter how you're getting online in China, surfing the web will be different than it is in your home country. You may or may not feel like the connection is slower than you're used to, but you'll definitely notice that many of your favorite sites are not accessible: Facebook, YouTube, Twitter, Flickr, Blogspot, Wordpress, Wikipedia (sometimes), The New York Times, and many more. Because of a spat between Google and the Chinese government in 2010, Google products like Gmail and Google Search can be unreliable. Unfortunately, these blocked sites are useful for travelers for keeping in touch with friends and family, keeping up with the news back home, organizing pictures, or writing blog updates.

Internet censorship in China is a government operation. Some sites may be blocked for political reasons – they may include content that is not favorable to the Chinese government. In other cases, Chinese websites lobby the government to block their international counterparts so that they can corner the domestic market. Whatever the reasons, this so-called "Great Firewall" is inconvenient and upsetting to travelers who are used to complete internet freedom. For some, the best solution is just to put away the computer and enjoy a trip spent offline. But for those who prefer or need to access the web freely, there is a relatively simple solution: Virtual Private Networks, or VPNs.

Simply put, a VPN is a program that allows you to hop over the Great Firewall by connecting to a proxy server outside of Mainland China, which allows you to access the internet as if you were in that location instead of in Beijing. Ironically, the websites for VPN providers are often blocked in China, so if you're determined to use one, it's smart to set it up before you leave home. Some reliable and popular VPN providers include **Astrill** (astrill.com, from $29.95 for 3 months), **StrongVPN** (strongvpn.com, from $21.00 for 3 months), and **Witopia** (witopia.net).

Telephone Access

Public phones

You may have a phone in your room if you're staying at a hotel or hostel. Local calls are usually free, but long-distance and international ones can be quite pricey. Check with the staff for rates before you start dialing. When you're out and about in the city, public phones are everywhere, and you can usually make calls from newspaper stands and small hole-in-the-wall shops for less than ¥1. Look for a China Unicom or China Mobile sign. There are also pay phones in many locations, but they take phone cards, not change.

Mobile phones

You may be able to use the mobile phone you use in your home country, unless it has been locked by your network (check with your phone company before you go, if your phone is locked, you can buy an inexpensive cell phone here for about ¥200-300). Either way, you'll need to purchase a local SIM card. These can be found in China Unicom and China Mobile outlets all over town, as well as in many grocery stores and some convenience stores. A SIM card will set you back between ¥40 and ¥100, usually with ¥50 of credit to start. When your initial credit runs out, you can recharge your minutes with credit-charging cards that you can buy practically on every corner.

Phone cards

No matter what phone you're calling from, phone cards offer the cheapest rates. There are two kinds of phone cards you should be aware of: IC cards and IP cards. You can buy both of these cards in convenience stores, newspaper stands, supermarkets, hotel lobbies, and other retail outlets throughout China. The Chinese word for "card" is *kǎ* (卡), so ask for an IC or IP *kǎ*, but note that they often only work in the region/province of purchase and also have an expiration date.

IC (Integrated Circuit) cards: These are prepaid cards you can use to make calls from payphones.

IP (Internet Phone) cards: For international calls on a mobile phone or a hotel phone, use one of these. IP cards offer a rate of ¥1.8 per minute to the United States and Canada and ¥3.2 to all other countries. Domestic long-distance calls are ¥0.3 per minute. IP cards usually work like a calling card in the West – you dial a number and input a PIN before dialing. Your card will have dialing instructions on the back side, and English-language service is usually available.

Dialing

To make an international call from China, dial: 00 + country code + area/region code + phone number.

International country dialing codes:

US & Canada: 1
China: 86
Macau: 853
UK: 44
Australia: 61
Hong Kong: 852
New Zealand: 64
Taiwan: 886

Area/Region calling codes:

Beijing: 10
Chengdu: 28
Fuzhou: 591
Guilin: 773
Hefei: 551
Kunming: 871
Nanchang: 791
Shanghai: 21
Shenzhen: 755
Urumqi: 991
Xiamen: 592
Changsha: 731
Chongqing: 23
Guangzhou: 20
Hangzhou: 571
Ji'nan: 531
Lhasa: 891
Nanjing: 25
Shenyang: 24
Tianjin: 22
Wuhan: 27
Xi'an: 29

Traveling with Kids

Let's face it, taking your kids to China isn't quite like packing up the minivan and driving to Disney World. But if the thought of long international flights, unfamiliar foods, crazy traffic and rumors of stifling air pollution weren't enough to deter you from visiting Beijing with kids, congratulations! You'll find that not only is it cleaner and safer than what you've heard, it's a fascinating and in some ways uniquely kid-friendly destination. Thanks in part to the country's One Child Policy, the Chinese shower attention on children, and in all likelihood, you and your family will be happily accommodated wherever you go (and maybe asked to pose for more pictures than a celebrity on the red carpet).

But what does the city even offer for kids to do? In this section, we'll first highlight some kid-pleasing Beijing attractions, and then get into common concerns and how you can best prepare for a worry-free trip.

Kid-Friendly Attractions

You don't necessarily need to tailor your entire itinerary to your kids. Many of Beijing's sights are visually exciting and offer huge open spaces for kids to run around and explore. But some won't appreciate the nuances of architecture or history the same way you will, and after a few days boredom might become an issue. The key to successfully touring Beijing with kids is to balance out the more adult-centric visits with something that the kids will love. For example, spend a few hours exploring the famous and historically rich Forbidden City as a family, then zip over to Beihai Park, just one block north, to rent colorful paddleboats and relax on an imperial lake. Everybody wins.

Another strategy is to keep your visits to the big sights short and simple. Take the Temple of Heaven: it's a gorgeous site where the emperors would make sacrifices to the heavens, but it might look pretty darn familiar to a kid who's already seen the Forbidden City. When visiting a site, do a tiny bit of research to choose one thing that your kids will get a kick out of, then check it out and leave. At the Temple of Heaven, for example, there's a special echo wall surrounding the Imperial Vault. It's 193 m (633 ft) in circumference, and if you stand at one side and whisper then the person on the opposite side can clearly hear it. Kids love it!

Your kids may surprise you with their ability to take interest in what they observe in a foreign culture. But for those temper tantrum moments when you really need a kid-oriented activity, check out one of the sites below.

Water Cube – When Beijing hosted the 2008 Olympics, the Water Cube, also known as the National Aquatics Center, was home to the swimming and synchronized swimming events. Swimmers at the Water Cube broke 25 world records that summer. After the Olympics, half of the stadium was converted into a water park with a wave pool, lazy river, spa area and 13 water slides and rides, including the Bullet Bowl, Speed Slide and Tornado. It's a little on the pricey side, but kids will have a blast. Once they're tired out, you can wander the Olympic grounds nearby and see the iconic "Bird's Nest" stadium.

> Hours: 10:00 – 22:00, tickets sold between 9:00 and 20:30.
> Admission: ¥200 for adults, ¥160 for kids
> Website: www.water-cube.com/en

For address, transportation and more info, please see page 129.

Chaoyang Park – There's a ton for kids to do in this expansive park on the east side of town. Kids can play in the big grassy fields and fly a kite in the free kite flying zone, and there's a range of boating options, a big merry-go-round, a roller coaster, bumper cars, sky swings and several large inflatable castles. On top of all this, the Sony Explora Science Museum is also located in the park. The lovely northwestern section of the park includes a lake, flower beds and grassy areas where families can enjoy a picnic. You can't beat the price.

> Hours: daily 6:00 – 22:00 (last entry at 21:00)
> Admission: ¥5

For address, transportation and more info, please see page 171.

Cooking classes for kids – Several venues in Beijing have noticed the demand for Chinese cooking classes for adults and created safe and fun versions for kids.

Usually, children as young as four can participate in the fun since the ingredients are all carefully chopped up and prepared beforehand, so all the kids have to do is join in. It's a great way to be exposed to Chinese culture in a more hands-on way. Check the Hutong (thehutong.com), and China Culture Center (chinaculturecenter.org) for the most up-to-date schedules if you think your little chef would enjoy it.

Beijing Aquarium and Zoo – Situated within the Beijing Zoo complex, this world class aquarium is home to a huge array of wonderful fish. There's also a shark tank, Amazonian Rainforest with piranhas, coral reefs, and a marine mammal section with dolphin and seal performances throughout the day. The aquarium gets high marks from visitors for its engaging displays and overall bright, clean feeling. The adjacent Beijing Zoo has a wide variety of animals, including the giant panda, the golden monkey, the white-lipped deer, the red-crowned crane, and many rare animals from other parts of the world. In contrast to the aquarium, many visitors find that the zoo is not up to Western standards and is not worth a lot of time, but checking out the giant pandas is at least worth a stop.

> Hours: 9:00-17:30 (Apr-Oct); 10:00 – 16:30 (Nov- Mar)
> Admission: ¥130 for adults
> Children below 1.2 m (3.9 ft) are free

Visitors who pay for the admission fee to the aquarium will also receive an entrance ticket for the Beijing Zoo and Panda Hall.

For address, transportation and more info, please see page 155.

Rickshaws through the hutongs – Central Beijing is home to an ever-decreasing number of ancient alleyways called hutongs. These narrow streets and their traditional courtyard homes represent a way of life that has mostly disappeared in Beijing, replaced by high-rise apartment buildings and big traffic-filled streets. Although the hutongs are rapidly being gentrified, developed, and torn down, there's still plenty to see, and you can really get an amazing glimpse of daily life. To make exploring the neighborhood more interesting for kids, you can hire a rickshaw – a bicycle with a big two-person seat on the back – to zip you around. You can try your hand at hiring a rickshaw by yourself but be prepared to negotiate hard or ask your hotel or hostel about arranging a formal rickshaw tour.

> Price: Varies
> Location: A good place to start exploring the hutongs is around the Drum and Bell Towers around the Gulou metro station.

Kung fu or acrobatics show – See page 188 for more information on the Chaoyang Acrobatic Show and the Legend of Kung Fu. Kids will be in awe of the performers, and it's a nice low-energy activity for when you're tired of walking.

The Great Wall – The Great Wall of China is a must while in Beijing with kids. Mutianyu is one of the best sections to visit with your children since it is the longest fully restored section of the wall that is open to visitors and has 22 watch towers. Your teenagers will love the cable car ride up and the optional toboggan ride down. Young children can still ride in a double toboggan with a parent. Older kids might enjoy the 10 km (6 mi) hike from Jinshanling to Simatai. There is even a zip line ride at Simatai to speed the way down. You might even choose to go the extra mile and plan a camping trip on the Great Wall. Several tour operators offer packages that provide all the hiking and camping gear you need to spend a night under the stars on the Wall.

See our section on the Great Wall (pg 50) for more details on how to get to various parts of the Wall. For camping, see Distractions (pg 263).

Beijing World Park – This undoubtedly cheesey attraction is nevertheless an awesome daytrip for kids. The Beijing World Park is a theme park with miniature replicas of famous landmarks from around the world. Haven't been to the Taj Mahal, Great Pyramids of Giza, or the leaning tower of Pisa yet? Check out the park and decide where your next family vacation will lead you.

> Hours: 8:00-17:00 (Apr 15-Oct 31); 8:00-16:30 (Nov 1-Apr 14)
> Admission: ¥65 per adult and ¥24 for children

For address, transportation and more info, please see page 160.

Before You Go: How to Prepare

Time your trip wisely. Travel during Chinese holidays? Forget about it. China's 1.4 billion people all seem to travel at the same time: during Lunar New Year every January or February, and during the National Day holiday in October. Lines for tourist attractions can stretch on for hours. Train stations are a mess. Adults can deal with it, but children may not be able to. Do consider visiting in the spring or fall, when extreme weather is less likely to be a factor. Bundling kids up to face the cold every time you go out will be a hassle, and likewise, the summer heat and humidity can sap the little ones' energy.

Get healthy before you go. Try to ensure that everyone is getting their vitamins and is in good shape before you embark on a long trip. If you're already prone to illness, twelve hours on a packed airplane can do you in.

Prepare in advance for medical issues. Check with your pediatrician or travel clinic to see if kids need extra vaccines or anti-malaria pills, depending on the exact destination. Many pharmacy staples that are easily available in your home town are tough to find in China, so pack accordingly. Also note emergency contacts for a major hospital – preferably an international one – in each destination city.

Examples of good things to bring include oral hydrating salts or electrolyte solution, hand sanitizer, Aspirin or Tylenol (whatever anti-fever/pain meds you usually use), anti-itch cream, hydrocortisone cream, Benadryl syrup, and children's sunscreen and mosquito repellent.

Figure out what to bring with you and what to buy in Beijing. It's smart to bring your own infant formula when traveling anywhere abroad, since switching brands suddenly can upset a baby's stomach. But if your luggage is lost or you run out while in China, don't panic, family doctors in Beijing regularly advise their patients that buying international brands such as Nestlé, Similac and Enfamil is safe. Ditto for diapers; unless your baby is very sensitive or has particular needs, you'll find imported diapers with little trouble in Beijing. Plus, many brands have Chinese counterparts, like Huggies and Pampers. They're not exactly like the ones back home, but are pretty much OK.

As for food, if your kid is picky, you're better off bringing his or her favorite snacks with you, as they might be hard to find and be expensive here. If your kid is a little more easygoing, there's a wide range of treats that they'll probably love. Heinz brand baby food is widely available, though the flavors may be a little unfamiliar. If you're looking for no-sugar-added or organic baby food, better to pack it with you. There's a wide variety of safe bottled water brands to give to kids or mix with formula, and a brand called Great Lakes makes 100% apple, orange and tomato juice that is widely available in small bottles and sometimes juice boxes.

Learn a little bit about Beijing before you leave. Rent movies that take place in China and watch the newspaper and TV for stories from Beijing. Have your kids think up questions they have about China and try to find the answers on Google. Basically, anything you can do to build excitement and curiosity for the trip will pay off.

Try to pick up a few phrases in Mandarin. Becoming fluent is obviously not a reasonable short-term goal, but learning a few key words can be fun. You might even find a Chinese language camp or class in your neighborhood that your kids could take before you go. Children pick up new languages much more easily than adults, and they might surprise you! An adorable 7-year-old with a few phrases in Chinese is an excellent bargaining tool in the markets of Beijing.

Give Chinese food a test run. The good news is that most Chinese restaurants have kid-friendly choices: it's hard to go wrong with pork dumplings or fried rice. But it's smart to hit up a few Chinese spots in your town before the trip. You'll find that Western Chinese food doesn't necessarily resemble Chinese food in Beijing, but it's a good warm-up for your kids' taste buds and can help them feel more adventurous.

Pack comfort food. Comfort food can turn a bad day into an incredible one. Stash some of your kid's favorites to keep them satisfied throughout the day. Comfort food also comes in handy since your child may not be accustomed to real Chinese food.

Time to Travel: The Flight

Time your flight wisely to maximize sleep. It's bound to be a grueling overnight flight to Beijing, but you can try to minimize the disruption to your kids' sleep schedules by choosing a flight that leaves later in the evening, when they're likely to be asleep anyway.

Check in early to select good seats. Online check-in becomes available 24 hours before departure, so make a point of logging on to check in and choose your family's seats. Try to avoid sitting near the restrooms, where a lot of foot traffic and doors opening and closing can disturb sleep. The ultimate score for traveling with kids is to be seated in the bulkhead, the row of seats with nothing in front but a wall. There's more legroom (or crawl room) and you won't have to worry about your kids kicking the seat in front of them.

Use the time to read about China. Reading about where you're going when you're actually on your way only adds to the excitement. Whether you choose our guidebooks, history books, or even Chinese children's stories in English, books can provide hours of entertainment while passing along tons of history.

Go high-tech. Even if you try to limit your kids' use of electronics at home, now is not the time to take away the DVDs or the Game Boy. You can confiscate the gadgets once you land and only pull them out again on long bus rides or for the flight home. Older kids might even have homework they need to keep up with if you're traveling during the school year, and the flight is a perfect opportunity to take care of it.

Bring snacks. A must to quell hunger pangs when no meal is in sight, or simply to keep them distracted. Don't forget to stay hydrated during the flight, even if it means getting up more often to use the bathroom. Getting up to stretch your legs is beneficial anyway.

On the Ground: Once You've Arrived

Treat jet lag with patience. The first three nights are the most difficult, and the second night is probably the worst. The best advice is to take it slow and sleep when they do. This might mean slowing down your sightseeing activities for the first couple of days. Don't push everyone too hard. There's a lot to see in Beijing, but you can't see it all in two weeks anyway. The time difference is a big adjustment, especially for little ones. Being tired and run down can lead to sickness, so make sure everyone gets rest and try to adjust slowly to the time difference.

Hope for the best, plan for the worst. Give your child a filled out copy of our Emergency Card (pg 39).

Don't leave home without tissues. Toilet paper is not provided in most bathrooms, and you never know when you'll need it. Likewise for Kleenex when you need to blow your nose or wipe your hands.

Plan for toilet drama. If you stay in nicer hotels and restaurants in Beijing, you may never see a squat toilet. But odds are you'll encounter one eventually. See our toilets section (pg 307) for more information on how to make using a squat toilet a relatively painless experience. Odds are, small children probably won't care, though older kids might.

Keep hands clean. That's good advice for all the travelers in your group, no matter their age. Bring along hand sanitizer and wet wipes (wipes are readily available in China too). Wash your hands and your kids' hands whenever you get a chance – it'll go a long way toward keeping you healthy.

Be prepared to face the paparazzi. This is less true in Beijing, where foreigners are a more regular sight, but foreign kids can attract a lot of attention in China. Notions of personal space are different than what you're used to. Some people might try to touch or pick your baby up. If you'd rather they didn't, just be polite and firm.

Watch the traffic. See our culture shock section (pg 318) for more information on how to be a safe pedestrian in Beijing. It's extremely important to keep an eye on little ones when you're out and about, and little kids will be better off in an infant carrier, in your arms, or in a stroller. It's not a good place to learn how to walk.

Use common sense with food and drink. See our food safety section (pg 305) for more information on how to stay safe (and full) during your visit.

Engage your kids in their cultural surroundings. Take the time to point out cultural differences that you notice and explain the reasons behind them. With a little guidance, kids tend to appreciate them rather than becoming grossed out or upset. Remember that it's good to get out of your comfort zone, no matter how old you are.

Hot Topics

Beijing on a Budget

The cost of living in Beijing has shot up in recent years, so it's not really the dirt-cheap destination that it once was. If you keep to a very tight budget, you can get by on about US$30 per day. And if money is no object, you'll find plenty of ways to spend it. Prices for transportation and attractions are pretty fixed, so the wiggle room in your budget comes from accommodation and food. Below, we've created three sample budgets for a day in Beijing visiting the Forbidden City and Beihai Park.

What you'll spend during your trip

	Pinching pennies	Middle of the road	Spare no expense
Hostel room	A dorm-style hostel room: ¥50	A private room at a hostel: ¥200	A high-end hotel room: ¥500
Breakfast	Baozi on the street: ¥8	Coffee and muffin at café: ¥40	The hotel's Western buffet: ¥150
Souvenirs at Forbidden City			¥80
Subway to Forbidden City	¥2	¥2	
Forbidden City ticket	¥60	¥60	¥60
Guide		Forbidden City audio guide: ¥40	Guided tour to Forbidden City with bus pickup: ¥250
Lunch	Noodle lunch: ¥15	Noodle lunch: ¥15	Three-course lunch in local restaurant: ¥100
Bottle of water	¥3	¥3	¥3
Walk to Beihai Park	¥0	¥0	¥0
Beihai entrance ticket	¥5	¥5	¥5
Renting a paddleboat at Beihai		¥50/30 minutes	¥50/30 minutes
Taxi to dinner		¥15	¥15
Dinner	Walk to dinner at a local restaurant: ¥30	At a Yunnan restaurant: ¥90	At an upscale Sichuan restaurant in Sanlitun: ¥300
One cocktail at a bar		¥40	¥200
Buy a few beers at a corner store and sit outside people-watching	¥8		
Back to hostel	Subway: ¥2	Taxi: ¥15	Taxi: ¥15
TOTAL	¥183 or US$29.80	¥575 or US$93.65	¥1,668 or US$271.70

Tips for saving money

Beijing is a great city to visit if you're on a budget. From playing badminton in a public park to grabbing a stool and enjoying a beer and some *chuan'er* on the sidewalk, much of the city's charm is available for free or almost free. If you're trying to see Beijing without breaking the bank, here are some general rules and tips for maximizing your money.

Accommodation

You want to have a safe and clean place to lay your head at the end of the day. But if you're really getting the most out of Beijing, your hotel will just be a place to crash and rest up for the next exciting day. If you're trying to cut costs, start here: the city is full of decent, reasonably priced hostels, and as a bonus, you can meet other travelers and exchange stories and information.

Skip cabs, bike or subway instead

Cabs are a bargain here compared to what they cost back home, but get too reliant on them and you'll break your budget, not to mention spend a lot of time sitting in traffic. The subway only costs ¥2, and renting a bike, though it's not free, is a great way of seeing the city while getting where you want to go.

Skip tour guides

Generally speaking, you get what you pay for when it comes to tour packages and tour guides. That means that if you have money to drop, you could end up with a knowledgeable, hardworking and honest tour guide who takes your sightseeing to the next level, but it also means that if you go cheap, you might end up with a dubious or disinterested tour guide who doesn't add much at all. If you're trying to save money, this is a good place to skimp.

Nothing imported

Your trip to Beijing is not a great time to develop a taste for cheese or high-end microbrews. While both are available here, like all imported products and products targeted at Western tastes, they'll cost you dearly. Indulging once in a while is one thing, but you'll save money and have a more authentic experience if you eat and drink like the locals.

Mandarin Phrasebook

Introduction

Chinese is one of the world's oldest and most unique languages. Though Chinese actually has a vast number of languages and dialects, it's the nationally standardized Mandarin dialect of Pǔtōnghuà (普通话) – which is based off of the Beijing dialect – that you will mostly encounter in Beijing. Putonghua is currently the official language of the People's Republic of China, Taiwan and Singapore, and is widely spoken in Hong Kong, Macau, Thailand, Malaysia and Indonesia. Since many in the PRC still don't speak fluent English, knowing a bit of Mandarin will most certainly make your trip much easier, so it's recommended to remember some key phrases and characters. But before you start memorizing countless strokes and confusing tones, there are a few other things about the language that are worth noting.

You may have already learned some of the following facts from our Language section in the Overview, but we'll go ahead and refresh your memory. First, more than one billion people, or roughly 12.5% of the world's population, speak Mandarin as their native tongue. It is therefore the most widely spoken language (in terms of native speakers) in the world today. Second, although there are more than 80,000 Chinese characters, most of them are not commonly used. Nonetheless, you still need to know about 5,000 to fully comprehend a newspaper, while an educated Chinese person knows more than 6,000. Third, Mandarin is a tonal language with four distinct tones and there's one neutral tone. Since many of the words in Mandarin sound alike, the only way to differentiate them is with tones. For example, if you say the word "ma," it can mean either mother (pronounced mā in the first tone) or horse (pronounced mǎ in the third tone); it's quite easy to call your dear mother a horse! Fourth, though most Chinese speak Mandarin, accents and dialects vary greatly from province to province and even village to village, making it extremely difficult to understand those with different regional dictions. Many times locals in different areas even speak local languages, like Cantonese in Hong Kong, which is a separate language from Mandarin and unintelligible to Chinese who are not natives of that particular province or city. Fifth, with so many twisting tones and a never ending list of characters, Mandarin is considered by many linguistic experts to be one of the hardest languages for a native English speaker to learn.

But wait, there's more. You'd still better be careful when speaking Mandarin since your meaning may not always translate well into the ears of native speakers. One expat with little knowledge of Mandarin traveled to the coast with his Chinese colleagues to watch the incoming high tide. Upon seeing the rushing current, his colleagues asked, "What do you think of the tide?" He responded, "I've never experienced such a high tide (gāocháo) before." He used the correct translation of *gāo* which means "high" and *cháo* which means "tide," but the crowd went silent followed by a long moment of awkwardness. After asking a Chinese friend, he discovered that the words *gāocháo* (高潮) when put together literally mean "orgasm," not "high tide," which should be pronounced as *dàcháo* (大潮), or "big tide." This man had told every single one of his colleagues that he had never experienced such an orgasm before!

Another traveler in a restaurant wanted to know how much for a bowl of dumplings, so he asked, *"Xiǎojiě, shuìjiào yīwǎn duōshǎo qián?"* The humiliated waitress ran away with her face planted in her hands. He later discovered that although his words were 100% correct, his tones were off. Instead of saying, "Miss, how much is one bowl of dumplings?" which should be pronounced *"Xiǎojiě, shuǐjiǎo yīwǎn duōshǎo qián?"* he asked the waitress, "Miss, how much does it cost for one night?" The waitress was mortified because he used two fourth tones in *shuìjiào*, which means "to sleep," instead of two third tones in *shuĭjiăo*, which means "dumplings." To make matters more difficult, the words *yīwăn* mean both "one night" (一晚) and "one bowl" (一碗) even though they are two different characters.

There are also other nuances in Chinese that can be confusing for the foreigner. When one fellow we know first got to China, he went to a bar and realized that bar tenders kept calling him *shuàigē* (帅哥), which means "handsome guy." He even checked the dictionary to make sure he understood them correctly, which he did. At first he had quite a nice confidence boost, but he soon noticed that not only were both men and women calling him handsome guy, they were also saying it to everyone else at the bar. Furthermore, all the waiters and waitresses were calling the women customers *měinǚ* (美 女), which means "beautiful woman." Despite the compliments he thought he was receiving, his confidence deflated when he discovered that "handsome man" and "beautiful woman" are common flattery terms loosely used to address someone you don't know, not to indicate how physically attractive one is.

Since it takes years of practice to master one of the world's most difficult languages, don't be discouraged if you embarrass yourself a couple of times, because it's going to happen at some point during your Mandarin career. For the beginner, we've provided some useful information, words and phrases to help get you around town.

Pronunciation

There are four tones and one neutral tone in Mandarin (see the diagram to the right). The first tone is high and flat (e.g. 妈 or mā for "mother"), as if you're singing a single note. The second tone starts at a middle pitch and rises to high (e.g. 麻 or má for "hemp"), as in a question like "Really?" The third tone starts low, dips even lower and then slightly rises (e.g. 马 or mă for "horse"). The fourth tone starts high and rapidly shoots to down (e.g. 骂 or mà for the verb "to scold"), as if you're giving a command to your dog (like "Sit!"). The fifth tone is neutral and pronounced without any intonation (e.g. 吗 or ma used as a question tag). Although tones are extremely important and can change the entire meaning of your sentence, sometimes the native speakers will be able to understand what you mean even if your tones are atrocious.

Pinyin

Pinyin is the romanized alphabetical system used for Chinese, and it's a great tool for foreigners learning how to pronounce a character. Many letters are pronounced the same way they are in English and the tonal markings (see the diagram below) are placed over the vowel in every syllable to indicate one of the four tones. Listed below is the phonetic guide for pinyin letters.

Vowels
a – as in "father"
ai – as in "aisle"
ao – as in "now"
e – as in "her"
ei – as in "weight"
i – as in "see"
ian – as in "yen"
ie – as in "yeah"
o – as in "more"
ou – as in "oh"
u – as in "flute"
ui – as in "spray"
uo – as in "whoa"
yu - as in "new"
ü – as in "new" but with closed lips

Consonants
The consonants *b, ch, d, f, hard g, h, j, k, l, m, n, p, s, sh, t, w,* and *y* are all pronounced the same as they are in English.

However, there are several exceptions:
z – as in the "ds" in "suds"
c – as in the "ts" in "bits"
q – as in the "ch" in "chase" but with tongue touching the teeth
x – a combination of the English pronunciation of "s" and "ch"
zh – as in the "dge" in "judge"

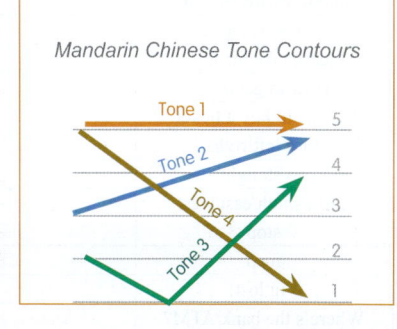

Mandarin Chinese Tone Contours

Basic Phrases

English	Pinyin	Chinese
Hello!	Nǐhǎo!	你好!
Goodbye!	Zàijiàn!	再见!
How are you?	Nǐhǎo ma?	你好吗?
I'm fine, and you?	Wǒ hěnhǎo, Nǐ ně?	我很好，你呢?
Excuse me (When speaking)…	Qǐngwèn…	请问……
Excuse me (When passing through)	Láojià…	劳驾……
I'm sorry.	Duìbùqǐ.	对不起。
Yes.	Shì.	是。
No.	Búshì.	不是。
Please!	Qǐng!	请!
Thank you!	Xièxiè!	谢谢!
You're welcome!	Bùkèqi!	不客气。
What's your name?	Nǐ jiào shénmē míngzi?	你叫什么名字?
My name is…	Wǒ jiào…	我叫……
Nice to meet you!	Jiàndào nǐ hěn gāoxìng!	见到你很高兴!
I (can't) speak Chinese.	Wǒ (bù) huì shuō zhōngwén.	我（不）会说中文。
I (don't) understand.	Wǒ (bù) míng bái.	我（不）明白。
Can you speak English?	Nǐ huì shuō Yīngyǔ ma?	你会说英语吗?
I (don't) want…	Wǒ (bù) yào…	我（不）要……
I like…	Wǒ xǐhuān…	我喜欢……
I don't like…	Wǒ bù xǐhuān…	我不喜欢……
Do you have…?	Nǐ yǒu méiyǒu?	你有没有……?
I don't know.	Wǒ bùzhīdào.	我不知道。
No problem!	Méi wèntí!	没问题!
Good (morning/evening)!	(Zǎoshang/Wǎnshang) hǎo!	(早上/晚上）好!
Good night!	Wǎn'ān!	晚安!
See you soon.	Yīhuì'er jiàn.	一会儿见。
See you tomorrow.	Míngtiān jiàn!	明天见!

Travel, Transport & Directions

taxi	chūzūchē	出租车
train/train station	huǒchē /huǒchēzhàn	火车 / 火车站
bus/ bus stop	gōngjiāo /gōngjiāozhàn	公交 / 公交站
airplane/ airport	fēijī /jīchǎng	飞机 / 机场
car	qìchē	汽车
metro/metro station	dìtiě /dìtiě zhàn	地铁 / 地铁站
Where is the…	…zài nǎ lǐ?	……在哪里?
Please take me to…	Qǐng dài wǒ qù…	请带我去……
How to get to…	…zěn me zǒu ?	……怎么走?
I'd like to buy a ticket.	Wǒ xiǎng mǎi piào.	我想买票。
turn left/right	zǒu zhuǎn /yòu zhuǎn	走转 / 右转
go straight	zhí zǒu	直走
north/south/east/west	běi /nán /dōng /xī	北 / 南 / 东 / 西
stop	tíng	停
map	dì tú	地图
I'm lost!	Wǒ mí lù le!	我迷路了!
Where's the bank/ATM?	Yínháng zài nǎlǐ ?	银行在哪里?

Famous Dishes

hot and sour shredded potato	suān là tǔdòu sī	酸辣土豆丝
stir fried bean curd with chili	mápó dòufǔ	麻婆豆腐
tomato and egg soup	xīhóngshì jīdàn tāng	西红柿鸡蛋汤
kung pao chicken	gōngbǎo jīdīng	宫保鸡丁
stir fried pork	dōngpō ròu	东坡肉
double cooked pork slices	huíguō ròu	回锅肉
sweet and sour pork	tángcù lǐjǐ	糖醋里脊
steamed stuffed bun	bāozi	包子
thin pancake	jiānbǐng	煎饼
wonton	húntún	馄饨
dumpling	jiǎozi	饺子
steamed rice	mǐfàn	米饭
fried rice	chǎofàn	炒饭
BBQ	shāokǎo	烧烤
deep fried breadstick	yóutiáo	油条
kebab	ròuchuàn	肉串
hot pot	huǒguō	火锅
noodles	miàn	面
fried noodles	chǎomiàn	炒面

Shopping

supermarket	chāoshì	超市
shop/store	shāngdiàn	商店
Where is the nearest store?	Zuìjìn de shāngdiàn zài nàlǐ?	最近的商店在哪里?
Where can I buy…?	Zài nàlǐ kěyǐ mǎi…?	在哪里可以买……?
How much is this?	Zhègè duōshǎo qián?	这个多少钱?
Too expensive!	Tài guì le!	太贵了!
I want it cheaper.	Wǒ yào piányí yīdiǎn.	我要便宜一点。
Can you give me a discount?	Nǐ kěyǐ dǎzhé ma?	你可以打折吗?
No, I really don't want it.	Bù, wǒ zhēnde bùyào.	不，我真的不要。
OK, I'll buy it.	Hǎode, wǒ yào mǎi.	好的，我要买。
clothing	fúzhuāng	服装
furniture	jiājù	家具
art	yìshù	艺术
bicycle	zìxíngchē	自行车
jewelry	zhūbǎo	珠宝

Question Words

Who?	Shuí?	谁?
What?	Shénme?	什么?
Where?	Nàlǐ?	哪里?
When/What time?	Shénme shíhòu?	什么时候?
Why?	Wèishén me?	为什么?
How?	Zěnme?	怎么?

Restaurant & Bar

I don't eat (peanuts).	Wǒ bù chī (huāshēng).	我不吃（花生）。
What's your specialty?	Nǐmen de tèsè shì shénme?	你们的特色是什么？
What do you recommend?	Nǐ tuījiàn shénmē?	你推荐什么？
Table for (two/four)	liǎng wèi / sì wèi	两位 / 四位
Waiter, check please!	Fúwùyuán, mǎidān!	服务员，买单！
Cheers!	Gānbēi!	干杯！
one bottle of (beer/water)	yīpíng (píjiǔ / shuǐ)	一瓶（啤酒 / 水）
breakfast	zǎofàn	早饭
lunch	zhōngfàn	中饭
dinner	wǎnfàn	晚饭
knife	dāo	刀
fork	chā	叉
spoon	sháo	勺
chopsticks	kuàizi	筷子
bowl	wǎn	碗
glass	bēizi	杯子
menu	càidān	菜单
I don't want it spicy.	Bù yào là.	不要辣。
I want it very spicy!	Wǒ yào hěn là!	我要很辣！
restaurant/bar	cāntīng / jiǔbā	餐厅 / 酒吧

Emergency

Leave me alone!	Bùyào dǎrǎo wǒ!	不要打扰我！
I don't want it.	Wǒ bùyào.	我不要。
Don't touch me.	Bùyào pèng wǒ!	不要碰我
Call the police!	Jiào jǐngchá ba!	叫警察吧！
Thief!	Xiǎotōu!	小偷！
It's an emergency!	Jǐnjí qíngkuàng!	紧急情况！
Call a doctor!	Jiào yīshēng ba!	叫医生吧！
I've been injured.	Wǒ shòushāng le.	我受伤了。
Help!	Jiùmìng!	救命！

Accommodation

hotel	jiǔdiàn / bīn'guǎn	酒店 / 宾馆
hostel	qīngnián lǚshè	青年旅舍
room	fángjiān	房间
single room	dānrén jiān	单人间
double room	shuāngrén jiān	双人间
dormitory	duōrén jiān (sùshè)	多人间（宿舍）
deposit	yājīn	押金
(private/public) bathroom	(sīrén / gōnggòng) yùshì / cèsuǒ	（私人 / 公共）浴室 / 厕所
I would like to check in.	Wǒ yào dēngjì.	我要登记。
I would like to check out.	Wǒ yào tuìfáng.	我要退房。
I have a reservation.	Wǒ yǒu yùdìng.	我有预订。

Drink

beer	píjiǔ	啤酒
coffee	kāfēi	咖啡
(green/black) tea	(lǜ / hóng) chá	（绿／红）茶
(hot/cold) water	(kāi / bīng) shuǐ	（开／冰）水
(orange) juice	(chéng) zhī	（橙）汁
milk	niúnǎi	牛奶
(red/white) wine	(hóng / bái) pútáo jiǔ	（红／白）葡萄酒
Chinese liquor	báijiǔ	白酒
cola	kělè	可乐
soy milk	dòujiāng	豆浆

Telephone & Internet

Where is the internet café?	Nǎlǐ yǒu wǎngba?	哪里有网吧？
Can I make a (international) call?	Wǒ kěyǐ dǎ (guójì) diànhuà ma?	我可以打（国际）电话吗？
How much is it for one hour?	Yīxiǎoshí duōshǎo qián?	一小时多少钱？
Do you have wi-fi?	Yǒuméiyǒu wúxiàn xìnhào?	有没有无线信号？
telephone number	diànhuà hàomǎ	电话号码
Internet	wǎngluò	网络
cell phone	shǒujī	手机
computer	diànnǎo	电脑

Beijing Popular Sights

Great Wall	Cháng Chéng	长城
Forbidden City	Gù Gōng	故宫
Tian'anmen Square	Tiān'ānmén Guǎngchǎng	天安门广场
Temple of Heaven	Tiān Tán	天坛
Summer Palace	Yíhé Yuán	颐和园
Old Summer Palace	Yuánmíng Yuán	圆明园
hutong	hútóng	胡同
Lama Temple	Yōnghé Gōng	雍和宫
Bell (Drum) Tower	Zhōng (Gǔ) Lóu	钟（鼓）楼
Houhai Lake	Hòu Hǎi	后海
798 Art District	Qījiǔbā Yìshùqū	798艺术区
Pianjiayuan Market	Pānjiāyuán Shìchǎng	潘家园市场
Sanlitun Bar Street	Sānlǐtún Jiǔba Jiē	三里屯酒吧街

Wishes & blessings

Happy birthday!	Shēngrì kuàilè!	生日快乐！
Happy New Year!	Xīnnián kuàilè!	新年快乐！
I love you!	Wǒ ài nǐ!	我爱你！
Good luck!	Zhù nǐ hǎoyùn!	祝你好运！
Have a good trip!	Yīlù shùnfēng!	一路顺风！
Congratulations!	Gōngxǐ!	恭喜！

Numbers

one	yī	一
two	èr	二
three	sān	三
four	sì	四
five	wǔ	五
six	liù	六
seven	qī	七
eight	bā	八
nine	jiǔ	九
ten	shí	十
eleven	shíyī	十一
twelve	shí'èr	十二
thirteen	shísān	十三
fourteen	shísì	十四
fifteen	shíwǔ	十五
sixteen	shíliù	十六
seventeen	shíqī	十七
eighteen	shíbā	十八
nineteen	shíjiǔ	十九
twenty	èrshí	二十
thirty	sānshí	三十
forty	sìshí	四十
fifty	wǔshí	五十
one Hundred	yībǎi	一百
one Thousand	yīqiān	一千
ten Thousand	yīwàn	一万
one Million	yībǎiwàn	一百万

Time / Date

January	yī yuè	一月
February	èr yuè	二月
March	sān yuè	三月
April	sì yuè	四月
May	wǔ yuè	五月
June	liù yuè	六月
July	qī yuè	七月
August	bā yuè	八月
September	jiǔ yuè	九月
October	shí yuè	十月
November	shíyī yuè	十一月
December	shí'èr yuè	十二月
Monday	xīngqī yī	星期一
Tuesday	xīngqī èr	星期二
Wednesday	xīngqī sān	星期三
Thursday	xīngqī sì	星期四
Friday	xīngqī wǔ	星期五
Saturday	xīngqī liù	星期六
Sunday	xīngqī ri / xīngqī tiān	星期日 / 星期天
Yesterday	zuótiān	昨天
Today	jīntiān	今天
Tomorrow	míngtiān	明天
One o'clock	yīdiǎn	一点
Two fifteen	liǎngdiǎn shíwǔ fēn	两点十五分
Three thirty	sān diǎn bàn	三点半
Four forty-five	sìdiǎn sìshiwǔ fēn	四点四十五分
What time is it?	Xiànzài jǐdiǎn?	现在几点?

Signs

Entrance	rùkǒu	入口
Exit	chūkǒu	出口
Open	yíngyè / kāimén	营业 / 开门
Closed	xiēyè / guānmén	歇业 / 关门
Toilets	cèsuǒ	厕所
Man	nán	男
Woman	nǚ	女

Food

chicken	jīròu	鸡肉
beef	niúròu	牛肉
pork	zhūròu	猪肉
duck	yāròu	鸭肉
lamb	yángròu	羊肉
seafood	hǎixiān	海鲜
fish	yú	鱼
fruit	shuǐguǒ	水果
apple	píngguǒ	苹果
banana	xiāngjiāo	香蕉
orange	chéngzi	橙子
mango	mángguǒ	芒果
watermelon	xīguā	西瓜
pineapple	bōluó	菠萝
vegetable	shūcài	蔬菜
green beans	biǎndòu	扁豆
mushroom	mógū	蘑菇
cucumber	huángguā	黄瓜
onion	yángcōng	洋葱
radish	luóbo	萝卜
egg	jīdàn	鸡蛋
tofu	dòufǔ	豆腐
bread	miànbāo	面包
salt	yán	盐
soy sauce	jiàngyóu	酱油
vinegar	cù	醋
sugar	táng	糖
pepper	hújiāofěn	胡椒粉
MSG	wèijīng	味精

Nationality

What country are you from?	Nǐ shì nǎguó rén?	你是哪国人?
I'm from…	Wǒ shì…rén.	我是……人。
America	Měiguó	美国
Canada	Jiānádà	加拿大
Mexico	Mòxīgē	墨西哥
Brazil	Bāxī	巴西
Ireland	Ài'ěrlán	爱尔兰
Great Britain	Yīngguó	英国
Spain	Xībānyá	西班牙
France	Fǎguó	法国
Germany	Déguó	德国
Italy	Yìdàlì	意大利
Sweden	Ruìdiǎn	瑞典
Russia	Éluósī	俄罗斯
Turkey	Tǔ'ěrqí	土耳其
South Africa	Nánfēi	南非
Egypt	Āijí	埃及
India	Yìndù	印度
Australia	Àodàlìyà	澳大利亚
New Zealand	Xīnxīlán	新西兰
Japan	Rìběn	日本
Korea	Hánguó	韩国
Vietnam	Yuènán	越南
Thailand	Tàiguó	泰国
Singapore	Xīnjiāpō	新加坡
Malaysia	Mǎláixīyà	马来西亚

Provinces & Cities

Provinces	Cities
Ānhuī 安徽	Héféi 合肥 ; Huángshān 黄山 ; Wúhú 芜湖
Běijīng 北京	
Chóngqìng 重庆	
Fújiàn 福建	Fúzhōu 福州 ; Xiàmén 厦门 ; Pútián 莆田 ; Quánzhōu 泉州
Gānsù 甘肃	Lánzhōu 兰州 ; Jiāyùguān 嘉峪关
Guǎngdōng 广东	Guǎngzhōu 广州 ; Dōngguǎn 东莞 ; Zhūhǎi 珠海 ; Shēnzhèn 深圳
Guǎngxī 广西	Nánníng 南宁 ; Guìlín 桂林 ; Běihǎi 北海 ; Bǎisè 百色
Guìzhōu 贵州	Guìyáng 贵阳 ; Ānshùn 安顺 ; Zūnyì 遵义
Hǎinán 海南	Hǎikǒu 海口 ; Sānyà 三亚
Héběi 河北	Shíjiāzhuāng 石家庄 ; Chéngdé 承德
Hēilóngjiāng 黑龙江	Hā'ěrbīn 哈尔滨
Hénán 河南	Zhèngzhōu 郑州 ; Kāifēng 开封 ; Luòyáng 洛阳
Hong Kong Xiānggǎng 香港	
Húběi 湖北	Wǔhàn 武汉 ; Jīngzhōu 荆州 ; Yíchāng 宜昌 ; Shénnóngjià 神农架
Húnán 湖南	Chángshā 长沙 ; Xiāngtán 湘潭 ; Zhāngjiājiè 张家界
Inner Mongolia Nèiměnggǔ 内蒙古	Hūhéhàotè 呼和浩特 (Hohhot); Bāotóu 包头 ; Hūlúnbèi'ěr 呼伦贝尔 (Hulunbuir); È'ěrduōsī 鄂尔多斯 (Ordos)
Jiāngsū 江苏	Nánjīng 南京 ; Sūzhōu 苏州 ; Wúxī 无锡 ; Chángzhōu 常州 ; Yángzhōu 扬州
Jiāngxī 江西	Nánchāng 南昌 ; Jǐngdézhèn 景德镇
Jílín 吉林	Chángchūn 长春 ; Yánbiān 延边
Liáoníng 辽宁	Shěnyáng 沈阳 ; Dàlián 大连
Macau Àomén 澳门	
Níngxià 宁夏	Yínchuān 银川
Qīnghǎi 青海	Xīníng 西宁
Shāndōng 山东	Jǐnán 济南 ; Qīngdǎo 青岛 ; Tài'ān 泰安 ; Wéifāng 潍坊 ; Wēihǎi 威海 ; Yāntái 烟台
Shànghǎi 上海	
Shānxī 山西	Tàiyuán 太原
Shǎnxī 陕西	Xī'ān 西安 ; Yán'ān 延安
Sìchuān 四川	Chéngdū 成都 ; Lèshān 乐山 ; Zìgòng 自贡 ; Yíbīn 宜宾
Táiwān 台湾	Táiběi 台北 (Taipei)
Tiānjīn 天津	
Tibet Xīzàng 西藏	Lāsà 拉萨 (Lhasa); Rìkāzé 日喀则 (Shigatse)
Xīnjiāng 新疆	Wūlǔmùqí 乌鲁木齐 (Urumqi); Tǔlǔfān 吐鲁番 (Turpan); Ākèsū 阿克苏 (Aksu); Hétián 和田 (Hotan); Kāshí 喀什 (Kashgar)
Yúnnán 云南	Kūnmíng 昆明 ; Lìjiāng 丽江 ; Dàlǐ 大理 ; Xīshuāngbǎnnà 西双版纳
Zhèjiāng 浙江	Hángzhōu 杭州 ; Níngbō 宁波 ; Shàoxīng 绍兴 ; Wēnzhōu 温州

Glossary

A

arhat (luóhàn; 罗汉) – Sanskrit for a Buddhist, especially a monk, who has attained enlightenment and is freed from the cycle of rebirth

bāguà (八卦) – literally "the eight trigrams;" a set of broken (yin) and solid (yang) lines formed into eight sets of three and used for divination practices and to describe the nature of universal events in Taoist philosophy

B

běidàjiē (北大街) – north avenue

běijiē (北街) – north street

běilù (北路) – north road

běizhàn (北站) – north railway (or bus) station

bīn'guǎn (宾馆) – tourist hotel

Bodhisattva (púsà; 菩萨) – Buddhist who has reached nirvana but remains on earth to help others achieve enlightenment

bówùguǎn (博物馆) – museum

C

CAAC (Zhōngguó Mínháng; 中国民航) – Civil Aviation Administration of China

cān'guǎn (餐馆) or **cāntīng** (餐厅) – restaurant; cafeteria

CCP (Zhōngguó Gòngchǎndǎng; 中国共产党) – Chinese Communist Party

Cháng Chéng (长城) – the Great Wall

chēpiào (车票) – train or bus ticket

Chiang Kai-shek (Jiǎng Jièshí; 蒋介石) (1887-1957) – anti-communist leader of the Kuomintang and head of the nationalist government from 1928 to 1949

CITS (Zhōngguó Guójì Lǚxíngshè; 中国国际旅行社) – China International Travel Service

Confucius (Kǒngzǐ, 孔子) (551-470 BCE) – legendary thinker, philosopher and scholar who developed the philosophy of Confucianism, a system of rules, moral values and code of conduct for civil and obedient society

cūn (村) – village

D

dàdào (大道) – boulevard; avenue

dàfàndiàn (大饭店) – large hotel

dàjiē (大街) – avenue

dàjiǔdiàn (大酒店) – large hotel

dàshà (大厦) – hotel; building; mansion

dàxué (大学) – university; college

Dèng Xiǎopíng (邓小平) (1904-1997) – paramount leader of the Chinese Communist Party from 1978 to 1992.

diàn (殿) – hall

dìtiě (地铁) – subway

dōngdàjiē (东大街) – east avenue

dōngjiē (东街) – east street

dōnglù (东路) – east road

dòngwùyuán (动物园) – zoo

dōngzhàn (东站) – east railway (or bus) station

E

erhu (èrhú; 二胡) – the Chinese fiddle; a two-stringed bow instrument originally used in folk music and now being applied to a spectrum of musical genres

F

fāpiào (发票) – receipt, usually from a restaurant, taxi or department store

fàndiàn (饭店) – hotel; restaurant

fēngjǐngqū (风景区) – scenic area

feng shui (fēng shuǐ; 风水) – also called geomancy, literally "wind and water;" the ancient art of arranging a space (i.e. buildings and objects) to maximize the flow of *qi* and harmonize humans with the surrounding environment

G

gé (阁) – pavilion; temple

gōng (宫) – palace

gōngyuán (公园) - park

gōu (沟) – gorge; valley

guān (观) – pass

guàn (观) – hall; temple

gùjū (故居) – former residence

H

hǎi (海) – sea

Hàn (汉) – China's dominant ethnic group, making up over 92% of the population

hé (河) – river

hú (湖) – lake

Huí (回) – a Chinese Muslim ethnicity

huǒchēzhàn (火车站) – train station

hutong (hútóng; 胡同) – a narrow alleyway, especially in Beijing

J

jiǎo (角) – a unit of Chinese currency; 10 jiao equals 1 yuan

jiàotáng (教堂) – church

jīchǎng (机场) – airport

jiē (街) – street

jié (节) – festival; celebration

jīn (斤) – a unit of weight; 1 jin

equals 500 g

jīngjù (京剧) – Beijing Opera

jì'niànbēi (纪念碑) – memorial

jì'niànguǎn (纪念馆) – memorial hall

jiǔdiàn (酒店) – hotel

K

kuài (块) – in spoken Chinese, the colloquial term for the currency yuan

Kuomintang (Guómíndǎng; 国民党) – the Nationalist Party under Chiang Kai-shek who were dominant for a time after the fall of the Qing Dynasty

kung fu (gōngfū; 功夫) – western word for the Chinese martial arts

L

lama (lǎma, 喇嘛) – a honorific title bestowed on a monk or nun of Tibetan Buddhism, especially those of the Tantric school

líng (陵) – tomb

lóu (楼) – tower; building

lù (路) – road

lǚdiàn (旅店) or **lǚguǎn** (旅馆) – guesthouse

lǚshè (旅舍) – hostel

M

mahjong (májiāng; 麻将) – a hugely popular Chinese game that involves engraved tiles and rabid gambling

Máo Zédōng (毛泽东) (1893-1976) – the early leader of the communist forces and founder of the PRC, he stood as the Chairman and de facto ruler of the Communist Party until his death.

mén (门) – door; gate

ménpiào (门票) – entrance ticket

miào (庙) – temple

mù (墓) – tomb

N

nándàjiē (南大街) – south avenue

nánjiē (南街) – south street

nánlù (南路) – south road

nánzhàn (南站) – south railway (or bus) station

nèidàjiē (内大街) – inner street

P

páilóu (牌楼) – traditional decorative archways

pīnyīn (拼音) – the official system for transliteration of Chinese characters into Roman script

PSB (gōng'ānjú; 公安局) – Public Security Bureau, the branch of the police force that manages foreigners in China

Q

qì (气) – vital energy; universal energy

qiáo (桥) – bridge

qìchēzhàn (汽车站) – bus station

qìgōng (气功) – exercises and meditation to channel and nurture qi

R

rénmín (人民) – the people; the people's

rénmínbì (人民币) – literally "the people's currency"; the official name of Chinese currency

RMB – abbreviation of renminbi

S

sānlúnchē (三轮车) – non-motorized three-wheeler

shān (山) – mountain; hill

shāngdiàn (商店) – shop; store

shěng (省) – province; provincial

shì (市) – city

shìchǎng (市场) – market

shòupiàochù (售票处) – ticket office

sì (寺) – temple; monastery

sìhéyuàn (四合院) – traditional courtyard home

stupa (fótǎ; 佛塔) – a usually ornate tower built as a repository for the cremated remains of important monks

Sun Yat-sen (Sūn Zhōngshān; 孙中山) (1866-1925) – first president of the Republic of China; considered by many to be the father of modern China, he is adored by communists and republicans alike

T

tǎ (塔) – pagoda

tai chi (tài jí; 太极) – a slow-moving martial art that also functions as a moving meditation

tíng (亭) – pavilion

W

wàidàjiē (外大街) – outer street

wǎngba (网吧) – internet bar

wēnquán (温泉) – hot springs

wǔshù (武术) – Chinese word for martial arts, today it mostly refers to martia – based performance acrobatics

wǔxiá (武侠) – martial hero

X

xiá (峡) – gorge

xiàn (县) – county

xiàng (巷) – alley

xīdàjiē (西大街) – west avenue

xījiē (西街) – west street

xīlù (西路) – west road

xīzhàn (西站) – west railway (or bus) station

Y

yáng (阳) – outward, giving, light and masculine energy; complimentary force to yin

yīn (阴) – inward, accepting, dark and feminine energy; complimentary force to yang

yīn yáng (阴阳) – as a whole, the complimentary forces of the universe that act in harmony to create existence

yóujú (邮局) – post office

yuán (元) – basic unit of Chinese currency

yuán (园) – garden

Z

zhāodàisuǒ (招待所) – guesthouse

zhíwùyuán (植物园) – botanical gardens

Zhōngguó (中国) – China

zhōnglù (中路) – middle road

Travel Resources

Embassies

Whether you have a problem, lose your passport or are looking to continue your trip and need a visa into another foreign country, all roads point towards the embassies. Luckily, Beijing is the political capital of the country, meaning just about every country is represented here and their embassies are just a short taxi ride away. Listed below are the names, locations, Chinese addresses, telephone numbers and fax numbers, email addresses and websites of foreign embassies in Beijing. (Show the Chinese address to taxi driver if you can't speak Chinese).

Australia, Embassy of
Address: 21 Dongzhimen Waidajie, Chaoyang District (东直门外大街 21 号)
Phone: 5140 4111
Email: embassy.beijing@dfat.gov.cn
Website: www.china.embassy.gov.au

Brazil, Embassy of the Federative Republic of
Address: 27 Guanghua Lu, Chaoyang District (光华路 27 号)
Phone: 6532 2881
Email: info@brazil.org.cn
Website: www.brazil.org.cn

Cambodia, Royal Embassy of
Address: Dongzhimen Waidajie, Chaoyang District (东直门外大街 9 号)
Phone: 6532 1889
Email: cambassy@public2.bta.net.cn

Canada, Embassy of
Address: 19 Dongzhimen Waidajie, Chaoyang District (东直门外 19 号)
Phone: 5139 4000
Email: canadaeuropa@dfait-maeci.gc.ca

France, Embassy of the Republic of
Address: 3 Dong San Jie, Sanlitun, Chaoyang District (三里屯东三街 3 号)
Phone: 8532 8080

Website: www.ambafrance-cn.org

Germany, Embassy of the Federal Republic of
Address: 17 Dongzhimen Waidajie, Chaoyang District (东直门外大街17号)
Phone: 8532 9000
Email: embassy@peki.diplo.de
Website: www.peking.diplo.de/Vertretung/peking/de/Startseite.html

India, Embassy of the Republic of
Address: 1 Ritan Donglu, Chaoyang District (朝阳区日坛东路1号)
Phone: 6532 1908
Email: webmaster@indianembassy.org.cn
Website: www.indianembassy.org.cn

Indian Visa Office:
Address: Room 706, Ruichen International Center, 13 Nongzhanguan Nanlu (朝阳区农展馆南路13号瑞辰国际中心706)
Tel: 6592 5377
Email: info.bj@blsindia-china.com
Website: beijing.blsindia-china.com

Indonesia, Embassy of the Republic of
Address: 4 Dongzhimen Waidajie, Chaoyang District (朝阳区东直门外大街4号)
Phone: 6532 5486; 6532 5487;
Email: set.indonesia.kbri@depRoad.go.id

Ireland, Embassy of
Address: 3 Ritan Donglu, Chaoyang District (日坛东路3号)
Phone: 6532 2691; 6532 2914
Email: beijingembassy@dfa.ie
Website: www.embassyofireland.cn

Israel, Embassy of
Address: 17 Tianze Lu, Chaoyang District (朝阳区天泽路17号)
Phone: 8532 0500
Website: beijing.mfa.gov.il

Italy, Embassy of the Republic of
Address: 2 Dong Er Jie, Sanlitun, Chaoyang District (三里屯东二街2号)
Phone: 8532 7600
Email: ambasciata.pechino@esteri.it

Japan, Embassy of
Address: 7 Ritan Lu, Chaoyang District (日坛路7号)
Phone: 6532 2361
Website: www.cn.emb-japan.go.jp

Kazakhstan, Embassy of the Republic of
Address: 9 Dong Liu Jie, Sanlitun, Chaoyang District (三里屯东6街9号)
Phone: 6532 6182; 6532 4189 ext 11
Email: kz@kazembchina.org
Website: www.kazembchina.org

Korea, Embassy of the Republic of
Address: 20 Dongfang Donglu, Chaoyang District (朝阳区东方东路20号)
Phone: 8531 0700
Email: chinawebmaster@mofat.go.kr
Website: china.koreanembassy.cn

Korea Visa office:
Address: 14 Liangmahe Nanlu (朝阳区亮马河南路14号塔园国外交办公大楼)
Phone: 6532 6774/6775
Email: chinaconsul@mofat.go.kr

Lao, Embassy of
Address: 11 Dong Si Jie, Sanlitun (三里屯东4街11号)
Administrative Office: 6532 1224
Culture & Education Office: 6532 5652
Commercial Office: 6532 3601

Malaysia, Embassy of
Address: 2 Liangmaqiao Beijie, Chaoyang District (朝阳区亮马桥北街2号)
Phone: 6532 2531; 6532 2532
Email: mwbjing@kln.gov.my
Website: www.kln.gov.my/web/chn_beijing/home

Mexican States, Embassy of the United
Address: 5 Dong Wu Jie, Sanlitun (三里屯东5街5号)
Phone: 6532 2574; 6532 2070; 6532 1947
Email: embmxchn@public.bta.net.cn

Mongolia, Embassy of
Address: 2 Xiushui Beijie (建国门外秀水北街2号)
Phone: 6532 1203; 6532 6513
Email: mail@mongolembassychina.org
Website: www.mongolembassychina.org

Nepalese Embassy, Royal
Address: 1 Xi Liu Jie, Sanlitun (三里屯路西6街1号)
Phone: 6532 1795
Email: beijing@nepalembassy.org.cn
Website: www.nepalembassy.org.cn

New Zealand, Embassy of
Address: 1 Ritan Dong Er Jie, Chaoyang District (日坛东二街1号)
Phone: 6532 7000
Email: enquiries@nzembassy.cn
Website: www.nzembassy.com/china

Pakistan, Embassy of the Islamic Republic of
Address: 1 Dongzhimen Waidajie, Chaoyang District (东直门外大街1号)
Phone: 6532 2504; 6532 2695; 6532 2072

Philippines, Embassy of the Republic of the
Address: 23 Xiushui Beijie (建国门外秀水北街23号)
Phone: 6532 1872; 6532 2451; 6532 2518
Email: main@philembassy-china.org

Russian Federation, Embassy of the
Address: 4 Bei Zhong Jie, Dongzhimen Nei (东直门内北中街4号)
Phone: 6532 2051; 6532 1381; 6532 1291

Email: embassy@russia.org.cn
Visa Office
Email: text@russia.org.cn
Website: www.russia.org.cn/eng

Singapore, Embassy of the Republic of
Address: 1 Xiushui Beijie, Chaoyang District (朝阳区秀水北街1号)
Phone: 6532 1115
Website: www.mfa.gov.sg/beijing
Visa Office: Phone: 6532 9380

South Africa, Embassy of the
Address: 5 Dongzhimen Waidajie, Dongcheng District (东直门外大街5号)
Phone: 6532 0171
Email: embassy@saembassy.org.cn

Spain, Embassy of
Address: 9 Sanlitun Lu, Chaoyang District (三里屯路9号)
Phone: 6532 1986; 6532 3629
Email: embesp@public.bta.net.cn, embespcn@mail.mae.es

Sri Lanka, Embassy of the Democratic Socialist Republic of
Address: 3 Jianhua Lu, Jianguomen Wai (建国门外建华路3号)
Phone: 6532 1861; 6532 1862
Email: lkembj@public3.bta.net.cn

Thai Embassy, Royal
Address: 40 Guanghua Lu (光华路40号)
Phone: 6532 1749; 6532 2151
Email: thaibej@public.bta.net.cn

United Kingdom of Great Britain and Northern Ireland, Embassy of the
Address: 11 Guanghua Lu, Jianguomen Wai (建国门外光华路11号)
Phone: 5192 4000 (General enquiries only); 8529 6083 (Consular assistance for British nationals)
Website: ukinchina.fco.gov.uk/en

United States of America, Embassy of the
Address: 55 Anjialou Lu (安家楼路55号)
Phone: 8531 3000
Email: amcitbeijing@state.gov
Website: beijing.usembassy-china.org.cn

American Citizen Services
Emergency Contact Number: 8531 4000
Email: AmCitBeijing@state.gov
Non-Immigrant Visas
Visa Information Call Center: 400 887 2333; 3881 4611

Vietnam, Embassy of the Socialist Republic of
Address: 32 Guanghua Lu, Jianguomen Wai (建国门外光华路32号)
Phone: 6532 1155

Consular Office: Phone: 6532 7038

Expat Websites

In such a diverse, vibrant city, there are new places popping up by the day, and various shows, concerts and special events light up the town every night of the week. To stay up to date with the best Beijing has to offer and get reviews on certain venues, check out some of these English language websites.

eChinaCities: www.echinacities.com/Beijing
City Weekend: www.cityweekend.com.cn/Beijing
The Beijinger: www.thebeijinger.com
Time Out Beijing: www.timeoutbeijing.com

Useful Telephone Numbers

Emergency calls

Fire: 119
Police: 110
First Aid/Ambulance: 120
Traffic Accident: 122
Beijing Public Security Bureau English Service: 8402 0101
International SOS Assistance: 6462 9100

Other useful numbers

BCNC Car Rental Toll-free: 800 810 9001
Beijing Customs: 6539 6114 (in Chinese)
Bus Hotline: 96166
Customer Complaint: 12315 or 96315 (in Chinese)
International Phone Directory: 115
Local Phone Directory: 114 (in Chinese)
Master Card: 6510 1090; 6510 1095
Public Transport Superpass Hotline: 8808 7733 (in Chinese)
Ticket Booking Hotline: 6417 7845 or 800 810 3721
Tourist Information: 6513 0828
Weather Forecast: 121121 (in Chinese)

Index

500Arhat Statues 144
798 Art District 123
798 Art Festival 20
798 Photo Gallery 126
798 Space 126
7 Days Inn 194

A

accommodation 32 see also sleeping
acrobatics 22, 185, 188, 297, 330
air ticket 32
air pollution 301-304
airport 40
Alcohol 206, 317
ambulance 349
Anchee Min 25
Ancient Observatory 136
apps 35-36, 304, 309-311
aquariums 155
Arts 22
Art Students 314-315
ATMs 36-37
Temple of Azure Clouds 148

B

Badachu Park 141
Bada Hutongs 113
Badaling 54
Bag Snatching 315
bargain 254
bars, see drinking
bathrooms, see toilets
beggars 316
Beidaihe 273-274
Beihai Park 107-109, 294, 334-335
Beijing Antique City 259
Beijing Aquarium 155
Beijing Bicycle 26
Beijing Botanic Gardens 170
Beijing Capital Museum 156
Beijing Coma 25
Beijingers 29-30
Beijing Festivals 20
Beijing Films 26
Beijing food 209
Beijing Layout 15
Beijing Museum of Natural History 157
Beijing opera 186-187
Beijing Overview 8-30
    Arts 22

Beijing Festivals 20
Beijing Layout 15
Characters 29
Crazy Beijing 17
Economy 10
Film 25
Food 11
Grammar 28
Holidays & Festivals 19
Hutongs 11
Language 26
Literatures 24
Mandarin 26
Music 22
Peking Opera 22
Politics 10
Population 12
Safety 14
The Car Boom 13
Tones 28
Tourism 13
Visual Arts 23
Weather 21
Beijingers 29-30
Beijing Planetarium 158
Beijing Reading List 25
Beijing Tokyo Art Projects(BTAP) 126
Beijing Wildlife Park 159
Beijing World Park 160
Beijing Zoo 161
Beiping 9, 93, 94
Bell Tower 100, 296
Bernardo Bertolucci 26
Big Bell Temple 142
Big Underpants 162
bike tour 99, 105-106
body language 324
Bookworm 261
Boxer Rebellion 8, 72, 81, 109
Buddhism 118-119
Bullet Train 46
bus 44
Business Etiquette 325-326

C

calligraphy 262
Caochangdi 126
Capital Airport, see airport
Car Boom 13
cathedrals 257
CCTV Building 162
cell phones 322, 328, 341
censorship 10, 24, 327-328

Chairman Mao Memorial Hall 91
Chang Ling 138
Chaoyang District 17
Chaoyang Park 171, 244
Chaoyang Theater 185
Characters 29
Chen Kaige 26
Chengde 275-277
Chiang Kai-shek 66, 93, 103,345
China Aviation Museum 163
China Red SandalwoodMuseum 164
Chinese Communist Party(CCP) 91, 93, 134, 345
Chinese Ethnic Culture Park165
Chinese Medicine 262
chopsticks 242
Circular Mound Altar 81
Temple of the City God 271
Cixi, Empress Dowager 8, 25,69, 72, 74, 93, 113, 114147, 150,
Cloisonné 262
Temple of Cloud Dwelling 149
communism 23, 77, 86, 104
Communist Party 10, 25, 26, 88, 91, 93, 134, 345, 346
Confucian Temple 121-122, 271
consulates 347-349
cooking classes 264
counterfeit bills 315-316
crazy Beijing 17
Ctrip 194
Cultural Revolution 22, 25, 26,72, 95, 120, 185, 206,243, 256, 274, 324
culture shock 318-322
currency 36-37, 309
customs regulations 5-6

D

Dashilar 257
Deng Xiaoping 24, 95, 124, 345
disabilities, travelers 38-39
distractions 263-265
Ditan Park 83-84
Dongcheng District 16, 192,194,
Donghuamen Night Market 211
Dongjiaomin Xiang 114
Dragon Boat Festival 19
Dream of the Red Chamber 166
drinking 243-251

Drum Tower 100

E

Earth Altar 83
eating 205-242
Echo Wall 81
Economy 10
Eight Outer Temples 276
electricity 35
Elong 194
embassies & consulates 347-349
embroideries & brocades 261
emergency 340
Emergency Card 39
English books 261
etiquette 323-326
Eunuch Museum 265
expat websites 349
express hotels 194
Exit and Entry Administration of Beijing Public Security Bureau 122

F

Farewell My Concubine, 26
female travelers 38
festivals 19
  Lantern Festival 19
  Dragon Boat Festival 19
  Mid-Autumn Festival 19
  National Day 19
  Spring Festival 19
  Tomb Sweeping Day 19
film 25
Five Pagoda Temple 143
flag-raising ceremony 89
food, see eating
food safety 305
food tips 206
Forbidden City 13, 16, 62-70, 78, 80, 86, 88-89, 92, 98-99, 105-106, 169, 184, 280, 282, 284-286, 291-292, 334, 341
foreign exchange 27
Former Residences
  Former Residence of Guo Moruo 104
  Former Residence of Mao Dun 135
  Former Residence of Mei Lanfang 104
  Former Residence of Lao She 135
  Former Residence of Li Dazhao 134
  Former Residence of Lu Xun 132
  Former Residence of Song Qingling 103
  Former Residence of Qi Baishi 134
Fragrant Hills Park 172
Front Gate 88, 92
Fucheng Street 212

G

798 Art District 123-126
Dashanzi, see 798 Art District
Gate of Heavenly Peace 88-97
Gate of Supreme Harmony 67
gay travelers 38, 249-250
Ghost Street 211
gifts 324-325, see also souvenirs
glossary 345-346
Golden River 169
Grammar 28
Grand View Garden 166
Temple of Great Awakening 150
Great Hall of the People 90
Great Wall 50-61,
  Badaling 54
  Gubeikou 59
  Huanghuacheng 58
  Jiankou 61
  Jinshanling 60
  Juyongguan 57
  Mutianyu 55
  Simatai 59
Great Firewall 10, 322, 328
Green Tree Inn 194
Guandi Temple 276
Guanyuan Pet Market 259
Gubeikou 59
Gui Jie 211
Guo Jinlong 10
Guozijian Street 114, 121

H

Haidian District 16
Hall of Prayer for Good Harvests 81-82
Hall of Supreme Harmony 67
Hanting Express 194
Han Chinese 12
Happy Valley Amusement Park 167
health 303
health insurance 36
hiking 52-61
Holidays & Festivals 19
Home Inn 194
Hongluo Temple 144
Hongqiao Pearl Market 258
Hot Pot 209, 213
Houhai Bar Street 244
Hu Jintao 77, 96
hukou 12
Huanghuacheng 58
Huguang Guild Hall 186
Hutong 11, 16, 18, 45, 99, 101, 102, 105, 106, 110-115, 134-135, 279-289, 296, 330, 341, 345

I

ice skating 73, 76
Imperial Archives 105
Imperial City 88, 92,

Imperial College 114, 116, 121, 296,
Imperial Garden 63, 69, 72, 77, 161, 294,
Imperial Mountain Resort 275
Imperial Vault of Heaven 79, 81
internet access 327-328
itineraries 31, 290-300

J

jade 262
Jade Islet 108
Jiang Wen.26
Jiankou 61
Jietai Temple 145
Jin Dynasty 57, 147, 152
Jingdong Grand Canyon 173
Jingshan Park 70
Jinshanling 60
Jinyu Hutong 114
Jiumen Snack Street 211
Ju'er Hutong 114
Jung Chang 25
Juyongguan 57

K

Kangxi, Emperor 137, 145, 275, 276
karaoke 243
Kids, traveling with 329-332
KTV 316
Kublai Khan 8
Kunming Lake 73
Kuomintang (KMT) 9, 93, 103, 345

L

Lacquer 262
Lama Temple 116-122
Language 26-29, 119, 262, 310, 318, 324, 331, 336-346
Lantern Festival 19
Lao She 25, 135, 187, 293
Laoshe Teahouse 187
Last Days of Old Beijing 25
Last Emperor 26
Last Empress 25
Legend of Kung Fu 188
lesbian travelers 38, 249-250
Liao Dynasty 8, 115, 145
Li Dazhao 134
liquor 262
Literatures 24
Liulichang Cultural Street 258
Liulichang Street 114-115
Liyuan Theater 186
Longqing Gorge 174
Longtanhu Park 175
Lucky Street 212
Lu Xun 132

M

Ma Jian 25
Maliandao Tea Market 258

Manchus 8, 52
Mandarin 26-29, 310, 318, 331, 336-346
Mao Dun 135
Mao'er Hutong 115
Mao Zedong 9, 25, 77, 87, 88, 91, 93, 94, 346
Marco Polo Bridge 137
Markets, see shopping
martial arts 22, 26, 187, 346
massage 264, 315
May Fourth Movement 132, 135
Mei Lanfang 22, 104
Meridian Gate 106
Michael Myer 25
Mid-Autumn Festival 19
Military Museum 168
Ming Dynasty 8, 51, 52, 111
Ming Tombs 13, 138, 292
mobile phones 259, 328
money 36-37, see also currency
Monument to the People's Heroes 90
Mo Yan 24
museums
National Museum of China 91
Beijing Capital Museum 156
Beijing Museum of Natural History 157
China Aviation Museum 163
China Red Sandalwood Museum 164
Military Museum 168
National Art Museum 189
Eunuch Museum 265
Watermelon Museum 265
Music 22
Beijing opera 22, 25, 186-187, 293, 345
Mutianyu 55

N

Nanjing 8, 9, 27, 65, 83, 136, 148, 328, 344
Nanluogu Xiang 12, 44, 101, 105-106, 110, 115, 256, 296, 298,
National Aquatics Center 129
National Art Museum 189
National Center for the Performing Arts 186, 190
National Day 19
National Museum of China 91
National People's Congress 90
National Stadium 129
Nightlife, see drinking
Niujie Mosque 146
Niujie Islamic Supermarket 224
Niujie Muslim Snack Street 212
North Putuo Film & TV City 191
numbers 326

O

Ocean Theater 155
Old Summer Palace 75-76
Olympics 127-130
  National Aquatics Center 129
  National Stadium 129
Olympic Forest Park 130
One-child policy 329
opera 22, 104, 140, 186, 187
Opium Wars 8, 72
Ordination Altar Temple 145
Ox Street Mosque 146

P

Page One 261
pailou 121, 346
painting 22, 67, 101, 115, 134, 189, 252, 255, 256, 262
palaces
  Forbidden City 13, 16, 62-70, 78, 80, 86, 88-89, 92, 98-99, 105-106, 169, 184, 280, 282, 284-286, 291-292, 334, 341
  Old Summer Palace 75-76
  Summer Palace 13, 17, 71-76,
  Workers' Cultural Palace 169
Panjiayuan Flea Market 256
parks & gardens
  Badachu Park 141
  Beihai Park 107-109, 294, 334-335
  Beijing Botanic Gardens 170
  Beijing Wildlife Park 159
  Beijing World Park 160
  Chaoyang Park 171, 244
  Chinese Ethnic Culture Park 165
  Ditan Park 83-84
  Fragrant Hills Park 172
  Grand View Garden 166
  Happy Valley Amusement Park 167
  Imperial Garden 63, 69, 72, 77, 161, 294,
  Jingshan Park 70
  Longtanhu Park 175
  Phoenix Hill Nature Park 176
  Purple Bamboo Garden 177
  Ritan Park 85
  Taoranting Park 179
  Temple of Heaven Park 78-82
  Tuanjiehu Park 181
  Western Hills National Forest Park 182
  Yuyuantan Park 183
  Zhongshan Park 86, 98, 105, 106, 184
Peking Duck 9, 11, 205, 209, 213, 292,
Peking Man Site 13, 139
Peking Opera 22, 104, 140, 190, 268,
Peking University 77
People's Liberation Army (PLA) 93, 124
phone cards 328
Phoenix Hill Nature Park 176
Pickpocket 315
Pinyin, see language
Pingyao 270-272
The Place 260
Pace Beijing Galleries 126
Pod Inn 194
police 349
politics 10
pollution 10, 17, 21, 36, 301-304
Poly Art Museum 76
Pool & Mulberry Tree Temple 147
population 12
porcelain 262
Prince Gong's Mansion 102, 140
Public Security Bureau (PSB) 122, 193, 346, 349
pubs & bars, see drinking
Pule Temple 276
Puning Temple 276
Purple Bamboo Garden 177
Putuozongcheng Temple 276
Puyi, Emperor 26, 66, 93, 103

Q

Qianmen 8, 92, 291, 293, 298
Qi Baishi 134
Qing Dynasty 8, 69, 93, 112, 115, 140, 210
Queyou Men 106
Quezuo Men 106

R

Temple of the Recumbent Buddha 151
Red Sorghum 26
Red Theater 188
religious services 39
rickshaw 99, 312-313, 330,
Rickshaw Boy 25, 135
Ritan Park 85

S

safety 14, 305-307
sandstorms 9, 15, 302
Sanlitun Bar Street 243
Sanlitun Village 260
scams 312-317
Shichahai area 98-104
  Drum & Bell Towers 100
  Former Residence of Guo Moruo 104
  Former Residence of Mei Lanfang 104
  Former Residence of Song Qingling 103
  Nanluogu Xiang 101

Prince Gong's Mansion 102, 140
Shichahai Bar Street 100
Yandai Xiejie 102
shopping 252-262
  Beijing Antique City 259
  Bookworm 261
  Dashilar 257
  Donghuamen Night Market 211
  Guanyuan Pet Market 259
  Hongqiao Pearl Market 258
  Liulichang Cultural Street 258
  Maliandao Tea Market 258
  Nanluogu Xiang 256
  Niujie Islamic Supermarket 224
  Page One 261
  Panjiayuan Flea Market 256
  Sanlitun Village 260
  Silk Street 255
  Solana 260
  The Place 260
  Tianyi Market 257
  Wangfujing 256
  Xidan 257
  Yashow Market 256
  Zhongguancun 259
  Zoo Market 258
shopping tips 253
silk 261
Silk Street 255
Solana 260
Songzhuang Art District 126
Spring Festival 19
Stone Flower Cave 178
Street Food 208, 211, 212, 306-307
subway 41-44
Temple of Sumeru, Happiness and Longevity 276
Summer Palace 13, 17, 71-76
Sun Yat-sen 9, 103, 148, 172, 184, 346
supermarkets 261-262, 305, 339
swimming 273, 329,

T

taboo 323-326
tai chi 179, 293, 346
Tanzhe Temple 147
Taoism 153,
Taoranting Park 179
taxi 45, 312, 313, 315, 316, 319, 338
tea 261
tea house 313
telephone 327-328
temples
  Big Bell Temple 142
  Confucian Temple 121-122, 271
  Eight Outer Temples 276
  Five Pagoda Temple 143
  Guandi Temple 276
  Hongluo Temple 144
  Lama Temple 116-122
  Ordination Altar Temple 145
  Ox Street Mosque 146
  Pool & Mulberry Tree Temple 147
  Pule Temple 276
  Puning Temple 276
  Putuozongcheng Temple 276
  Temple of Azure Clouds 148
  Temple of City God 271
  Temple of Cloud Dwelling 149
  Temple of Great Awakening 150
  Temple of Heaven 13, 78-85, 293, 341
  Temple of Recumbent Buddha 151
  Temple of Sumeru, Happiness and Longevity 276
  Temple of Vast Succor 152
  Tianhou Temple 268
  White Cloud Temple 153
  White Dagoba Temple 154
Ten Ferries Scenic Area 180
theaters
  Chaoyang Theater 185
  Huguang Guild Hall 186
  Laoshe Teahouse 187
  Liyuan Theater 186
  National Center for the Performing Arts 186, 190
  Red Theater 188
  Tiandi Theater 185
  Tianqiao Acrobatic Theater 185
theft 37, 315
Tiandi Theater 185
Tianhou Temple 268
Tianjin 267-269
Tianqiao Acrobatic Theater 185
Tianyi Market 257
Tian Zhuangzhuang 26
tipping 40
toilets 307-309
Tomb Sweeping Festival 19
Tones 28
Tourism 13
Tian'anmen Square 86-97
Tian'anmen Tower 89, 92-97
transportation 40-48, 309-310
  airport 40
  bicycle 45
  bus 44
  subway 41
  taxi 45
  train 46
  Yikatong 41
travel stories 278-289
Tsinghua University 77
Tuanjiehu Park 181

U

Ullens Center for Contemporary Art (UCCA) 126
UNESCO 13, 64, 72, 81, 138, 139, 270, 275, 294,

V

Vairochana Pavilion 147
Temple of Vast Succor 152
visas 31-34, 347-349
Visual Arts 23

W

Wang Anshun 10
Wangfujing 256
Wangfujing Snack Street 211
Wang Xiaoshuai 26
Watermelon Museum 265
water safety 305
Weather 21
Western Hills National Forest Park 182
White Cloud Temple 153
White Dagoba Temple 154
wi-fi 327
Wild Swans 25
Workers' Cultural Palace 169
Workers' Stadium 243
Wudaokou 244
Wuta Temple 143

X

Xicheng District 16, 193, 201
Xidan 257
Xijiaomin Xiang 115
Xi Jinping 10, 24, 77
Xiannong Altar 85

Y

Yandai Xiejie 102, 115
Yanjing 8
Yashow Market 256
Yellow Earth 26
Yikatong 41
Yinding Bridge 98, 100, 102
Yongle, Emperor 8, 65, 66,70, 80, 92, 101, 121, 136, 138, 142, 143, 184,
Yuan Dynasty 8
Yuyuantan Park 183

Z

Zhang Yimou 26
Zhaoheng Gate 79, 81
Zhongguancun 259
Zhongshan Park 86, 98, 105, 106, 184
Zoo Market 258

Notes

Notes

Notes

Notes

Behind the scenes

This is the first edition of Panda Guides' *Beijing* guidebook and it was written by a team of expert Beijing expat writers who come from all corners of the English speaking world. Apart from their writings, this book was produced in Panda Guides' Beijing office with assistance from the Panda Guides headquarters in Toronto, Canada. It was produced by the following:

Commissioning Editor – **Grant Dou**

Managing Editors – **Trey Archer, Robert Linnet**

Managing Layout Designers – **Liu Qingli, Alice Harris**

Coordinating Cartographer – **Yan Laiyong**

Managing Cartographers – **Ding Zhicheng, Jessie Li**

Assistant Cartographers – **Feng Lili, Paul Taylor**

Proofreaders – **Elmer Chen, Robynne Tindall, Douglas Smith, Tina Johnson**

Internal Image Research – **Ellen Wong, Aaron Clarke**

Mandarin Content – **Xue Xue**

Office Assistant – **Li Lan, Zhang Qin**

Writers – **Robert Linnet, Trey Archer, Emily Umhoefer, Grant Dou**

A special thanks also goes out to **Danny Shao**, **Chen Chen**, **Chang Zhengong**, **Ellen Hou**, **Jason Yu**, **Han Fei**, **Liu Quanzu**, **Zhao Yong**, **Li Weixing**, **Yang Haibin**, **Wang Lei**, **Abel Thompson**, **Jeffery Scott**, **Lawrence Anderson** and **Jackie Lee**. Your work and help are greatly appreciated.

And last but not least, thank you to everyone along the way who helped us research this book. From the farmer on the street who pointed us in the right direction to the business man who gave us a ride when it was raining outside; none of this would have been possible without the people of China. 谢谢你们！ Xie Xie!

PANDA GUIDES

The Panda Ambassadors Program

Do you want an all-inclusive paid trip to China? Of course you do! By following the Panda, you can do just that, so keep reading to learn about the incredible Panda Ambassadors Program.

Once a year we will choose 20 lucky individuals to have the Chinese adventure of a lifetime. The selection process is simple. All you have to do is buy any Panda Guides travel book (*Beijing, Shanghai, Hong Kong* or *China*), go to our website to enter the six-digit code found on the inside of the front cover, then wait to see if your number is selected. All winners will be announced on our website and contacted through email in April. That's it!

Each winner gets a free two-week trip to China – transportation, accommodation and meals will be paid for by Panda Guides Publishing Inc. The only thing you have to do is purchase your visa, a flight and any extra souvenirs you'll want during your visit. The total value of this amazing package is ¥15,000 (roughly US$2,500).

A certified Panda Guides tour guide will bring the selected winners on a journey through a fascinating part of the country. It could be the ancient Silk Road along China's great northwest, a tropical retreat in the southern Canton region, or a river cruise through the Yangtze River. The journey will change once a year to ensure the scenery stays fresh, but no matter where you end it up, we guarantee it will be a wonderful trip!

Unfortunately, sometimes the real world gets in the way of our leisure time. But don't worry, all winners will have a three-year window to take their trip. If the winner still cannot take their free trip during this time, they can give it to someone else.

As you can see, through our Panda Ambassadors Program, Panda Guides is more than just a guide, it's an experience. In fact, we want you to enjoy your travel experience so much that we're willing to pay for it. So come along and let us welcome you to China, we hope to see you here soon.

See our website **www.pandaguides.com/pandaambassadors** for more.

123456

This number only serves as an example. Please see the inside of the front cover for the actual code.

The Authors

Robert Linnet

Born in Denver, CO, Robert received his BA in Linguistics from the nearby University of Colorado. After growing up admiring ancient Taoist philosophies and the furious fists of Bruce Lee and Gordon Liu, he came to China in 2009 for a summer stint at a martial arts school and a month of travel. Utterly smitten with the country, he hurried back in the summer of 2010 and has made it his home ever since. Robert has traveled to more than 20 cities throughout China, practices kettlebell and Baji Chuan kung fu, and is obsessed with adding to the thousands of Chinese characters he currently reads and writes. Though he resides in Beijing, he recently made a trip to his girlfriend Chen Chen's hometown of Xi'an to marry her. Robert speaks fluent Mandarin and French and is working on adding Shaanxi Hua (the dialect of Xi'an) to the list.

Trey Archer

Trey Archer is from Lake Charles, Louisiana and studied International Affairs at the George Washington University. While backpacking Latin America in 2007, he declared while hitchhiking by boat from Colombia to Panama that he'd pursue a career in travel writing after graduation instead of entering the world of diplomacy. Since then he has traveled to nearly 100 countries, speaks Spanish, Portuguese and Mandarin fluently, and has lived in nine different nations. In his free time he practices various martial arts (especially muay Thai), keeps up with the New Orleans Saints, cycles and is still obsessed with traveling. He's been in China for six years and has visited almost every province, but currently he resides in the hutongs of Beijing.

Emily Umhoefer

Emily Umhoefer is a Milwaukee, Wisconsin native who arrived in Beijing two years ago after a stint as a staffer on Capitol Hill in Washington, DC. As a writer, she's worked on everything from nonfiction political bestsellers to poems and press releases and now, this guide. Having worked as a wilderness trip leader in Tanzania, Ecuador, Costa Rica, and Colorado, Emily loves the outdoors, and on a beautiful summer day you'll find her exploring Beijing by bike and joining the old men in Speedos to take a dip in Houhai.

Grant Dou

Grant was born in Jiangsu Province and spent the first 30 years of his life in China. After receiving a PhD in Hydraulic Structural Engineering and teaching as a college professor, he moved to Toronto in 2002 to become a successful writer and publisher. Since then he has lived and traveled throughout North America, China and other Asian cities, so much that he often thinks with a Western mind and sees through local eyes. Grant recently moved back to China and currently resides in Beijing with his lovely wife; though he still experiences bits of reverse culture shock every once in a while.